CHILTON BOOK COMPANY

REPAIR & TUNE-UP GUIDE

CORVETTE 1984 to 1986

All U.S. and Canadian "new" body style Corvettes from 1984

President LAWRENCE A. FORNASIERI
Vice President and General Manager JOHN P. KUSHNERICK
Editor-in-Chief KERRY A. FREEMAN, S.A.E.
Senior Editor RICHARD J. RIVELE, S.A.E.
Editor RICHARD T. SMITH

CHILTON BOOK COMPANY
Radnor, Pennsylvania
19089

SAFETY NOTICE

Proper service and repair procedures are vital to the safe, reliable operation of all motor vehicles, as well as the personal safety of those performing repairs. This book outlines procedures for servicing and repairing vehicles using safe, effective methods. The procedures contain many NOTES, CAUTIONS and WARNINGS which should be followed along with standard safety procedures to eliminate the possibility of personal injury or improper service which could damage the vehicle or compromise its safety.

It is important to note that repair procedures and techniques, tools and parts for servicing motor vehicles, as well as the skill and experience of the individual performing the work vary widely. It is not possible to anticipate all of the conceivable ways or conditions under which vehicles may be serviced, or to provide cautions as to all of the possible hazards that may result. Standard and accepted safety precautions and equipment should be used during cutting, grinding, chiseling, prying or any other process that can cause material removal or projectiles.

Some procedures require the use of tools specially designed for a specific purpose. Before substituting another tool or procedure, you must be completely satisfied that neither your personal safety nor the performance of the vehicle will be endangered.

Although the information in this guide is based on industry sources and is as complete as possible at the time of publication, the possibility exists that the manufacturer made later changes which could not be included here. While striving for total accuracy, Chilton Book Company cannot assume responsibility for any errors, changes, or omissions that may occur in the compilation of this data.

PART NUMBERS

Part numbers listed in this reference are not recommendations by Chilton for any product by brand name. They are references that can be used with interchange manuals and aftermarket supplier catalogs to locate each brand supplier's discrete part number.

SPECIAL TOOLS

Special tools are recommended by the vehicle manufacturer to perform their specific job. Use has been kept to a minimum, but where absolutely necessary they are referred to in the text by the part number of the tool manufacturer. These tools can be purchased, under the appropriate part number, through the Service Tool Division, Kent-Moore Corporation, 29784 Little Mack, Roseville, MI 48066-2298. In Canada, contact Kent-Moore of Canada, Ltd., 2395 Cawthra Mississauga, Ontario, Canada L5A 3P2. Before substituting any tool for the one recommended, read the SAFETY NOTICE at the top of this page.

ACKNOWLEDGMENTS

The Chilton Book Company expresses its appreciation to the Chevrolet Motor Division, General Motors Corporation for their generous assistance.

Information has been selected from Chevrolet shop manuals, owners manuals, service bulletins, and technical training manuals.

Published in Radnor, Pennsylvania 19089 by Chilton Book Company

Manufactured in the United States of America
4567890 54321098

Chilton's Repair & Tune-Up Guide: Corvette 1984–86
ISBN 0-8019-7682-0 pbk.
Library of Congress Catalog Card No. 85-47982

CONTENTS

1 General Information and Maintenance

2 Tune-Up and Performance Maintenance

3 Engine and Engine Overhaul

4 Emission Controls and Fuel System

5 Chassis Electrical

6 Drive Train

7 Suspension and Steering

8 Brakes

9 Body and Trim

10 Troubleshooting

Quick Reference Specifications For Your Vehicle

Fill in this chart with the most commonly used specifications for your vehicle. Specifications can be found in Chapters 1 through 3 or on the tune-up decal under the hood of the vehicle.

Tune-Up

Firing Order ______

Spark Plugs:

Type ______

Gap (in.) ______

Torque (ft. lbs.) ______

Idle Speed (rpm) ______

Ignition Timing (°) ______

Vacuum or Electronic Advance (Connected/Disconnected) ______

Valve Clearance (in.)

Intake ______ **Exhaust** ______

Capacities

Engine Oil Type (API Rating) ______

With Filter Change (qts) ______

Without Filter Change (qts) ______

Cooling System (qts) ______

Manual Transmission (pts) ______

Type ______

Automatic Transmission (pts) ______

Type ______

Front Differential (pts) ______

Type ______

Rear Differential (pts) ______

Type ______

Transfer Case (pts) ______

Type ______

FREQUENTLY REPLACED PARTS

Use these spaces to record the part numbers of frequently replaced parts.

PCV VALVE	OIL FILTER	AIR FILTER	FUEL FILTER
Type ______	Type ______	Type ______	Type ______
Part No. ______	Part No. ______	Part No. ______	Part No. ______

General Information and Maintenance

1

HOW TO USE THIS BOOK

Chilton's Repair & Tune-Up Guide for the Corvette is intended to help you learn more about the inner working of your vehicle and save you money in it's upkeep and operation.

The first two chapters will be the most used, since they contain maintenance and tune-up information and procedures. Studies have shown that a properly tuned and maintained car can get at least 10% better gas mileage than an out-of-tune car. The other chapters deal with the more complex systems of your car. Operating systems from engine through brakes are covered to the extent that the average do-it-yourselfer becomes mechanically involved. This book will not explain such things as rebuilding the differential for the simple reason that the expertise required and the investment in special tools make this task uneconomical. It will give you detailed instructions to help you change your own brake pads and shoes, replace points and plugs, do many more jobs that will save you money, give you personal satisfaction and help you avoid expensive problems.

A secondary purpose of this book is a reference for owners who want to understand their car and/or their mechanics better. In this case, no tools at all are required.

Before removing any bolts, read through the entire procedure. This will give you the overall view of what tools and supplies will be required. There is nothing more frustrating that having to walk to the bus stop on Monday morning because you were short one bolt on Sunday afternoon. So read ahead and plan ahead. Each operation should be approached logically and all procedures thoroughly understood before attempting any work.

All chapters contain adjustments, maintenance, removal/installation and repair or overhaul procedures. When repair is not considered practical, we tell you how to remove the part and then how to install the new or rebuilt replacement. In this way, you at least save the labor costs. Backyard repair of such components as the alternator is just not practical.

Two basic mechanic's rules should be mentioned: One, whenever the left-side of the vehicle or engine is referred to, it is meant to specify the driver's-side of the vehicle. Conversely, the right-side of the vehicle means the passenger's-side. Secondly, most screws and bolts are removed by turning them counterclockwise and/or tightened by turning them clockwise.

Safety is always the most important rule. Constantly be aware of the dangers involved in working on an automobile and take the proper precautions. (See the section in this chapter "Servicing Your Vehicle Safely" and the SAFETY NOTICE on the acknowledgment page).

Pay attention to the instructions provided. There are 3 common mistakes in mechanical work:

1. Incorrect order of assembly, disassembly or adjustment. When taking something apart or putting it together, doing things in the wrong order usually just costs extra time, however, it CAN break something. Read the entire procedure before beginning the disassembly. Do everything in the order in which the instructions say you should do it, even if you can't immediately see a reason for it. When you're taking something apart that is very intricate (for example, a carburetor), you might want to draw a picture of how it looks when assembled at one point, in order to make sure you get everything back in its proper position. (We will supply exploded views whenever possible). When making adjustments, especially tune-up adjustments, do them in order. Often, one adjustment affects another and you cannot expect satisfactory results unless each adjust-

ment is made only when it cannot be changed by any other.

2. Overtorquing (or undertorquing). While it is more common for overtorquing to cause damage, undertorquing can cause a fastener to vibrate loose causing serious damage. Especially, when dealing with aluminum parts, pay attention to torque specifications and utilize a torque wrench in assembly. If a torque figure is not available, remember that if you are using the right tool to do the job, you will probably not have to strain yourself to get a fastener tight enough. The pitch of most threads is so slight that the tension you put on the wrench will be multiplied many, many times in actual force on what you are tightening. A good example of how critical torque is can be seen in the case of spark plug installation, especially where you are putting the plug into an aluminum cylinder head. Too little torque can fail to crush the gasket, causing leakage of combustion gases and consequent overheating of the plug and engine parts. Too much torque can damage the threads or distort the plug, which changes the spark gap.

NOTE: *There are many commercial products available for ensuring that fasteners won't come loose, even if they are not torqued just right (a very common brand is "Locite®"). If you're worried about getting something together tight enough to hold but loose enough to avoid mechanical damage during assembly, one of these products might offer substantial insurance. Read the label on the package and make sure the product is compatible with the materials, fluids and etc. involved before choosing one.*

3. Crossthreading occurs when a part such as a bolt is screwed into a nut or casting at the wrong angle and forced. Crossthreading is more likely to occur if access is difficult. It helps to clean and lubricate fasteners, then start threading with the part to be installed going straight in. Start the bolt, spark plug or etc. with your fingers. If you encounter resistance, unscrew the part and start over again at a different angle until it can be inserted and turned several turns without much effort. Keep in mind that many parts, especially spark plugs, use tapered threads so that gentle turning will automatically bring the part you're threading to the proper angle if you don't force it or resist a change in angle. Don't put a wrench on the part until it's been turned a couple of turns by hand. If you suddenly encounter resistance, and the part has not been seated fully, don't force it. Pull it back out and make sure it's clean and threading properly.

NOTE: *Always take your time and be patient, once you have some experience working on your vehicle, it will become an enjoyable hobby.*

TOOLS AND EQUIPMENT

Naturally, without the proper tools and equipment, it is impossible to properly service your vehicle. It would be impossible to catalog each tool that you would need to perform each or any operation in this book. It would also be unwise for the amateur to rush out and buy an expensive set of tools on the theory that he may need one or more of them at sometime.

The best approach is to proceed slowly, gathering a good quality set of tools that are used most frequently. Don't be misled by the low cost of bargain tools. It is far better to spend a little more for better quality. Forged wrenches, 6 or 12 point sockets and fine tooth ratchets are by far preferable to their less expensive counterparts. As any good mechanic can tell you, there are few worse experiences than trying to work on a vehicle with bad tools. Your monetary savings will be far outweighed by frustration and mangled knuckles.

Begin accumulating tools that are used most frequently; those associated with routine maintenance and tune-up.

In addition to the normal assortment of screwdrivers and pliers you should have the following tools for routine maintenance jobs:

1. SAE (or Metric) or SAE/Metric wrenches – sockets and combination open end/box end wrenches in sizes from 1/8" (3mm) to 3/4" (19mm) and a spark plug socket (13/16 or 5/8 in. depending on plug type).

NOTE: *If possible, buy various length socket drive extensions. One break in this department is that the metric sockets available in the U.S. will all fit the ratchet handles and extensions you may already have (1/4", 3/8" and 1/2" drive).*

2. Jackstands, for support
3. Oil filter wrench
4. Oil filler spout, for pouring oil
5. Grease gun, for chassis lubrication
6. Hydrometer, for checking the battery
7. A container for draining oil
8. Many rags for wiping up the inevitable mess.

In addition to the above items there are several others that are not absolutely necessary but handy to have around. These include oil dry, a transmission funnel and an usual supply of lubricants, antifreeze and fluids, although these can be purchased as needed. This is a basic list for routine maintenance but only your personal needs and desires can accurately determine your list of tools. If you are serious

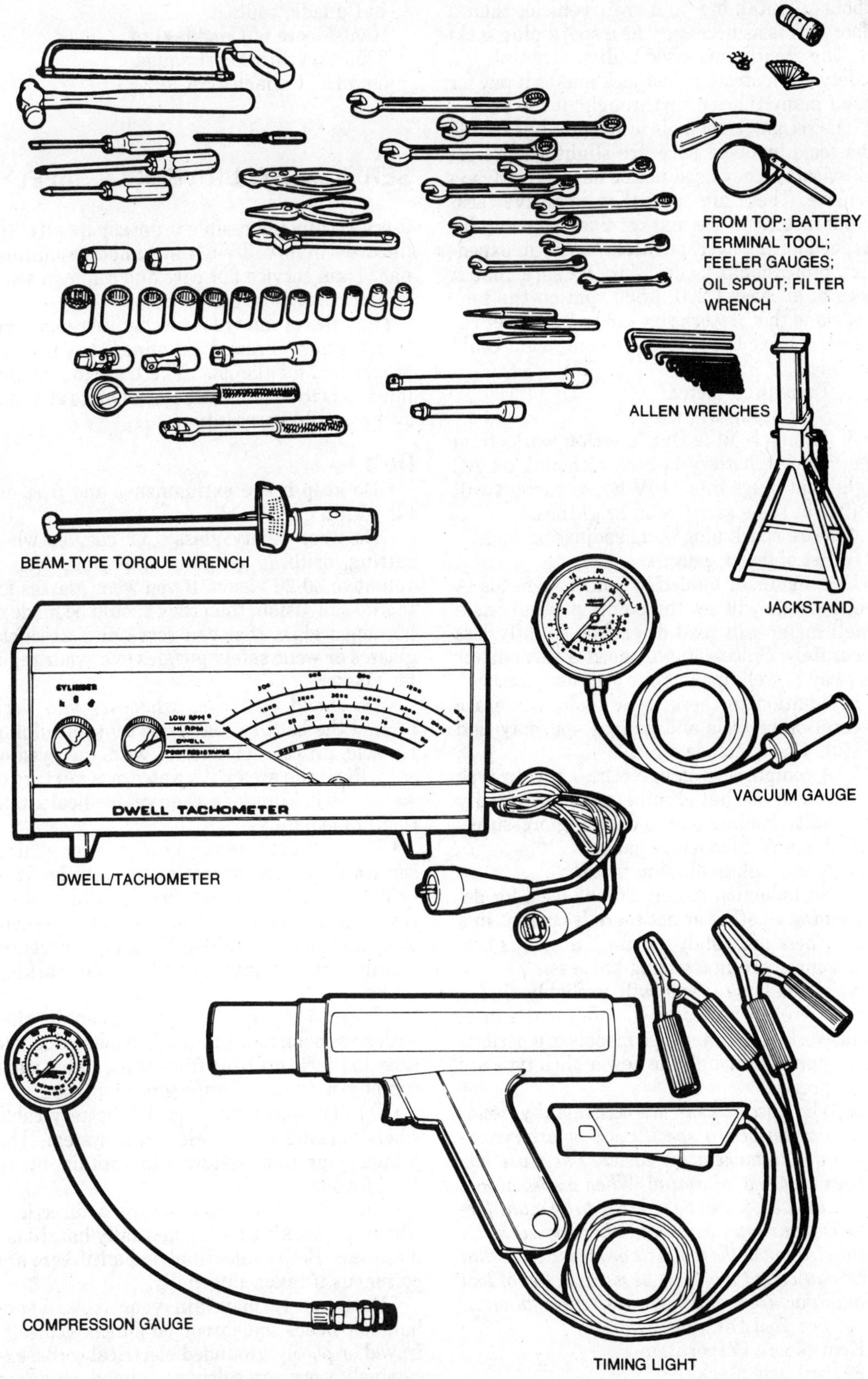

You need only a basic assortment of hand tools and test instruments for most maintenance and repair jobs

about maintaining your own vehicle, then a floor jack is as necessary as a spark plug socket. The greatly increased utility, strength and safety of a hydraulic floor jack makes it pay for itself many times over throughout the years.

The second list of tools is for tune-ups. While the tools involved here are slightly more sophisticated, they need not be outrageously expensive. There are several inexpensive tack/dwell meters on the market that are every bit as good for the average mechanic as an expensive professional model. Just be sure that it goes to at least 1,200–1,500 rpm on the tach scale and that it works on 4, 6 or 8 cylinder engines. A basic list of tune-up equipment could include:

1. Tach-dwell meter.
2. Spark plug wrench.
3. Timing light (a DC light that works from the vehicle's battery is best, although an AC light that plugs into 110V house current will suffice at some sacrifice in brightness).
4. Wire spark plug gauge/adjusting tools.
5. Set of feeler gauges.

Here again, be guided by your own needs. A feeler gauge will set the points as easily as a dwell meter will read dwell but slightly less accurately. Since you will need a tachometer anyway ... well, make your own decision.

In addition to these basic tools, there are several other tools and gauges you may find useful. These include:

1. A compression gauge. The screw-in type is slower to use but eliminates the possibility of a faulty reading due to escaping pressure.
2. A manifold vacuum gauge.
3. A test light, volt/ohm meter.
4. An induction meter. This is used for determining whether or not there is current in a wire. These are handy for use if a wire is broken somewhere in a wiring harness.

As a final note, you will probably find a torque wrench necessary for all but the most basic work. The beam type models are perfectly adequate, although the newer click type are more precise.

NOTE: *Special tools are occasionally necessary to perform a specific job or are recommended to make a job easier. Their use has been kept to a minimum. When a special tool is indicated, it will be referred to by manufacturer's part number, and, where possible, an illustration of the tool will be provided so that an equivalent tool may be used. A list of tool manufacturers and their addresses follows:*

Service Tool Division
Kent-Moore Corporation
29784 Little Mack
Roseville, MI 48066-2298

In Canada, contact:
Kent-Moore of Canada, Ltd.
2395 Cawthra Mississauga
Ontario, Canada L5A 3P2.

SERVICING YOUR VEHICLE SAFELY

It is virtually impossible to anticipate all of the hazards involved with automotive maintenance and service but care and common sense will prevent most accidents.

The rules of safety for mechanics range from "don't smoke around gasoline," to "use the proper tool for the job." The trick to avoiding injuries is to develop safe work habits and take every possible precaution.

Do's

• Do keep a fire extinguisher and first aid kit within easy reach.

• Do wear safety glasses or goggles when cutting, drilling, grinding or prying, even if you have 20-20 vision. If you wear glasses for the sake of vision, then they should be made of hardened glass that can serve also as safety glasses or wear safety goggles over your regular glasses.

• Do shield your eyes whenever you work around the battery. Batteries contain sulphuric acid. In case of contact with the eyes or skin, flush the area with water or a mixture of water and baking soda, then get medical attention immediately.

• Do use safety stands for any under vehicle service. Jacks are for raising the vehicle. Safety stands are for making sure the vehicle stays raised until you want it to come down. Whenever the vehicle is raised, block the wheels remaining on the ground and set the parking brake.

• Do use adequate ventilation when working with any chemicals. Like carbon monoxide, the asbestos dust resulting from brake lining wear can be poisonous in sufficient quantities.

• Do disconnect the negative battery cable when working on the electrical system. The primary ignition system can contain up to 40,000 volts.

• Do follow the manufacturer's directions whenever working with potentially hazardous materials. Both brake fluid and antifreeze are poisonous if taken internally.

• Do properly maintain your tools. Loose hammer heads, mushroomed punches/chisels, frayed or poorly grounded electrical cords, excessively worn screwdrivers, spread wrenches (open end), cracked sockets, slipping ratchets and/or faulty droplight sockets cause accidents.

- Do use the proper size and type of tool for the job being done.
- Do when possible, pull on a wrench handle rather than push on it and adjust your stance to prevent a fall.
- Do be sure that adjustable wrenches are tightly adjusted on the nut or bolt and pulled so that the face is on the side of the fixed jaw.
- Do select a wrench or socket that fits the nut or bolt. The wrench or socket should sit straight, not cocked.
- Do strike squarely with a hammer—avoid glancing blows.
- Do set the parking brake and block the drive wheels if the work requires that the engine be running.

Dont's

- Don't run an engine in a garage or anywhere else without proper ventilation—EVER! Carbon monoxide is poisonous. It takes a long time to leave the body and can build up a deadly supply of it in your system by simply breathing in a little every day. You may not realize you are slowly poisoning yourself. Always use power vents, windows, fans or open the garage doors.
- Don't work around moving parts while wearing a necktie or other loose clothing. Short sleeves are much safer than long, loose sleeves and hard-toed shoes with neoprene soles protect your toes and give a better grip on slippery surfaces. Jewelry such as watches, fancy belt buckles, beads or body adornment or any kind is not safe working around a vehicle. Long hair should be hidden under a hat or cap.
- Don't use pockets for tool boxes. A fall or bump can drive a screwdriver deep into your body. Even a wiping cloth hanging from the back pocket can wrap around a spinning shaft or fan.
- Don't smoke when working around gasoline, cleaning solvent or other flammable material.
- Don't smoke when working around the battery. When the battery is being charged, it gives off explosive hydrogen gas.
- Don't use gasoline to wash your hands. There are excellent soaps available. Gasoline may contain lead, and lead can enter the body through a cut, accumulating in the body until you are very ill. Gasoline also removes all the natural oils from the skin so that bone dry hands will suck up oil and grease.
- Don't service the air conditioning system unless you are equipped with the necessary tools and training. The refrigerant, R-12, is extremely cold and when exposed to the air, will instantly freeze any surface it comes in contact with, including your eyes. Although the refrigerant is normally non-toxic, R-12 becomes a deadly poisonous gas in the presence of an open flame. One good whiff of the vapors from burning refrigerant can be fatal.

HISTORY

In 1984 a new generation of Corvette was born, it is known as the best handling production vehicle in the world today. The only engine available is the L83–350 V8 with Cross-Fire Injection (CFI), which features twin throttle bodies equipped with throttle body mounted Electronic Fuel Injectors and a specially designed manifold to blend and deliver the air/fuel mixture more efficiently.

Two transmissions are offered: The THM 700-R4 automatic (standard) or the 83mm, 4-speed manual with automatic overdrive (optional). The power rack/pinion steering and suspension package combine to provide precision and predictability at all speeds, along with the highest lateral acceleration figure (0.95G) ever recorded for a production model at the GM Proving Grounds. The new design is more aerodynamic than ever, with a drag coefficient of 0.34. The instrument panel features a long list of liquid crystal analog display and digital instrumentation.

In 1985, the L98–350 V8 engine introduced a new fuel system which included the use of straight tail pipes. The Tuned Port Injection (TPI) system replaced the 1984 Cross-Fire Injection (CFI) system to provide a 19% increase in horsepower. The TPI system utilizes a newly designed intake system, using a single throttle body (on the intake plenum) and individual fuel injectors (located at each intake valve).

The 1986 model ushered in the return of the Roadster (Convertible), after a 10 year absence, and captured the Indy 500 Pace Car title. For the Roadster, a number of structural changes differentiate it from the Coupe. New equipment includes: An anti-lock braking system, an anti-theft system (which allows the engine to start ONLY after the computer reads a familiar value embedded in the ignition key), new aluminum cylinder heads (designed to shed 40 lbs. and increase the compression ratio) with centrally located copper core spark plugs, an upshift indicator light (for increased fuel economy, a high center mounted brake light, a new dual exhaust system utilizing 3 monolithic catalytic converters (to maximize the emission controls during the engine warmup), all new cast alloy wheels and a newly tilted instrument cluster (to reduce glare).

SERIAL NUMBER IDENTIFICATION

Vehicle

The vehicle serial number plate is located on the top left-side of the instrument panel (1984 and later). The vehicle serial number identifies the body style, model year, assembly plant, engine usage and production number.

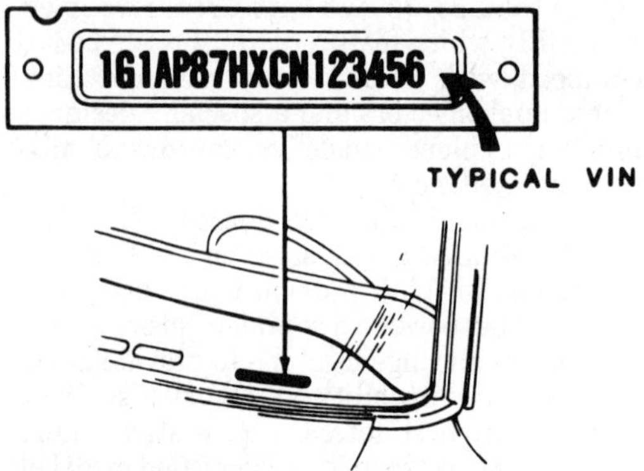

View of the vehicle identification number

Body

The service parts identification label is located on the center of the chassis floor, behind the seats (1984 and later). It relates the body, trim, paint and parts information.

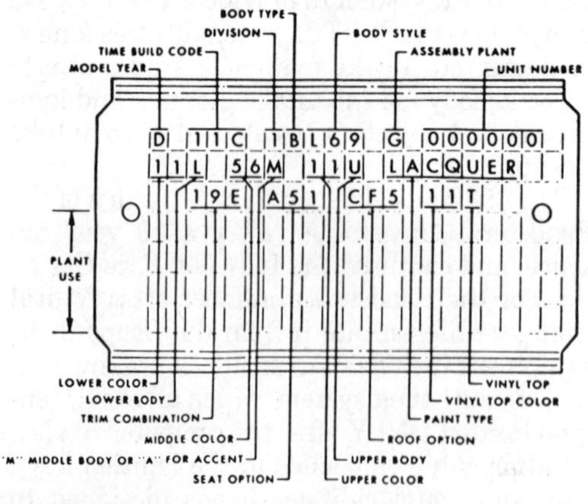

View of the body identification number

Engine

All Corvette engine identification numbers are stamped on a pad of the engine block which is located at the lower front-edge of the right-side cylinder head. The first letter designates the plant in which the engine was manufactured and the numbers which follow identify the production date. The two or three letter suffix identifies the engine type and related equipment. On 1984 and later models, if the engine in the vehicle is known to be original, the eighth digit of the serial number may also identify the engine used in the vehicle.

Engine Identification

Year	Engine	Mfg.	Code
1984	350-V8 EFI	Chev.	ZFC, ZFD, ZFF, ZFN, ZFM
1985	350-V8 TPI	Chev.	ZDF, ZJB, ZJC, ZJJ, ZJK
1986	350-V8 TPI	Chev.	ZJH, ZKA, ZKD, ZJS, ZJW

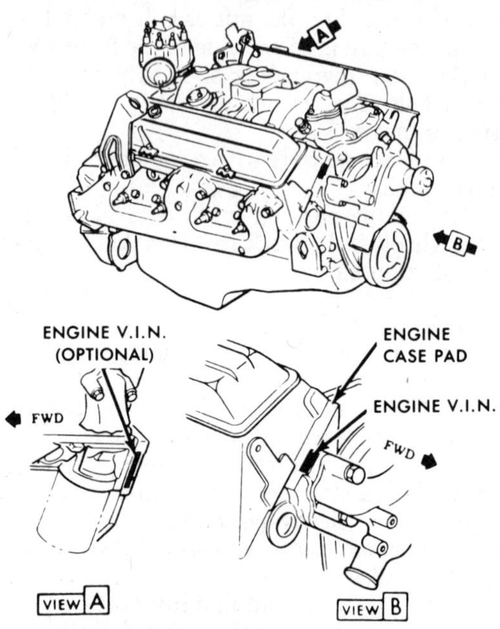

Typical engine serial number location

Transmission

NOTE: *In 1986, an upshift indicator light was installed on the dash, to provide maximum fuel economy and low emission quality.*

FOUR-SPEED MANUAL (WITH AUTOMATIC OVERDRIVE)

1985 and Later

The transmission serial numbers are located on the front right-side of the bell housing or on the rear left-side (optional) of the final drive case.

The newly designed 4-plus-3-spd. manual transmission with computer controlled overdrive, provides 4-spd. manual operation or 3-spd. overdrive (except 1st gear). The shifting

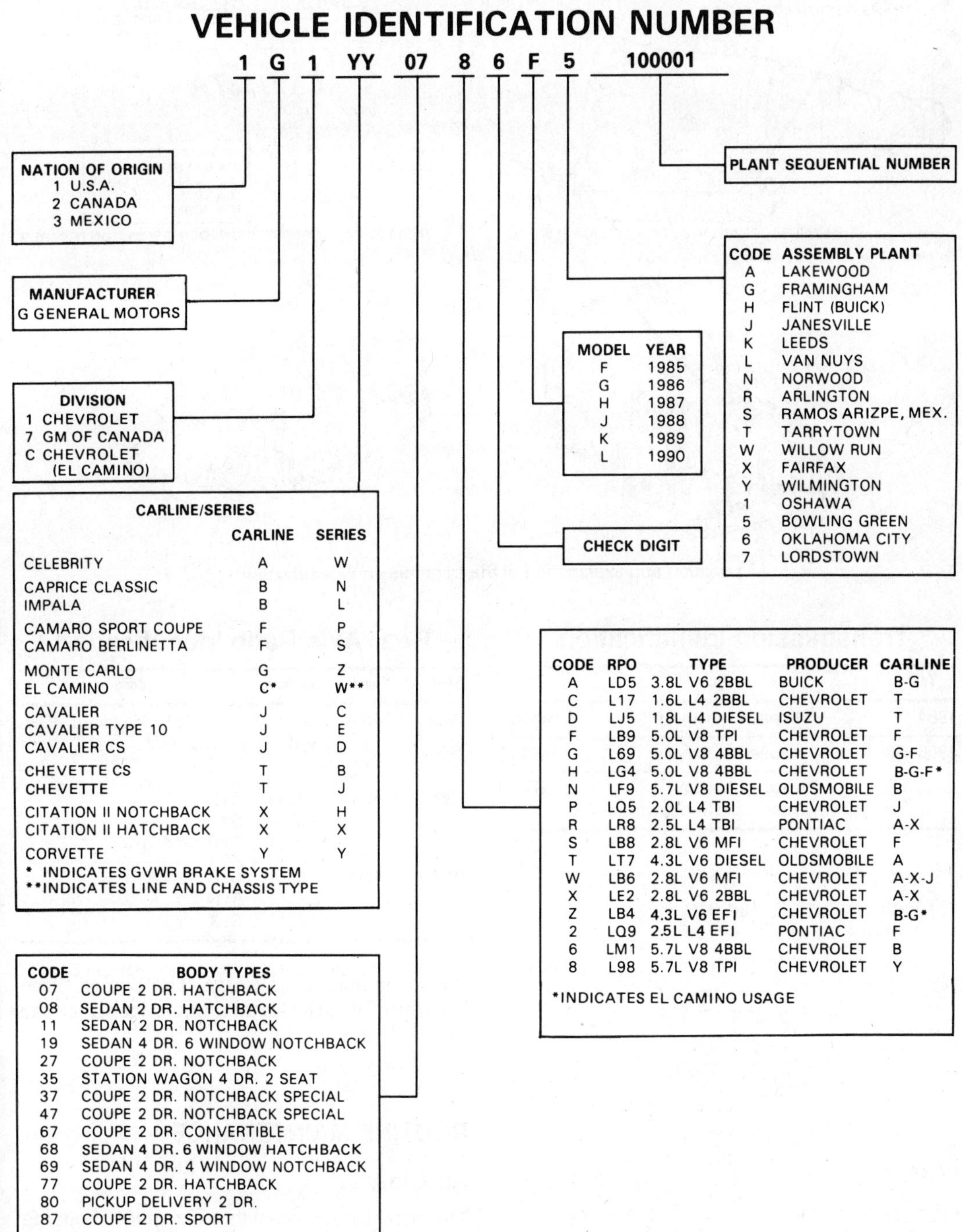

VEHICLE IDENTIFICATION NUMBER

1 G 1 YY 07 8 6 F 5 100001

NATION OF ORIGIN

1 U.S.A.
2 CANADA
3 MEXICO

MANUFACTURER

G GENERAL MOTORS

DIVISION

1 CHEVROLET
7 GM OF CANADA
C CHEVROLET (EL CAMINO)

CARLINE/SERIES

	CARLINE	SERIES
CELEBRITY	A	W
CAPRICE CLASSIC	B	N
IMPALA	B	L
CAMARO SPORT COUPE	F	P
CAMARO BERLINETTA	F	S
MONTE CARLO	G	Z
EL CAMINO	C*	W**
CAVALIER	J	C
CAVALIER TYPE 10	J	E
CAVALIER CS	J	D
CHEVETTE CS	T	B
CHEVETTE	T	J
CITATION II NOTCHBACK	X	H
CITATION II HATCHBACK	X	X
CORVETTE	Y	Y

* INDICATES GVWR BRAKE SYSTEM
**INDICATES LINE AND CHASSIS TYPE

CODE	BODY TYPES
07	COUPE 2 DR. HATCHBACK
08	SEDAN 2 DR. HATCHBACK
11	SEDAN 2 DR. NOTCHBACK
19	SEDAN 4 DR. 6 WINDOW NOTCHBACK
27	COUPE 2 DR. NOTCHBACK
35	STATION WAGON 4 DR. 2 SEAT
37	COUPE 2 DR. NOTCHBACK SPECIAL
47	COUPE 2 DR. NOTCHBACK SPECIAL
67	COUPE 2 DR. CONVERTIBLE
68	SEDAN 4 DR. 6 WINDOW HATCHBACK
69	SEDAN 4 DR. 4 WINDOW NOTCHBACK
77	COUPE 2 DR. HATCHBACK
80	PICKUP DELIVERY 2 DR.
87	COUPE 2 DR. SPORT

PLANT SEQUENTIAL NUMBER

CODE	ASSEMBLY PLANT
A	LAKEWOOD
G	FRAMINGHAM
H	FLINT (BUICK)
J	JANESVILLE
K	LEEDS
L	VAN NUYS
N	NORWOOD
R	ARLINGTON
S	RAMOS ARIZPE, MEX.
T	TARRYTOWN
W	WILLOW RUN
X	FAIRFAX
Y	WILMINGTON
1	OSHAWA
5	BOWLING GREEN
6	OKLAHOMA CITY
7	LORDSTOWN

MODEL	YEAR
F	1985
G	1986
H	1987
J	1988
K	1989
L	1990

CHECK DIGIT

CODE	RPO	TYPE	PRODUCER	CARLINE
A	LD5	3.8L V6 2BBL	BUICK	B-G
C	L17	1.6L L4 2BBL	CHEVROLET	T
D	LJ5	1.8L L4 DIESEL	ISUZU	T
F	LB9	5.0L V8 TPI	CHEVROLET	F
G	L69	5.0L V8 4BBL	CHEVROLET	G-F
H	LG4	5.0L V8 4BBL	CHEVROLET	B-G-F*
N	LF9	5.7L V8 DIESEL	OLDSMOBILE	B
P	LQ5	2.0L L4 TBI	CHEVROLET	J
R	LR8	2.5L L4 TBI	PONTIAC	A-X
S	LB8	2.8L V6 MFI	CHEVROLET	F
T	LT7	4.3L V6 DIESEL	OLDSMOBILE	A
W	LB6	2.8L V6 MFI	CHEVROLET	A-X-J
X	LE2	2.8L V6 2BBL	CHEVROLET	A-X
Z	LB4	4.3L V6 EFI	CHEVROLET	B-G*
2	LQ9	2.5L L4 EFI	PONTIAC	F
6	LM1	5.7L V8 4BBL	CHEVROLET	B
8	L98	5.7L V8 TPI	CHEVROLET	Y

*INDICATES EL CAMINO USAGE

Explanation of the vehicle identification number

combination provides a total of 7 forward gear operations.

TURBO HYDRA-MATIC FOUR-SPEED

1984 and Later

The THM 700-R4, 4-spd automatic transmission serial numbers are located on the rear right-side of the transmission case, above the oil pan.

Rear Axle

All Corvette have the rear axle serial number located on the bottom surface of the carrier at

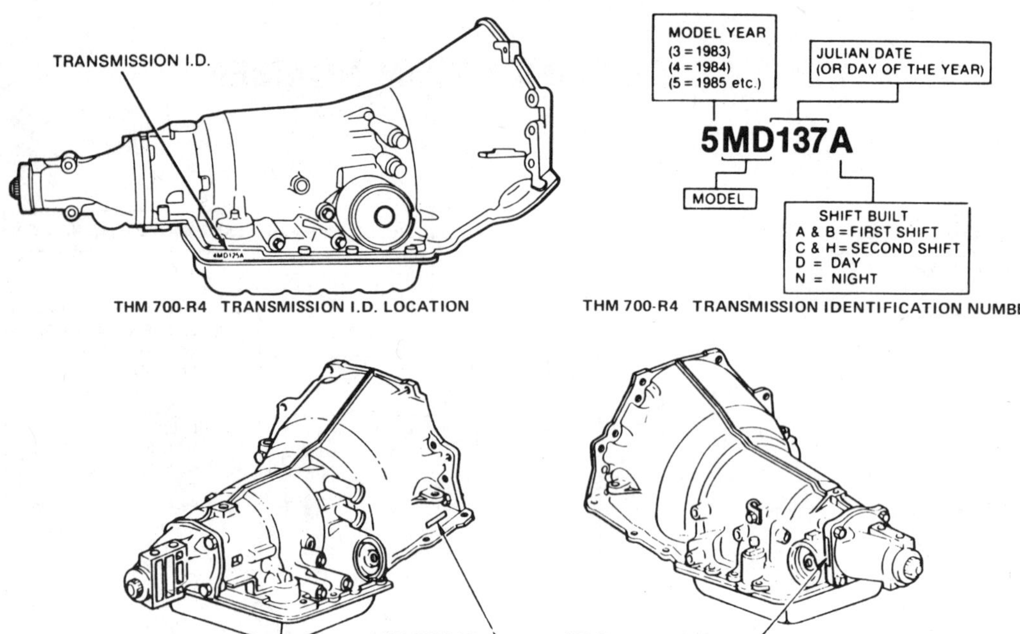

Location and explanation of the transmission identification

Transmission Identification

Year	Type	Code
1984	4-speed Automatic	MD8
1985–86	4-speed Automatic	MD8
	4-speed Manual (Automatic Overdrive)	MK2

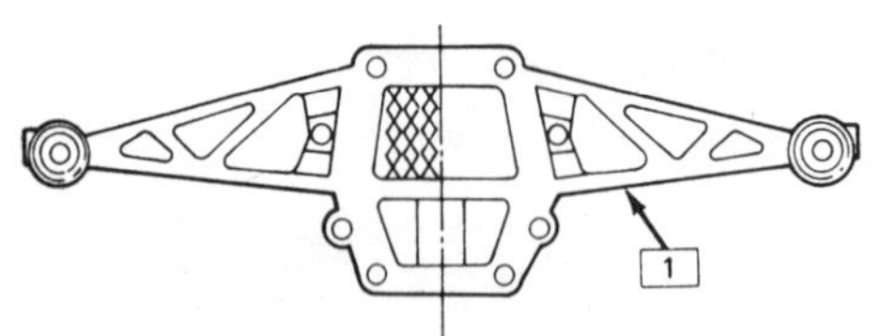

Location and explanation of the rear axle identification plate

Rear Axle Ratio Identification

Year	Prefix	Axle Ratio	Code
1984	DANA	3.07 3.31	4CC, 4CF, 4CH, 4CJ, 4CN, 4CS, 4YJ 4CB, 4CK, 4CR
1985	DANA	2.73:1 2.87:1 3.07:1	5YN 5YY 5YB, 5YX, 5YJ
1986	DANA	2.59:1 2.73:1 3.07:1	6YB 5YN 5YX

the cover mounting flange. The two or three letter prefix in the serial number identifies the rear axle gear ratio.

ROUTINE MAINTENANCE

Air Cleaner

The air cleaner consists of a metal housing with a replaceable paper filter and the necessary hoses connecting it to the crankcase ventilation system. The air cleaner cover is held by knurled nuts on all models. The factory recommends that the filter be replaced once every 30,000 miles. Inspection and replacement should come more often when the vehicle is operated under dusty conditions. To check the effectiveness of your paper element, remove the air cleaner assembly, if the idle speed in-

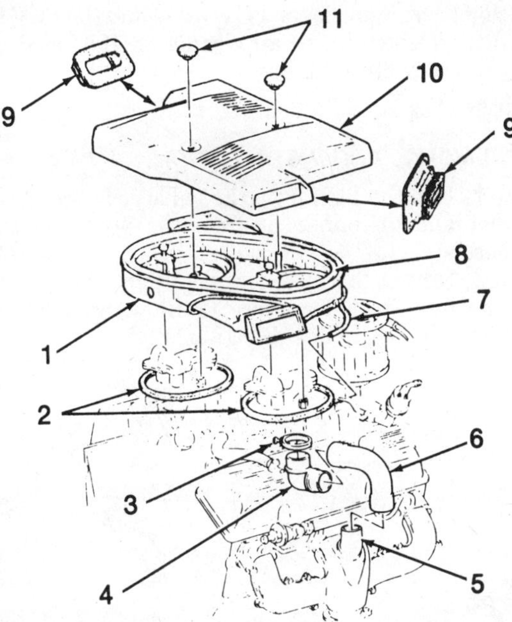

1. Air cleaner assembly
2. Gasket
3. Hose clamp
4. Heat stove adapter
5. Heat stove
6. Heat stove tube
7. Manifold vacuum hose
8. Air filter element
9. Hood seal
10. Air cleaner cover
11. Knurl nuts

Air cleaner assembly—1984 TBI shown

creases noticeably, the element is restricting airflow and should be replaced.

REMOVAL AND INSTALLATION

1. Remove the air cleaner top knurled nuts and lift off the top.
2. Remove the filter from inside the filter housing.
3. Clean the inside of the air cleaner housing before reinstalling the air filter.
4. To install, reverse the removal procedures.

Fuel Filter

The fuel filter is in the fuel feed line attached next the right frame rail.

CAUTION: *Before removing any component of the fuel system, be sure to reduce the fuel pressure in the system.*

REMOVAL AND INSTALLATION

1984

1. Loosen the hose clamps and slide the clamps away from the filter.
2. Gently twist and pull the hoses free of the filter pipes.
3. Remove the filter-to-frame mounting bolt and discard the old filter.

NOTE: *When installing a new filter, pay attention to the direction the fuel must flow through it.*

3. Install a new filter onto the frame, slide the hoses and clamps back into position. Tighten the clamps, start the engine and check for leaks.

1985 and Later

1. Using two wrenches, remove the fuel lines from the filter.
2. Remove the filter-to-frame mounting bolt and discard the old filter.

NOTE: *When installing a new filter, pay attention to the direction the fuel must flow through it.*

3. Install a new filter onto the frame. Using two wrenches, tighten the fuel lines onto the filter. Start the engine and check for leaks.

Positive Crankcase Ventilation (PCV)

The PCV valve is attached to the valve cover by a rubber grommet and connected to the air cleaner/carbon canister (1984) or the intake manifold (1985 and later) through a ventila-

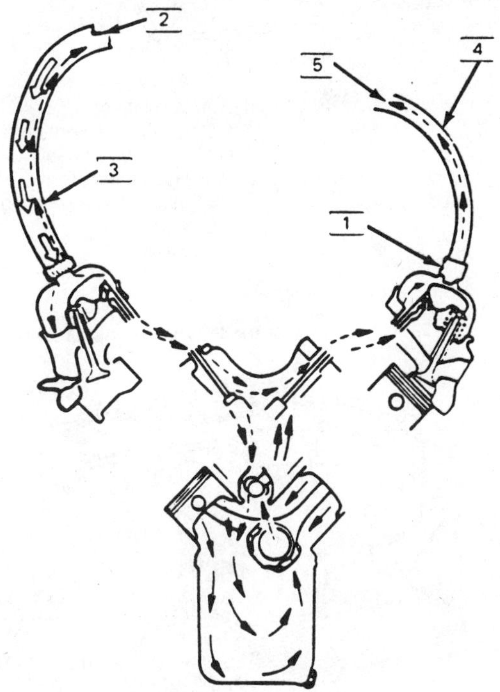

1. PCV valve
2. To throttle body
3. Crankcase vent hose
4. PCV valve hose
5. To intake manifold

View of the PCV and the exhaust gas flow

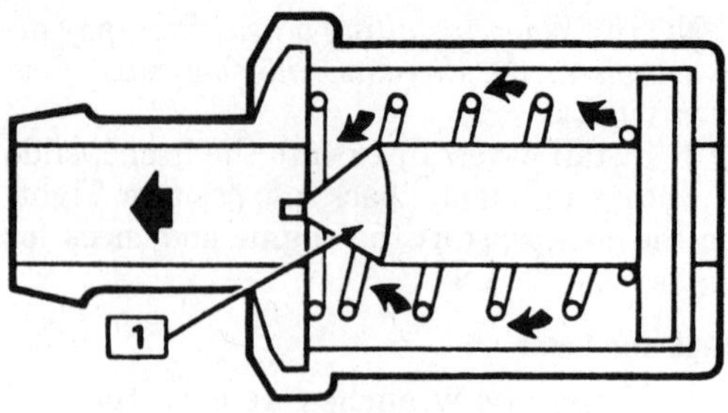

Sectional view of the PCV valve

tion hose. Replace the PCV valve and the PCV filter (located in the air cleaner on 1984 models) every 30,000 miles.

REMOVAL AND INSTALLATION

1. Pull the PCV from the valve cover grommet and disconnect it from the ventilation hose(s).

2. Inspect the valve for operation: (1) Shake it to see if the valve is free; (2) Blow through it (air will pass in one direction only).

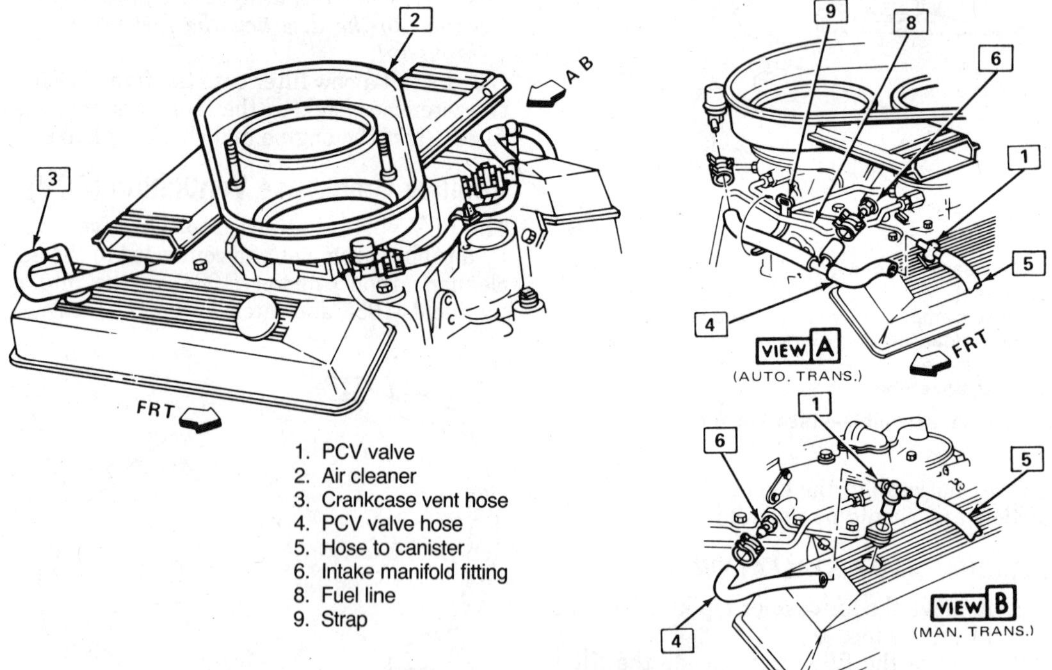

View of the PCV valve installation on the 1984 Cross-Fire Injection system

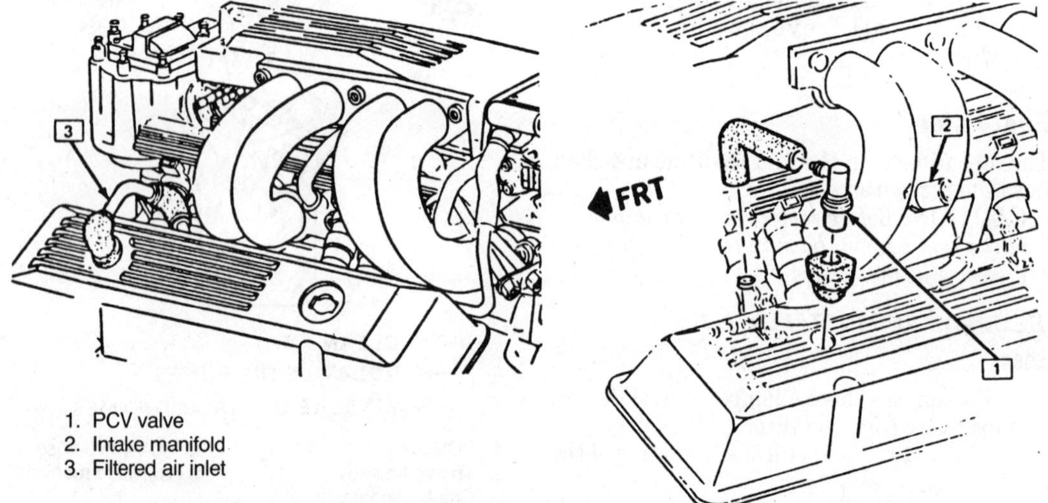

View of the PCV valve installation on the 1985 and later Throttle Port Injection system

NOTE: *When replacing the PCV valve, it is recommended to use a new one.*

3. To install, reverse the removal procedures.

Evaporative Canister

To limit gasoline vapor discharge into the air, this system is designed to trap fuel vapors, which normally escape from the fuel tank and the intake manifold. Vapor arrest is accomplished through the use of the charcoal canister. This canister absorbs fuel vapors and stores them until they can be removed to be burned in the engine. Removal of the vapors from the canister to the engine is accomplished by a computer controlled canister solenoid. In addition to the modifications and the canister, the fuel tank requires a non-vented gas cap. The domed fuel tank positions a vent high enough above the fuel to keep the vent pipe in the vapor at all times. The single vent pipe is routed directly to the canister. From the canister, the vapors are routed to the PCV system, where they will be burned during normal combustion.

REMOVAL AND INSTALLATION

1. Disconnect and mark the charcoal canister vent hoses.
2. Remove the canister-to-bracket bolt.
3. Lift the canister from the bracket.

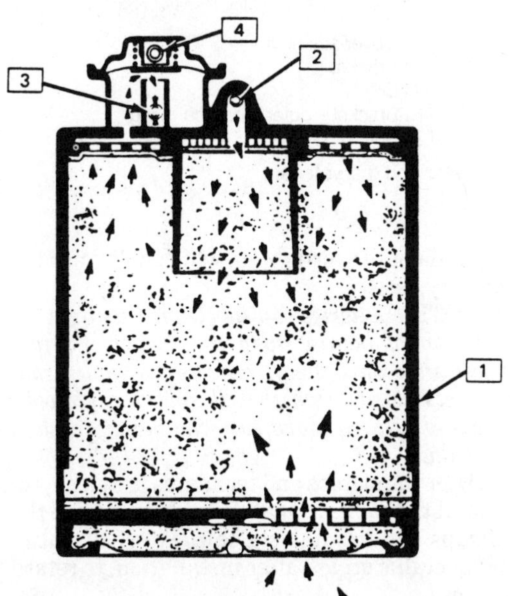

1. Charcoal canister
2. To fuel tank
3. Purge valve (to ported vacuum)
4. Control valve (to manifold vacuum)

Cross-sectional view of the charcoal canister

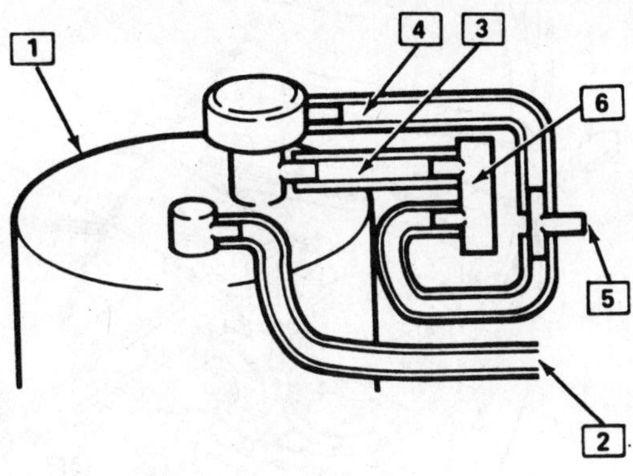

1. Charcoal canister
2. To fuel tank
3. To manifold (purge valve)
4. To manifold vacuum (control valve)
5. To manifold vacuum
6. Canister solenoid (ECM controlled)

View of the charcoal canister hoses and solenoid

NOTE: *When installing the canister, be sure that the hose connectors (on top of the canister) are facing the left fender.*

4. To install, reverse the removal procedures.

CHARCOAL CANISTER SOLENOID REPLACEMENT

1. Disconnect the negative battery cable.
2. Remove the solenoids retaining bolt, the cover and the solenoid.
3. Disconnect the electrical connector and the hoses from the solenoid.
4. To install, reverse the removal procedures.

FILTER REPLACEMENT

The filter in the bottom of the carbon canister which is located in the engine compartment should be removed and replaced every 30,000 miles or 24 months.

1. Refer to the "Charcoal Canister, Removal and Installation" procedures, in this section and remove the canister from it's bracket.
2. At the bottom of the canister, grasp the filter with your fingers and pull it out.
3. To install, use a new filter and reverse the removal procedures.

Battery

All Corvettes have a "Maintenance Free" battery as standard equipment, eliminating the need for fluid level checks and the possibility of specific gravity tests. Never-the-less, the battery does require some attention.

Once a year, the battery terminals and the cable clamps should be cleaned. Remove the

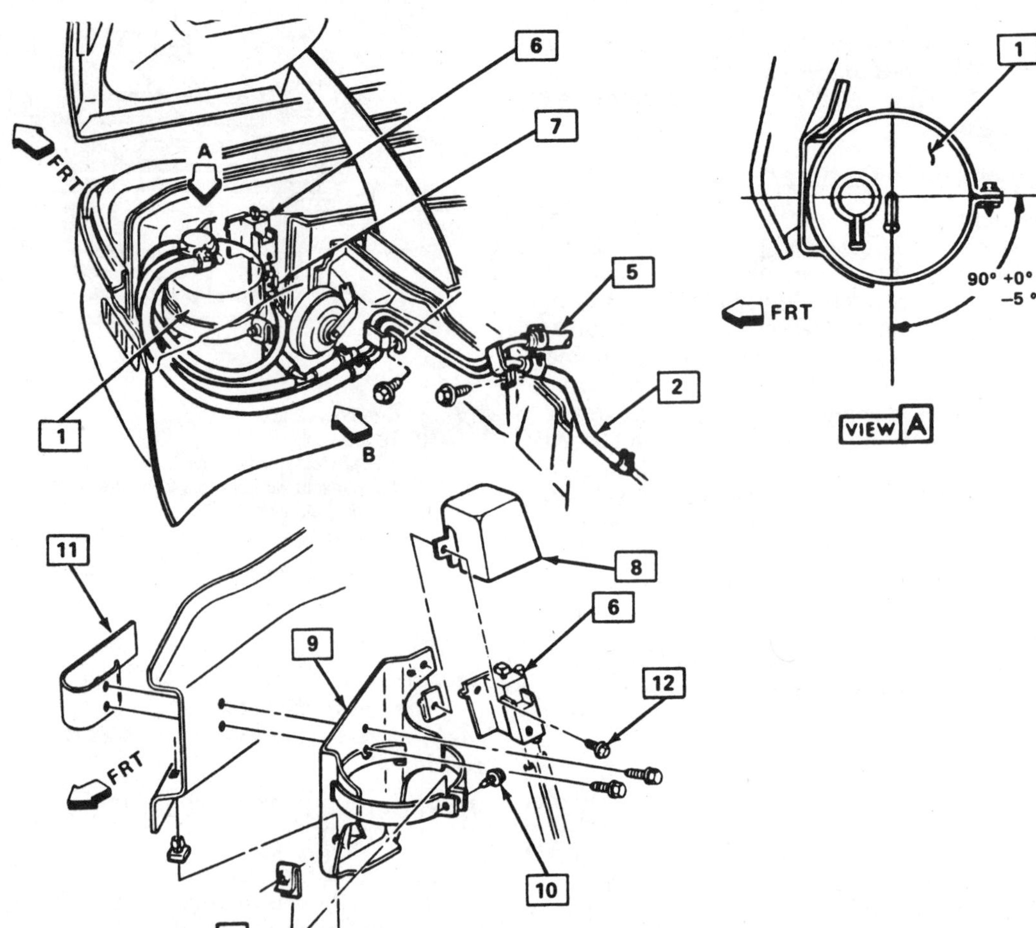

1. Fuel vapor canister
2. Hose—vapor pipe to fuel tank
5. Hose—to manifold
6. Fuel vapor canister solenoid
7. Frt. lamp harness—connector to solenoid
8. Cover solenoid
9. Bracket
10. Bolt
11. Bracket—outer lamp mounting
12. Bolt

Exploded view of the charcoal canister and the solenoid

side terminal bolts and the cables, negative cable first. Clean the cable clamps and the battery terminals with a wire brush until all corrosion, grease, etc. is removed and the metal is shiny. It is especially important to clean the inside of the clamp thoroughly, since a small deposit of foreign material or oxidation there will prevent a sound electrical connection and inhibit either starting or charging. Special tools are available for cleaning the side terminal clamps and terminals.

Before installing the cables, loosen the battery hold-down clamp, remove the battery and check the battery tray. Clear it of any debris and check it for soundness. Rust should be wire-brushed away and the metal given a coat of anti-rust paint. Replace the battery and tighten the hold-down clamp securely but be careful not to overtighten, which will crack the battery case.

NOTE: *Batteries can be cleaned using a solution of baking soda and water. Surface coatings on battery cases can actually conduct electricity which will cause a slight voltage drain, so make sure the battery case is clean.*

After the clamps and terminals are clean, reinstall the cables, negative cable last. Give the clamps and terminals a thin external coat of nonmetallic grease after installation, to retard corrosion.

Check the cables at the same time that the terminals are cleaned. If the cable insulation is cracked, broken or the ends are frayed, the cable should be replaced with a new one of the same length and gauge.

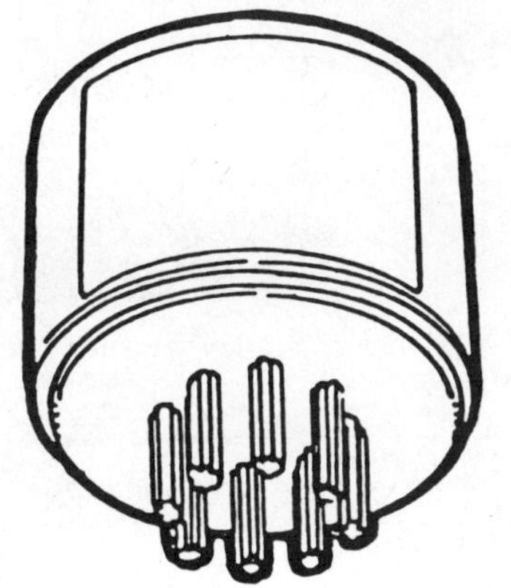

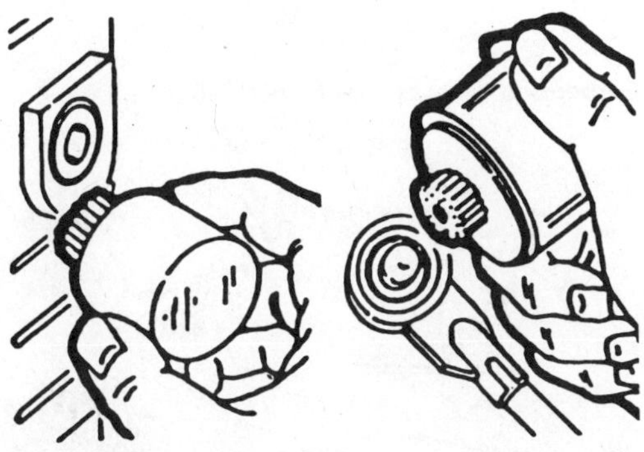

Using a special tool for cleaning the side terminals and clamps

NOTE: *Keep flames or sparks away from the battery. It gives off explosive hydrogen gas. The battery electrolyte contains sulphuric acid. If you should get any on your skin or in your eyes, flush the affected areas with plenty of clear water. If it lands in your eyes, seek medical help immediately.*

Testing the Maintenance-Free Battery

Maintenance-free batteries, do not require normal attention as far as fluid level checks are concerned. However, the terminals require periodic cleaning, which should be performed at least once a year.

The sealed-top battery cannot be checked for charge in the normal manner, since there is no provision for access to the electrolyte. To check the condition of the battery:

1. If the indicator eye on top of the battery is dark, the battery has enough fluid. If the eye is lit, the electrolyte fluid is too low and the battery must be replaced.
2. If a green dot appears in the middle of the eye, the battery is sufficiently charged. Proceed to Step 4. If no green dot is visible, charge the battery as in Step 3.
3. Charge the battery at this rate:

NOTE: *DO NOT charge the battery for more than 50 amp/hours. If the green dot appears or if the electrolyte squirts out of the vent hole, stop the charge and proceed to Step 4.*

It may be necessary to tip the battery from side-to-side to get the green dot to appear after charging.

CAUTION: *When charging the battery, the electrical system and control unit can be quickly damaged by improper connections, high-output battery chargers or incorrect service procedures.*

4. Connect a battery load tester and a voltmeter across the battery terminals (the battery cables should be disconnected from the battery). Apply a 300 amp load to the battery for 15 seconds to remove the surface charge. Remove the load.
5. Wait 15 seconds to allow the battery to recover. Apply the appropriate test load, as specified in the following chart:

BATTERY	TEST LOAD (AMPS)
70-315	150
70-355	170
75-500	250

A listing the various testing loads

Apply the load for 15 seconds while reading the voltage. Disconnect the load.

6. Check the results against the following chart. If the battery voltage is at or above the specified voltage for the temperature listed,

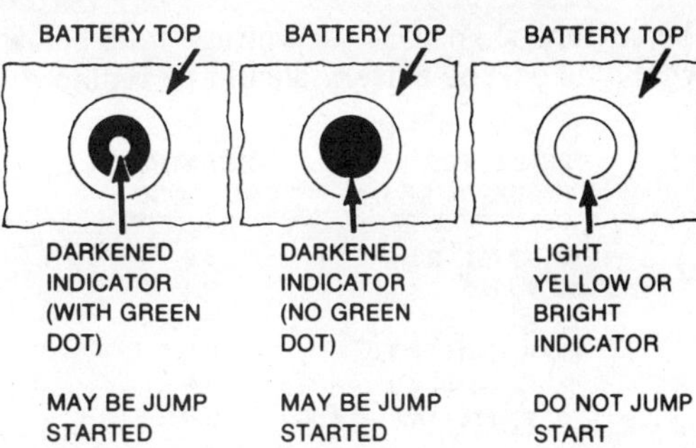

Maintenance-free batteries contain their own built-in hydrometer

Charging Rate Amps	Time
75	40 min
50	1 hr
25	2 hr
10	5 hr

Various charging rates

the battery is good. It the voltage falls below what's listed, the battery should be replaced.

ESTIMATED TEMPERATURE	MINIMUM VOLTAGE
70° F. (21° C.)	9.6
50° F. (10° C.)	9.4
30° F. (0° C.)	9.1
15° F. (−10° C.)	8.8
0° F. (−18° C.)	8.5
0° F. (BELOW: −18° C.)	8.0

Rating the battery voltage against temperature

Drive Belt

INSPECTION

Check the drive belt every 6,000 miles for evidence of wear such as cracking, fraying and incorrect tension. Determine the belt tension at a point halfway between the pulleys by pressing on the belt with moderate thumb pressure. The belt should deflect about ¼" at this point. If the deflection is found to be too much or too little, loosen the mounting bolts and make the adjustments.

Measuring fan belt tension

ADJUSTING TENSION

On all 1984 and later engines, a single serpentine belt is used to drive all accessories formerly driven with V-belts. Belt tension is maintained by a spring loaded tensioner which has the ability to maintain belt tension over a broad range of belt lengths. There is an indicator to make sure the tensioner is adjusted to within its operating range.

1. Loosen the tensioner pulley mounting bolt.

2. Using a ½" breaker bar and a Belt Tension Gauge tool No. BT-7825 or J-23600, insert the breaker bar into the square hole in the tensioner arm and the tension gauge between the alternator and the A.I.R. pump. Turn the breaker bar and adjust the drive belt tension to 120-140 lbs.

3. While holding the correct tension on the tensioner pulley, tighten the pulley mounting bolt. Remove the tensioner gauge.

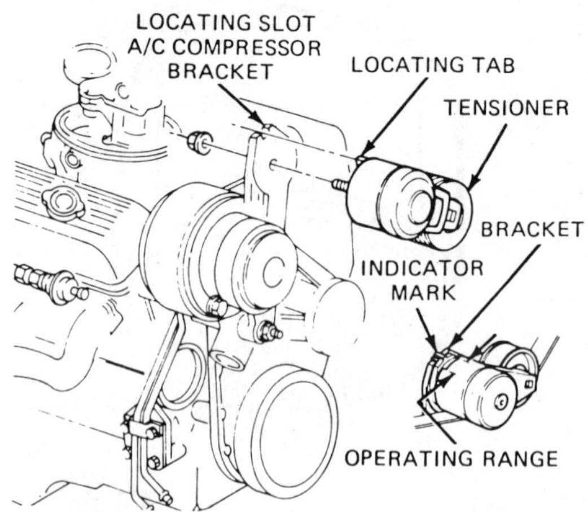

Serpentine drive belt tensioner—1984 and later

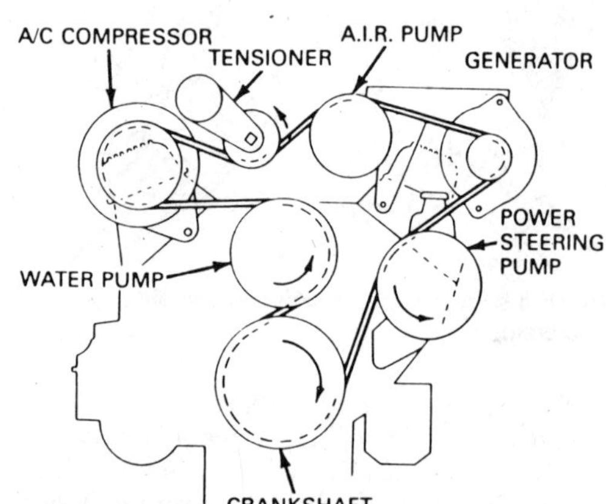

Serpentine drive belt installation—1984

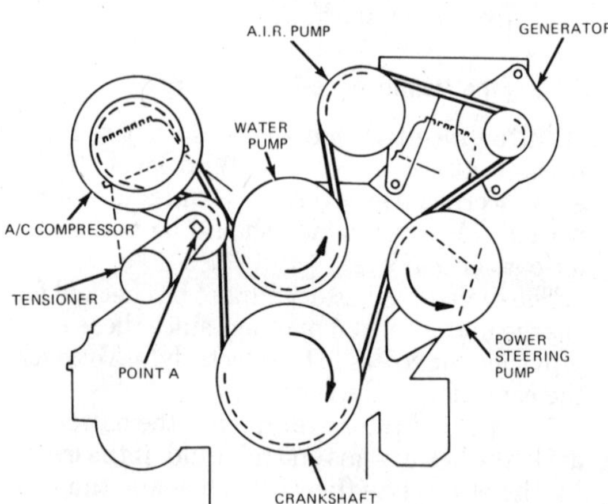

Serpentine drive belt installation—1985 and later

REMOVAL AND INSTALLATION

1. Loosen the tensioner pulley mounting bolt.

2. Turn the pulley to reduce the tension on the drive belt.

HOW TO SPOT WORN V-BELTS

V-Belts are vital to efficient engine operation—they drive the fan, water pump and other accessories. They require little maintenance (occasional tightening) but they will not last forever. Slipping or failure of the V-belt will lead to overheating. If your V-belt looks like any of these, it should be replaced.

Cracking or weathering

This belt has deep cracks, which cause it to flex. Too much flexing leads to heat build-up and premature failure. These cracks can be caused by using the belt on a pulley that is too small. Notched belts are available for small diameter pulleys.

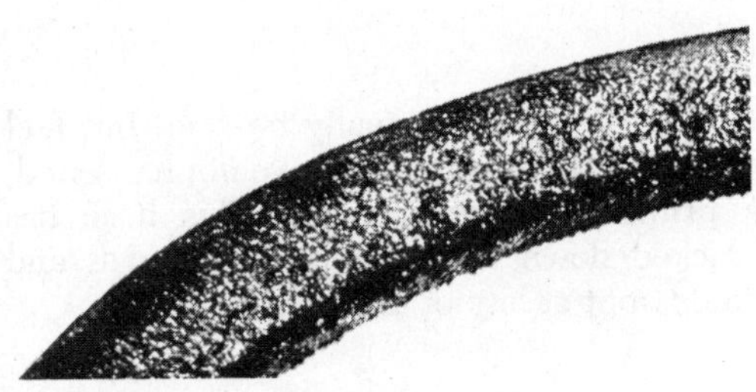

Softening (grease and oil)

Oil and grease on a belt can cause the belt's rubber compounds to soften and separate from the reinforcing cords that hold the belt together. The belt will first slip, then finally fail altogether.

Glazing

Glazing is caused by a belt that is slipping. A slipping belt can cause a run-down battery, erratic power steering, overheating or poor accessory performance. The more the belt slips, the more glazing will be built up on the surface of the belt. The more the belt is glazed, the more it will slip. If the glazing is light, tighten the belt.

Worn cover

The cover of this belt is worn off and is peeling away. The reinforcing cords will begin to wear and the belt will shortly break. When the belt cover wears in spots or has a rough jagged appearance, check the pulley grooves for roughness.

Separation

This belt is on the verge of breaking and leaving you stranded. The layers of the belt are separating and the reinforcing cords are exposed. It's just a matter of time before it breaks completely.

HOW TO SPOT BAD HOSES

Both the upper and lower radiator hoses are called upon to perform difficult jobs in an inhospitable environment. They are subject to nearly 18 psi at under hood temperatures often over 280°F., and must circulate nearly 7500 gallons of coolant an hour—3 good reasons to have good hoses.

Swollen hose

A good test for any hose is to feel it for soft or spongy spots. Frequently these will appear as swollen areas of the hose. The most likely cause is oil soaking. This hose could burst at any time, when hot or under pressure.

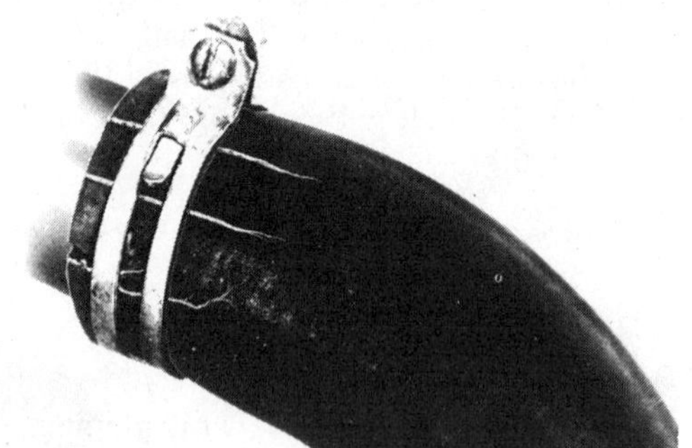

Cracked hose

Cracked hoses can usually be seen but feel the hoses to be sure they have not hardened; a prime cause of cracking. This hose has cracked down to the reinforcing cords and could split at any of the cracks.

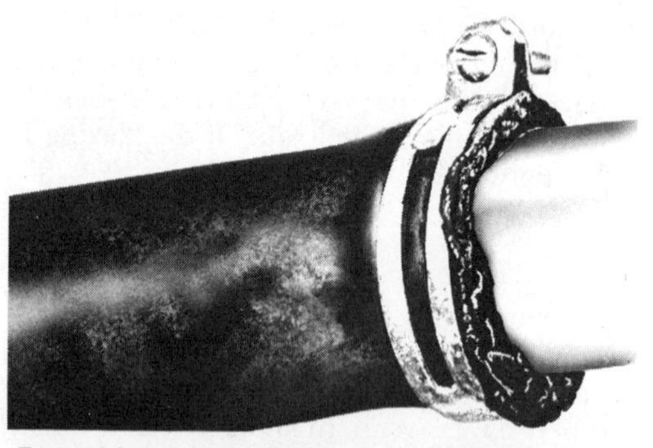

Frayed hose end (due to weak clamp)

Weakened clamps frequently are the cause of hose and cooling system failure. The connection between the pipe and hose has deteriorated enough to allow coolant to escape when the engine is hot.

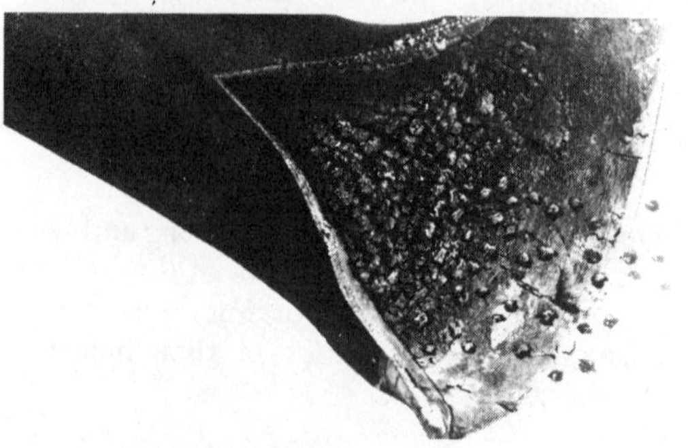

Debris in cooling system

Debris, rust and scale in the cooling system can cause the inside of a hose to weaken. This can usually be felt on the outside of the hose as soft or thinner areas.

3. Slip the drive belt from the tensioner pulley and remove it from the engine.

4. To install, reverse the removal procedures. Adjust the belt tension.

Hoses

The upper/lower radiator hoses and all of the heater hoses should be checked for deterioration, leaks and loose hose clamps every 15,000 miles.

REMOVAL AND INSTALLATION

1. Drain the cooling system.
2. Loosen the hose clamps at each end of the hose.
3. Working the hose back and forth, slide it off it's connection and then install a new hose, if necessary.
4. To install, reverse the removal procedures.

NOTE: *Always make sure that the hose clamps are beyond the bead and placed in the center of the clamping surface before tightening them.*

Air Conditioning

NOTE: *This book contains simple testing procedures for your vehicle's air conditioning system. More comprehensive testing, diagnosis and service procedures may be found in CHILTON'S GUIDE TO AIR CONDITIONING SERVICE AND REPAIR, book part number 7580, available at your local retailer.*

SAFETY PRECAUTIONS

There are two particular hazards associated with air conditioning systems and they both relate to the refrigerant gas:

1. The refrigerant gas is an extremely cold substance. When exposed to air, it will instantly freeze any surface it comes in contact with, including your eyes.
2. Although normally non-toxic, refrigerant gas becomes highly poisonous in the presence of an open flame. Inhalation of the vapor formed by burning refrigerant can be fatal. Keep all forms of fire (including cigarettes) well clear of the air conditioning system.

Any repair work to an air conditioning system should be left to a professional. DO NOT, under any circumstances, attempt to loosen or tighten any fittings or perform any work other than that outlined here.

CHECKING FOR OIL LEAKS

Refrigerant leaks show up as oily areas on the various components because the compressor oil is transported around the entire system along with the refrigerant. Look for oily spots on all the hoses and lines, especially on the hose and tubing connections. If there are oily deposits, the system may have a leak, have it checked by a qualified repairman.

NOTE: *A small area of oil on the front of the compressor is normal and no cause for alarm.*

CHECKING THE COMPRESSOR BELT

Refer to the "Drive Belts" section in this chapter.

KEEP THE CONDENSER CLEAR

Periodically inspect the front of the condenser for bent fins or foreign material (dirt, buts, leaves, etc.). If any cooling fins are bent, straighten them carefully with needle-nose pliers. You can remove any debris with a stiff bristle brush or hose.

OPERATE THE A/C SYSTEM PERIODICALLY

A lot of A/C problems can be avoided by simply running the air conditioner at least once a week regardless of the season. Simply let the system run for at least 5 minutes a week (even in the winter) and you'll keep the internal parts lubricated as well as preventing the hoses from hardening.

REFRIGERANT LEVEL CHECK

The first order of business when checking the sight glass is to find the sight glass. It will either be in the head of the receiver/drier or in one of the metal lines leading from the top of the receiver/drier. Once you've found it, wipe it clean and proceed as follows:

1. With the engine and the air conditioning system running, look for the flow of refrigerant through the sight glass. If the air conditioner is working properly, you'll be able to see a continuous flow of clear refrigerant through the sight glass, with perhaps an occasional bubble at very high temperatures.
2. Cycle the air conditioner ON and OFF to

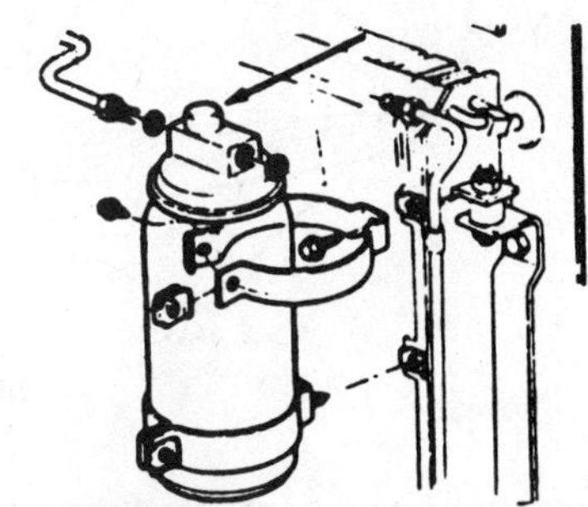

Air conditioning sight glass

make sure what you are seeing is clear refrigerant. Since the refrigerant is clear, it is possible to mistake a completely discharged system for one that is fully charged. Turn the system OFF and watch the sight glass. If there is refrigerant in the system, you'll see bubbles during the off cycle. If you observe no bubbles when the system is running and the air flow from the unit in the vehicle is delivering cold air, everything is OK.

3. If you observe bubbles in the sight glass while the system is operating, the system is low on refrigerant. Have it checked by a professional.

4. Oil streaks, in the sight glass are an indication of trouble. Most of the time, if you see oil in the sight glass, it will appear as a series of streaks, although occasionally it may be a solid stream of oil. In either case, it means that part of the charge has been lost.

Windshield Wipers

For maximum effectiveness and longest element life, the windshield and wiper blades should be kept clean. Dirt, tree sap, road tar and so on will cause streaking, smearing and blade deterioration if left on the glass. It is advisable to wash the windshield carefully with a commercial glass cleaner at least once a month. Wipe off the rubber blades with the wet rag, afterwards.

If the blades are found to be cracked, broken or torn, they should be replaced immediately. Replacement intervals will vary with usage, although ozone deterioration usually limits blade life to about one year. If the wiper pattern is smeared, streaked or if the blade chatters across the glass, the elements should be replaced. It is easiest and most sensible to replace the elements in pairs.

REFILL REPLACEMENT

1. The wiper blades are retained to the wiper arms by one of two methods:

   a. A press-type release tab, which, when depressed, allows the blade to be separated from the arm.

   b. A coil spring retainer. By inserting an appropriate tool on the top of the spring and pressing downward, the blade can be separated from the arm.

2. The rubber wiper element can be replaced separately from the blade, which is usually less expensive than replacing both blade and

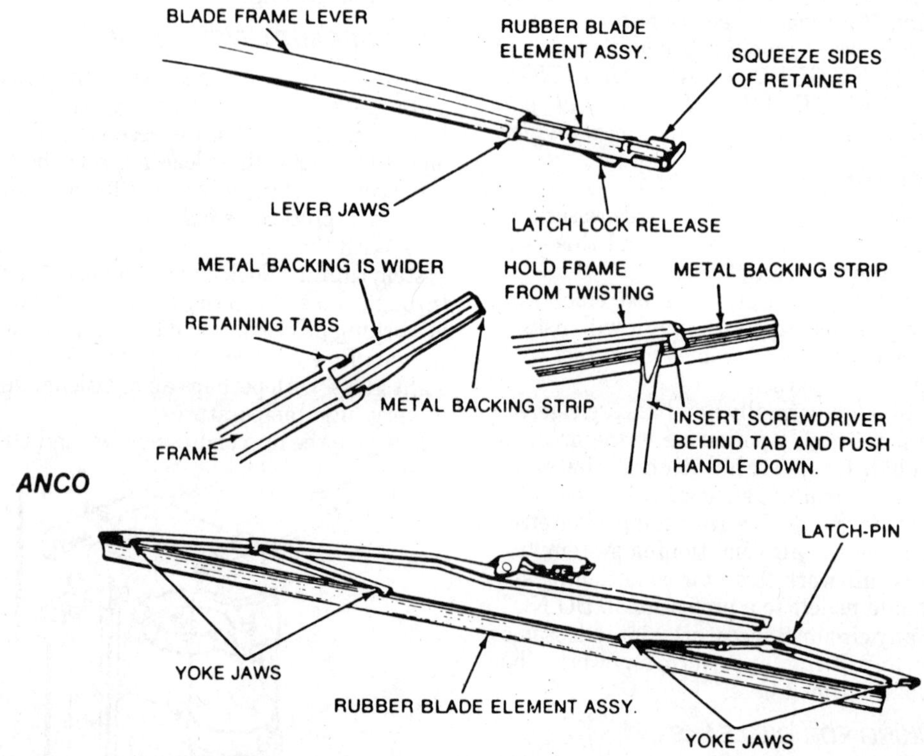

The rubber element can be changed without replacing the entire blade assembly; your vehicle may have either one of these types of blades

element. As with the blades, two methods are used to retain the rubber element to the blade:

a. A press-type button is used which, when depressed, releases the element, which can be slid off the blade.

b. A squeeze clip is used. Squeezing the clip allows the element to be pulled from the blade. Replacements are simply slid back into place. Be sure both arms are engaged.

Tires

TIRE ROTATION

Tire wear can be equalized by switching the position of the tire about every 6000 miles. Including a conventional spare in the rotation pattern can give up to 20% more tire life.

CAUTION: *DO NOT include the new "Space Saver®" or temporary spare tires in the rotation pattern.*

There are certain exceptions to tire rotation, however. Studded snow tires should not be rotated and radials should be kept on the same side of the vehicle (maintain the same direction of rotation). The belts on radial tires get set in a pattern. If the direction of rotation is reversed, it can cause rough ride and vibration.

NOTE: *When radials or studded snows are taken off the vehicle, mark them, so you can maintain the same direction of rotation.*

INFLATION PRESSURE

The inflation is the most ignored item of auto maintenance. Gasoline mileage can drop as much as 0.8% for every 1 pound/square inch (psi) of under inflation.

Two items should be a permanent fixture in every glove compartment: a tire pressure gauge and a tread depth gauge. Check the tire air pressure (including the spare) regularly with a pocket type gauge. Kicking the tires won't tell you a thing and the gauge on the service station air hose is notoriously inaccurate.

The tire pressures recommended for your vehicle are usually found on the glove-box door or in the owner's manual. Ideally, inflation pressure should be checked when the tires are cool. When the air becomes heated it expands and the pressure increases. Every 10° rise (or drop) in temperature means a difference of 1 psi, which also explains why the tire appears to lose air on a very cold night. When it is impossible to check the tires "cold," allow for pressure build-up due to heat. If the "hot" pressure exceeds the "cold" pressure by more than 15 psi, reduce your speed, load or both. Otherwise internal heat is created in the tire. When the heat approaches the temperature at which the tire was cured, during manufacture, the tread can separate from the body.

CAUTION: *Never counteract excessive pressure build-up by bleeding off air pressure (letting some air out). This will only further raise the tire operating temperature.*

Before starting a long trip with lots of luggage, you can add about 2–4 psi to the tires to make them run cooler but never exceed the maximum inflation pressure on the side of the tire.

TREAD DEPTH

All tires have 8 built-in tread wear indicator bars that show up as ½" wide smooth bands across the tire when $^{1}/_{16}$" of tread remains. The appearance of tread wear indicators means

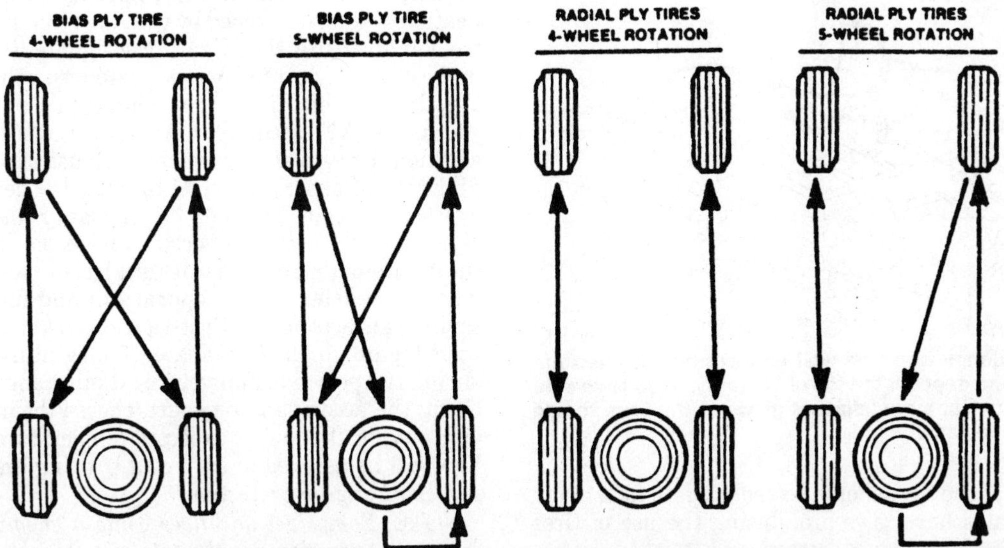

Tire rotation diagrams; note that radials should not be cross-switched

Tread wear indicators will appear when the tire is worn out

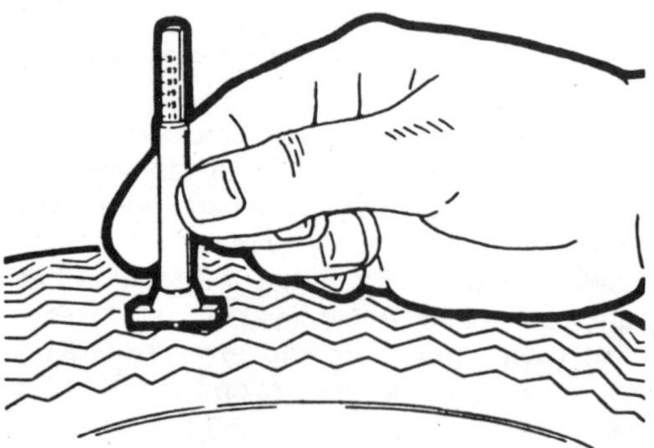

Tread depth can be checked with an inexpensive gauge

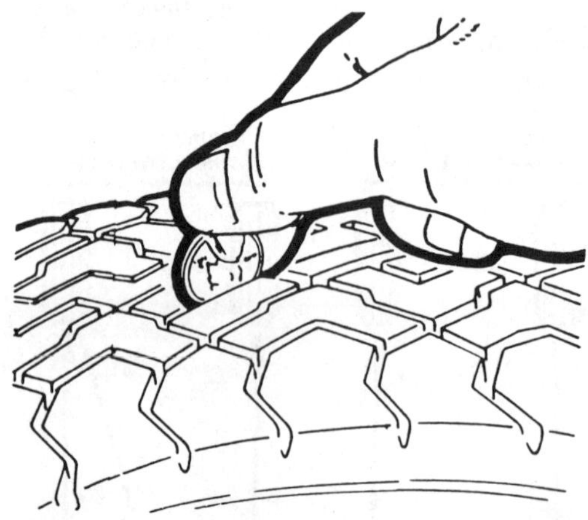

A penny works as well as anything for checking tread depth; if the top of Lincoln's head is visable in two or more adjacent grooves, the tires should be replaced

that the tires should be replaced. In fact, many states have laws prohibiting the use of tires with less than $^1/_{16}$" tread.

You can check your own tread depth with an inexpensive gauge or by using a Lincoln head penny. Slip the Lincoln penny into several into several tread grooves. If you can see the top of Lincoln's head in 2 adjacent grooves, the tires have less than $^1/_{16}$" tread left and should be replaced. You can measure snow tires in the same manner by using the "tails" side of the Lincoln penny. If you can see the top of the Lincoln memorial, it's time to replace the snow tires.

TIRE STORAGE

Store the tires at proper inflation pressures if they are mounted on wheels. All tires should be kept in a cool, dry place. If they are stored in the garage or basement, DO NOT let them stand on a concrete floor, set them on strips of wood.

ALUMINUM WHEELS

CAUTION: *If your vehicle has aluminum wheels, be very careful when using any type of cleaner on either the wheels or the tires. Read the label on the package of the cleaner to make sure that it will not damage aluminum.*

NOTE: *The optional 16 in. cast aluminum wheels on 1984 and later models are designated for right, left, front or rear installation depending on the cooling fins. Rear wheels are one inch wider than the front.*

FLUIDS AND LUBRICANTS

Fuel And Engine Oil

For 1984 and later vehicles, use ONLY SF rated oils. It is O.K. to use an SF oil with a combination rating, such as SF/CC. Under the classification system developed by the American Petroleum Institute, the SF rating designates the highest quality oil for use in passenger vehicles. In view of this, it is recommended that you use an SF rated oil in ANY Corvette. In addition, Chevrolet recommends the use of an SF/Energy Conserving oil. Oils labeled "Energy Conserving (or Saving)," "Fuel (Gas or Gasoline) Saving," etc. are recommended due to their superior lubricating qualities (less friction = easier engine operation) and fuel saving characteristics. Pick your oil viscosity with regard to the anticipated temperatures during the period before your next oil change. Using the accompanying chart, choose the oil viscosity for the lowest expected temperature. You will be assured of easy cold starting and sufficient engine protection.

NOTE: *Some fuel additives contain chemicals that can damage the catalytic converter and/or oxygen sensor. Read all of the labels*

Oil Viscosity Selection Chart

	Anticipated Temperature Range	SAE Viscosity
Multi-grade	Above 32°F	10W–40 10W–50 20W–40 20W–50 10W–30
	May be used as low as −10°F	10W–30 10W–40
	Consistently below 10°F	5W–20 5W–30
Single-grade	Above 32°F	30
	Temperature between +32°F and −10°F	10W

carefully before using any additive in the engine or fuel system.

Fuel should be selected for the brand and octane which performs best with your engine. Judge a gasoline by its ability to prevent "pinging," it's engine starting capabilities (cold and hot) and general all-weather performance. As far as the octane rating is concerned, refer to the "General Engine Specifications" chart in Chapter 3 to find your engine and its compression ratio. If the compression ratio is 9.0:1 or lower, in most cases a regular unleaded grade of gasoline can be used.

If the compression ratio is 9.0:1–10.0:1, use a premium grade of unleaded fuel. Vehicles with a compression ratio higher than 10.0:1 (check the engine chart) should use a premium unleaded fuel, if it is available.

CAUTION: *Unleaded fuel MUST be used in 1984 and later vehicles. Use of leaded fuel in these vehicles will render the catalytic converter ineffective and damage the oxygen sensor.*

Engine

The mileage figures given in your owner's manual are the Chevrolet recommended intervals for oil and filter changes assuming average driving. If your Corvette is being used under dusty, polluted or off-road conditions, change the oil and filter sooner than specified. The same thing goes for vehicles driven in stop-and-go traffic or only for short distances.

Always drain the oil after the engine has been running long enough to bring it to operating temperature. Hot oil will flow easier and more contaminants will be removed along with the oil than if it were drained cold. You will need a large capacity drain pan, which you can purchase at any store which sells automotive parts. Another necessity is a container for the used oil. You will find that plastic bottles, such as those used for bleach or fabric softener, make excellent storage jugs. One ecologically desirable solution to the used oil disposal problem is to find a cooperative gas station owner who will allow you to dump your used oil into his tank. Another is to keep the oil for use around the house as a preservative on fences, railroad tie borders, etc.

Chevrolet recommends changing both the oil and filter during the first oil change and the filter every other oil change thereafter. For the small price of an oil filter, it's cheap insurance to replace the filter at every oil change. One of the larger filter manufacturers points out in it's advertisements that not changing the filter leaves one quart of dirty oil in the engine. This claim is true and should be kept in mind when changing your oil.

OIL LEVEL CHECK

The engine oil level is checked with the dipstick, which is located the right-side of the engine.

NOTE: *The oil should be checked before the engine is started or 5 minutes after the engine has been shut OFF. This gives the oil time to drain back to the oil pan and prevents an inaccurate oil level reading.*

Remove the dipstick from its tube, wipe it clean and insert it back into the tube. Remove it again and observe the oil level. It should be maintained between the "Full" and "Add" marks without going above "Full" or below "Add."

CAUTION: *DO NOT overfill the crankcase. It may result in oil-fouled spark plugs, oil leaks caused by oil seal failure or engine damage due to foaming of the oil.*

OIL AND FILTER CHANGE

1. Operate the engine until it reaches normal operating temperature.
2. Raise and support the front of the vehicle jackstands.
3. Slide a drain pan of at least 6 quarts capacity under the oil pan.
4. Loosen the drain plug. Turn it out by hand by keeping an inward pressure on the plug as you unscrew it. Oil won't escape past the threads and you can remove it without being burned by hot oil.

NOTE: *Dispose of waste oil properly. Don't pollute the environment. Avoid prolonged skin contact with used oil directly or from oil-saturated clothing.*

5. Allow the oil to drain completely and then install the drain plug. Don't overtighten the plug or you'll be buying a new pan or a trick replacement plug for damaged threads.

6. Using a strap wrench, remove the oil filter. Keep in mind that it's holding about one quart of dirty, hot oil.
7. Empty the old filter into the drain pan and dispose of the filter.
8. Using a clean rag, wipe off the filter adapter on the engine block. Be sure that the rag doesn't leave any lint which could clog an oil passage.
9. Coat the rubber gasket on the filter with fresh oil. Spin it onto the engine by hand. When the gasket touches the adapter surface give it another ½–¾ turn; no more or you'll squash the gasket and cause it to leak.
10. Refill the engine with the correct amount of new oil. See the "Capacities" chart.
11. Crank the engine over several times and then start it. If the oil pressure gauge shows zero, shut the engine OFF and find out what's wrong.
12. If the oil pressure is OK and there are no leaks, shut the engine OFF and lower the vehicle.
13. Wait a few minutes and check the oil level. Add oil, as necessary, to bring the level up to the Full mark.

Manual Transmission With Automatic Overdrive – 1985 And Later

FLUID RECOMMENDATIONS

NOTE: *The 4-speed overdrive transmission uses two types of fluid.*

Main Housing

Fill the main transmission housing with SAE-80W-GL5 or SAE-80W-90-GL5 multipurpose gear lubricant.

Overdrive Housing

Fill the overdrive (extension) housing with Dexron II® automatic transmission fluid.

LEVEL CHECK

Main Housing

Remove the filler plug from the passenger's-side of the transmission (the upper plug if the transmission has two plugs). The oil should be level with the bottom edge of the filler hole. This should be checked at least once every 6,000 miles and more often if any leakage or seepage is observed.

Overdrive Housing

Remove the filler plug from the driver's-side of the overdrive (extension) housing. The oil should be level with the bottom edge of the filler hole. The fluid should be changed every 30,000 miles and refilled more often if any leakage or seepage is observed.

DRAIN AND REFILL

Main Housing

Under normal conditions, the transmission fluid should not be changed.

1. Raise and support the vehicle on jackstands.
2. Place a fluid catch pan under the transmission.
3. Remove the bottom plug and drain the fluid.
4. Install the bottom plug and refill the transmission housing.

Overdrive Housing and Filter

1. Raise and support the vehicle on jackstands.
2. Place a fluid catch pan under the overdrive housing.
3. Remove the oil pan bolts from the front and side of the pan. Loosen the rear bolts 4 turns. Using a small pry bar, carefully pry the front of the pan loose and drain the fluid.
4. Remove the rear bolts and the pan, then drain the remaining fluid.
5. Using solvent, clean the pan and blow it dry.
6. Remove the oil filter from the overdrive housing.
7. Using a putty knife, clean the gasket mounting surfaces.
8. To install, use a new filter and RTV sealant, then reverse the removal procedures. Torque the oil pan bolts to 6–8 ft. lbs. Refill the overdrive housing.

NOTE: *When installing the oil pan, install it when the sealant is still wet.*

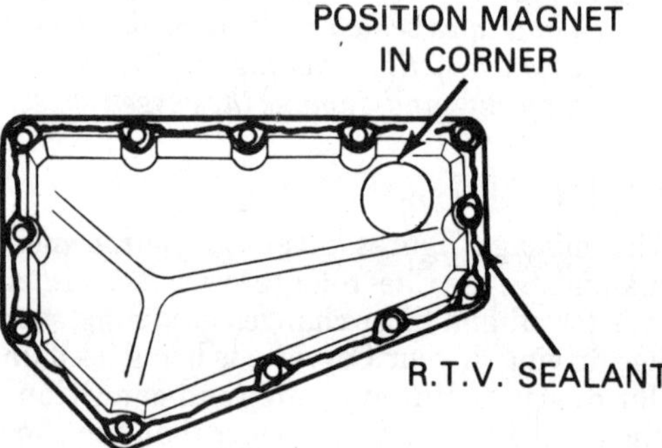

View of the 4-speed manual transmission's overdrive housing oil pan

Automatic Transmission

FLUID RECOMMENDATIONS

When adding fluid or refilling the transmission, use Dexron II® Automatic Transmission Fluid.

LEVEL CHECK

Before checking the fluid level of the transmission, drive the vehicle for at least 15 miles to warm the fluid.

1. Place the vehicle on a level surface, apply the parking brake and block the front wheels.
2. Start the engine and move the selector through each range, then place it in Park.

   NOTE: *When moving the selector through each range, DO NOT race the engine.*

3. With the engine running at a low idle, remove the transmission's dipstick to check the fluid level.
4. The level should be at the Full Hot mark of the dipstick. If not, add fluid.

   CAUTION: *DO NOT overfill the transmission, damage to the seals could occur. Use Dexron®II Automatic Transmission Fluid. One pint raises the level from "Add" to "Full."*

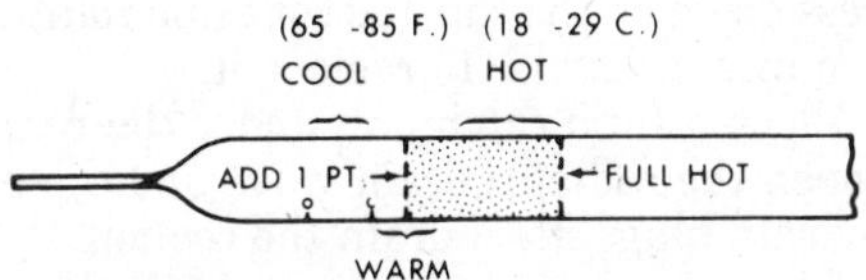

Automatic transmission dipstick

DRAIN AND REFILL

The vehicle should be driven 15 miles to warm the transmission fluid before the pan is removed.

NOTE: *The fluid should be drained while the transmission is warm.*

1. Raise and support the front of vehicle on jackstands.
2. Place a drain pan under the transmission pan.
3. Remove the pan bolts from the front and the sides, then loosen the rear bolts 4 turns.
4. Using a small pry bar, pry the pan from the transmission. This will allow the pan to partially drain. Remove the remaining pan bolts and lower the pan from the transmission.

   NOTE: *If the transmission fluid is dark or or has a burnt smell, transmission damage is indicated. Have the transmission checked professionally.*

5. Empty the pan, remove the gasket material and clean with a solvent.
6. Using a putty knife, clean gasket mounting surfaces.
7. To install the oil pan, use a new gasket and sealant, then reverse the removal procedures. Torque the pan bolts to 8 ft. lbs. in a criss-cross pattern.
8. Using Dexron®II Automatic Transmission Fluid, add it through the filler tube. See the Capacities Chart to determine the proper amount of fluid to be added.

   CAUTION: *DO NOT OVERFILL the transmission. Foaming of the fluid and subsequent transmission damage due to slippage will result.*

9. With the gearshift lever in PARK, start the engine and let it idle. DO NOT race the engine.
10. Apply the parking brake and move the gearshift lever through each position. Return the lever to PARK and check the fluid level with the engine idling. The level should be between the two dimples on the dipstick, about ¼" below the ADD mark. Add fluid, if necessary.
11. Check the fluid level after the vehicle has been driven enough to thoroughly warm the transmission.

PAN AND FILTER SERVICE

1. Refer to the "Drain and Refill" procedures in this section and remove the oil pan.
2. Remove the screen and the filter from the valve body.
3. Install a new filter using a new gasket or O-ring.

   NOTE: *If the transmission uses a filter having a fully exposed screen, it may be cleaned and reused.*

4. To install the oil pan, use a new gasket and sealant, then reverse the removal procedures. Torque the pan bolts to 8 ft. lbs. in a criss-cross pattern. Refill the transmission.

Drive Axle

Two types of rear axles are used: Model 36 (7⅞" ring gear) for automatic transmissions and Model 44 (8½" ring gear) for manual transmissions.

FLUID RECOMMENDATIONS

CAUTION: *Never use standard differential lubricant in a positraction differential.*

Always use GM Rear Axle Fluid No. 1052271. Before refilling the rear axle, add 4 ounces of GM Fluid No. 1052358.

LEVEL CHECK

The lubricant level should be checked at each chassis lubrication and maintained at the bottom of the filler plug hole. Special positraction oil must be used in this differential.

1. Raise and support the vehicle on jackstands. Be sure that the vehicle is level.
2. Remove the filler plug, located at the right-side of the differential carrier.

3. Check the fluid level, it should be level with the bottom of the filler plug hole, add fluid (if necessary).
4. Replace the filler plug.

DRAIN AND REFILL

Refer to "Fluid Recommendations" in this section for information on when to change the fluid.

1. Run the vehicle until the lubricant reaches operating temperature.
2. Raise and support the vehicle on jackstands. Be sure that the vehicle is level.
3. Using a floor jack, support the drive axle. Position a drain pan under the rear axle.
4. Remove the carrier cover beam from the rear of the drive axle and drain the lubricant.
5. Using a putty knife, clean the gasket mounting surfaces.
6. To install, use a new gasket, sealant and reverse the removal procedures.
7. Torque the carrier beam cover-to-rear axle bolts in a criss-cross pattern to 21–24 ft. lbs. (Model 36) or 32–38 ft. lbs. (Model 44). Using a suction gun or a squeeze bulb, install the fluids through the filler plug hole. Install the filler plug.

Cooling System

At least once every 2 years, the engine cooling system should be inspected, flushed, and refilled with fresh coolant. If the coolant is left in the system too long, it loses its ability to prevent rust and corrosion. If the coolant has too much water, it won't protect against freezing.

FLUID RECOMMENDATIONS

Using a good quality of ethylene glycol antifreeze (one that will not effect aluminum), mix it with water until a 50–50 antifreeze solution is attained.

LEVEL CHECK

NOTE: *When checking the coolant level, the radiator need not be removed, simply check the coolant tank.*

Check the coolant recovery bottle (with the built-in dipstick). With the engine Cold, the coolant should be at the "Full Cold" mark on the dipstick (tank ¼ full). With the engine warm, the coolant should be at the "Full Warm" mark on the dipstick (tank ½ full). If necessary, add fluid to the recovery bottle.

DRAIN AND REFILL

CAUTION: *To avoid injuries from scalding fluid and steam, DO NOT remove the radiator cap while the engine and radiator are still HOT.*

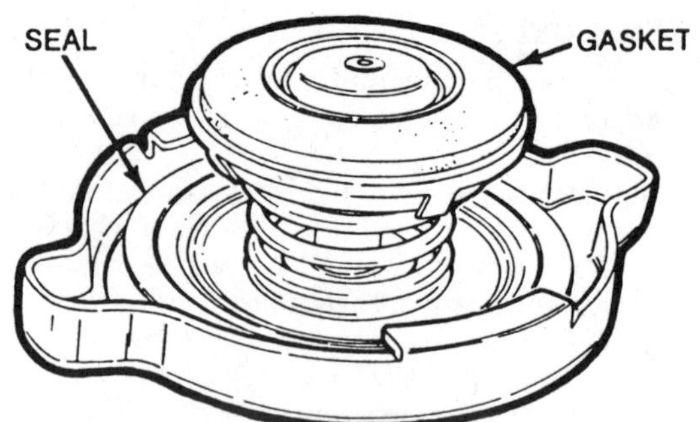

Check the radiator cap's rubber gasket and metal seal for deterioration at least once a year

1. When the engine is cool, remove the radiator cap using the following procedures.
   a. Slowly rotate the cap counterclockwise to the detent.
   b. If any residual pressure is present, WAIT until the hissing noise stops.
   c. After the hissing noise has ceased, press down on the cap and continue rotating it counterclockwise to remove it.
2. Place a fluid catch pan under the radiator, open the radiator drain valve and the engine drain plugs, then drain the coolant.
3. Close the drain valve and install the engine drain plugs.
4. Empty the coolant reservoir and flush it.
5. Using the correct mixture of antifreeze, fill the radiator to the bottom of the filler neck and the coolant tank to the Full mark.
6. Install the radiator cap (make sure that the arrows align with the overflow tube).
7. Run the engine until it reaches the operating temperatures, allow it to cool, then check the fluid level and add fluid (if necessary).

FLUSHING AND CLEANING THE SYSTEM

1. Refer to the "Drain and Refill" procedures in this section, then drain the cooling system.
2. Close the drain valve and install the engine drain plugs, then add sufficient water to the cooling system.
3. Run the engine, then drain and refill the system. Perform this procedure several times, until the fluid (drained from the system) is clear.
4. Empty the coolant reservoir and flush it.
5. Using the correct mixture of antifreeze, fill the radiator to the bottom of the filler neck and the coolant tank to the Full mark.
6. Install the radiator cap (make sure that the arrows align with the overflow tube).

Master Cylinder

FLUID RECOMMENDATIONS

Use only heavy-duty Delco Supreme 11 or DOT-3 brake fluid.

LEVEL CHECK

The brake fluid level should be inspected every 6 months.

1. Remove the master cylinder reservoir caps.
2. The fluid should be ¼" from top of the reservoir, if necessary, add fluid.
3. Replace the reservoir caps.

Power Steering Pump

The power steering pump reservoir is located at the front left-side of the engine.

FLUID RECOMMENDATIONS

Use GM Power Steering Fluid No. 10500176 or equivalent.

NOTE: *Avoid using automatic transmission fluid in the power steering unit, except in an emergency.*

LEVEL CHECK

The power steering fluid should be checked at least every 6 months. There is a Cold and a Hot mark on the dipstick. The fluid should be check when the engine is warm and turned OFF. If necessary, add fluid to the power steering pump reservoir.

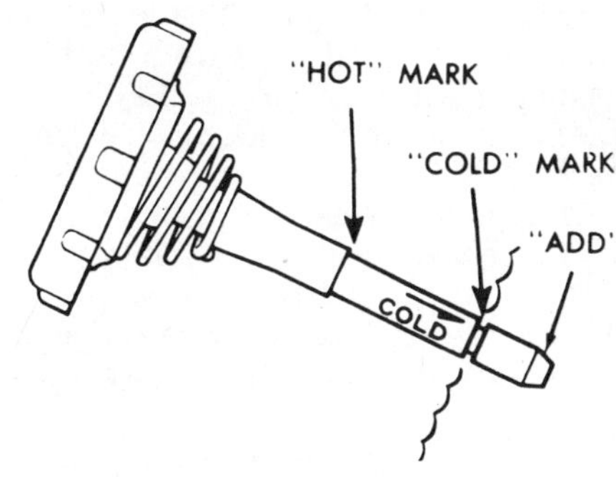

Power steering dipstick

Hydraulic Clutch

FLUID RECOMMENDATIONS

Use only heavy-duty Delco Supreme 11 or DOT-3 brake fluid.

LEVEL CHECK

The hydraulic clutch reservoir should be checked at least every 6 months.

Chassis Greasing

Chassis greasing can be performed with a pressurized grease gun or it can be performed at home by using a hand-operated grease gun. Wipe the grease fittings clean before greasing in order to prevent the possibility of forcing any dirt into the component.

Body Lubrication

HOOD LATCH AND HINGES

Clean the latch surfaces and apply clean engine oil to the latch pilot bolts and the spring anchor. Use the engine oil to lubricate the hood hinges as well. Use a chassis grease to lubricate all the pivot points in the latch release mechanism.

DOOR HINGES

The gas tank filler door, car door and rear hatch hinges should be wiped clean and lubricated with clean engine oil. Silicone spray also works well on these parts but must be applied more often. Use engine oil to lubricate the hatch lock mechanism, the lock bolt and striker. The door lock cylinders can be lubricated easily with a shot of silicone spray or one of the many dry penetrating lubricants commercially available.

PARKING BRAKE LINKAGE

Use chassis grease on the parking brake cable where it contacts the guides, links, levers and pulleys. The grease should be a water resistant one for durability under the vehicle.

ACCELERATOR LINKAGE

Lubricate the throttle body lever, the cable and the accelerator pedal lever (at the support inside the vehicle) with clean engine oil.

TRANSMISSION SHIFT LINKAGE

Lubricate the shift linkage with water resistant chassis grease which meets GM specification No. 6031M or equivalent.

Wheel Bearings

Once every 30,000 miles, clean and repack wheel bearings with a GM Wheel Bearing Grease No. 1051344 or equivalent. Use only enough grease to completely coat the rollers. Remove any excess grease from the exposed surface of the hub and seal.

NOTE: *The front wheel bearings are not serviceable. When the wheel bearing needs to be replaced, replace the hub/wheel bearing assembly as a unit.*

REMOVAL AND INSTALLATION

1. Raise and support the front of the vehicle on jackstands.
2. Remove the tire/wheel assembly.
3. Remove the hub/bearing assembly-to-steering knuckle bolts and the assembly from the vehicle.
4. To install, use a new hub/bearing assembly and reverse the removal procedures.

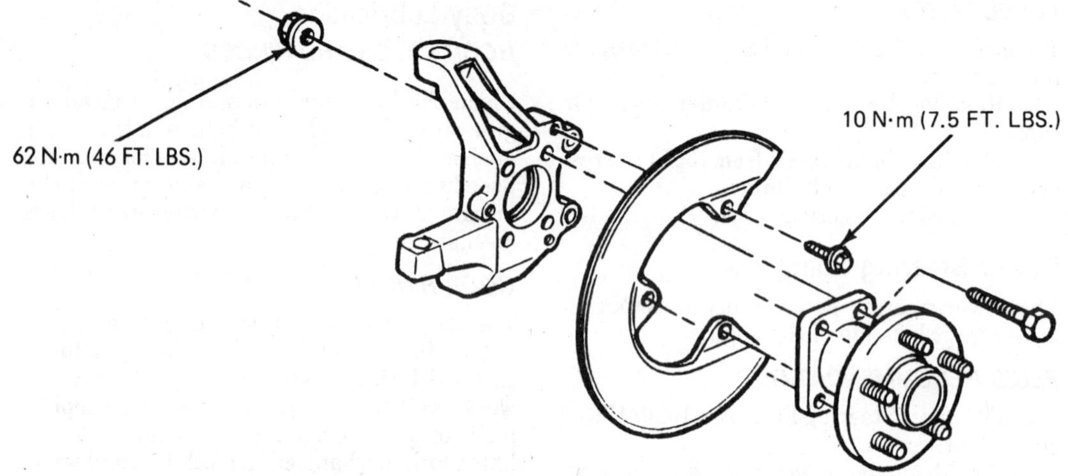

Exploded view of the hub/wheel bearing assembly

Torque the hub/bearing assembly-to-steering knuckle bolts to 46 ft. lbs.

PUSHING AND TOWING

DO NOT push or tow your Corvette to start it. Unusually high catalytic converter and exhaust system temperatures may result, which under extreme conditions may ignite the interior floor-covering material above the converter.

NOTE: *When towing your Corvette, DO NOT tow it with all four wheels on the ground.*

Corvettes may be towed at speeds up to 35 mph and distances not over 50 miles with the driveshaft in place, if no engine/drive-line damage is present. If engine/drive-line damage is known or suspected, the driveshaft should be disconnected before towing.

To be sure that no damage will occur to your vehicle, consult any GM dealer or professional tow truck service for towing instructions.

NOTE: *To avoid damage to the fiberglass springs when raising the vehicle, DO NOT allow the lifting equipment to come into contact with the springs.*

JUMP STARTING

The following procedure is recommended by the manufacturer. Be sure that the booster battery is a 12 volt with a negative ground.

CAUTION: *DO NOT attempt this procedure on a frozen battery. It will probably explode. DO NOT attempt it on a sealed Delco Freedom battery showing a light color in the charge indicator. Be certain to observe correct polarity connections. Failure to do so will result in almost immediate alternator and regulator destruction. Never allow the jumper cable ends to touch each other.*

1. Position the 2 vehicles so that they are not touching. Set the parking brake and place the automatic transmission in Park or the manual transmission in Neutral. Turn off the lights, heater and other electrical loads.
2. Remove the vent caps from both the booster and discharged battery. Lay a cloth over the open vent cells of each battery. This is not necessary on batteries equipped with sponge type flame arrestor caps and it is not possible on sealed Freedom batteries.
3. Attach one cable to the positive (+) terminal of the booster battery and the other end to the positive terminal of the discharged battery.
4. Attach one end of the remaining cable to the negative (-) terminal of the booster battery and the other end to the alternator bracket (about 18 inches from the discharged battery). DO NOT attach to the negative terminal of discharged batteries.
5. Start the engine of the vehicle with the booster battery. Start the engine of the vehicle with the discharged battery. If the engine will no start, disconnect the batteries as soon as possible. If this is not done, the two batteries will soon reach a state of equilibrium, with both too weak to start an engine. This will not be a problem if the engine of the booster vehicle is kept running fast enough. Lengthy cranking can overheat and damage the starter.
6. Reverse the above steps to disconnect the booster and discharged batteries. Be certain to remove negative connections first.
7. Dispose of the cloths. They may have battery acid on them.

JUMP STARTING A DEAD BATTERY

The chemical reaction in a battery produces explosive hydrogen gas. This is the safe way to jump start a dead battery, reducing the chances of an accidental spark that could cause an explosion.

Jump Starting Precautions

1. Be sure both batteries are of the same voltage.
2. Be sure both batteries are of the same polarity (have the same grounded terminal).
3. Be sure the vehicles are not touching.
4. Be sure the vent cap holes are not obstructed.
5. Do not smoke or allow sparks around the battery.
6. In cold weather, check for frozen electrolyte in the battery. Do not jump start a frozen battery.
7. Do not allow electrolyte on your skin or clothing.
8. Be sure the electrolyte is not frozen.

CAUTION: *Make certain that the ignition key, in the vehicle with the dead battery, is in the OFF position. Connecting cables to vehicles with on-board computers will result in computer destruction if the key is not in the OFF position.*

Jump Starting Procedure

1. Determine voltages of the two batteries; they must be the same.
2. Bring the starting vehicle close (they must not touch) so that the batteries can be reached easily.
3. Turn off all accessories and both engines. Put both cars in Neutral or Park and set the handbrake.
4. Cover the cell caps with a rag—do not cover terminals.
5. If the terminals on the run-down battery are heavily corroded, clean them.
6. Identify the positive and negative posts on both batteries and connect the cables in the order shown.
7. Start the engine of the starting vehicle and run it at fast idle. Try to start the car with the dead battery. Crank it for no more than 10 seconds at a time and let it cool off for 20 seconds in between tries.
8. If it doesn't start in 3 tries, there is something else wrong.
9. Disconnect the cables in the reverse order.
10. Replace the cell covers and dispose of the rags.

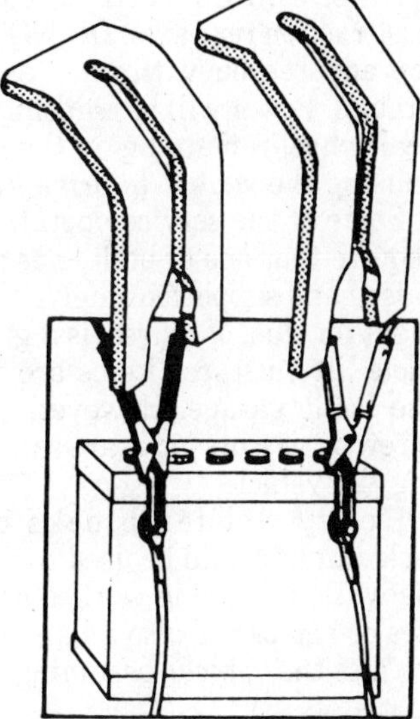

Side terminal batteries occasionally pose a problem when connecting jumper cables. There frequently isn't enough room to clamp the cables without touching sheet metal. Side terminal adaptors are available to alleviate this problem and should be removed after use.

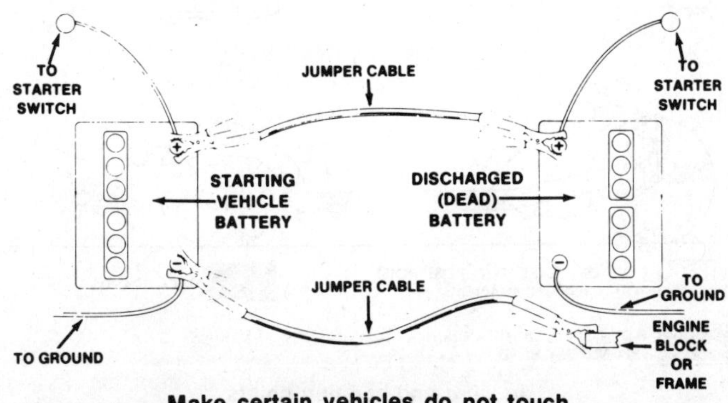

Make certain vehicles do not touch

This hook-up for negative ground cars only

CAUTION: *The use of any "hot shot" type of jumper system in excess of 12 volts can damage the electronic control units or cause the discharged battery to explode.*

JACKING

The jack supplied with the Corvette was meant for changing tires. It was not meant to support a vehicle while you crawl under it and work. Whenever it it necessary to get under a vehicle to perform service operations, always be sure that it is adequately supported, preferably by jackstands at the proper points. Always block the wheels when changing tires.

Since the Corvette is equipped with a positraction rear axle, DO NOT run the engine for any reason with one rear wheel off the ground. Power will be transmitted through the rear wheel remaining on the ground, possibly causing the vehicle to drive itself off the jack.

Some of the service operations in this book require that one or both ends of the vehicle be raised and supported safely. The best arrangement for this, of course, is a grease pit or a vehicle lift but these items are seldom found in the home garage. However, small hydraulic, screw or scissors jacks are satisfactory for raising the vehicle.

Heavy wooden blocks or adjustable jackstands should be used to support the vehicle while it is being worked on. Drive-on trestles or ramps are also a handy and a safe way to raise the vehicle, assuming their capacity is adequate. These can be bought or constructed from suitable heavy timbers or steel.

In any case, it is always best to spend a little extra time to make sure that your Corvette is lifted and supported safely.

CAUTION: *Concrete blocks are not recommended. They may crumble if the load is not evenly distributed. Boxes and milk crates of any description must not be used. Shake the vehicle a few times to make sure the jackstands are securely supporting the weight before crawling under.*

HOW TO BUY A USED CAR

Many people believe that a two or three year old used vehicle is a better buy than a new vehicle. This may be true. The new vehicle suffers the heaviest depreciation in the first two years but is not old enough to present a lot of costly repair problems. Whatever the age of the used vehicle you might want to buy, this section and a little patience will help you select one that should be safe and dependable.

TIPS

1. First decide what model you want and how much you want to spend.
2. Check the used car lots and your local newspaper ads. Privately owned vehicles are usually less expensive, however you will not get a warranty that, in most cases, comes with a used vehicle purchased from a lot.

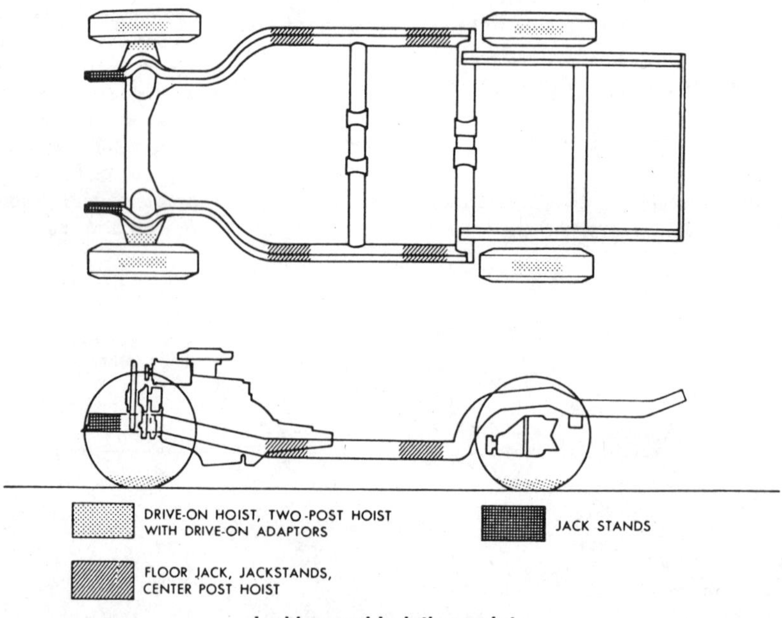

Jacking and hoisting points

Maintenance Intervals

Maintenance	1984 and later
Air Cleaner (Check and Clean) Paper element ①	 30,000 mi (replace)
PCV Valve (Replace)	30,000 mi.
Evaporative Canister Replace filter	 24 mo/30,000 mi.
Engine Oil Check Replace	 each fuel stop 12 mo/7500 mi. ④
Engine Oil Filter (Replace)	every other oil change
Fuel Filter Replace	 15,000 mi.
Powerglide Transmission Fluid Check Replace	—
Turbo Hydra-Matic Fluid & Filter Check fluid Change fluid Replace	 each eng. oil change 100,000 mi. ③ 100,000 mi. ③
Manual Transmissions (All) Check lubricant Add lubricant	 7500 mi. as necessary
Battery Lubricate terminal felt washer Clean terminals Check electrolyte level	 — as necessary not necessary
Coolant level	each fuel stop
Rear Axle Level Check Replace	 7500 mi. 1st 7500 mi. ⑤

Maintenance Intervals

Maintenance	1984 and later
Brake Fluid (Master Cylinder) Check fluid level Add liquid	 7500 mi. as necessary
Manual Steering Gear Lubricant Check level Add lubricant	⑥
Power Steering Reservoir Check fluid level Add fluid	 each eng. oil change as necessary
Rotate Tires	1st 7500 mi. Then every 15,000 mi.
Chassis Lubrication	12 mo/7500 mi.
Drive Belts Check and adjust (as necessary)	12 mo/15,000 mi
Rear Wheel Bearings Lubricate	15,000 ② 30,000

NOTE: *Heavy-duty operation (trailer towing, prolonged idling, severe stop-and-start driving) should be accompanied by a 50% increase in maintenance. Cut the interval in half for these conditions. Figures given are maintenance intervals when service should be performed.*

① Paper element air cleaners should be rotated 180° each time they are checked (except special performance open-element air cleaners).

② Severe service. Front wheels are not serviceable.

③ If operated under any of the conditions listed in the preceding note, change the fluid every 15,000 mi.

④ More often under severe conditions.

⑤ Change every 7500 mi. if vehicle is used for trailer towing.

⑥ Factory sealed; maintenance not required, but check for fluid leakage.

Capacities

Year	V.I.N. Code	Model (cu in.)	Engine Crankcase Add 1 Qt for New Filter	Transmission Pts to Refill after Draining: Manual 3-spd	Manual 4-spd	Automatic	Differential (pts)	Fuel Tank (gal)	Cooling System (qts)	Max Coolant Pressure (psi)
1984	L83	350	4	—	2.1 ①	8.0	4.0	20	14.5	15
1985–86	L98	350	4	—	2.1 ①	8.0	4.0	20	14.5	15

① 3.45 pts. with overdrive unit

3. Never shop at night. The glare of the lights make is easy to miss faults on the body caused by accident or rust repair.

4. Try to get the name and phone number of the previous owner. Contact him/her and ask about the vehicle. If the owner of the lot refuses this information, look for a vehicle somewhere else.

NOTE: *A private seller can tell you about the vehicle and maintenance. Remember, however, there's no law requiring honesty from private citizens selling used vehicles. There is a law that forbids the tampering with or turning back the odometer mileage. This includes both the private citizen and the lot owner. The law also requires that the seller or anyone transferring ownership of the vehicle must provide the buyer with a signed statement indicating the mileage on the odometer at the time of transfer.*

5. Write down the year, model and serial number before you buy any used vehicle. Then dial 1-800-424-9393, the toll free number of the National Highway Traffic Safety Administration, and ask if the vehicle has ever been included on any manufacturer's recall list. If so, make sure the needed repairs were made.

6. Use the "Used Car Checklist" in this section and check all the items on the used vehicle you are considering. Some items are more important than others. You know how much money your can afford for repairs, and, depending on the price of the vehicle, may consider doing any needed work yourself. Beware, however, of trouble in areas that will affect operation, safety or emission. Problems in the "Used Car Checklist" break down as follows:

1–8: Two or more problems in these areas indicate a lack of maintenance. You should beware.

9–13: Indicates a lack of proper care, however, these can usually be corrected with a tune-up or relatively simple parts replacement.

14–17: Problems in the engine or transmission can be very expensive. Walk away from any vehicle with problems in both of these areas.

7. If you are satisfied with the apparent condition of the vehicle, take it to an independent diagnostic center or mechanic for a complete check. If you have a state inspection program, have it inspected immediately before purchase or specify on the bill of sale that the sale is conditional on passing the state inspection.

8. Road test the vehicle – refer to the "Road Test Checklist" in this section. If your original evaluation and the road test agree – the rest is up to you.

USED CAR CHECKLIST

1. *Mileage:* Average mileage is about 12,000 miles per year. More than average mileage may indicate hard usage. The catalytic converter may need converter service at 50,000 miles.

2. *Paint:* Check around the tail pipe, molding and windows for overspray indicating that the vehicle has been repainted.

3. *Rust:* Check the fenders, doors, rocker panels, window molding, wheelwells, floorboards, under the floormats and in the trunk for any signs of rust. Any rust at all will be a problem. There is no way to check the spread of rust, except to replace the part of panel.

4. *Body Appearance:* Check the moldings, the bumpers, grille, vinyl roof, glass, doors, trunk lid and body panels for general overall condition. Check for misalignment, loose hold down clips, ripples, scratches in the glass, rips or patches in the top. Mismatched paint, welding in the trunk, severe misalignment of the body panels or ripples may indicate crash work.

5. *Leaks:* Get down and look under the vehicle. There should be no normal "leaks", other than water from the air conditioning condenser.

6. *Tires:* Check the tire air pressure. A common trick is to pump the tire pressure up to

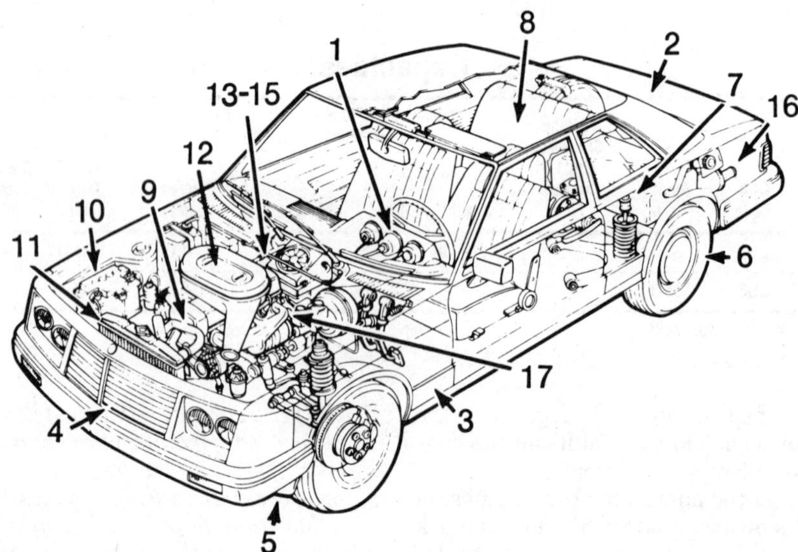

You should check these points when buying a used car. The "Used Car Checklist" gives an explanation of the numbered items

make the vehicle roll easier. Check the tread wear, open the trunk and check the spare too. Uneven wear is a clue that the front end needs alignment. See the troubleshooting chapter for clues to the causes of tire wear.

7. *Shock Absorbers:* Check the shock absorbers by forcing downward sharply on each corner of the vehicle. Good shocks will not allow the vehicle to bounce more than twice after you let go.

8. *Interior:* Check the entire interior. You're looking for an interior condition that agrees with the overall condition of the vehicle. Reasonable wear is expected but be suspicious of the new seat covers on sagging seats, new pedal pads and worn armrests. These indicate an attempt to cover up hard use. Pull back the carpets and look for evidence of water leaks or flooding. Look for missing hardware, door handles, control knobs and etc. Check the lights and signal operations. Make sure all accessories (air conditioner, heater, radio and etc.) work. Check the windshield wiper operation.

9. *Belts and Hoses:* Open the hood and check all the belts and hoses for wear, cracks or weak spots.

10. *Battery:* Low electrolyte level, corroded terminals and/or cracked case indicate a lack of maintenance.

11. *Radiator:* Look for corrosion or rust in the coolant indicating a lack of maintenance.

12. *Air Filter:* A dirty air filter usually means a lack of maintenance.

13. *Ignition Wires:* Check the ignition wires for cracks, burned spots or wear. Worn wires will have to be replaced.

14. *Oil Level:* If the oil level is low, chances are the engine uses oil or leaks. Beware of water in the oil (cracked block), excessively thick oil (used to quiet a noisy engine) or thin, dirty oil with a distinct gasoline smell (internal engine problems).

15. *Automatic Transmissions:* Pull the transmission dipstick out when the engine is running. The level should read "Full" and the fluid should be clear or bright red. Dark brown or black fluid that has distinct brunt odor, signals a transmission in need of repair or overhaul.

16. *Exhaust:* Check the color of the exhaust smoke. Blue smoke indicates, among other problems, worn rings. Black smoke can indicate burnt valves or fuel injection problems. Check the exhaust system for leaks. It can be expensive to replace.

17. *Spark Plugs:* Remove one of the spark plugs (the most accessible will do). An engine in good condition will show plugs with a light tan or gray deposit on the firing tip. See the color Tune-Up tips section for spark plug conditions.

ROAD TEST CHECK LIST

1. *Engine Performance:* The vehicle should be peppy whether cold or warm, with adequate power and good pickup. It should respond smoothly through the gears.

2. *Brakes:* They should provide quick, firm stops with no noise, pulling or brake fade.

3. *Steering:* Sure control with no binding, harshness or looseness and no shimmy in the wheel should be expected. Noise or vibration from the steering wheel when turning the vehicle means trouble.

4. *Clutch (Manual Transmission):* Clutch action should give quick, smooth response with easy shifting. The clutch pedal should have about 1–1½" of free-play before it disengages the clutch. Start the engine, set the parking brake, place the transmission in first gear and slowly release the clutch pedal. The engine should begin to stall when the pedal is ½–¾ of the way up.

5. *Automatic Transmission:* The transmission should shift rapidly and smoothly, with no noise, hesitation or slipping.

6. *Differential:* No noise of thumps should be present. Differentials have no "normal" leaks.

7. *Driveshaft, Universal Joints:* Vibration and noise could mean driveshaft problems. Clicking at low speed or coast conditions means worn U-joints.

8. *Suspension:* Try hitting bumps at different speeds. A vehicle that bounces has weak shock absorbers. Clunks mean worn bushings or ball joints.

9. *Frame:* Wet the tires and drive in a straight line. Tracks should show two straight lines, not four. Four tire tracks indicate a frame bent by collision damage. If the tires can not be wet for this purpose, have a friend drive along behind you to see if the vehicle appears to be traveling in a straight line.

Tune-Up and Performance Maintenance

Tune-Up Specifications

Year	V.I.N. Code	Model	Spark Plugs Type	Spark Plugs Gap (in.)	Distributor Point Dwell (deg)	Distributor Point Gap (in.)	Basic Ignition Timing (deg BTDC)	Valves Clearance (in.) Intake	Valves Clearance (in.) Exhaust	Valves Intake Opening (deg BTDC)	Idle Speed (rpm)	Normal Fuel Pressure (psi)
1984	L83	205 hp	R45TS	0.045	Electronic		②	①	①	NA	②	9–13
1985	L98	230 hp	R43CTS	0.045	Electronic		②	①	①	NA	②	9–13
1986	L98	230 hp	R43CTS	0.035	Electronic		②	①	①	NA	②	9–13

NA—Not Available
① Hydraulic lifters—one turn down from zero lash
② Use the specification listed on the tune-up sticker under the hood.

TUNE-UP PROCEDURES

This section gives specific procedures on how to tune-up your Corvette. It is intended to be as complete and as basic as possible. Those who are familiar with the steps involved in a tune-up may wish to skip the following procedures and use the generalized section in Chapter 10. However, it is felt that nothing would be lost by first reading over this section. Perhaps the best procedure to follow would be to read both sections before starting your tune-up.

Spark Plugs

A typical spark plug consists of a metal shell surrounding a ceramic insulator. A metal electrode extends downward through the center of the insulator and protrudes a small distance. Located at the end of the plug and attached to the side of the outer metal shell is the side electrode. The side electrode bends in at a 90° angle so that its tip is even with and parallel to the tip of the center electrode. The distance between these two electrodes (measured in thousandths of an inch) is called the spark plug gap. The spark plug in no way produces a spark but merely provides a gap across which the current can arc. The coil produces anywhere from 20,000–40,000 volts which travels to the distributor where it is distributed through the spark plug wires to the spark plugs. The current passes along the center electrode and jumps the gap to the side electrode, then it ignites the air/fuel mixture in the combustion chamber.

SPARK PLUG HEAT RANGE

Spark plug heat range is the ability of the plug to dissipate heat. The longer the insulator (or the farther it extends into the engine), the hotter the plug will operate; the shorter the insulator the cooler it will operate. A plug that absorbs little heat and remains too cool will quickly accumulate deposits of oil and carbon since it is not hot enough to burn them off. This leads to plug fouling and consequently to misfiring. A plug that absorbs too much heat will have no deposits but (due to the excessive heat) the electrodes will burn away quickly and in some instances, preignition may result. Preignition takes place when plug tips get so hot that they glow sufficiently to ignite the fuel/air mixture before the actual spark occurs. This early ignition will usually cause a pinging during low speeds and heavy loads.

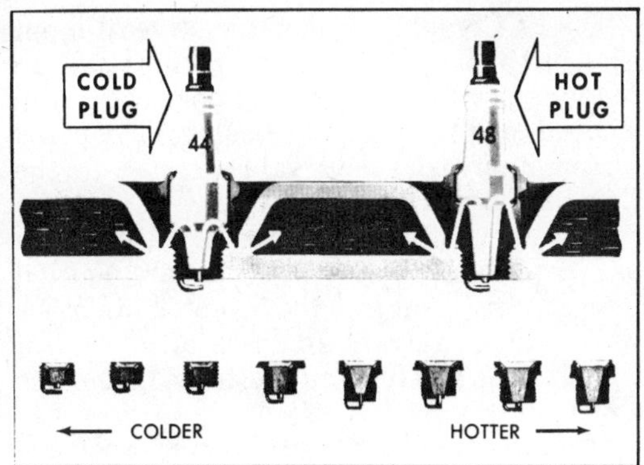

Spark plug heat range, the higher the number the hotter the plug

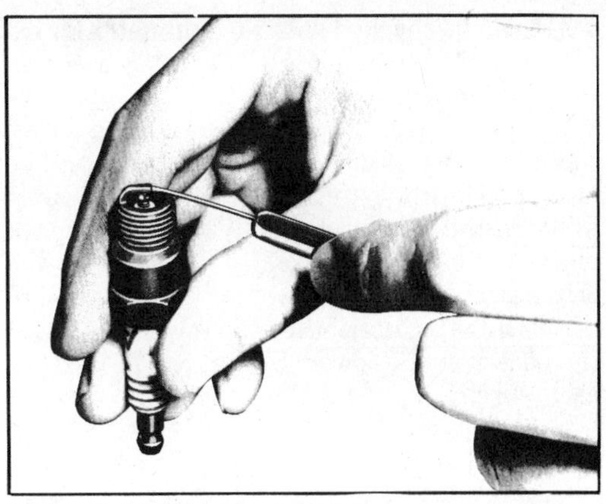

Check the gap with a round wire gauge

The general rule of thumb for choosing the correct heat range when picking a spark plug is: if most of your driving is long distance, high speed travel – use a colder plug; if most of your driving is stop and go – use a hotter plug. Original equipment plugs are compromise plugs but most people never have the occasion to change their plugs from the factory-recommended heat range.

REMOVAL AND INSTALLATION

Normally, a set of spark plugs requires replacement about every 20,000–30,000 miles on vehicles equipped with an High Energy Ignition (HEI) system. Any vehicle which is subjected to severe conditions will need more frequent plug replacement.

Under normal operation, the plug gap increases about 0.001 in. for every 1,000–2,000 miles. As the gap increases, the plug's voltage requirement also increases. It requires a greater voltage to jump the wider gap and about 2–3 times as much voltage to fire a plug at high speeds than at idle.

When you are removing the spark plugs, work on one at a time. Don't start by removing the plug wires all at once, for unless you number them, they may become mixed up. Take a minute before you begin and number the wires with tape. The best location for numbering the wires is near the distributor cap.

1. Twist the spark plug boot ½ turn and remove the boot/wire from the plug. DO NOT pull on the wire itself as this will ruin the wire.
2. If possible, use a brush or rag to clean the area around the spark plug. Make sure that all the dirt is removed so that none will enter the cylinder after the plug is removed.
3. Remove the spark plug using a ⅝" spark plug socket. Turn the socket counterclockwise to remove the plug. If the engine has aluminum cylinder heads, be extremely careful when removing the plugs. If any plug turns with difficulty, spray a penetrating lubricant (Liquid Wrench®, WD-40® or etc.) around the plug threads and reseat the plug. Wait a couple of minutes for the oil to work it's way through the threads and then "nurse" the plug out about ¼ turn at a time. Be sure to hold the socket straight on the plug to avoid breaking the plug or rounding off the hex on the plug.
4. Once the plug is out, check it against the plugs shown on the *Color Insert on Spark Plug Analysis* to determine engine condition. This is crucial since plug readings are vital signs of engine condition.
5. Use a round wire feeler gauge to check the plug gap. The correct size gauge should pass through the electrode gap with a slight drag. If you are in doubt, try one size smaller and/or one larger. The smaller gauge should go through easily while the larger one shouldn't go through at all. If the gap is incorrect, use the electrode bending tool on the end of the gauge to adjust the gap. When adjusting the gap, always bend the side electrode. The center electrode is non-adjustable.
6. If the engine has cast-iron heads, squirt a DROP of penetrating oil onto the plug threads and install the plug. If the engine has aluminum heads, apply a small amount of anti-seize compound to the plug threads and carefully install the plugs. Turn the plugs in by hand until they are snug.
7. When the plug is finger tight, tighten it with a wrench.
8. Install the plug boot firmly over the plug. Proceed to the next plug.

Spark Plug Wires

Visually inspect the spark plug cables for burns, cuts or breaks in the insulation. Check the spark plug boots and the nipples on the distributor cap and coil. Replace any damaged wiring. If no physical damage is obvious, the wires can be checked with an ohmmeter for excessive resistance. *Refer to the Color Insert on Spark Plug Analysis.*

When installing a new set of spark plug wires, replace the wires one at a time so there will be no mixup. Start by replacing the longest cable first. Install the boot firmly over the spark plug. Route the wire exactly the same as the original. Insert the distributor end of the wire firmly into the distributor cap tower, then seat the boot over the tower. Repeat the process for each wire.

Firing Orders

NOTE: *To avoid confusion, remove and tag the wires one at a time, for replacement.*

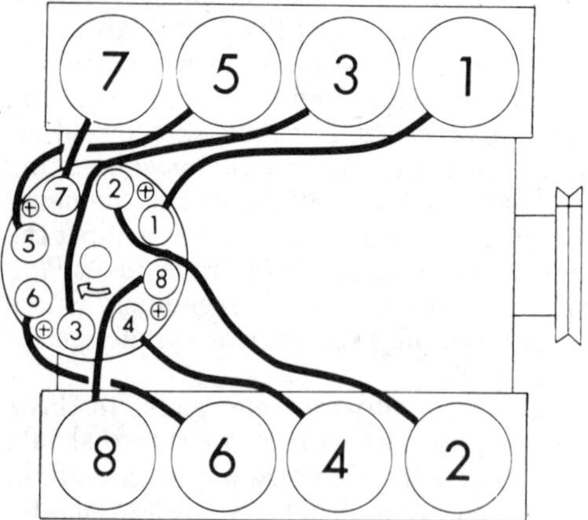

1984–86 HEI

Electronic Ignition

NOTE: *This book contains simple testing procedures for your Corvette's electronic ignition. More comprehensive testing on this system and other electronic control systems on your vehicle can be found in CHILTON'S GUIDE TO ELECTRONIC ENGINE CONTROLS, book part number 7535, available at your local retailer.*

The Electronic Concentrated Engine Control System is used on all engines. This system employs a microcomputer which controls fuel injection, spark timing, exhaust gas recirculation (EGR), idle speed, fuel pump operation and mixture ratio feedback. Electrical signals from each sensor are fed into the computer and each actuator is controlled by an electrical pulse with a duration that is computed in the microcomputer. When engine malfunctions occur, the use of an ECCS analyzer is necessary to accurately diagnose the problem.

The ECCS analyzer monitors several input and output signals that are emitted in response to various engine operating and stopped conditions. Input signals are compared to computerized signal values stored in the Central Electronic Control Unit (CECU) while output signals are monitored to ensure they are properly attuned before they are emitted from the CECU unit to the actuators. In other words, this analyzer analyzes all electrical signals that are transmitted to and from the CECU unit.

Since this analyzer would be very expensive to purchase, any suspected malfunction of the engine cannot be corrected by an obvious visual inspection, this should be left to a qualified repair shop that contains this equipment.

TROUBLESHOOTING

1. Turn the ignition switch OFF. Disconnect the fusible link connector for the fuel injection wiring harness. Be sure the ignition is OFF before doing this. Disconnect the cold start valve wiring harness connector. Disconnect the high tension lead (coil-to-distributor) at the distributor and hold it 1/8–1/4" away from the cylinder head with a pair of insulated pliers and a heavy glove. When the engine is cranked, a spark should be observed. If not, check the lead and replace as necessary. If there is still no spark, go on with the following system checks.
2. Make a check of the power supply circuit. Turn the ignition OFF. Disconnect the connector from the top of the IC unit. Turn the ignition ON. Measure the voltage at each terminal of the connector in turn by touching the probe of positive lead of the voltmeter to one of the terminals and touching the probe of the negative lead of the voltmeter to a ground, such as the engine. In each case, battery voltage should be indicated. If not, check all of the wiring, the ignition switch and all connectors for breaks, corrosion, discontinuity and etc., then repair as necessary.
3. Check the primary windings of the ignition coil. Turn the ignition OFF. Disconnect the harness connector from the negative coil terminal. Use an ohmmeter to measure the resistance between the positive and negative coil terminals. If resistance is 0.84–1.02 Ω, the coil is OK; replace it, if the reading is far from this range.
4. If the power supply, circuits, wiring and coil are in good shape, check the IC unit and pick-up coil as follows:
   a. Turn the ignition OFF.
   b. Remove the distributor cap and ignition rotor.
   c. Using an ohmmeter, measure the resis-

tance between the two terminals of the pick-up coil, where they attach to the IC unit. Measure the resistance by reversing the polarity of the probes. If approximately 400 Ω are indicated, the pick-up coil is OK but the IC unit is bad and must be replaced.

5. If the resistance is other than 400 Ω, proceed with the following:

a. Be certain the two pin connector to the IC unit is secure.

b. Turn the ignition ON.

c. Measure the voltage at the ignition coil's negative terminal.

d. Turn the ignition OFF.

CAUTION: *Remove the tester probe from the coil negative terminal before switching the ignition OFF, to prevent burning out the tester.*

e. If 0 voltage is indicated, the IC unit is bad and must be replaced.

6. If battery voltage is indicated, remove the IC unit from the distributor, by proceeding as follows:

a. Disconnect the battery ground (negative) cable.

b. Remove the distributor cap and ignition rotor.

c. Disconnect the harness connector from the top of the IC unit.

d. Remove the two screws securing the IC unit to the distributor.

e. Disconnect the two pick-up coil wires from the IC unit.

CAUTION: *Pull the connectors free with a pair of needlenose pliers. DO NOT pull on the wires to detach the connectors.*

f. Remove the IC unit.

7. Measure the resistance between the terminals of the pick-up coil. It should be approximately 400 Ω. If so, the pick-up coil is OK and the IC unit is bad. If the resistance is other than 400 Ω, the pick-up coil is bad and must be replaced.

HEI SYSTEM TACHOMETER HOOKUP

Connect one tach lead to the "TACH" terminal on the side of the distributor and the other to ground. Some tachometers must be connected to the "TACH" terminal and the battery positive terminal. Not all tachometers will operate correctly with the HEI system. Check with the manufacturer if there is any doubt.

CAUTION: *The "TACH" terminal should never be connected to ground.*

When connecting a remote starter switch, disconnect the "BATT" terminal.

Ignition Timing

1. Warm the engine to normal operating temperature.

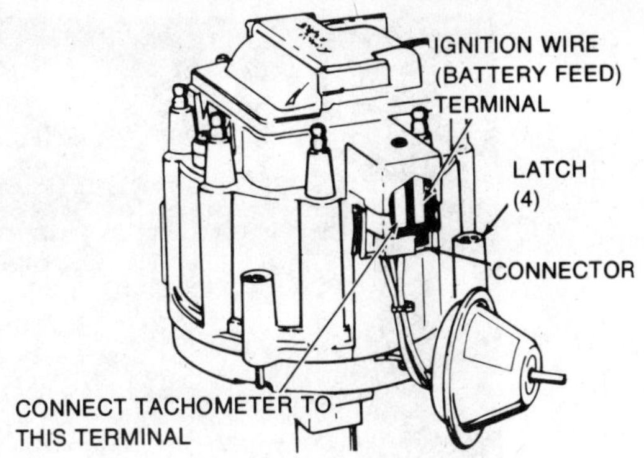

Hook up one tach lead to the tachometer terminal on the HEI system

2. Connect a timing light according to the timing light manufacturers instructions. DO NOT use a timing light which requires piercing of the spark plug lead. Use ONLY an inductive pickup type timing light.

NOTE: *Timing lights requiring a 12 volt DC power source (battery) may be connected as follows: Connect the positive timing light lead to the BAT terminal of the alternator; the negative timing light lead to a good engine ground.*

CAUTION: *Be careful not to ground the positive lead to the alternator case.*

3. Disconnect the EST BYPASS wire from the distributor, by performing the following:

a. Trace the four wires from the distributor housing which join at a common multi-connector, close to the distributor.

b. Follow the tan wire with a black strip (EST BYPASS wire) from the multi-connector. Past the multi-connector, the EST BYPASS wire has its own, single connector.

NOTE: *Disconnect the 4-terminal EST connector to operate in the bypass timing mode.*

c. Separate this connector before adjusting the timing. While the EST BYPASS wire is disconnected, the CHECK ENGINE light on the instrument panel will illuminate. After adjusting the timing, reconnect the EST BYPASS connector; the CHECK ENGINE light will go out.

NOTE: *An Electronic Spark Control (ESC) is incorporated into the distributor which retards the spark advance when engine detonation occurs. If the controller fails, the result could be no ignition, no retard or full retard. Some engines will also have a magnetic timing probe hole for use with electronic timing equipment. Consult the manufacturer's instructions for the use of this equipment.*

4. Locate the timing plate (metal plate marked in graduations) which is attached to the timing cover. Locate the single mark on

1. Positive (+) connection at the alternator BAT terminal
2. Negative (−) connection at a good engine ground

12VDC timing light power connections on a typical, externally regulated Delcotron

the vibration damper (one groove). Clean both the timing plate and the damper marking. Use chalk to accentuate the marks, if necessary.

5. Be sure that all the wiring and tools are clear of the fan and drive belts. Start the engine and allow it to idle. Aim the timing light at the marks and note where the vibration damper mark aligns with the timing plate.

NOTE: *The 0° mark on the plate is the Top Dead Center (TDC) mark and all the Before Top Dead Center (BTDC) marks are on the "before" (advance) side of the 0° mark or the After Top Dead Center (ATDC) marks are on the "after" (retard) side of the 0° mark.*

6. Loosen the distributor clamp (hold-down) bolt and slowly rotate the distributor as neces-

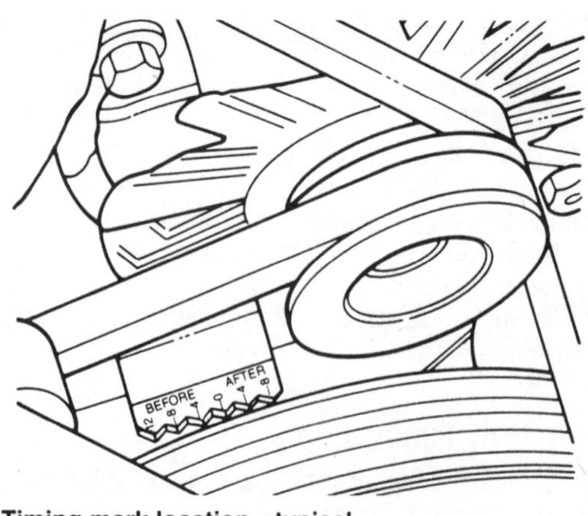

Timing mark location—typical

CHECK ENGINE lamp location. This lamp will be illuminated while the EST BYPASS wire is disconnected

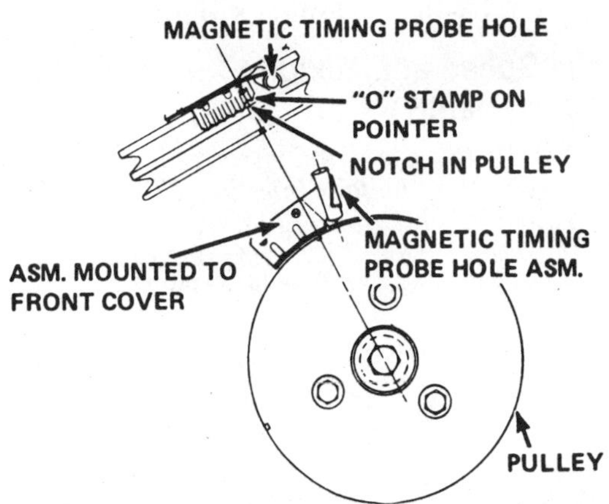

View of the timing marks and the magnetic timing probe hole, located at the front of the engine

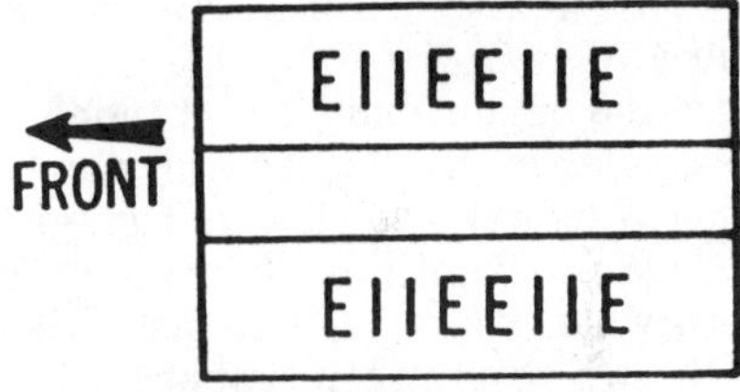

Valve arrangement of the 350 engine

sary until the damper mark is aligned with the specified mark of the timing plate. Tighten the hold-down bolt and recheck the timing.

7. Turn the engine OFF and remove the timing light.

Valve Lash

These engines are equipped with hydraulic lifters which VERY rarely need adjustment of the valve lash. If the vehicle runs well and there is no audible "clicking" in the valve train, leave it alone. This is because removal of the valve covers on vehicles equipped with air conditioning, various emission controls, cruise control, etc., can be a major project in itself.

On air conditioned models, the A/C compressor must be moved out of the way to gain access to one of the valve covers. DO NOT disconnect the refrigerant lines to move the compressor. After the cover is removed, either move the compressor to retighten the belt or remove the belt completely so that it will not tangle while the engine is running.

If wiring is attached to metal clips on the valve cover, carefully bend each clip to free the wire from the valve cover. If corrugated plastic tubing containing wiring is attached to the valve cover with plastic clips, the clips can be undone by gently twisting the upper part of the clip while holding the lower section. If the clip must be removed, press the lower most arms of the clips together with needle nose pliers and push upward.

If the vehicle uses a PCV valve pressed into the valve cover grommet, pull the valve from the grommet and remove the valve from the hose. Plug the hose with an old bolt to prevent a vacuum leak.

Should it be necessary to remove additional components to gain access to the valve covers, note the wire and/or vacuum hose connection locations and sizes of the bolts which retain the component(s).

ADJUSTMENT

1. Purchase oil stopper clips for the rocker arms. These are available at most auto parts stores. These clips are installed either over (metal style) or in (plastic style) the rocker arm oiling hole located at the pushrod end of the rocker arm.

   NOTE: *If these clips are not installed, both you and your Corvette will become oil soaked when the engine is started.*

2. Start the engine and allow it to reach normal operating temperature.
3. Remove the valve covers. If you have only 8 oil stopper clips, remove only one valve cover and adjust the valves. Then adjust the valves on the other side after the first cover has been reinstalled.
4. Start the engine and allow it to idle.
5. Slowly loosen the rocker arm nut until the rocker arm starts to clatter. Tighten the nut (clockwise) just until the clatter stops. This position is what is termed "zero lash." Slowly tighten the nut ¼ turn then wait about 10 seconds for the idle to smooth out. Repeat this until the nut is tightened one full turn past zero lash.

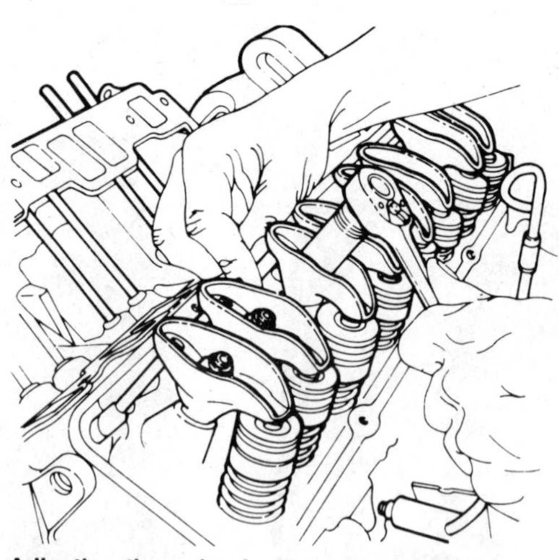

Adjusting the valve lash on a hydraulic lifter engine

   CAUTION: *WAIT until the engine smooths out after each ¼ turn past zero lash. Impatience in this case can cause engine damage due to valve interference. Repeat step 5 for each remaining valve.*

6. Remove the oil stopper clips.
7. To reinstall, use new valve cover gaskets and reverse the removal procedures.

Idle Speed and Mixture Adjustment

NOTE: *Idle speed and mixture adjustments, for the Throttle Body Injection (TBI) and the Tuned Port Injection (TPI) systems, are set at the factory. Any adjustments should be made by an authorized GM dealer ONLY.*

Engine and Engine Overhaul 3

UNDERSTANDING THE ENGINE ELECTRICAL SYSTEM

The engine electrical system can be broken down into three separate and distinct systems – (1) the starting system; (2) the charging system; (3) the ignition system.

NOTE: *See "Troubleshooting" for typical diagnosis procedures.*

Battery and Starting System

The battery is the first link in the chain of mechanisms which work together to provide cranking of the automobile engine. In most modern vehicles, the battery is a lead-acid electrochemical device consisting of six two-volt (2V) subsections connected in series so the unit is capable of producing approximately 12V of electrical pressure. Each subsection (cell) consists of a series of positive and negative plates held a short distance apart in a solution of sulfuric acid and water. The two types of plates are of dissimilar metals. A chemical reaction takes place which produces current flow from the battery, when it's positive and negative terminals are connected to an electrical appliance such as a lamp or motor. The continued transfer of electrons would eventually convert the sulfuric acid in the electrolyte to water and make the two plates identical in chemical composition. As electrical energy is removed from the battery, it's voltage output tends to drop. Thus, measuring battery voltage and battery electrolyte composition are two ways of checking the ability of the unit to supply power. During the starting of the engine, electrical energy is removed from the battery. However, if the charging circuit is in good condition and the operating conditions are normal, the power removed from the battery will be replaced by the alternator which will force electrons back into the battery, reversing the normal flow and restoring the battery to it's original chemical state.

The battery and starting motor are linked by very heavy electrical cables designed to minimize resistance to the flow of current. Generally, the major power supply cable that leaves the battery goes directly to the starter, while other electrical system needs are supplied by a smaller cable. During the starter operation, power flows from the battery to the starter, then is grounded through the vehicle's frame and the battery's negative ground strap.

The starting motor is a specially designed, direct current electric motor capable of producing a very great amount of power for it's size. One thing that allows the motor to produce a great deal of power is it's tremendous rotating speed. It drives the engine through a tiny pinion gear (attached to the starter's armature), which drives the very large flywheel ring gear at a greatly reduced speed. Another factor allowing it to produce so much power is that only intermittent operation is required of it. Thus, little allowance for air circulation is required and the windings can be built into a very small space.

The starter solenoid is a magnetic device which employs the small current supplied by the starting switch circuit of the ignition switch. This magnetic action moves a plunger, which mechanically engages the starter and electrically closes the heavy switch which connects it to the battery. The starting switch circuit consists of the starting switch (contained within the ignition switch), a transmission neutral safety switch or clutch pedal switch and wiring necessary to connect these with the starter solenoid or relay.

The pinion (small gear) is mounted to a one-way drive clutch. This clutch is splined to the starter armature shaft. When the ignition switch is moved to the Start position, the solenoid plunger slides the pinion toward the flywheel ring rear via a collar and spring. If the teeth on the pinion and flywheel match properly, the pinion will engage the flywheel immediately. If the gear teeth butt one another, the spring will be compressed and will force the gears to mesh as soon as the starter turns far enough to allow them to do so. As the solenoid plunger reaches the end of its travel, it closes the contacts that connect the battery to the starter, then the engine is cranked.

As soon as the engine starts, the flywheel ring rear begins turning fast enough to drive the pinion at an extremely high rate of speed. At this point, the one-way clutch allows the pinion to spin faster than the starter shaft so that the starter will not operate at excessive speed. When the ignition switch is released from the starter position, the solenoid is de-energized, the spring (contained within the solenoid assembly) pulls the pinion out of mesh and interrupts the current flow to the starter.

The Charging System

The charging system provides electrical power for operation of the vehicle's ignition, starting system and all of the electrical accessories. The battery serves as an electrical surge or storage tank, storing (in chemical form) the energy originally produced by the alternator. The system also provides a means of regulating the alternator output to protect the battery from being overcharged and the accessories from being destroyed.

The storage battery is a chemical device incorporating parallel lead plates in a tank containing a sulfuric acid-water solution. Adjacent plates are slightly dissimilar and the chemical reaction of the two dissimilar plates produces electrical energy when the battery is connected to a load such as the starter motor. The chemical reaction is reversible, so that when the alternator is producing a voltage (electrical pressure) greater than that produced by the battery, electricity is forced into the battery and it is returned to it's fully charged state.

Alternators are used on the modern automobile for they are lighter, more efficient, rotate at higher speeds and have fewer brush problems. In an alternator, the field rotates while all of the current produced passes only through the stator windings. The brushes bear against the continuous slip rings; this causes the current produced to periodically reverse the direction of it's flow. Diodes (electrical one-way switches) block the flow of current from traveling in the wrong direction. A series of diodes are wired together to permit the alternating flow of the stator to be converted to a pulsating but unidirectional flow at the alternator output. The alternator's field is wired in series with the voltage regulator.

SAFETY PRECAUTIONS

Observing these precautions will ensure safe handling of the electrical system components and will avoid damage to the vehicle's electrical system:

1. Be absolutely sure of the polarity of a booster battery before making connections. Connect the cables positive-to-positive and negative-to-negative. Connect the positive cables first and the last connection to a ground on the body of the booster vehicle, so that arcing cannot ignite the hydrogen gas that may have accumulated near the battery. Even a momentary connection of a booster battery with polarity reserved may damage alternator diodes.
2. Disconnect both vehicle battery cables before attempting to charge a battery.
3. Never ground the alternator output or battery terminal. Be cautious when using metal tools around a battery to avoid creating a short circuit between the terminals.
4. Never run an alternator without load unless the field circuit is disconnected.
5. Never attempt to polarize an alternator.
6. Never disconnect components with the ignition ON.

High Energy Ignition (HEI) System

The HEI system operates in basically the same manner as the conventional ignition system, with the exception of the type of "switching device" used. A toothed iron timer core is mounted on the distributor shaft which rotates inside of an electronic pole piece. The pole piece has internal teeth (corresponding to those on the timer core) which contains a permanent magnet and pick-up coil (not to be confused with the ignition coil). The pole piece senses the magnetic field of the timer core teeth and sends a signal to the ignition module which electronically controls the primary coil voltage. The ignition coil operates in basically the same manner as a conventional ignition coil (though the ignition coils DO NOT interchange).

NOTE: *The HEI systems uses a condenser which is primarily used for radio interference purposes.*

None of the electrical components used in the HEI systems are adjustable. If a component is found to be defective, it must be replaced.

PRECAUTIONS

Before going on to troubleshooting, it might be a good idea to take note of the following precautions:

Timing Light Use

Inductive pick-up timing lights are the best kind to use. Timing lights which connect between the spark plug and the spark plug wire occasionally give false readings.

Spark Plug Wires

The plug wires are of a different construction than conventional wires. When replacing them, make sure to use the correct wires, since conventional wires won't carry the voltage. Also, handle them carefully to avoid cracking or splitting them and never pierce them.

Tachometer Use

Not all tachometers will operate or indicate correctly. While some tachometers may give a reading, this does not necessarily mean the reading is correct. In addition, some tachometers hook up differently from others. If you can't figure out whether or not your tachometer will work on your vehicle, check with the tachometer manufacturer.

System Testers

Instruments designed specifically for testing the HEI system are available from several tool manufacturers. Some of these will even test the module.

ENGINE ELECTRICAL

Ignition Coil

TESTING

1. Remove the electrical connector from the distributor cap and the distributor cap from the distributor, then invert it.
2. Using an ohmmeter (set on the low scale), connect one probe to the "C" terminal and the other probe to the "B+" terminal. The reading should be zero or almost zero, if not, replace the the coil.
3. Using an ohmmeter (set on the high scale), perform the following test:
   a. Connect one probe to the "B+" terminal and the other probe to the cap's center terminal; the reading should not be infinite.
   b. Connect one probe to the "Ground" terminal and the other probe to the cap's center terminal; the reading should not be infinite.
   c. If both readings are infinite, replace the ignition.

REMOVAL AND INSTALLATION

1. Remove the distributor cap.
2. Remove the ignition coil cover-to-cap screws and lift the cover from the cap.

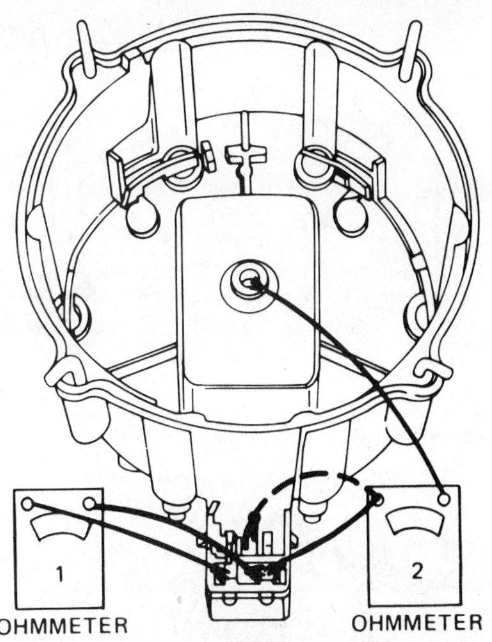

Testing the ignition coil with an ohmmeter

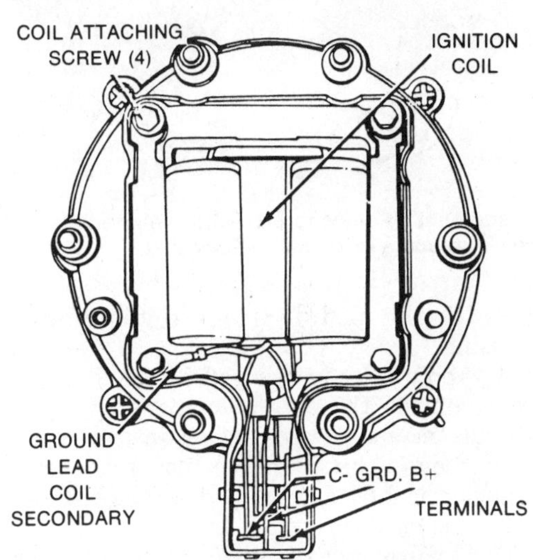

Ignition coil mounted in the HEI distributor cap

3. Remove the ignition coil-to-cap screws and lift the coil and the lead from the cap.
4. To install, reverse the removal procedures.

Ignition Module

REMOVAL AND INSTALLATION

1. Remove the distributor cap and the rotor from the distributor.
2. Carefully disconnect the wiring from the module.
3. Remove the two module retaining screws

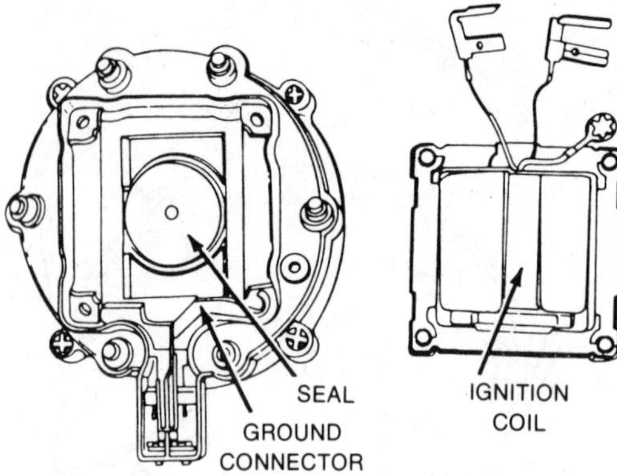

After removing the coil, check the condition of the arc seal

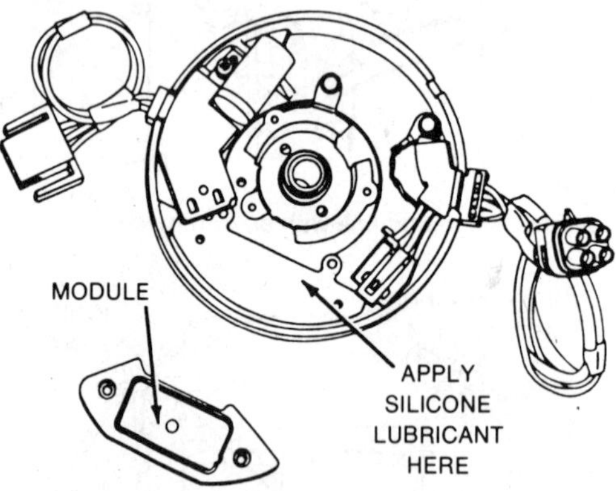

Placement of silicone dielectric compound prior to HEI module installation—see text

and lift the module from the distributor housing.

4. Apply a light coating of silicone dielectric compound to the distributor housing in the module mounting area before installing the new module. The silicone compound is used to transfer heat from the module to the distributor housing. If this compound is not used, the module will overheat, causing failure of the ignition system.

NOTE: *Silicone compounds are available strictly for this purpose–DO NOT use a regular silicone lubricant or sealer.*

5. Install the new module, using the accompanying illustration as a guide to establish the best possible module connections.

NOTE: *Many HEI failures have been attributed to poor module connections. Inspect the wires, terminals, connectors for damage and follow the accompanying illustration.*

6. Install the rotor and the distributor cap as previously outlined.

NOTE: *Items previously listed are the only items of the HEI distributor which are serviceable with the distributor installed. Other services will require distributor removal and disassembly.*

Distributor

REMOVAL

1. Rotate the engine until the timing mark on the damper pulley is aligned with the Top Dead Center TDC (0°) mark on the timing plate scale.
2. Remove the air cleaner assembly and the ignition shielding. Disconnect the negative battery cable.
3. With the ignition switch in the OFF position, disconnect the feed wire and the tachometer lead from the distributor cap, by releasing the connector retaining tabs and pulling downward on the connector(s).
4. Remove the distributor cap and move it out of the way. Disconnect the four-wire ECM harness connector from the distributor.

CAUTION: *Never allow the "Tach" terminal to touch ground.*

5. Locate the locking tabs of the spark plug wire retaining ring (on the distributor cap). Move each of the two locking tabs outward to release the retaining ring. With the plug wires still attached to the ring, carefully remove the retaining ring from the distributor cap and move the ring (with the wires still attached) out of the way.
6. Check that the firing tip of the rotor is pointing to the No. 1 terminal of the distributor cap; if it is not, rotate the engine one full revolution and again align the timing marks. Recheck the position of the rotor.
7. Remove the distributor hold-down bolt and clamp, then lift the distributor from the engine.

INSTALLATION

Undisturbed Engine

1. Clean the distributor and intake manifold mounting surfaces and check the condition of the O-ring, replace it if necessary.
2. Position the distributor in the engine without engaging it. Align the distributor housing-to-engine alignment marks which were made during the removal procedures. Position the rotor firing tip slightly counterclockwise of the corresponding distributor housing mark; remember, the rotor will turn slightly during installation.
3. Engage the distributor to the engine by moving it downward. The rotor should turn to it's proper alignment position. If it does not, lift the distributor enough to disengage the drive gear, reposition the rotor and lower the distributor.

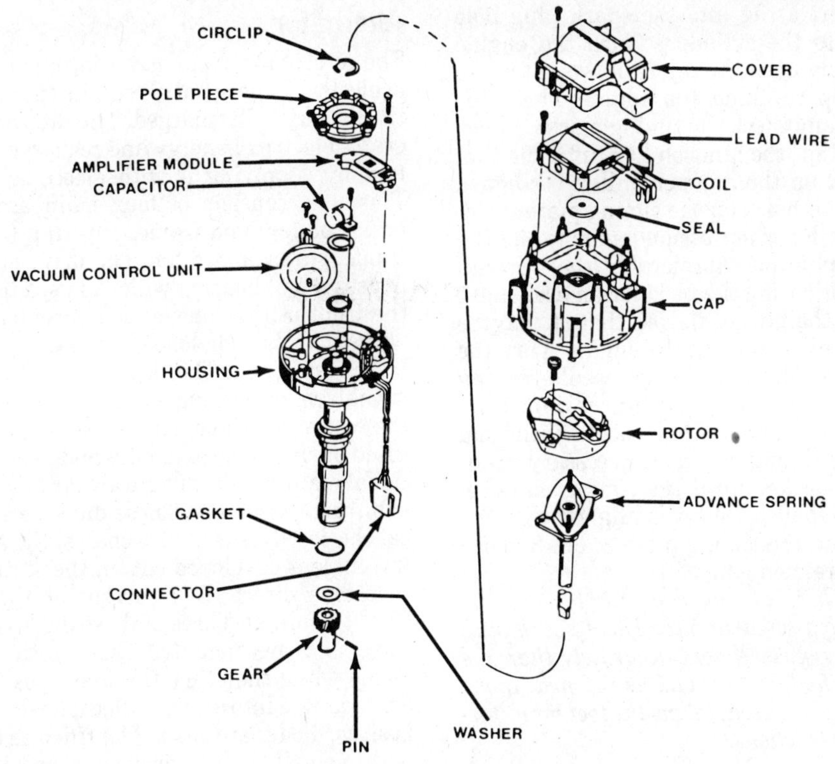

Exploded view of the HEI distributor

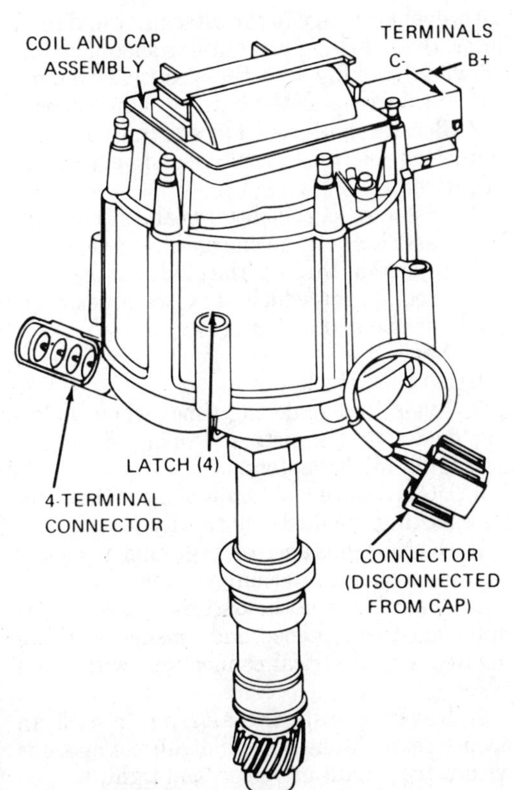

View of the HEI distributor

4. Install the distributor hold-down clamp and lightly tighten the bolt.

5. Make sure that the rotor retaining screws are tight and install the distributor cap.

6. Install the electrical connectors to the distributor.

7. Install the plug wire retaining ring. Press the ring downward until the two locking tabs engage. Make sure that the plug wire terminals are firmly seated on the distributor cap terminals.

8. Install the air cleaner and reconnect the battery cables.

9. Adjust the ignition timing and tighten the distributor hold-down bolt. Reinstall the ignition shielding.

Disturbed Engine

1. Remove the No. 1 spark plug, turn the crankshaft to position the No. 1 piston to the TDC of the compression stroke. The various methods are as follows:

a. Hold your finger over the spark plug hole and have an assistant turn the engine over slowly. When you feel compression, watch the timing marks. Stop turning the engine as soon as the timing mark on the crankshaft balancer is aligned with the 0° mark on the timing plate scale.

b. Insert a rag into the spark plug hole (NOT into the cylinder). Turn the engine over slowly until the rag is blown out of the hole. Stop cranking the engine when this happens and check the timing marks. If necessary, "tap" the ignition key until the timing mark on the damper pulley is aligned with the 0° mark on the timing plate scale.

c. Attach a compression gauge to the No. 1 spark plug hole (preferably the screw-in type; eliminating the need for an assistant). Position the gauge dial so that it may be viewed while cranking the engine. Turn the engine over until the gauge needle reading increases, indicating compression. Stop cranking the engine when this happens and check the timing marks. If necessary, "tap" the ignition key until the timing mark on the crankshaft balancer is aligned with the 0° mark on the timing plate scale. Remove the compression gauge.

NOTE: *There are tools available commercially which screw into the No. 1 spark plug hole and register (more accurately than the above methods) when TDC is reached. If one of these tools is used, follow the tool manufacturer's instructions.*

2. Reinstall the No. 1 spark plug and connect the plug wire. With the distributor out of the vehicle and the distributor cap installed, locate the No. 1 distributor cap terminal and chalk mark it's position on the distributor housing. Remove the distributor cap.

3. Position the distributor into the engine block with the firing tip of the rotor pointing to the mark made during Step 2.

4. As the distributor drive gear engages, the rotor will turn slightly. If the distributor housing does not sit properly on the block, the oil pump shaft is not engaging with the distributor shaft. In this case, you can do one of two things:

a. Remove the distributor and turn the oil pump driveshaft with a long screwdriver to align the pump driveshaft slot with the "blade" of the distributor shaft. This is done strictly by visual approximation.

b. Apply downward pressure on the distributor housing (NOT the rotor) and have someone "tap" the ignition key to slowly turn the engine over until the distributor falls into it's proper position. After doing this, it is recommended that you recheck the timing by repeating steps 1 and 2.

5. Install the distributor hold-down bolt and clamp. Lightly tighten the retaining bolt.

6. Connect the electrical connectors to the distributor.

7. Adjust the ignition timing. Install the ignition shielding.

Alternator

The alternator supplies a continuous amount of electrical energy at all engine speeds to keep the battery fully charged. The alternator generates electrical energy and recharges the battery by supplying it with electrical current. This unit consists of four main assemblies: drive (pulley) end frame, slip ring (rear) end frame, stator and rotor. The drive end frame houses a ball bearing which is used to support the front of the rotor and is large enough to withstand the side loads imposed on the rotor by the drive belt. The slip ring end frame uses a small roller bearing which is used to support the rear of the rotor. These bearings are lubricated during their assembly and need no additional maintenance. There are six diodes in the end frame assembly. These diodes are electrical check valves that also change the alternating current developed within the stator windings to a direct (DC) current at the output (BAT) terminal. Three of these diodes are negative and are mounted flush with the end frame while the other three are positive and are mounted into a strip called a heat sink. The positive diodes are easily identified as the ones within small cavities or depressions.

ALTERNATOR PRECAUTIONS

To prevent damage to the alternator and regulator, the following precautions should be taken when working with the electrical system.

1. Never reverse the battery connections.
2. Booster batteries for starting must be connected positive-to-positive and negative-to-negative.
3. Disconnnect the battery cables before using a fast charger; the charger has a tendency to force current through the diodes in the opposite direction for which they were designed. This burns out the diodes.
4. Never use a fast charger as a booster for starting the vehicle.
5. Avoid long soldering times when replacing diodes or transistors. Prolonged heat is damaging to alternators.
6. DO NOT use test lamps of more than 12V for checking the diode continuity.
7. DO NOT short across or ground any of the terminals on the alternator.
8. The polarity of the battery and the alternator must be matched and considered before making any electrical connections within the system.
9. Never operate the alternator with an open circuit. Make sure that all connections within the circuit are clean and tight.
10. Disconnect the battery terminals when performing any service on the electrical sys-

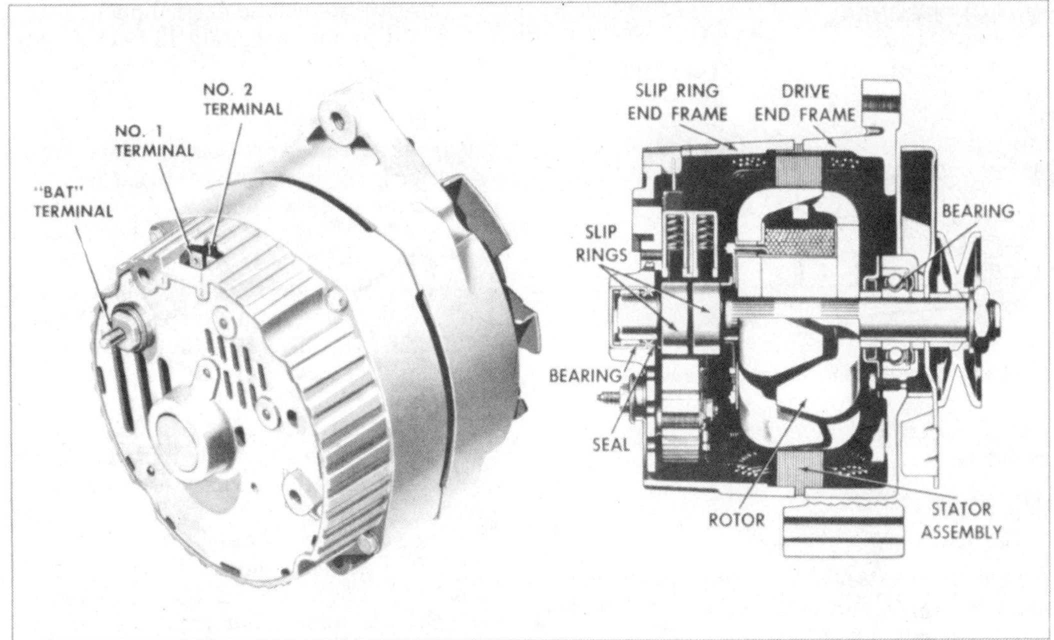

Internally regulated Delcotron

tem. This will eliminate the possibility of accidental reversal of polarity.

11. Disconnect the battery ground cable if arc welding is to be done on any part of the vehicle.

REMOVAL AND INSTALLATION

1. Disconnect the negative battery cable at the battery; this will prevent damaging the alternator diodes.
2. Remove the air cleaner flex duct and the adjusting brace bolt.
3. Disconnect the wiring from the rear of the alternator (bolt-on and push-in connectors).
4. Loosen the lower alternator bolt and remove the upper (adjustment) bolt. Slip the drive belt off of the pulley.
5. Remove the pivot bolt and lift the alternator out of its mounting brackets.
6. To install, reverse the removal procedures. Adjust the drive belt to the proper tension.

Voltage Regulator

The voltage regulator is mounted inside of the alternator and is non-adjustable, it must be replaced, if defective.

REMOVAL AND INSTALLATION

1. Refer to the "Alternator, Removal and Installation" procedures, in this section and remove the alternator from the vehicle.
2. Scribe a line on the alternator case from front-to-rear which will aid in attaining the proper relationships between components during assembly.
3. Remove the four through-bolts which join the end frame assemblies.
4. Separate the end frames by carefully prying between the drive (front) end frame and the stator. DO NOT pry between the slip ring (rear) end frame and the stator. The stator is wired to the rectifier bridge which is attached within the rear end frame.
5. Disconnect the three stator wire terminals at the rectifier bridge connections.
6. Remove the stator from the slip ring end frame. It may be necessary to carefully pry the stator from the frame.
7. Remove the three screws which retain the brush holder and regulator. Note the positions of the two screws which are equipped with plastic insulating washers - these screws MUST be installed in their original locations.

   NOTE: *Some alternators also have a resistor which is installed between the regulator and brush ground terminals. Note it's position and reinstall it in the same manner.*
8. Lift the brush holder/regulator from the alternator frame.
9. Before installing the regulator, push the brushes into the holder and insert a straightened paper clip through the holes (provided in the holder) to hold the brushes in position. The paper clip is removed after the alternator is assembled.

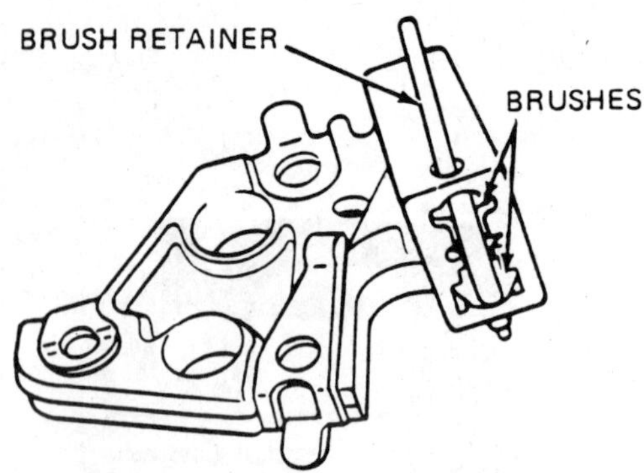

Retaining the brushes in the voltage regulator

10. To install, reverse the removal procedures.

VOLTAGE TESTING

On The Vehicle

Though other tests of the internal voltage regulator exist, the following test is quite accurate and requires a minimum of tools.

NOTE: *The following test must be performed with the engine at normal operating temperature.*

1. Attach one lead of a voltmeter to the "BAT" terminal of the alternator and the other lead to a good ground.

2. Start the engine and operate it at about 1500 rpm.

INSERT SCREWDRIVER
GROUND TAB TO
END FRAME

TAB

END
FRAME
HOLE

Ground this tab to test the alternator voltage output—internally regulated Delcotron only

3. Observe the voltmeter reading:

a. If it is approximately 13.5–15.2 volts, the regulator is properly limiting the voltage to the battery.

b. If the voltage is above about 15.2 volts, replace the voltage regulator as previously described.

c. If the voltage is below 13 volts, locate the test hole in the rear end frame of the alternator. Insert a screwdriver into the test hole about 3/4" to depress the field grounding tab. Under no circumstances should you push the screwdriver further than 1 inch into the alternator. If the voltage reading increases as the screwdriver is put into the test hole, the alternator is functioning properly and the regulator must be replaced. If the voltage reading did not increase with the insertion of the screwdriver, the alternator must be disassembled and tested.

NOTE: *If the test hole is not accessible, remove the alternator and test the following components: rotor, stator, rectifier bridge, diode trio and brushes (1/4" minimum length). Replace any component which may be defective. If these components are OK, replace the voltage regulator.*

Off The Vehicle

NOTE: *This test requires the use of a fast charger.*

1. Refer to the "Voltage Regulator, Removal and Installation" procedures, in this section and remove the regulator from the alternator.

2. Connect voltmeter and fast charger to battery.

3. Connect regulator and test light as shown, observing battery polarity.

4. The test light should be on when connected.

5. Turn ON the fast charger and slowly increase the charge rate. Check the voltmeter and make sure that the test light goes out at a minimum of 13.5 volts and a maximum of 16.0 volts.

Battery

REMOVAL AND INSTALLATION

1. Remove the negative battery cable and then the positive battery cable.

2. Remove the battery retainer screw and the retainer. Remove the battery from the vehicle.

3. To install, reverse the removal procedures. Torque the battery cables to 19 ft. lbs. (12 Nm). Coat the battery terminals with a non-metallic grease.

Alternator and Regulator Specifications

	Alternator				Regulator						
						Field Relay			Regulator		
		Field Current Draw	Output @ Generator RPM			Air Gap	Point Gap	Volts to	Air Gap	Point Gap	Volts at
Year	Model	@ 12V	2000	5000	Model	(in.)	(in.)	Close	(in.)	(in.)	125°
1984	1105513	4.0–4.5	—	97A ①	Integrated with alternator						13.8–14.8
1985	1105450	4.0–4.5	—	108A ①	Integrated with alternator						13.8–14.8
1986	1105678	4.0–4.5	—	105A ①	Integrated with alternator						13.8–14.8

① @ 80°F with carbon pile load used for maximum output.

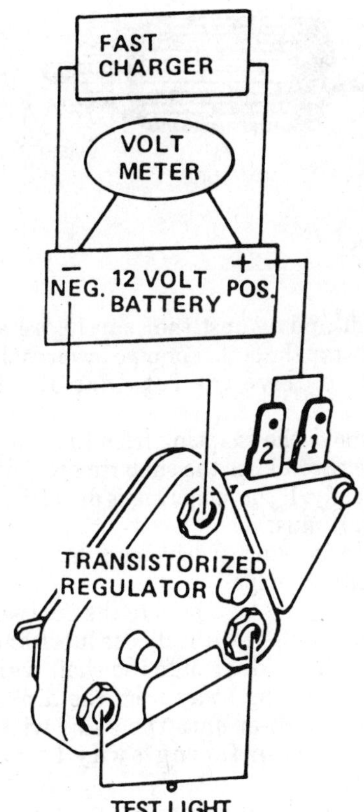

Testing voltage regulator on the bench

Starter

REMOVAL AND INSTALLATION

1. Disconnect the negative battery cable.
2. Raise and support the front of the vehicle on jackstands.
3. Disconnect the wiring from the starter solenoid. Replace each connector nut as the terminals are removed as the thread sizes differ between connectors. Note or tag the wiring positions to avoid improper connections during installation.
4. Remove the front starter support bracket and the flywheel cover.

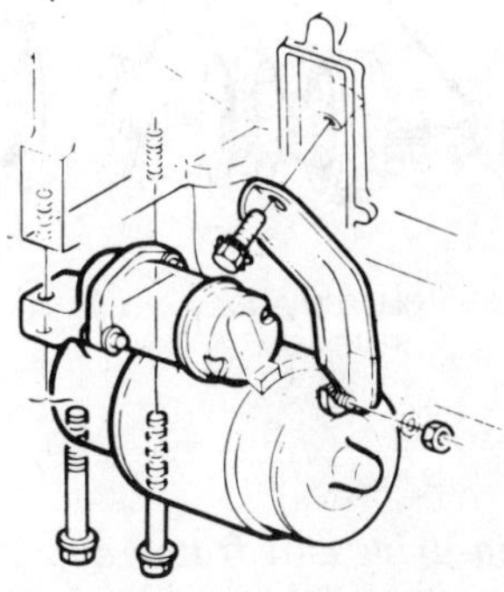

Removing the starter from the vehicle

5. Loosen the two main starter mounting bolts, support the starter and remove the bolts. Lower the starter front end first and remove the starter.
6. To install, reverse the removal procedures. Torque the starter-to-engine bolts to 25–35 ft. lbs.

SOLENOID REPLACEMENT

1. Remove the screw and washer from the motor connector strap terminal.
2. Remove the two solenoid retaining screws.
3. Twist the solenoid clockwise to remove the solenoid flange key from the keyway in the housing. Remove the solenoid.
4. To reinstall the unit, place the return spring on the plunger and place the solenoid body on the drive housing. Push the solenoid inward and turn counterclockwise to engage the flange key. Install and tighten the solenoid-to-starter screws, then the screw and washer which secure the strap terminal.

OVERHAUL

Drive Replacement

1. Disconnect the field coil strap(s) from the solenoid.

NOTE: *Scribe alignment marks on the field*

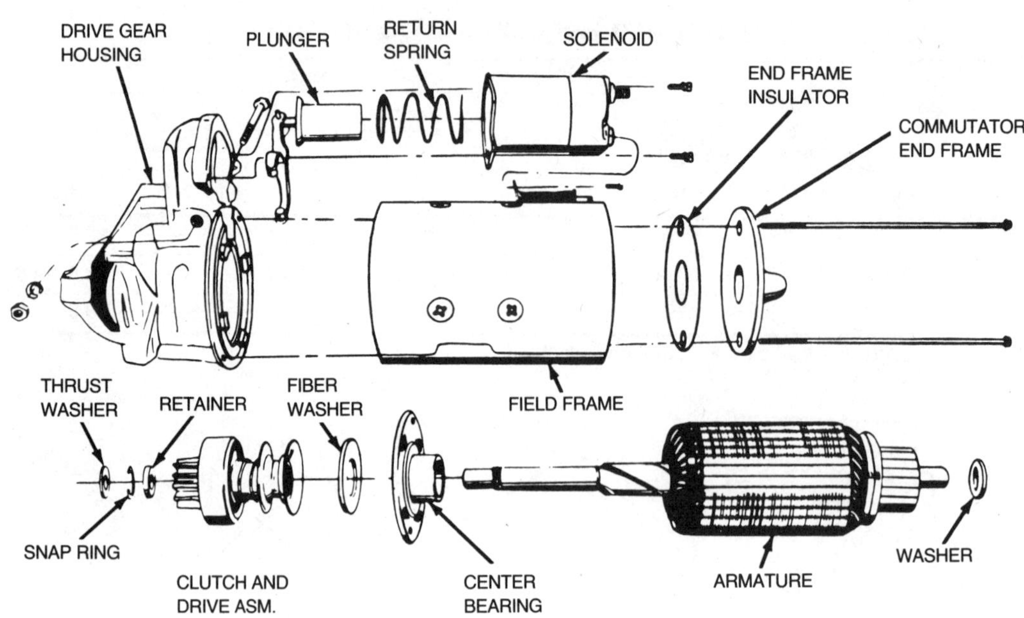

Exploded view of the starter

housing-to-drive end frame and the field housing-to-commutator end frame.

2. Remove the two starter through bolts. Separate the commutator end frame, field frame, drive housing and armature from each other.

3. Slide the thrust collar off of the end of the armature shaft.

4. Slide a 5/8" deep socket or a piece of pipe of suitable size over the drive end of the armature shaft and against the snapring retainer. Carefully tap the socket or pipe towards the armature to drive the retainer off of the snapring.

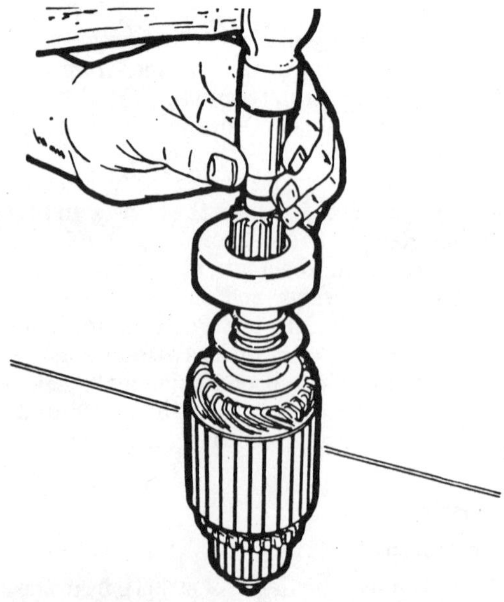

Use a piece of pipe to drive the retainer toward the snap-ring

5. Remove the snapring from the armature shaft. Be careful, for the snap ring will distort rather easily. If the snap ring is distorted after removal, it must be replaced.

6. Slide the starter drive and retainer from the armature shaft.

7. To reassemble, lubricate the drive end of the armature shaft with silicone lubricant and slide the starter drive onto the shaft with the pinion gear facing away from the armature. Slide the retainer onto the shaft with the cupped portion facing away from the armature.

8. Support the armature assembly in a vertical fashion with the drive end pointing upward. Position the snap ring on the top of the shaft, and carefully place a block of wood on the snap ring. Keep the snap ring centered. Tap the block of wood to drive the snap ring onto the shaft. Using a deep socket that will fit around the shaft without interference and yet contact the snap ring, force the snap ring downward into it's groove on the shaft.

9. Place the thrust washer on the shaft. Using two pairs of pliers as shown in the accompanying illustration, force the snapring retainer over the snapring and engage it with the thrust washer.

10. Lubricate the drive housing bushing with silicone lubricant. Install the armature and clutch assembly into the drive housing,

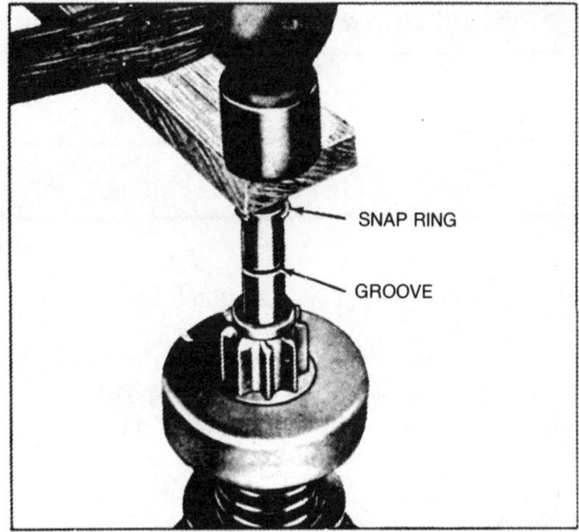

Forcing snap-ring over the armature shaft

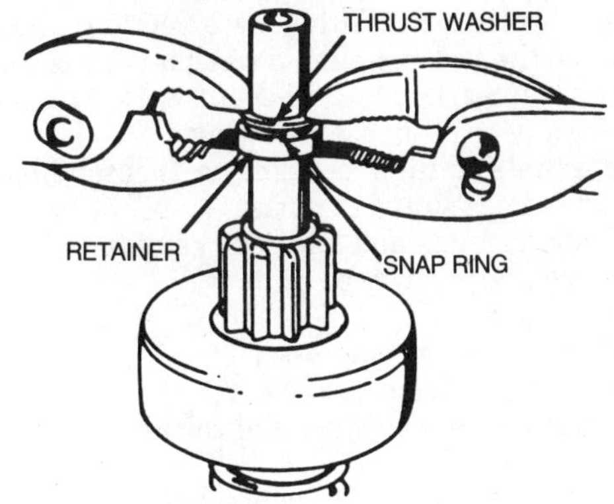

Snap-ring installation

engaging the solenoid shift lever with the clutch and position the front end of the armature shaft into the drive housing bushing.

11. Apply a sealing compound (GM No. 1050026 or equivalent) to the drive housing around the area where the field frame mates with the housing.

12. Slide the field-frame assembly over the armature and guide the brushes over the armature commutator. Continue to push the field frame in until the frame mates with the drive housing. Work slowly and carefully to prevent brush damage.

13. Lubricate the bushing in the commutator end frame with silicone lubricant, being careful not to get the lubricant on surrounding components.

14. Place the leather washer onto the armature shaft and slide the commutator end frame over the shaft and into position against the field frame. Line up the bolt holes, then install and tighten the two starter through bolts.

NOTE: *If replacement of the starter drive fails to cure improper engagement of the starter pinion to the flywheel, there are probably defective parts in the solenoid and/or shift lever. In this case, it would probably be best to take the starter assembly (incl. solenoid) where a pinion clearance check can be made. If the pinion clearance is incorrect, disassemble the solenoid and shift lever. Inspect these parts and replace as necessary.*

Brush Replacement

1. Disconnect the field coil strap(s) from the solenoid.

NOTE: *Scribe alignment marks on the field housing-to-drive end frame and the field housing-to-commutator end frame.*

2. Remove the two starter through bolts. Separate the commutator end frame, field frame, drive housing and armature from each other.

3. Replace the brushes one at a time to avoid having to mark the wiring, by performing the following steps:

   a. Remove the brush retaining screw and the old brush.

   b. Install the new brush in the same direction (large end towards the end of the field frame).

   c. Position the wire connector on the top of the brush, line up the holes and reinstall the screw. Make sure the screw is snug enough to ensure good contact.

4. Lubricate the drive housing bushing with silicone lubricant. Install the armature and clutch assembly into the drive housing, engaging the solenoid shift lever with the clutch and position the front end of the armature shaft into the drive housing bushing.

5. Apply a sealing compound (GM No. 1050026 or equivalent) to the drive housing around the area where the field frame mates with the housing.

6. Slide the field-frame assembly over the armature and guide the brushes over the armature commutator. Continue to push the field frame in until the frame mates with the drive housing. Work slowly and carefully to prevent brush damage.

7. Lubricate the bushing in the commutator end frame with silicone lubricant, being careful not to get the lubricant on surrounding components.

8. Place the leather washer onto the armature shaft and slide the commutator end frame over the shaft and into position against the field frame. Line up the bolt holes, then install and tighten the two starter through bolts.

NOTE: *If replacement of the starter drive fails to cure improper engagement of the starter pinion to the flywheel, there are probably defective parts in the solenoid and/or shift*

Battery and Starter Specifications

Year	Engine	Battery Cold Crank (Amps)	Starter Amps	Starter Volts	Starter RPM
1984–86	350	500	70–110	10.6	6,500–10,700

lever. In this case, it would probably be best to take the starter assembly (incl. solenoid) where a pinion clearance check can be made. If the pinion clearance is incorrect, disassemble the solenoid and shift lever. Inspect these parts and replace as necessary.

ENGINE MECHANICAL

Description

The two induction systems offered for this engine are the "Cross-Fire Injection" (CFI) which consists of two opposed throttle body fuel injection units and the "Tuned Port Injection" (TPI) which consists of a single throttle body and multiple fuel injectors (one for each cylinder).

The 350 cu. in. engines is equipped with a forged crankshaft. The cylinders are numbered front to rear with cylinders 1, 3, 5 and 7 on the left-bank and 2, 4, 6 and 8 on the right-bank. The firing order is 1-8-4-3-6-5-7-2. Both the crankshaft and camshaft are supported by five bearings. Viewed from the front, crankshaft rotation is clockwise. Lubrication is full pressure and a gear type oil pump feeds the system through a full flow oil filter. Both the oil pump and the distributor are driven by the camshaft. The main oil gallery pressurizes the bearings via the crankshaft and camshaft. The valve lifter oil gallery provides oil to the lifters which, in turn, feed the rocker arms through the hollow pushrods.

Engine Overhaul Tips

Most engine overhaul procedures are fairly standard. In addition to specific parts replacement procedures and complete specifications for your individual engine, this chapter also is a guide to accept rebuilding procedures. Examples of standard rebuilding practice are shown and should be used along with specific details concerning your particular engine.

Competent and accurate machine shop services will ensure maximum performance, reliability and engine life.

On most instances it is more profitable for the do-it-yourself mechanic to remove, clean and inspect the component, buy the necessary parts and deliver these to a shop for actual machine work.

On the other hand, much of the rebuilding work (crankshaft, block, bearings, piston rods, and other components) is well within the scope of the do-it-yourself mechanic.

TOOLS

The tools required for an engine overhaul or parts replacement will depend on the depth of your involvement. With a few exceptions, they will be the tools found in a mechanic's tool kit (see Chapter 1). More in-depth work will require any or all of the following:

- a dial indicator (reading in thousandths) mounted on a universal base
- micrometers and telescope gauges
- jaw and screw-type pullers
- scraper
- valve spring compressor
- ring groove cleaner
- piston ring expander and compressor
- ridge reamer
- cylinder hone or glaze breaker
- Plastigage®
- engine stand

Use of most of these tools is illustrated in this chapter. Many can be rented for a one-time use from a local parts jobber or tool supply house specializing in automotive work.

Occasionally, the use of special tools is called for. See the information on Special Tools and Safety Notice in the front of this book before substituting another tool.

INSPECTION TECHNIQUES

Procedures and specifications are given in this chapter for inspecting, cleaning and assessing the wear limits of most major components. Other procedures such as Magnaflux® and Zyglo® can be used to locate material flaws and stress cracks. Magnaflux® is a magnetic process applicable only to ferrous materials. The Zyglo® process coats the material with a fluorescent dye penetrant and can be used on any material Check for suspected surface cracks can be more readily made using spot check dye. The dye is sprayed onto the suspected area, wiped off and the area sprayed with a developer. Cracks will show up brightly.

OVERHAUL TIPS

Aluminum has become extremely popular for use in engines, due to its low weight. Observe the following precautions when handling aluminum parts:

• Never hot tank aluminum parts (the caustic hot tank solution will eat the aluminum.

• Remove all aluminum parts (identification tag, etc.) from engine parts prior to the tanking.

• Always coat threads lightly with engine oil or anti-seize compounds before installation, to prevent seizure.

• Never over-torque bolts or spark plugs especially in aluminum threads.

Stripped threads in any component can be repaired using any of several commercial repair kits (Heli-Coil®, Microdot®, Keenserts®, etc.).

When assembling the engine, any parts that will be frictional contact must be prelubed to provide lubrication at initial start-up. Any product specifically formulated for this purpose can be used, but engine oil is not recommended as a prelube.

When semi-permanent (locked, but removable) installation of bolts or nuts is desired, threads should be cleaned and coated with Loctite® or other similar, commercial non-hardening sealant.

REPAIRING DAMAGED THREADS

Several methods of repairing damaged threads are available. Heli-Coil® (shown here), Keenserts® and Microdot® are among the most widely used. All involve basically the same principle – drilling out stripped threads, tapping the hole and installing a prewound insert – making welding, plugging and oversize fasteners unnecessary.

Two types of thread repair inserts are usually supplied – a standard type for most Inch Coarse, Inch Fine, Metric Course and Metric Fine thread sizes and a spark lug type to fit most spark plug port sizes. Consult the individual manufacturer's catalog to determine exact applications. Typical thread repair kits will contain a selection of prewound threaded inserts, a tap (corresponding to the outside diameter threads of the insert) and an installation tool. Spark plug inserts usually differ because they require a tap equipped with pilot threads and a combined reamer/tap section. Most manufacturers also supply blister-packed thread repair inserts separately in addition to a master kit containing a variety of taps and inserts plus installation tools.

Before effecting a repair to a threaded hole, remove any snapped, broken or damaged bolts or studs. Penetrating oil can be used to free frozen threads; the offending item can be removed with locking pliers or with a screw or stud extractor. After the hole is clear, the thread can be repaired, as follows:

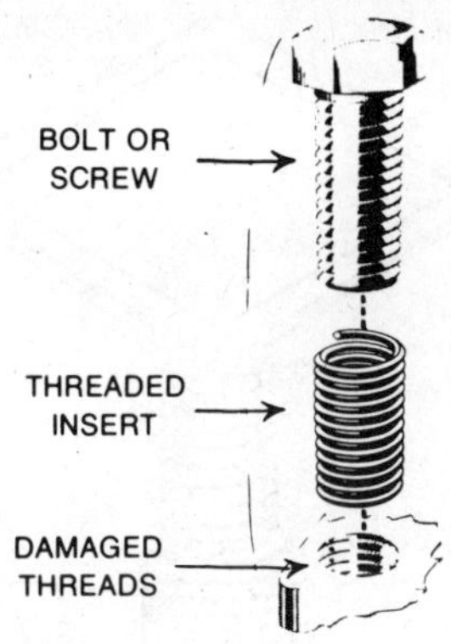

Damaged bolt holes can be repaired with thread repair inserts

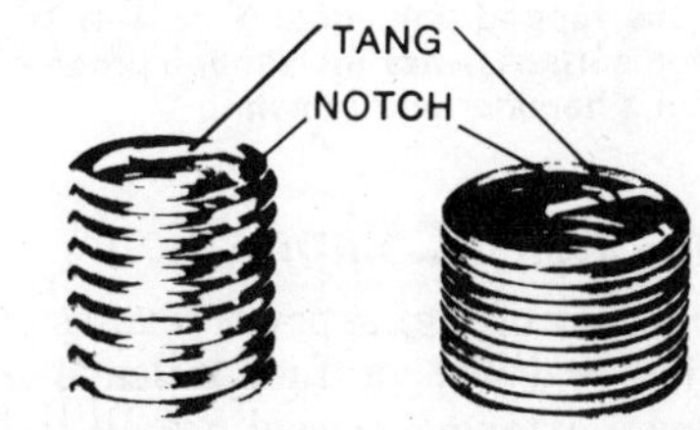

Standard thread repair insert (left) and spark plug thread insert (right)

Drill out the damaged threads with specified drill. Drill completely through the hole or to the bottom of a blind hole

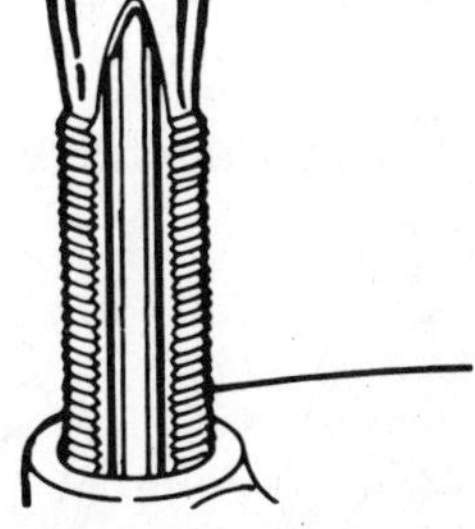

With the tap supplied, tap the hole to receive the thread insert. Keep the tap well oiled and back it out frequently to avoid clogging the threads

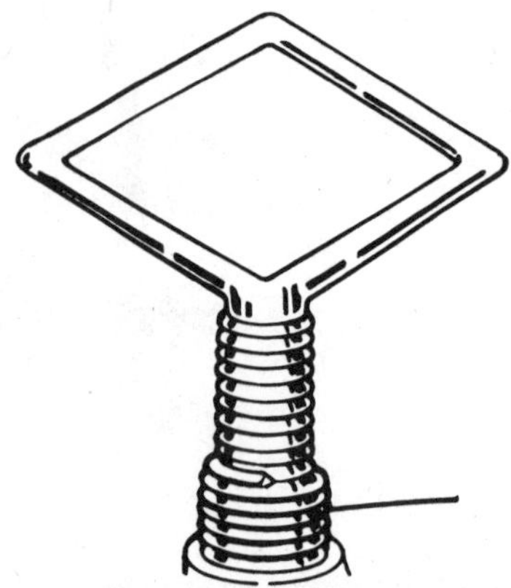

Screw the threaded insert onto the installation tool until the tang engages the slot. Screw the insert into the tapped hole until it is ¼–½ turn below the top surface. After installation break off the tang with a hammer and punch

Checking Engine Compression

A noticeable lack of engine power, excessive oil consumption and/or poor fuel mileage measured over an extended period are all indicators of internal engine wear. Worn piston rings, scored or worn cylinder bores, blown head gaskets, sticking or burnt valves and worn valve seats are all possible culprits here. A check of each cylinder's compression will help you locate the problems.

As mentioned in the Tools and Equipment section of Chapter 1, a screw-in type compression gauge is more accurate that the type you simply hold against the spark plug hole, although it takes slightly longer to use. It's worth it to obtain a more accurate reading. Follow the procedures below for gasoline and diesel engine trucks.

1. Warm up the engine to normal operating temperature.
2. Remove all spark plugs.
3. Disconnect the high tension lead from the ignition coil.
4. Fully open the throttle, either by operating the carburetor throttle linkage by hand or by having an assistant floor the accelerator pedal.

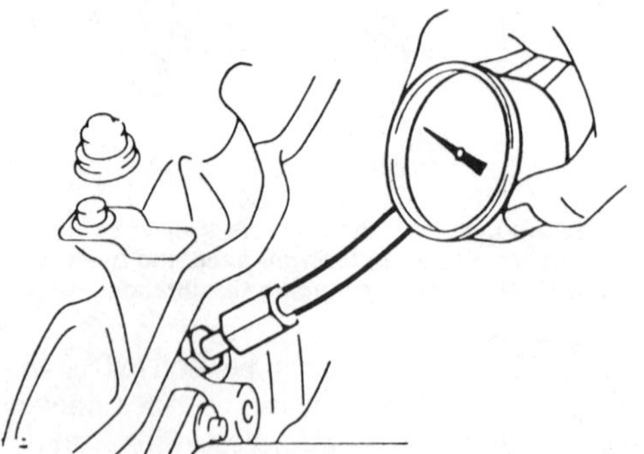

The screw-in type compression gauge is more accurate

5. Screw the compression gauge into the No. 1 spark plug hole until the fitting is snug.

NOTE: *Be careful not to crossthread the plug hole. On aluminum cylinder heads use extra care, as the threads in these heads are easily ruined.*

6. Ask an assistant to depress the accelerator pedal fully on both carbureted and fuel injected trucks. Then, while you read the compression gauge, ask the assistant to crank the engine two or three times in short bursts using the ignition switch.
7. Read the compression gauge at the end of each series of cranks, and record the highest of these readings. Repeat this procedure for each of the engine's cylinders. Compare the highest reading of each cylinder to the compression pressure specification in the Tune-Up Specifications chart in Chapter 2. The specs in this chart are maximum values.

NOTE: *A cylinder's compression pressure is usually acceptable if it is not less than 80% of maximum. The difference between each cylinder should be no more than 12–14 pounds.*

8. If a cylinder is unusually low, pour a tablespoon of clean engine oil into the cylinder through the spark plug hole and repeat the compression test. If the compression comes up after adding the oil, it appears that the cylinder's piston rings or bore are damaged or worn. If the pressure remains low, the valves may not be seating properly (a valve job is needed), or the head gasket may be blown near that cylinder. If compression in any two adjacent cylinders is low and if the addition of oil doesn't help the compression, there is leakage past the head gasket. Oil and coolant water in the combustion chamber can result from this problem. There may be evidence of water droplets on the engine dipstick when a head gasket has blown.

Engine

REMOVAL AND INSTALLATION

1984 (CFI)

1. Using a scribing tool, mark the relationship between each hood hinge and the hood, then remove the hood.
2. Disconnect the negative battery cable.
3. Remove the air cleaner assembly.
4. From the AIR check valve, disconnect the management, the right and the left hoses.
5. Place a fluid catch pan under the radiator, then loosen the radiator drain petcock and drain the cooling system.
6. At the front of the engine, loosen the al-

General Engine Specifications

Year	V.I.N. Code	Engine Displacement (cu in.)	Fuel Delivery System	Horsepower @ rpm■	Torque @ rpm (ft. lbs.)■	Bore and Stroke (in.)	Compression Ratio	Oil Pressure @ 2000 rpm
1984	L83	350	TBI ①	205 @ 4300	290 @ 2800	4.000 x 3.480	9.0:1	50–65
1985	L98	350	TPI ②	230 @ 4000	330 @ 3200	4.000 x 3.480	9.0:1	50–65
1986	L98	350	TPI ②	230 @ 4000	330 @ 3200	4.000 x 3.480	9.5:1	50–65

① Throttle Body Injection (Cross Fire Injection)
② Turned Port Injection

Valve Specifications

Year	V.I.N. Code	Engine Displacement (cu in.)	Seat Angle (deg)	Face Angle (deg)	Spring Test Pressure (lbs. @ in.)	Spring Installed Height (in.)	Stem to Guide Clearance (in.)		Stem Diameter (in.)	
							Intake	Exhaust	Intake	Exhaust
1984	L83	350	46	45	①	②	0.0010–0.0027	0.0010–0.0027	N.A.	N.A.
1985–86	L98	350	46	45	①	②	0.0010–0.0027	0.0010–0.0027	N.A.	N.A.

N.A.—Not Available
① Closed: 76–84 lbs. @ 1.70 in. (Intake); 76–84 lbs. @ 1.61 in. (Exhaust)
Open: 194–206 lbs. @ 1.25 in. (Intake); 194–206 lbs. @ 1.16 in. (Exhaust)
② 1 23/32 in. (Intake); 1 19/32 in. (Exhaust)

Camshaft Specifications

(All measurements in inches)

Year	V.I.N. Code	Engine	Eng. Mfg.	Journal Diameter					Bearing Clearance	Lobe Lift		Camshaft End Play
				1	2	3	4	5		Intake	Exhaust	
1984	L83	350	Chev.			1.8682–1.8692			—	0.2733	0.2820	0.004–0.012
1985–86	L98	350	Chev.			1.8682–1.8692			—	0.2733	0.2820	0.004–0.012

Crankshaft and Connecting Rod Specifications

All measurements are given in inches

Year	V.I.N. Code	Engine	Crankshaft				Connecting Rod		
			Main Brg Journal Dia	Main Brg Oil Clearance	Shaft End-Play	Thrust on No.	Journal Diameter	Oil Clearance	Side Clearance
1984	L83	350	①	②	0.002–0.006	5	2.0988–2.0998	0.0013–0.0035	0.008–0.014
1985–86	L98	350	①	②	0.002–0.006	5	2.0988–2.0998	0.0013–0.0035	0.008–0.014

① No. 1: 2.4484–2.4493
No. 2, 3, 4: 2.4481–2.4490
No. 5: 2.4479–2.4488
② No. 1: 0.0008–0.0020
No. 2, 3, 4: 0.0011–0.0023
No. 5: 0.0017–0.0032

Piston and Ring Specifications

(All measurements are given in inches. To convert inches to metric units, refer to the Metric Information section.)

Year	V.I.N. Code	Engine Type/ Disp. cu. in.	Piston-to-Bore Clearance	Ring Gap			Ring Side Clearance		
				Top Compression	Bottom Compression	Oil Control	Top Compression	Bottom Compression	Oil Control
1984	L83	350	0.0025–0.0035	0.010–0.020	0.010–0.020	0.015–0.055	0.0012–0.0032	0.0012–0.0032	0.002–0.007
1985–86	L98	350	0.0025–0.0035	0.010–0.020	0.010–0.020	0.015–0.055	0.0012–0.0032	0.0012–0.0032	0.002–0.007

Torque Specifications

(All readings in ft. lbs.)

Year	V.I.N. Code	Engine No. Cyl. Displacement (cu. in)	Eng. Mfg.	Cylinder Head Bolts	Rod Bearing Bolts	Main Bearing Bolts	Crankshaft Bolts	Flywheel to Crankshaft Bolts	Manifold	
									Intake	Exhaust
1984	L83	350	Chev.	65	45	80	60	60	35	20
1985–86	L98	350	Chev.	65	45	80	60	60	35	20

ternator adjusting bolt and remove the drive belt.

7. At the air conditioning (A/C) compressor, remove the rear braces (one at the intake and one at the exhaust) and disconnect the wiring electrical connectors.

8. From the AIR pump, remove the pulley, the AIR management valve adaptor, the pump-to-engine bolts and the pump.

9. From the thermostat housing, remove the upper radiator hose and the power steering reservoir brace.

10. At the alternator, remove the electrical connectors, the alternator brace and the alternator.

11. At the intake manifold, remove the AIR pipe and the power steering brace.

12. At the power steering pump, remove the reservoir brace and the lower bracket, then move the reservoir, the brace, the pump and the A/C wire loom toward the front of the vehicle.

13. Remove the fuel inlet and return lines.

14. At the water pump, remove the A/C compressor and idler pulley bracket nuts.

15. At the A/C compressor, remove the lower mounting bolt, move the bracket forward and remove the upper bolt, then move the compressor aside.

16. Near where the mechanical fuel pump is normally mounted, remove the lower bracket of the fuel lines.

17. Remove the idler pulley bracket.

18. At the water pump, remove the lower radiator and the heater hoses. Move the hoses and the fuel lines aside.

19. At the throttle bodies, remove the accelerator, the TV and the cruise control brackets, then label and disconnect the electrical connectors.

20. Disconnect the front ground stud, the coolant sensor and the EGR solenoid, then label and disconnect the vacuum hoses.

21. From the valve cover clip, remove the wiring harness. Move the AIR management valve, the AIR pipe and the wiring harness to the back right-side of the engine.

22. From the intake cover stud, remove the tachometer filter and the ground wires.

23. From the distributor, disconnect the electrical connectors, remove the distributor cap from the distributor. Disconnect the spark plug wires from the spark plugs, then the distributor cap/wire assembly from the vehicle.

24. From the intake manifold, remove the heater hose. Mark the distributors position and remove the distributor from the engine.

25. Remove the oil sending unit, the rear intake manifold bolt and the wire bracket.

26. At the front of the engine, remove the crankshaft pulley (for clearance purposes).

27. Raise and support the front of the vehicle on jackstands.

28. Remove the crossover pipe from the exhaust manifold, the catalytic convertor and the hanger.

29. From the right exhaust manifold, remove the converter air management pipe.

30. Remove the starter wires and the oxygen sensor wire.

31. Disconnect the coolant sensor from the cylinder head and the bracket from the block.

32. Disconnect the wiring harness from the oil pan, the front of the block, the coolant and oil temperature sensors, then the oxygen sensor.

33. Remove the engine ground strap from the rear of the block (above the oil filter).

34. Remove the flywheel cover and the torque converter-to-flywheel bolts, then push the torque converter back into the transmission.

35. Remove the bellhousing-to-engine bolts from the right-side; remove the lower bolt, then the upper bolt (in order to gain access to the center bolt). Remove the bellhousing-to-engine bolts from the left-side, including the ground wire.

36. Using a floor jack and a block of wood (for protection), support the engine and remove the engine-to-mount bolts from both sides, then lower the engine and remove the floor jack. Remove the jackstands and lower the vehicle.

37. Using a floor jack, support the transmission.

38. Secure the engine to a vertical lifting device, then carefully remove the engine from the transmission and the vehicle. Secure the engine onto a work stand.

39. To install, reverse the removal procedures. Check the systems for leaks.

1985–86 (TPI)

1. Using a scribing tool, mark the relationship between each hood hinge and the hood, then remove the hood.
2. Disconnect the negative battery cable.
3. Remove the air cleaner assembly.
4. Place a fluid catch pan under the radiator, then loosen the radiator drain petcock and drain the cooling system.
5. At the front of the engine, loosen the alternator adjusting bolt and remove the drive belt.
6. From the A/C compressor, disconnect the electrical connections and remove the braces from the back-side.

NOTE: *Many of the fuel feed and return lines are under high pressure, the fittings are of a screw coupling type with O-rings.*

7. Remove the fuel lines by performing the following procedures:

   a. Reduce the pressure in the fuel system before disconnecting the fittings.

   b. Use a backup wrench to loosen the fittings.

   c. Always check the O-rings for cuts or damage and replace them (if necessary).

   d. If replacing any of the fuel lines, ALWAYS use steel tubing (NOT copper or aluminum).

8. At the A/C compressor, remove the bracket-to-engine bolts, the compressor-to-bracket bolt, the bracket and move the compressor aside.
9. Disconnect the heater hoses, then the upper radiator hose from the thermostat housing.
10. Near where the mechanical fuel pump is normally mounted, remove the fuel line clip.
11. At the intake manifold, remove the PFI electrical harness, the cruise control, detent cable/bracket and accelerator cables.
12. At the distributor, remove the shield, the distributor cap, the 4-wire connector and the distributor.
13. At the oil pressure sending unit, remove the electrical connector(s) and the unit.
14. Label and disconnect the necessary vacuum hoses and electrical connectors.
15. At the power steering rack/pinion, disconnect the power steering hoses.
16. At the front of the engine, remove the crankshaft pulley.
17. Disconnect the AIR hose from the converter check valve.
18. Move the fuel lines aside. Disconnect the radiator hose from the water pump and the power steering reservoir bracket.
19. Raise and support the front of the vehicle on jackstands.
20. Disconnect the AIR pipe from the exhaust manifold and the catalytic converter.
21. Disconnect the hanger and the heat shields from the "Y" exhaust pipe and the catalytic converter. Remove the "Y" exhaust pipe from the exhaust manifold and the catalytic converter.
22. Disconnect the wire from the oxygen sensor.
23. Remove the flywheel cover. If equipped with an automatic transmission, remove the torque converter-to-flywheel bolts and slide the converter toward the transmission.
24. Remove the engine-to-mount thru bolts and the bellhousing-to-engine bolts. Lower the vehicle.
25. Disconnect the knock sensor wire, the ground cable from the block, the positive battery from the battery (remove the cable from the vehicle).
26. Remove the right-rear intake manifold bolt and install a lift hook.
27. Using a floor jack, support the transmission.
28. Using a vertical lifting device, secure it to the engine, separate the engine from the

transmission and remove the engine from the vehicle. Secure the engine onto a work stand.

29. To install, reverse the removal procedures. Check the systems for leaks.

Rocker Arm Cover

REMOVAL AND INSTALLATION

Right-Side

1984 WITH CFI

1. Disconnect the negative battery cable.
2. Remove the air cleaner.
3. Disconnect the AIR hose from the exhaust check valve.
4. At the TBI units, disconnect the fuel inlet and return lines.
5. Loosen the alternator adjusting bolt and remove the drive belt.
6. At the A/C compressor, remove the two rear braces and the lower mounting bolt.
7. At the water pump, remove the idler pulley brackets.
8. At the A/C compressor, slide the compressor mounting bracket forward, disconnect the electrical connectors, then remove the mounting bolt and the compressor.
9. Remove the rocker arm cover bolts. At the rear of the cylinder head, bend the bracket and remove the rocker arm cover.
10. Using a putty knife, clean the gasket mounting surfaces.
11. To install, use RTV sealant (apply a 1/8" bead around the cover sealing edge, going around the bolt holes) and reverse the removal procedures. Torque the rocker arm cover-to-cylinder head to 50 inch lbs.

NOTE: *When applying the RTV sealant, keep the sealant out of the bolt holes; this could cause a hydraulic condition which could ruin the cylinder head.*

1985–86 WITH TPI

1. Disconnect the negative battery cable.
2. Remove the fresh air pipe.
3. Disconnect any necessary electrical connections.
4. Remove the rocker arm cover bolts and the cover from the engine.
5. Using a putty knife, clean the gasket mounting surfaces.
6. To install, use RTV sealant (apply a 1/8" bead around the cover sealing edge, going around the bolt holes) and reverse the removal procedures. Torque the rocker arm cover-to-cylinder head to 50 inch lbs.

NOTE: *When applying the RTV sealant, keep the sealant out of the bolt holes; this could cause a hydraulic condition which could ruin the cylinder head.*

Left-Side

1984 WITH CFI

1. Disconnect the negative battery cable.
2. Remove the air cleaner.
3. Disconnect the PCV valve and the hose from the intake manifold and the rocker arm cover.
4. At the intake manifold, disconnect the brake vacuum pipe.
5. Loosen the alternator adjusting bolt and remove the drive belt.
6. Disconnect the radiator hose bracket from the alternator brace.
7. Remove the alternator mounting bolts and move the alternator aside.
8. Remove the rocker arm cover-to-cylinder head bolts.
9. Disconnect and label the spark plug wires.
10. At the rear of the cylinder head, bend the bracket and remove the rocker arm cover.
11. Using a putty knife, clean the gasket mounting surfaces.
12. To install, use RTV sealant (apply a 1/8" bead around the cover sealing edge, going around the bolt holes) and reverse the removal procedures. Torque the rocker arm cover-to-cylinder head to 50 inch lbs.

NOTE: *When applying the RTV sealant, keep the sealant out of the bolt holes; this could cause a hydraulic condition which could ruin the cylinder head.*

1985–86 WITH TPI

1. Disconnect the negative battery cable.
2. Remove the air cleaner. Drain the cooling system to a level below the upper radiator hose.
3. Disconnect the PCV valve and hose from the intake manifold and the rocker arm cover.
4. From the thermostat housing, remove the upper radiator hose.
5. Remove the rocker arm cover bolts and the cover from the engine.
6. Using a putty knife, clean the gasket mounting surfaces.
7. To install, use RTV sealant (apply a 1/8" bead around the cover sealing edge, going around the bolt holes) and reverse the removal procedures. Torque the rocker arm cover-to-cylinder head to 50 inch lbs.

NOTE: *When applying the RTV sealant, keep the sealant out of the bolt holes; this could cause a hydraulic condition which could ruin the cylinder head.*

Rocker Arm

REMOVAL AND INSTALLATION

1. Refer to the "Rocker Arm Cover, Removal and Installation" procedures in this section and remove the rocker arm covers.
2. Remove the rocker arm nuts, the rocker arm ball washers, the rocker arms and the push rods.

NOTE: *When removing the rocker arm parts, be sure to keep them in order so that they may be installed in their same locations. Before installing the rocker arms and/or the rocker arm balls, be sure to coat the bearing surfaces with Molykote® or equivalent.*

3. Install the push rods; make sure that the rods seat in the lifter sockets.
4. Install the rocker arms, the rocker arm ball washers and the nuts, then tighten the rocker arm nuts until all of the lash is removed.
5. To adjust the valves, perform the following procedures:

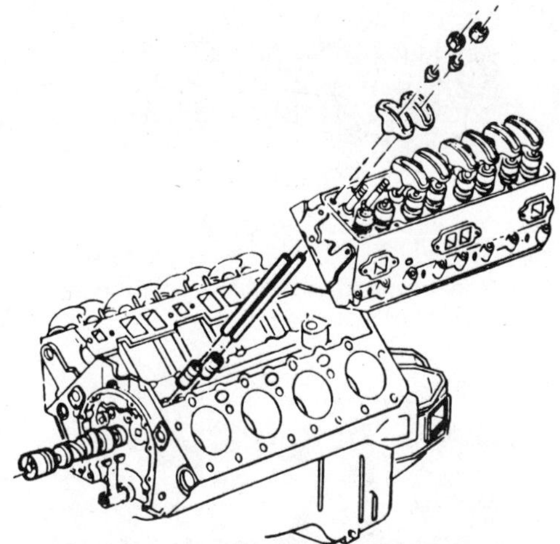

Removing the rocker arm assemblies

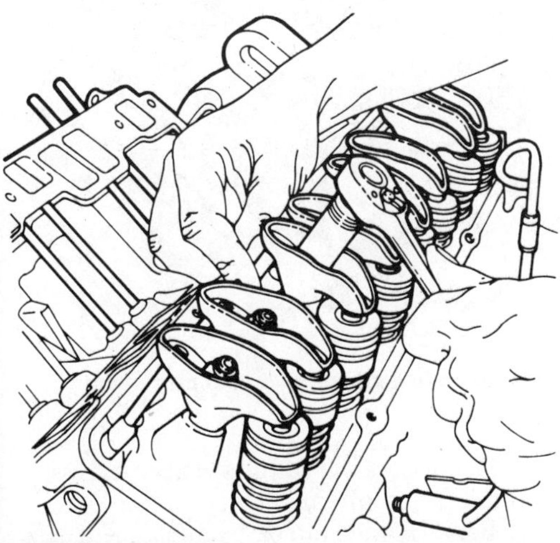

Adjusting the valves

a. Turn the crankshaft to position the No. 1 cylinder at the TDC of it's compression stroke and the timing mark on the damper pulley is aligned with the 0° mark on the timing plate.

NOTE: *Check the valves of the No. 1 cylinder, if they are loose, the engine is positioned on the compression stroke of the No. 6 cylinder. To correct this situation, turn the crankshaft 1 full revolution, then align the timing mark on the damper pulley with the 0° mark on the timing plate.*

b. With the engine positioned on the compression stroke of the No. 1 cylinder, adjust the exhaust valves of the No. 1, 3, 4, 8 cylinders and the intake valves of the No. 1, 2, 5, 7 cylinders.

c. To adjust the valves, back out the adjusting nut until lash is felt at the push rod (rotate the rod), then turn in the adjusting nut until the lash is removed. After the lash has been removed, turn the nut in 1 additional full turn (to center the lifter plunger).

d. Turn the crankshaft 1 full turn, then align the timing mark on the damper pulley with the 0° mark on the timing plate. With the engine in this position, adjust the exhaust valves of the No. 2, 5, 6, 7 cylinders and the intake valves of the No. 3, 4, 6, 8 cylinders.

6. To install the rocker arm covers, use sealant and reverse the removal procedures.

Thermostat

REMOVAL AND INSTALLATION

1. Disconnect the negative battery cable.
2. Remove the air cleaner.
3. Drain the cooling system to a level below the upper radiator hose.
4. Remove the upper radiator hose from the thermostat housing.
5. Remove the thermostat housing mounting bolts, the housing and the thermostat.

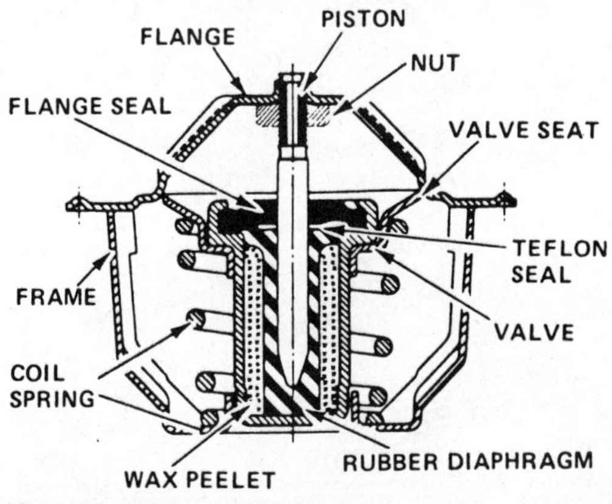

Cross-sectional view of the thermostat

6. Using a putty knife, clean the gasket mounting surfaces.

7. To install, use RTV sealant (apply a 1/8" bead around the sealing surface of the intake manifold) and reverse the removal procedures. Torque the thermostat housing-to-intake manifold to 18–23 ft. lbs. Refill the cooling system. Start the engine and check for leaks.

Intake Manifold

REMOVAL AND INSTALLATION

1984 With CFI

1. Disconnect the negative battery cable. Remove the air cleaner.

2. Drain the cooling system to a level below the intake mainfold.

3. Reduce the pressure in the fuel system, then disconnect the fuel inlet and return lines.

4. Label and disconnect the necessary vacuum hoses and electrical connectors.

5. Disconnect the accelerator, the cruise control and the detent cables, then disconnect the cable from the accelerator bracket.

6. Remove the intake cover nuts/bolts and the cover from the intake manifold.

7. Disconnect the radiator hose from the thermostat housing and the alternator brace.

8. Remove the distributor cap. Using a scribing tool, mark the relationship of the rotor to the distributor and the distributor to the engine.

9. At the rear of the intake manifold, disconnect the heater hose.

10. Loosen the alternator adjusting bolt and remove the drive belt.

11. Remove the AIR pump pulley, the AIR pump valve adapter, the AIR pump-to-engine bolts and the AIR pump.

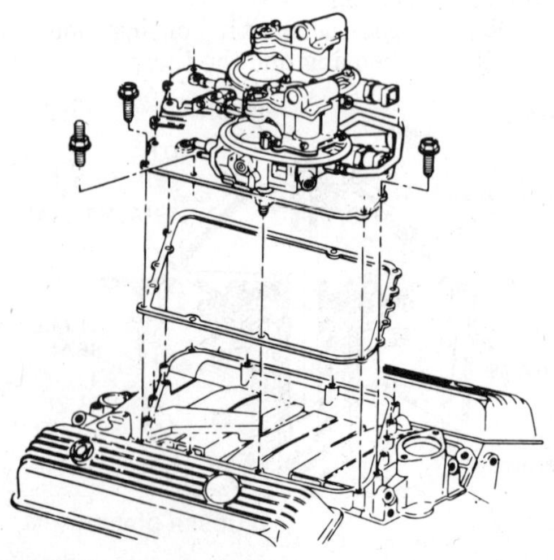

1984 TBI plate installation

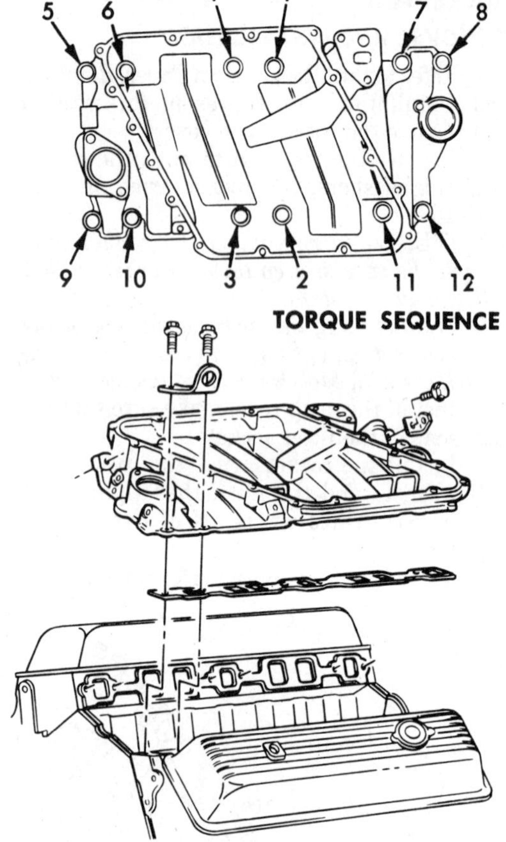

1984 intake manifold installation and torque sequence

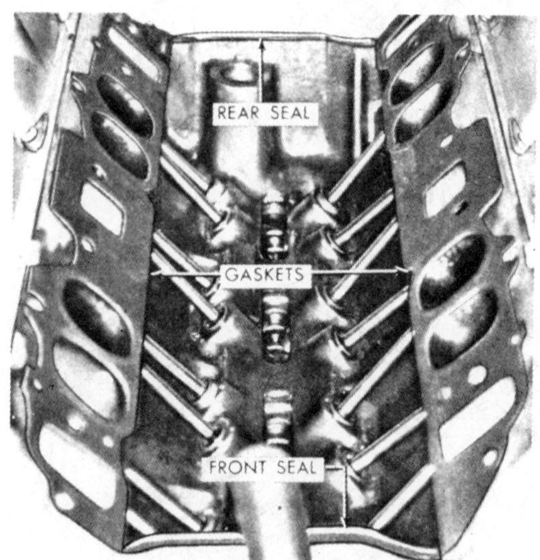

Intake manifold gasket and seal placement

12. Disconnect the coolant temperature sensor electrical connector.

13. Remove the intake manifold bolts and the manifold from the engine.

14. Using a putty knife, clean the gasket mounting surfaces.

15. To install, use a new gasket (bend the tab flush with the rear face of the cylinder), RTV sealant (apply a $^{3}/_{16}$ in. on the front and rear ridges of the cylinder case), Loctite® (on the bolt threads) and reverse the removal procedures. Torque the intake manifold-to-engine bolts to 35 ft. lbs. and the intake cover-to-intake manifold bolts to 15–25 ft. lbs. Refill the cooling system. Start the engine and check for leaks.

1985–86 With TPI

1. Disconnect the negative battery cable. Remove the air cleaner.
2. Drain the cooling system to a level below the intake manifold.
3. Refer to the "Tuned Port Injection (TPI)" in the Fuel System of Chapter 4, then remove the Mass Air Flow Sensor, the Plenum, the Intake Runners and the Fuel Rail.
4. Label and disconnect the necessary vacuum hoses and electrical connectors.
5. Remove the distributor cap. Using a scribing tool, mark the relationship of the rotor to the distributor and the distributor to the engine.
6. At the rear of the intake manifold, disconnect the heater hose.
7. Loosen the alternator adjusting bolt and remove the drive belt.
8. Remove the AIR pump-to-engine bracket bolts and the AIR pump.

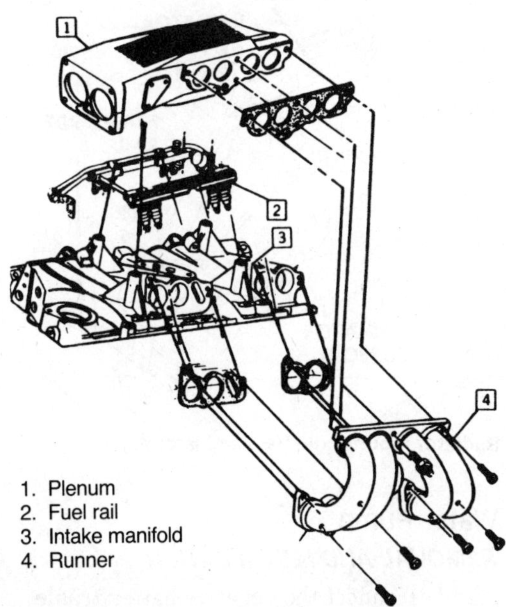

Exploded view of the Tuned Port Injection TPI (1985 and later)

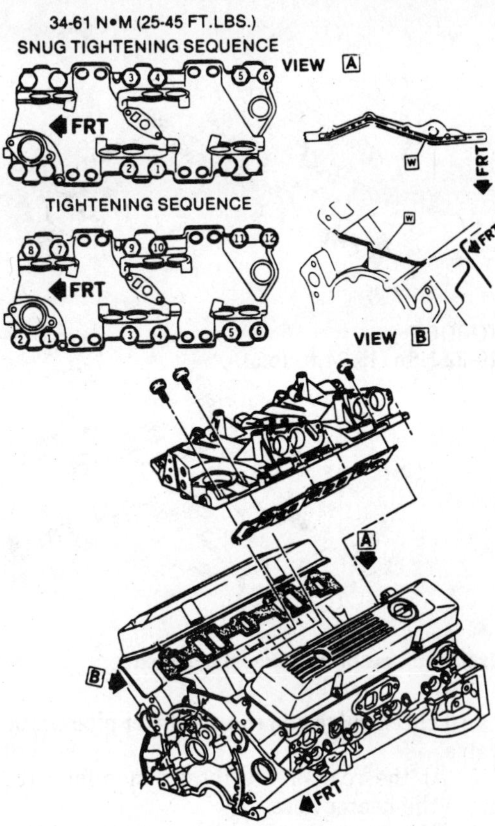

View of the intake manifold and the torquing sequence for the Tuned Port Injection (TPI) engine (1985 and later)

9. Disconnect the coolant temperature sensor electrical connector.
10. Remove the intake manifold bolts and the manifold from the engine.
11. Using a putty knife, clean the gasket mounting surfaces.
12. To install, use a new gasket (bend the tab flush with the rear face of the cylinder), RTV sealant (apply a $^{3}/_{16}''$ on the front and rear ridges of the cylinder case), Loctite® (on the bolt threads) and reverse the removal procedures. Torque the intake manifold-to-engine bolts to 25–45 ft. lbs. Refill the cooling system. Start the engine and check for leaks.

Exhaust Manifold

REMOVAL AND INSTALLATION

Right-Side

1. Disconnect the negative battery cable.
2. Remove the air cleaner. Place a fluid catch pan under the radiator and drain the cooling system.
3. At the rear of the A/C compressor, remove the brace and allow it to hang.
4. Disconnect the AIR hose from the ex-

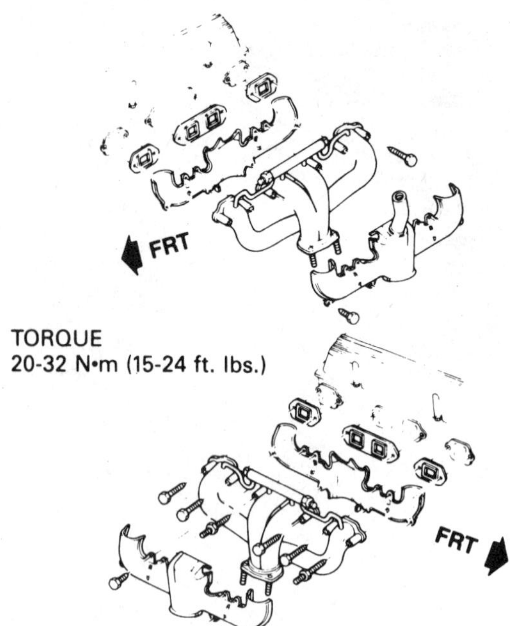

Exploded view of the exhaust manifold

haust check valve and the converter pipe check valve.

5. At the rear of the intake manifold, remove the heater hose.

6. Disconnect the spark plug wires from the spark plugs and the valve covers, then remove the spark plugs.

7. From the right cylinder head, remove the temperature sending unit.

8. Raise and support the front of the vehicle on jackstands.

9. At the exhaust manifold, remove the exhaust pipe, the AIR pipe and the two rear exhaust manifold bolts.

10. Remove the dipstick and the dipstick tube from the exhaust manifold. Lower the vehicle.

11. Remove the exhaust manifold-to-engine bolts and the manifold, then discard the gasket.

12. Using a putty knife, clean the gasket mounting surfaces.

13. To install, use a new gasket and reverse the removal procedures. Torque the exhaust manifold-to-engine bolts to 15–24 ft. lbs. Refill the cooling system. Start the engine and check for leaks.

Left-Side

1. Disconnect the negative battery cable. Remove the air cleaner.

2. Disconnect the PCV hose from the intake manifold and the rocker arm cover, then the AIR hose from the exhaust check valve.

3. From the rear of the alternator, remove the brace at the exhaust manifold and allow it to hang.

4. Raise and support the front of the vehicle on jackstands.

5. Disconnect the exhaust pipe from the exhaust manifold. Lower the vehicle.

6. Remove the exhaust manifold bolts and the manifold.

7. Using a putty knife, clean the gasket mounting surfaces.

8. To install, use a new gasket and reverse the removal procedures. Torque the exhaust manifold-to-engine bolts to 15–24 ft. lbs.

Radiator

REMOVAL AND INSTALLATION

1. Disconnect the negative battery cable.

2. Place a fluid catch pan under the radiator and drain the cooling system.

3. Remove the upper, the lower and the overflow radiator hoses.

4. Remove the A/C accumulator and move it aside; DO NOT disconnect the fluid lines.

5. If equipped with an automatic transmission, disconnect and plug the oil cooler lines from the radiator.

6. Disconnect the electrical connector from the fan and the shroud, then remove the fan (to gain access to the lower cooler line).

7. Remove the upper shroud bolts, the shroud and the radiator.

8. To install, reverse the removal procedures. Refill the cooling system. Start the engine and check for leaks.

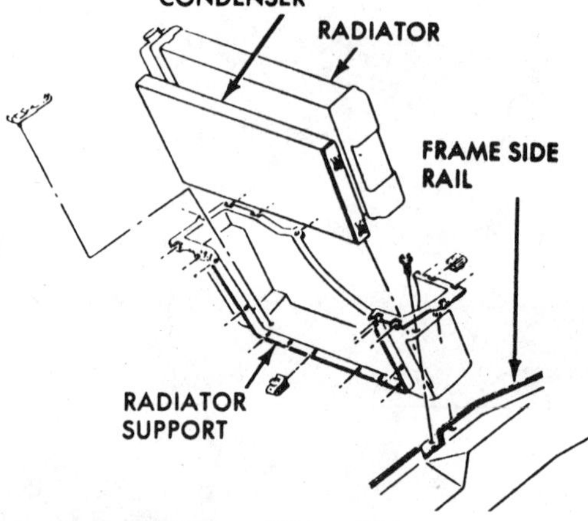

Radiator mounting—1984 and later

Water Pump

REMOVAL AND INSTALLATION

1. Disconnect the negative battery cable.

2. Place a fluid catch pan under the radiator and drain the cooling system.

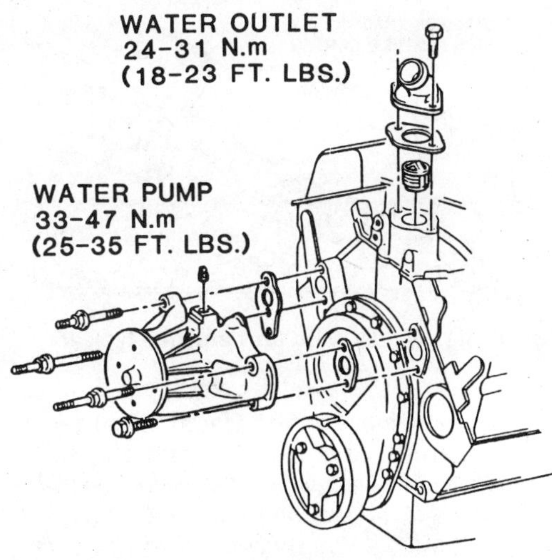

Exploded view of the water pump

3. Loosen the alternator adjusting bolt and remove the drive belt.

4. Remove the water pump and the AIR pump pulleys.

5. Remove the air management valve adapter and the AIR pump.

6. Reduce the pressure in the fuel system, then remove the fuel inlet and return lines.

7. At the A/C compressor, disconnect the electrical connectors, then remove the rear braces, the lower mounting bolt, the compressor and the idler pulley bracket nuts.

8. Remove the left and right AIR hoses from the check valve.

9. Remove the AIR pipe from the intake manifold and the power steering pump reservoir.

10. Remove the power steering reservoir bracket along with the alternator's top bolt.

11. Remove the lower AIR bracket from the water pump.

12. At the water pump, remove the lower radiator and heater hoses.

13. Remove the water pump-to-engine bolts and the water pump.

14. Using a putty knife, clean the gasket mounting surfaces.

15. To install, use a new gasket and reverse the removal procedures. Torque the water pump-to-engine bolts to 25–35 ft. lbs. Refill the cooling system. Start the engine and check for leaks.

Cylinder Head

REMOVAL AND INSTALLATION

1. Refer to the "Rocker Arm, Removal and Installation," the "Intake Manifold, Removal and Installation" and the "Exhaust Manifold, Removal and Installation" procedures in this section, then remove the rocker arms, the intake manifold and the exhaust manifold (depending on which cylinder head is being removed) from the enigne.

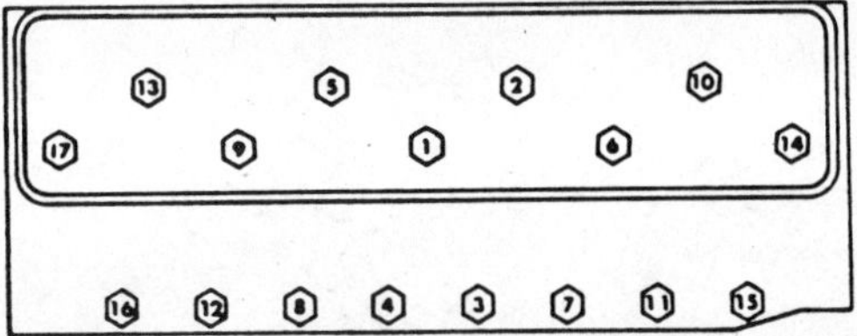

Small block V8 cylinder head bolt tightening sequence

2. Remove the cylinder head bolts, the cylinder head(s) and the gasket(s) (discard the gasket).

3. Using a putty knife, clean the gasket mounting surfaces.

4. To install, use new gasket(s) and reverse the removal procedures. The head gasket is installed with the bead up.

NOTE: *If a steel head gasket is used, coat both sides of the gasket (thinly and evenly) with sealer. Clean the bolt threads, apply sealing compound No. 1052080 or equivalent and install the bolts finger tight.*

5. Torque the head bolts a little at a time, in the sequence, to 60–75 ft. lbs. Adjust the valves.

CLEANING AND INSPECTION

1. Refer to the "Valves, Removal and Installation" procedures in this section and remove the valve assemblies from the cylinder head.

2. Using a small wire power brush, clean the carbon from the combustion chambers and the valve ports.

3. Inspect the cylinder head for cracks in the exhaust ports, combustion chambers or external cracks to the water chamber.

4. Thoroughly clean the valve guides using a suitable wire bore brush.

NOTE: *Excessive valve stem to bore clearance will cause excessive oil consumption and may cause valve breakage. Insufficient clearance will result in noisy and sticky functioning of the valve and disturb engine smoothness.*

5. Measure valve stem clearance as follows:

a. Clamp a dial indicator on one side of the cylinder head rocker arm cover gasket rail.

b. Locate the indicator so that movement of the valve stem from side to side (crosswise to the head) will cause a direct movement of the indicator stem. The indicator stem must contact the side of the valve stem just above the valve guide.

Measuring valve stem clearance with dial gauge

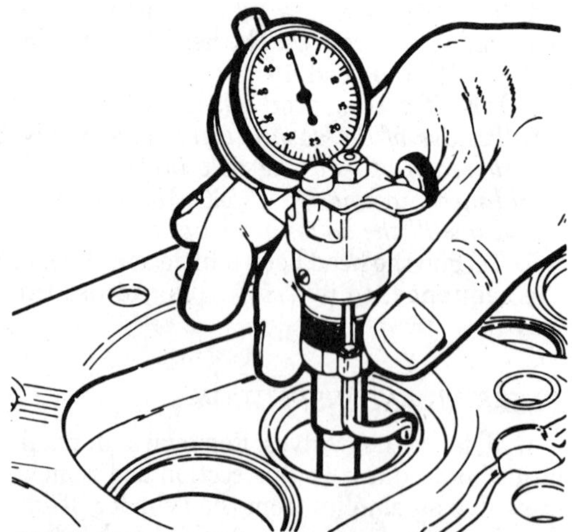

Checking valve seat concentricity with run-out gauge

c. Prop the valve head about $^1/_{16}$″ off the valve seat.

d. Move the stem of the valve from side to side using light pressure to obtain a clearance reading. If the clearance exceeds specifications, it will be necessary to ream (for oversize valves) or knurl (raise the bore for original valves) the valve guides.

6. Inspect rocker arm studs for wear or damage.

7. Install a dial micrometer into the valve guide and check the valve seat for concentricity.

RESURFACING

1. Using a straightedge, check the cylinder head for warpage.

2. If warpage exceeds 0.003 in. in a 6 in. span, or 0.006 in. over the total length, the cylinder head must be resurfaced. Resurfacing can be performed at most machine shops.

NOTE: *When resurfacing the cylinder heads, the intake manifold mounting position is altered and must be corrected by machining a proportionate amount from the intake manifold flange.*

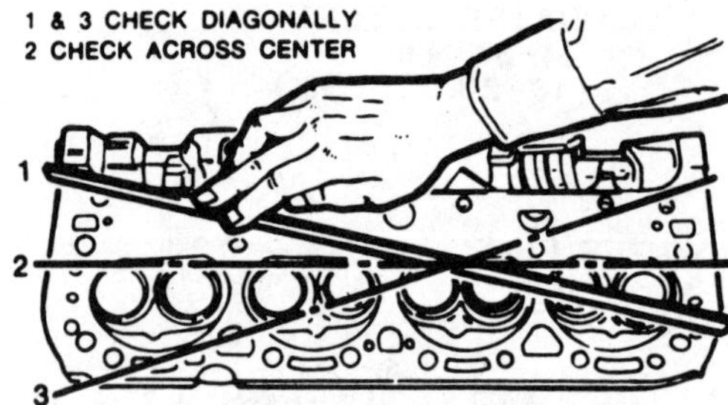

Checking cylinder head for warpage—typical

Valves

REMOVAL AND INSTALLATION

NOTE: *Invert the cylinder heads and number the valve faces (front-to-rear), using a permanent felt-tip marker.*

1. Refer to the "Cylinder Head, Removal and Installation" procedures in this section and remove the cylinder heads from the engine.

2. Remove valve rocker arm nuts, the ball washers and the rocker arms (if not previously done).

3. Using a Valve Spring Compressor tool No. J-15062, compress the valve springs and remove stem keys. Release the compressor tool and the rotators or spring caps, the oil shedders, the springs and the damper assembly, then remove the oil seals and the valve spring shims.

Using a valve spring compressor to compress the valve spring

4. Remove the valves from cylinder head and place them in a rack in their proper sequence so that they can be assembled in their original positions. Discard any bent or damaged valves.

5. To install, use new oil seals and reverse the removal procedures. Refer to the "Rocker Arm, Removal and Installation" procedures in this section and adjust the valve lash.

INSPECTION

Inspect the valve faces and seats (in the head) for pits, burned spots and other evidence of poor seating. If a valve face is in such bad shape that the head of the valve must be ground in order to true up the face, discard the valve because the sharp edge will run too hot. The correct angle for the valve face is 45°. We recommend that the refacing be done by a reputable machine shop.

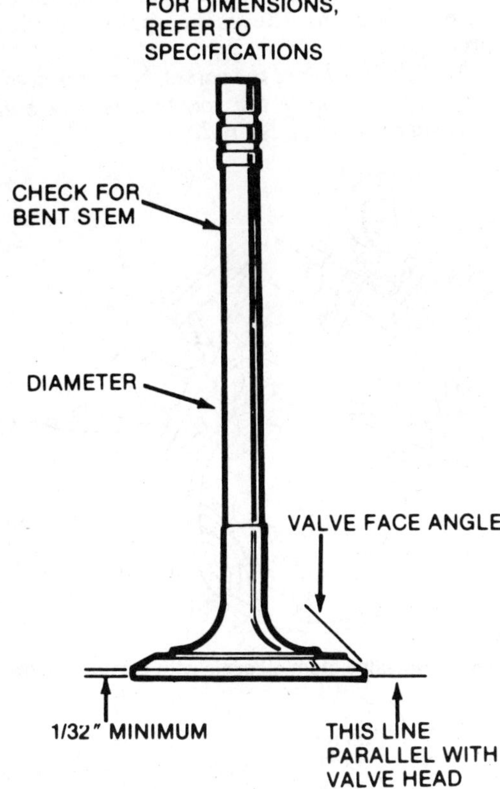

Critical valve dimensions

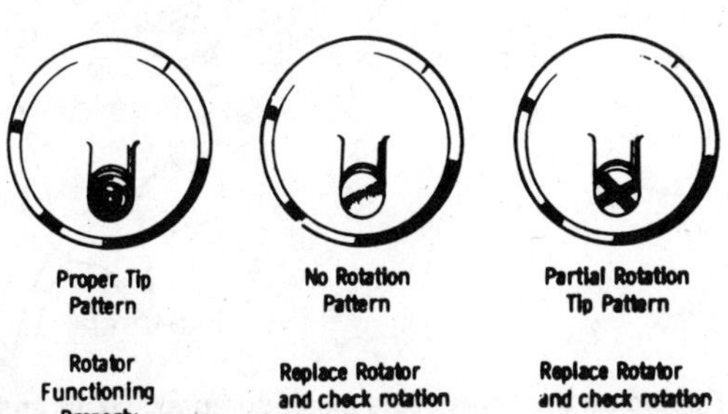

Typical valve stem wear patterns

Check the valve stem for scoring and burned spots. If not noticeably scored or damaged, clean the valve stem with solvent to remove all gum and varnish. Clean the valve guides using solvent and an expanding wire-type valve guide cleaner. If you have access to a dial indicator for measuring the valve stem-to-guide clearance, mount it so that the stem of the indicator is at 90° to the valve stem and as closes to the valve guide as possible. Move the valve off it's seat and measure the valve guide-to-stem clearance by rocking the stem back and forth to actuate the dial indicator. Measure the valve stems using a micrometer and compare to specifications to determine whether stem or guide wear is responsible for the excess clearance. If a dial indicator and micrometer are not available to you, take the cylinder head and valves to a reputable machine shop for inspection.

These engines are equipped with valve rotators, which double as valve spring caps. In normal operation, the rotators put a certain degree of wear on the tip of the valve stem; this wear appears as concentric rings on the stem tip. However, if the rotator is not working properly, the wear may appear as straight notches or "X" patterns across the valve stem tip. Whenever the valves are removed from the cylinder head, the tips should be inspected for improper pattern, which could indicate valve rotator problems. Valve stem tips will have to be ground flat if the rotator patterns are severe.

RESURFACING

1. Using a wire power brush, clean the carbon and deposits from the valves.

2. Using a valve grinding machine, grind a new valve face on the valve head and trim the valve stem to the proper length.

NOTE: *If the edge of the valve face is ground to a thickness of less than* $\frac{1}{32}$*", discard the valve.*

LAPPING THE VALVES

When the valve faces and seats have been refaced and re-cut or if they are determined to be in good condition, the valves must be "lapped in" to ensure efficient sealing when the valve closes against the seat.

1. Invert the cylinder head so that the combustion chambers are facing up.

2. Lightly lubricate the valve stems with

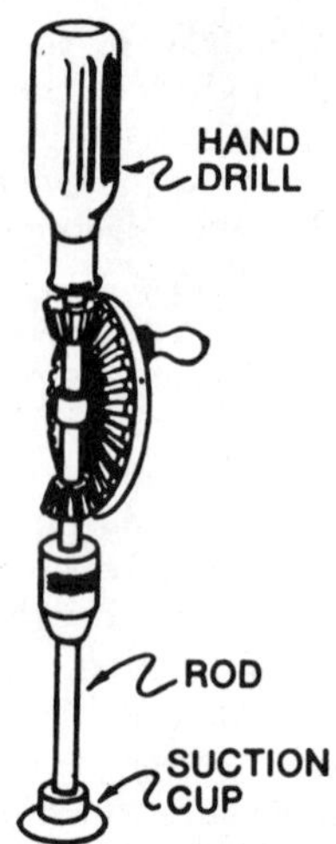

Fabricated valve lapping tool

Lapping the valve and seat by hand—typical

clean oil and coat the valve seats with valve grinding compound. Install the valves in the head as numbered.

3. Attach the suction cup of a valve lapping tool to a valve head. Moisten the suction cup to securely attach the tool to the valve.

4. Rotate the tool between the palms, changing position and lifting the tool often to prevent grooving. Lap the valve until a smooth, polished seat is evident (you may have to add a bit more compound after some lapping is done).

5. Remove the valve, the tool and ALL traces of grinding compound with solvent-soaked rag or rinse the head with solvent.

NOTE: *Valve lapping can also be done by fastening a suction cup to a piece of drill rod in a hand "egg-beater" type drill. Proceed as above, using the drill as a lapping tool. Due to the higher speeds involved when using the hand drill, care must be exercised to avoid grooving the seat. Lift the tool and change direction of rotation often.*

Valve Springs

REMOVAL AND INSTALLATION

NOTE: *The following procedures apply to the cylinder heads installed on the engine. Access to an air compressor and the purchase of certain tools are required.*

1. Refer to the "Rocker Arm Cover, Removal and Installation" procedures in this section and remove the rocker arm cover.

2. Remove the spark plug from the cylinder which is being serviced, then set the cylinder on TDC of the compression stroke.

3. Install an Air Line Adaptor tool No. J-23590 and apply air pressure to the cylinder. The compressed air is used to hold the valves in place during the valve spring service procedures.

NOTE: *If either of the valves, being serviced, are open, remove the rocker arm, the ball washer and the push rod.*

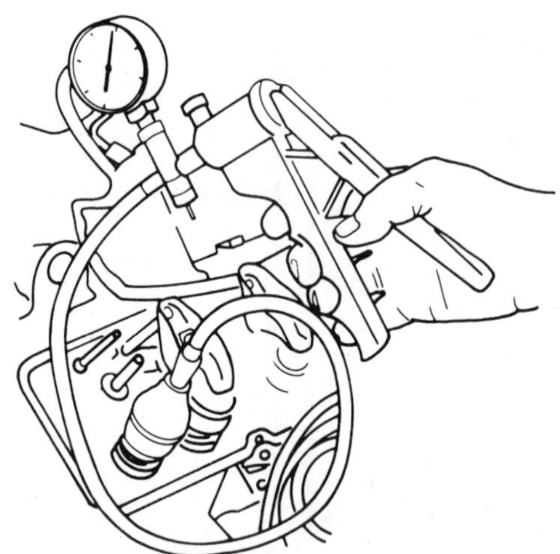

Checking valve stem oil seals with vacuum tester

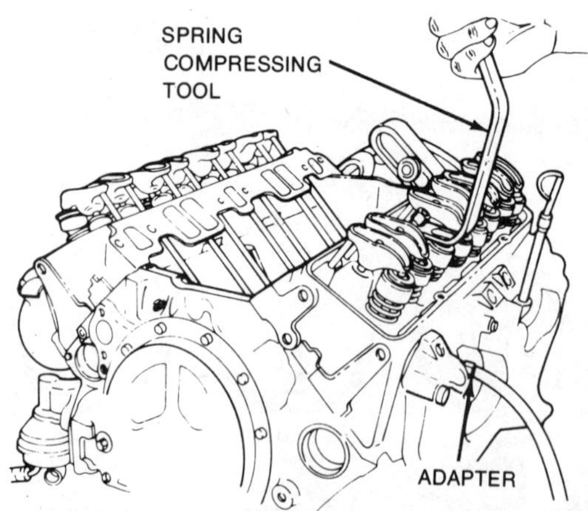

Replacing the valve seals using compressed air and a special valve spring compressing tool—small block shown, big block similar

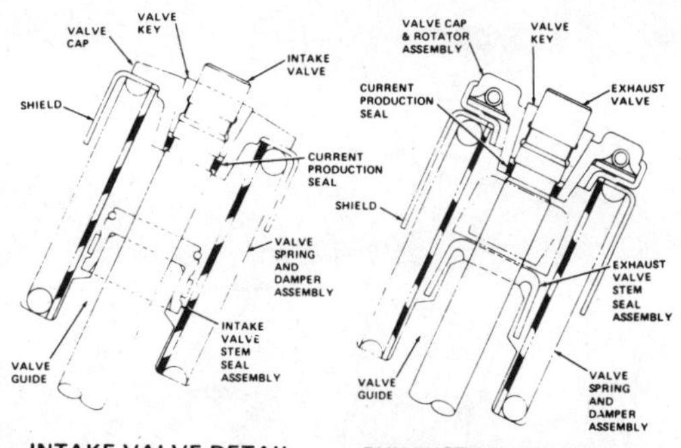

O-ring type valve seal placement. Note the optional seal types are shown as dotted lines.

4. Using the Valve Spring Compressor tool No. J-5892, compress the valve spring, remove the valve keepers, the valve cap, the spring and the damper; be sure to remove the valve stem seal.
5. Inspect the valve spring tension, squareness and height.
6. To install, use new oil seals and reverse the removal procedures.

INSPECTION

1. With the rocker arm removed and using a graduated scale, measure the installed height of the spring (valve closed). Measure from the top of the shim or the spring seat to the top of the oil shedder. If this is found to exceed the specified height, install a valve spring seat shim approximately $1/16$" thick. At no time should the spring be shimmed to give an installed height under the minimum specified.
2. Using a Valve Spring Tester tool No. J-8056 (spring removed), check the valve spring tension. The springs should be compressed to the specified height and checked against the specifications chart. They should be replaced if not within 10 lbs. of the specified load (without dampers).
3. Using a combination square (with the spring) on a flat surface, check the squareness of the spring.

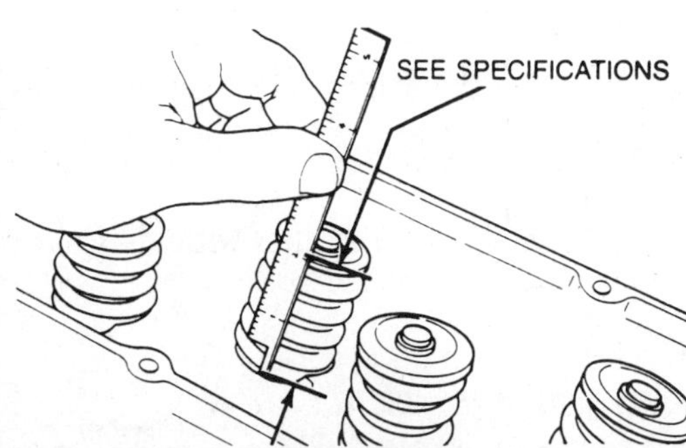

Measuring valve spring installed height

Checking valve spring tension—typical

Valve Seats

The valve seats are an integral part of the cylinder head and are not replaceable. The only service performed to the seat is reconditioning. Reconditioning will provide two important factors: First, allowing the valves to seal off the compression chamber to provide maximum power and performance. Secondly, to provide good valve-to-seat contact, which allows maximum cooling of the valve heads.

REFACING

1. Refer to the "Valve, Removal and Installation" procedures in this section and remove the valves from the cylinder head.
2. Using a drill equipped with a wire brush, clean all of the carbon from the combustion chambers and valve ports.
3. Contact a reputable automotive machine shop and have the valve seat refaced to specifications.
4. Before installing the valves, be sure to lap them into the seats.

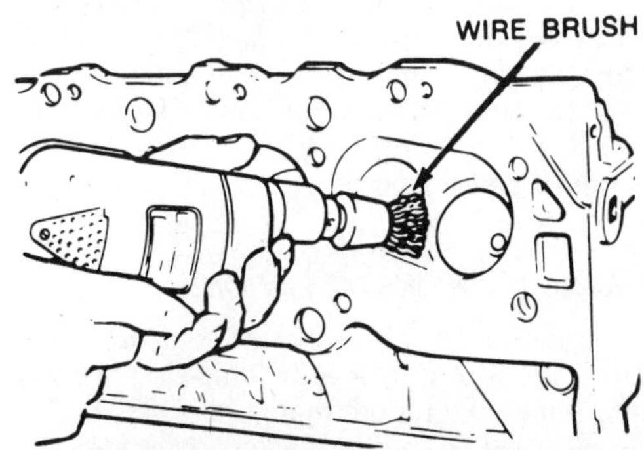

Removing the carbon from the cylinder head using a wire brush and a drill

Valve Guides

The valve guides are an integral part of the cylinder head and are not replaceable. The only service performed to the guides is to ream them to the next largest oversize valve diameter.

NOTE: *Excessive valve stem to bore clearance will cause excessive oil consumption and may cause valve breakage. Insufficient clearance will result in noisy and sticky functioning of the valve and disturb engine smoothness.*

RESURFACING

1. Refer to the "Valve, Removal and Installation" procedures in this section and remove the valves from the cylinder head.
2. Using a valve guide wire brush tool, thoroughly clean the valve guides.

NOTE: *Any cutting, knurling or reaming operations should be performed by a reputable automotive machine shop.*

3. After the valve guide repair, reinstall the valve into the cylinder head.

KNURLING

Valve guides which are not excessively worn or distorted may , in some cases, be knurled. Knurling is a process in which metal is displaced and raised, thereby reducing the clearance. Knurling also provides excellent oil control.

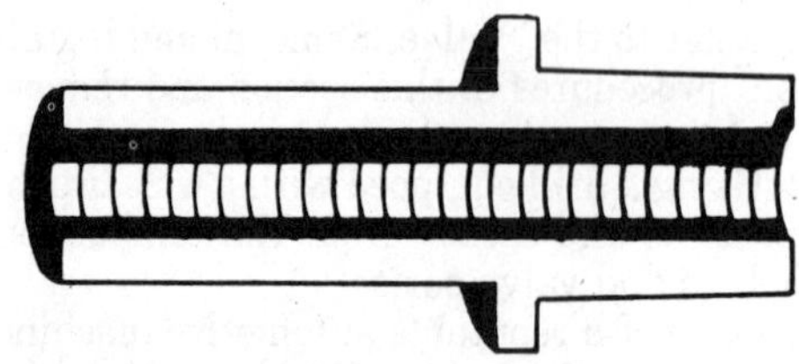

Cutaway view of knurled valve guide

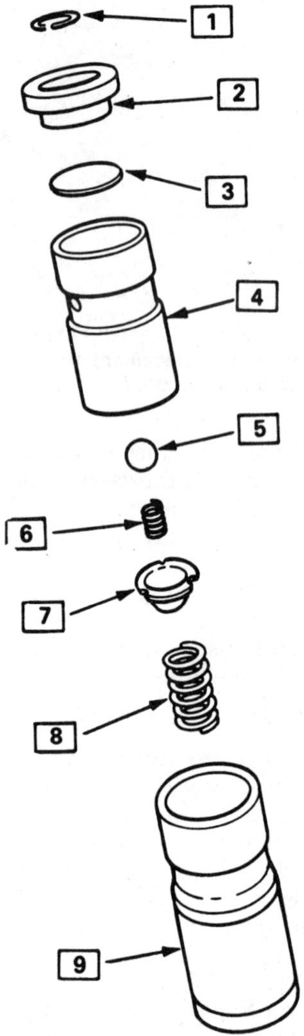

1. Retainer spring
2. Push rod seat
3. Rocker feed metering valve
4. Plunger
5. Ball check valve
6. Ball check valve spring (high ball lifter only)
7. Ball check valve retainer
8. Plunger spring
9. Lifter body

Exploded view of the hydraulic lifter

Valve Lifters

NOTE: *The hydraulic valve lifters very seldom require attention. The lifters are extremely simple in design, readjustments are not necessary and servicing requires only that care and cleanliness be exercised in the handling of the parts.*

REMOVAL AND INSTALLATION

1. Refer to the "Intake Manifold, Removal and Installation" procedures in this section and remove the intake manifold.
2. Remove the valve rocker arms and the pushrods.
3. Remove the valve lifters, then place the rocker arms, the ball washers, the push rods and the lifters in order, so that they may be installed in the same location from which they were removed.
4. To install, coat the lifter with Molykote® and reverse the removal procedures.

Oil Pan

REMOVAL AND INSTALLATION

1. Disconnect the negative battery cable. Remove the dipstick.

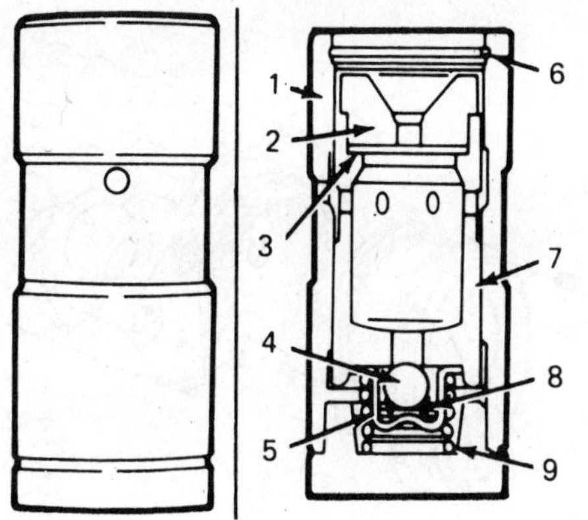

1. Lifter Body
2. Push Rod Seat
3. Metering Valve
4. Check Ball
5. Check Ball Retainer
6. Push Rod Seat Retainer
7. Plunger
8. Check Ball Spring
9. Plunger Spring

Typical hydraulic valve lifter showing internal components

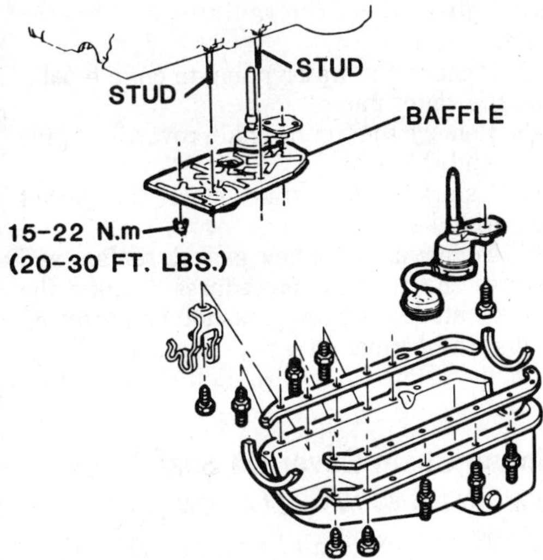

Exploded view of the oil pan

2. Raise and support the front of the vehicle on jackstands.
3. Place a fluid catch pan under the engine, remove the oil pan plug and drain the engine oil.
4. Disconnect the electrical connectors from the starter. Remove the starter brace nut, the starter bolts and remove the starter.
5. Remove the flywheel cover.
6. Remove the oil pan bolts and the oil pan.
7. Using a putty knife, clean the gasket mounting surfaces.
8. To install, use new oil pan gaskets and seals, then reverse the removal procedures. Torque the oil pan bolts to 80 inch lbs. Refill the engine with new oil. Start the engine and check for leaks.

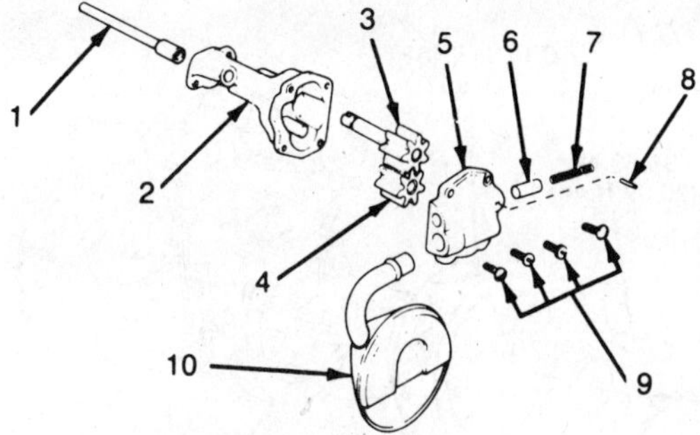

1. Shaft extension
2. Pump body
3. Drive gear and shaft
4. Idler gear
5. Pump cover
6. Pressure regulator valve
7. Pressure regulator spring
8. Retaining pin
9. Screws
10. Pickup screen and pipe

Exploded view of the oil pump

Oil Pump

REMOVAL AND INSTALLATION

1. Refer to the "Oil Pan, Removal and Installation" procedures in this section and remove the oil pan.
2. Remove the oil pump-to-rear bearing cap bolt, the pump and the extension shaft.
3. Clean and inspect the cracks, damage and/or excessive wear.

NOTE: *The oil pump is not serviceable. If any problem with the pump exist, it must be replaced.*

4. To install, reverse the removal procedures. Torque the pump-to-rear main bearing cap bolts to 65 ft. lbs.

Timing Chain Cover

REMOVAL AND INSTALLATION

1. Disconnect the negative battery cable.
2. Drain the cooling system. Remove the radiator, the fan shroud and the fan (if necessary).
3. Loosen the alternator adjusting bolt and remove the drive belt from the pulleys.
4. Remove the crankshaft pulley-to-crankshaft damper bolts and the pulley.
5. Using ONLY the Wheel Puller tool No. J-23523, press the crankshaft damper from the crankshaft.
6. Remove the AIR pump pulley, the AIR management valve adapter, the AIR pump-to-engine bolts and the AIR pump.
7. Reduce the pressure in the fuel system, then remove the fuel inlet and return lines

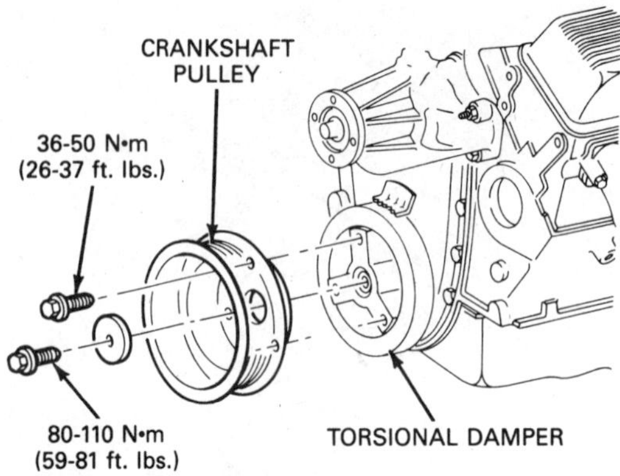

Exploded view of the crankshaft pulley

Removing the vibration damper using a puller

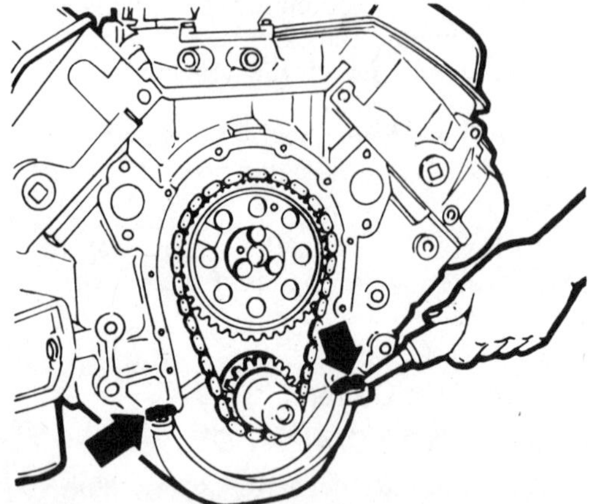
Apply sealer to the front pads at the area shown (V8)

from the TBI units (1984) or the TPI fuel rail (1985 and later).

8. At the A/C compressor, remove the rear braces, the lower mounting bolt and the bracket nuts from the water pump, then slide the compressor mounting bracket forward and remove the compressor mounting bolt. Disconnect the compressor electrical connectors and move it aside (DO NOT disconnect the A/C lines).

9. Disconnect the AIR hose from the right exhaust manifold and remove the compressor mounting bracket.

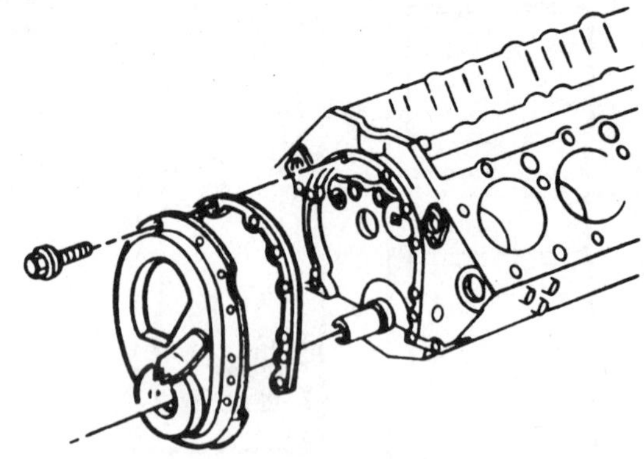
Timing cover and gasket—typical

10. Remove the upper AIR pump bracket (with the power steering reservoir) and the lower AIR pump bracket.

11. Drain the cooling system. At the water pump, disconnect the radiator and heater hoses.

12. Remove the water pump-to-engine bolts and the water pump.

13. Remove the timing chain cover-to-engine bolts and the cover.

14. Using a putty knife, clean the gasket mounting surfaces.

15. To install, use a new gasket, sealant and reverse the removal procedures. Torque the crankshaft damper-to-crankshaft bolt to 59–81 ft. lbs., the damper pulley-to-crankshaft damper bolts to 26–37 ft. lbs. Refill the cooling system.

Timing Chain Cover Oil Seal

REMOVAL AND INSTALLATION

NOTE: *When installing the new oil seal, be sure to position the open end of the seal toward the inside of the cover.*

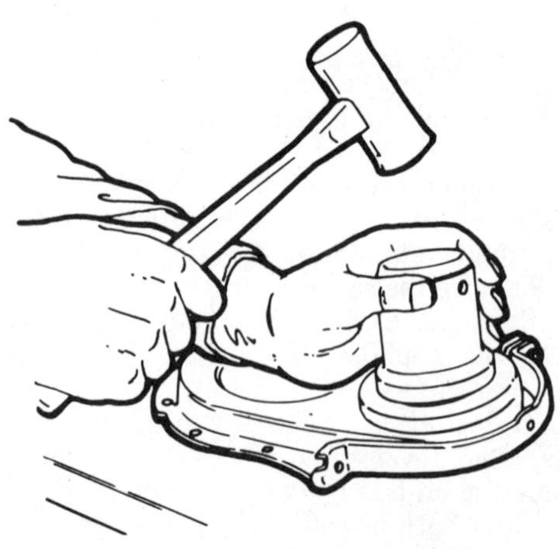
Seal installation with the cover removed

Cover Removed

1. Refer to the "Timing Chain Cover, Removal and Installation" procedures in this section and remove the timing chain cover.
2. Using a medium sized pry bar, pry the oil seal from the timing chain cover.
3. Using the Seal Installation tool No. J-23042, drive the new seal into the cover until it seats.
4. Using engine oil, lubricate the lip of the new seal.
5. To complete the installation, reverse the removal procedures.

Cover Installed

1. Refer to the "Timing Chain Cover, Removal and Installation" procedures in this section and remove the crankshaft damper.
2. Using a medium sized pry bar, pry the oil seal from the timing chain cover.
3. Using engine oil, lubricate the lip of the new seal.
4. Using the Seal Installation tool No. J-23042, drive the new seal into the cover until it seats.
5. To complete the installation, reverse the removal procedures.

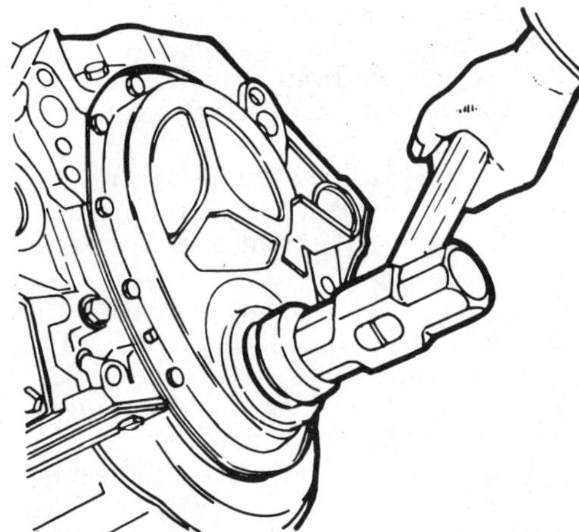
Seal installation with the cover installed

Timing Chain

REMOVAL AND INSTALLATION

1. Refer to the "Timing Chain Cover, Removal and Installation" procedures in this section and remove the timing chain cover.
2. Rotate the crankshaft to align the timing marks on the camshaft and the crankshaft sprockets.
3. Remove the camshaft sprocket-to-camshaft bolts and camshaft sprocket (with the chain from the engine.

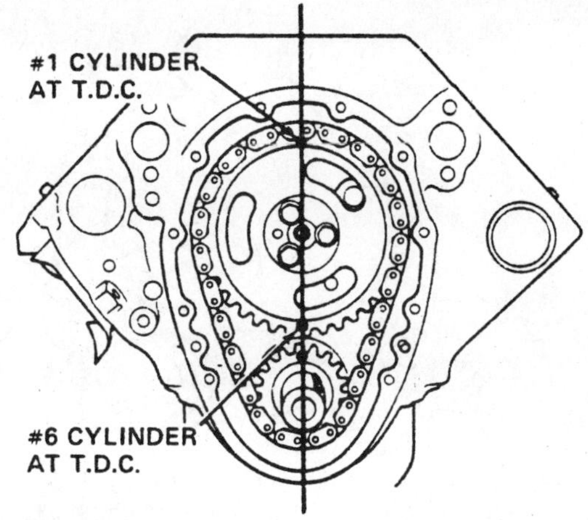

Timing mark alignment

4. To install, reverse the removal procedures.

Camshaft

REMOVAL AND INSTALLATION

1. Refer to the "Timing Chain, Removal and Installation" and the "Rocker Arm, Removal and Installation" procedures in this section, then remove the timing chain, the rocker arms, the ball washers, the push rods and the hydraulic lifters.
2. Disconnect the A/C high pressure line bracket from the right frame rail, DO NOT disconnect the A/C hoses.
3. Install two long bolts into the camshaft threaded holes (for leverage) and pull the camshaft through the front of the engine.

NOTE: *When removing the camshaft, be careful not to damage the camshaft bearings, the camshaft journals or lobes.*

4. Clean and inspect the camshaft.
5. To install, lubricate the camshaft with engine oil and reverse the removal procedures. Torque the camshaft sprocket-to-camshaft bolts to 20 ft. lbs.

INSPECTION

Degrease the camshaft (using solvent) and clean out all of the holes. Visually inspect the cam lobes and the bearing journals for excessive wear. If a lobe is questionable, check all the lobes by performing the following procedures:

a. If a journal or lobe is worn, the camshaft must be reground or replaced.

NOTE: *If a journal is worn, there is a good chance that the bushings are worn.*

b. If the lobes and journals appear intact, place the front and rear journals in V-blocks and rest a dial indicator on the center jour-

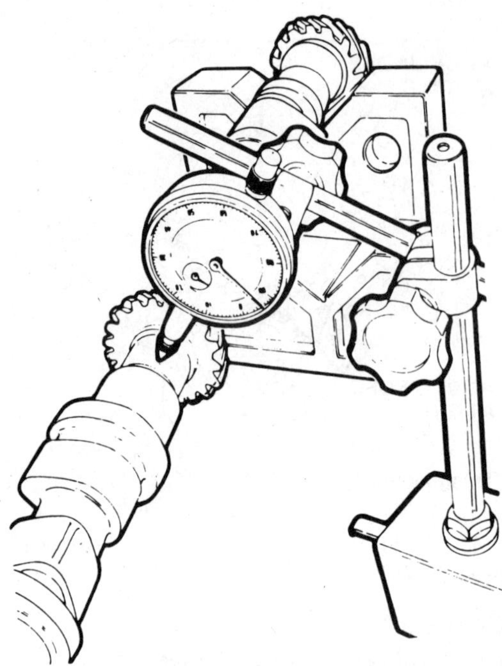
Checking the camshaft for straightness

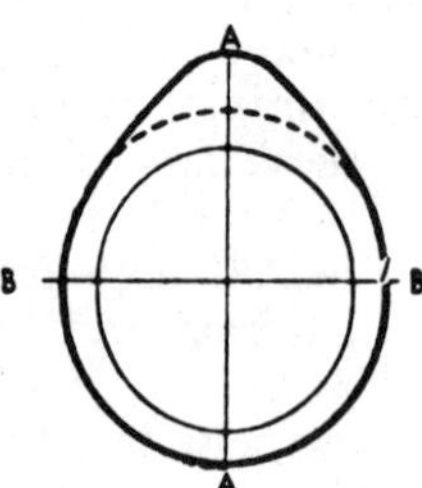

Measuring the camshaft lobe

nal. Rotate the camshaft to check the straightness. If the deviation exceeds 0.001 in., replace the camshaft.

c. Using a micrometer, check the camshaft lobes by measuring the lobes from nose-to-base and again at 90° (see illustration).

NOTE: *The lift is determined by subracting the second measurement from the first. If all exhaust and intake lobes are not identical, the camshaft must be replaced or reground.*

Camshaft Bearings

NOTE: *The camshaft must be removed in order to replace the camshaft bearings.*

REMOVAL AND INSTALLATION

NOTE: *To perform this procedure, it is recommended to remove the engine from the vehicle.*

To remove the camshaft bearing, the camshaft, the lifters, the flywheel, the rear camshaft ex-

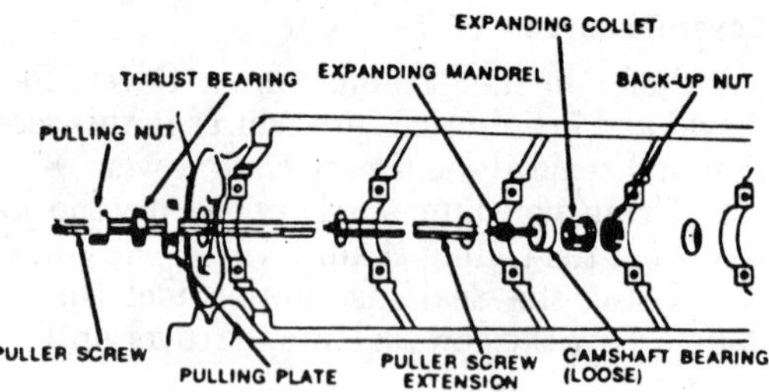

View of the camshaft bearing replacement tool

pansion plug and the crankshaft must be removed.

The camshaft bearings can be replaced with the engine completely or partially disassembled. To replace the bearings without complete disassembly, remove the camshaft and the crankshaft leaving the cylinder heads attached and the pistons in place. Before removing the crankshaft, tape the threads of the connecting rod bolts to prevent damage to the crankshaft. Fasten the connecting rods against the sides of the engine, so that they will not be in the way while replacing the camshaft bearings.

If excessive wear is indicated or if the engine is being completely rebuilt, the camshaft bearings should be replaced as follows:

1. Drive the camshaft rear plug from the block.
2. Assemble the Bearing Puller tool No. J-6098 with it's shoulder on the bearing to be removed.
3. Gradually, tighten the puller nut until the bearing is removed. Remove the remaining bearings, leaving the front and the rear for last.
4. To remove the front and rear bearing, reverse the position of the tool, so as to pull the bearings in toward the center of the block.
5. To install the new bearings, leave the tool in this position, pilot the new front and rear bearings on the installer, then pull them into position.
6. Return the tool to it's original position and pull the remaining bearings into position.

NOTE: *Ensure that the oil holes align when installing the bearings.*

7. Replace the camshaft rear plug and stake it into position to aid retention.
8. To complete the installation, reverse the removal procedures.

Pistons And Connecting Rods

REMOVAL AND INSTALLATION

1. Refer to the "Oil Pump, Removal and Installation" and the "Cylinder Head, Removal and Installation" procedure in this section,

then remove the oil pump and the cylinder heads.

2. For the cylinder being serviced, turn the crankshaft until the piston is at the bottom of stroke, then place a clean shop cloth on top of the piston.

3. Using a Ridge Reamer tool, remove the ridge and/or any deposits from the upper end of the cylinder bore.

NOTE: *Make sure that the piston top and the cylinder bore are absolutely clean before removing the piston assembly.*

4. Match-mark the connecting rod cap-to-connecting rod with a scribe; each cap must be reinstalled on the proper rod in the proper direction. Remove the connecting rod bearing cap and the rod bearing. Number the top of each piston with silver paint or a felt-tip pen for later assembly.

5. Remove the connecting rod cap and install 3/8" pieces of rubber tubing onto the connecting rod studs.

6. Turn the crankshaft to position the piston/connecting rod assembly at the top of the cylinder travel. Using a hammer handle, drive the piston/connecting rod assembly out through the top of the cylinder.

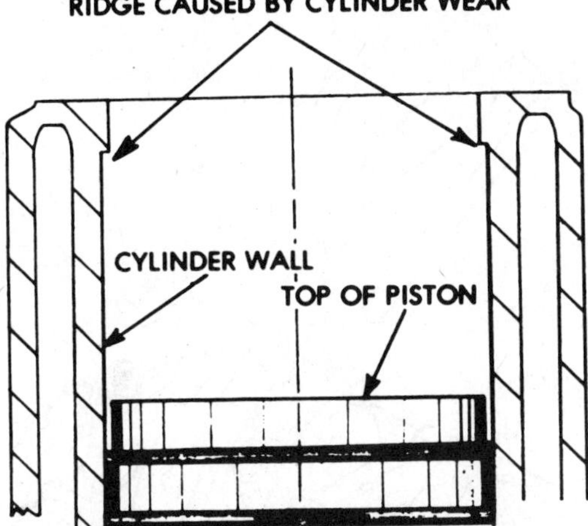

Wear ridge must be removed before piston removal

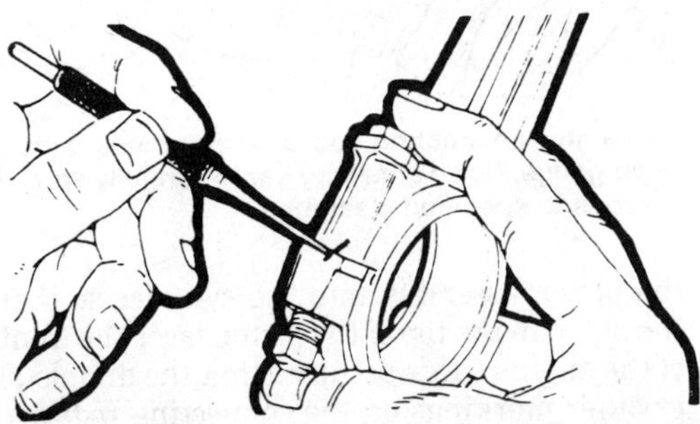

Scribe a matchmark on the connecting rod and cap

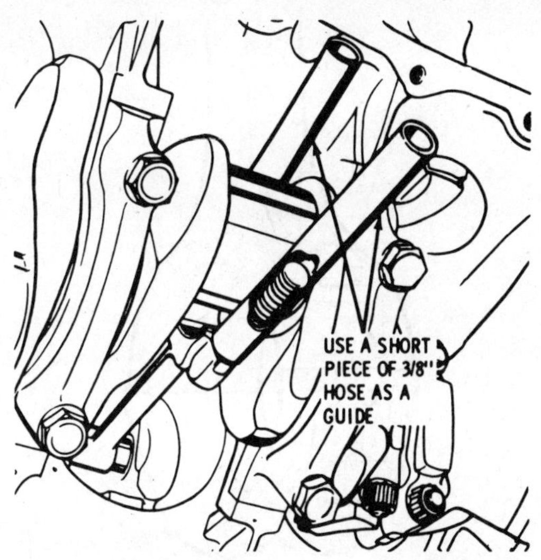

Fabricate rod bolt guides out of rubber hose to prevent damage to crankshaft journals when removing or installing pistons

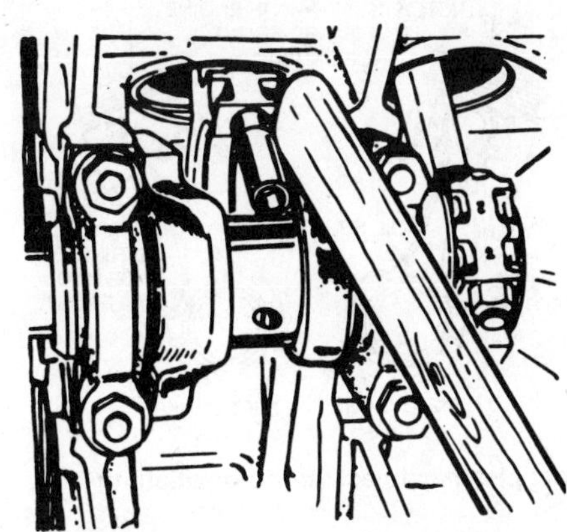

Carefully tap the piston and rod assembly out of the cylinder bore with a wooden hammer handle

7. Place the rod bearing and cap back on the connecting rod, then install the nuts temporarily. Using a number stamp or punch (if not already done), stamp the cylinder number on the side of the connecting rod and cap; this will help keep the proper piston and rod assembly arranged for the proper cylinder.

8. Remove the remaining pistons in the similar manner. The notch on top of the piston will face the front of the engine during reassembly. The chamfered corners of the bearing caps should face toward the front of the left bank and toward the rear of the right bank. The boss on the connecting rod should face toward the front of the engine (right bank) or toward the rear of the engine (left bank).

9. Using a Ring Expander tool, remove the piston rings, clean and inspect the piston and the ring land areas, then replace the piston rings with a new set.

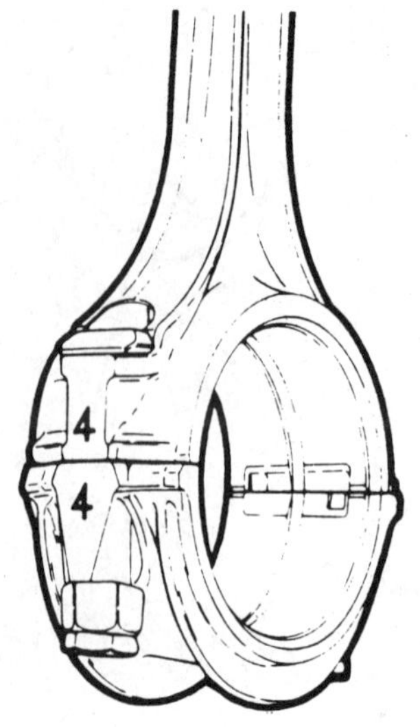

Stamped number matchmarks on connecting rod and cap

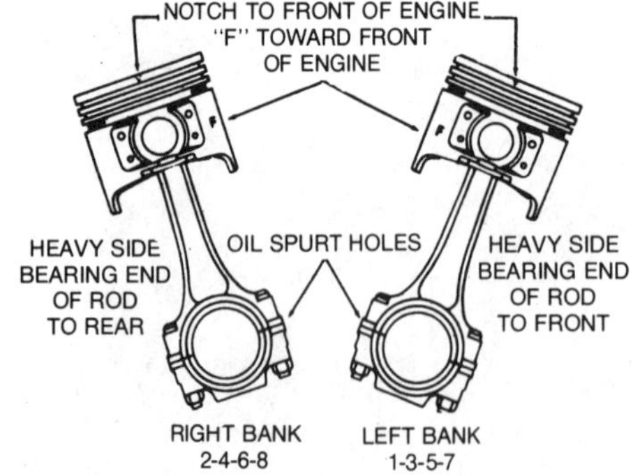

Correct piston/connecting rod positioning

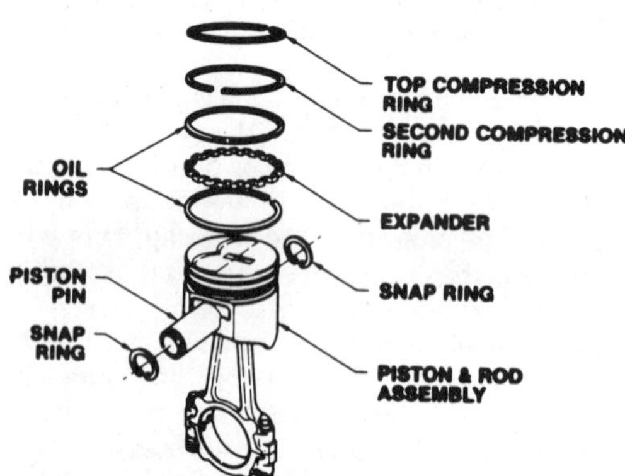

Piston rings and wrist pin

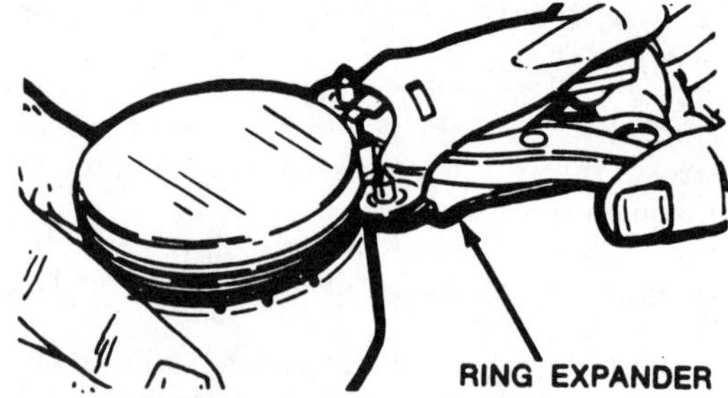

Removing the piston rings with expander tool

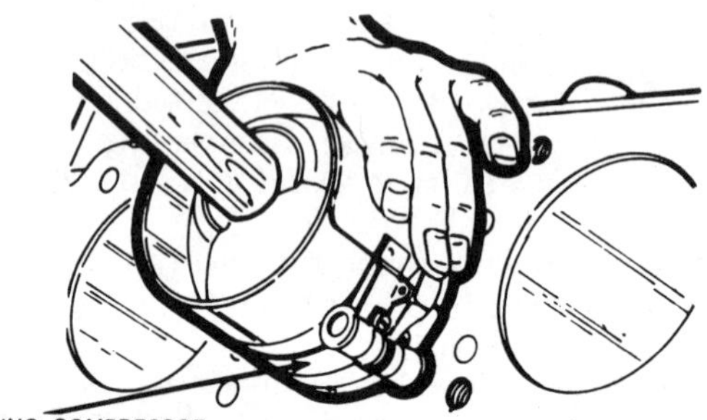

Install piston ring compressor, then tap the piston into the cylinder bore carefully. Make sure the piston front marks are correctly positioned when installing

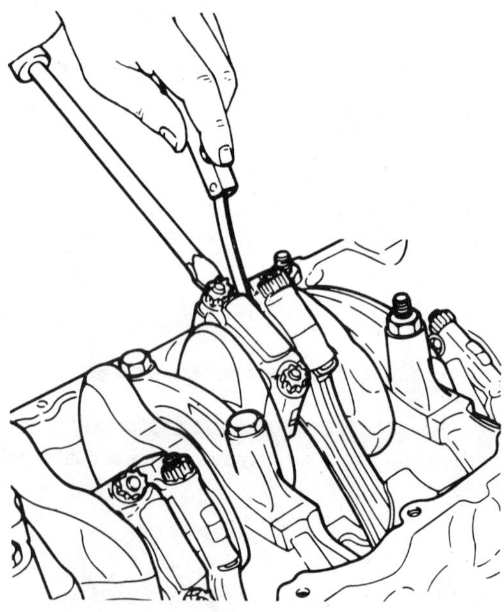
Check the connecting rod side clearance with a feeler gauge. Use a small pry bar to carefully spread the rods to specified clearance

10. Using a cylinder hone and light cutting oil, hone (break the glaze) the cylinder walls. If the cylinders are oblong shaped or have deep scratches, have the engine cylinders must be bored.

11. Using the Ring Compressor tool, insert the piston assembly into the cylinder so that the notch in the top of the piston faces the front of the engine–this assumes that the dimple(s) or other markings on the connecting rods are in correct relation to the piston notch(s).

12. Under the engine, coat each crank journal with clean engine oil. Pull the connecting rod, with bearing shell in place, into position against the crankshaft journal.

13. Remove the rubber hoses. Install the bearing cap and the cap nuts, then torque to 45 ft. lbs.

NOTE: *When more than one rod/piston assembly are being installed, the connecting rod cap attaching nuts should only be tightened enough to keep each rod in position until all have been installed. This will ease the installation of the remaining piston assemblies.*

14. Using a feeler gauge, check the clearance between the sides of the connecting rods and the crankshaft. Using a small pry bar, spread the rods slightly to insert the gauge. If the clearance is below the minimum tolerance, the rod may be machined to provide adequate clearance. If the clearance is excessive, substitute an unworn rod and recheck. If the clearance is still outside specifications, the crankshaft must be welded, reground or replaced.

15. To complete the installation, reverse the removal procedures.

CLEANING AND INSPECTION

Pistons

1. Using solvent, thoroughly clean all of the carbon and varnish from the piston.

CAUTION: *DO NOT use a wire brush or caustic solvent (acids, etc.) on the pistons.*

2. Using a ring groove cleaning tool, clean the ring grooves (DO NOT cut too deeply); make sure that the ring oil holes and the slots are clean.

3. Inspect the pistons for scuffed (damaged) skirts and wavy (worn) ring land areas, then for cracked ring land areas, skirts, pin bosses and/or eroded areas at the top of the piston.

4. Inspect the land areas for nicks or burrs that might cause the rings to hang up.

5. Using a micrometer, measure the piston skirt (across the center line of the piston pin) for clearance.

6. Using a telescoping gauge, an inside micrometer or a dial micrometer, perform the following procedures to check the cylinder bore:

a. Measure the cylinder bore diameter at a ¼" (below the cylinder head surface), at the midway and at the bottom of the cylinder travel.

b. Then, turn the measuring device 90° and measure the cylinder bore diameter; the difference between the two measurements is the piston clearance. If the piston-to-cylinder clearance is within or slightly below specifications, hone the cylinder walls to break the glaze and/or to true the cylinder.

7. If the cylinder bore taper is greater than 0.005 in. or the out-of-round is greater than 0.003 in., it is advisable to bore the cylinders for the next oversize pistons and ring set.

NOTE: *Cylinder block boring should be performed by a reputable machine shop equipped with the proper equipment.*

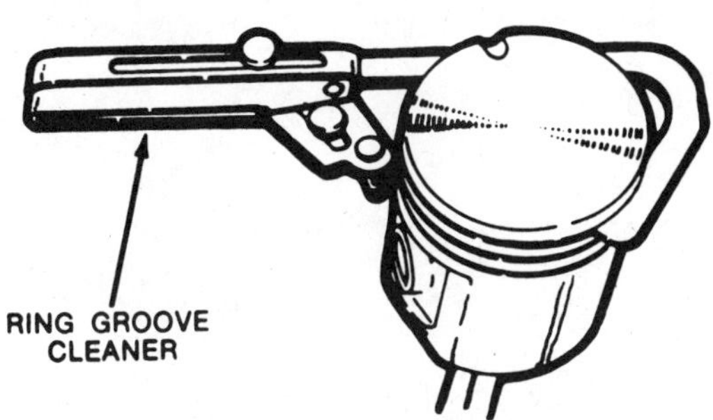

Clean the piston ring grooves with a suitable tool

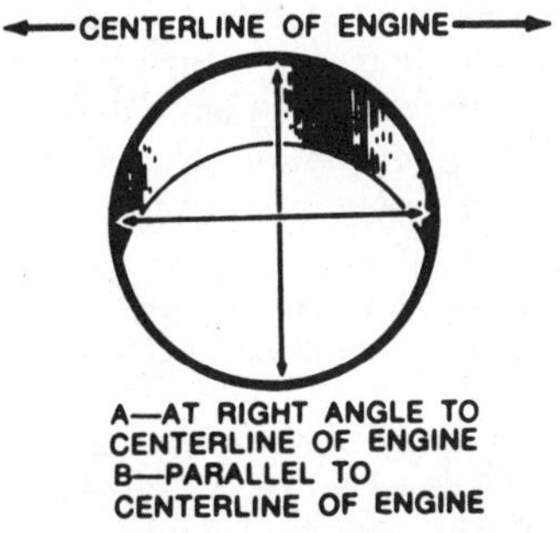

Cylinder bore measuring points

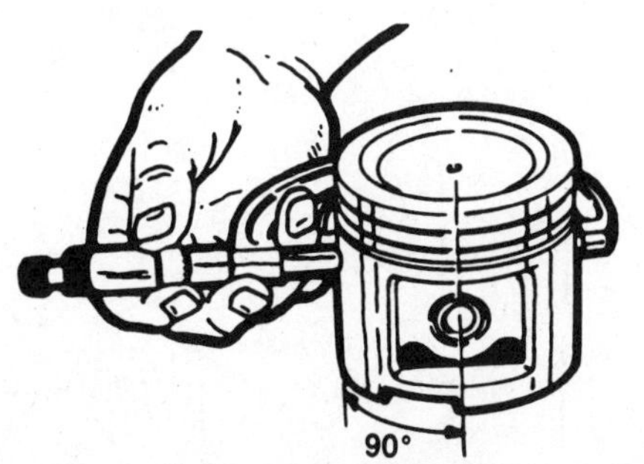

Measure the piston with a micrometer

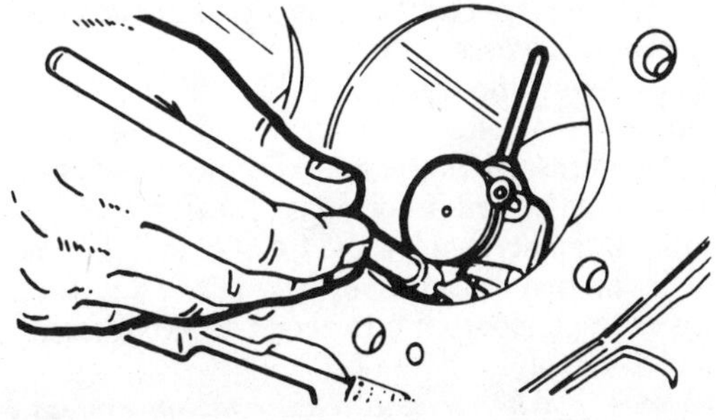

Measure cylinder bore with dial gauge

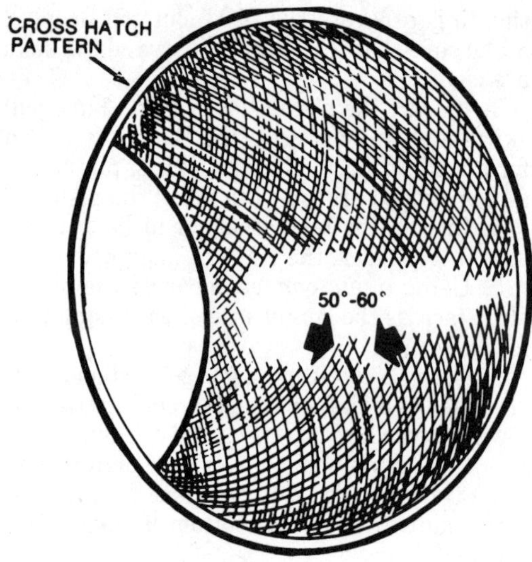

Correct cylinder bore honing pattern

Connecting Rods

1. Using solvent, wash the connecting rods, then blow dry with compressed air.
2. Inspect the connecting rods for nicks or cracks, then check them for twisted or bent conditions.
3. If any of the damaged conditions exist, replace the connecting rods.

PISTON PIN REPLACEMENT

1. Using an arbor press, the Fixture/Support Assembly tool No. J-24086-20 and the Piston Pin Removal tool No. J-24086-8, place the piston assembly in the fixture/support tool and press the pin from the piston assembly.

   NOTE: *The piston and the piston pin are a matched set which are not serviced separately.*
2. Using solvent, wash the varnish and oil from the parts, then inspect the parts for scuffing or wear.
3. Using a micrometer, measure the diameter of the piston pin. Using a inside micrometer or a dial bore gauge, measure the diameter of the piston bore.

   NOTE: *If the piston pin-to-piston clearance is in excess of 0.001 in., replace the piston and piston pin assembly.*
4. Before installation, lubricate the piston pin and the piston bore with engine oil.
5. To install the piston pin into the piston assembly, use an arbor press, the Fixture/Support Assembly tool No. J-24086-20 and the Piston Pin Installation tool No. J-24086-9, then press the piston pin into the piston/connecting rod assembly.

   NOTE: *When installing the piston pin into the piston/connecting rod assembly and the*

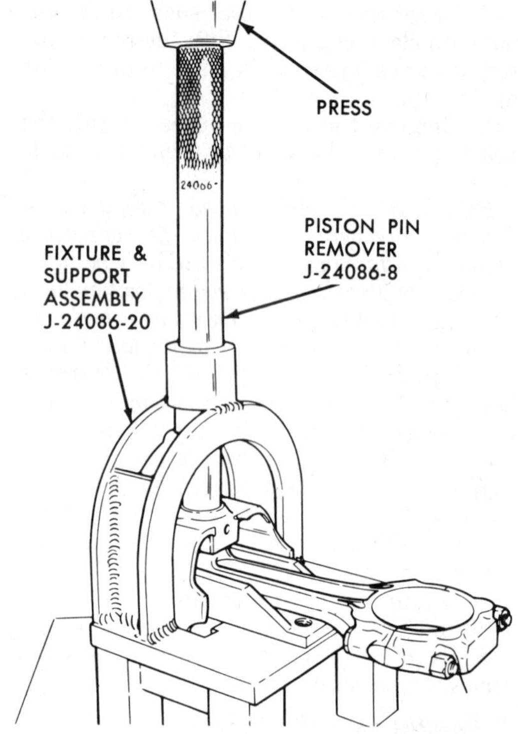

Removing the piston pin from the piston assembly

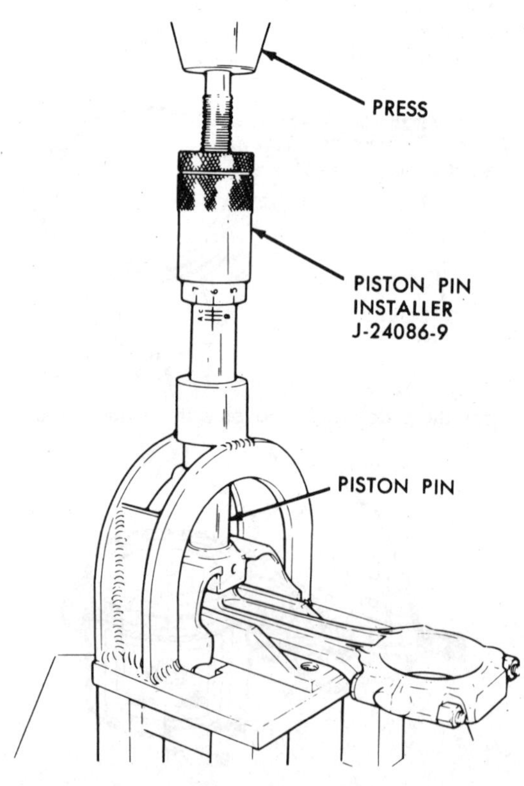

Installing the piston pin into the piston assembly

installation tool bottoms onto the support assembly, DO NOT exceed 5000 lbs. of pressure for structural damage may occur to the tool.

6. After installing the piston pin, make sure that the piston has freedom of movement with the piston pin. The piston/connecting rod assembly is ready for installation into the engine block.

PISTON RING REPLACEMENT AND SIDE CLEARANCE MEASUREMENT

Check the pistons to see that the ring grooves and oil return holes have been properly cleaned. Slide a piston ring into its groove and check the side clearance with a feeler gauge. Make sure the feeler gauge is inserted between the ring and its lower land (lower edge of the groove), because any wear that occurs forms a step at the inner portion of the lower land. If the piston grooves have been worn to the extent that relatively high steps exist on the lower land, the piston should be replaced, because these will interfere with the operation of the new rings and ring clearances will be excessive. Piston rings are not furnished in oversize widths to compensate for ring groove wear.

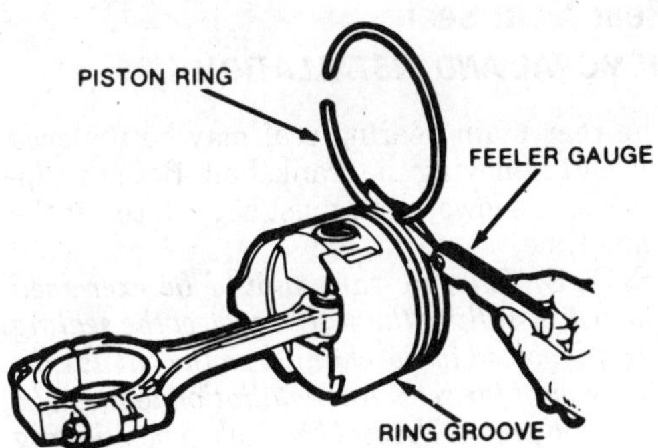

Measure piston ring side clearance with feeler gauge

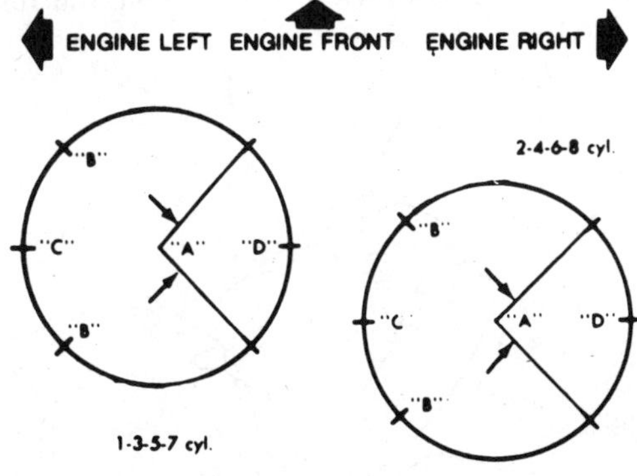

Piston ring gap location—all engines

Install the rings on the piston, bottom ring first, using a piston ring expander. There is a high risk of breaking or distorting the rings and/or scratching the piston, if the rings are installed by hand or other means.

Position the rings on the piston as illustrated; spacing of the various piston ring gaps is crucial to the proper oil retention and cylinder wear. When installing the new rings, refer to the installation diagram furnished with the new parts.

CHECKING RING END GAP

The piston ring end gap should be checked while the rings are removed from the pistons. Incorrect end gap indicates that the wrong size rings are being used; ***ring breakage could result.***

1. Compress the new piston ring into a cylinder (one at a time).
2. Squirt some clean oil into the cylinder so that the ring and the cylinder wall (the top 2 in.) are coated.
3. Using an inverted piston, push the ring approximately 1 in. below the top of the cylinder.
4. Using a feeler gauge, measure the ring gap and compare it to the "Ring Gap" chart in this chapter. Carefully remove the ring from the cylinder.

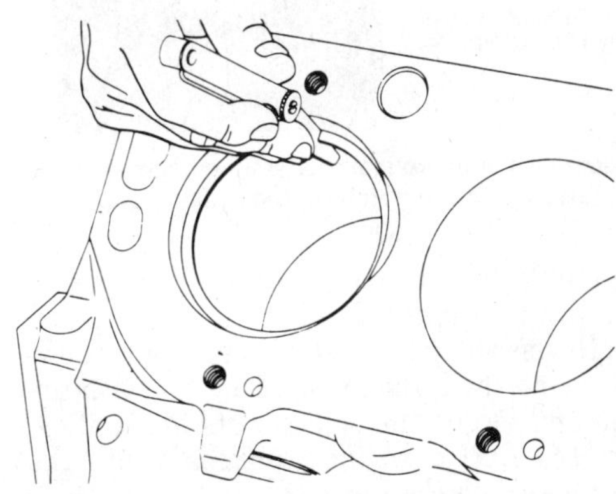
Measure piston ring end gap with feeler gauge

ROD BEARING REPLACEMENT

Replacement bearings are available in standard size and undersize (for reground crankshafts). Connecting rod-to-crankshaft bearing clearance is checked using Plastigage® at either the top or the bottom of each crank journal. The Plastigage® has a range of 0.001–0.003 in.

1. Remove the rod cap with the bearing shell. Completely clean the bearing shell and

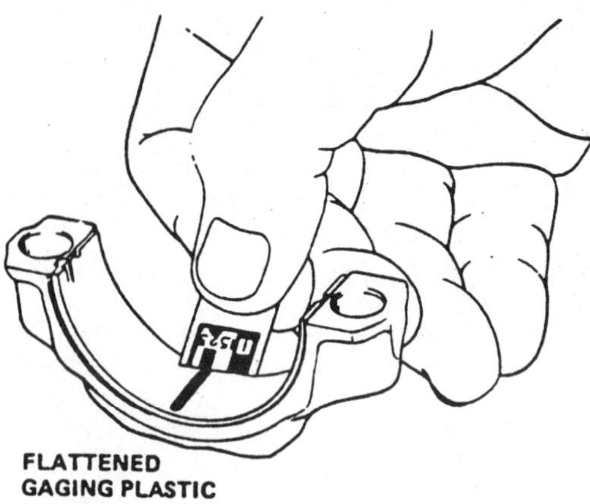

Check rod bearing clearance with Plastigage or equivalent

Undersize marks are stamped on the bearing shells. The tang fits in the notch on the rod and cap

the crank journal, blow any oil from the oil hole in the crankshaft; place the Plastigage® lengthwise along the bottom center of the lower bearing shell, then install the cap with the shell and torque the bolt or nuts to specification. DO NOT turn the crankshaft with the Plastigage® on the bearing.

2. Remove the bearing cap with the shell. The flattened Plastigage® will be found sticking to either the bearing shell or the crank journal. DO NOT remove it yet.

3. Use the scale printed on the Plastigage® envelope to measure the flattened material at its widest point. The number within the scale which most closely corresponds to the width of the Plastigage® indicates the bearing clearance in thousandths of an inch.

4. Check the specifications chart in this chapter for the desired clearance. It is advisable to install a new bearing if the clearance exceeds 0.003 in.; however, if the bearing is in good condition and is not being checked because of bearing noise, bearing replacement is not necessary.

5. If you are installing new bearings, try a standard size, then each undersize in order until one is found that is within the specified limits when checked for clearance with Plastigage®; each undersize shell has its size stamped on it.

6. When the proper size shell is found, clean off the Plastigage®, oil the bearing thoroughly, reinstall the cap with its shell and torque the rod bolt nuts to specifications.

NOTE: *With the proper bearing selected and the nuts torqued, it should be possible to move the connecting rod back and forth freely on the crank journal as allowed by the specified connecting rod end clearance. If the rod cannot be moved, either the rod bearing is too far undersize or the rod is misaligned.*

Rear Main Seal

REMOVAL AND INSTALLATION

The rear main bearing seal may be replaced without removing the crankshaft. Both the upper and the lower seals must be replaced at the same time.

NOTE: *Extreme care should be exercised when installing the seal to protect the sealing bead located in the channel on the outside diameter of the seal. An installation tool can be used to protect the seal bead when positioning the seal.*

1. Refer to the "Oil Pump, Removal and Installation" procedures in this section and remove the oil pump.

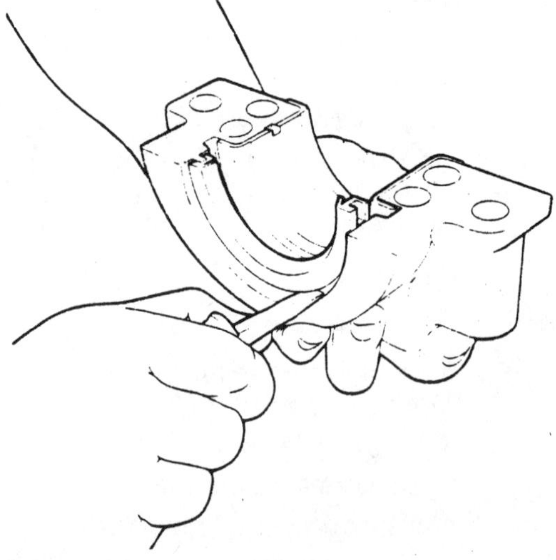

Removing the lower half of the rear main oil seal

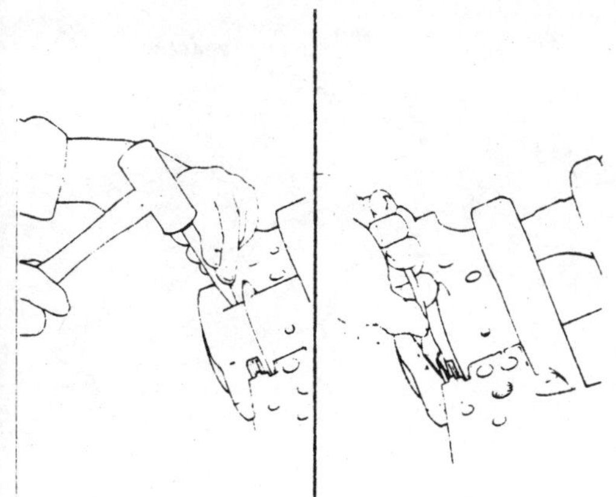
Removing the upper half of the rear main oil seal

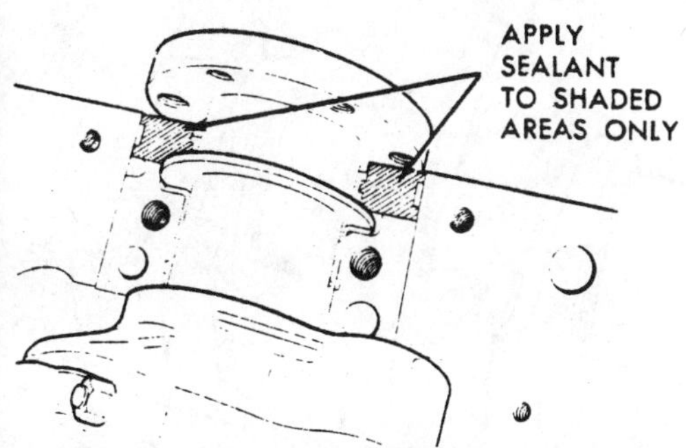

Before installing the rear bearing cap, apply sealer to the rear main seal as indicated

2. Remove the rear main bearing cap and pry the seal from the bottom with a small pry bar.

3. Remove the upper seal with a small hammer and a brass pin punch. Tap on one end of the seal until the opposite end can be gripped with a pair of pliers.

4. Clean the bearing cap and the crankshaft.

5. Coat the lips and the bead of the seal with a light engine oil. DO NOT get oil on the seal ends.

6. Insert the new seal into the bearing cap, rolling it into place with your finger and thumb. Press lightly on the seal, so that the seal tangs on the cap don't cut the bead on the back of the seal.

7. Lubricate the lip of the new oil seal and slowly push it into place while turning the crankshaft. Make sure that the seal tangs don't cut the bead on the back of the seal.

8. To install, use a new oil pan gasket and reverse the removal procedures. Torque the main bearing cap to 10–12 ft. lbs. Refill the engine with oil.

Crankshaft And Main Bearings

Crankshaft servicing literally makes or breaks any engine; especially a high performance one such as the Corvette.

The most critical maintenance operation is the replacement of the crankshaft main bearings. These bearings are of the precision insert design and do not require adjustment through shims. They are offered in undersizes of 0.001 in., 0.002 in., 0.009 in., 0.010 in., 0.020 in. and 0.030 in.

Despite the advent of these inserts and accompanying precision machine work, it does happen that sizing mistakes are made and no crankshaft should be installed in a block without checking the clearances. One of the simplest means of doing so is to use the Plastigage® method. This is a wax-like plastic material that is formed into precision threads. It will compress evenly between two surfaces, without damage and when measured, will indicate the actual clearance.

It is easier to check the bearing clearance with the engine removed from the vehicle and the block inverted. This ensures that the crank is resting against the upper bearing shells. If Plastigage® is to be used on an engine still in the vehicle, it will be necessary to support the crankshaft at both ends so that the clearance between the crankshaft and the upper bearing shells is eliminated.

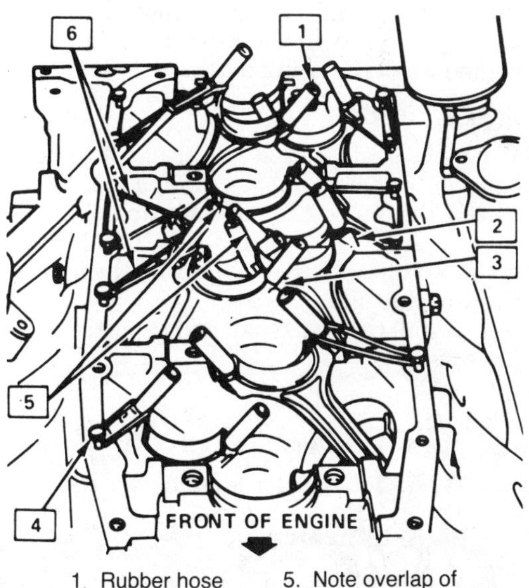

Support the connecting rods with rubber bands and install rubber rod bolt caps when crankshaft is removed

REMOVAL

1. Drain the engine oil and remove the engine from the vehicle. Mount the engine on a work stand in a suitable working area. Invert the engine, so that the oil pan is facing upward.
2. Remove the front (timing) cover, the timing chain and the sprockets.
3. Remove the oil pan and the oil pump.
4. Stamp the cylinder number on the machined surfaces of the bolt bosses of the connecting rods and the caps for identification when reinstalling. If the pistons are to be removed (eventually) from the connecting rod, mark the cylinder number on the pistons with silver paint or a felt-tip pen for proper cylinder identification and cap-to-rod location.
5. Remove the connecting rod caps. Install lengths of rubber hose on each of the connecting rod bolts, to protect the crank journals when the crank is removed.
6. Mark the main bearing caps with a number punch or punch so that they can be reinstalled in their original positions.
7. Remove the main bearing caps.
8. Note the position of the keyway in the crankshaft so it can be installed in the same position.
9. Install rubber bands between a bolt on each connecting rod and oil pan bolts that have been reinstalled in the block (see illustration). This will keep the rods from banging on the block when the crank is removed.
10. Carefully lift the crankshaft out of the block. The rods will pivot to the center of the engine when the crank is removed.

INSTALLATION

When the main bearing clearance has been checked, the bearings examined and/or replaced, the crankshaft can be installed.

1. Thoroughly clean the upper and lower bearing surfaces, then lubricate them with clean engine oil.
2. Install the crankshaft and the main bearing caps.

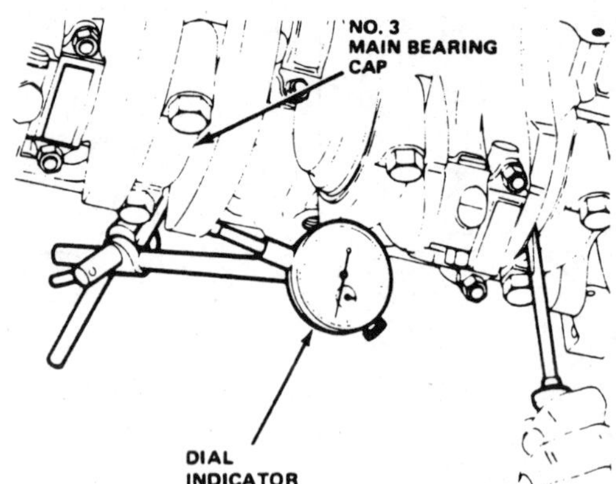

Measure crankshaft end play with a dial indicator

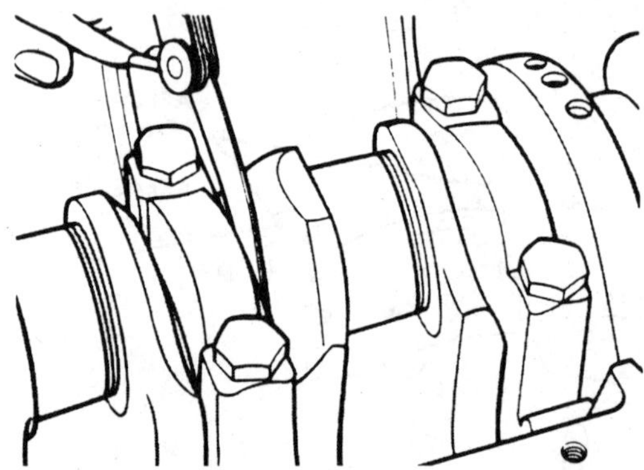
Use a feeler gauge to check crankshaft end play during assembly

NOTE: *Dip all of the main bearing cap bolts in clean oil and torque the main bearing caps to specifications (see the "Crankshaft and Connecting Rod" chart in this chapter to determine which bearing is the thrust bearing).*

3. Tighten the thrust bearing bolts finger tight.
4. To align the thrust bearing, pry the crankshaft the extent of its axial travel several times, holding the last movement toward the front of the engine. Add thrust washers if required for proper alignment. Torque the thrust bearing cap to specifications.

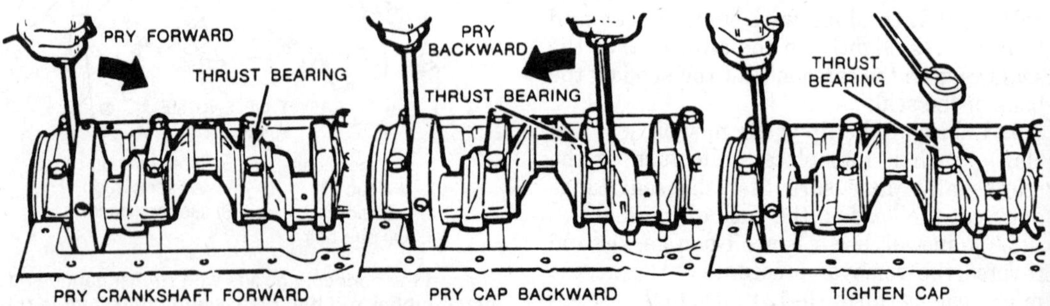

Align thrust bearing as illustrated. Torque caps to specifications

5. To check the crankshaft end-play, pry the crankshaft to the extreme rear of its axial travel, then to the extreme front of its travel. Using a feeler gauge, measure the end-play at the front of the rear main bearing. The end-play may also be measured at the thrust bearing.

6. Install a new rear main bearing oil seal in the cylinder block and the main bearing cap. Torque the main bearing cap bolts to 80 ft. lbs.

7. To complete the installation, reverse the removal procedures.

CLEANING AND INSPECTION

The crankshaft main bearings are shell-type inserts that do not utilize shims and cannot be adjusted. The bearings are available in various standard and undersizes; if the main bearing clearances are found to be excessive, a new bearing (both upper and lower halves) is required.

NOTE: *Factory-undersized crankshafts are marked, sometimes with a "9" and/or a large spot of light green paint; the bearing caps also will have the paint on each side of the undersized journal.*

Generally, the lower half of the bearing shell (except the No. 1 bearing) shows greater wear and fatigue. If the lower half (only) shows the effects of normal wear (no heavy scoring or discoloration), it can usually be assumed that the upper half is also in good shape; conversely, if the lower half is heavily worn or damaged, both halves should be replaced. ***Never replace one bearing half without replacing the other.***

MEASURING MAIN BEARING CLEARANCE

The main bearing clearance can be checked both with the crankshaft in or out of the vehicle.

If the engine block is still in the vehicle, the crankshaft should be supported both front and rear (by the damper and the flywheel) to remove clearance from the upper bearing. The total clearance can then be measured between the lower bearing and the journal.

If the block has been removed from the vehicle (and inverted), the crank will rest on the upper bearings and the total clearance can be measured between the lower bearing and the journal. Clearance is checked in the same manner as the connecting rod bearings, using the Plastigage® method.

NOTE: *The crankshaft bearing caps and the bearing shells should NEVER be filed flush with the cap-to-block mating surface to adjust for wear in the old bearings. Always install new bearings.*

1. If the crankshaft has been removed, install it (engine removed from the vehicle). If the engine is still in the vehicle, remove the oil pan and the oil pump. Remove the rear bearing cap and wipe all of the oil from the crank journal and the bearing cap.

2. Place a strip of Plastigage® the full width of the bearing (parallel to the crankshaft) on the journal.

NOTE: *Plastigage® is soluble in oil; therefore, oil on the journal or bearing could result in erroneous readings.*

CAUTION: *DO NOT rotate the crankshaft while the gaging material is between the bearing and the journal.*

3. Install the bearing cap and evenly torque the cap bolts to specifications.

4. Remove the bearing cap. The flattened Plastigage® will be sticking to either the bearing shell or the crank journal.

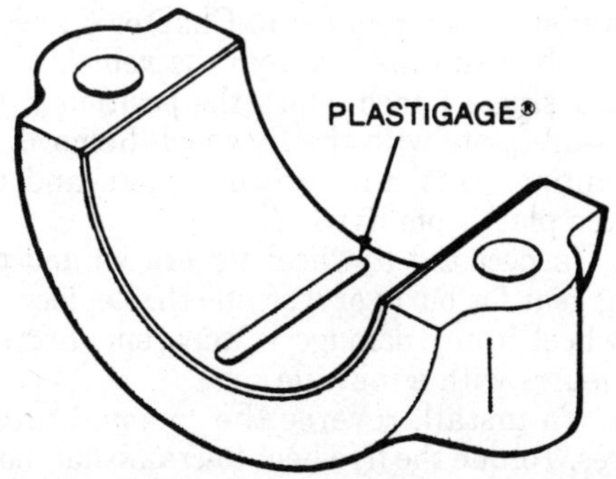

Plastigage installed on main bearing caps correctly

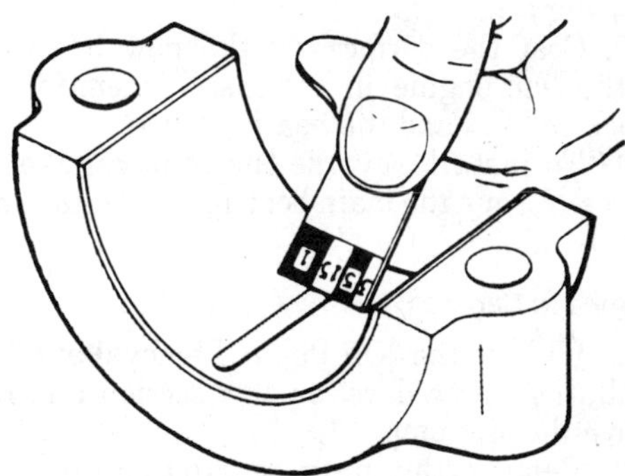
Measure main bearing clearance by comparing flattened strip to Plastigage scale as shown

Check main bearing saddle alignment with straightedge

5. Using the graduated scale on the Plastigage® envelope, measure the material at its widest point. *If the flattened Plastigage® tapers toward the middle or ends, there is a difference in clearance indicating the bearing or journal has a taper, low spot or other irregularity. If this is indicated, measure the crank journal with a micrometer.*

6. If the bearing clearance is within specifications, the bearing insert is in good shape. Replace the insert if the clearance is not within specifications. *Always replace both the upper and the lower inserts as a unit.*

7. Standard, 0.001 in. or 0.002 in. undersize bearings should produce the proper clearance. If these sizes still produce too sloppy a fit, the crankshaft must be reground for use with the next undersize bearing. Recheck all of the clearances after installing the new bearings.

8. Replace the rest of the bearings in the same manner. After all of the bearings have been checked, rotate the crankshaft to make sure there is no excessive drag. When checking the No. 1 main bearing, loosen the accessory drive belts (engine in the vehicle) to prevent a tapered reading with the Plastigage®.

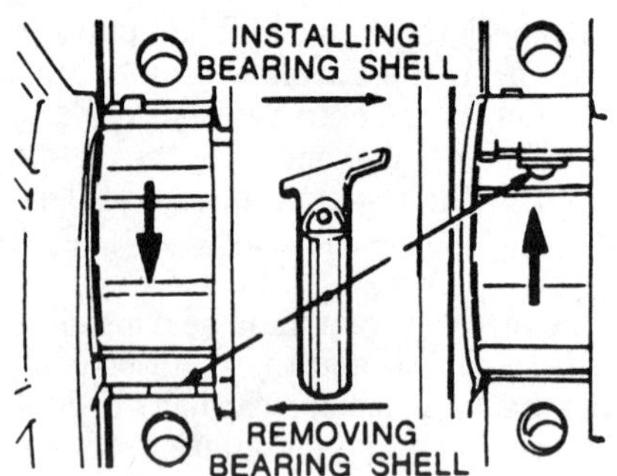

Use a roll-out pin as illustrated to remove bearing shells

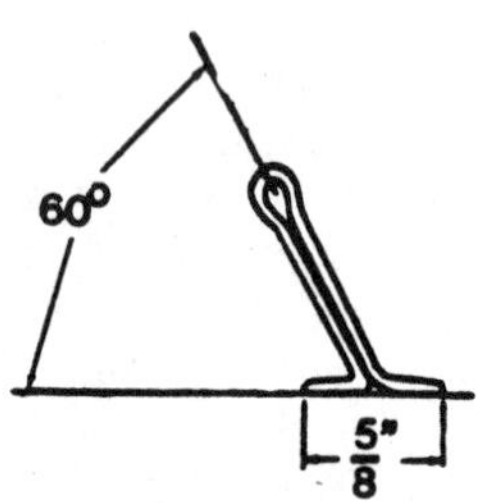

Fabricate a roll-out pin as illustrated, if necessary

MAIN BEARING REPLACEMENT

Engine Out of Car

1. Refer to the "Crankshaft, Removal and Installation" procedures in this section, then remove and inspect the crankshaft.

2. Remove the main bearings from the bearing saddles in the cylinder block and the main bearing caps.

3. Coat the surfaces of the new bearings with clean engine oil and install them in the block saddles and the bearing caps.

4. To install, reverse the removal procedures. Torque the main bearing cap bolts to 80 ft. lbs.

Engine in Car

1. Refer to the "Oil Pump, Removal and Installation" procedures in this section and remove the oil pump.

2. Remove the main bearing cap (of the bearing that needs to be replaced) and the bearing from the cap.

3. Using a bearing roll-out pin (or one fabricated from a cotter pin), install it into the crankshaft journal oil hole.

4. Rotate the crankshaft clockwise (as viewed from the front of the engine) and roll the upper bearing shell out of the block.

5. Using a new upper replacement bearing, lubricate it and insert the plain (unnotched) end between the crankshaft and the indented or notched side of the block. Roll the bearing into place, making sure that the oil holes are aligned. Remove the roll pin from the oil hole.

6. Using a new lower replacement bearing, lubricate and install it into the main bearing cap. Install the cap, making sure that it is positioned in the proper direction with the matchmarks in alignment.

7. To complete the installation, reverse the removal procedures. Torque the main bearing cap bolts to 80 ft. lbs.

Flywheel

REMOVAL AND INSTALLATION

The ring gear is an integral part of the flywheel and is not replaceable.

1. Refer to the "Transmission, Removal and Installation" procedures in Chapter 6 and remove the transmission from the vehicle.

2. Using a punch, mark the position of the pressure plate with the flywheel. Remove the mounting bolts, the pressure plate and the clutch plate from flywheel.

3. Inspect the flywheel for cracks and the ring gear for burrs or worn teeth. Replace the flywheel if any damage is apparent. Remove the burrs with a mill file.

4. To install, reverse the removal procedures. Torque the flywheel-to-crankshaft bolts to 60 ft. lbs. and the pressure plate-to-flywheel bolts to 30 ft. lbs.

EXHAUST SYSTEM

Exhaust "Y" Pipes

REMOVAL AND INSTALLATION

Front

1. Raise the support the front of the vehicle on jackstands.
2. At the front pipe-to-convertor intersection, remove the front heat shield bolts and raise the heat shield, then remove the exhaust pipe hanger clamp from the exhaust pipe.
3. Remove the front pipe-to-catalytic convertor bolts and separate the pipe from the convertor.
4. At the right-side of the front "Y" pipe, disconnect the convertor air pipe brackets.
5. Disconnect the front "Y" pipe from the exhaust manifolds. Remove the front pipe from the vehicle.
6. To install, use a new gasket and reverse the removal procedures.

Rear

1. Raise and support the rear of the vehicle on jackstands.

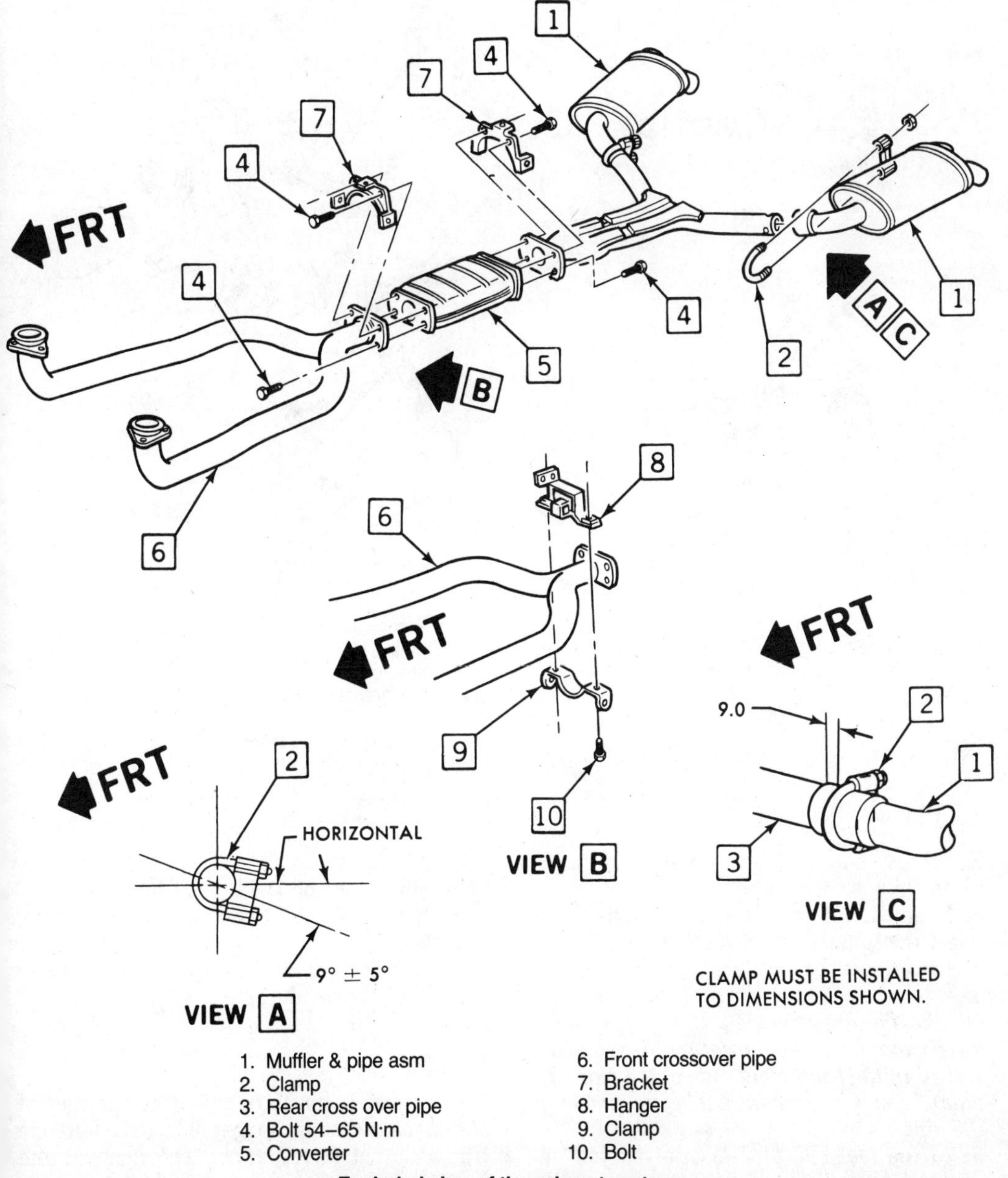

1. Muffler & pipe asm
2. Clamp
3. Rear cross over pipe
4. Bolt 54–65 N·m
5. Converter
6. Front crossover pipe
7. Bracket
8. Hanger
9. Clamp
10. Bolt

Exploded view of the exhaust system

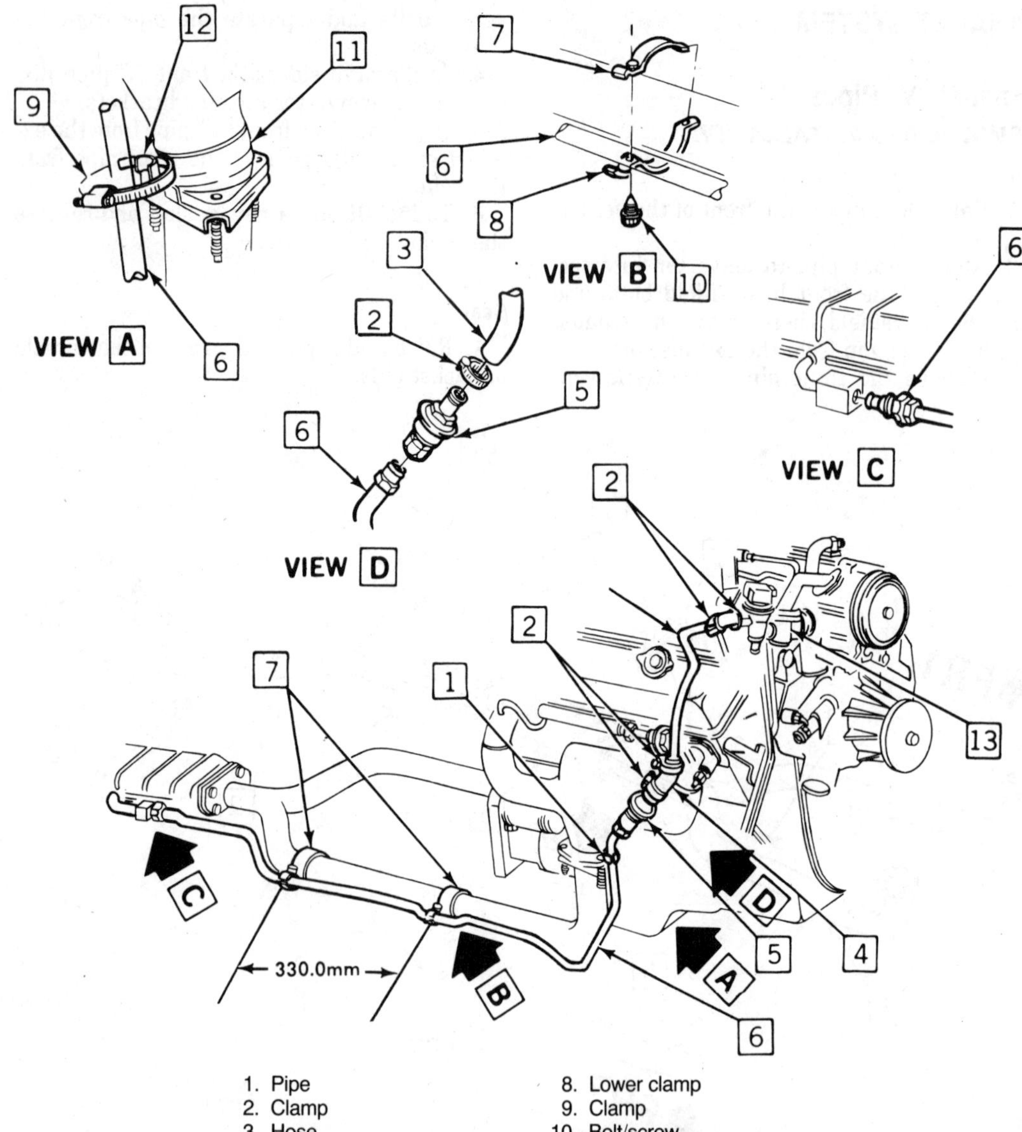

1. Pipe
2. Clamp
3. Hose
4. Hose
5. Valve asm
6. Pipe asm
7. Upper clamp
8. Lower clamp
9. Clamp
10. Bolt/screw
11. Exhaust manifold
12. Bracket
13. Air management valve

Exploded view of the air pipe system

2. Remove both muffler-to-rear "Y" pipe retaining clamps.

3. If muffler-to-vehicle hangers exist, disconnect the hangers from the mufflers.

4. Disconnect the mufflers from the rear "Y" pipe.

NOTE: *The export models are equipped with an Exhaust Overtemperature Sensor (installed in the front right-side of the rear "Y" pipe), be sure to disconnect it before removing the pipe.*

5. At the rear "Y" pipe-to-catalytic convertor intersection, disconnect the retaining bolts and separate the rear "Y" pipe from the catalytic convertor and the hanger bracket.

6. Remove the rear "Y" pipe from the vehicle.

7. To install, use a new gasket and reverse the removal procedures.

Muffler

There are two mufflers built into the rear of the exhaust system: a right-side and a left-side (these do not interchange). The removal and installation procedures apply to both mufflers.

REMOVAL AND INSTALLATION

1. Raise and support the rear of the vehicle on jackstands.
2. Remove the muffler-to-rear "Y" pipe retaining clamp.
3. If a muffler-to-vehicle hanger exists, disconnect the muffler from the hanger.
4. Separate the muffler from the rear "Y" pipe.
5. To install, coat the slip joints with exhaust system sealer and reverse the removal procedures. Install the retaining clamps at a 9° angle below the horizontal centering line.

Catalytic Convertor

The catalytic convertor is employed as an emission control device, to reduce the harmful pollutants in the exhaust gases to CO_2 and water vapor. The convertor is not serviceable and experiences a long life with the use of unleaded fuel.

REMOVAL AND INSTALLATION

1. Raise and the support the vehicle on jackstands.
2. If the catalytic convertor is equipped with an air pipe, disconnect the pipe from the convertor.
3. At the front pipe-to-convertor intersection, remove the front heat shield bolts and raise the heat shield.
4. Remove the front pipe-to-catalytic convertor bolts and separate them.
5. At the rear "Y" pipe-to-catalytic convertor intersection, disconnect the retaining bolts and separate the rear "Y" pipe from the catalytic convertor and the hanger bracket.
6. Remove the catalytic convertor by sliding it downwards and away from the vehicle.
7. To install, use new gaskets and reverse the removal procedures.

Emission Controls and Fuel System

EMISSION CONTROLS

Due to the complex nature of modern electronic engine control systems comprehensive diagnosis and testing procedures fall outside the confines of this repair manual. For complete information on diagnosis testing and repair procedures concerning all modern engine and emission control systems, please refer to *CHILTON'S GUIDE TO ELECTRONIC ENGINE CONTROLS*.

Crankcase Ventilation System

OPERATION

In this system, crankcase vapors are drawn into the intake manifold to be burned in the combustion chambers; instead of merely venting the crankcase vapors into the atmosphere. An added benefit to engines equipped with this system is that the engine oil will tend to stay cleaner for a longer period of time; therefore, if you notice that the oil in your engine becomes dirty very easily, check the functioning of the PCV valve. Engines which use a PCV system are calibrated to run richer, to compensate for the added air which accompanies the crankcase vapors to the combustion chambers. If the PCV valve or line is clogged, the engine idle will tend to be rough due to the excessively rich mixture. Maintenance is covered in Chapter 1.

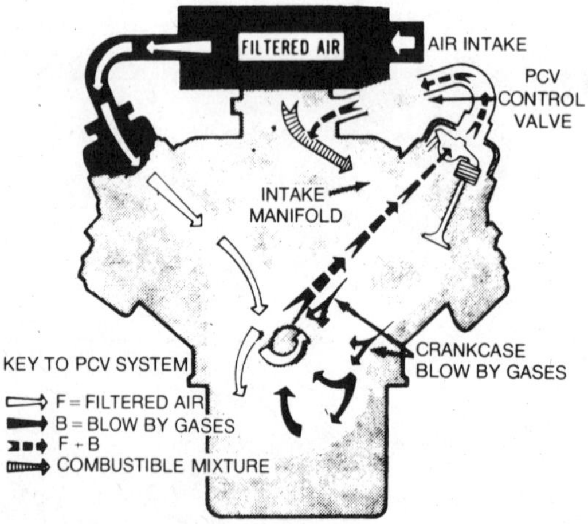

Schematic of the PCV system

TESTING

1. Remove the PCV valve from the rocker arm cover.
2. Operate the engine at idle speed.
3. Place your thumb over the end of the valve to check for vacuum. If no vacuum exists, check the valve, the hoses or the manifold port for a plugged condition.
4. Remove the valve from the hose(s), then shake it and listen for a rattling of the check needle (inside the valve); the rattle means the valve is working. If no rattle is heard, replace the valve.

REMOVAL AND INSTALLATION

1. Pull the PCV valve from the rocker arm cover grommet.
2. Remove the hose(s) from the PCV valve.
3. Shake the valve to make sure that it is not plugged.
4. To install, reverse the removal procedures.

Air Injection Reactor (AIR)

OPERATION

The AIR system uses both an air control valve and an air switching valve. Both the control and switching valves are controlled by the Electronic Control Module (ECM) of the computer controlled emissions system. When the engine is cold, the ECM energizes an air control solenoid, which allows air to flow to the air switching valve. The air switching valve is then energized which directs the air injection to the exhaust manifolds. When the engine warms, the ECM de-energizes the air switching valve, which changes the point of air injection from the exhaust manifolds to the catalytic converter. The extra air at the converter permits the converter to more effectively decrease exhaust emission levels. During deceleration and wide open throttle operation, air is directed to the air cleaner (1984) or silencer (1985 and later).

TESTING

Air Injection Pump

1. Check for proper drive belt tension.
2. Make sure that the pump is not seized.
3. Remove the air hoses, accelerate the engine to 1,500 rpm and check for air flow from the hose outlets.

Check Valves

1. Disconnect the hose from the valve and unscrew the valve from the injection manifold assembly.
2. Blow into each side of the valve: air should pass only in one direction; if air passes through the valve in both directions, replace the valve. Check each valve in the same manner.

REMOVAL AND INSTALLATION

Air Injection Pump

1. Compress the drive belt to keep the pump pulley from turning, then loosen the pump pulley bolts.
2. Lift the drive belt tensioner, then remove the drive belt.
3. Unscrew the mounting bolts and then remove the pump pulley.
4. If necessary, use a pair of needle nose pliers to pull the fan filter from the hub.
5. Remove the hoses, the vacuum lines and the electrical connectors from the Air Control Valve.
6. Unscrew the pump mounting bolts and then remove the pump.
7. To install, reverse the removal procedures. Torque the pump pulley bolts to 100 inch lbs. Be sure to adjust the drive belt tension after installing it.

Check Valve(s)

1. Remove the clamp and disconnect the hose from the valve.
2. Unscrew the valve from the air injection pipe.
3. The test the valve(s); air should pass only in one direction.
4. To install, reverse the removal procedures.

Air Control Valve

1. Disconnect the negative battery cable.

NOTE: *On the 1984 models, remove the air cleaner.*

2. Tag and disconnect the air outlet hoses from the valve.
3. Bend back the lock tabs and then remove the bolts holding the elbow to the valve.
4. Tag and disconnect the electrical connectors and vacuum hoses at the valve. Remove the control valve.

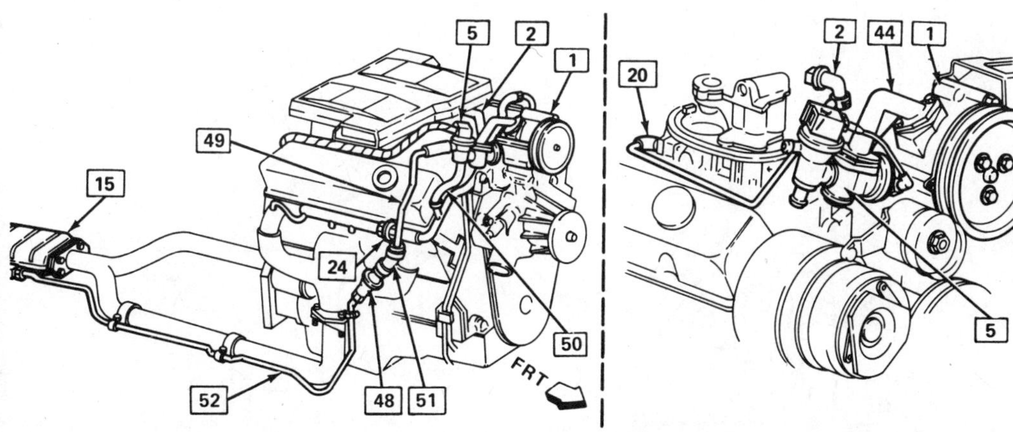

1. Air pump
2. Control valve diverter hose
5. Control valve
15. Catalytic converter
42. Air pump pulley
44. Control valve adapter
48. Cat. conv. air injection check valve
49. Pipe, air injection cat. conv. check vale
50. Control valve hose
51. Cat. conv. air injection check valve hose
52. Cat. conv. air injection check valve pipe

View of the 1984 AIR system, later years are similar

5. To install, reverse the removal procedures.

Air Switching Valve

The switching valve is replaced in basically the same manner as the control valve.

Thermostatic Air Cleaner (THERMAC)—1984 Only

OPERATION

This system is designed to improve driveability and exhaust emissions when the engine is cold. Components added to the basic air cleaner assembly include a temperature sensor (connected to a manifold vacuum source), vacuum diaphragm motor (connected to the temperature sensor) and an inlet damper door (installed in the air cleaner inlet snorkel). Additional components of the system include an exhaust manifold-mounted heat stove and a hot air duct running from the heat source to the underside of the air cleaner snorkel.

When the engine is cold, the temperature sensor allows vacuum to pass through to the vacuum diaphragm motor. The vacuum acting on the vacuum motor causes the motor to close the damper door, which prohibits the introduction of cold, outside air to the air cleaner. The intake vacuum then pulls hot air, generated by the exhaust manifold, through the hot air duct and into the air cleaner. This heated air supply helps to more effectively vaporize the fuel mixture entering the engine. As the engine warms, the temperature sensor bleeds off vacuum to the vacuum motor, allowing the damper door to gradually open.

The usual problems with this system are leaking vacuum lines (which prevent proper operation of the sensor and/or motor); torn or rusted-through hot air ducts and/or rusted-through heat stoves (either condition will allow the introduction of too much cold air to the air cleaner). Visually check and replace these items as necessary. Should the system still fail to operate properly, disconnect the vacuum line from the vacuum motor and apply at least 7 in. Hg of vacuum directly to the motor from an outside vacuum source; the damper door should close. If the door does not close, either the vacuum motor is defective or the damper door and/or linkage is binding. If the door closes, but then gradually opens (with a steady vacuum source), the vacuum motor is defective.

TESTING

Vacuum Motor

1. With the engine Off, disconnect the hose from the vacuum diaphram motor.
2. Using a vacuum source, apply 7 in. Hg to the vacuum motor; the door should close and block off the outside air, completely.
3. Bend the vacuum hose (to trap the vacuum in the motor) and make sure that the door stays closed; if not, replace the vacuum motor.

NOTE: *Before replacing the vacuum motor (if defective), be sure to check the motor linkage, for binding.*

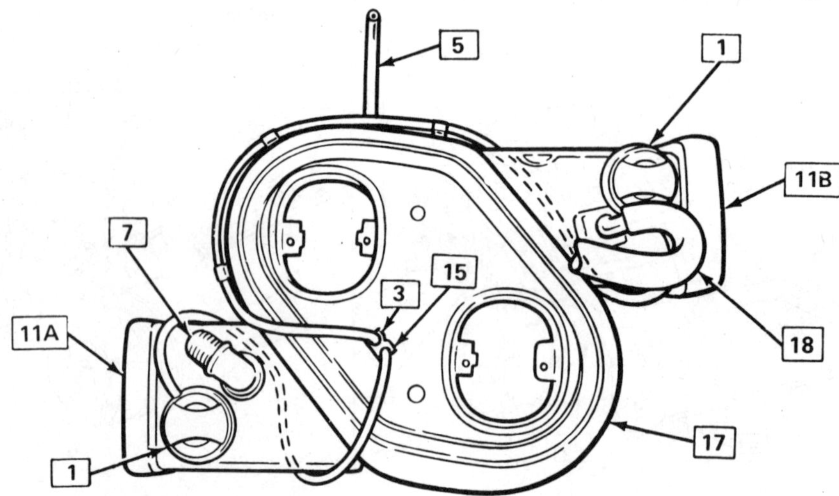

1. Vacuum diaphragm motor
3. Temperature sensor
5. Vacuum hose (to manifold vacuum)
7. Heat stove adapter
11A. Snorkel (left side)
11B. Snorkel (right side)
15. Sensor retainer
17. Air cleaner asm
18. Crankcase vent hose

View of the thermostatic air cleaner—1984 only

4. If the vacuum motor is OK and the problem still exists, check the temperature sensor.

Temperature Sensor

1. Remove the air cleaner cover and place a thermometer near the temperature sensor; the temperature MUST BE below 86°F (30°C). When the temperature is OK, replace the air cleaner.
2. Start the engine and allow it to idle. Watch the vacuum motor door, it should close immediately (if the engine is cool enough).
3. When the vacuum motor door starts to open, remove the air cleaner cover and read the thermometer, it should be about 131°F (55°C).
4. If the door does not respond correctly, replace the temperature sensor.

REMOVAL AND INSTALLATION

Vacuum Motor

1. Remove the air cleaner.
2. Disconnect the vacuum hose from the motor.
3. Drill out the spot welds with a ⅛" hole, then enlarge as necessary to remove the retaining strap.
4. Remove the retaining strap.
5. Lift up the motor and cock it to one side to unhook the motor linkage at the control damper assembly.
6. Install the new vacuum motor as follows:
   a. Drill a $^{7}/_{64}$" hole in the snorkel tube as the center of the vacuum motor retaining strap.
   b. Insert the vacuum motor linkage into the control damper assembly.
   c. Use the motor retaining strap and a sheet metal screw to secure the retaining strap and motor to the snorkel tube.
   NOTE: *Make sure the screw does not interfere with the operation of the damper assembly; shorten the screw, if necessary.*

Temperature Sensor

1. Remove the air cleaner.
2. Disconnect the hoses from the sensor.
3. Pry up the tabs on the sensor retaining clip and remove the clip and sensor from the air cleaner.
4. To install, reverse the removal procedures.

Evaporative Emission Control (EEC)

OPERATION

The EEC system is designed to reduce the amount of escaping gasoline vapors to the atmosphere. Fuel vapors are directed through lines to a canister containing an activated charcoal filter; unburned fuel vapor is trapped here until the engine is started. When the engine is started, the canister is purged by air drawn in by the manifold vacuum. The air/fuel vapor mixture is drawn into the engine and burned.

The purge control solenoid is installed in the vacuum line between the charcoal canister and the PCV valve (mounted on the driver's-side fender, under the hood). The ECM of the computerized emissions system controls the action of the purge control solenoid. Depending upon various conditions of operation, the ECM will either energize or de-energize the solenoid. When the solenoid is energized, vacuum is not available to draw fuel vapors from the canister; when de-energized, vacuum draws the canister vapors into the intake tract of the engine. The solenoid is mounted on the drivers-side fender, inside the engine compartment.

TESTING

Charcoal Canister

1. Remove the lower tube of the canister (purge valve) and install a short length of tube, then try to blow through it (little or no air should pass).
2. Using a vacuum source, apply 15 in. Hg to the upper tube of the canister (purge valve). The diaphragm should hold the vacuum for at least 20 seconds, if not replace the canister.

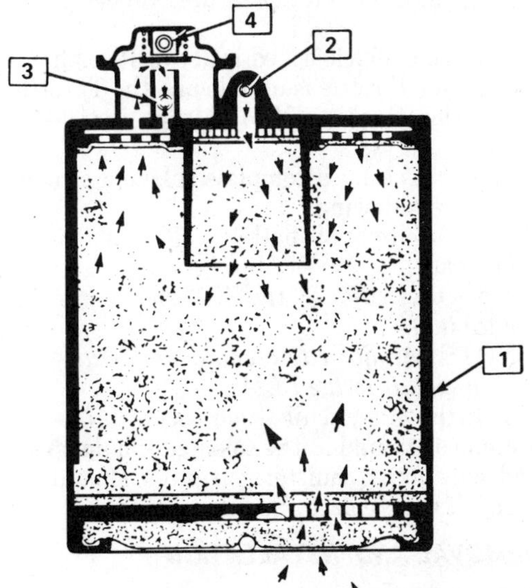

1. Charcoal canister
2. To fuel tank
3. Purge valve (to manifold)
4. Control valve (to manifold vacuum)

Cross-sectional view of the carbon canister

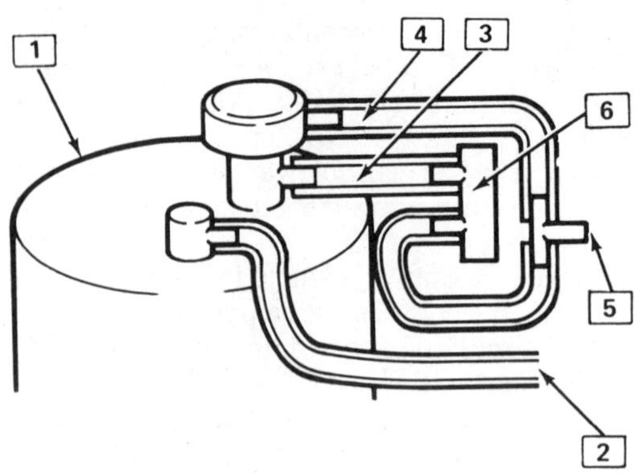

1. Charcoal canister
2. To fuel tank
3. To manifold (purge valve)
4. To manifold vacuum (control valve)
5. To manifold vacuum
6. Canister solenoid (ECM controlled)

View of the carbon canister hose routing

3. While holding the vacuum on the upper tube, blow through the lower tube (air should now pass); if not, replace the canister.

Charcoal Canister Solenoid

1. Check to see if the solenoid is open or closed; it will be open if one or more of the following conditions are met:
   a. The diagnostic test terminal is grounded with the engine stopped.
   b. The engine is run more than 1 minute from being cold.
   c. The coolant temperature is above 105°F (75°C).
   d. The vehicle speed is above 15 mph.
   e. The throttle is off idle and the Throttle Position Sensor (TPS) voltage is 0.9–1.0 volts.
2. To check for a complete solenoid circuit, check the following:
   a. On circuit 39, battery voltage should be present.
   b. On circuit 428, the ECM should provide a ground.
   NOTE: *A shorted solenoid may cause an open circuit in the ECM.*
3. If the 428 circuit (from the ECM) is not grounded, ground it (the solenoid should open) and check the canister purge (it should be open); if not, replace the solenoid.

REMOVAL AND INSTALLATION

Charcoal Canister

1. Label and disconnect the hoses from the canister.
2. Loosen the retaining bolt and remove the canister from the vehicle.
   NOTE: *If necessary to replace the canister filter, simply pull the filter from the bottom of the charcoal filter and install a new one.*
3. To install, reverse the removal procedures.

Charcoal Canister Solenoid

1. Disconnect the negative battery cable.
2. Remove the solenoid cover bolt, the cover and the solenoid.
3. Disconnect the electrical connector and the hoses from the solenoid.
4. To install, reverse the removal procedures.

Exhaust Gas Recirculation (EGR)

OPERATION

All engines are equipped with exhaust gas recirculation (EGR). This system consists of a metering valve, a vacuum line to the intake manifold and cast-in exhaust gas passages in the intake manifold. The EGR valve is controlled by manifold vacuum, which accordingly opens and closes to admit exhaust gases into the fuel/air mixture. The exhaust gases lower the combustion temperature and reduce the amount of oxides of nitrogen (NOx) produced. The valve is closed at idle between the two extreme throttle positions.

The vacuum to the EGR valve is controlled by EGR solenoid (controlled by the ECM), Thermal Vacuum Switch (TVS), the Throttle Position Sensor (TPS) and the Manifold Pressure Sensor (MAP)—1984 or Mass Air Flow Sensor (MAF)—1985 and later. Vacuum to the EGR valve is restricted until the engine is hot.

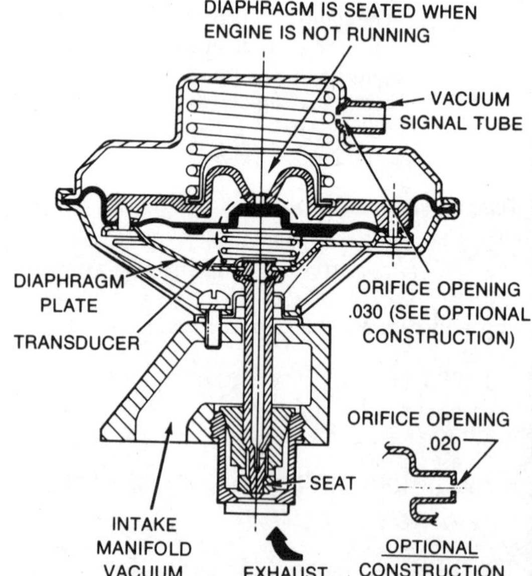

Cross section of a negative backpressure EGR valve

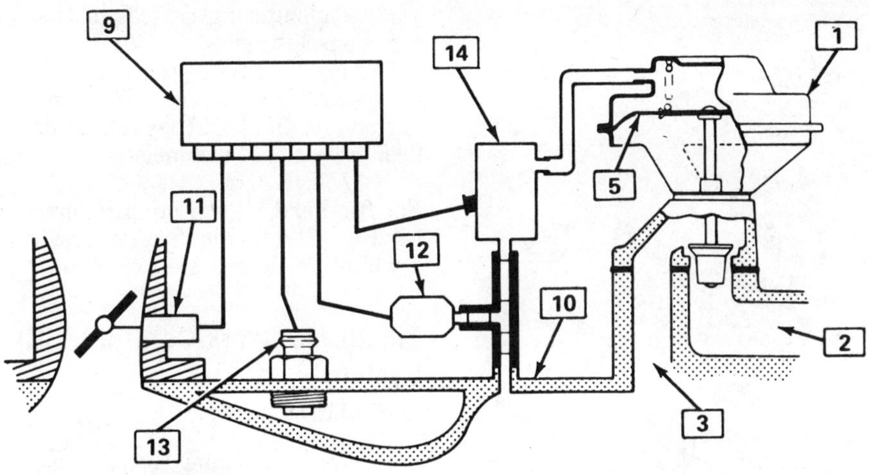

1. EGR valve
2. Exhaust gas
3. Intake air
5. Diaphragm
9. Electronic control module
10. Manifold vacuum
11. Throttle position sensor
12. Manifold pressure sensor
13. Coolant temperature sensor
14. EGR control solenoid

EGR valve control layout—1984 only

This prevents the stalling and lumpy idle which would result if EGR occurred when the engine was cold.

TESTING

EGR Valve

1. Remove the vacuum hose from the EGR valve.
2. Using a vacuum source, connect it to the EGR valve hose fitting and apply 10 in. Hg; the valve should lift off of its seat, if not, replace the EGR valve.

EGR Solenoid

1. Disconnect the electrical connector from the solenoid.
2. Using an ohmmeter, measure the solenoid's resistance, it should be more than 20 Ω. If less than 20 Ω, replace the solenoid and possibly the ECM.

REMOVAL AND INSTALLATION

EGR Valve

1. Remove the air cleaner (1984 models) or the plenum (1985 and later).
2. Detach the vacuum hose from the EGR valve.
3. Unfasten the mounting bolts and the EGR valve from the manifold.
4. To install, use a new gasket and reverse the removal procedures. Torque the EGR valve-to-manifold bolts to 14 ft. lbs.

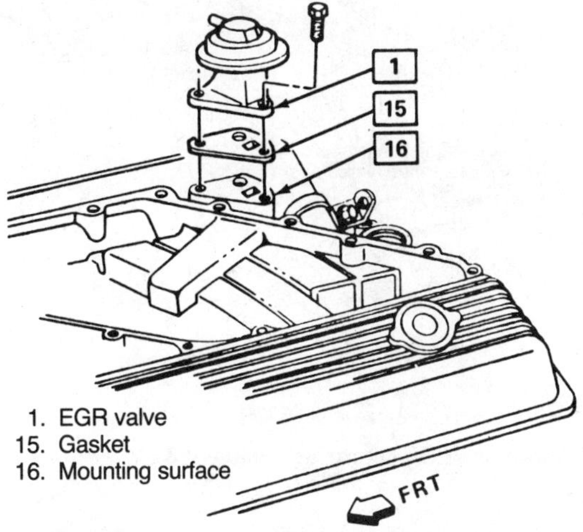

1. EGR valve
15. Gasket
16. Mounting surface

Exploded view of the EGR valve—1984 only

EGR Solenoid

1. Disconnect the negative battery cable.

   NOTE: *On the 1984 models, remove the air cleaner.*
2. Disconnect the electrical connector and the vacuum hoses from the solenoid.
3. Remove the mounting nut and the solenoid.
4. To install, reverse the removal procedures. Torque the solenoid mounting nut to 17 ft. lbs.

Coolant Temperature Sensor (CTS)

1. Drain the radiator to a level below the coolant temperature sensor.

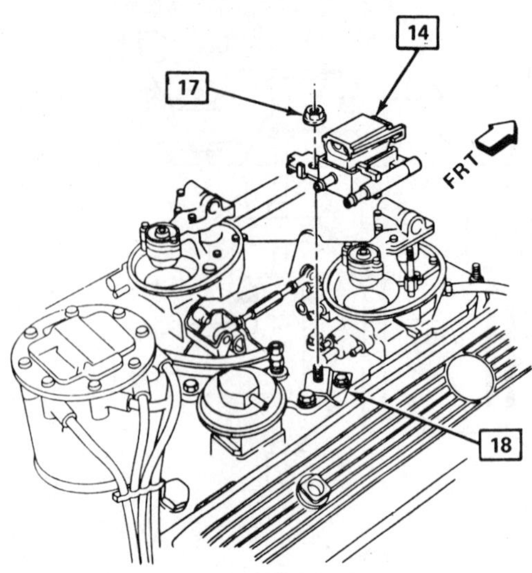

14. EGR solenoid
17. Nut
18. Bracket

View of the EGR control solenoid—1984 only

1. EGR solenoid

View of the EGR control solenoid—1985 and later

2. Disconnect the electrical connector from the sensor, then remove the sensor from the engine.

3. To install, apply sealer to the threaded portion of the new switch and reverse the removal procedure. Torque the CTS to 15 ft. lbs.

Electronic Spark Timing (EST) System

The EST system does not have vacuum or mechanical spark advance mechanisms, as these functions are controlled electronically by the distributor module assembly and the ECM of the computer emissions system.

The purpose of the EST system is to precisely adjust the spark timing according to specific engine operating conditions, as sensed by the various monitoring devices of the computer emissions system.

Because the EST system is directly tied into the computer emissions system, service, testing, and repair should be performed by a qualified, professional technician.

For further EST system information, refer to the "Electronic Spark Control (ESC) System" in this section.

Electronic Spark Control (ESC) System

OPERATION

Since varying octane levels of gasoline can cause detonation (spark knock) in the high performance engines, causing piston and ring rattle or vibrate, the ESC system has been added to the engine to remedy the knocking situation by retarding the spark timing by as much as 20°; this allows the engine to maximize the spark advance to improve the fuel economy and driveability.

A sensor is mounted on the block (near the cylinders) to detect the knock and send the information to the ECM. The ECM adjusts the Electronic Spark Timing (EST) to reduce the spark knock. If no signal is received from the ESC sensor, the ECM provides normal spark advance.

Loss of the signal, through a bad ESC sensor, ESC module or a poor ground, will cause the engine to operate sluggishly and cause a Code 43 (to be set).

TESTING

1. With the engine operating at 1,500 rpm, tap on the engine block in the area of the knock sensor, the engine rpm should drop.

NOTE: *The the speed does not drop, the timing is not retarding or it is retarded all of the time.*

2. Disconnect the ESC module connector (the engine rpm should drop); after 4 seconds, the "CHECK ENGINE" light should turn ON and the Code 43 will be stored.

3. Using a digital voltmeter (set on the low AC scale), check the knock sensor voltage; low or no voltage will indicate an open circuit at terminal "E" or a bad sensor.

4. Check the "CHECK ENGINE" light and the Code 43 in the ESC system. If no light turns ON, the ECM is not retarding the engine spark for there may be voltage on the "B7" terminal or the ECM may be faulty, replace the ECM.

5. Disconnect the electrical connector from the knock sensor; if the rpm increases with the

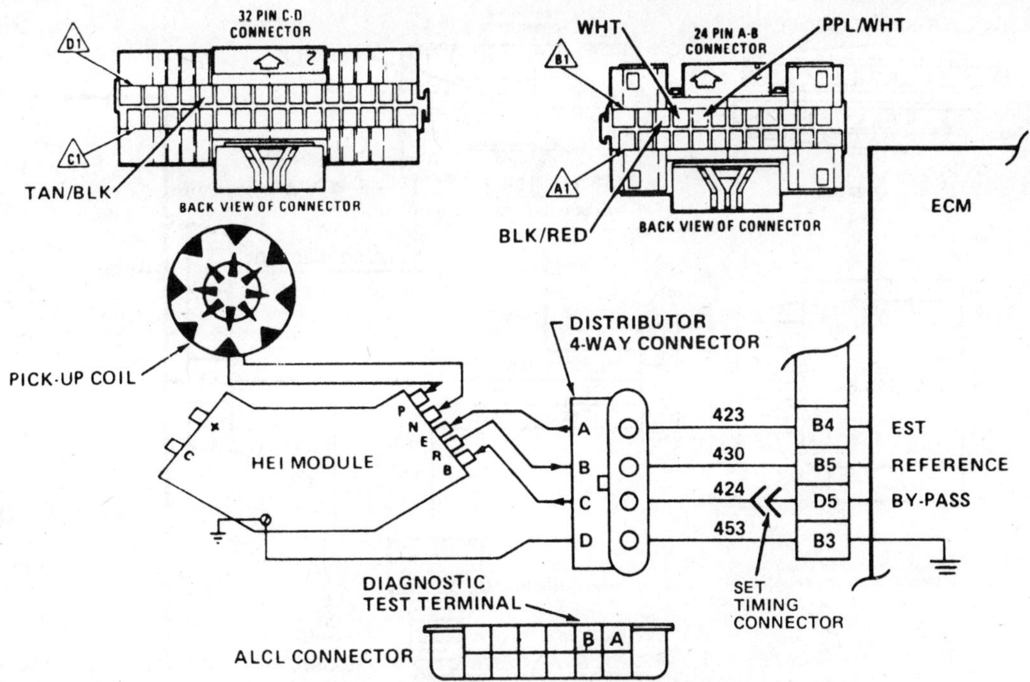

Schematic of the electronic spark timing system

sensor disconnected, the sensor is bad and should be replaced.

REMOVAL AND INSTALLATION

Knock Sensor

1. Disconnect the negative battery cable.
2. Raise and support the vehicle on jackstands.
3. Disconnect the electrical connector from the knock sensor.
4. Remove the knock sensor from the engine block.
5. To install, apply teflon tape to the threads and reverse the removal procedures.

ESC Module

1. At the heater fan housing, disconnect the electrical connector from the ESC module.
2. Remove the mounting bolts and the module from the vehicle.
3. To install, reverse the removal procedures.

Electronic Control Module (ECM)

The fuel/emission system capabilities are greatly extended through the use of additional

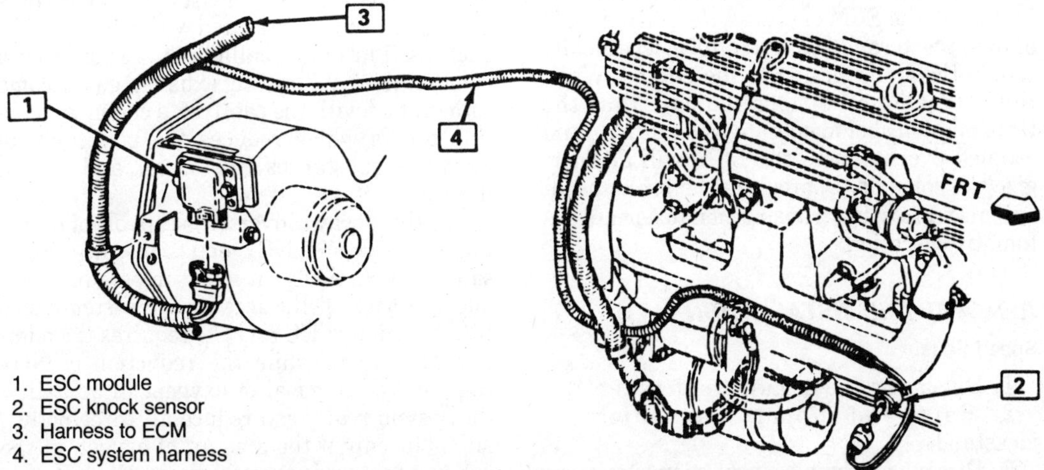

View of the electronic spark control components

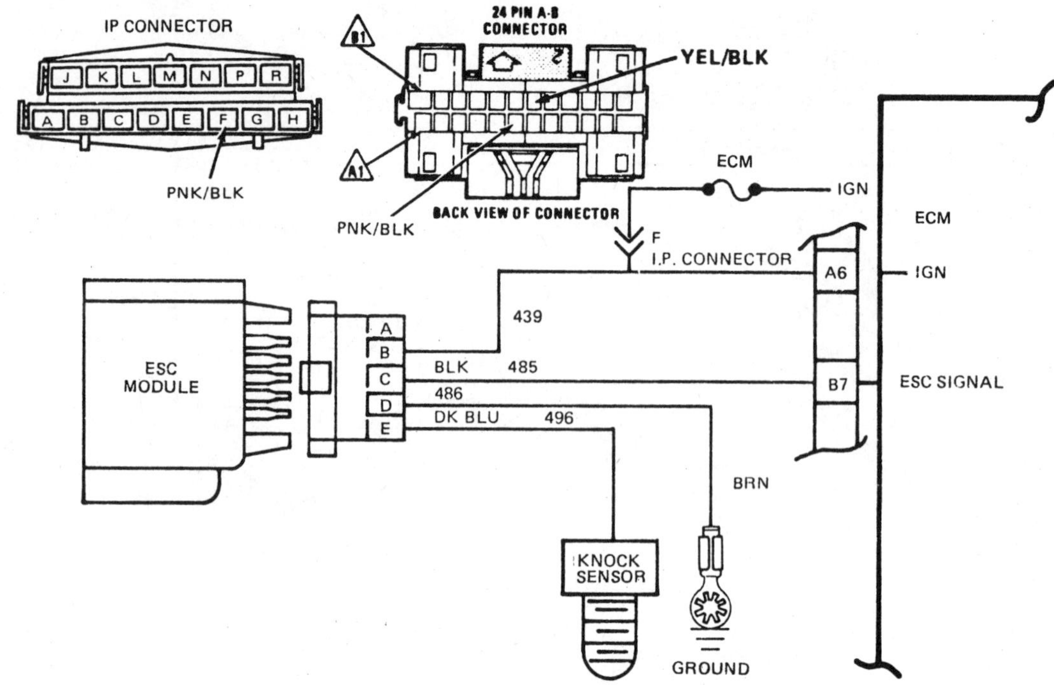

View of the electronic spark control wiring diagram

sensors and increased control capacities of the ECM and PROM units.

The ECM system also controls the AIR, EGR, Electronic Spark Timing (EST), Torque Converter Clutch (TCC) systems, the fresh air induction and fuel injection systems.

Transmission Converter Clutch (TCC) System

All vehicles equipped with an automatic transmission use the TCC system. The ECM controls the converter by means of a solenoid mounted in the outdrive housing of the transmission. When the vehicle speed reaches a certain level, the ECM energizes the solenoid and allows the torque converter to mechanically couple the transmission to the engine. When the operating conditions indicate that the transmission should operate as a normal fluid coupled transmission, the ECM will de-energize the solenoid. Depressing the brake pedal will also return the transmission to normal automatic operation.

REMOVAL AND INSTALLATION

Speed Sensor

1. Disconnect the negative battery cable.
2. Raise and support the vehicle on jackstands.
3. Disconnect the electrical connector from the speed sensor.
4. Remove the sensor-to-transmission retaining bolt and retainer.
5. Remove the speed sensor, the oil seal and the speedometer gear from the transmission.
6. To install, lubricate the oil seal with transmission oil and reverse the removal procedures. Torque the speed sensor-to-transmission bolt to 3.5 ft. lbs.

Catalytic Converter

The catalytic converter is a muffler-like container, located midway in the exhaust system, to aid in the reduction of exhaust emissions. The catalyst element consists of a honeycomb monolithic substrate coated with noble metals, such as: Platinum, palladium, rhodium or a combination. When the exhaust gases come into contact with the catalyst, a chemical reaction occurs which reduces the pollutants to harmless substances like water and carbon dioxide.

The three-way converter is capable of reducing HC, CO and NOx emissions; all at the same time. In theory, it seems impossible to reduce all three pollutants in one system since the reduction of HC and CO requires the addition of oxygen, while the reduction of NOx calls for the removal of oxygen. In actuality, the system really can reduce all three pollutants, but only if the amount of oxygen in the exhaust system is precisely controlled. Due to this precise oxygen control requirement, the

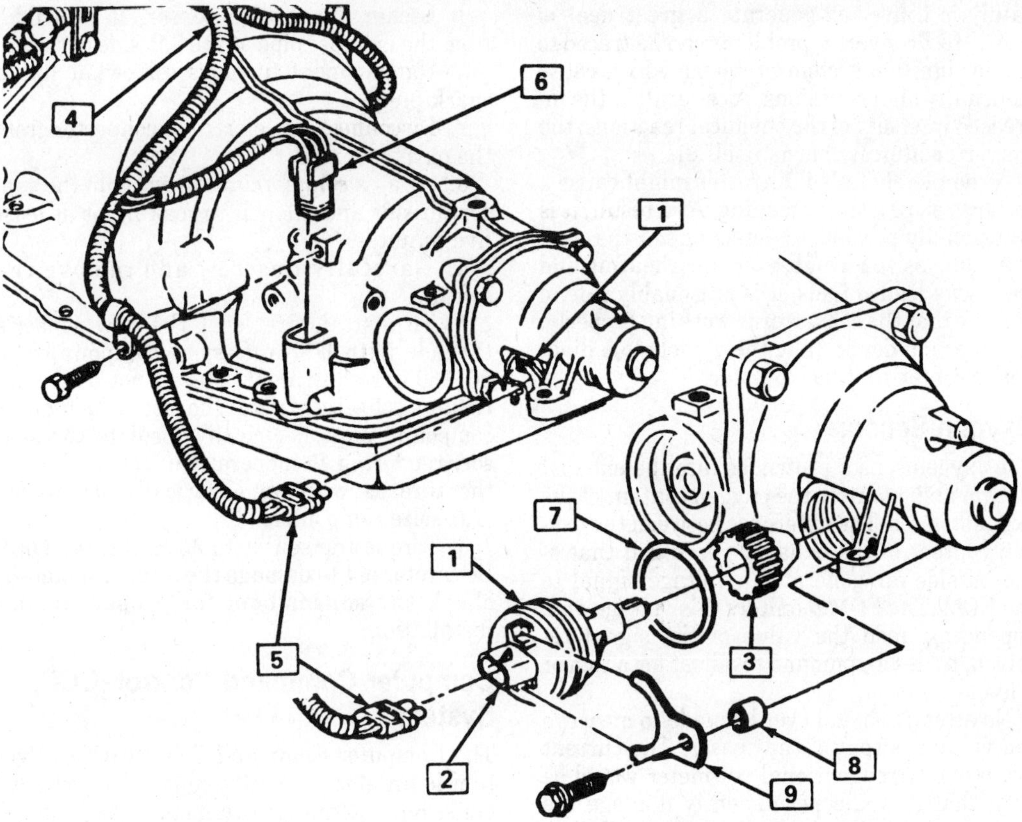

1. Speedo buffer sensor
2. Sensor connector
3. Speedo driven gear
4. ECM harness
5. ECM harness connector to speedo buffer sensor
6. ECM harness connector to T.C.C.
7. Oil seal
8. Spacer
9. Retainer

Exploded view of the speedo Buffer Sensor—transmission converter clutch

three-way converter system is used only in conjunction with an oxygen sensor system.

There are no service procedures required for the catalytic converter, although the converter body should be inspected occasionally for damage.

PRECAUTIONS

1. Use only unleaded fuel.
2. Avoid prolonged idling; the engine should run no longer than 20 min. at curb idle and no longer than 10 min. at fast idle.
3. Do not disconnect any of the spark plug leads while the engine is running.
4. Make engine compression checks as quickly as possible.

CATALYST TESTING

At the present time there is no known way to reliably test the catalytic converter operation in the field. The only reliable test is a 12 hour and 40 min. "soak" test (CVS) which must be done in a laboratory.

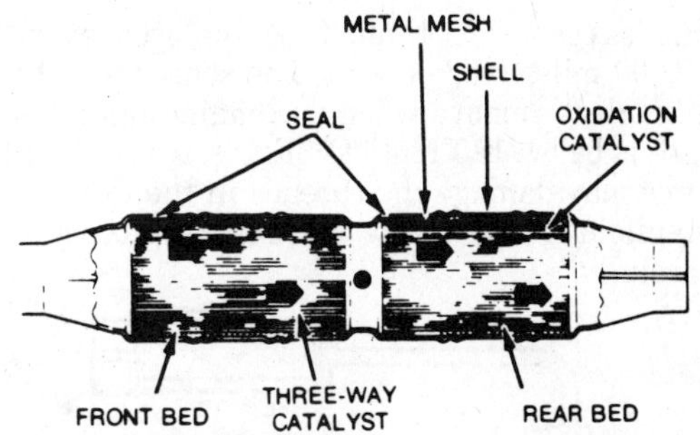

Cutaway view of the typical three-way catalytic converter

An infrared HC/CO tester is not sensitive enough to measure the higher tailpipe emissions from a failing converter. Thus, a bad converter may allow enough emissions to escape so that the vehicle is no longer in compliance with Federal or State standards, but will still not cause the needle on a tester to move off zero.

The chemical reactions which occur inside a

catalytic converter generate a great deal of heat. Most converter problems can be traced to fuel or ignition system problems which cause unusually high emissions. As a result of the increased intensity of the chemical reactions, the converter literally burns itself up.

A completely failed converter might cause a tester to show a slight reading. As a result, it is occasionally possible to detect one of these.

As long as you avoid severe overheating and the use of leaded fuels, it is reasonably safe to assume that the converter is working properly. If you are in doubt, take the vehicle to a diagnostic center that has a tester.

Oxygen Sensor

The oxygen sensor protrudes into the exhaust stream and monitors the oxygen content of the exhaust gases. The difference between the oxygen content of the exhaust gases and that of the outside air generates a voltage signal to the ECM. The ECM monitors this voltage and, depending upon the value of the signal received, issues a command to adjust for a rich or a lean condition.

No attempt should ever be made to measure the voltage output of the sensor. The current drain of any conventional voltmeter would be such that it would permanently damage the sensor. No jumpers, test leads or any other electrical connections should ever be made to the sensor. Use these tools ONLY on the ECM side of the wiring harness connector AFTER disconnecting it from the sensor.

REMOVAL AND INSTALLATION

The oxygen sensor must be replaced every 30,000 miles (48,000 km). The sensor may be difficult to remove when the engine temperature is below 120°F (48°C). Excessive removal force may damage the threads in the exhaust manifold or pipe; follow the removal procedure carefully.

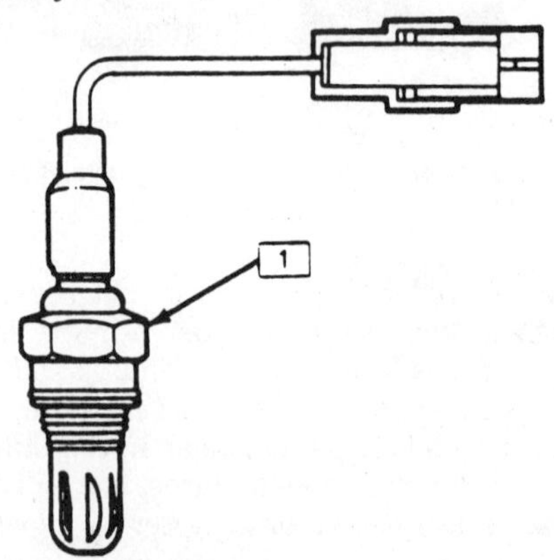

View of the oxygen sensor

1. Locate the oxygen sensor. It protrudes from the exhaust pipe at the left-side of the engine compartment (it looks somewhat like a spark plug).
2. Disconnect the electrical connector from the oxygen sensor.
3. Spray a commercial solvent onto the sensor threads and allow it to soak in for at least five minutes.
4. Carefully unscrew and remove the sensor.
5. To install, first coat the new sensor's threads with GM anti-sieze compound No. 5613695 or equivalent. This is not a conventional anti-seize paste. The use of a regular compound may electrically insulate the sensor, rendering it inoperative. You must coat the threads with an electrically conductive anti-seize compound.
6. Torque the sensor to 30 ft. lbs. (42 Nm). Be careful not to damage the electrical pigtail; check the sensor boot for proper fit and installation.

Computer Command Control (CCC) System

The Computer Command Control (CCC) System is an electronically controlled exhaust emission system that can monitor and control a large number of interrelated emission control systems. It can monitor many engine/vehicle operating conditions and then use the information to control the various engine related systems. The "System" is thereby making constant adjustments to maintain good vehicle performance under all normal driving conditions while at the same time allowing the catalytic converter to effectively control the emissions of HC, CO and NOx.

OPERATION

Electronic Control Module (ECM)

The Electronic Control Module (ECM) is the control center of the fuel control system. It constantly monitors various information from the sensors and controls the systems that affect the vehicle performance. The ECM has two

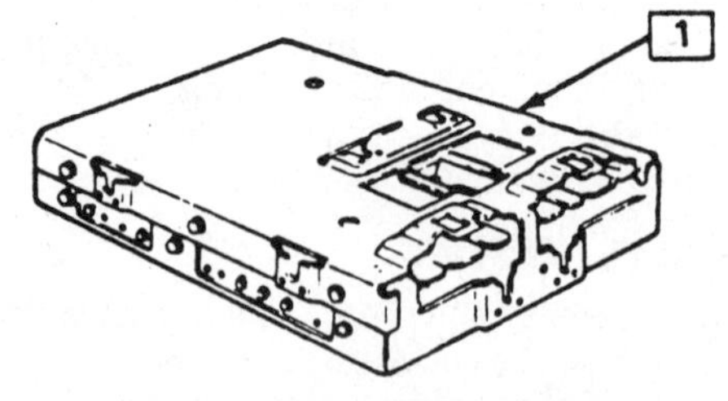

1. Electronic control module (ECM)

Electronic Control Module (ECM)

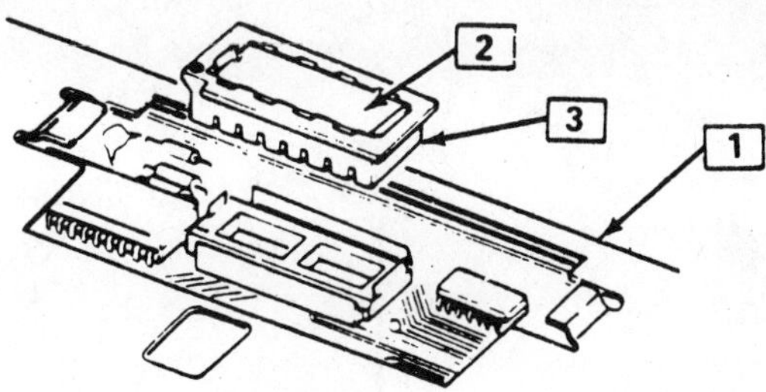

1. ECM
2. Prom (engine calibrator)
3. Prom carrier

Programmable Read Only Memory (PROM)

parts: A Controller (the ECM without the PROM) and a separate calibrator (the PROM). The ECM is located behind the instrument panel's console trim plate.

Programmable Read Only Memory (PROM)

To allow the Controller to be used in many different vehicles, a device called a Calibrator or Programmable Read Only Memory (PROM) is used. The PROM which is located inside the ECM, stores information such as: the vehicle's weight, engine, transmission, axle ratio and many other specifications. Since the PROM stores specific information, it is important that the correct one be used in the right vehicle.

NOTE: *Due to the intricacy of the system, it is advised to have a qualified mechanic perform any testing, adjusting or replacement of the system components.*

Throttle Position Sensor (TPS)

The throttle position sensor is mounted on the throttle body and is used to supply throttle position information to the ECM. The ECM memory stores an average of operating conditions with the ideal air/fuel ratios for each of these conditions. When the ECM receives a signal that indicates throttle position change, it immediately shifts to the last remembered set of operating conditions that resulted in an ideal air/fuel ratio control. The memory is continually being updated during normal operations.

FUEL INJECTION SYSTEM

Electric Fuel Pump

An electric impeller-type fuel pump is designed to deliver a constant flow of fuel to the throttle body mounted injector units (1984) or the fuel injectors (1985 and later).

On the 1984 – CFI engines, the fuel pressure is regulated at the pressure regulator and compensator units, both of which are integrated with the throttle body injection units.

On the 1985 and later – TPI engines, the fuel pressure is regulated at the rear of the fuel rail by the pressure regulator.

The pump is mounted inside the fuel tank as part of the fuel gauge sending unit, it is replaced independently of the sending unit.

REMOVAL AND INSTALLATION

Cross-Fire Injection (CFI) – 1984

1. Disconnect the negative battery cable.
2. Remove the fuel filler door and cap.
3. Remove the fuel filler neck housing and drain hose.
4. Disconnect the fuel lines and electrical connector from the sending unit/pump assembly, then remove the sending unit/pump assembly-to-fuel tank screws.
5. Remove the sending unit/pump assembly and the gasket.
6. Separate the pump from the sending unit.
7. To install, reverse the removal procedures. Start the engine and check for fuel leaks.

CAUTION: *DO NOT connect the battery until all other steps have been completed.*

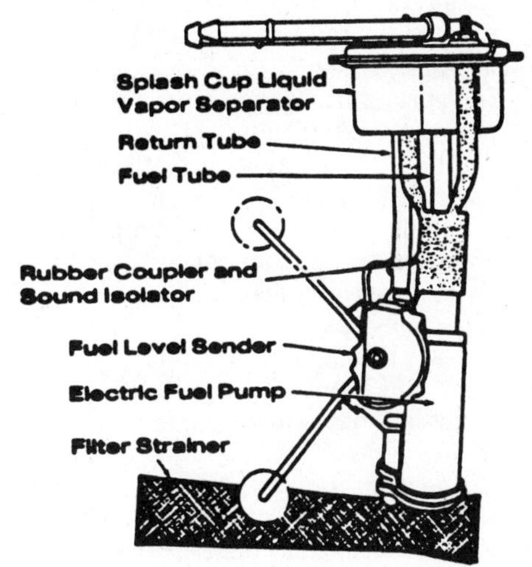

View of the cross-fire injection fuel pump assembly—1984

Tuned Port Injection (TPI) – 1985 and Later

The fuel system is under pressure, it must be relieved before removing any lines from the fuel system.

1. To release the fuel pressure, perform the following procedures:
   a. On top of the right-side fuel rail, remove the fuel pressure connector cap.
   b. Using the Fuel Gauge tool No. J-34730-1, connect it to the fuel pressure connector;

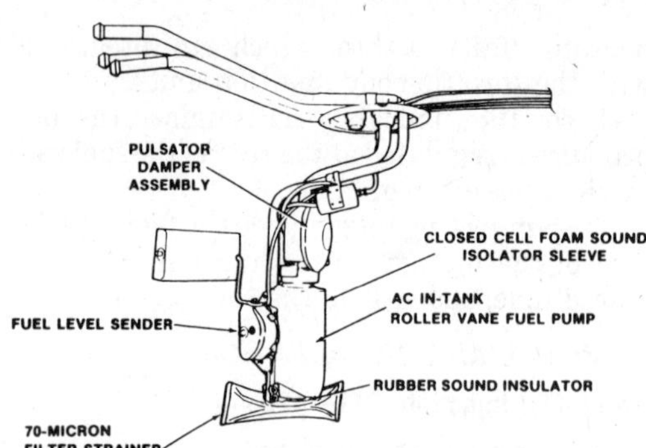

View of the tuned port injection fuel pump assembly—1985 and later

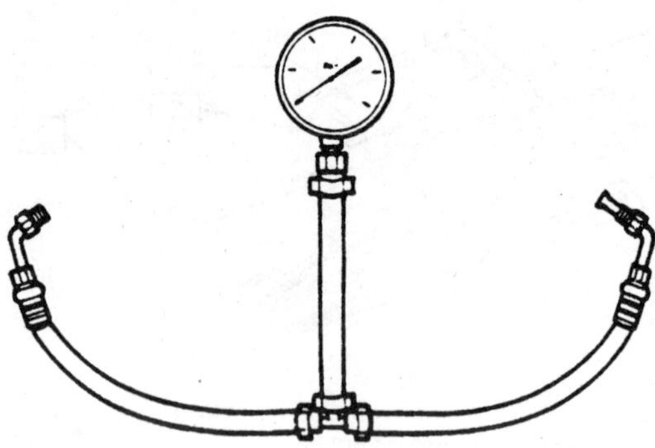

Fuel pressure gauge used to test the fuel pressure TBI models

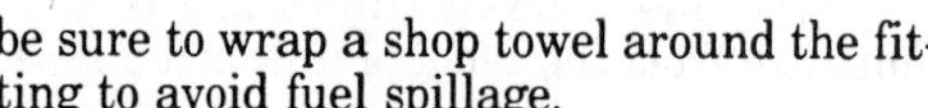

be sure to wrap a shop towel around the fitting to avoid fuel spillage.

c. Place the bleed hose into a fuel container, open the valve and bleed off the excess fuel.

2. Disconnect the negative battery cable.
3. Remove the fuel filler door and cap.
4. Remove the fuel filler neck housing and drain hose.
5. Disconnect the fuel lines and electrical connector from the sending unit/pump assembly, then remove the sending unit/pump assembly-to-tank screws.
6. Remove the sending unit/pump assembly and the gasket.
7. To separate the pump from the sending unit, perform the following.
   a. Push the fuel pump up into the pulsator.
   b. Pull the bottom of the pump outward (away) from the bottom support; be careful not to damage the rubber insulator and filter during removal.
   c. When the pump is clear of the bottom support, pull it out of the pulsator.
8. To install, use a new gasket and reverse the removal procedures. Start the engine and check for leaks.

CAUTION: *DO NOT connect the battery until all other steps have been completed.*

TESTING

CFI System – 1984

NOTE: *A special Fuel Pressure Gauge tool No. J-29658 is required to safely perform this test.*

1. Remove the air cleaner assembly and plug the THERMAC vacuum port at the TBI unit.
2. Remove the fuel tube installed between the TBI units.

NOTE: *Use two line wrenches of the appropriate sizes to disconnect each fitting; one wrench to hold the large fitting, the other to loosen the smaller fitting.*

CAUTION: *A small amount of fuel will be released from the connections.*

3. Using the Pressure Gauge tool No. J-29658, install it between the two TBI units.
4. Turn the ignition switch ON and check for fuel leakage at the gauge arrangement. If leakage is noted, turn the ignition switch OFF and correct the leak.
5. Start the engine and read the fuel pressure on the gauge, it should be 9–13 psi. Turn the engine OFF. Replace the fuel pump if the pressure is not within this range.
6. Remove the fuel pressure gauge, install the fuel tube assembly and check for leaks.
7. To complete the installation, reverse the removal procedures.

TPI System – 1985 and Later

NOTE: *A special Fuel Pressure Gauge tool No. J-34730-1 is required to safely perform this test.*

1. At the right-side of the fuel rail, remove the fuel pressure connector cap.
2. Using a shop cloth, wrap it around the fuel pressure connector (to absorb any excess fuel).
3. Using the Pressure Gauge tool No. J-34730-1, connect it to the fuel pressure connector.
4. Turn the ignition switch ON and read the pressure gauge, the pressure should be 34–39 psi.
5. Start the engine, if the fuel pressure falls (another problem exists), check the following components to determine the problem:
   a. The intank fuel pump check valve may not be holding.
   b. A possible leaking hose at the pump connection.
   c. A leaking fuel pressure regulator valve.

d. The injectors (cold start valve also) may be sticking open.

6. To install, reverse the removal procedures.

Throttle Body

DESCRIPTION

CFI System – 1984

The Model 400 Electronic Fuel Injection (EFI) system is a computer controlled system that uses a pair of Throttle Body Injection (TBI) units, which are mounted on a single manifold cover. Since each TBI feeds the cylinders on the opposite side of the engine, the system has acquired the name of Cross-Fire Injection (CFI).

Fuel is supplied by an electric fuel pump located in the fuel tank, to the front TBI fuel accumulator. From the accumulator, it is carried to the rear TBI fuel pressure regulator by a connecting tube. Unused fuel is sent to the fuel tank through a separate return line.

Fuel is supplied to the engine through electronically pulsed injector valves located in the throttle body.

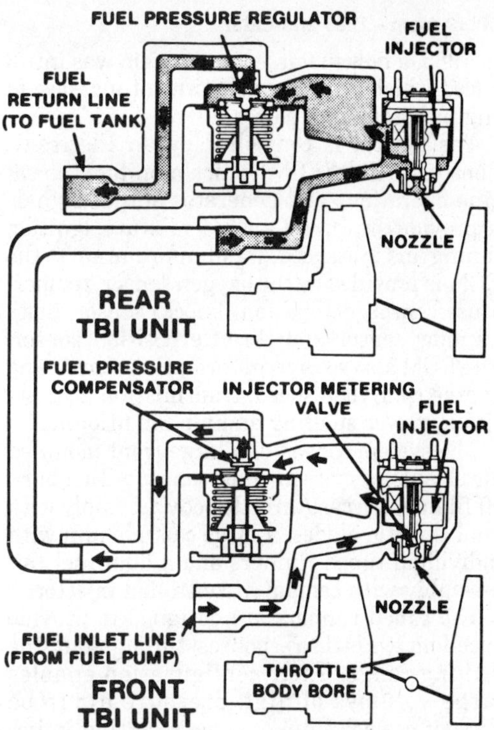

TBI fuel flow schematic

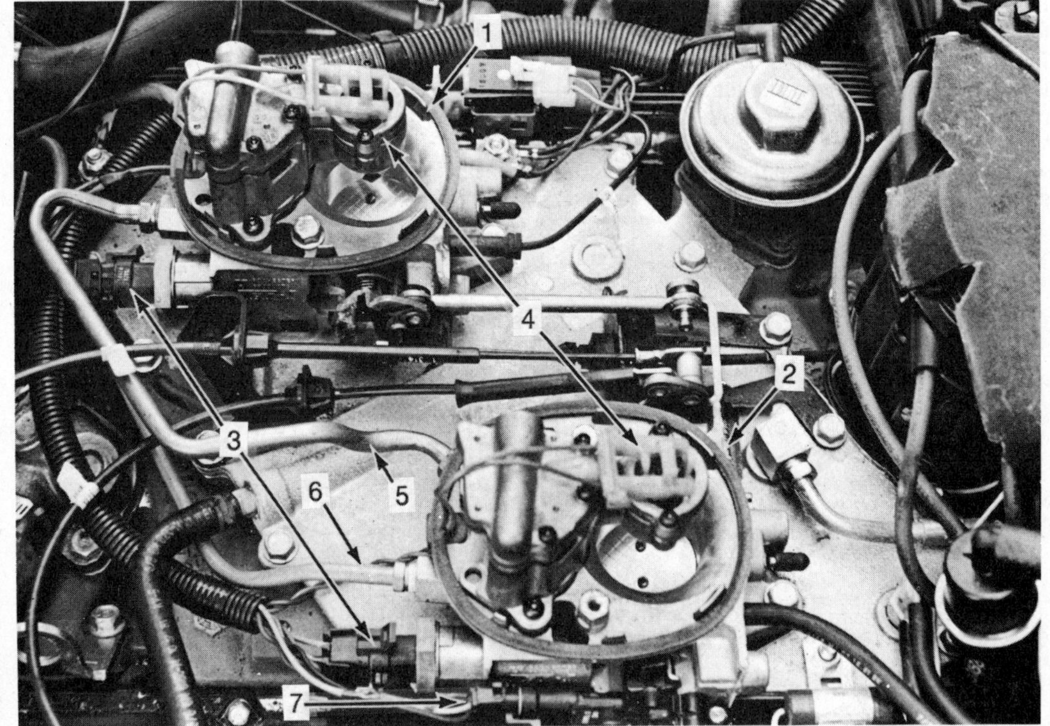

1. Front TBI unit
2. Rear TBI unit
3. Idle air control (IAC) motors
4. Fuel injectors
5. Fuel balance line
6. Fuel return line

Throttle Body Injection (TBI) system nomenclature

TPI System—1985 and Later

In 1985, a new fuel injection system was introduced which provides a significant increase in engine torque and power.

The system is controlled by an Electronic Control Module (ECM) which monitors the engine operations and generates output signals to provide the correct air/fuel mixture, ignition timing and idle speed. Input information to the ECM is provided by the oxygen sensor, temperature sensor, detonation (knock) sensor, mass air flow sensor and throttle position sensor. The ECM also receives information concerning engine rpm, road speed, transmission gear position, power steering and air conditioning.

The system consist of a large front mounted air cleaner, a mass air flow sensor with a burn off filament, a cast throttle body assembly with dual throttle blades, a large cast plenum with individual tuned runners and a dual fuel rail assembly with computer controlled injectors.

The tuned runners are designed to provide excellent throttle responses through-out the driving range. Their configuration enables large volumes of high pressure air to be present at each intake valve, resulting in improved cylinder charging and operation efficiency.

The system uses Bosch injectors, one at each intake port, rather than the single injector found on the earlier throttle body system. The injectors are mounted on a fuel rail and are activated by a signal from the electronic control module. The injector is a solenoid-operated valve which remains open depending on the width of the electronic pulses (length of the signal) from the ECM; the longer the open time, the more fuel is injected. In this manner, the air/fuel mixture can be precisely controlled for maximum performance with minimum emissions.

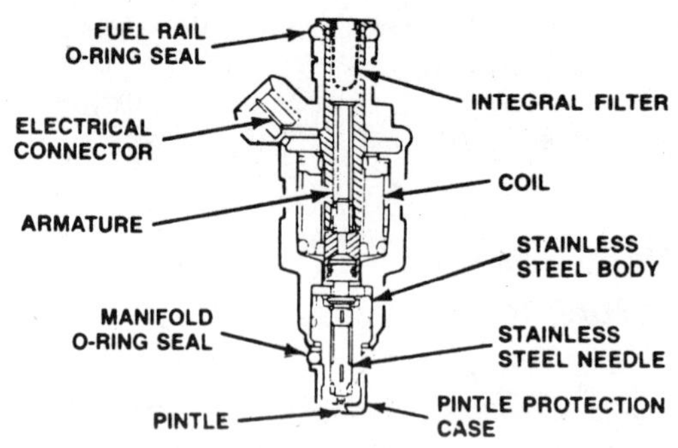

Cross-sectional view of the fuel injector—1985 and later

Fuel is pumped from the tank by a high pressure fuel pump, located inside the fuel tank. It is a positive displacement roller vane pump. The impeller serves as a vapor separator and precharges the high pressure assembly. A pressure regulator maintains 44 psi in the fuel line to the injectors and the excess fuel is fed back to the tank. A fuel accumulator is used to dampen the hydraulic line hammer in the system created when all injectors open simultaneously.

The Mass Air Flow Senor is used to measure the mass of air that is drawn into the engine cylinders. It is located just ahead of the air throttle in the intake system and consists of a heated film which measures the mass of air rather that just the volume. A resistor is used to measure the temperature of the incoming

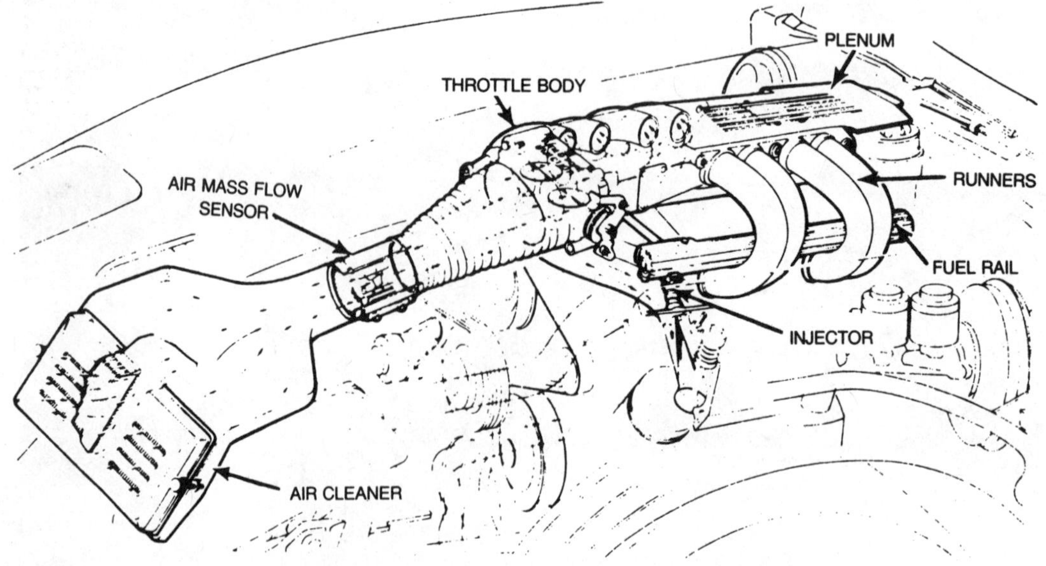

View of the Tuned Port Injection (TPI) system—1985 and later

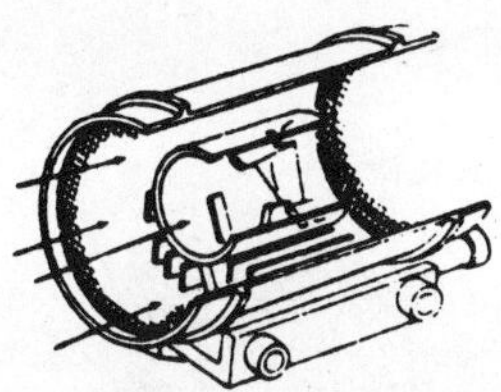

Sectional view of the Air Mass Flow sensor—TPI system

air and the air mass sensor maintains the temperature of the film at 75°F above the ambient temperature. As the ambient (outside) air temperature rises, more energy is required to maintain the heated film at the higher temperature and the control unit uses this difference in required energy to calculate the mass of the incoming air. The control unit uses this information to determine the duration of fuel injection pulse, timing and EGR.

The throttle body incorporates an idle air control (IAC) that provides for a bypass channel through which air can flow. It consists of an orifice and pintle which is controlled by the ECM through a stepper motor. The IAC provides air flow for idle and allows additional air during cold start until the engine reaches operating temperature. As the engine temperature rises the opening through which air passes is slowly closed.

The throttle position sensor (TPS) provides the control unit with information on the throttle position, in order to determine injector pulse width and hence correct the mixture. The TPS is connected to the throttle shaft on the throttle body and consists of a potentiometer with one end connected to a 5.0 volt source from the ECM and the other to ground. A third wire is connected to the ECM to measure the voltage output from the TPS which changes as the throttle valve angle is changed (accelerator pedal moves). At the closed throttle position, the output is low (approx. 0.4 volts); as the throttle valve opens, the output increases to a maximum 5.0 volts at wide open throttle (WOT). The TPS can be misadjusted open, shorted or loose and if it is out of adjustment, the idle quality or WOT performance may be poor. A loose TPS can cause intermittent bursts of fuel from the injectors and an unstable idle because the ECM thinks the trouble is moving. This should cause a trouble code to be set. Once a trouble code is set, the ECM will use a preset value for TPS and some vehicle performance may return. A small amount of engine coolant is routed through the throttle assembly to prevent freezing inside the throttle bore during cold operation.

REMOVAL AND INSTALLATION

CFI System – 1984

FRONT TBI UNIT

1. Disconnect the negative battery cable.
2. Remove the air cleaner assembly, noting the connection points of the vacuum lines.
3. Disconnect the electrical connectors from the injector and the idle air control motor.
4. Disconnect the vacuum lines from the TBI unit, noting the connection points.

   NOTE: *During installation, refer to the underhood emission control information decal for vacuum line routing information.*
5. Disconnect the transmission detent cable from the TBI unit.
6. Disconnect the fuel inlet (feed) and fuel balance line connections from the front TBI unit.
7. Disconnect the throttle control rod between the two TBI units.
8. Unbolt and remove the TBI unit.
9. To install, reverse the removal procedures. Torque the TBI bolts to 8–14 ft. lbs.

REAR TBI UNIT

1. Disconnect the negative battery cable.
2. Remove the air cleaner assembly, noting the connection points of the vacuum lines.
3. Disconnect the electrical connectors from the injector, the idle air control motor and the throttle position sensor.
4. Disconnect the vacuum lines from the TBI unit, noting the connection points. During installation, refer to the underhood emission control information decal for vacuum line routing information.
5. Disconnect the throttle and cruise control (if equipped) cables from the TBI unit.
6. Disconnect the fuel return and balance line connections from the rear TBI unit.
7. Disconnect the throttle control rod between the two units.

   CAUTION: *On the rear TBI unit, the throttle rod bearing is permanently attached the throttle lever stud. If the rod and bearing need to be replaced, the entire throttle body MUST BE replaced.*
8. Unbolt and remove the TBI unit.
9. To install, reverse the removal procedures. Torque the TBI bolts to 8–14 ft. lbs.

BOTH TBI UNITS/MANIFOLD COVER

1. Disconnect the negative battery cable. Remove the air cleaner.
2. Disconnect the electrical connectors from the injectors, the IAC assembly and the TPS, then the wiring harness from the TBIs.
3. Label and disconnect the vacuum hoses from the TBI assembly.

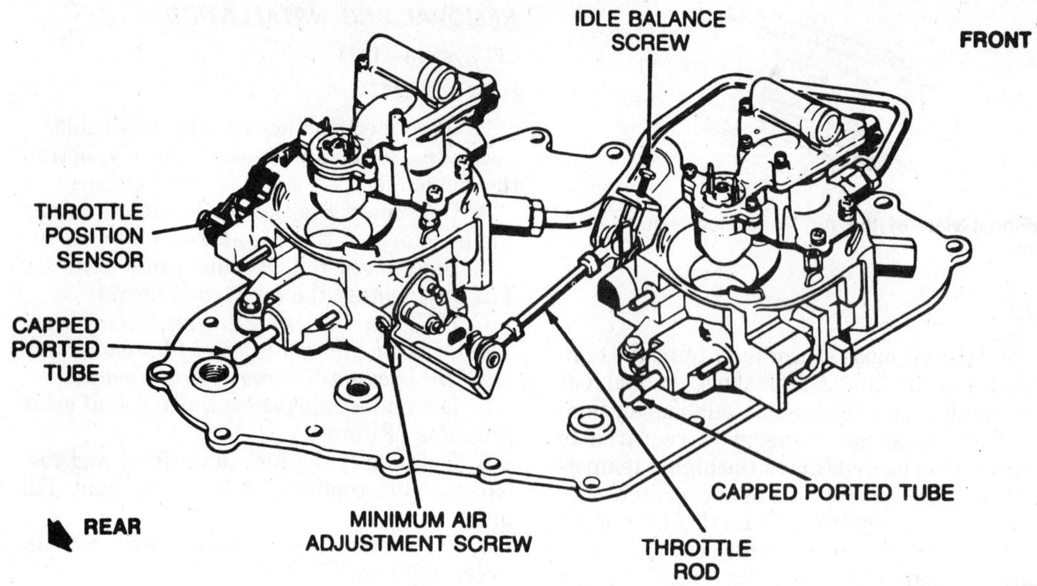

Cross-Fire Injection (CFI) System—Twin Throttle Body Injectors (TBI)

4. Remove the throttle cable, the transmission detent and the cruise control cable.

CAUTION: *Before removing the fuel line, be sure to cover the line with a shop cloth to collect the excess fuel.*

5. Remove the fuel inlet and return lines from the TBIs.

NOTE: *When removing the fuel lines from the TBIs, be sure to use two wrenches to prevent loosening the retaining nuts.*

6. Remove the TBI assembly/manifold cover bolts and the assembly from the engine.

NOTE: *When removing the TBI assembly, be careful not to damage the "swirl" plates, located beneath the throttle plates.*

7. Using a putty knife, clean the gasket mounting surfaces.
8. To install, use a new gasket and reverse the removal procedures. Torque the TBI assembly/manifold cover-to-intake manifold bolts to 12–18 ft. lbs.

THROTTLE POSITION SENSOR (TPS)

1. Disconnect the negative battery cable. Remove the air cleaner.
2. Disconnect the electrical harness connector from the TPS.
3. Remove the TPS-to-throttle body screws and the TPS from the throttle body.
4. To install, reverse the removal procedures. Adjust the TPS.

IDLE AIR CONTROL (IAC) VALVE

1. Disconnect the negative battery cable. Remove the air cleaner.
2. Disconnect the electrical harness connector from the IAC.
3. Unscrew the IAC from the throttle body.

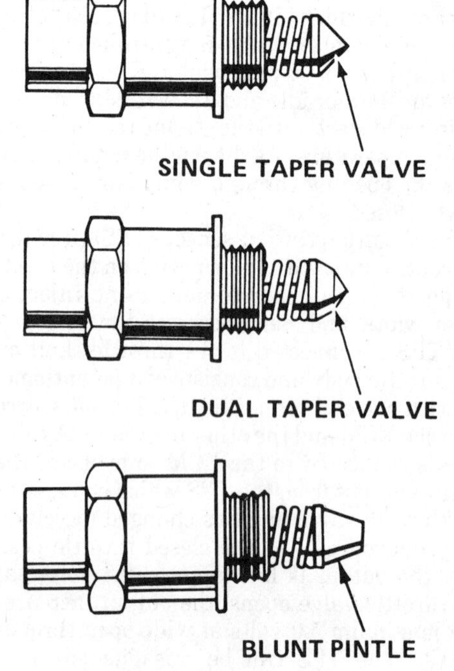

Idle air control valve designs

NOTE: *If installing a new IAC valve, be sure you are installing one of the same design that was removed.*

4. To install, reverse the removal procedures. If the idle speed is not correct, drive the vehicle to 30 mph (to adjust it).

TPI System – 1985 and Later

THROTTLE BODY

1. Disconnect the negative battery cable.
2. Remove the air inlet duct. Disconnect the

CHILTON'S FUEL ECONOMY & TUNE-UP TIPS

55 WAYS TO IMPROVE FUEL ECONOMY

Tune-up • Spark Plug Diagnosis • Emission Controls

Fuel System • Cooling System • Tires and Wheels

General Maintenance

CHILTON'S FUEL ECONOMY & TUNE-UP TIPS

Fuel economy is important to everyone, no matter what kind of vehicle you drive. The maintenance-minded motorist can save both money and fuel using these tips and the periodic maintenance and tune-up procedures in this Repair and Tune-Up Guide.

There are more than 130,000,000 cars and trucks registered for private use in the United States. Each travels an average of 10-12,000 miles per year, and, and in total they consume close to 70 billion gallons of fuel each year. This represents nearly ⅔ of the oil imported by the United States each year. The Federal government's goal is to reduce consumption 10% by 1985. A variety of methods are either already in use or under serious consideration, and they all affect you driving and the cars you will drive. In addition to "down-sizing", the auto industry is using or investigating the use of electronic fuel delivery, electronic engine controls and alternative engines for use in smaller and lighter vehicles, among other alternatives to meet the federally mandated Corporate Average Fuel Economy (CAFE) of 27.5 mpg by 1985. The government, for its part, is considering rationing, mandatory driving curtailments and tax increases on motor vehicle fuel in an effort to reduce consumption. The government's goal of a 10% reduction could be realized — and further government regulation avoided — if every private vehicle could use just 1 less gallon of fuel per week.

How Much Can You Save?

Tests have proven that almost anyone can make at least a 10% reduction in fuel consumption through regular maintenance and tune-ups. When a major manufacturer of spark plugs sur-

TUNE-UP

1. Check the cylinder compression to be sure the engine will really benefit from a tune-up and that it is capable of producing good fuel economy. A tune-up will be wasted on an engine in poor mechanical condition.

2. Replace spark plugs regularly. New spark plugs alone can increase fuel economy 3%.

3. Be sure the spark plugs are the correct type (heat range) for your vehicle. See the Tune-Up Specifications.

Heat range refers to the spark plug's ability to conduct heat away from the firing end. It must conduct the heat away in an even pattern to avoid becoming a source of pre-ignition, yet it must also operate hot enough to burn off conductive deposits that could cause misfiring.

The heat range is usually indicated by a number on the spark plug, part of the manufacturer's designation for each individual spark plug. The numbers in bold-face indicate the heat range in each manufacturer's identification system.

Manufacturer	**Typical Designation**
AC	R **45** TS
Bosch (old)	WA **145** T30
Bosch (new)	HR **8** Y
Champion	RBL **15** Y
Fram/Autolite	41**5**
Mopar	P-**62** PR
Motorcraft	BRF-**42**
NGK	BP **5** ES-15
Nippondenso	W **16** EP
Prestolite	14GR **5** 2A

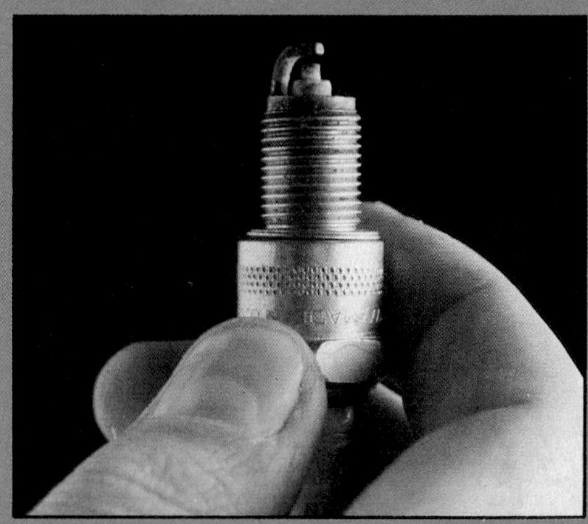

Periodically, check the spark plugs to be sure they are firing efficiently. They are excellent indicators of the internal condition of your engine.

On AC, Bosch (new), Champion, Fram/Autolite, Mopar, Motorcraft and Prestolite, a higher number indicates a hotter plug. On Bosch (old), NGK and Nippondenso, a higher number indicates a colder plug.

4. Make sure the spark plugs are properly gapped. See the Tune-Up Specifications in this book.

5. Be sure the spark plugs are firing efficiently. The illustrations on the next 2 pages show you how to "read" the firing end of the spark plug.

6. Check the ignition timing and set it to specifications. Tests show that almost all cars have incorrect ignition timing by more than 2°.

veyed over 6,000 cars nationwide, they found that a tune-up, on cars that needed one, increased fuel economy over 11%. Replacing worn plugs alone, accounted for a 3% increase. The same test also revealed that 8 out of every 10 vehicles will have some maintenance deficiency that will directly affect fuel economy, emissions or performance. Most of this mileage-robbing neglect could be prevented with regular maintenance.

Modern engines require that all of the functioning systems operate properly for maximum efficiency. A malfunction anywhere wastes fuel. You can keep your vehicle running as efficiently and economically as possible, by being aware of your vehicle's operating and performance characteristics. If your vehicle suddenly develops performance or fuel economy problems it could be due to one or more of the following:

PROBLEM	POSSIBLE CAUSE
Engine Idles Rough	Ignition timing, idle mixture, vacuum leak or something amiss in the emission control system.
Hesitates on Acceleration	Dirty carburetor or fuel filter, improper accelerator pump setting, ignition timing or fouled spark plugs.
Starts Hard or Fails to Start	Worn spark plugs, improperly set automatic choke, ice (or water) in fuel system.
Stalls Frequently	Automatic choke improperly adjusted and possible dirty air filter or fuel filter.
Performs Sluggishly	Worn spark plugs, dirty fuel or air filter, ignition timing or automatic choke out of adjustment.

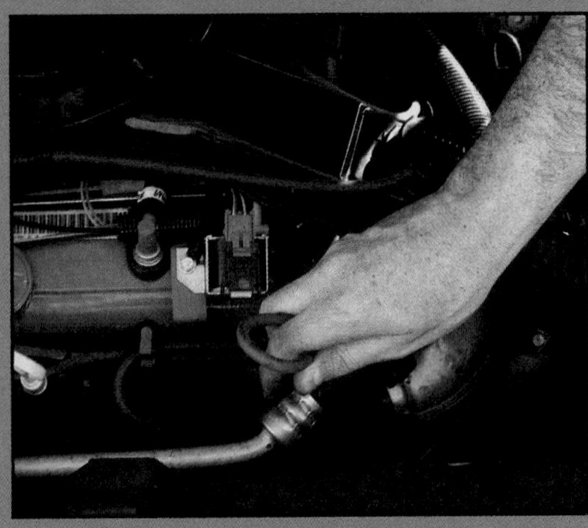

Check spark plug wires on conventional point type ignition for cracks by bending them in a loop around your finger.

Be sure that spark plug wires leading to adjacent cylinders do not run too close together. (Photo courtesy Champion Spark Plug Co.)

7. If your vehicle does not have electronic ignition, check the points, rotor and cap as specified.

8. Check the spark plug wires (used with conventional point-type ignitions) for cracks and burned or broken insulation by bending them in a loop around your finger. Cracked wires decrease fuel efficiency by failing to deliver full voltage to the spark plugs. One misfiring spark plug can cost you as much as 2 mpg.

9. Check the routing of the plug wires. Misfiring can be the result of spark plug leads to adjacent cylinders running parallel to each other and too close together. One wire tends to pick up voltage from the other causing it to fire "out of time".

10. Check all electrical and ignition circuits for voltage drop and resistance.

11. Check the distributor mechanical and/or vacuum advance mechanisms for proper functioning. The vacuum advance can be checked by twisting the distributor plate in the opposite direction of rotation. It should spring back when released.

12. Check and adjust the valve clearance on engines with mechanical lifters. The clearance should be slightly loose rather than too tight.

SPARK PLUG DIAGNOSIS

Normal

APPEARANCE: This plug is typical of one operating normally. The insulator nose varies from a light tan to grayish color with slight electrode wear. The presence of slight deposits is normal on used plugs and will have no adverse effect on engine performance. The spark plug heat range is correct for the engine and the engine is running normally.
CAUSE: Properly running engine.
RECOMMENDATION: Before reinstalling this plug, the electrodes should be cleaned and filed square. Set the gap to specifications. If the plug has been in service for more than 10-12,000 miles, the entire set should probably be replaced with a fresh set of the same heat range.

Incorrect Heat Range

APPEARANCE: The effects of high temperature on a spark plug are indicated by clean white, often blistered insulator. This can also be accompanied by excessive wear of the electrode, and the absence of deposits.
CAUSE: Check for the correct spark plug heat range. A plug which is too hot for the engine can result in overheating. A car operated mostly at high speeds can require a colder plug. Also check ignition timing, cooling system level, fuel mixture and leaking intake manifold.
RECOMMENDATION: If all ignition and engine adjustments are known to be correct, and no other malfunction exists, install spark plugs one heat range colder.

Photos Courtesy Fram Corporation

Oil Deposits

APPEARANCE: The firing end of the plug is covered with a wet, oily coating.
CAUSE: The problem is poor oil control. On high mileage engines, oil is leaking past the rings or valve guides into the combustion chamber. A common cause is also a plugged PCV valve, and a ruptured fuel pump diaphragm can also cause this condition. Oil fouled plugs such as these are often found in new or recently overhauled engines, before normal oil control is achieved, and can be cleaned and reinstalled.
RECOMMENDATION: A hotter spark plug may temporarily relieve the problem, but the engine is probably in need of work.

Carbon Deposits

APPEARANCE: Carbon fouling is easily identified by the presence of dry, soft, black, sooty deposits.
CAUSE: Changing the heat range can often lead to carbon fouling, as can prolonged slow, stop-and-start driving. If the heat range is correct, carbon fouling can be attributed to a rich fuel mixture, sticking choke, clogged air cleaner, worn breaker points, retarded timing or low compression. If only one or two plugs are carbon fouled, check for corroded or cracked wires on the affected plugs. Also look for cracks in the distributor cap between the towers of affected cylinders.
RECOMMENDATION: After the problem is corrected, these plugs can be cleaned and reinstalled if not worn severely.

MMT Fouled

APPEARANCE: Spark plugs fouled by MMT (Methycyclopentadienyl Maganese Tricarbonyl) have reddish, rusty appearance on the insulator and side electrode.

CAUSE: MMT is an anti-knock additive in gasoline used to replace lead. During the combustion process, the MMT leaves a reddish deposit on the insulator and side electrode.

RECOMMENDATION: No engine malfunction is indicated and the deposits will not affect plug performance any more than lead deposits (see Ash Deposits). MMT fouled plugs can be cleaned, regapped and reinstalled.

High Speed Glazing

APPEARANCE: Glazing appears as shiny coating on the plug, either yellow or tan in color.

CAUSE: During hard, fast acceleration, plug temperatures rise suddenly. Deposits from normal combustion have no chance to fluff-off; instead, they melt on the insulator forming an electrically conductive coating which causes misfiring.

RECOMMENDATION: Glazed plugs are not easily cleaned. They should be replaced with a fresh set of plugs of the correct heat range. If the condition recurs, using plugs with a heat range one step colder may cure the problem.

Ash (Lead) Deposits

APPEARANCE: Ash deposits are characterized by light brown or white colored deposits crusted on the side or center electrodes. In some cases it may give the plug a rusty appearance.

CAUSE: Ash deposits are normally derived from oil or fuel additives burned during normal combustion. Normally they are harmless, though excessive amounts can cause misfiring. If deposits are excessive in short mileage, the valve guides may be worn.

RECOMMENDATION: Ash-fouled plugs can be cleaned, gapped and reinstalled.

Detonation

APPEARANCE: Detonation is usually characterized by a broken plug insulator.

CAUSE: A portion of the fuel charge will begin to burn spontaneously, from the increased heat following ignition. The explosion that results applies extreme pressure to engine components, frequently damaging spark plugs and pistons.

Detonation can result by over-advanced ignition timing, inferior gasoline (low octane) lean air/fuel mixture, poor carburetion, engine lugging or an increase in compression ratio due to combustion chamber deposits or engine modification.

RECOMMENDATION: Replace the plugs after correcting the problem.

Photos Courtesy Champion Spark Plug Co.

EMISSION CONTROLS

13. Be aware of the general condition of the emission control system. It contributes to reduced pollution and should be serviced regularly to maintain efficient engine operation.

14. Check all vacuum lines for dried, cracked or brittle conditions. Something as simple as a leaking vacuum hose can cause poor performance and loss of economy.

15. Avoid tampering with the emission control system. Attempting to improve fuel econ-

FUEL SYSTEM

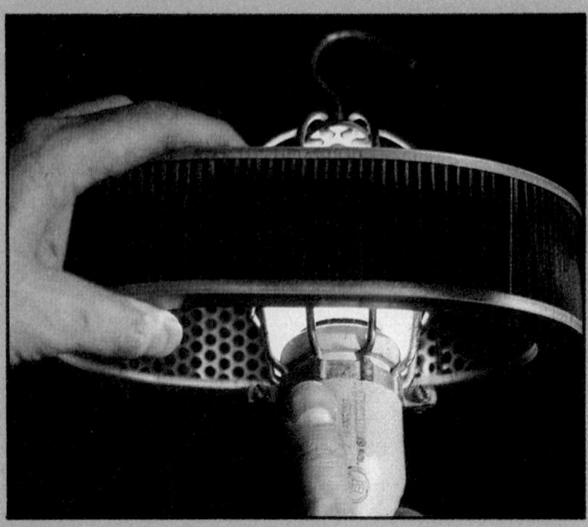

Check the air filter with a light behind it. If you can see light through the filter it can be reused.

Extremely clogged filters should be discarded and replaced with a new one.

18. Replace the air filter regularly. A dirty air filter richens the air/fuel mixture and can increase fuel consumption as much as 10%. Tests show that ⅓ of all vehicles have air filters in need of replacement.

19. Replace the fuel filter at least as often as recommended.

20. Set the idle speed and carburetor mixture to specifications.

21. Check the automatic choke. A sticking or malfunctioning choke wastes gas.

22. During the summer months, adjust the automatic choke for a leaner mixture which will produce faster engine warm-ups.

COOLING SYSTEM

29. Be sure all accessory drive belts are in good condition. Check for cracks or wear.

30. Adjust all accessory drive belts to proper tension.

31. Check all hoses for swollen areas, worn spots, or loose clamps.

32. Check coolant level in the radiator or expansion tank.

33. Be sure the thermostat is operating properly. A stuck thermostat delays engine warm-up and a cold engine uses nearly twice as much fuel as a warm engine.

34. Drain and replace the engine coolant at least as often as recommended. Rust and scale

TIRES & WHEELS

38. Check the tire pressure often with a pencil type gauge. Tests by a major tire manufacturer show that 90% of all vehicles have at least 1 tire improperly inflated. Better mileage can be achieved by over-inflating tires, but never exceed the maximum inflation pressure on the side of the tire.

39. If possible, install radial tires. Radial tires deliver as much as ½ mpg more than bias belted tires.

40. Avoid installing super-wide tires. They only create extra rolling resistance and decrease fuel mileage. Stick to the manufacturer's recommendations.

41. Have the wheels properly balanced.

omy by tampering with emission controls is more likely to worsen fuel economy than improve it. Emission control changes on modern engines are not readily reversible.

16. Clean (or replace) the EGR valve and lines as recommended.

17. Be sure that all vacuum lines and hoses are reconnected properly after working under the hood. An unconnected or misrouted vacuum line can wreak havoc with engine performance.

---

23. Check for fuel leaks at the carburetor, fuel pump, fuel lines and fuel tank. Be sure all lines and connections are tight.

24. Periodically check the tightness of the carburetor and intake manifold attaching nuts and bolts. These are a common place for vacuum leaks to occur.

25. Clean the carburetor periodically and lubricate the linkage.

26. The condition of the tailpipe can be an excellent indicator of proper engine combustion. After a long drive at highway speeds, the inside of the tailpipe should be a light grey in color. Black or soot on the insides indicates an overly rich mixture.

27. Check the fuel pump pressure. The fuel pump may be supplying more fuel than the engine needs.

28. Use the proper grade of gasoline for your engine. Don't try to compensate for knocking or "pinging" by advancing the ignition timing. This practice will only increase plug temperature and the chances of detonation or pre-ignition with relatively little performance gain.

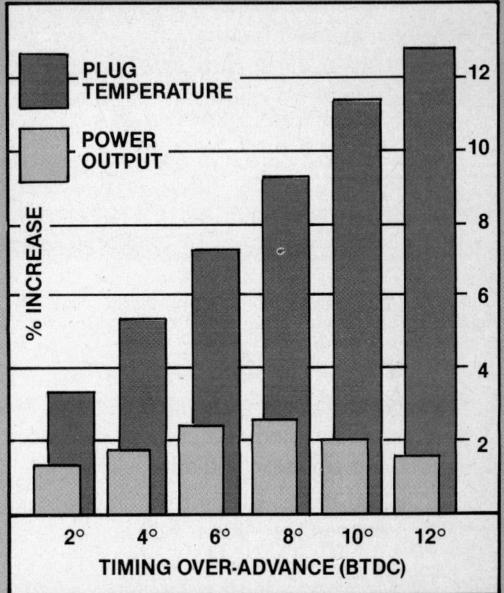

Increasing ignition timing past the specified setting results in a drastic increase in spark plug temperature with increased chance of detonation or preignition. Performance increase is considerably less. (Photo courtesy Champion Spark Plug Co.)

---

that form in the engine should be flushed out to allow the engine to operate at peak efficiency.

35. Clean the radiator of debris that can decrease cooling efficiency.

36. Install a flex-type or electric cooling fan, if you don't have a clutch type fan. Flex fans use curved plastic blades to push more air at low speeds when more cooling is needed; at high speeds the blades flatten out for less resistance. Electric fans only run when the engine temperature reaches a predetermined level.

37. Check the radiator cap for a worn or cracked gasket. If the cap does not seal properly, the cooling system will not function properly.

---

42. Be sure the front end is correctly aligned. A misaligned front end actually has wheels going in differed directions. The increased drag can reduce fuel economy by .3 mpg.

43. Correctly adjust the wheel bearings. Wheel bearings that are adjusted too tight increase rolling resistance.

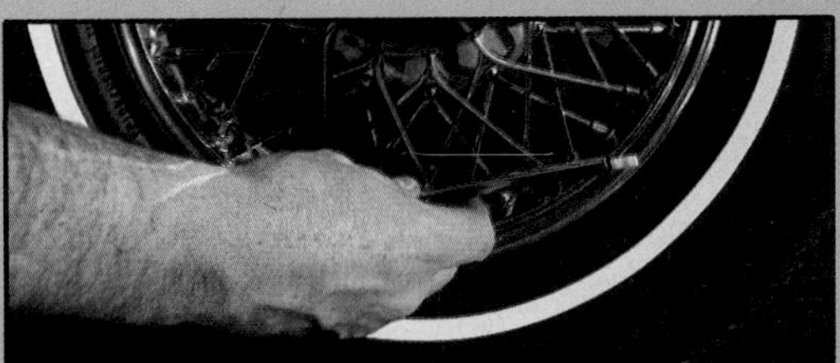

Check tire pressures regularly with a reliable pocket type gauge. Be sure to check the pressure on a cold tire.

GENERAL MAINTENANCE

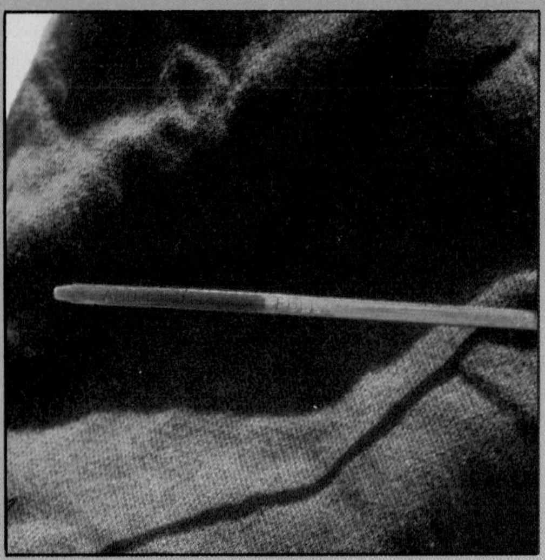

Check the fluid levels (particularly engine oil) on a regular basis. Be sure to check the oil for grit, water or other contamination.

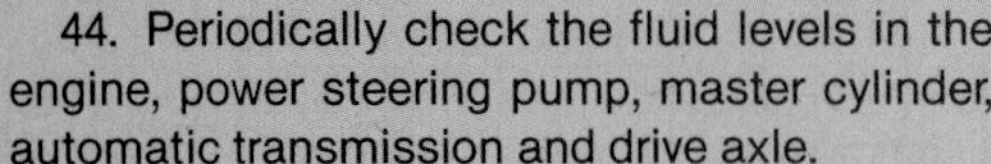

A vacuum gauge is another excellent indicator of internal engine condition and can also be installed in the dash as a mileage indicator.

44. Periodically check the fluid levels in the engine, power steering pump, master cylinder, automatic transmission and drive axle.

45. Change the oil at the recommended interval and change the filter at every oil change. Dirty oil is thick and causes extra friction between moving parts, cutting efficiency and increasing wear. A worn engine requires more frequent tune-ups and gets progressively worse fuel economy. In general, use the lightest viscosity oil for the driving conditions you will encounter.

46. Use the recommended viscosity fluids in the transmission and axle.

47. Be sure the battery is fully charged for fast starts. A slow starting engine wastes fuel.

48. Be sure battery terminals are clean and tight.

49. Check the battery electrolyte level and add distilled water if necessary.

50. Check the exhaust system for crushed pipes, blockages and leaks.

51. Adjust the brakes. Dragging brakes or brakes that are not releasing create increased drag on the engine.

52. Install a vacuum gauge or miles-per-gallon gauge. These gauges visually indicate engine vacuum in the intake manifold. High vacuum = good mileage and low vacuum = poorer mileage. The gauge can also be an excellent indicator of internal engine conditions.

53. Be sure the clutch is properly adjusted. A slipping clutch wastes fuel.

54. Check and periodically lubricate the heat control valve in the exhaust manifold. A sticking or inoperative valve prevents engine warm-up and wastes gas.

55. Keep accurate records to check fuel economy over a period of time. A sudden drop in fuel economy may signal a need for tune-up or other maintenance.

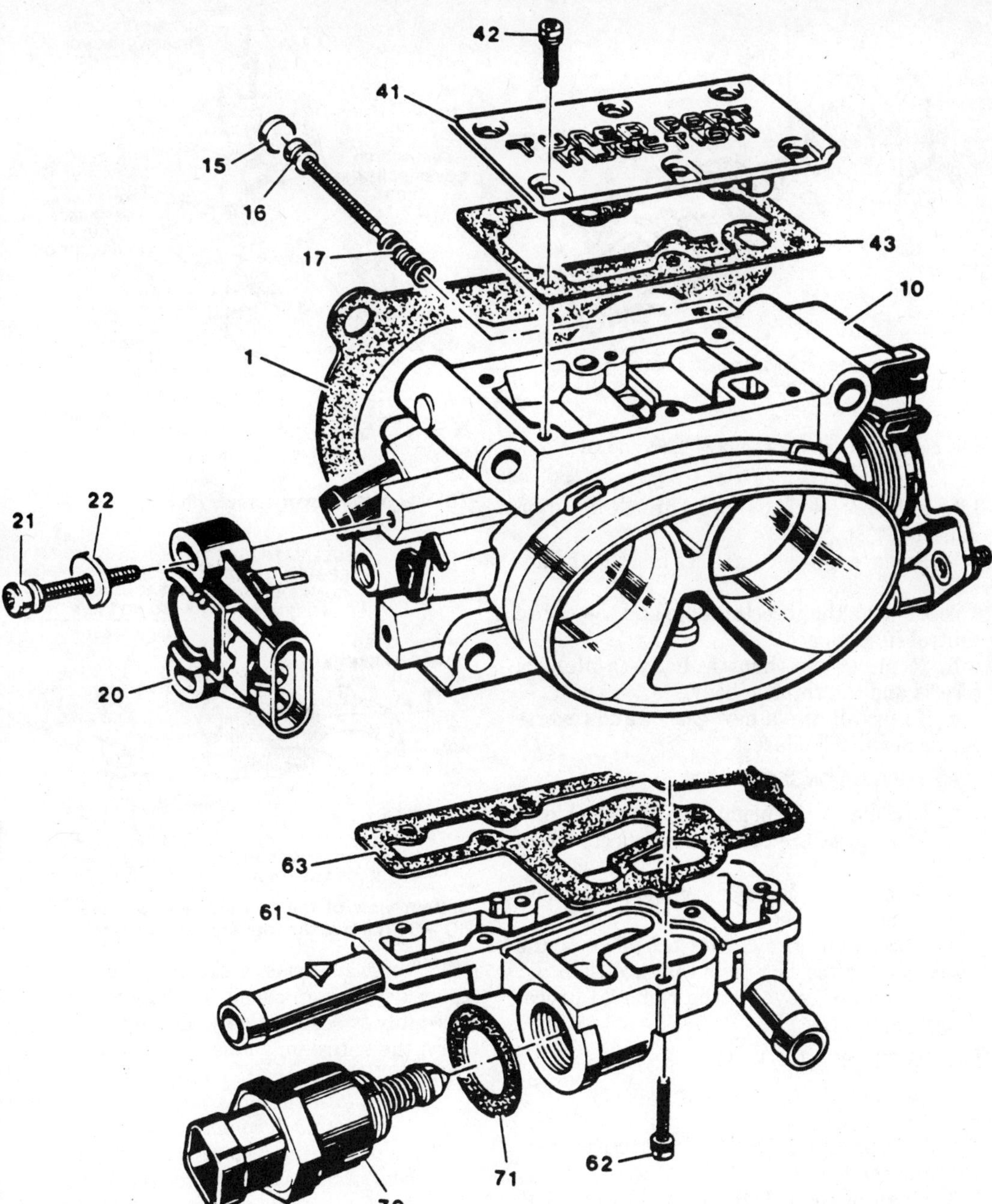

45. Attaching screw
46. O-ring—coolant cover to throttle body
60. Idle air/vacuum signal housing assembly
65. Screw assembly—idle air/vacuum signal assembly
66. Screw assembly—idle air/vacuum signal assemly
67. Gasket—idle air/vacuum signal assembly
70. Valve assembly—idle air control (IAC)
71. Gasket—IAC valve assembly
22. Retainer—TPS attaching screw
41. Cover—clean air
42. Screw assembly—clean air cover attaching
43. Gasket—clean air cover
61. IACV/coolant cover assembly
62. Screw assembly—IACV cover assembly to throttle body
63. Gasket—IACV/coolant cover to throttle body
70. Valve assembly—idle air control (IAC)
71. Basket—IAC valve assembly
1. Gasket—flange
10. Throttle body assembly
15. Plug—idel stop screw
16. Screw assembly—idle stop
17. Spring—idle stop screw
20. Sensor—throttle position (TPS)
21. Screw assembly—TPS attaching

Exploded view of the Tuned Port Injection (TPI) throttle body

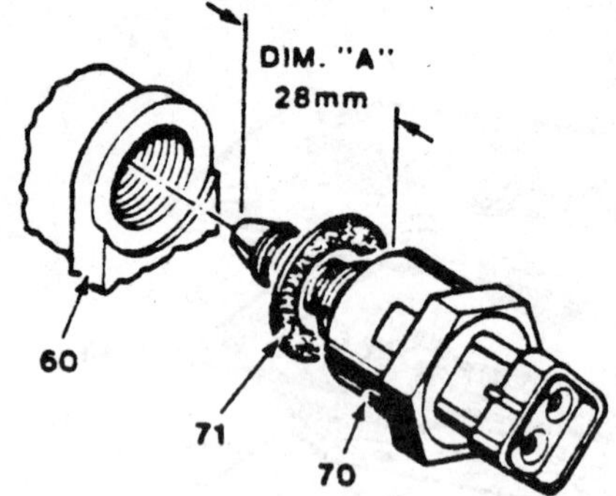

60. Idle air/vacuum signal housing
70. Idel air control valve (IAC)
71. IAC gasket

Idle air control valve assembly—1985 and later

Idle Air Control (IAC) and Throttle Position Sensor (TPS).

3. Remove the vacuum lines and the coolant hoses.
4. Remove the throttle cable and the cruise control (if equipped).
5. Remove the throttle body-to-plenum screws and the throttle body.
6. To install, use a new gasket and reverse the removal procedures.

THROTTLE POSITION SENSOR (TPS)

1. Disconnect the negative battery cable.
2. Disconnect the electrical connector from the TPS.
3. Remove the canister control valve hose from the throttle body.
4. Remove the screws, the lockwashers, the retainers and the TPS from the throttle body.
5. To install, reverse the removal procedures. Adjust the TPS.

IDLE AIR CONTROL (IAC) VALVE

1. Disconnect the negative battery cable. Remove the air cleaner.
2. Disconnect the electrical harness connector from the IAC.
3. Unscrew the IAC from the throttle body.

NOTE: *If installing a new IAC valve, be sure you are installing one of the same design that was removed.*

4. Adjust the pintle-to-housing length to 1⅛" (28mm).
5. To install, reverse the removal procedures. Torque the IAC valve to 13 ft. lbs.

INJECTOR REPLACEMENT

CFI System—1984 Only

NOTE: *If both TBI units are to be disassembled, DO NOT mix parts between either unit.*

1. Remove the fuel meter cover assembly

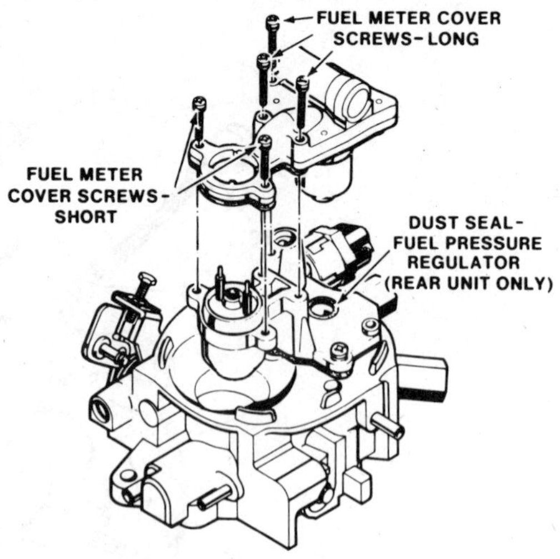

TBI fuel meter cover screws (five)

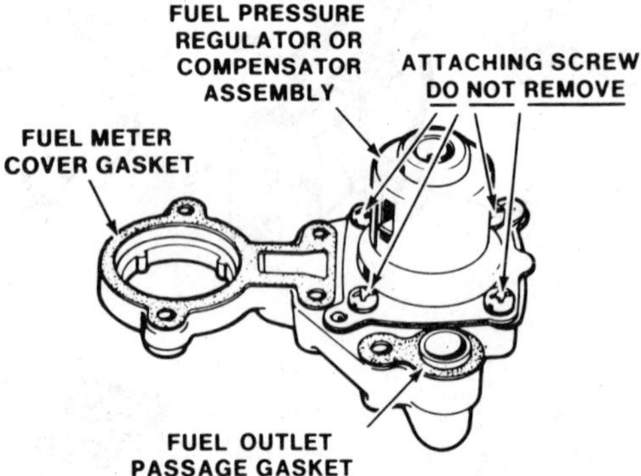

Bottom view of the fuel meter cover assembly—DO NOT remove the four screws indicated

(five screws). Remove the gaskets after the cover has been removed. The fuel meter cover assembly is serviced only as a unit. If necessary, the entire unit must be replaced.

CAUTION: *DO NOT remove the four screws which retain the pressure regulator (rear unit) or pressure compensator (front unit). There is a spring beneath the cover which is under great pressure. If the cover is accidentally released, personal injury could result. DO NOT immerse the fuel meter cover in any type of cleaning solvent.*

2. Remove the foam dust seal from the meter body of the rear unit.

NOTE: *If the injectors are to be removed from both TBI units, mark them so that they may be reinstalled in their original units.*

3. To remove the fuel injector from the throttle body, perform the following procedures:
   a. Use a screwdriver and a rod to lift the fuel injector from the throttle body.
   b. Use a twisting motion when removing the fuel injector.

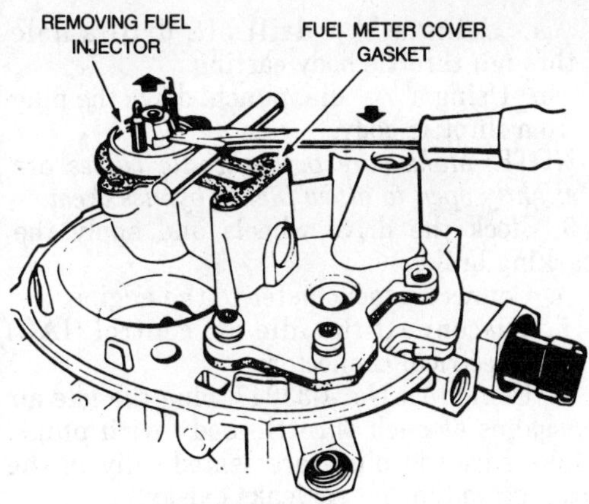

Removing the fuel injector—cross-fire injection—1984

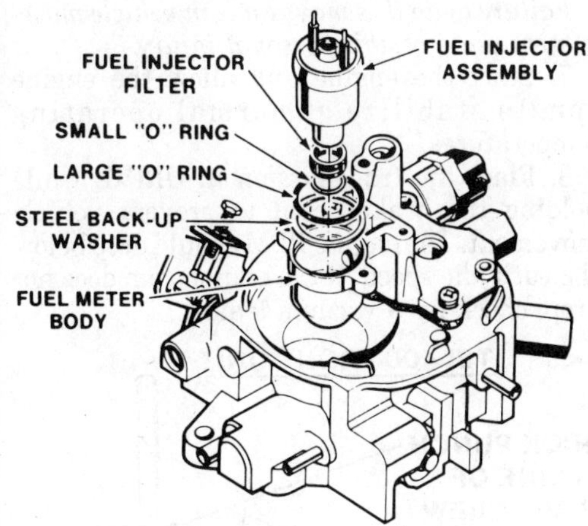

Fuel injector installation

4. Remove the filter from the base of the injector by rotating it back and forth.

5. Remove the O-ring and the steel washer from the top of the fuel meter body, then the small O-ring from the bottom of the injector cavity.

6. To install, use new gaskets, seals and filter, then reverse the removal procedures.

ADJUSTMENTS

Throttle Position Sensor (TPS)

CFI SYSTEM – 1984

NOTE: *An accurate digital voltmeter is needed to perform this adjustment.*

1. Remove the air cleaner.
2. Disconnect the electrical harness connector from the TPS. Using 3 jumper wires (6 in. long), reconnect the electrical harness to the TPS with the jumper wires.
3. Remove the TPS attaching screws and apply thread locking compound to the screws. Reinstall the screws loosely.
4. Turn the ignition ON (engine stopped) and measure the voltage between the A and B terminals of the TPS. Rotate the TPS to obtain a voltmeter reading of 0.45–0.60 volts (closed throttle). Tighten the screws.

NOTE: *If the adjustment specifications cannot be met, replace the TPS.*

5. Turn the ignition OFF and reverse the removal procedures.

TPI SYSTEM – 1985 AND LATER

NOTE: *An accurate digital voltmeter is needed to perform this adjustment.*

1. Disconnect the electrical harness connector from the TPS. Using 3 jumper wires (6 in.

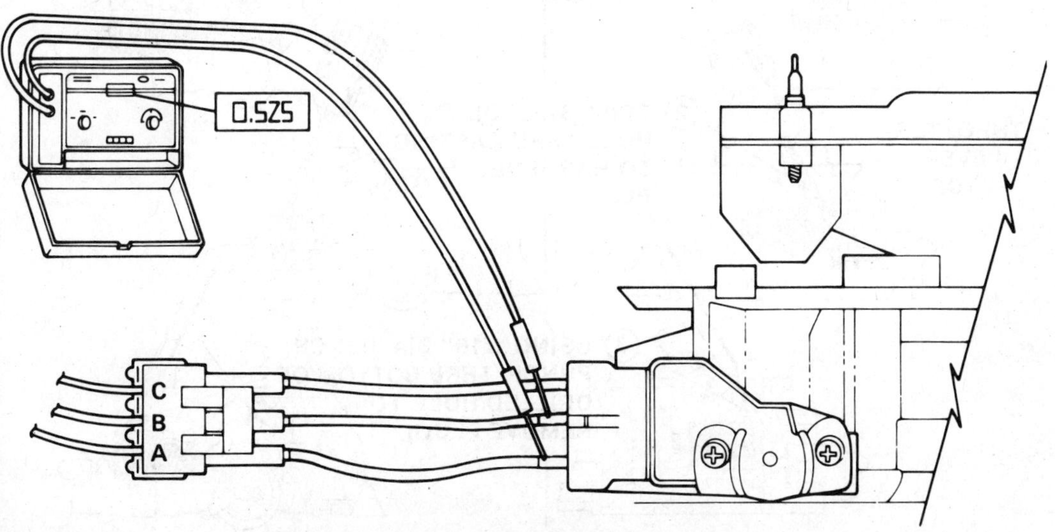

Throttle position sensor adjustment—see text

long), reconnect the electrical harness to the TPS with the jumper wires.

2. Remove the TPS attaching screws and apply thread locking compound to the screws. Reinstall the screws loosely.

3. Turn the ignition ON (engine stopped) and measure the voltage between the A and B terminals of the TPS. Rotate the TPS to obtain a voltmeter reading of 0.465–0.615 volts (closed throttle). Tighten the screws.

NOTE: *If the adjustment specifications cannot be met, replace the TPS.*

4. Turn the ignition OFF and reverse the removal procedures.

Minimum Idle and Throttle Valve Synchronizing

CFI SYSTEM–1984

The throttle position of each throttle body must be balanced so that the throttle plates are synchronized and open simultaneously. Adjustment should be performed only when a manifold cover, TBI unit or throttle body has been replaced.

1. Remove the air cleaner and plug the thermostatic air cleaner (THERMAC) vacuum port on the rear TBI unit.

2. Remove the tamper resistant plugs covering both TBI stop screws, by performing the following procedures:

a. Using a $^5/_{32}$" drill bit, drill a hole through throttle body casting.

b. Using a $^1/_{16}$" dia. punch, drive the plug from throttle body.

NOTE: *Make sure both throttle valves are slightly open to allow fuel to bypass them.*

3. Block the drive wheels and apply the parking brake.

4. Connect a tachometer to the engine.

5. Disconnect the idle air control (IAC) valve electrical connectors.

6. Using tool No. J-33047, plug the idle air passages of each throttle body with plugs. Make sure the plugs are seated fully in the passage so that no air leaks exist.

CAUTION: *To prevent the engine from running at a high rpm, be sure the ignition switch is OFF and transmission is in NEUTRAL before connecting the IAC valves or removing/installing idle air passage plugs. Failure to do this may result in vehicle movement and possible personal injury.*

7. Start the engine and allow the engine rpm to stabilize at normal operating temperatures.

8. Place the transmission in DRIVE while holding the brake pedal to prevent vehicle movement. The engine RPM should drop below the curb idle speed. If the engine rpm does not drop, check for a vacuum leak.

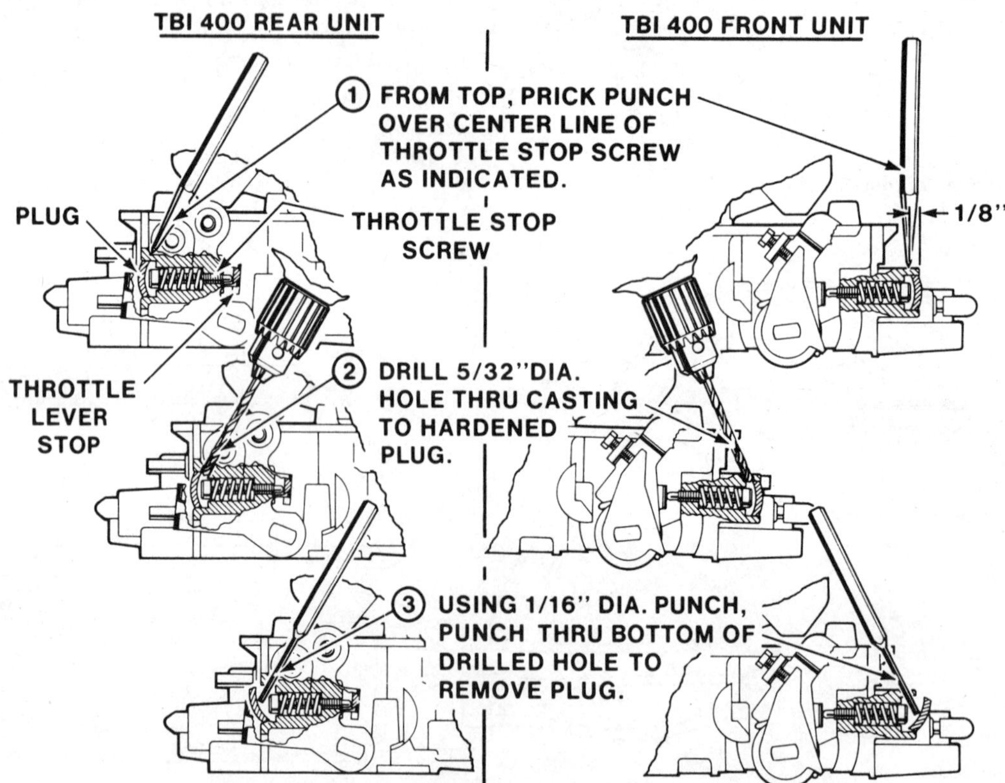

Removing the throttle stop screw plugs

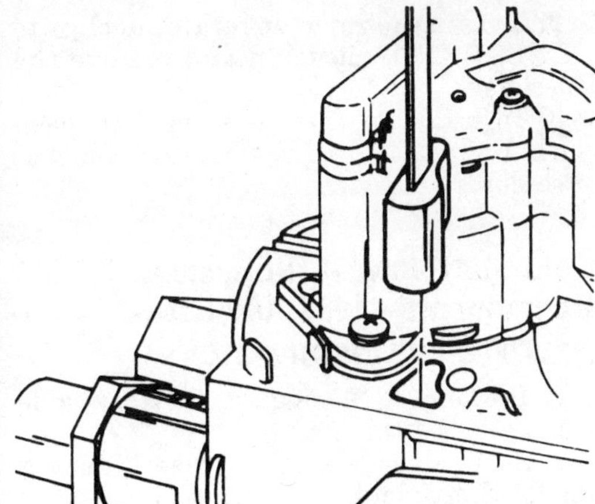
Plug the idle air passages of each throttle body as shown

9. Remove the cap from the ported tube on the rear TBI unit and connect a water manometer tool No. J-23951.

10. Adjust the rear unit throttle stop screw to obtain approximately 6 in. of water as read on the manometer. If not able to adjust to this level, check that the front unit throttle stop is not limiting throttle travel.

11. Remove the manometer from the rear unit and install the cap on the ported vacuum tube.

12. Remove the cap from the ported vacuum tube on the front TBI unit and install the manometer as before. If the reading is not the same as the rear unit, proceed as follows:

a. Locate the throttle synchronizing screw and collar on the front TBI unit. The screw retaining collar is welded to the throttle lever to discourage tampering with this adjustment.

b. If the collar is in place, grind off the weld from the screw collar and the throttle lever.

c. Using an Allen wrench, block possible movement of the throttle lever, relieving the force of the heavy spring against the throttle synchronizing screw, to prevent the levers from coming into contact.

NOTE: *If the lever is not blocked before the throttle synchronizing screw is removed, the screw may be damaged and reinstallation will be done only with great difficulty.*

d. Remove the screw and the collar, then discard the collar.

e. Reinstall the throttle synchronizing screw, using thread locking compound.

f. Adjust the screw to obtain 6 in. of water on the manometer.

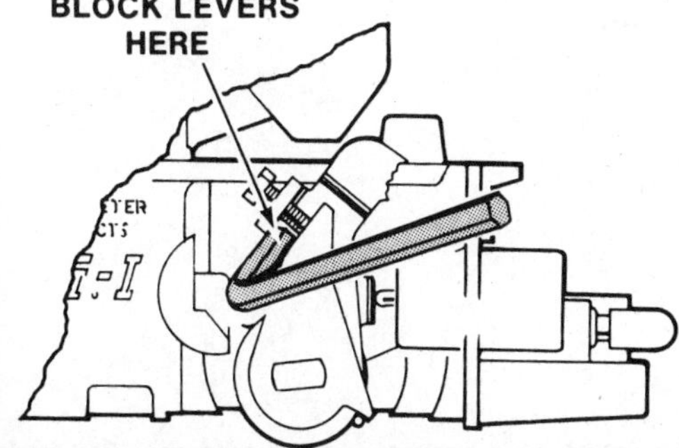

Block throttle lever movement as shown

13. Remove the manometer from the ported tube and reinstall the cap.

14. Adjust the rear throttle stop screw to obtain 475 rpm, with the transmission in DRIVE and the parking brake applied. On manual transmission models, leave the gear selector in NEUTRAL.

15. Turn the ignition OFF and place the automatic transmission in NEUTRAL.

16. Adjust the front throttle stop screw to obtain 0.005 in. clearance between the front throttle stop screw and the throttle lever tang.

17. Remove idle air passage plugs and reconnect IAC valves.

18. Start the engine. It may run at a high rpm but the engine speed should decrease when the idle air control valves close the air passages. Stop the engine when the rpm decreases.

19. The throttle position sensor (TPS) voltage should be checked and adjusted, if necessary. See "TPS Adjustment" for procedures.

20. Install the air cleaner gasket, connect the vacuum line to the TBI unit and install the air cleaner.

21. Reset the idle speed control motors by driving the vehicle to 30 mph.

TPI SYSTEM – 1985 AND LATER

1. Remove the idle stop screw plug by piercing it with an awl.

2. With the idle air control motor connected, ground the diagnostic connector.

3. Turn the ignition ON and wait 30 seconds, DO NOT start the engine.

4. Disconnect the idle air control connector with the ignition ON.

5. Remove the ground from the diagnostic connector and start the engine.

6. If equipped with an automatic transmission, place it in Drive (parking brake engaged) and adjust the idle stop screw to 400 rpm. If equipped with a manual transmission, place it in Neutral and adjust the idle stop screw to 450 rpm.

7. Turn the ignition OFF and reconnect the idle air control motor connector.

8. Remove the throttle position sensor (TPS)

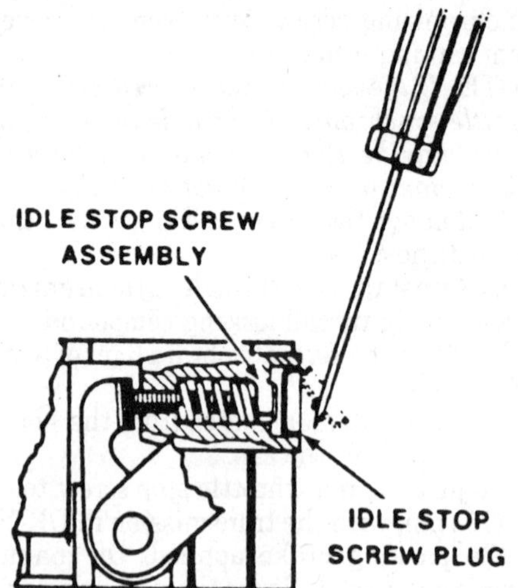

Removing the idle stop screw plug—TPI system—1985 and later

connector and install 3 jumper wires between the connector and the sensor. Connect a digital voltmeter to terminals "A" and "B".

9. Turn the ignition ON and adjust the sensor to 0.465–0.615 volts.

10. Tighten the screws, remove the jumper wires with the ignition OFF and reconnect the harness connector.

11. Start the engine and check for proper idle operation.

Fuel Injectors–TPI System Components–1985 And Later

REMOVAL AND INSTALLATION

1. Refer to the "Fuel Rail and Pressure Regulator, Removal and Installation" procedures in this section and remove the fuel rail.

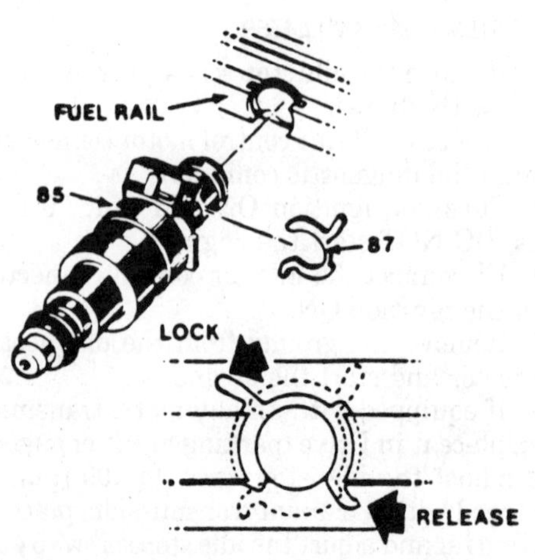

85. Injector—port
87. Clip—injector retainer

Removing the fuel injector from the fuel rail—1985 and later

2. Rotate the injector retaining clips to "UNLOCKED" position and remove the injectors.

3. To install, use new the O-rings (coat them with engine oil) and reverse the removal procedures.

Cold Start Valve–TPI System Components–1985 And Later

REMOVAL AND INSTALLATION

1. Disconnect the negative battery cable and brake booster line.

2. Relieve the fuel pressure, then disconnect the fuel line from the fuel rail.

3. Disconnect the wiring harness.

4. Remove the PCV pipe retaining screws.

5. Remove cold start valve retaining bolts and the valve.

6. To install, use new O-rings (coat them with engine oil) and reverse the removal procedures.

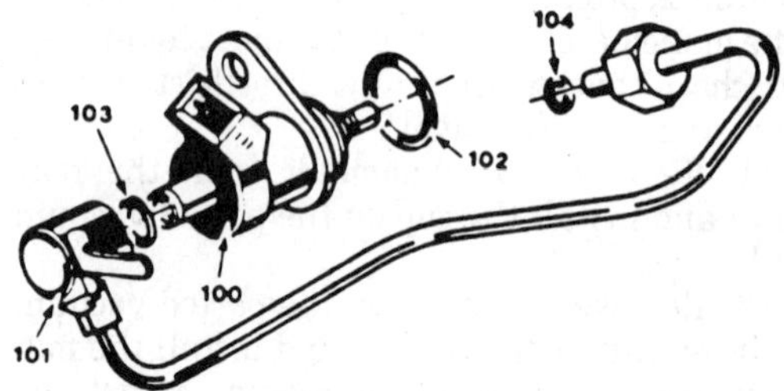

100. Valve—cold start
101. Tube and body assembly
102. O-ring seal—valve
103. O-ring seal—body
104. O-ring seal—tube

Exploded view of the cold start valve assembly—1985 and later

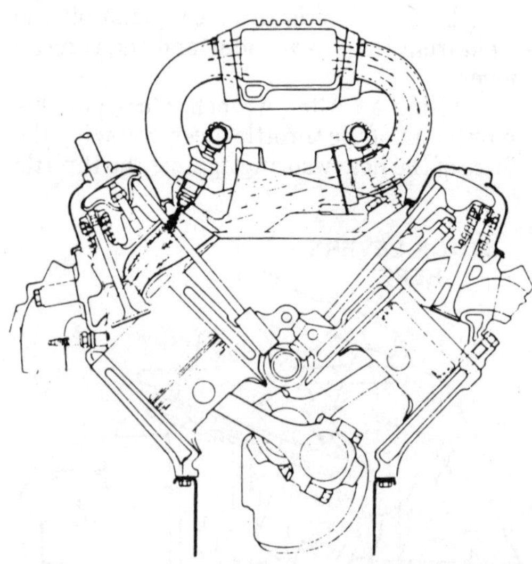

Cross-sectional view of the TPI system—1985 and later

Plenum – TPI System – 1985 and Later

REMOVAL AND INSTALLATION

1. Disconnect the negative battery cable.
2. Remove the throttle cable, thermal vacuum connector and the cruise control cable, if equipped.
3. Remove the cable retaining bracket.
4. Remove the Throttle Position Sensor (TPS) and the Idle Air Control (IAC) connectors.
5. Remove the throttle body bolts and the throttle body.
6. Remove the brake booster pipe, the vacuum hose and the PCV valve fresh air pipe.
7. Remove the right runners, the plenum retaining bolts and the plenum.
8. Using a putty knife, clean the gasket mounting surfaces.
9. To install, use new gaskets and reverse the removal procedures.

Fuel Rail – TPI System – 1985 And Later

REMOVAL AND INSTALLATION

NOTE: *When servicing the fuel system, be sure to relieve the pressure of the fuel system and drain the fuel into an approved container. DO NOT allow dirt or other contaminants to enter the system.*

1. Refer to the "Plenum, Removal and Installation" procedures in this section and remove the plenum.

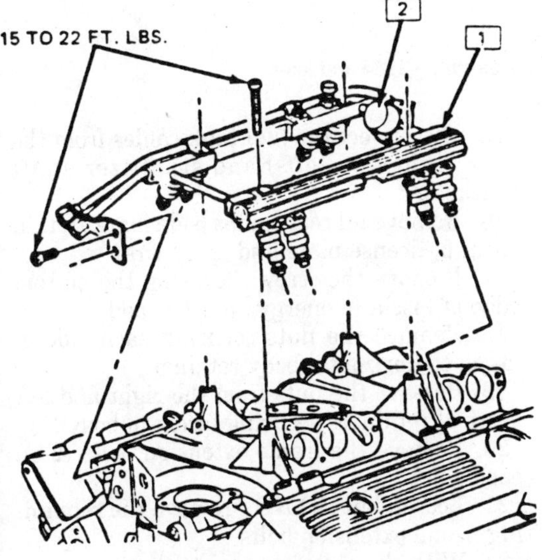

Exploded view of the fuel rail—TPI system—1985 and later

2. Remove the fuel lines and the cold start valve. Remove the injector wiring harness connectors.
3. Remove the fuel rail retaining bolts, the fuel rail and the injectors.
4. To install, use new O-rings (coat them with engine oil) on the injectors and reverse the removal procedures.
5. Turn the ignition switch ON and OFF (several times) and inspect for leaks.

Fuel Tank

REMOVAL AND INSTALLATION

CAUTION: *Exercise extreme caution while servicing the fuel tank. Service the tank only in a well ventilated area. DO NOT smoke or use any type of drop light in the service area.*

NOTE: *It is best to run the tank as low on fuel as possible prior to removing the tank. If the filler cap requires replacement, only a cap with the same features should be used. Failure to use the correct cap can result in a serious malfunction of the system. Allow the fuel level to fall below 1/4 tank for this procedures. The fuel tank consists of a tough, pliable polyethylene liner inside a steel container.*

1. Remove the negative battery cable.
2. Drain fuel from the tank into a suitable safety can.
3. Remove the fuel tank filler door as an assembly.
4. Remove the fuel tank filler neck housing and drain hose. Use clean rags to catch any fuel left in the lines.
5. Disconnect the fuel feed hose, fuel return hose, vapor hose and electrical connector from the fuel meter and pump assembly. The fuel

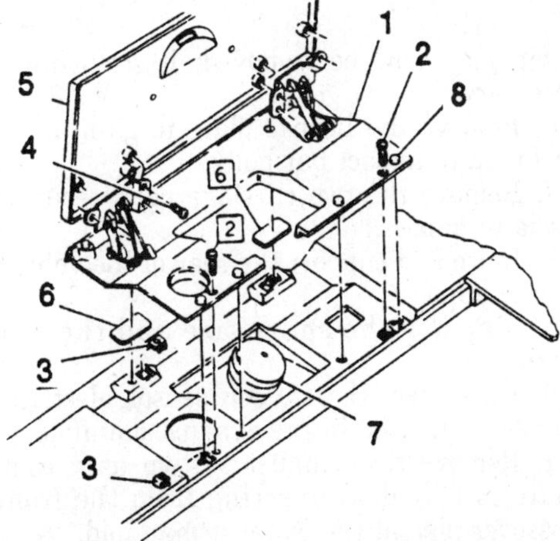

Fuel filler door assembly—1984 and later

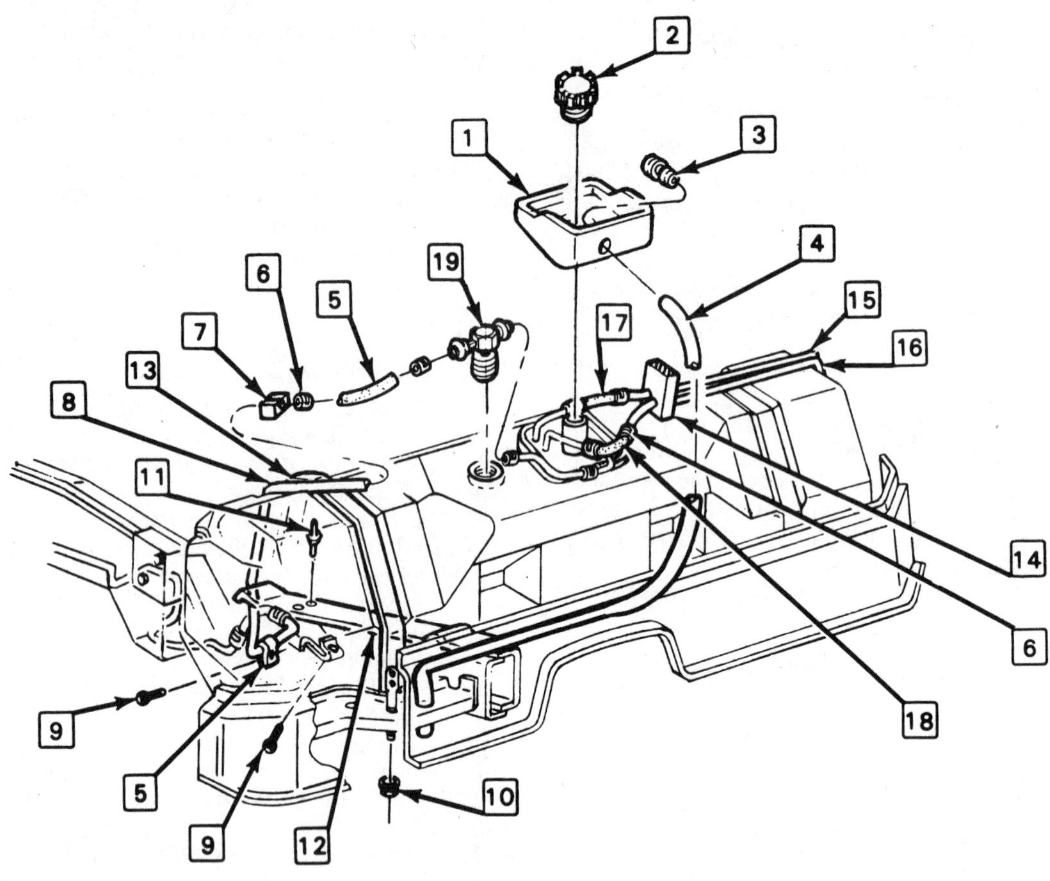

1. Filler neck housing
2. Fuel cap
3. Nipple
4. Drain hose
5. Vapor hose
6. Clamp
7. Retainer
8. Vapor pipe
9. Bolt
10. Nut
11. Rivet
12. Support
13. Strap
14. Retainer
15. Fuel feed pipe
16. Fuel return pipe
17. Fuel feed hose
18. Fuel return hose
19. Fuel vapor connector

Exploded view of the fuel tank assembly—1984 and later

pump may now be removed, if servicing is necessary.

6. Remove the license plate to gain access for fascia to impact bar bolts.
7. Remove the two carriage bolts securing fascia to impact bar.
8. Raise and support the rear of the vehicle on jackstands.
9. Remove the spare tire and the tire carrier.
10. Disconnect the oxygen sensor electrical connector, located in the exhaust manifold.
11. Remove the exhaust system as a complete unit by disconnecting from the front crossover pipe at the exhaust manifold.
12. Remove both inner rear fender braces and panels.
13. Disconnect the antenna ground strap.
14. Remove the bolt securing the fuel vapor pipe to the left-hand fuel tank strap.
15. Disconnect the fuel tank cables from the rear right and left-hand stabilizer shaft brackets.
16. Remove all rear lamps (side marker, tail, backup, license plate and spare tire).
17. Remove the screws securing the bottom edge of fascia to energy absorber pad.
18. Remove the nuts securing each side of fascia to horizontal body retainer.
19. Remove the nuts from the right and left vertical retainers securing fascia to body.
20. Remove the frame extension bolts (2 on each side).
21. Loosen but DO NOT remove the remaining frame extension bolts.
22. With the aid of an assistant, remove the remaining bolts and pull the fuel tank and frame assembly rearward pushing the cover outward. Tilt the assembly down to remove and clear the cover.

23. Remove tank straps and the tank. If fuel tank is being replaced transfer cables, fuel meter and pump, and fuel vapor connector to new tank.

24. To install, reverse the removal procedures. Make sure all connections are tight.

NOTE: *A woven plastic filter is located on the lower end of the fuel pickup pipe in the fuel tank. This filter prevents dirt from entering the fuel line and also stops water unless the filter becomes completely submerged in water. This filter is self cleaning and normally requires no maintenance. Fuel stoppage at this point indicates that the fuel tank contains an abnormal amount of sediment or water; the tank should therefore be thoroughly cleaned. If trouble is due to contaminated fuel or foreign material that has been put into the tank, it can usually be cleaned.*

CLEANING THE FUEL SYSTEM

CAUTION: *This procedure will not remove fuel vapor. DO NOT attempt any repair on tank or filler neck where heat or flame is required.*

1. Disconnect the negative battery cable and the engine electrical harness from the HEI distributor.

NOTE: *Be sure to keep a dry chemical (Class B) fire extinguisher near the work area.*

2. Remove in-line fuel filter and inspect for dirt, rust or contamination. If the filter is plugged, replace but DO NOT install until fuel lines are cleared.

3. Siphon fuel from the tank into a clean fuel container.

4. Remove fuel meter/fuel pump, located under the filler door.

5. Using a wet sponge, wipe inside liner clean of all foreign material. Rinse out the sponge often when wiping the liner. Wipe dry. DO NOT use harsh chemicals when cleaning.

6. Inspect the strainer on the fuel tank meter/fuel pump. If dirty or clogged, replace with a new strainer.

7. Disconnect the inlet fuel line at the throttle body (1984) or fuel rail (1985 and later) and apply air pressure in direction of the fuel flow.

8. Apply air pressure in direction of fuel flow form fuel tank to filter.

9. Disconnect return fuel line at throttle body (1984) or fuel rail (1985 and later) and apply air pressure from the engine to fuel tank.

10. Connect all of the fuel lines and install the fuel filter. If the lines are damaged, see below.

11. To install the fuel tank meter/fuel pump, use a new gasket.

12. Connect the fuel lines, fuel vapor pipe and electrical connector; make sure the connections are tight.

13. Connect negative battery cable and add fuel. DO NOT reuse contaminated fuel.

14. Start engine and check for fuel leaks. Dispose of contaminated fuel properly.

Fuel feed, return and emission pipes or hoses are secured to the under body with clamp and screw assemblies. Flexible hoses are located at the fuel tank, fuel vapor and return lines. The pipes should be inspected occasionally for leaks, kinks or dents. Replace any excessively corroded lines.

NOTE: *Fuel and vapor hoses are specially manufactured. If replacement becomes necessary, it is important to use only replacement hoses meeting the manufacturer's specifications. Hoses not meeting minimum specifications could cause early part failure or failure to meet emission standards.*

DO NOT use copper or aluminum tubing to replace steel tubing. These materials DO NOT have satisfactory durability to withstand normal vehicle vibrations. DO NOT use rubber hose within 4 in. of any part of the exhaust system or within 10 in. of the catalytic converter. When making repairs, cut a piece of fuel hose about 4 in. longer than a portion of the line removed. If more than a 6 in. length of pipe is removed, use a combination of steel pipe and hose so that the hose lengths will not be more than 10 in.

Follow the same routing as the original pipe and always use screw type hose clamps. Slide the hose clamps over the replacement part and push the hose an equal amount onto each portion of fuel pipe. Tighten the clamps on each side of the repair but DO NOT overtighten. The pipes must be properly secured to the frame to prevent chafing, which could wear hole in the line.

Chassis Electrical

5

UNDERSTANDING BASIC ELECTRICITY

For any electrical system to operate, it must make a complete circuit. This simply means that the power flow from the battery must make a complete circle. When an electrical component is operating, power flows from the battery to the component, passes through the component causing it to perform its function (lighting a light bulb, for example) and then returns to the battery through the ground of the circuit. This ground is usually (but not always) the metal part of the vehicle on which the electrical component is mounted.

Perhaps the easiest way to visualize this is to think of connecting a light bulb (with two wires attached to it) to the battery. The battery has two posts (negative and positive). If one of the two wires (attached to the light bulb) is attached to the negative post of the battery and the other wire is attached to the positive post of the battery, you would have a complete circuit. Current from the battery would flow out of one post, through the wire (attached to it) and then to the light bulb, causing it to light. It would then leave the light bulb, travel through the other wire and return to the other post of the battery.

The normal automotive circuit differs from this simple example in two ways. First, instead of having a return wire from the bulb to the battery, the light bulb returns the current to the battery through the chassis of the vehicle. Since the negative battery cable is attached to the chassis and the chassis is made of electrically conductive metal, the chassis of the vehicle can serve as a ground wire to complete the circuit. Secondly, most automotive circuits contain switches to turn components ON and OFF as required.

There are many types of switches but the most common simply serves to prevent the passage of current when it is turned OFF. Since the switch is a part of the circle necessary for a complete circuit, it operates to leave an opening in the circuit and thus an incomplete or open circuit, when it is turned OFF.

Some electrical components which require a large amount of current to operate also have a relay in their circuit. Since these circuits carry a large amount of current, the thickness of the wire (gauge size) in the circuit is also greater. If this large wire were connected from the component to the control switch on the instrument panel and then back to the component, a voltage drop would occur in the circuit. To prevent this potential drop in voltage, an electromagnetic switch (relay) is used. The large wires in the circuit are connected from the battery to one side of the relay and from the opposite side of the relay to the component. The relay is normally open, preventing current from passing through the circuit. An additional, smaller, wire is connected from the relay to the control switch for the circuit. When the control switch is turned ON, it grounds the smaller wire from the relay and completes the circuit. This closes the relay and allows current to flow from the battery to the component. The horn, headlight and starter circuits are three which use relays.

You have probably noticed how the vehicle's instrument panel lights get brighter the faster you rev the engine. This happens because the alternator (which supplies current to the battery) puts out more current at speeds above idle. This is normal. However, it is possible for larger surges of current to pass through the electrical system. If this surge of current were to reach an electrical component, it could burn the component out. To prevent this from happening, fuses are connected in the current supply wires of most of the major electrical systems. The fuse serves to head off the surge at the pass. When an electrical current of excessive power passes through the component's fuse, the fuse blows out and breaks the circuit, saving it from destruction.

The fuse also protects the component from damage if the power supply wire to the component is grounded before the current reaches the component.

There is another important rule to the complete circle circuit. ***Every complete circuit from a power source must include a component which is using the power from the power source.*** If you were to disconnect the light bulb (from the previous example of a light bulb being connected to the battery by two wires together – take our word for it – don't try it) the result would literally be shocking. A similar thing happens (on a smaller scale) when the power supply wire to a component or the electrical component itself becomes grounded before the normal ground connection for the circuit. To prevent damage to the system, the fuse for the circuit blows to interrupt the circuit – protecting the components from damage. Because grounding a wire from a power source makes a complete circuit – less the required component to use the power – this phenomenon is called a short circuit. The most common causes of short circuits are: the rubber insulation on a wire breaking or rubbing through to expose the current carrying core of the wire to a metal part of the vehicle or a shorted switch.

Some electrical systems on the vehicle are protected by a circuit breaker which is, basically, a self-repairing fuse. When either of the above described events take place in a system which is protected by a circuit breaker, the circuit breaker opens the circuit the same way a fuse does. However, when either the short is removed from the circuit or the surge subsides, the circuit breaker resets itself and does not have to be replaced as a fuse does.

The final protective device in the chassis electrical system is a fuse link. A fuse link is a wire that acts as a fuse. It is connected between the starter relay and the main wiring harness for the vehicle. This connection is under the hood, very near a similar fuse link which protects all the chassis electrical components. It is the probable cause of trouble when none of the electrical components function, unless the battery is disconnected or dead.

Electrical problems generally fall into one of three areas:

1. The component that is not functioning is not receiving current.
2. The component itself is not functioning.
3. The component is not properly grounded.

Problems that fall into the first category are by far the most complicated. It is the current supply system to the component which contains all the switches, relays, fuses and etc.

The electrical system can be checked with a test light and a jumper wire. A test light is a device that looks like a pointed screwdriver with a wire attached to it. It has a light bulb inside its handle. A jumper wire is a piece of insulated wire with an alligator clip attached to each end.

If a light bulb is not working, you must follow a systematic plan to determine which of the three causes is the villian.

1. Turn ON the switch that controls the inoperable bulb.
2. Disconnect the power supply wire from the bulb.
3. Attach the ground wire on the test light to a good metal ground.
4. Touch the probe end of the test light to the end of the power supply wire that was disconnected from the bulb. If the bulb is receiving current, the test light will turn ON.

NOTE: *If the bulb is one which works only when the ignition key is turned on (turn signal), make sure the key is turned ON.*

If the test light does not turn ON, then the problem is in the circuit between the battery and the bulb. As mentioned before, this includes all the switches, fuses and relays in the system. The problem is an open circuit between the battery and the bulb. If the fuse is blown and, when replaced, immediately blows again, there is a short circuit in the system which must be located and repaired. If there is a switch in the system, bypass it with a jumper wire. This is done by connecting one end of the jumper wire to the power supply wire into the switch and the other end of the jumper wire to the wire coming out of the switch. If the test light turns ON with the jumper wire installed, the switch or whatever was bypassed is defective.

NOTE: *Never substitute the jumper wire for the bulb, as the bulb is the component required to use the power from the power source.*

5. If the bulb in the test light turns ON, the current is getting to the bulb that is not working in the vehicle. This eliminates the first of the three possible causes. Connect the power supply wire and connect a jumper wire from the bulb to a good metal ground. Do this with the switch which controls the bulb turned ON and also the ignition switch turned ON (if it is required for the light to work). If the bulb works with the jumper wire installed, then it has a bad ground. This is usually caused by the metal area on which the bulb mounts to the vehicle being coated with some type of foreign matter or rust.
6. If neither test located the source of the trouble, then the light bulb itself is defective.

The above test procedures can be applied to any of the components of the chassis electrical system by substituting the component that is not working for the light bulb. Remember that for any electrical system to work, all connections must be clean and tight.

HEATER

Blower Motor

REMOVAL AND INSTALLATION

1. Raise the hood and disconnect the negative battery cable.
2. Remove the front wheel house rear panel and move the wheel house seal aside.
3. Remove the motor cooling tube.
4. Remove the relay.
5. Remove the blower motor-to-case screws.
6. Remove the blower motor and impeller assembly.
7. To install, reverse the removal procedures. Make sure all electrical connections are clean and tight.

Heater Core

REMOVAL AND INSTALLATION

1. Raise the hood and disconnect the negative battery cable.
2. Remove the instrument cluster bezel including the tilt wheel lever and dash pad.
3. Remove the A/C air duct and disconnect the flex hose.
4. Remove the right-side acoustic panel.
5. Remove the side window defroster flex hose.
6. Remove the side window defroster duct mounting screws and disconnect the extension.
7. Remove the temperature control cable and bracket assembly at the heater cover. Disconnect the heater door control shaft.
8. Remove the electronic control module (ECM) and disconnect the electrical connectors. Make sure the ignition is switched OFF when removing ECM connectors.
9. Remove the tubular support brace from the door pillar to the instrument panel reinforcement brace.
10. Remove the heater core cover mounting screws.
11. Remove the heater pipe and the heater water control bracket attaching screws.
12. Cut the heater hose at the heater core inlet and outlet connection. The heater hoses should be replaced when installing the core.
13. Remove the heater core. Be careful of any coolant left in the core when handling.
14. To install, reverse the removal procedures. Refill the cooling system.

Control Head

REMOVAL AND INSTALLATION

1. Raise the hood and disconnect the negative battery cable.
2. Remove the instrument cluster bezel, the tilt wheel lever and the center bezel (above the console).
3. Remove the control head-to-carrier screws.

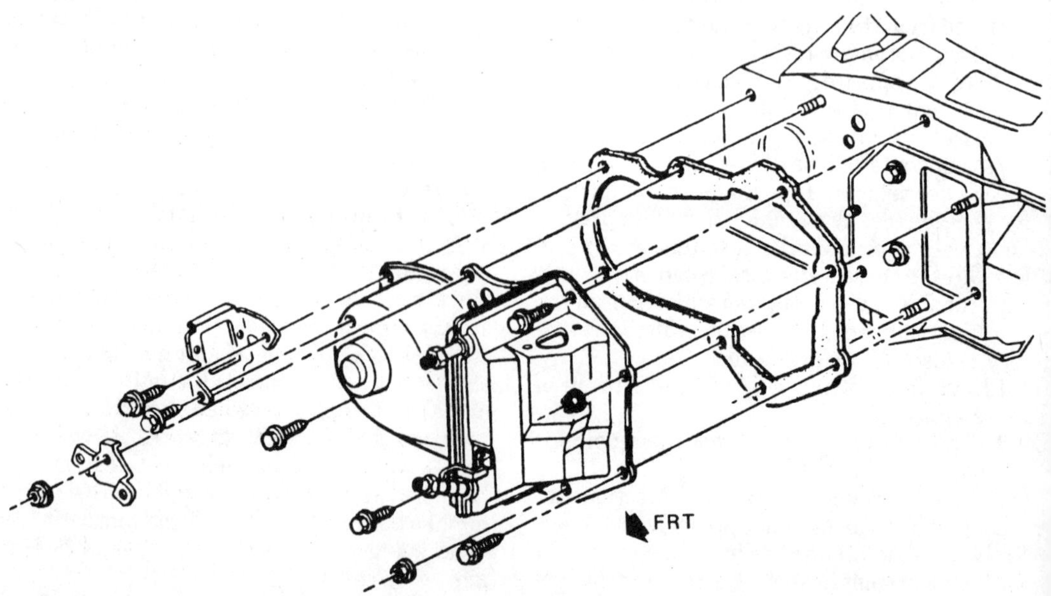

Exploded view of the blower motor assembly

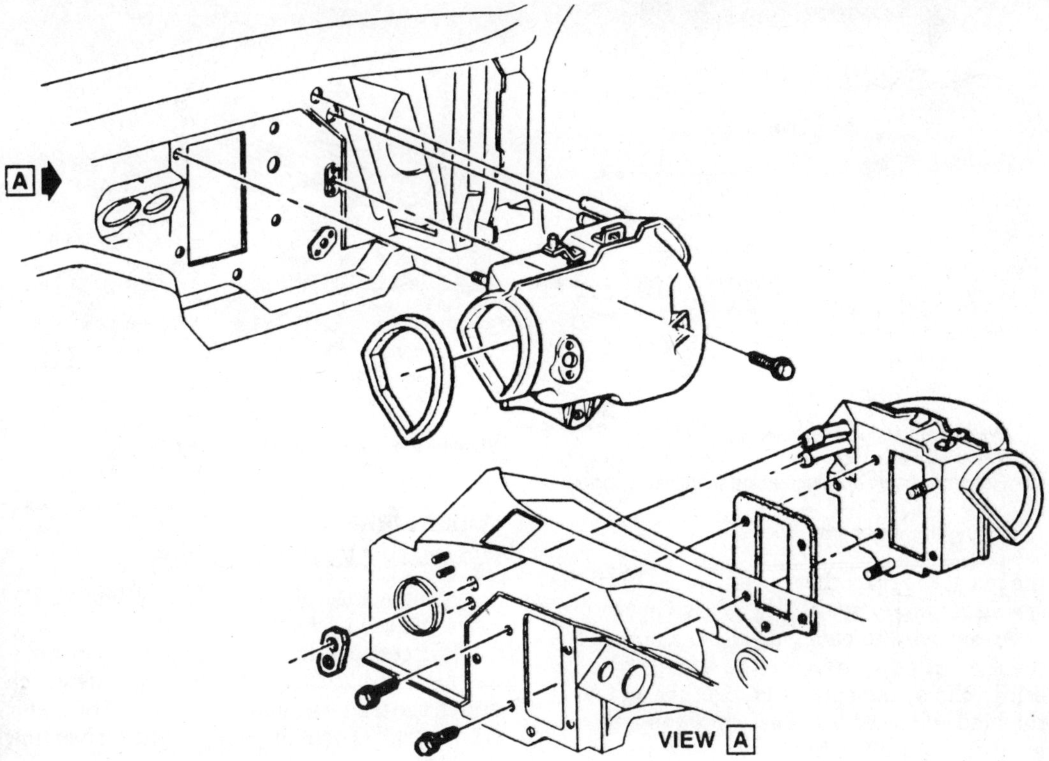

Exploded view of the heater core

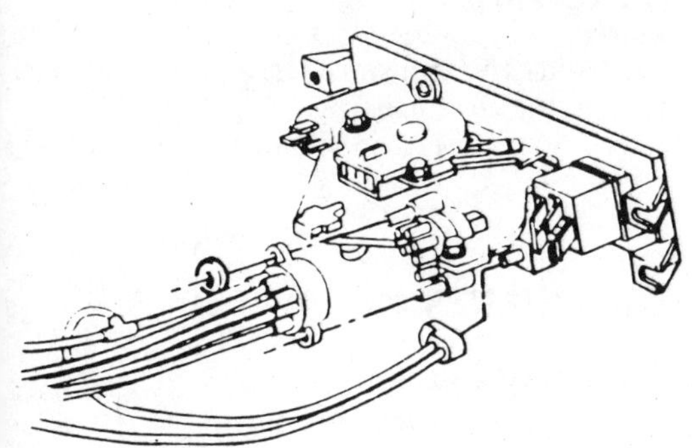

View of the control head

4. Rotate the control head, then disconnect the electrical connectors, the temperature control cable and vacuum hoses.

5. Remove the control head from the vehicle.

6. To install, reverse the removal procedures. Check the control head operation.

RADIO

REMOVAL AND INSTALLATION

There are several different types of radio and/or cassette sound systems available. One thing all sound systems have in common are ungrounded speakers. Installing add-on components that utilize the original speakers may cause damage to both the speakers and the added component.

1. Disconnect the negative battery cable.

2. Remove the headlight switch knob and the steering wheel tilt lever.

3. Remove the instrument panel cluster bezel and the center trim panel (above the console).

4. Remove the radio-to-carrier screws, pull the radio outward and disconnect the electrical connectors.

5. Remove the radio from the instrument panel.

6. To install, reverse the removal procedures.

WINDSHIELD WIPERS

Blade and Arm

REMOVAL AND INSTALLATION

If the wiper assembly has a press type release tab at the center, simply depress the tab and remove the blade. If the blade has no release tab, use a screwdriver to depress the spring at the center; this will release the assembly. To install the assembly, position the blade over

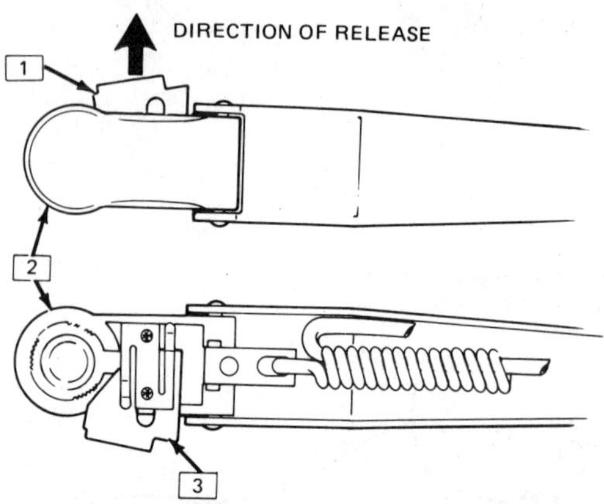

1. Wiper arm retainer (released position)
2. Wiper arm assembly
3. Retainer shown from underside (released position)

Removing the wiper arm

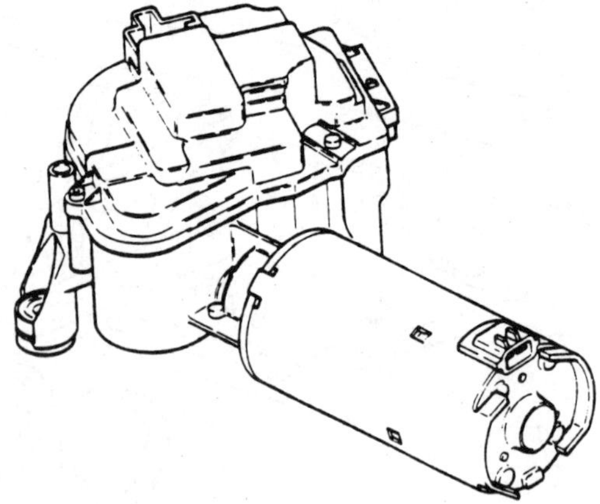

View of the wiper motor assembly

the pin at the tip of the arm and press until the spring retainer engages the groove in the pin.

To remove the element, either depress the release button or squeeze the spring type retainer clip at the outer end together and slide the blade element out. Just slide the new element in until it latches.

1. Remove the washer hoses from their connections.
2. Pull the wiper arm away from the windshield (this allows the retainer to be moved).
3. Pull the retainer away from the transmission spindle and the wiper arm off the spindle.
4. To install, reverse the removal procedures. Be sure that the motor is in the Park position before installing the arms.

Wiper Motor

REMOVAL AND INSTALLATION

1. Raise the hood and install fender covers.
2. Remove the wiper arms.
3. Remove the air inlet leaf screen.
4. Turn the ignition ON and activate the wiper switch. Allow the motor to rotate the crank arm to a position between 4 and 5 o'clock as viewed from the passenger compartment. Turn OFF the ignition to stop the crank arm in this position.
5. Disconnect the negative battery cable.
6. Disconnect the upper motor electrical connectors.
7. Remove the wiper motor-to-cowl mounting bolts.
8. With the crank arm in the position described above, the wiper motor may be easily removed from the vehicle. Disconnect the lower electrical connector as the motor is removed.
9. To install, reverse the removal procedures.

Wiper Linkage

REMOVAL AND INSTALLATION

1. Remove the wiper arms and blades. Remove the cowl screen or grille.
2. Disconnect the wiring from the wiper motor. Loosen, but do not remove the nuts which attach the transmission drive link to the motor crank arm. Then disconnect the drive link from the arm.
3. Remove the transmission-to-body mounting screws from both right and left-sides of the vehicle.
4. Guide the transmission and linkage out through the cowl opening.
5. To install, reverse the removal procedures.

INSTRUMENTS AND SWITCHES

Instrument Cluster

REMOVAL AND INSTALLATION

1. Disconnect the negative battery cable.
2. Remove the spring-loaded light switch knob and the light switch nut.
3. Remove the steering column trim cover.
4. Remove the two steering column attaching bolts and lower the steering column to provide access.
5. Remove the cluster bezel front and left-side screws, then the cluster bezel from the instrument panel.
6. Remove the cluster-to-instrument panel screws.
7. Pull the cluster carefully rearward to get at the cluster electrical connectors.
8. Remove the instrument cluster.

NOTE: *At this point, the odometer may be removed for service.*

9. To install, reverse the removal proce-

dures. Make sure all electrical connections are tight and properly plugged together.

Instrument Panel

REMOVAL AND INSTALLATION

Pad

1. Disconnect the negative battery cable.
2. Remove the instrument panel cluster bezel and the steering column tilt lever.
3. Remove the 5 instrument panel-to-carrier screws and the 2 instrument panel pad-to-defroster duct screws.
4. Pull the instrument panel from the carrier, disconnect the electrical connectors from the speakers and remove the panel from the vehicle.
5. To install, reverse the removal procedures.

Carrier

1. Refer to the "Instrument Panel Pad, Removal and Installation" procedures in this section and remove the pad from the vehicle.
2. Remove the 4 left and the 4 right close out panel screws. Disconnect the electrical connectors from the courtesy lights, then remove the panels.
3. Remove the instrument panel trim (right-side) and the fuse cover.
4. Remove the 4 upper dash brace screws and the braces. Remove the A/C flexible duct hose and duct from the right-side.
5. At the right-side, remove the 2 instrument panel-to-side glass defroster hose screws, the trim pad and the lower carpet panel.
6. Remove the radio.
7. At the center cluster, remove the 4 cluster-to-carrier screws, disconnect the electrical connectors and the center cluster.

NOTE: *When removing the electrical connectors from the center cluster, the metal retaining clips are located at the rear-side of the connectors.*

8. Remove the 4 main cluster screws, the console bezel and the shift handle; be sure to disconnect the bulb connector.
9. Remove the 4 A/C control-to-instrument panel screws and push the control back through the opening.
10. Remove the headlight switch attaching nut, the fog lamp switch and the hood release handle trim piece.
11. At the steering column, remove the trim cover and the 2 column mounting bolts.
12. At the instrument panel carrier, remove the carrier-to-console bolts and disconnect the fuse block.
13. At the instrument panel carrier, remove the A/C ducts from the center and the left-side, then the 2 defroster-to-carrier duct screws.
14. At the rear of the instrument panel carrier, remove the odometer harness screws and the left defroster hose from the column brace.
15. Remove the instrument panel carrier from the vehicle.
16. To install, reverse the removal procedures.

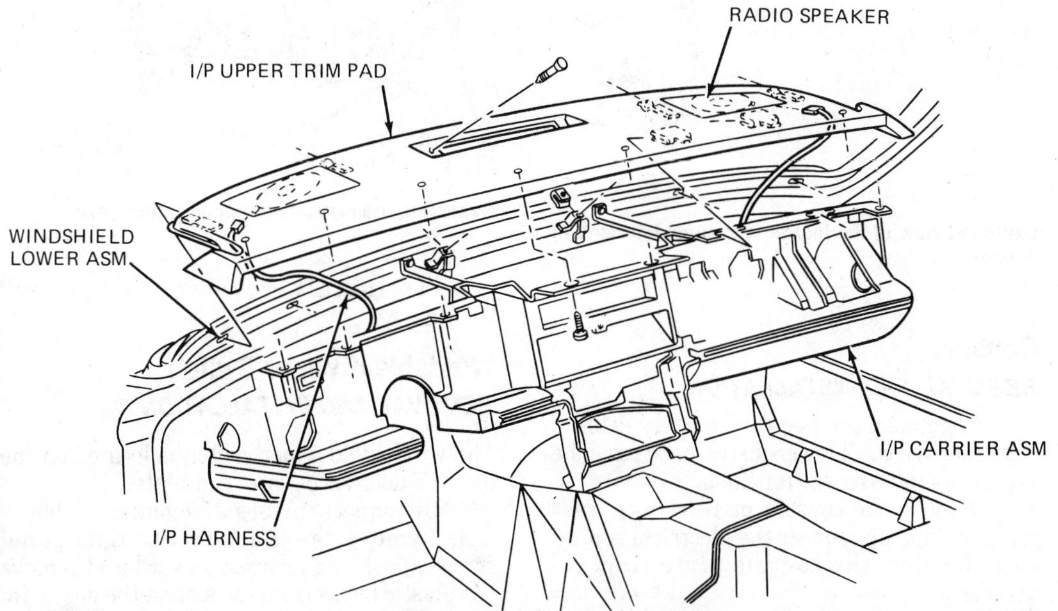

Exploded view of the instrument panel pad

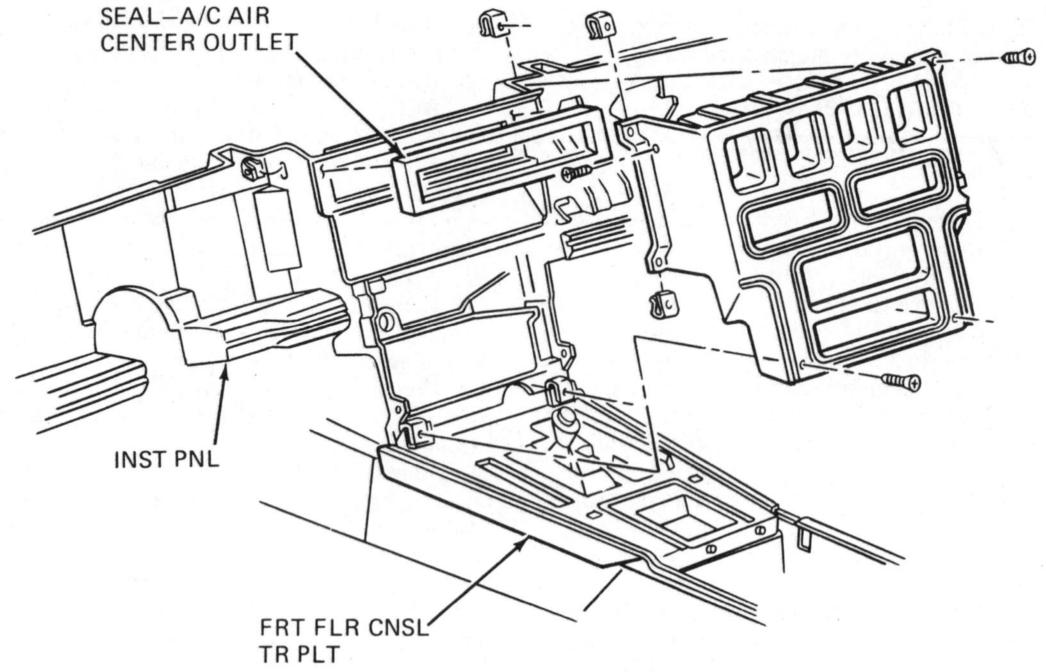

Removing the accessory trim plate assembly

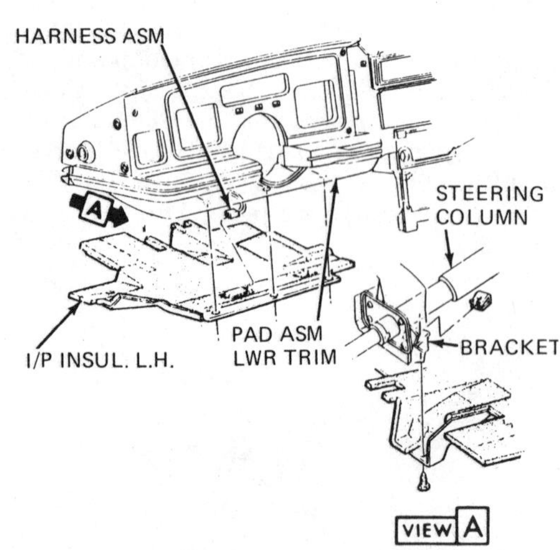

Exploded view of the instrument panel left-hand insulator

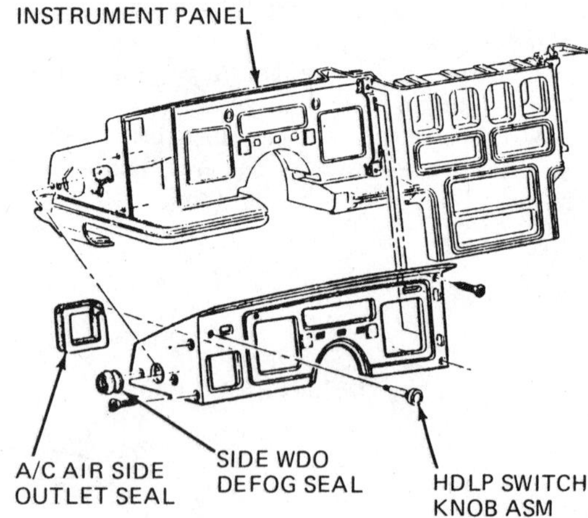

Removing the instrument panel cluster bezel

Console

REMOVAL AND INSTALLATION

1. Disconnect the negative battery cable.
2. Remove the 2 lower instrument panel bezel screws and the shifter knob.
3. Remove the console plate screws, raise the plate and disconnect the electrical connectors. Remove the console plate from the vehicle.
4. Remove the console compartment-to-vehicle screws and the console from the vehicle.
5. To install, reverse the removal procedures.

Windshield Wiper Switch

REMOVAL AND INSTALLATION

The windshield wiper switch is located on the driver's door accessory trim plate.

1. Disconnect the negative battery cable.
2. Remove the 2 armrest-to-trim panel screws, push the armrest inward and remove the plastic hooks from the slot on the door trim panel.
3. Remove the 5 accessory trim panel-to-

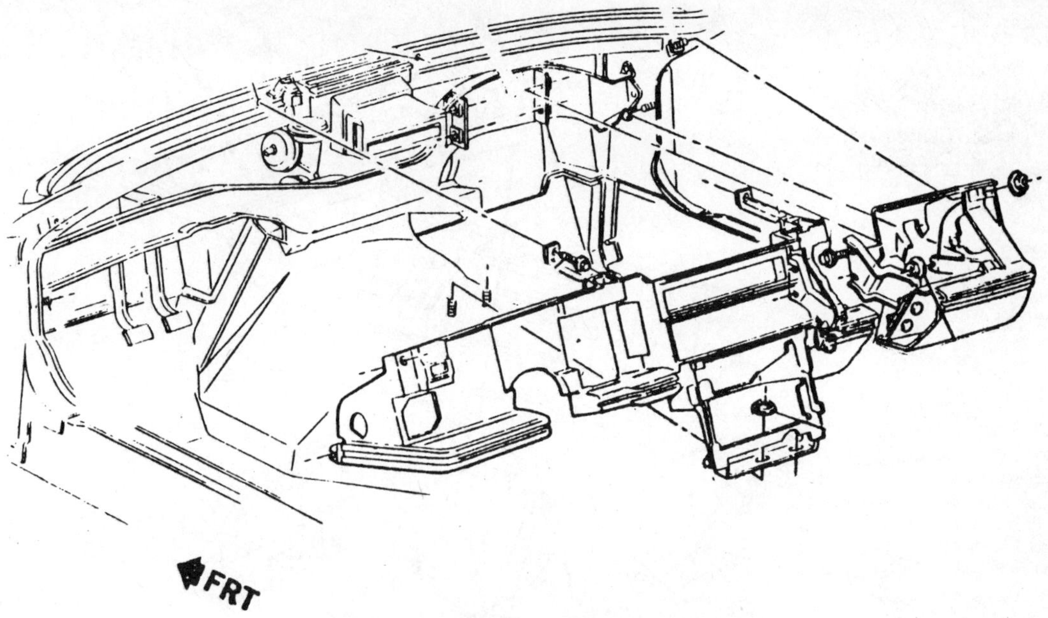

Exploded view of the instrument panel carrier

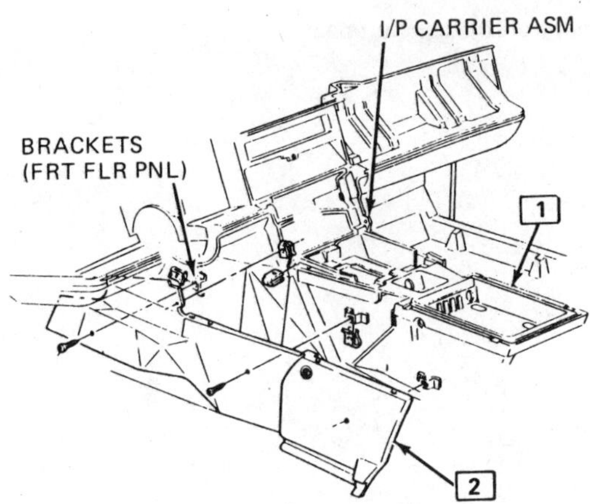

1. Console asm—frt flr
2. Panel asm—frt flr cnsl side trim

Exploded view of the front floor console side trim panel

door screws; one screw is located behind the door handle.

4. Pull the accessory trim panel outward and disconnect the electrical connectors from the trim panel.
5. Remove the windshield wiper switch from the accessory trim panel.
6. To install, reverse the removal procedures.

Headlight Switch

The headlight switch is located at the left-side of the instrument panel.

REMOVAL AND INSTALLATION

1. Refer to the "Instrument Panel Carrier, Removal and Installation" procedures in this section and remove the headlight switch from the instrument panel.
2. To install, reverse the removal procedures.

LIGHTING

Headlights

REMOVAL AND INSTALLATION

1. Open the hood and actuate the headlight switch to raise the headlights to the OPEN position.
2. Disconnect the negative battery cable.
3. Remove the headlight bezel retaining screws and remove the bezel.
4. Using a cotter pin removal tool, disengage the spring from the retaining ring.
5. Rotate the right headlight clockwise and the left headlight counterclockwise to release it from the aiming pins.
6. Disconnect the electrical connector and remove the retaining ring.
7. To install, reverse the removal procedures.

NOTE: *When installing the sealed beam unit, make sure the number (molded into the lens) is at the top.*

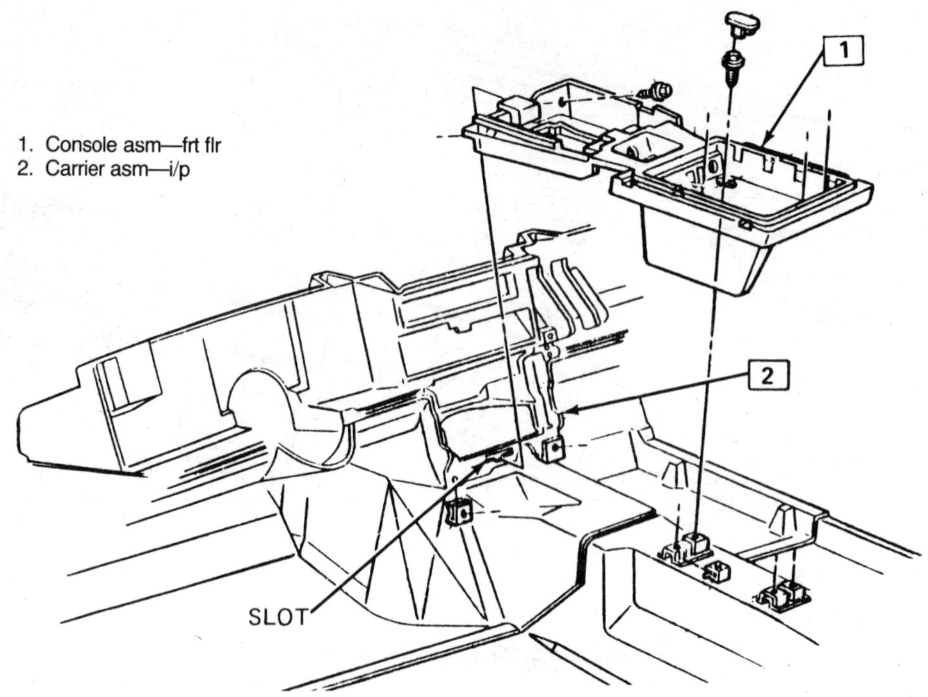

Exploded view of the front floor console compartment

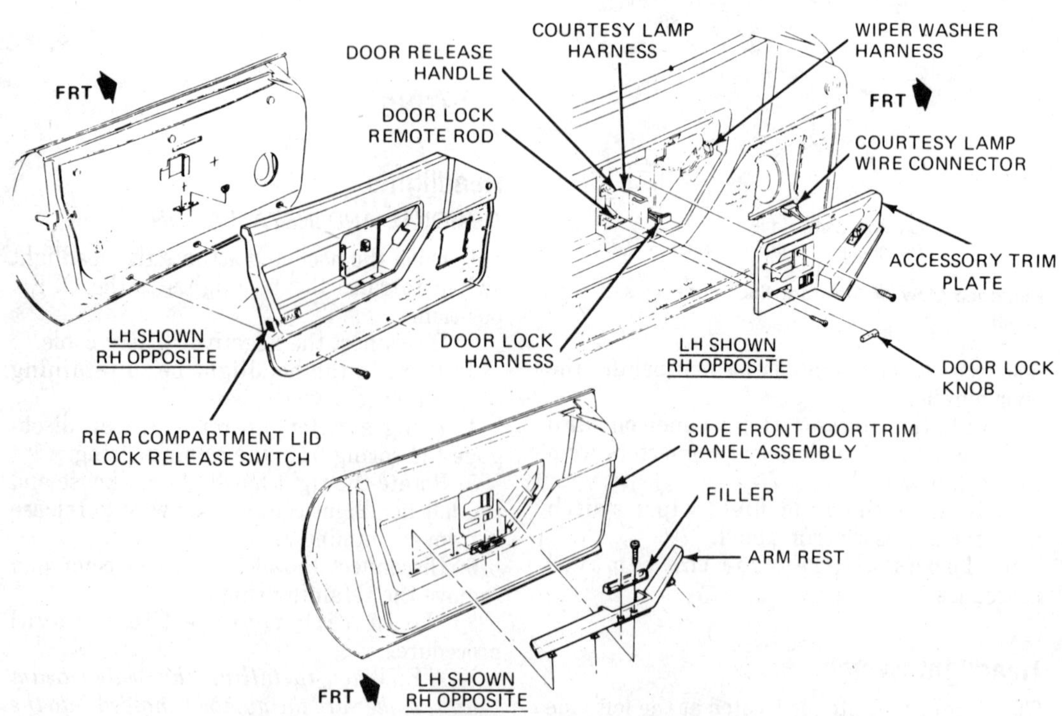

Exploded view of the door trim panel and accessory trim plate

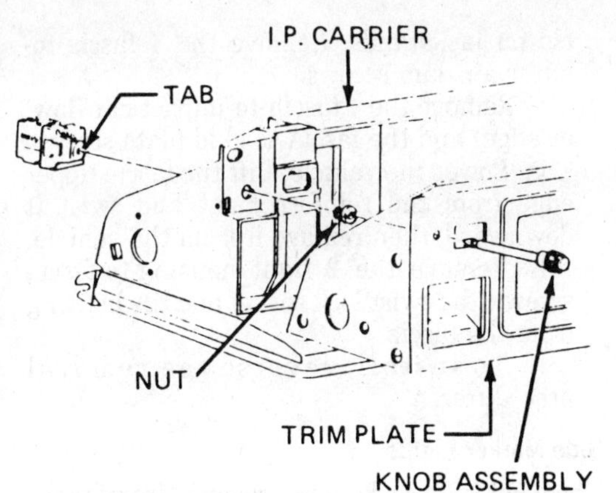

Exploded view of the headlight switch assembly

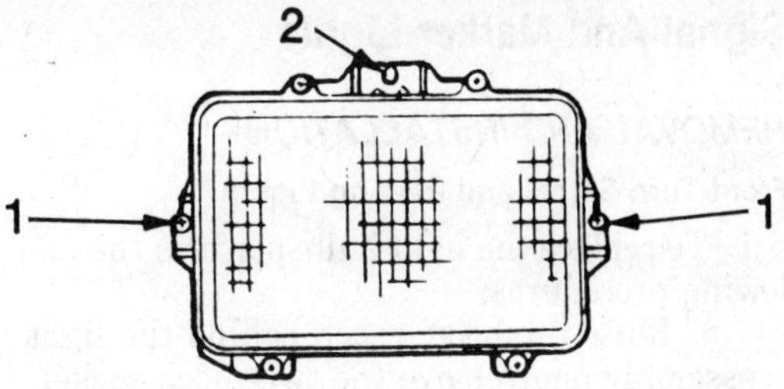

Location of horizontal (1) and vertical (2) adjustment screws

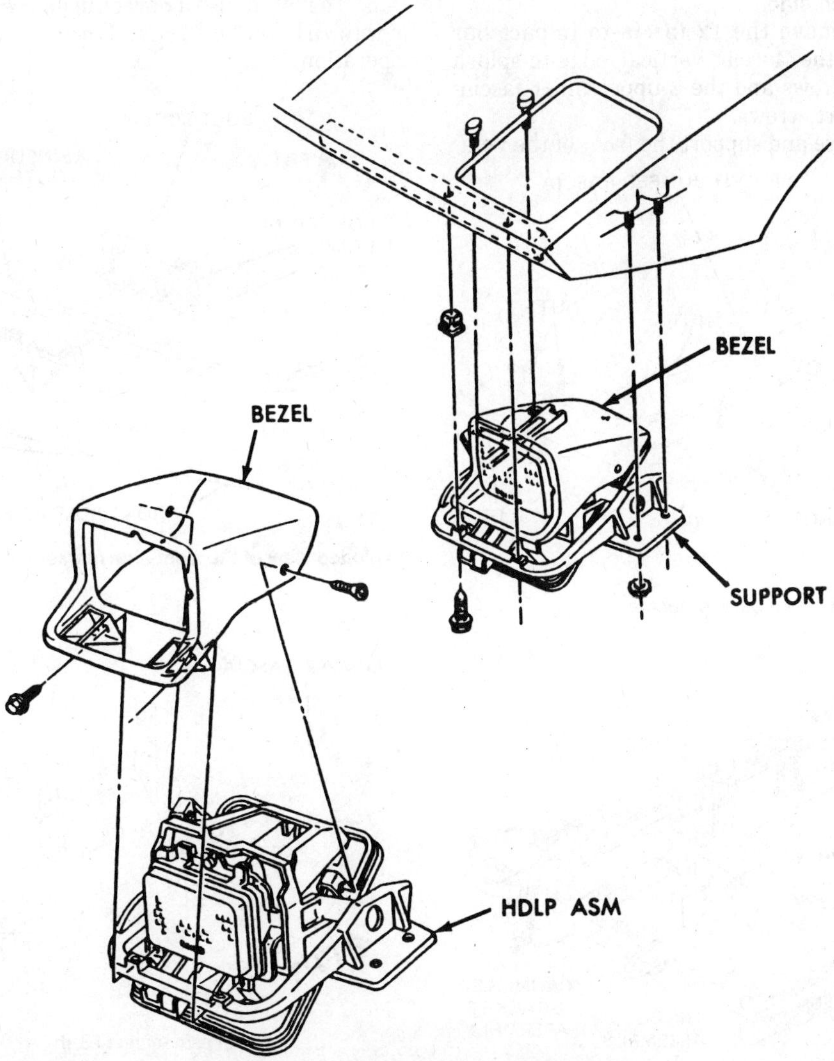

Headlamp assembly—1984 and later models

Signal And Marker Lights

REMOVAL AND INSTALLATION

Front Turn Signal and Parking Lights

1. To replace the light bulb, perform the following procedures:
   a. Raise the hood, reach behind the light assembly and remove the twist-lock socket.
   b. Remove the bulb from the socket.
   c. To install, use a new bulb and reverse the removal procedures.
2. To remove the light housing, perform the following procedures:
   a. Raise the hood and disconnect the negative battery cable.
   b. Disconnect the bulbs from the parking and the side marker lights.
   c. Remove the wheelhouse seal from the upper edge of the fascia, then the 4 screws from each side.
   d. Remove the 12 fascia-to-impact bar screws, the 4 rear vertical edge-to-splash shield screws and the 2 upper inner fascia-to-support screws.
   e. Raise and support the front of the vehicle on jackstands. Remove the 4 fascia-to-outer air dam screws.
   f. Remove the 4 fascia-to-impact bar (lower edge) and the fascia-to-skid plate screws.
   g. Lower the vehicle. Lift the fascia upper edge from the reinforcement and twist it downward, then remove it from the vehicle.
   h. Remove the 2 light housing-to-fascia screws, the twist lock socket and the housing from the fascia.
   i. To install, reverse the removal procedures.

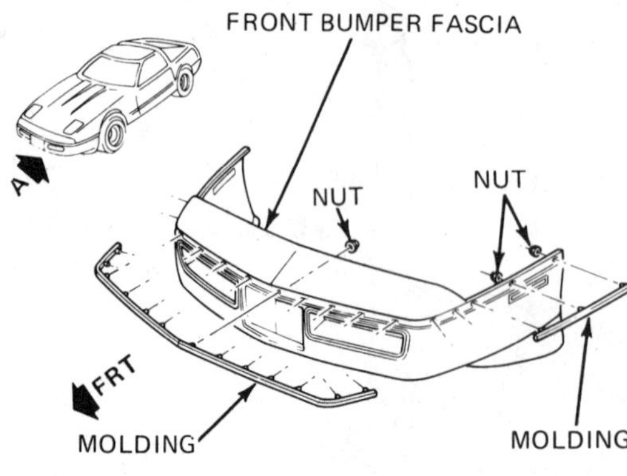

Removing the front bumper fascia

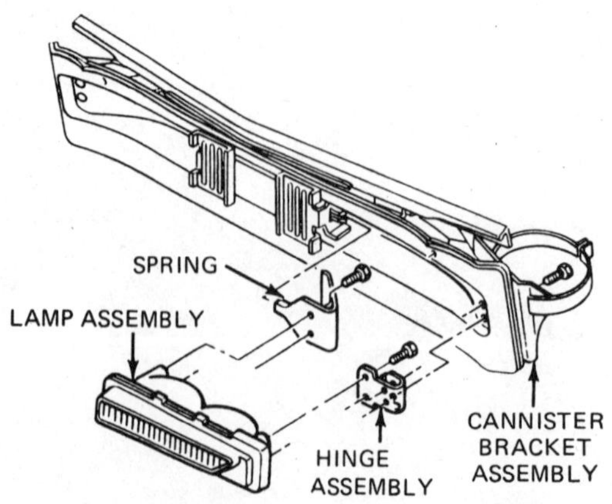

Removing the turn singal/parking light housing

Side Marker Lights

The front bulb sockets are reached from under the front fender. The rear bulb sockets are reached from inside the cargo area.

1. Turn the bulb socket 90° counterclockwise and pull it out.
2. Remove the bulb from the socket.
3. To install, use a new bulb and reverse the removal procedures. Check the lamp operation.

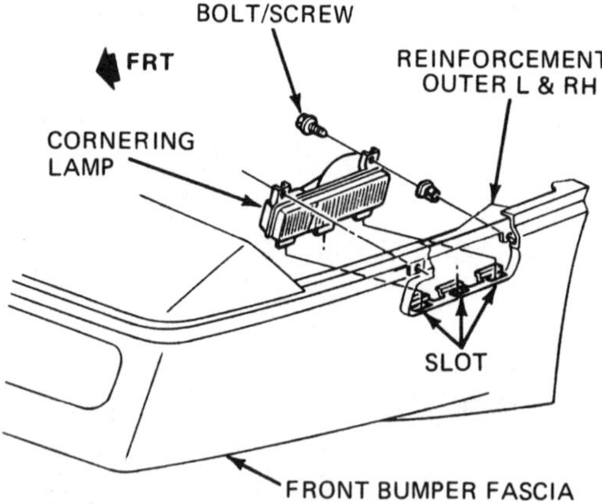

Exploded view of the front side marker light

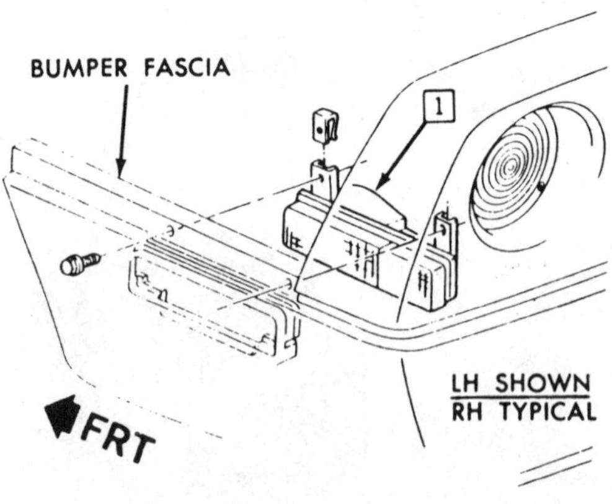

Exploded view of the rear side marker light

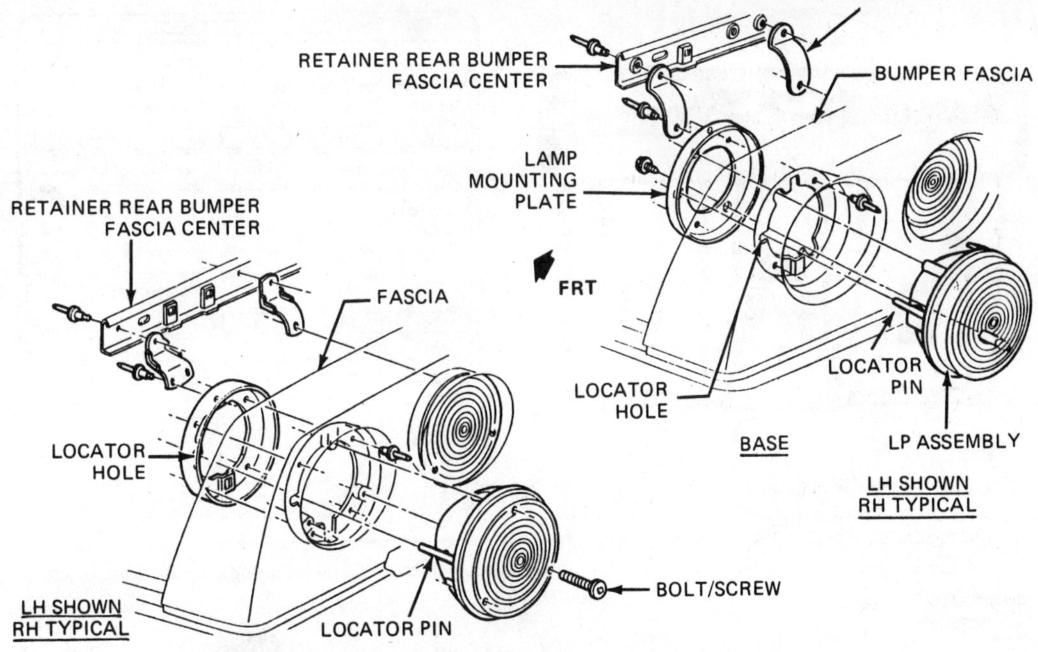

Exploded view of the rear turn signal, brake and parking light assembly

Rear Turn Signal, Brake and Parking Lights

1. Raise the rear hatch lid.
2. Turn the bulb socket and pull it out.
3. Remove the bulb from the socket.
4. To install, use a new bulb and reverse the removal procedures. Check the lamp operation.

CIRCUIT PROTECTION

Fusible Links

In addition to fuses, the wiring harness incorporates fusible links to protect the wiring. Fusible links are sections of wire, with special insulation, designed to melt under electrical overload. There are four different gauge sizes used. The links are marked on the insulation with the wire gauge size because of the heavier insulation which makes the link appear a heavier gauge than it actually is.

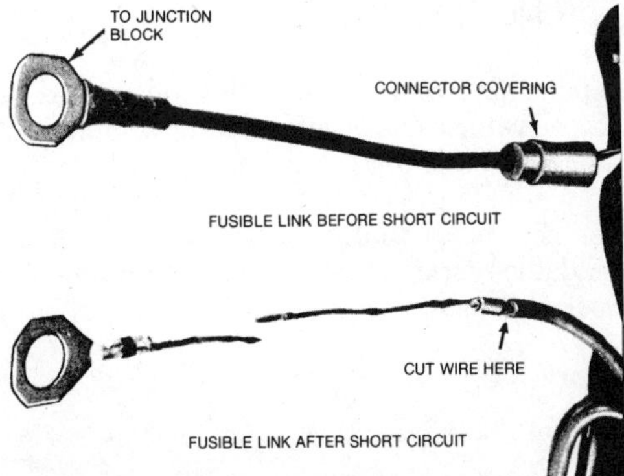

Fusible link (© Chevrolet Motor Division)

REPLACEMENT

1. Disconnect the negative battery cable.
2. Locate the burned out link.
3. Strip away the melted insulation and cut the burned link ends from the wire.
4. Strip the wire back ½" to allow soldering of the new link.
5. Using a new fusible link 4 gauges smaller than the protected circuit (approx. 10 in. long), solder it into the circuit.

   NOTE: *Whenever splicing a new wire, always bond the splice with rosin core solder, then cover with electrical tape. Using acid core solder may cause corrosion.*
6. Tape and seal all splices with silicone to weatherproof repairs.
7. After taping the wire, tape the electrical harness leaving an exposed 5 in. loop of wire.
8. Reconnect the battery.

Circuit Breakers

A circuit breaker is an electrical switch which breaks the circuit in case of an overload. The circuit breaker is located on the right-side of the fuse panel. The circuit breaker will remain open until the short or overload condition in the circuit is corrected.

To test for blown mini-fuse:
1. Pull fuse out and check visually
2. With the circuit activated use a test light across the points shown

Blown fuse

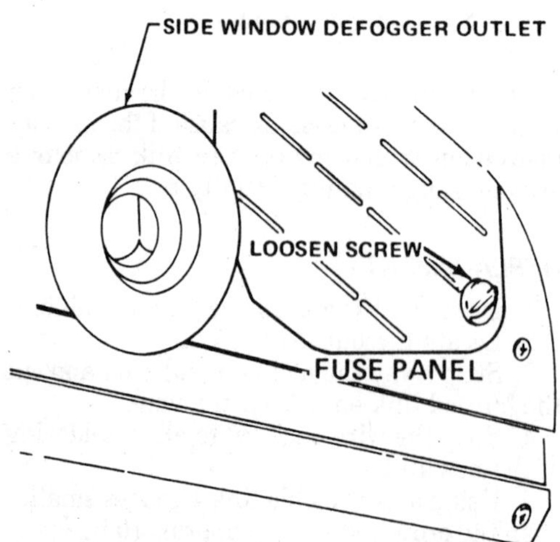

Location of the fuse panel at the right-hand side of the instrument panel

Fuses and Flashers

Fuses are located on the junction box (inside the instrument panel) at the right-side of the instrument panel, near the right door. Each fuse receptacle is marked as to the circuit it protects and the correct amperage of the fuse.

An in-line fuse block is located in the wiring harness, behind the instrument panel.

The Convenience Center is a swing-down unit located on the underside of the instrument panel, near the steering column. The swing-down feature provides central location and easy access to buzzers, relays and flasher units. All units are serviced by plug-in replacement.

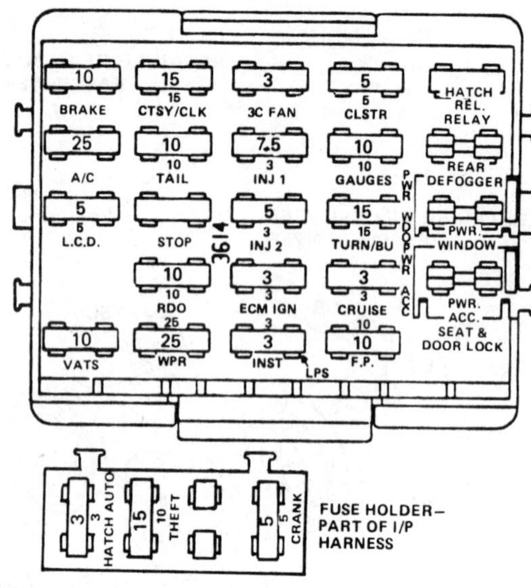

View of the fuse panel and the in-line fuse block

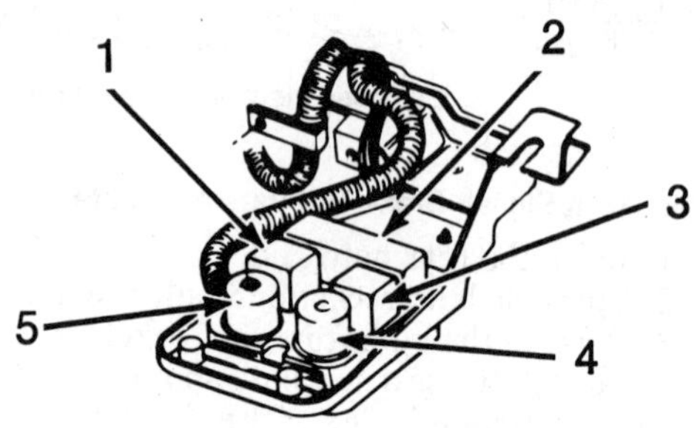

1. Horn relay
2. Warning buzzer
3. Electric choke relay
4. Hazard flasher
5. Turn signal flasher

Convenience center and components—typical

WIRING DIAGRAMS

Wiring diagrams are not included in this book. As the vehicles have become more complex and available with longer option lists, wiring diagrams have grown in size and complexity. It has become virtually impossible to provide a readable reproduction of a wiring diagram in a book this size.

Drive Train 6

MANUAL TRANSMISSION

Identification

The vehicle uses a new, computer-controlled 4-speed overdrive manual transmission, which is essentially a combination of two separate transmissions. The first is a conventional 4-speed (83mm) manual system with a 1:1 ratio in 4th gear. The second is a 2-speed (overdrive) system electronically controlled by the Electronic Control Module (ECM), which operates with a 1:1 and a 0.68:1 or a 0.59:1 ratio. By combining these two transmissions, the complete unit is actually capable of operating with seven separate gear ratios. The 2-speed or overdrive unit performs its function using a planetary gear system in combination with two sets of clutch packs.

The operation of these clutch packs is controlled by a hydraulic circuit which causes the movement of the main finger plate via piston and accumulator assembly. The accumulator is used to regulate the speed at which the piston moves, and thus, the speed of the complete shift from direct to overdrive or vice-versa. This also serves to reduce shock-loading during speed shifting. The ECM is programmed to control the shift solenoid and thus, the entire overdrive unit. It does this by monitoring both vehicle speed and throttle position. The overdrive mode cannot occur when the 4-speed transmission is in 1st gear. Overdrive is automatically engaged at speeds above 110 mph. The overdrive mode can be forced off by means of a switch on the vehicle console.

Adjustments

LINKAGE

1. Disconnect the negative battery cable.
2. Remove the left seat from the vehicle. If equipped with power seats, disconnect the electrical leads.
3. Remove the shift knob and the console cover.
4. Remove the glove box lock.
5. Remove the left side panel from the console and the shifter cover.
6. Loosen the adjusting nuts on the shifter rods.
7. With the transmission and shifter in the neutral positions, install the alignment pin in shifter as illustrated.
8. Equalize the swivels on all 3 shift levers. Hand tighten the forward and rear adjusting nuts at the same time with equal force. Do this for all 3 shifter rods, then torque the forward and rear adjusting nuts at the same time to specifications.

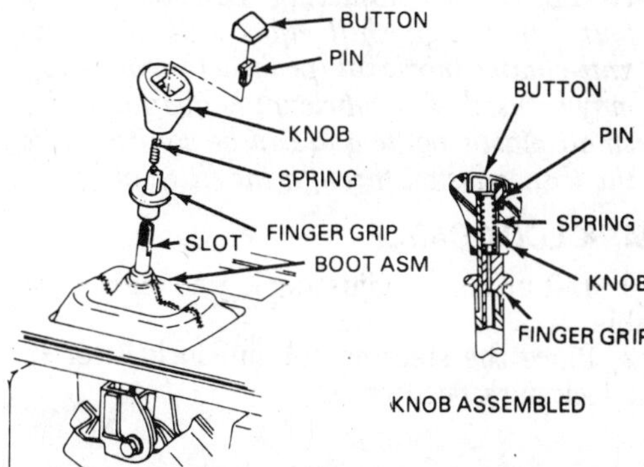

1. INSTALL FINGER GRIP ASM ONTO LEVER AND BRACKET ASM, ALIGNING TANG OF FINGER GRIP INTO SLOT OF LEVER AND BRACKET ASM SEATING FINGER GRIP ASM TO SHOULDER ON LEVER AND BRACKET ASM.
2. INSTALL SPRING INTO HOLE OF LEVER AND BRACKET ASM.
3. ASSEMBLE KNOB BY TURNING CLOCKWISE ONTO THREADS OF LEVER AND BRACKET ASM UNTIL FIRMLY SEATED IN PLACE. SLOT OF KNOB MUST BE IN LINE WITH SLOT OF LEVER AND BRACKET ASM.
4. ALIGN AND FIRMLY SEAT PIN INTO "T" SLOT OF KNOB AND SLOT OF LEVER AND BRACKET ASM.
5. ALIGN AND ASSEMBLE BUTTON INTO GROOVE OF KNOB THEN FIRMLY SEAT BUTTON IN PLACE AS SHOWN.

Shifter knob removal

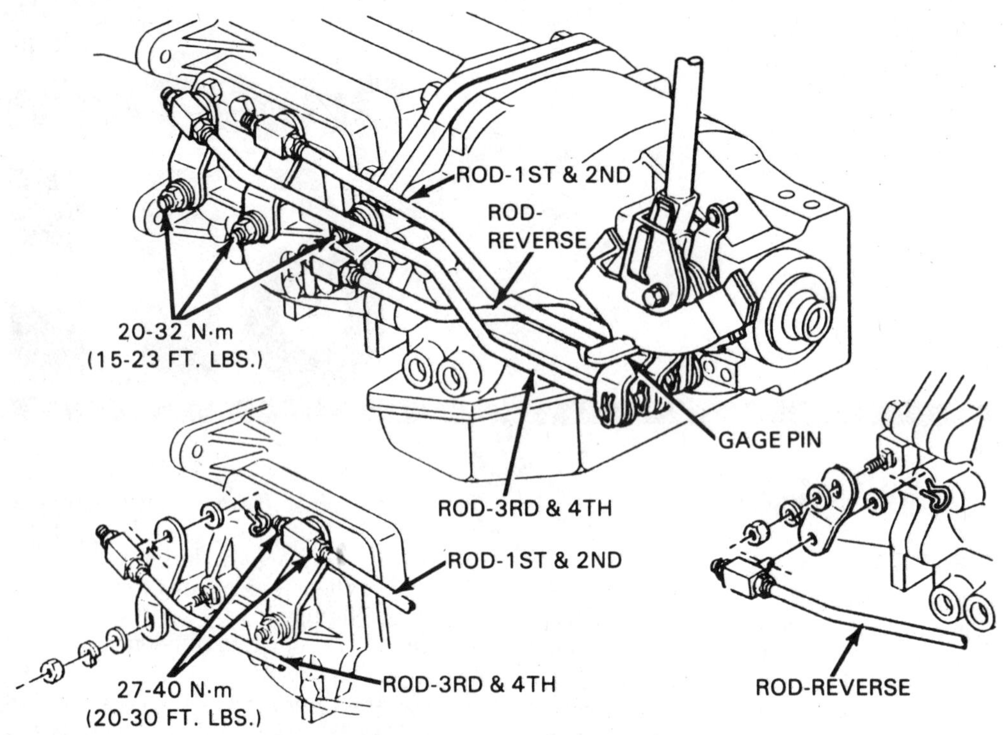

Linkage adjustments—4-speed overdrive transmission

9. To install the components, reverse the removal procedures. Lubricate all linkage pivot points.

NOTE: *If, after adjusting the linkage, it is found that high shift effort still exists, an anti-chatter lubricant (positraction additive) may be used. The lubricant is available in a small plastic bottle and can be squirted into the transmission through the filler plug.*

PARK LOCK CABLE

1. Lift up on the adjusting key to release the cable.
2. Place the steering column lock lever in the lock park position.
3. Shift the transmission into the reverse gear position.
4. Insert the gauge against the reverse stop and pull the reverse lever until the reverse pawl contacts the gauge.
5. Push down on the adjusting key to set the cable.
6. Remove the gauge, pull back on the shift lever, then insure that the pawl hits the stop and locks the shifter in the reverse position.

THROTTLE VALVE (TV) CABLE

1. If the cable has been removed and installed, check to see that the cable slider is in

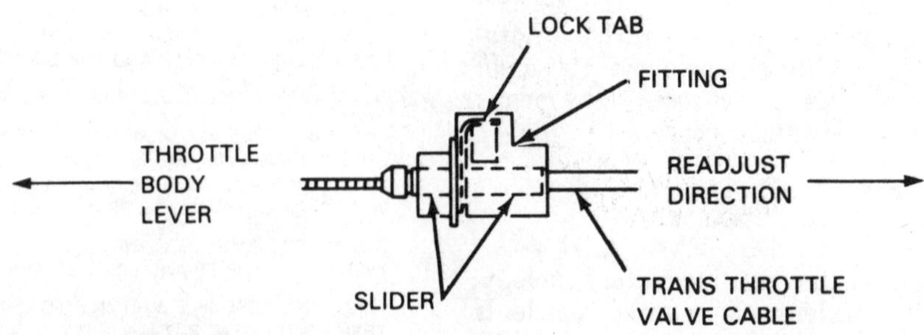

Adjusting the throttle valve cable lock—manual transmission

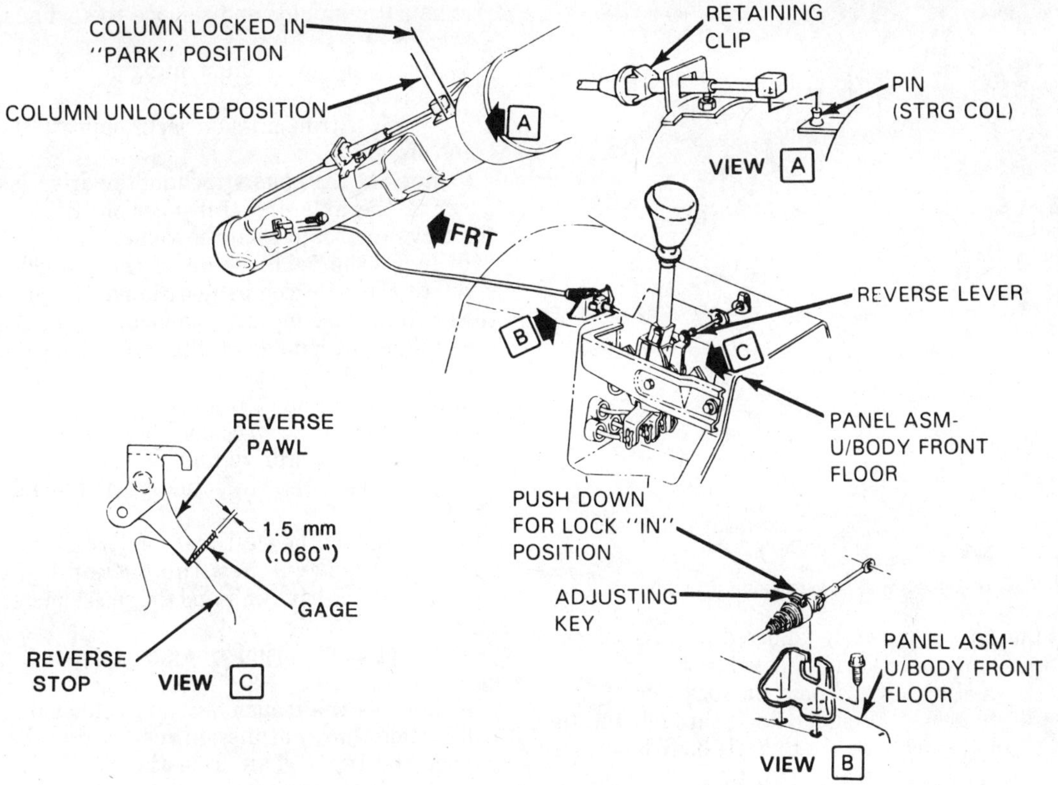

Adjusting the park lock cable—manual transmission

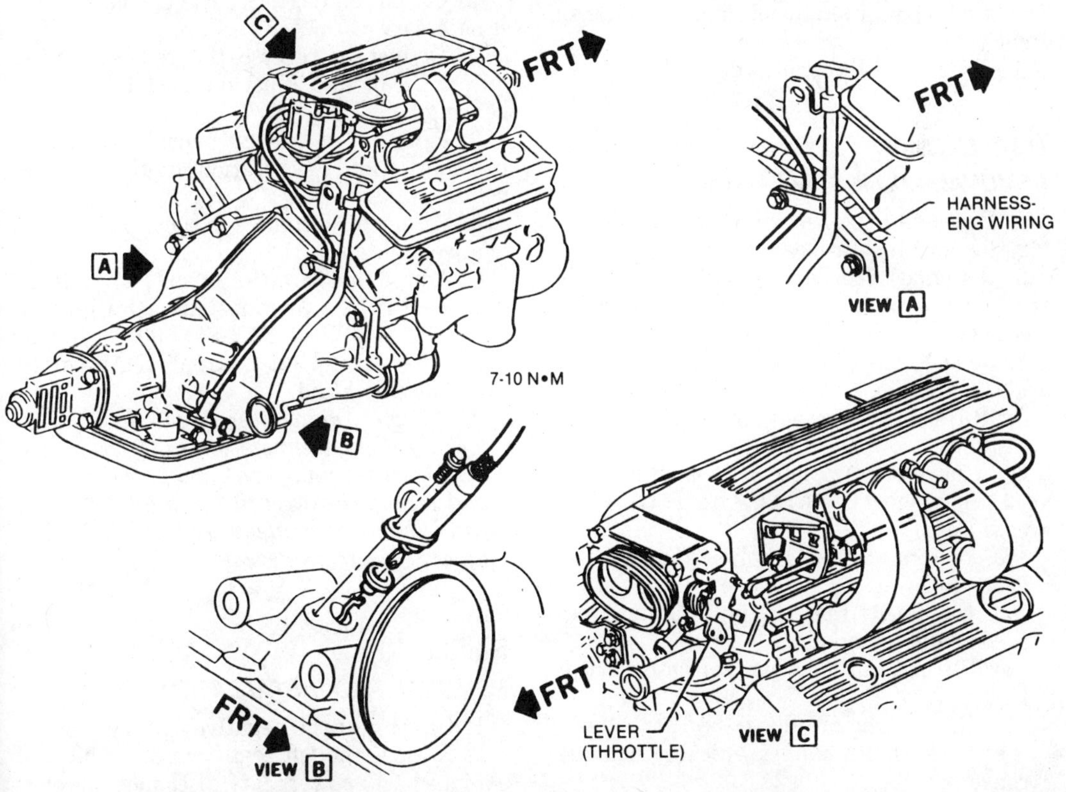

Adjusting the throttle valve cable—manual transmission

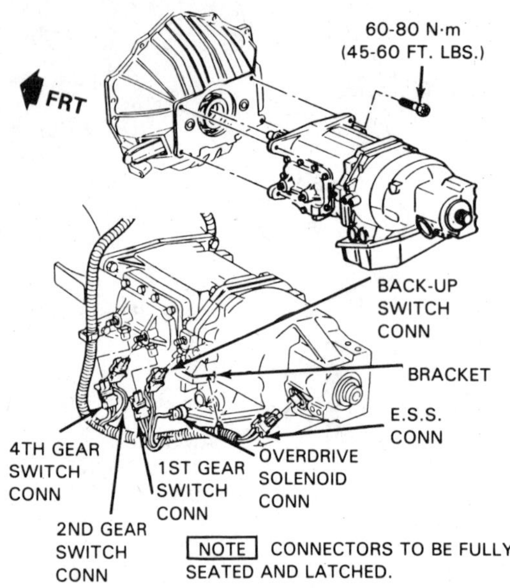

View of the manual transmission attachments

the zero or the fully adjusted position; if not, perform the following procedures:

a. Depress and hold the lock tab.

b. Move the slider back through the fitting (away from the throttle body lever) until it stops against the fitting.

c. Release the lock tab.

2. Rotate the throttle lever to the Full Throttle Stop position to obtain a minimum of 1 click.

3. Release the throttle lever

Transmission

REMOVAL AND INSTALLATION

1. Disconnect the negative battery cable.
2. Remove the air cleaner assembly.
3. Disconnect the Throttle Valve (TV) cable at the left throttle body unit (CFI) or throttle lever (TPI).
4. Remove the distributor cap and lay it aside.
5. Raise and support the vehicle on jackstands.
6. Remove the complete exhaust system assembly by performing the following procedures:

a. Disconnect the AIR pipe from the catalytic converter.

b. Disconnect the AIR pipe clamps from the exhaust manifold.

c. Disconnect the oxygen sensor electrical lead.

d. Remove the muffler-to-hanger bolts.

e. Remove the hanger bracket from the converter.

f. Disconnect the exhaust pipes from the exhaust manifolds and remove the exhaust system.

7. Remove the exhaust hanger from the transmission.
8. Using a transmission jack, support the transmission.
9. Remove the bolts attaching the driveline beam at the axle and transmission. Remove the driveline beam from the vehicle.
10. Mark the relationship of the propeller shaft to the axle companion flange. Remove the trunnion bearing straps and disengage the rear universal joint from the axle. Slide the propeller shaft slip yoke out from the overdrive unit and remove shaft from the vehicle.
11. Disconnect the oil cooler lines and the TV cable from the overdrive unit.
12. Disconnect the shift linkage at the side cover.
13. Disconnect the electrical connectors from the side cover switches, the backup light switch, the overdrive unit and the speedometer sensor.
14. Lower the transmission and support the engine.
15. Remove the transmission-to-bellhousing bolts. Slide the transmission rearward to disengage the input shaft from the clutch. Remove the transmission from the vehicle.
16. Inspect the clutch components for signs of wear or heat damage. See the Clutch Section, if necessary.
17. To install, reverse the removal procedures. Clean and repack the clutch release bearing.
18. Refer to the Rear Suspension Section for installation and specifications for the driveline beam.
19. Torque all fasteners to specifications. Do not overtighten.
20. Adjust the Throttle Valve (TV) cable.
21. Refill the transmission with fluid–(4 Speed) SAE-80W or SAE-80W-90 GL-5 gear lube–Overdrive Unit Dexron® II Automatic Transmission Fluid.

CAUTION: *Do not over-torque the bolts attaching the driveline beam to the transmission. Over-torquing can damage the bushing and seal in the overdrive unit and result in fluid leakage. Inadequate fluid level will damage the transmission.*

Shifter

REMOVAL AND INSTALLATION

1. Disconnect the negative battery cable.
2. Remove the left seat from the vehicle. If equipped with power seats, disconnect the electrical leads.

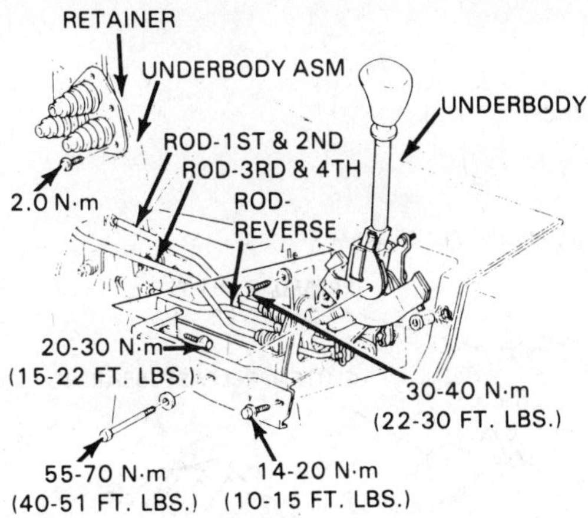

Shifter assembly removal

3. Remove the shifter lever knob and the glove box lock.
4. At the console, remove the left-side panel and the shifter cover.
5. At the shifter, remove the 3 control rods, the park lock cable, the cross bolt, the mounting bracket, the shifter-to-body panel bolt and the shifter assembly.
6. To install the components, reverse the removal procedures. Adjust the shift linkage and the Park Lock cable.

Oil Pan and Filter – Overdrive Unit

REMOVAL AND INSTALLATION

1. Raise and support the vehicle on jackstands.
2. With drain pan placed under overdrive oil pan, remove oil pan attaching bolts from the front and side of pan.
3. Loosen rear pan attaching bolts approximately four turns.
4. Carefully pry oil pan loose, allowing fluid to drain.
5. Remove remaining bolts and the oil pan.
6. Drain fluid from oil pan. Clean the pan with solvent and dry thoroughly with clean compressed air.
7. Remove the filter from the transmission.
8. To install, use a new filter, RTV sealant and reverse the removal procedures. Refill with Dexron®II automatic transmission fluid. DO NOT overfill.

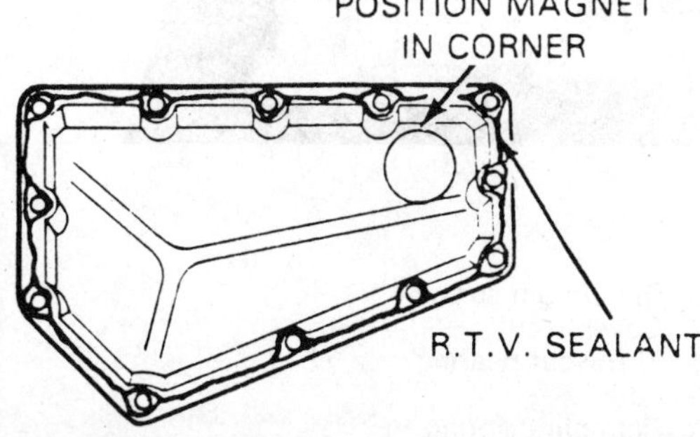

Place magnet as shown when installing the oil pan on the overdrive unit

CLUTCH

The vehicles use a hydraulic clutch system which consists of a master and a slave cylinder. When pressure is applied to the clutch pedal (pedal depressed), the push rod contacts the plunger and pushes it up the bore of the master cylinder. In the first $\frac{1}{32}$" of movement, the center valve seal closes the port to the fluid reservoir tank and as the plunger continues to move up the bore of the cylinder, the fluid is forced through the outlet line to the slave cylinder mounted on the clutch housing. As fluid is pushed down the pipe from the master cylinder, this in turn forces the piston in the slave cylinder outward. A push rod is connected to the slave cylinder and rides in the pocket of the clutch fork. As the slave cylinder piston moves rearward the push rod forces the clutch fork and release bearing to disengage the pressure plate from the clutch disc. On the return stroke (pedal released), the plunger moves back as a result of the return pressure of the clutch. Fluid returns to the master cylinder and the final movement of the plunger lifts the valve seal off the seat, allowing an unrestricted flow of fluid between system and reservoir.

A piston return spring in the slave cylinder preloads the clutch linkage and assures contact of the release bearing with the clutch release fingers at all times. As the driven disc wears, the diaphragm spring fingers move rearward forcing the release bearing, fork and push rod to move. This movement forces the slave cylinder piston forward in its bore, displacing hydraulic fluid up into the master cylinder reservoir, thereby providing the "self-adjusting" feature of the hydraulic clutch linkage system.

Before attempting to repair the clutch, transmission, hydraulic system or related linkages for any reason other than an obvious failure, the problem and probable cause should be identified. A large percentage of clutch and manual transmission problems are manifested by shifting difficulties such as high shift effort, gear clash and grinding or transmission blockout. When any of these problems occur, a careful analysis of these difficulties should be made, then the basic checks and adjustments

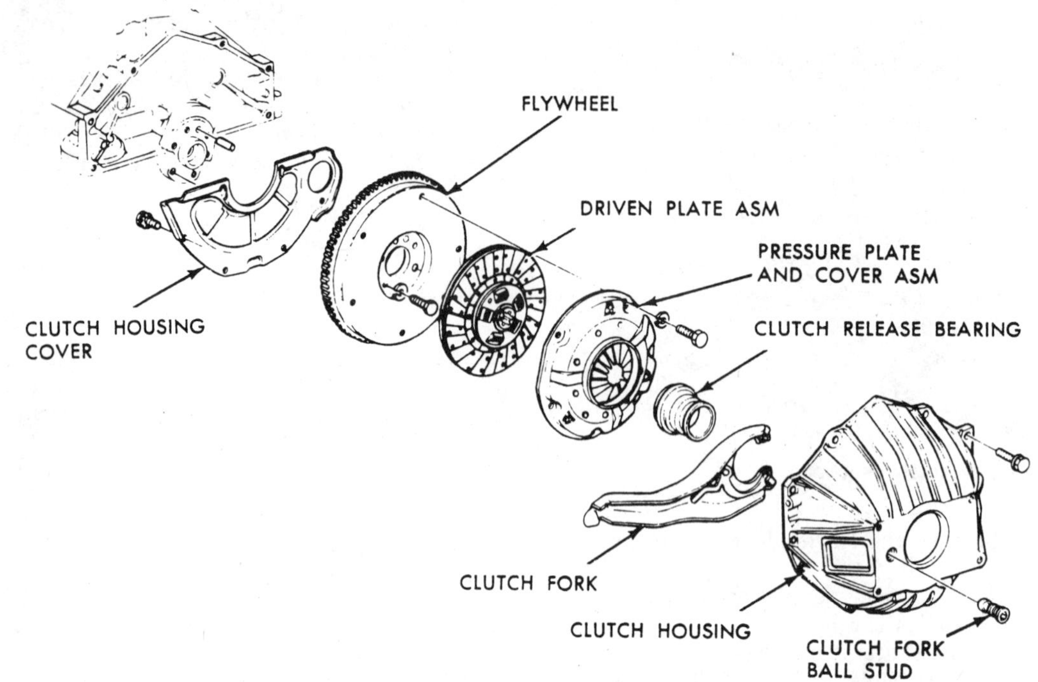

Typical clutch assembly

performed before removing the clutch or transmission for repairs. Run the engine at a normal idle with transmission in Neutral (clutch engaged). Disengage the clutch, wait about 10 seconds and shift the transmission into Reverse (no grinding noise should be heard). A grinding noise indicates incorrect clutch travel, lost motion, clutch misalignment or internal problems such as failed dampers, facings, cushion springs, diaphragm spring fingers, pressure plate drive straps, pivot rings or etc.

Adjustments

Since the hydraulic system provides automatic clutch adjustment, no adjustment of the clutch linkage or pedal height is required.

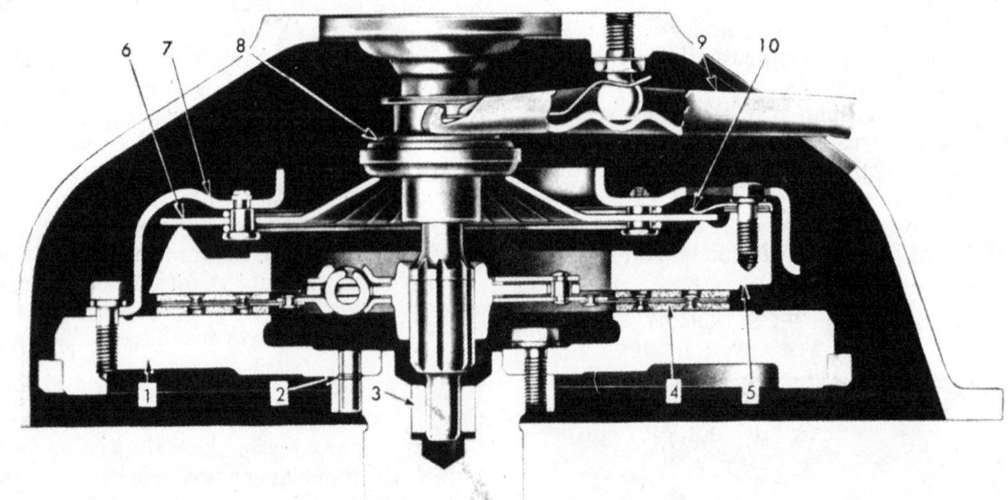

1. Flywheel
2. Dowel hole
3. Pilot bushing
4. Driven disc
5. Pressure plate
6. Diaphragm spring
7. Cover
8. Throwout bearing
9. Fork
10. Retracting spring

Cutaway of single disc clutch

Driven Disc And Pressure Plate

REMOVAL AND INSTALLATION

CAUTION: *The clutch driven disc contains asbestos, which has been determined to be a cancer causing agent. Never clean the clutch surfaces with compressed air! Avoid inhaling any dust from any clutch surface! When cleaning the clutch surfaces, use a commercially available brake cleaning fluid.*

1. Refer to the "Transmission, Removal and Installation" procedures in this section and remove the transmission from the vehicle.
2. Remove the slave cylinder attaching bolts and the bell housing.
3. Slide the clutch fork from the ball stud and remove the fork from the dust boot.

NOTE: *The ball stud is threaded into the clutch housing and is easily replaced.*

4. Install the Clutch Pilot tool No. J-5824 into the clutch plate to support it during removal.
5. The flywheel and clutch cover are marked with X's for correct assembly, if these are not visible, scribe new marks.
6. Gradually loosen the clutch-to-flywheel bolts one turn at a time until all spring pressure is released.
7. Remove the bolts and remove the clutch assembly.
8. To install, crank the engine over by hand until the X-mark on the flywheel is on the bottom.
9. Position the clutch disc and pressure plate in the same relative location as removed and support with the clutch pilot tool.

NOTE: *The clutch disc is installed with the damper springs and slinger toward the transmission.*

10. Rotate the clutch assembly until the X-marks on the flywheel and clutch assembly align. Align the cover bolt holes with those in the flywheel.
11. Install the bolts, then tighten evenly and gradually. Install the remaining bolts.
12. Remove the clutch pilot tool.
13. Lubricate the ball socket on the clutch fork and reinstall on the ball stud.
14. Pack the recess on the inside of the throwout bearing collar and the throwout groove with graphite grease.
15. Install the bell housing and the slave cylinder.
16. Install the throwout bearing on the fork. Lubricate the bearing groove.
17. To complete the installation, reverse the removal procedures. Lubricate and adjust the transmission shift linkages.

NOTE: *The clutch pilot bearing is an oil impregnated type bearing pressed into the crankshaft. This bearing requires attention when the clutch is removed from the vehicle, at which time it should be cleaned and inspected for excessive wear or damage and should be replaced (if necessary).*

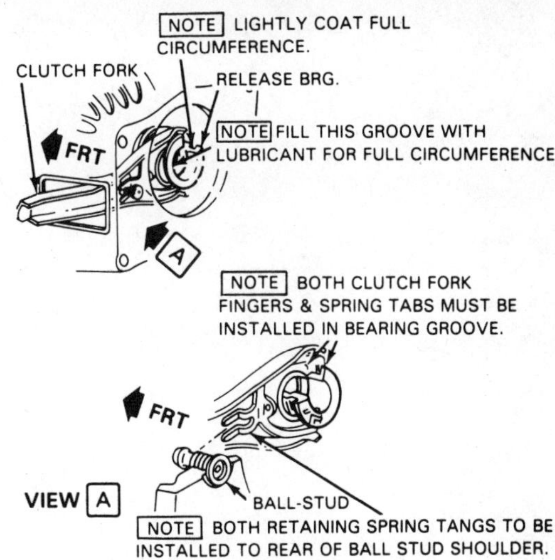

Clutch release bearing lubrication points—typical

Master Cylinder

REMOVAL AND INSTALLATION

1. Disconnect negative battery cable.
2. Remove hush panel from under dash.
3. Disconnect push rod from clutch pedal.
4. Disconnect hydraulic line from the clutch master cylinder.
5. Remove the mounting bolts for the master cylinder from the front of the dash assembly. Remove master cylinder and overhaul (if necessary).
6. To install, reverse the removal procedures. Torque the master cylinder-to-front of dash bolts to 15–22 ft. lbs. (20–30 Nm). Fill master cylinder with new hydraulic fluid con-

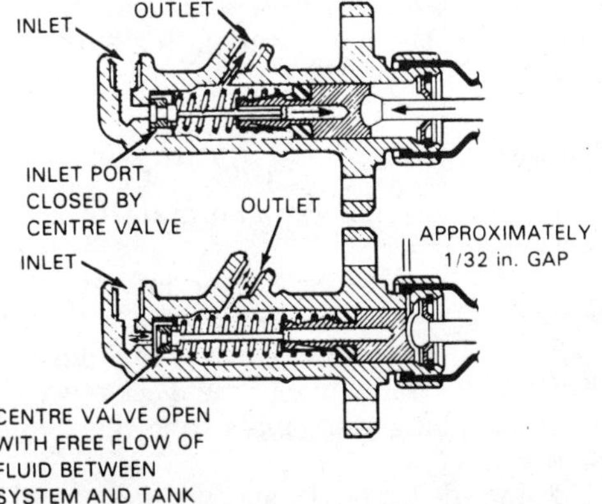

Cross section of the master cylinder of the hydraulic clutch system

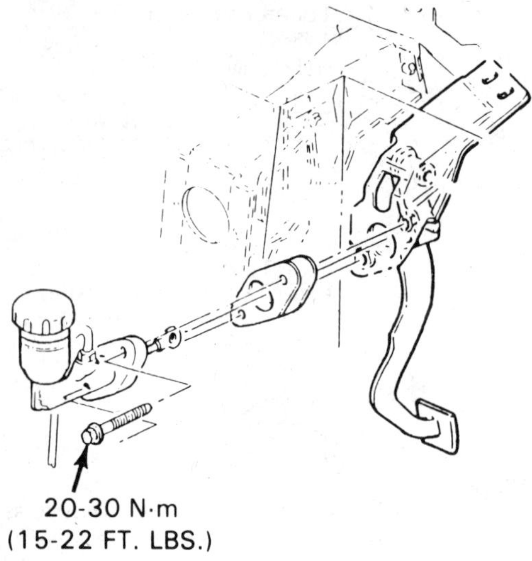

Clutch master cylinder mounting

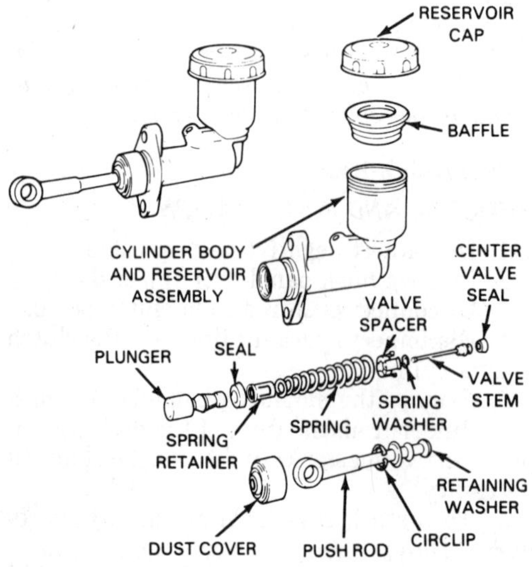

Exploded view of clutch master cylinder

forming to Dot 3 or Dot 4 specifications. Bleed and check the hydraulic clutch system for leaks.

OVERHAUL

1. Remove filler cap and drain fluid from master cylinder.
2. Pull back the dust cover and remove the circlip.
3. Remove retaining washer and push rod. Tap the master cylinder on a block of wood to eject the plunger assembly from the cylinder bore.
4. Lift the tab on the spring retainer and remove the spring assembly from the plunger.
5. Compress the spring to free the valve stem from the keyhole of the spring retainer.
6. Remove the spring, valve spacer and spring washer from the valve stem and the valve seal from the valve head.
7. Remove the seal carefully from the plunger, ensuring no damage occurs to the plunger surfaces.
8. Replace the seals and clean the remaining parts in clean brake fluid. Inspect the cylinder bore for visible scores, ridges and that it's smooth to the touch. Replace the master cylinder if any of the above conditions exist.
9. Fit the plunger seal to the plunger.
10. Fit the valve seal, smallest diameter leading to the valve head.
11. Position the spring washer on the valve stem so that it flares away from the valve stem shoulder and follow with valve spacer, legs (first) and spring.
12. Fit the spring retainer to the spring, then compress the spring until the valve stem passes through the key hole slot and engages in the center.
13. Fit the spring to the plunger and press the spring retainer tab to secure it.
14. Lubricate the seals and the cylinder bore with new hydraulic brake fluid conforming to Dot 3 or Dot 4 specifications.
15. Insert the plunger assembly, valve end leading into the cylinder bore (easing the entrance of the plunger seal).
16. Position the push rod and retaining washer into the cylinder bore. Install a new circlip to retain the push rod. Install dust cover onto the master cylinder. Lubricate the inside of the dust cover with Girling Rubber Grease or equivalent.

NOTE: *Be careful not to use any lubricant that will deteriorate rubber dust covers or seals.*

Slave Cylinder

REMOVAL AND INSTALLATION

1. Disconnect negative battery cable.
2. Raise and support the vehicle on jackstands.
3. Disconnect the hydraulic line from slave cylinder.
4. Remove the slave cylinder-to-clutch housing bolts.
5. Remove the push rod and the slave cylinder from the vehicle, then overhaul it (if necessary).
6. To install, reverse the removal procedures. Lubricate leading end of the slave cylinder with Girling Rubber Lube or equivalent. Torque mounting bolts to 20–30 ft. lbs. (26–40 Nm). Fill master cylinder with new brake fluid

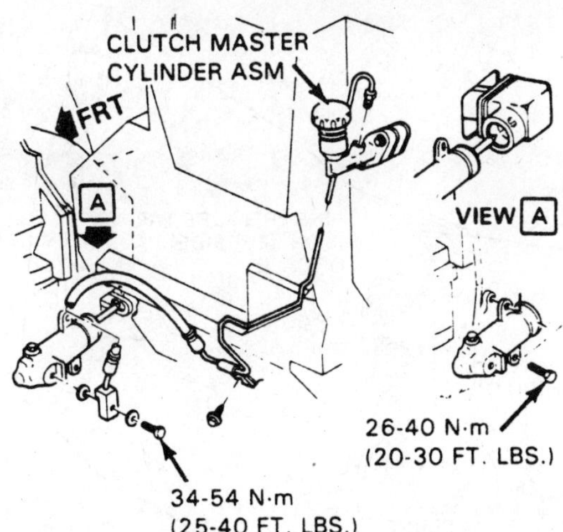

Clutch slave cylinder

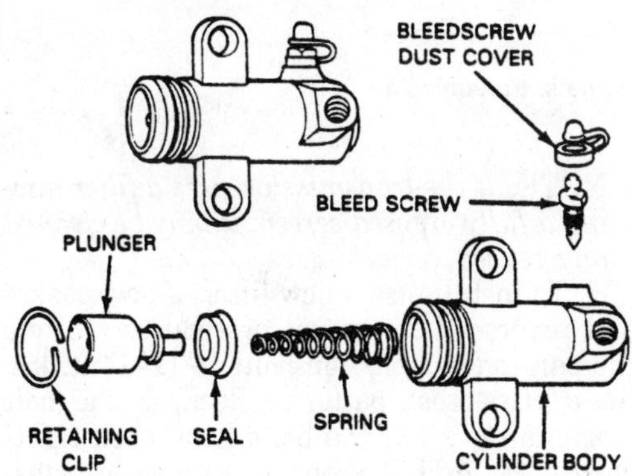

Exploded view of slave cylinder

conforming to Dot 3 or Dot 4 specifications. Bleed the hydraulic system.

OVERHAUL

1. Remove pushrod and dust cover from the slave cylinder, then inspect the cover for damage or deterioration.
2. Remove the retaining ring.
3. Tap the slave cylinder on a block of wood to eject the piston and seal.
4. Replace the seals and clean the remaining parts in clean brake fluid. Inspect the cylinder bore for visible scores, ridges and that it's smooth to the touch. Replace the slave cylinder if any of the above conditions exist.
5. Lubricate the seal and the piston bore with new brake fluid conforming to Dot 3 or Dot 4 specifications.
6. Position spring on piston.
7. Install the piston into the cylinder bore (easing the entrance of the plunger seal).
8. Install the retaining clip.

BLEEDING THE HYDRAULIC CLUTCH

Bleeding air from the hydraulic clutch system is necessary whenever any part of the system has been disconnected or the fluid level (in the reservoir) has been allowed to fall so low that air has been drawn into the master cylinder.

1. Fill master cylinder reservoir with new brake fluid conforming to Dot 3 or Dot 4 specifications.

   CAUTION: *Never, under any circumstances, use fluid which has been bled from a system to fill the reservoir as it may be aerated, have too much moisture content and possibly be contaminated.*
2. Raise and support the vehicle on jackstands.
3. Remove the slave cylinder attaching bolts.
4. Hold slave cylinder at approximately 45° with the bleeder at highest point. Fully depress clutch pedal and open the bleeder screw.
5. Close the bleeder screw and release clutch pedal.
6. Repeat the procedure until all of the air is evacuated from the system. Check and refill master cylinder reservoir as required to prevent air from being drawn through the master cylinder.

   NOTE: *Never release a depressed clutch pedal with the bleeder screw open or air will be drawn into the system.*

AUTOMATIC TRANSMISSION

Identification

The THM 700-R4 is a fully automatic transmission which provides 4 forward gears and a reverse gear. The oil pressure and shifting points are controlled by the throttle opening (via a Throttle Valve (TV) cable). An overdrive unit is used to provide better fuel economy.

Fluid Pan And Filter

REMOVAL AND INSTALLATION

NOTE: *The fluid should be drained with the transmission is warm.*

1. Raise and support the front of the vehicle with jackstands.
2. Place a drain pan under the transmission oil pan.
3. Remove the pan bolts from front and sides of the pan, then loosen the rear bolts 4 turns.
4. Using a small pry bar, pry the oil pan loose and allow the pan to partially drain. Remove the remaining pan bolts and carefully lower the pan away from the transmission.

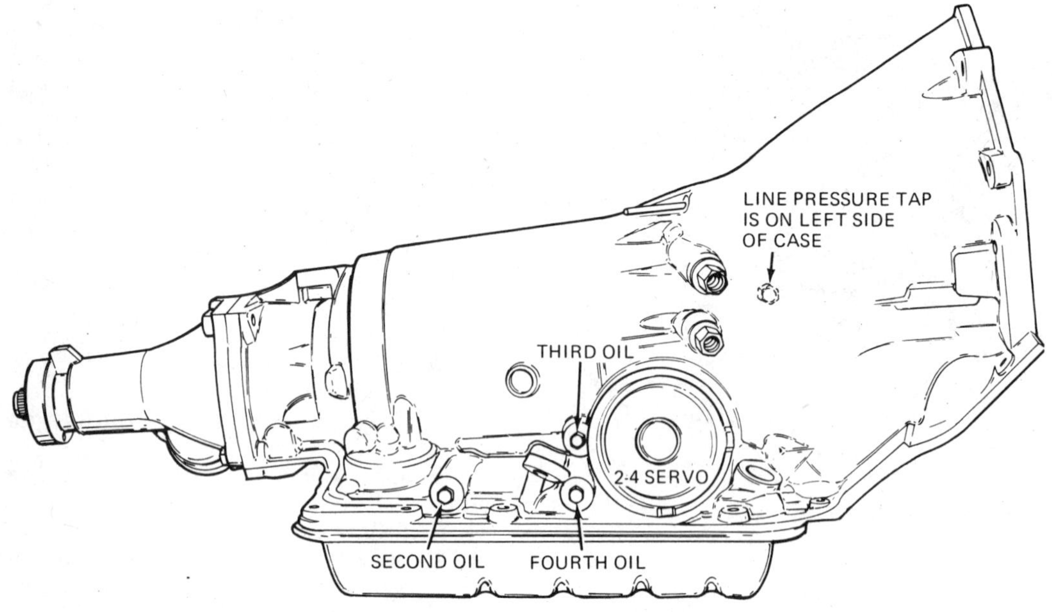

View of the THM 700-R4 automatic transmission

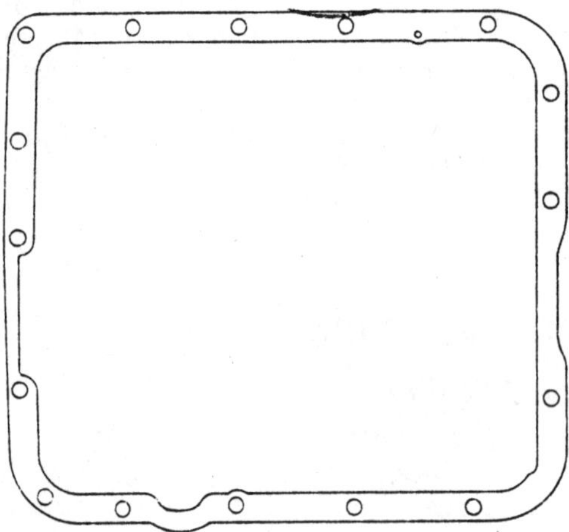

Turbo Hydra-Matic 700-R4

NOTE: *If the transmission fluid is dark or has a burnt smell, transmission damage is indicated. Have the transmission checked professionally.*

CAUTION: *If the pan sticks, carefully tap sideways on the pan with a rubber or plastic mallet to break it loose; DO NOT dent the pan.*

5. Empty and wash the pan in solvent, then blow dry with compressed air.
6. Using a putty knife, clean the gasket mounting surfaces.
7. Remove the transmission filter from the valve body. The filter may have either a fibrous or screen filtering element and is retained by one or two fasteners.

NOTE: *If the transmission uses a filter having a fully exposed screen, it may be cleaned and reused.*

8. To install, use a new filter, a new gasket and reverse the removal procedures. Torque the pan-to-transmission bolts to 12–14 ft. lbs. (in a criss-cross pattern). Recheck the bolt torque after all of the bolts have been tightened once. Add Dexron® II automatic transmission fluid through the filler tube.

CAUTION: *DO NOT OVERFILL the transmission; foaming of the fluid and subsequent transmission damage due to slippage will result.*

9. With the gearshift lever in PARK, start the engine and let it idle; DO NOT race the engine.
10. Move the gearshift lever through each position, holding the brakes. Return the lever to PARK and check the fluid level with the engine idling. The level should be between the two dimples on the dipstick, about 1/4" below the ADD mark. Add fluid, if necessary.
11. Check the fluid level after the vehicle has been driven enough to thoroughly warm up the transmission. Details are given under Fluid Level Checks earlier in Chapter 1. If the transmission is overfilled, the excess must be drained off. Use a suction pump, if necessary.

Adjustments

SHIFT LINKAGE

1. Raise and support the vehicle on jackstands.

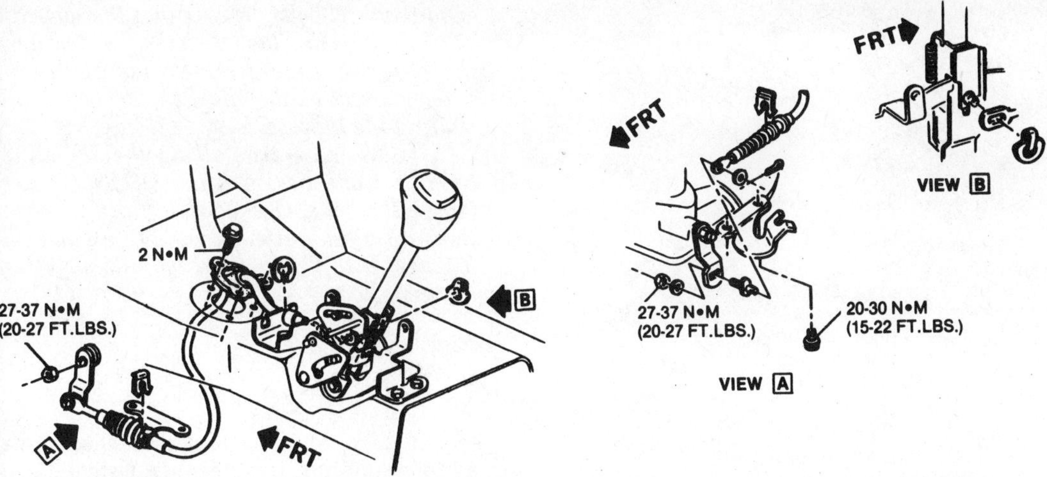

Adjusting the shift control cable

2. Disconnect the transmission control cable at the transmission lever. Rotate the transmission lever clockwise to the last detent position.

3. Push the shifter lever as far forward as possible, in the Park position.

4. Check the alignment of the control cable hole against the transmission lever stud. If the cable hole aligns with the stud, attach the cable with the washer and retaining pin; the adjustment is OK. If the stud and hole do not align, loosen the stud mounting nut and slide the stud as necessary to align it with the cable hole. Tighten the stud nut and attach the cable with the washer and retaining pin.

5. Lower the vehicle.

THROTTLE LINKAGE

Throttle Valve (TV) Cable

If the TV cable is broken, sticky, misadjusted or incorrect part for the model, the vehicle may exhibit various malfunctions, such as: delayed or full throttle shifts.

1. On the 1984 models, remove the air cleaner.

2. If the cable has been removed and installed, check to see that the cable slider is in the zero or the fully adjusted position; if not, perform the following procedures:

a. Depress and hold the lock tab.

b. Move the slider back through the fitting (away from the throttle body lever) until it stops against the fitting.

c. Release the lock tab.

3. Rotate the throttle lever to the Full Throttle Stop position to obtain a minimum of 1 click.

4. Release the throttle lever

PARK LOCK CABLE

1. Remove the shift lever plate from the console.

2. Lift up on the adjusting key to release the cable.

3. Place the steering column lock lever in the Locked position.

4. Place the shift lever in the rearward direction against the Park Stop position.

5. Push down on the adjusting key to set the cable.

6. Install the console shift lever plate.

Transmission

REMOVAL AND INSTALLATION

1. Raise the hood and place covers on both fenders.

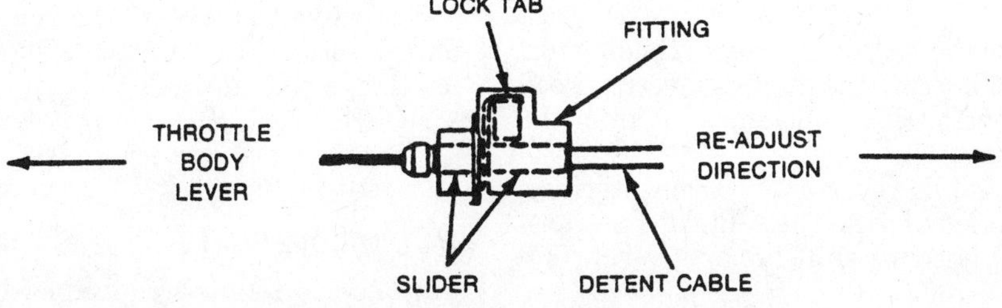

Throttle Valve (TV) cable adjustment

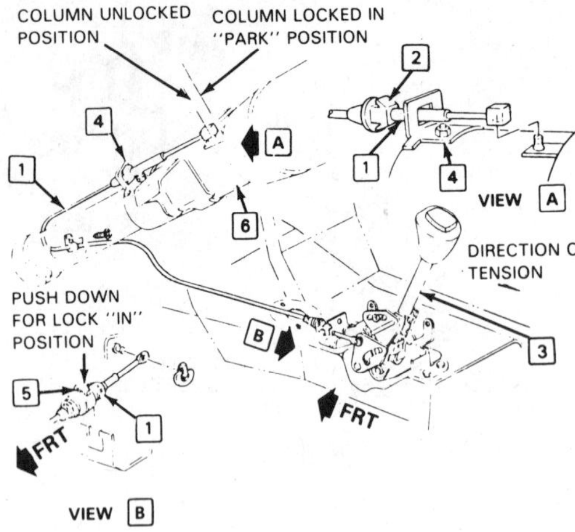

Adjusting the park lock cable

2. Disconnect the Throttle Valve (TV) cable from the throttle lever.
3. Remove the transmission oil dipstick and the dipstick tube bolt (if accessible).
4. Raise and support the vehicle on jackstands.
5. Disconnect the speedometer cable, the shift linkage and all of the electrical leads from the transmission, then any clips retaining the electrical leads to the case.
6. Remove the flywheel cover, then mark the flywheel and the torque converter to maintain balance during installation.
7. Remove the torque converter-to-flywheel bolts.
8. Remove the front section of the exhaust system.
9. Using a transmission jack, place it under, secure and raise the transmission slightly.
10. Remove the driveline beam and the driveshaft.
11. Lower the transmission to gain access to the oil cooler lines and the TV cable attachments.
12. Disconnect and plug the oil cooler and TV cable openings.
13. Using a vertical hoist, secure and support the engine. Remove the transmission-to-engine bolts.
14. Separate the transmission from the engine, be careful not to damage any cables, lines or linkage.
15. Using the Torque Converter Holding tool No. J-21366, secure the torque converter. Lower the transmission and remove it from the vehicle.
16. To install, reverse the removal procedures. Check and/or add new fluid to the transmission. Adjust the shift linkage and the TV cable.

NOTE: *When installing the torque converter-to-flywheel bolts, be sure that the converter's weld nuts are flush with the flywheel and the converter rotates freely (by hand). Install a new oil seal on the oil filler tube before installing the tube.*

CAUTION: *When installing the driveline beam-to-transmission bolts, DO NOT over torque the bolts. Over torquing can damage the transmission extension and result in fluid leakage. Insufficient fluid may damage the transmission.*

DRIVELINE

The vehicle uses two types of driveshafts: one made of aluminum and the other of steel. Each shaft is installed in the conventional manner.

The driveshaft is a balanced unit, it should be kept free of undercoating and other foreign material which may upset the balance.

Driveshaft and Universal Joints

REMOVAL AND INSTALLATION

1. Raise and support the vehicle on jackstands.
2. Remove the complete exhaust system by performing the following procedures:
    a. Disconnect the AIR pipe from the catalytic converter.
    b. Disconnect the AIR pipe clamps from the exhaust pipe.
    c. Disconnect the electrical connector from the oxygen sensor.
    d. Remove the muffler-to-hanger bolts.
    e. Disconnect the exhaust pipes from the exhaust manifold and remove the exhaust system.
3. Remove the support beam-to-axle/transmission bolts and the beam from the vehicle.
4. Mark the driveshaft-to-companion flange relationship so that it may be reinstalled in its original position. Remove the trunnion bearing strap bolts from the driveshaft.
5. Using tape, wrap the bearing cups to the trunnion to prevent losing the bearing rollers.
6. Push the front yoke into the transmission and remove the driveshaft by pulling it down and to the rear.
7. To install, reverse the removal procedures. Torque the trunnion strap-to-companion flange bolts to 12 ft. lbs.

NOTE: *Check the universal joints and replace damaged or worn units.*

U-JOINT OVERHAUL

The universal joints are lubed-for-life (without grease fittings). Whenever universal joints are

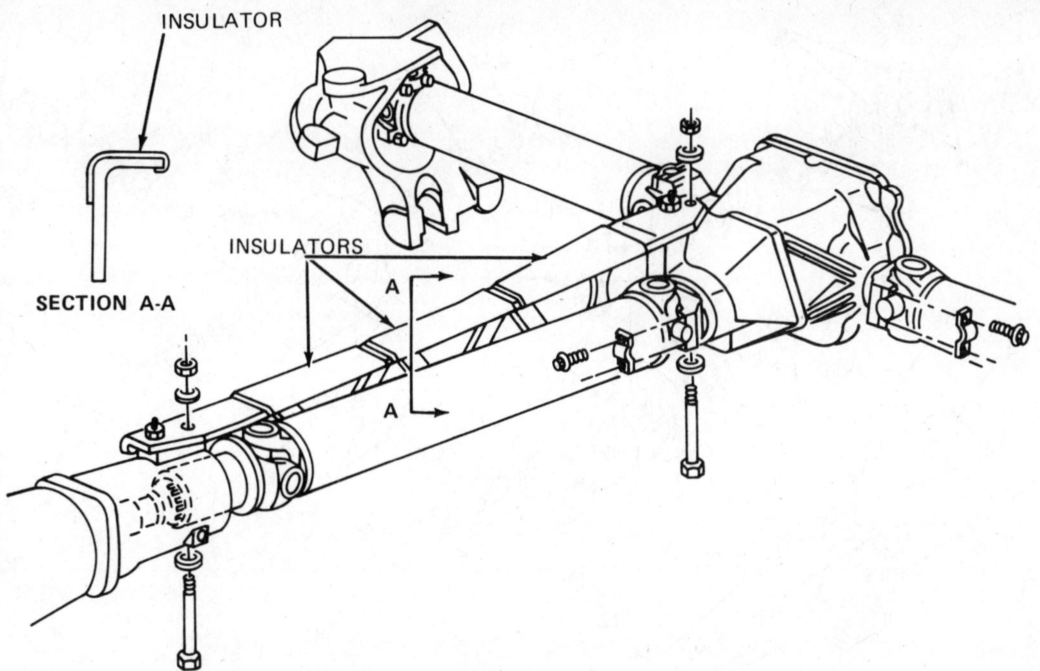

View of the driveshaft and the support beam

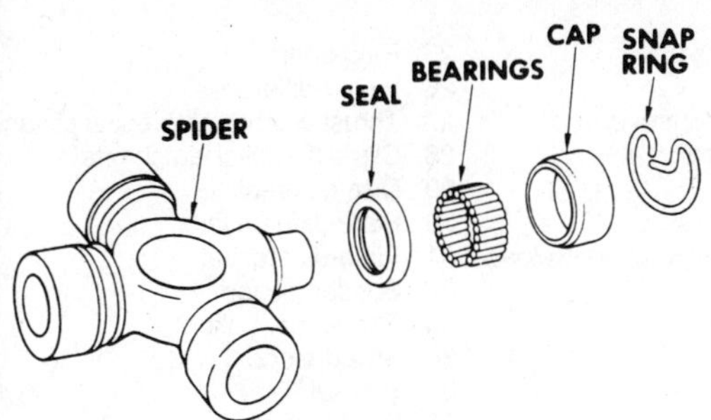

Typical universal joint assembly

removed from the vehicle, they should be checked and regreased.

1. Remove the bearing lock rings from the universal joint and the universal joint from the driveshaft. These can sometimes be tapped out but stubborn joints must be pressed out.
2. Remove the bearing cups and seals, being careful not to lose any roller bearings.
3. Inspect the cups and trunnion ends for damage or wear. Ensure that all bearing rollers are present. Replace the rubber seals.
4. Clean the cups and rollers. Repack the cup with grease and reassemble the joint.

REAR AXLE

Identification

Two types of Dana rear axle carriers (made of aluminum) are used on the Corvette: Model 36 (7⅞" ring gear) for automatic transmissions and Model 44 (8½" ring gear) for manual transmissions.

The identification number is located on the bottom surface of the carrier at the cover mounting flange.

Determining Axle Ratio

An axle ratio is obtained by dividing the number of teeth on the drive pinion gear into the number of teeth on the ring gear. For instance, on a 3.07:1 ratio, the driveshaft will turn 3.07 times for every turn of the rear wheels.

The most accurate way to determine the axle ratio is to drain the differential, remove the cover and count the number of teeth on the ring and pinion.

An easier method is raise and support the rear of the vehicle on jackstands. Make a chalk mark on the rear wheel and the driveshaft. Block the front wheels and put the transmission in Neutral. Turn the rear wheel one complete revolution and count the number of turns made by the driveshaft. The number of driveshaft rotations is the axle ratio. More accuracy can be obtained by going more than one tire revolution and dividing the result by the number of tire rotations.

The axle ratio is also identified by the axle serial number prefix on the axle; the axle ratios are listed in the dealer's parts books according to the prefix number.

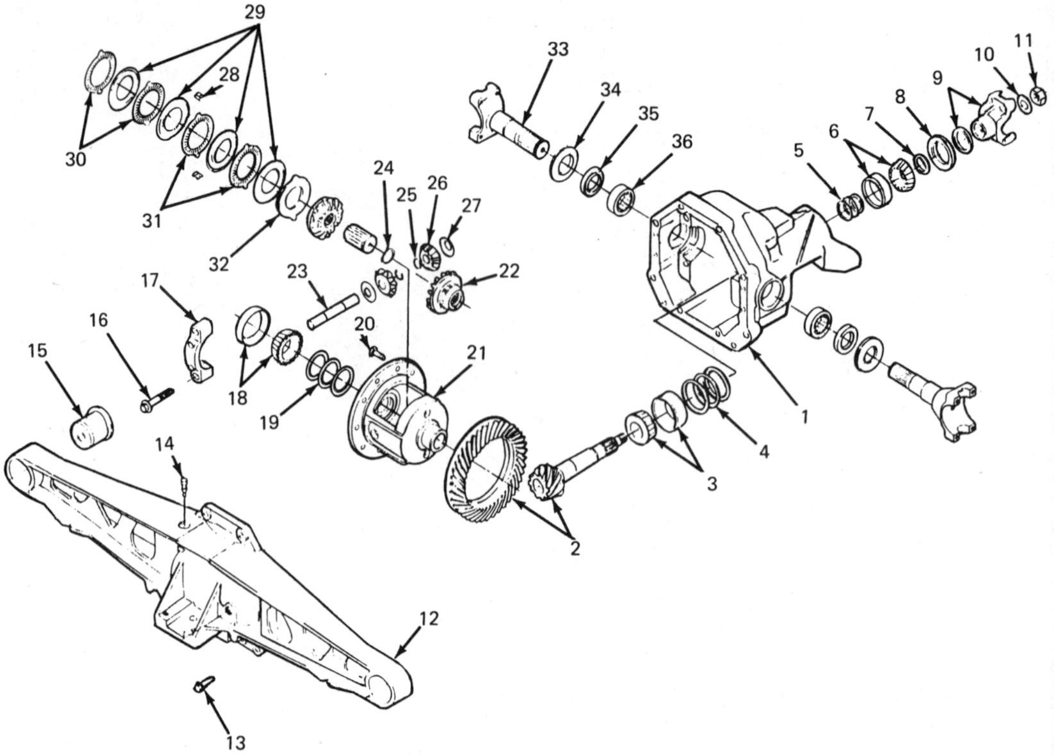

1. Carrier
2. Ring & pinion gear
3. Bearing-inner pinion
4. Shims-pinion adjusting
5. Shims-pinion bearing preload
6. Bearing-outer pinion preload
7. Slinger-pinion outer
8. Seal-pinion outer
9. Assembly-end yoke
10. Washer-pinion nut
11. Nut-pinion
12. Arm-lower control cover assembly
13. Screw-carrier cover
14. Vent-breather
15. Bushing-lower control arm
16. Screw-bearing cap
17. Cap-bearing
18. Bearing-differential
19. Shims-differential bearing preload
20. Screw-ring gear
21. Case-differential
22. Gear-differential side
23. Shaft-differential
24. Ring-snap
25. Ring-snap
26. Pinion-differential
27. Thrust washer-differential pinion
28. Clip-differential clutch retainer
29. Disc-differential
30. Plate-differential
31. Plate-differential
32. Spacer-dished
33. Shaft-inner yoke
34. Shield-stone
35. Seal-oil
36. Bearing-inner yoke shaft

Exploded view of the differential

Drive Axle Shaft

REMOVAL AND INSTALLATION

1. Raise and support the rear of the vehicle on jackstands.
2. Remove the rear wheel/tire assembly.
3. Disconnect the leaf spring and the tie-rod end from the knuckle
4. Place a scribe match-mark on the cam bolt and on the mounting bracket so that their relationship will be properly maintained during assembly.
5. Remove the cam bolt and separate the spindle support rod form the carrier mounting bracket.
6. Remove the drive axle shaft trunnion straps from the spindle and the side gear yoke.
7. Pull outward on the wheel/tire assembly,

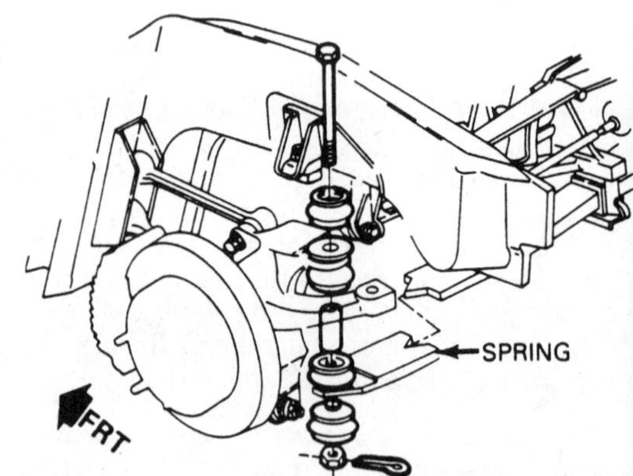

1. Brake pedal support
2. Switch
3. Switch bracket
4. Clip
5. Brake pedal
6. Acutator

Removing the leaf spring from the knuckle

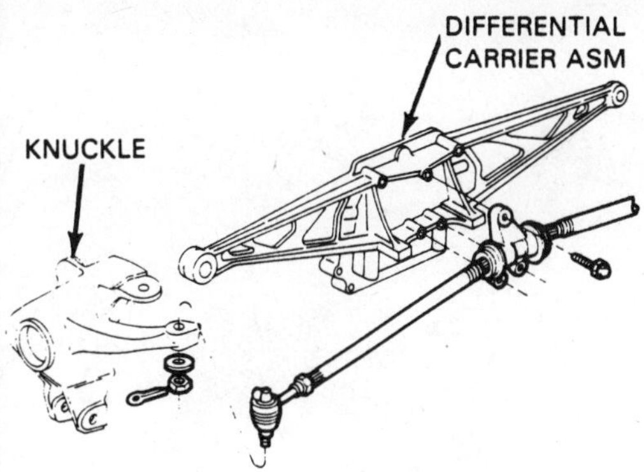

Removing the tie-rod end from the knuckle

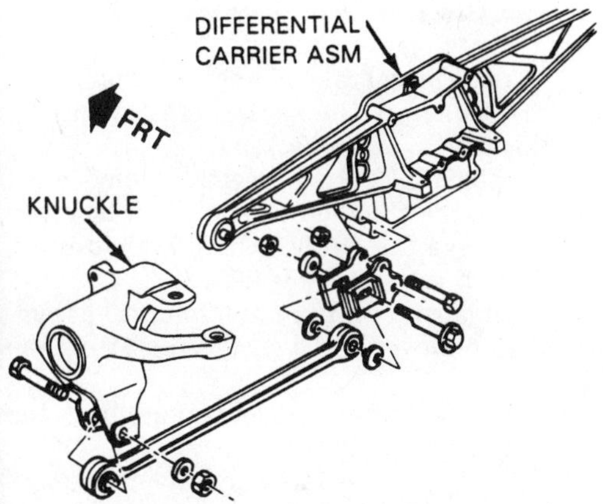

Removing the spindle support rod from the carrier mounting bracket

then remove the drive axle shaft and the plastic stone shield.

8. If necessary, replace the univeral joints.
9. To install, reverse the removal procedures. Realign the cam bolt scribe mark with the mark on the bracket. Check and/or adjust the rear suspension alignment.

Differential Carrier

REMOVAL AND INSTALLATION

1. Remove the air cleaner and the distributor cap from the distributor.
2. Raise and support the vehicle on jackstands.
3. Remove the spare tire cover support hooks, the cover and the spare tire.
4. Remove the exhaust system by performing the following procedures:
   a. Disconnect the AIR pipe from the catalytic converter and the AIR pipe clamps from the exhaust pipe.
   b. Disconnect the electrical lead from the oxygen sensor.
   c. Remove the muffler-to-hanger bolts.

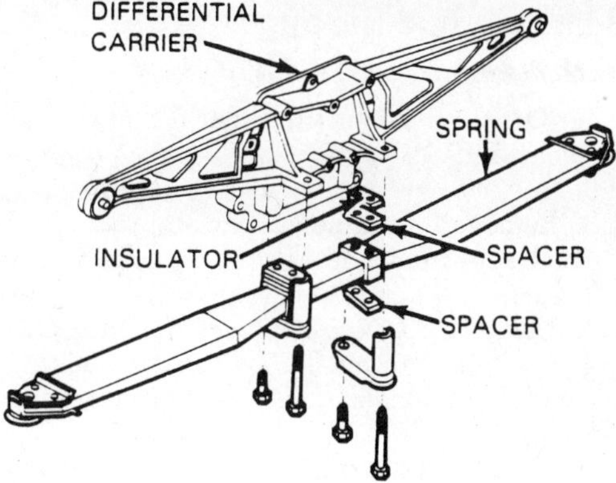

Removing the leaf spring from the differential carrier

   d. Remove the hanger bracket at the catalytic converter.
   e. Disconnect the exhaust pipes from the exhaust manifolds, then remove the exhaust system.
5. Disconnect the leaf spring from the knuckles and remove the leaf spring-to-carrier cover bolts, then remove the leaf spring from the vehicle.
6. Using a scribing tool, mark the cam bolts-to-bracket. Remove the cam bolts, then the mounting bracket from the carrier.
7. Disconnect the tie-rods from the knuckles.
8. Remove the drive axle shaft trunnion straps from the side gear yokes. Push the wheel/tire assemblies outward and disengage the trunnions from the side gear yokes.
9. Remove the driveshaft-to-pinion flange trunnion straps. Push the driveshaft forward (to disengage from the pinion flange) and tie the shaft to the support beam.
10. Using a floor jack, support the transmission.
11. Remove the differential carrier cover/beam-to-frame bracket bolts.
12. Remove the support beam-to-differential carrier bolts and the differential carrier from the vehicle.
13. To install, apply sealant to the top/bottom of the support beam mounting surfaces and reverse the removal procedures. Torque the cover beam-to-carrier bolts to 21–24 ft. lbs. (model 36) or 32–38 (model 44), the trunnion strap-to-pinion bolts to 15–20 ft. lbs., the trunnion strap-to-yoke bolts to 22–30 ft. lbs., the carrier cover beam-to-body bolts to 81–96 ft. lbs., the support beam-to-transmission bolts to 33–40 ft. lbs. and the support beam-to-carrier bolts to 51–67 ft. lbs.
14. Check and adjust the rear suspension. Check and/or add fluid to the differential carrier.

Rear Hub And Bearing

REMOVAL AND INSTALLATION

1. Raise and support the rear of the vehicle on jackstands.
2. Remove the rear wheel/tire assembly.
3. Remove the brake caliper and rotor.
4. Disconnect the leaf spring from the knuckle.
5. Using tool J-34161, remove the hub/bearing assembly-to-knuckle bolts, the backing plate and the hub/bearing assembly from the vehicle.
6. Remove cotter pin, the spindle nut and washer from the spindle.
7. Remove the hub/bearing assembly from the vehicle. Support the parking brake backing plate.
8. If necessary, replace the hub wheel bearing.
9. To install, use a new seal and reverse the removal procedures. Torque the hub/bearing assembly-to-knuckle bolts to 59–73 ft. lbs. and the spindle nut to 81 ft. lbs.

NOTE: *Before adjusting the rear suspension alignment, be sure to have the weight of the vehicle resting of it wheels.*

10. Check and/or adjust the rear suspension alignment.

Rear Wheel Spindle

REMOVAL AND INSTALLATION

1. Raise and support the rear of the vehicle on jackstands.
2. Remove the rear wheel/tire assembly.

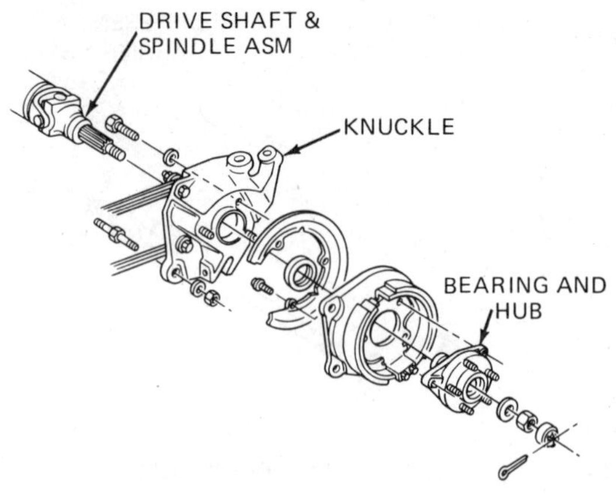

Exploded view of the rear wheel assembly

3. Remove the brake caliper and rotor.
4. Disconnect the leaf spring from the knuckle
5. At the hub/bearing assembly, remove the cotter pin, the spindle nut and the washer.
6. Remove the drive axle shaft trunnion straps from the spindle yoke.
7. Pull outward on the hub/knuckle assembly, then remove the drive axle shaft from the spindle.
8. Remove the rear wheel spindle from the hub/bearing assembly.
9. If necessary, replace the univeral joints.
10. To install, reverse the removal procedures. Torque the spindle-to-hub/bearing assembly nut to 81 ft. lbs. and the drive axle shaft-to-spindle trunnion strap bolts to 22-29 ft. lbs. Check and/or adjust the rear suspension alignment.

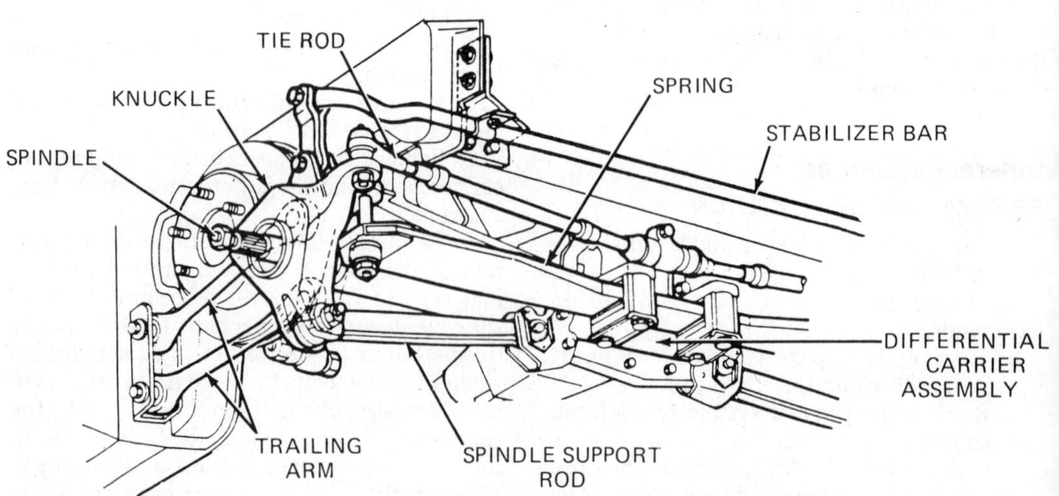

View of the rear wheel suspension assembly

Suspension and Steering 7

FRONT SUSPENSION

The front suspension uses aluminum for all its major components. These include forged aluminum arms and knuckles and replaces conventional coil springs with a lighter, more durable transverse fiberglass monoleaf spring. Other elements of the front suspension system include long life stabilizer link bushings and the use of spindle offset. Spindle offset is achieved by moving the center of the wheel rearward from the conventional location on line through the ball joints.

The displacement contributes to the directional sense. Combined with +3° caster, spindle offset gives an effect similar to higher caster without the poor responsiveness.

Transverse Leaf Spring

REMOVAL AND INSTALLATION

1. Raise and support the front of the vehicle on jackstands.
2. Remove the wheel and tire assemblies.
3. Remove both spring protectors and the spring mounting nuts, then push the bolts up.
4. Install the Spring Compressing tool No. J-33432 or equivalent.
5. Using the Ball Joint Removal tool No. J-33436-9, disconnect the lower ball joints.
6. Compress the leaf spring tool.
7. Remove the lower shock/stabilizer bracket-to-lower control arm bolts, the lower shock/stabilizer-to-bracket bolts and the bracket from the vehicle.

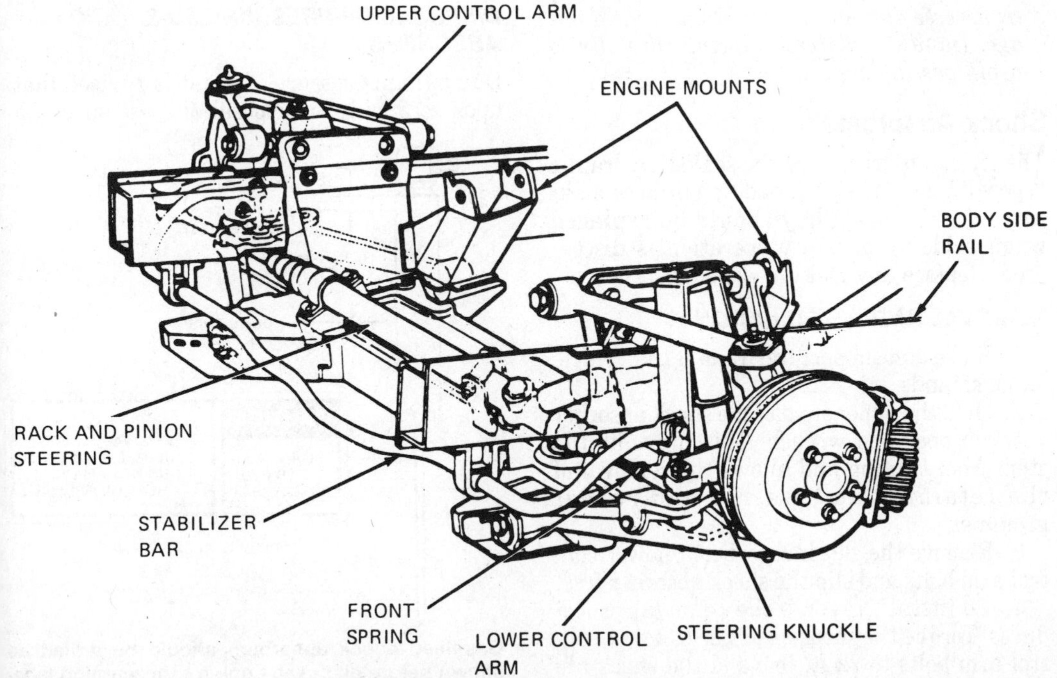

Front suspension on 1984 and later models

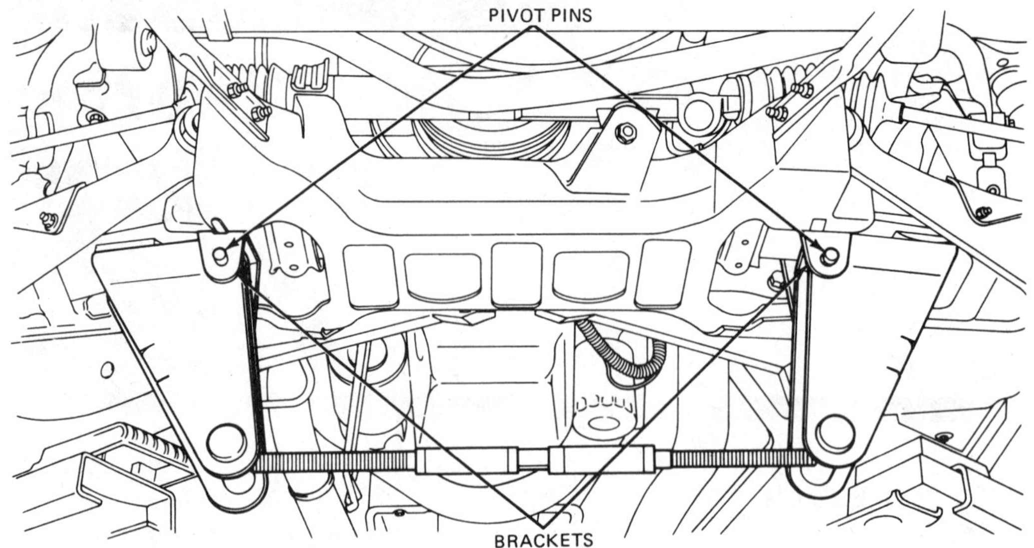

Transverse leaf spring removal requires the use of a spring compressor as shown. The pivot pins are removable so that the bracket may be placed over the top of the spring. See text for OEM tool numbers

8. Release and remove the Leaf Spring Compressor tool.
9. Using an assistant, pull both of the lower control down to the full travel position, then remove the spring; be careful not to scratch the spring.
10. Install the spring by reversing the removal procedure. Torque all nuts and bolts to specifications and check the front end alignment.

NOTE: *During removal and installation of transverse spring take care to prevent damage. Handle compressed spring carefully to avoid possible injury.*

Shock Absorbers

The shock absorbers are the sealed, hydraulic type with no provision for adding fluid or making adjustments. They should be replaced when evidence of faulty operation is discovered. Replace any leaking shock absorber.

REMOVAL AND INSTALLATION

1. Raise and support the front of the vehicle on jackstands.
2. Hold the upper stem of the shock absorber with an open-end wrench. This prevents the stem from turning and allows the removal of the retaining nut, washer and rubber grommet.
3. Remove the shock absorber-to-lower control arm bolts and slip the shock absorber free.
4. To install, reverse the removal procedures. Torque the shock absorber-to-lower control arm bolts to 22 ft. lbs. and the shock absorber-to-chassis nut to 19 ft. lbs.

BOUNCE TEST

Each shock absorber can be tested by bouncing the corner of the vehicle until the maximum up and down movement is obtained. Release the vehicle. It should stop bouncing in 1–2 bounces. Compare both front corners or both rear corners but do not compare the front to the rear. If one corner bounces longer than the other it should be inspected for damage and possibly be replaced.

DISPOSAL OF PRESSURIZED SHOCK ABSORBERS

Due to high pressure of gas it is advised that, upon scrapping or disposal of these shock ab-

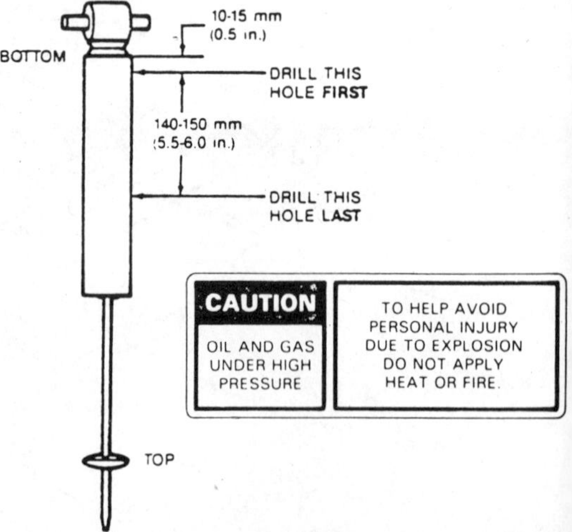

Gas-filled shock absorbers should be drilled as shown before disposal. Look for the warning label to identify gas shocks on 1984 and later models

sorbers, the pressure be released. This is carried out as follows:

1. Clamp shock in vise with piston rod pointing down.
2. Measure approx. 0.5 in. (10–15mm) from bottom of shock and drill an approx. 5mm hole so the gas can escape.
3. Measure approx. 5.5–6.0 in. (140–150mm) from first hole and drill a approx. 5mm hole to facilitate drainage of oil. Drain all oil from shock absorber.
4. Dispose of the shock absorber.

Upper Ball Joint

INSPECTION

Erratic front suspension behavior or alignment difficulties suggest possible excessive ball-joint wear. To check the upper ball joint, perform the following procedures:

1. Raise and support the front of the vehicle on jackstands (as near as possible to the lower ball joint) so that the front suspension hangs freely.
2. Position a dial indicator against the bottom of the wheel rim.
3. Grasping the wheel assembly (top and bottom), push the bottom of the tire IN and pull the top of the tire OUT. Read the dial indicator.
4. Reverse the push/pull procedure and read the dial indicator.
5. The horizontal deflection should not be more than 0.125 in. (3.18mm).
6. If the dial indicator reading exceeds 0.125 in. (3.18mm) or if any ball joint looseness (ball joint disconnected from the steering knuckle) is detected, replace the ball joint.

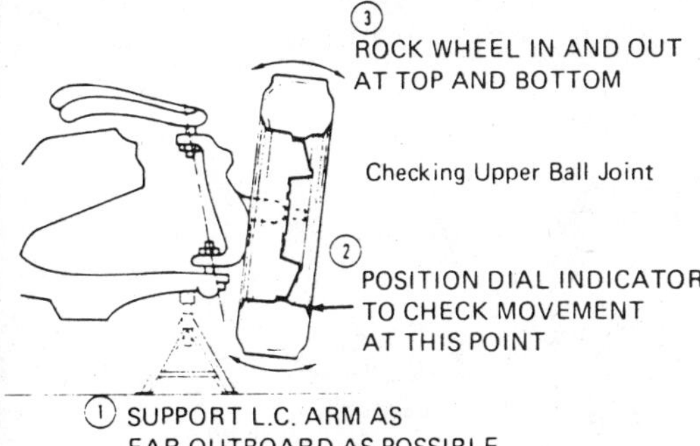

Inspecting the upper wheel bearing

REMOVAL AND INSTALLATION

Replacement of the ball joints may be done without removing the control arms from the vehicle.

1. Raise and support the front of the vehicle on jackstands. Remove the wheel/tire assembly. Be sure that the lift is positioned so that the front suspension will hang freely.
2. Remove the stabilizer link from the lower control arm.
3. Remove the cotter pin, the nut and washer from the upper ball joint.
4. Using the Ball Joint Removal tool No. J-33436-9, separate the top ball joint from the steering knuckle and let the knuckle and the wheel hub hang unsupported.

NOTE: *The upper ball joint assembly is riveted to the upper control arm.*

5. To remove the upper ball joint-to-upper control arm rivets, perform the following procedures:
   a. Using a center punch, place a punch mark on the rivet heads.
   b. Using an ⅛" drill bit, drill into the bodies of the rivets.

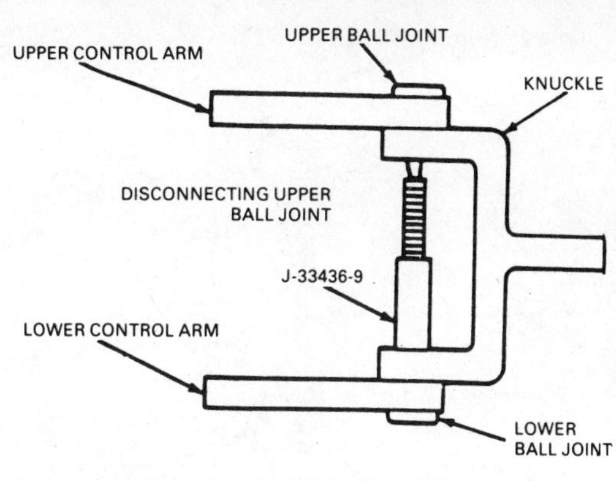

Separating the upper ball joint from the steering knuckle

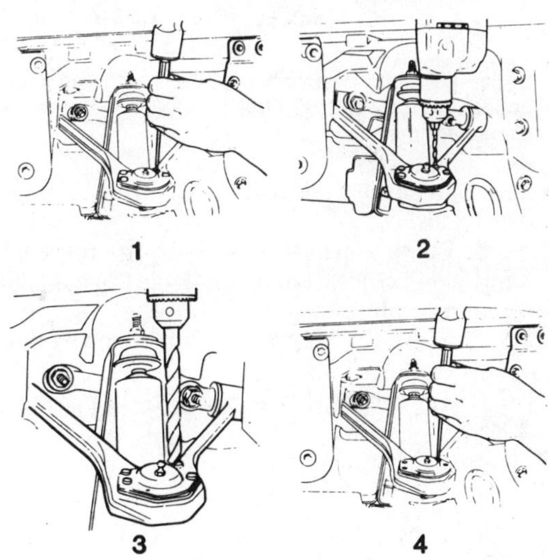

Removing the upper ball joint-to-upper control arm rivets

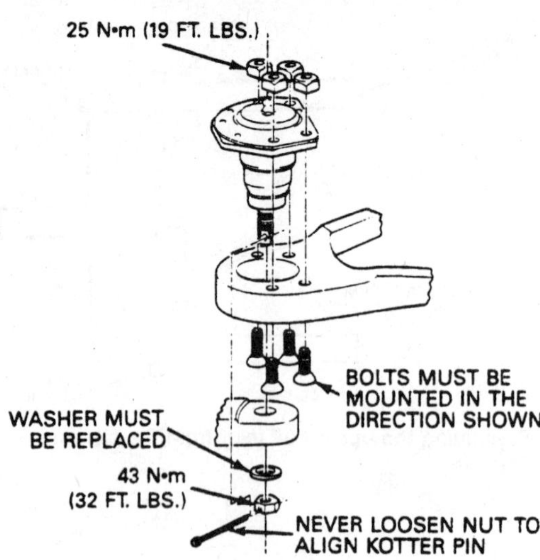

Upper ball joint installation. OEM rivets must be drilled and replaced with bolts supplied with the replacement part

c. Using a ⅜–½″ drill bit, drill off the rivet heads.

d. Using a drift punch, drive the remaining rivet bodies from the ball joint-to-control arm assembly.

6. Remove the upper ball joint from the upper control arm.

7. Using a putty knife, clean the upper control arm mounting surface. Check for signs of cracks or other damage.

8. Measure the thread diameter of the kit-supplied mounting bolts and drill out the control arm rivet holes to the appropriate size (if necessary).

9. To install, use a new ball joint and a new cotter pin, then reverse the removal procedures. Torque the upper ball joint-to-upper control arm bolts to 19 ft. lbs. (25 Nm) and the upper ball joint-to-steering knuckle nut to 32 ft. lbs. (43 Nm).

Lower Ball Joint

INSPECTION

The lower control arm ball joint is equipped with a visual wear indicator. With the weight of the vehicle resting on the tires, measure the distance between the ball joint housing socket and the grease fitting-to-ball joint housing socket mating surface, found on the bottom side of the ball joint. A difference in measurement of more than 0.050 in. (1.27mm) indicates replacement of the lower ball joint.

REMOVAL AND INSTALLATION

Replacement of the ball joints may be done without removing the control arms from the vehicle.

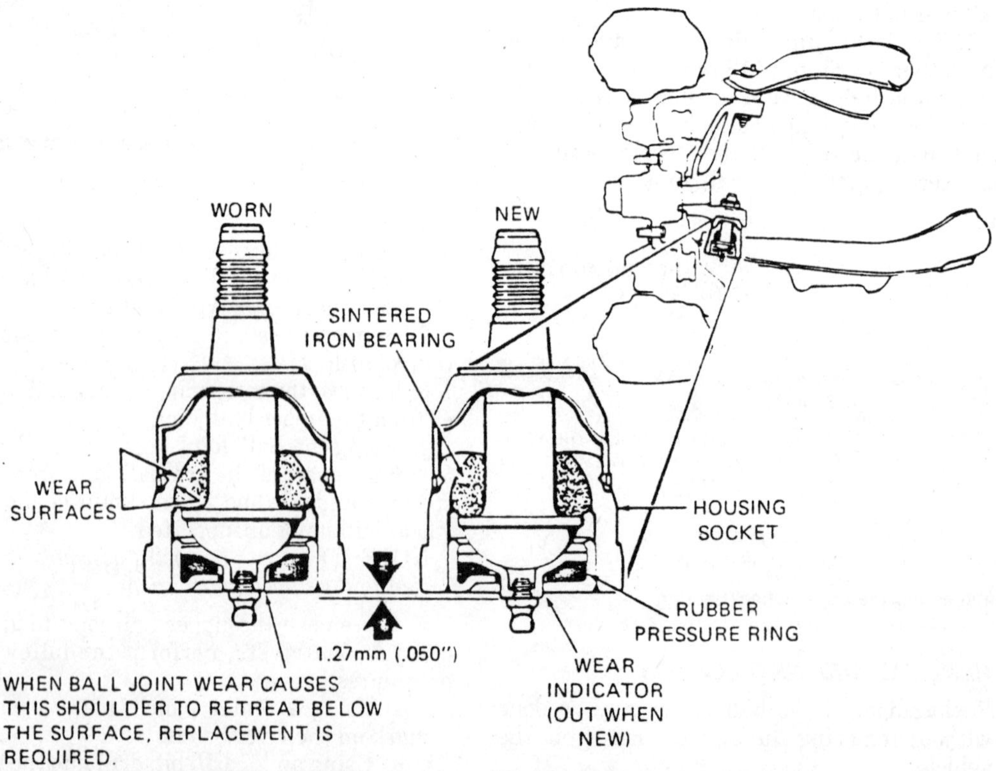

WORN

NEW

SINTERED IRON BEARING

WEAR SURFACES

HOUSING SOCKET

RUBBER PRESSURE RING

1.27mm (.050")

WEAR INDICATOR (OUT WHEN NEW)

WHEN BALL JOINT WEAR CAUSES THIS SHOULDER TO RETREAT BELOW THE SURFACE, REPLACEMENT IS REQUIRED.

Typical ball joint inspection, showing how to check wear indicator

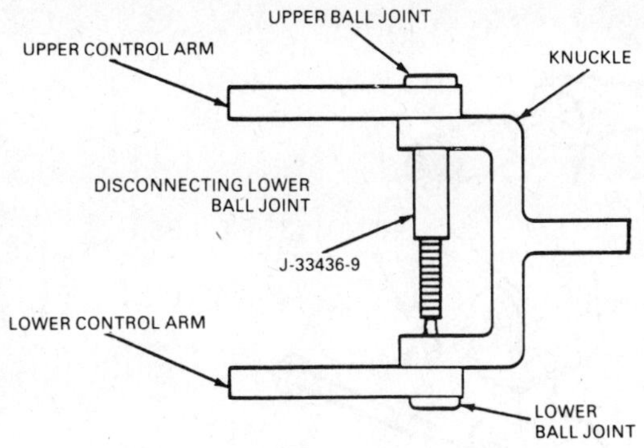

Separating the lower ball joint from the steering knuckle

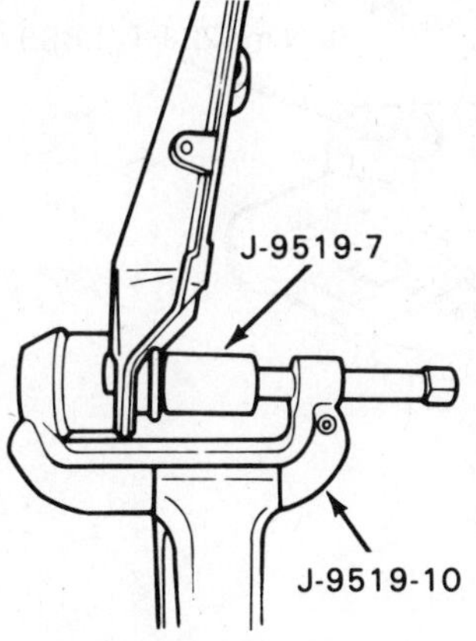

Removing the lower ball joint from the lower control arm

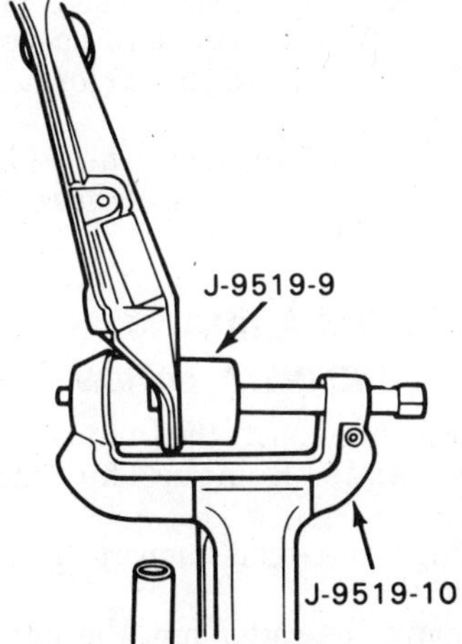

Installing a new lower ball joint into the lower control arm

1. Raise and support the front of the vehicle on jackstands. Remove the wheel/tire assembly. Be sure that the jackstands are positioned so that the front suspension will hang freely.

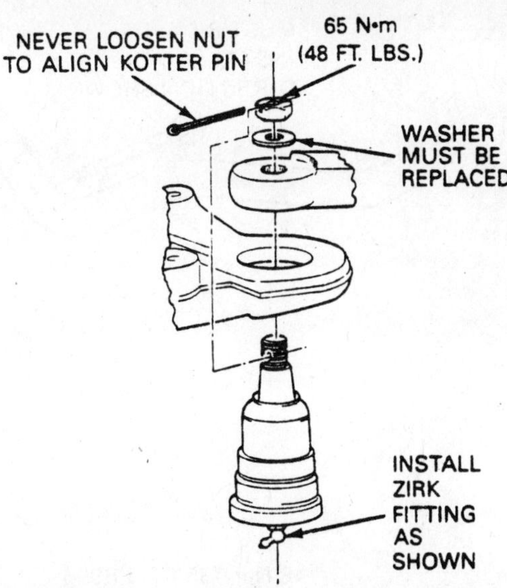

Lower ball joint installation—typical

2. Remove the stabilizer link from the lower control arm.
3. Remove the cotter pin, the nut and washer from the lower ball joint.
4. Using the Ball Joint Removal tool No. J-33436-9, separate the lower ball joint/lower control arm assembly from the steering knuckle.
5. Using the Ball Joint Removal tools No. J-9519-7 and No. J-9519-10, press the lower ball joint from the lower control arm.
6. Clean the mounting surface on the lower control arm and check for signs of cracks or other damage.
7. Using the Ball Joint Installation tools No. J-9519-9 and tool No. J-9519-10, press a new lower ball joint into the lower control arm, until it is seated.
8. To complete the installation procedures, reverse the removal procedures. Torque the lower ball joint-to-steering knuckle nut to 48 ft. lbs. (65 Nm). Install a new cotter pin.

Stabilizer Bar

REMOVAL AND INSTALLATION

The stabilizer bar is rubber-mounted to the frame in two locations and attaches to the lower control arms through two links.

1. Raise and support the vehicle vehicle on jackstands.
2. Disconnect the end links from the stabilizer bar.
3. Remove the stabilizer bar-to-frame retainers, then remove the stabilizer bar from the vehicle.

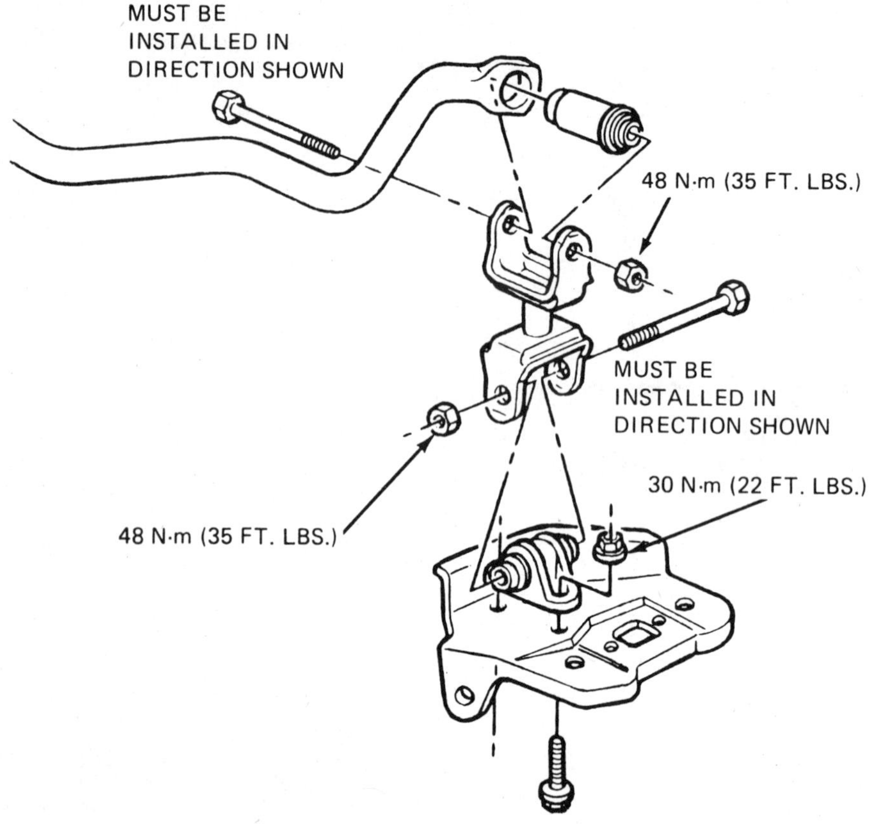

Stabilizer shaft linkage

4. To install, reverse the removal procedures and adjust the trim height.

NOTE: *Hand-tighten all connections until the bar and links are fully assembled.*

5. To adjust the trim height, perform the following procedures:

a. Tighten all of the connections and lower the vehicle.

b. Check and/or adjust the tire pressure; the fuel tank and cooling system MUST BE full.

c. With your hands, raise the front of the vehicle and allow it to settle at least 3 times.

d. With your hands, push down on the front of the vehicle and allow it to rise.

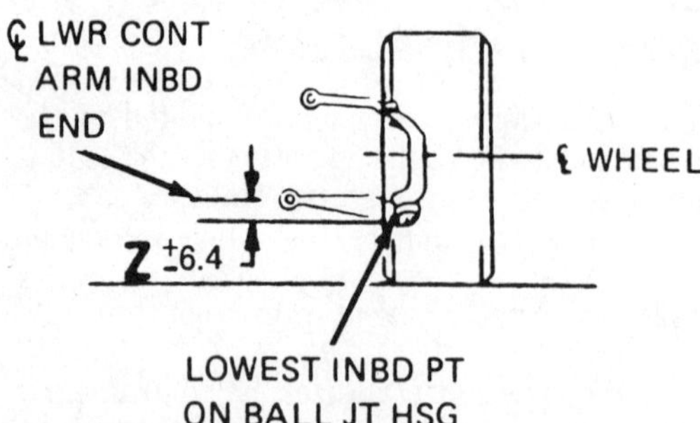

Adjusting the front suspension height

e. Check the "Z" height (distance from the center of the lower control arm-to-frame bolt to the bottom of the lower control arm's ball joint); the dimension should be 1.58–2.07 in. (40.1–52.6mm) for standard suspension or 1.78–2.28 in. (45.1–57.9mm) for heavy duty suspension.

7. Raise and support the vehicle on jackstands, then tighten all of the connections.

Upper Control Arm

REMOVAL AND INSTALLATION

1. Raise and support the front of the vehicle on jackstands. Remove the wheel/tire assembly.

2. Using a jackstand, support the lower control arm.

3. Remove the cotter pin, the nut and the washer from the upper control arm-to-steering knuckle ball joint.

4. Using the Ball Joint Disconnecting tool No. J-33436, disconnect the upper ball joint from the steering knuckle.

5. Count the shims at each end of the cross-shaft, then unbolt it from the frame and remove the upper control arm.

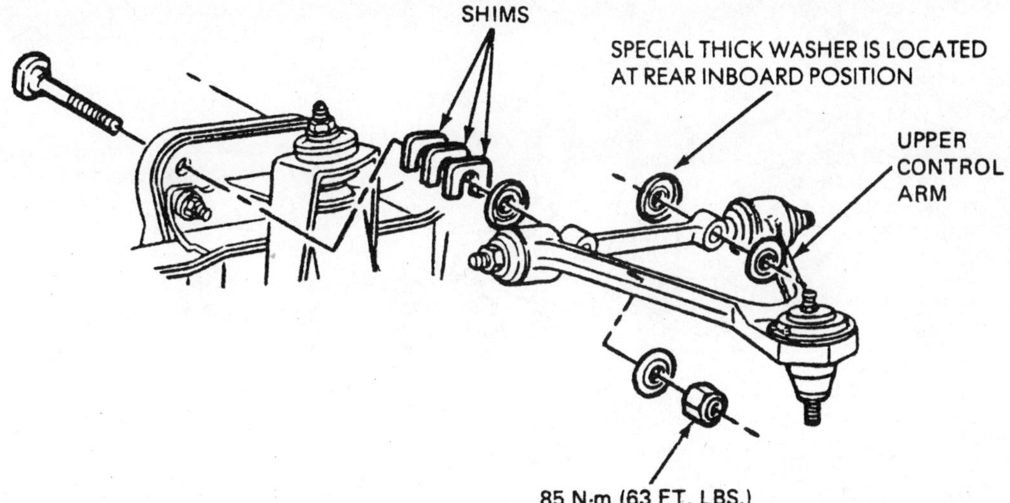

Upper control arm chassis mounting

6. To install, reverse the removal procedure. Check the front end alignment. Torque the upper control arm-to-chassis bolts to 63 ft. lbs. (85 Nm). and the upper control arm ball joint-to-steering knuckle nut to 32 ft. lbs. (43 Nm).

Lower Control Arm

REMOVAL AND INSTALLATION

1. Raise and support the front of the vehicle on jackstands. Remove the wheel/tire assembly.
2. Remove the front transverse leaf spring protector.
3. Using the Spring Compressor tool No. J-33432, compress the transverse leaf spring.
4. Disconnect the stabilizer bar and the shock absorber from the lower shock absorber mounting bracket. Remove the lower shock absorber mounting bracket from the lower control arm.
5. Remove the cotter pin, the nut and the washer from the lower control arm-to-steering knuckle ball joint.
6. Using the Ball Joint Disconnecting tool No. J-33436, disconnect the lower ball joint from the steering knuckle.
7. Remove the lower control arm-to-chassis bolts and the control arm from the vehicle.
8. To install, reverse the removal procedures. Adjust the suspension to curb height and torque the bolts. Torque the lower control arm-to-chassis bolts to 96 ft. lbs. (130 Nm), the lower ball joint-to-steering knuckle nut to 48 ft. lbs. and shock absorber bracket-to-lower control arm bolts to 22 ft. lbs.

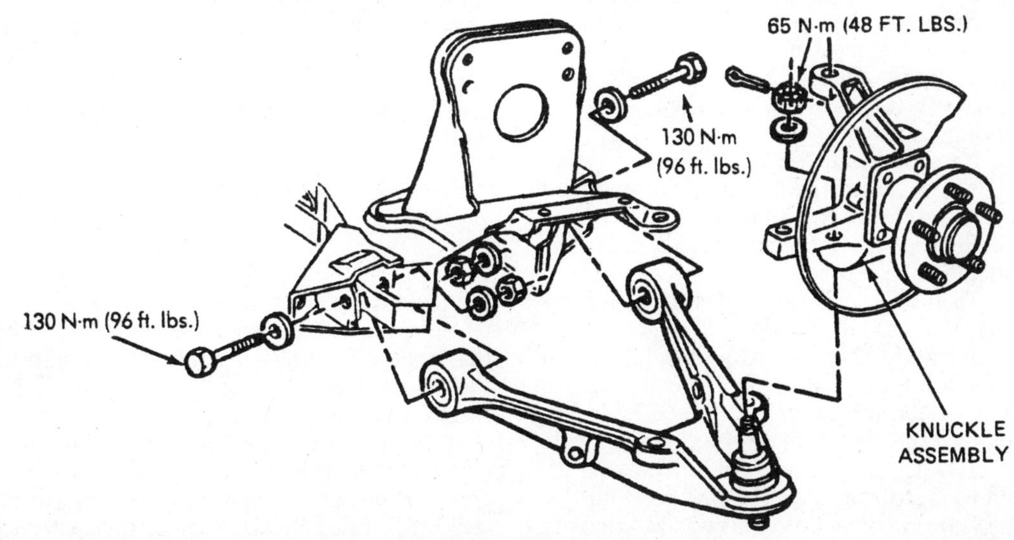

Lower control arm assembly

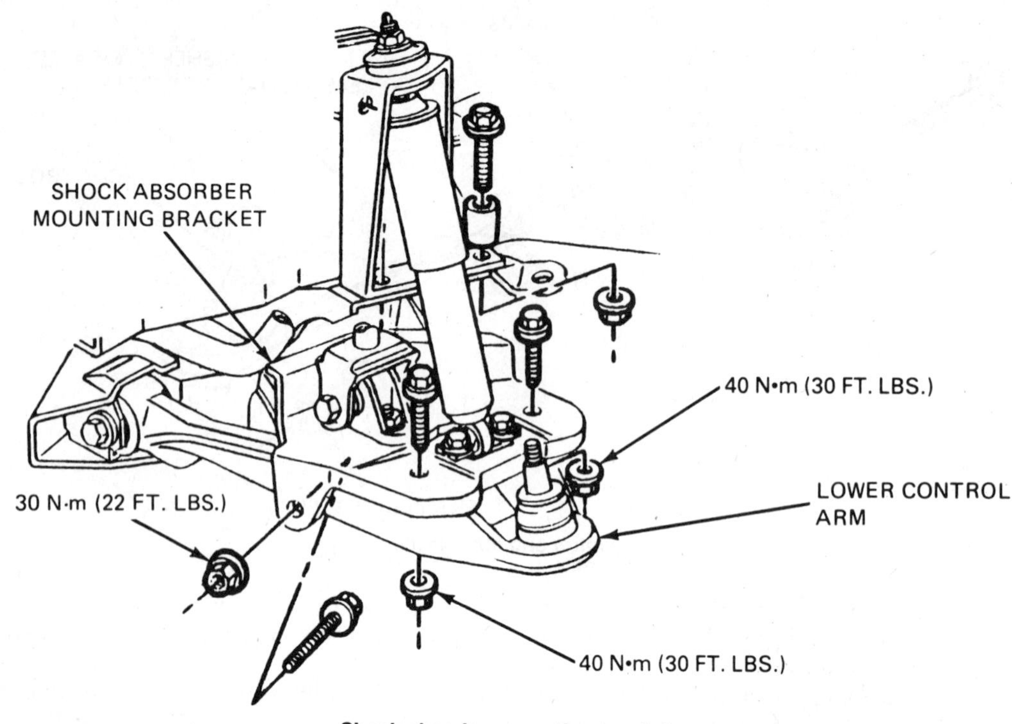

Shock absorber mounting bracket

Steering Knuckle

REMOVAL AND INSTALLATION

1. Raise and support the front of the vehicle with jackstands under the lower control arm.
2. Remove the wheel/tire assembly, brake caliper (support it on a wire), the brake disc, the hub/bearing assembly and the splash shield.
3. Remove the cotter pin, the ball joints/tie-rod end-to-steering knuckle nuts and washer.
4. Using the Tie-Rod End Removal tool No. J-24319-01, separate the tie-rod end from the steering knuckle.
5. Using the Ball Joint Removal tool No. J-33436-9, separate the upper and lower ball joints from the steering knuckle.
6. Remove the steering knuckle from the vehicle.
7. To install, use new cotter pins and reverse the removal procedures. Torque the upper stud nut to 32 ft. lbs. (43 Nm) and the lower stud nut to 48 ft. lbs. (65 Nm), the splash shield-to-steering knuckle screws to 7.5 ft. lbs. (10 Nm), the tie-rod end-to-steering knuckle nut to 32 ft. lbs. (43 Nm), the hub/bearing assembly-to-steering knuckle bolts to 46 ft. lbs. (62 Nm) and the brake caliper-to-steering knuckle bolts to 133 ft. lbs. (180 Nm).

Front Hub And Bearing

REMOVAL AND INSTALLATION

1. Raise and support the front of the vehicle with jackstands under the lower control arm.
2. Remove the wheel/tire assembly, brake caliper (support it on a wire), the brake disc.
3. Remove the hub/bearing assembly from the steering knuckle.
4. To install, reverse the removal procedures. Torque the hub/bearing assembly-to-steering knuckle bolts to 46 ft. lbs. (62 Nm) and the brake caliper-to-steering knuckle bolts to 133 ft. lbs. (180 Nm).

Front End Alignment

CASTER ADJUSTMENT

Caster is the measured angle between a true vertical line passing through the center of the wheel and a line drawn through the center of the upper and lower ball joints. Adjustments to the caster angle are made by the insertion of shims between the upper control arm pivot shaft and the frame bracket. Moving the shims (front-to-rear) will decrease the positive caster. Insertion and removal of a $\frac{1}{32}''$ shim will effect a $\frac{1}{4}°$ caster change. Adjust the caster to specifications.

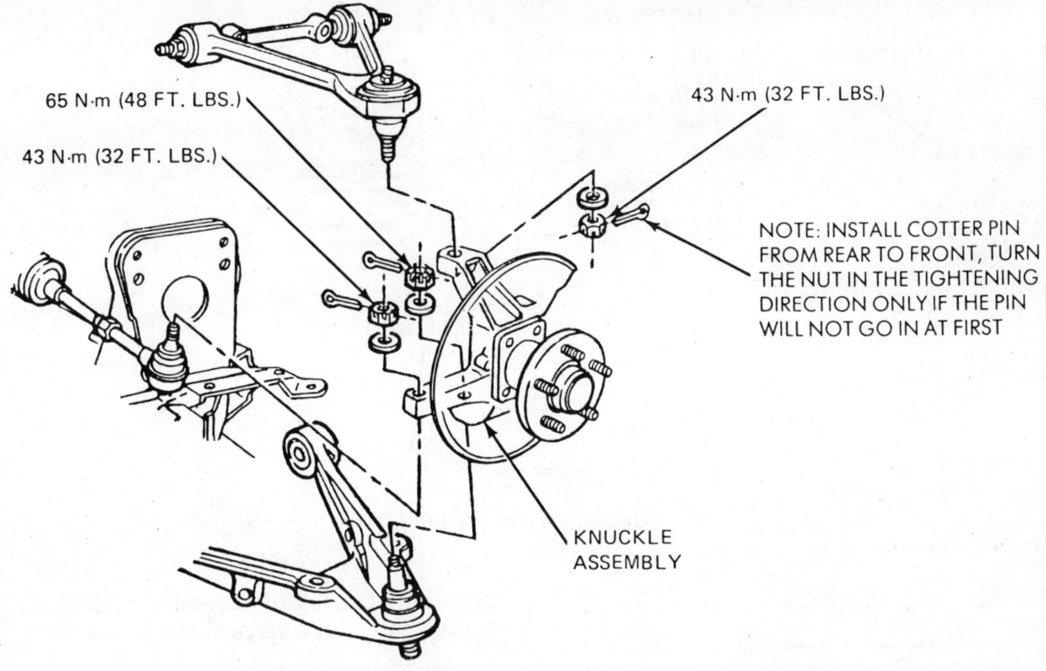

Exploded view of the steering knuckle

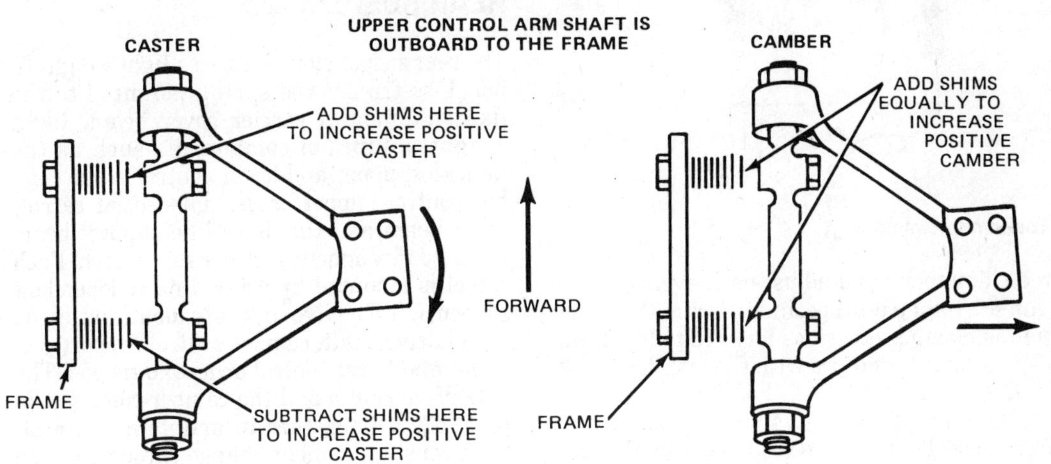

Adjusitng the camber and caster positions—front suspension

CAMBER ADJUSTMENT

Camber is the measurement in degrees of the outward or inward tilt of the top of the wheel/tire assembly in relation to the true vertical. Tilting the top of the tire away from the centerline of the vehicle is called the positive camber; tilting toward the vehicle centerline is the negative camber. Camber adjustment is made by adding or removing shims equally at both bolts. Camber and caster adjustment may be made at the same time. A $^{1}/_{32}$ in. shim will effect a $^{1}/_{6}°$ change in camber. Adjust the camber to specifications.

TOE-IN ADJUSTMENT

Toe-in is the measurement in inches of the inward direction of the wheel fronts from a line drawn through the horizontal center of the wheel, parallel to the centerline of the vehicle. Toe-in is expressed as the difference in measurement between the extreme front and rear of the wheel pair.

Two methods of setting toe-in may be employed. In the first, position the steering gear at the high point and mark the 12 o'clock position on the steering shaft, with the wheel in the straight-ahead position. Loosen both tie-

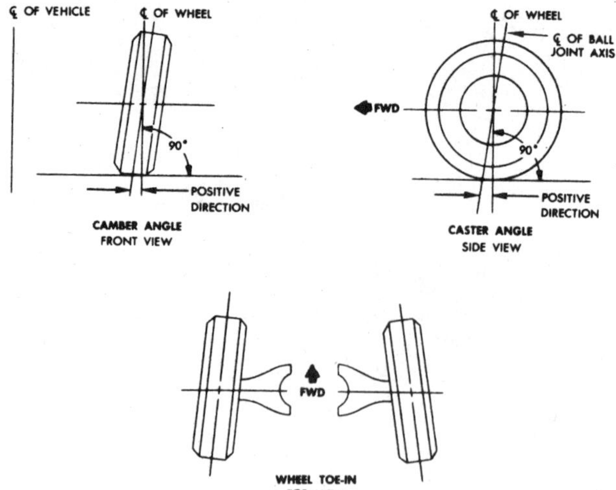

Caster, camber, toe-in

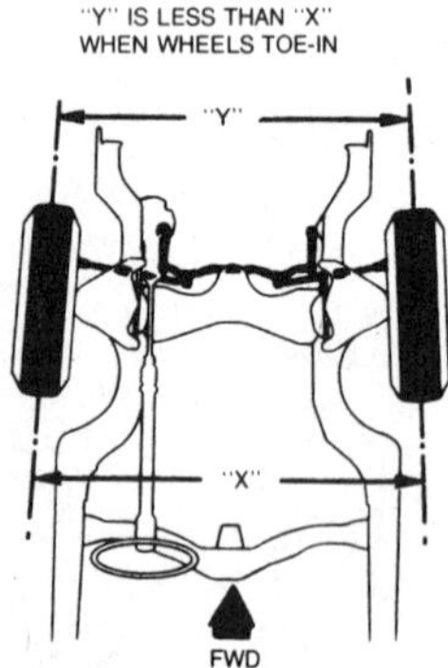

Toe-in adjustment

rod clamp bolts and adjust each evenly to obtain the total toe-in specified. Secure the inner tie-rod clamp protrusions forward to 90° down to prevent interference with the stabilizer link bolt.

If a tram gauge is available, position the front wheels straight-ahead. Loosen the tie-rod clamp on one end and adjust the one rod to the total specified toe-in. Loosen the other tie-rod clamp, then rotate both rods (in the same amount in the same direction) to position the steering gear at the high point and the wheels straight ahead. Secure the inner tie-rod clamps with the bolts down and horizontal. Secure the outer bolts vertical and to the rear.

REAR SUSPENSION

The rear suspension features a light weight fiberglass transverse spring mounted to the fixed differential carrier cover beam. Light weight aluminum components such as the knuckles, upper and lower control arms, camber control support rods, differential carrier cover beam and the drive line support beam are used throughout the rear suspension. Each wheel is mounted by a five link independent suspension. The five links are identified as the wheel drive shaft, camber control support rod, upper and lower control arms and tie-rod. The axle drive shafts and the camber control support rods act together in maintaining an almost constant camber change throughout the entire arc of the wheel travel. Fore-aft motion of the wheel is controlled by the upper and lower control arms. Each rear wheel has a short spindle, hub/bearing assembly and knuckle contained at the rear of the upper and lower control arms. The knuckle also acts as a mount

Wheel Alignment Specifications

All measurements stated in degrees, unless noted

Year	Front Wheel Caster		Front Wheel Camber		Rear Wheel Camber		Toe-in (in.)	
	Range	Preferred	Range	Preferred	Range	Preferred	Front Wheel	Rear Wheel
1984–86	2½P–3½P	3	³⁄₁₀P–1³⁄₁₀P	⅘P	⅒N–⁹⁄₁₀P	⅖P	¹⁄₂₀–¼	⅒–⅕

N—Negative
P—Positive

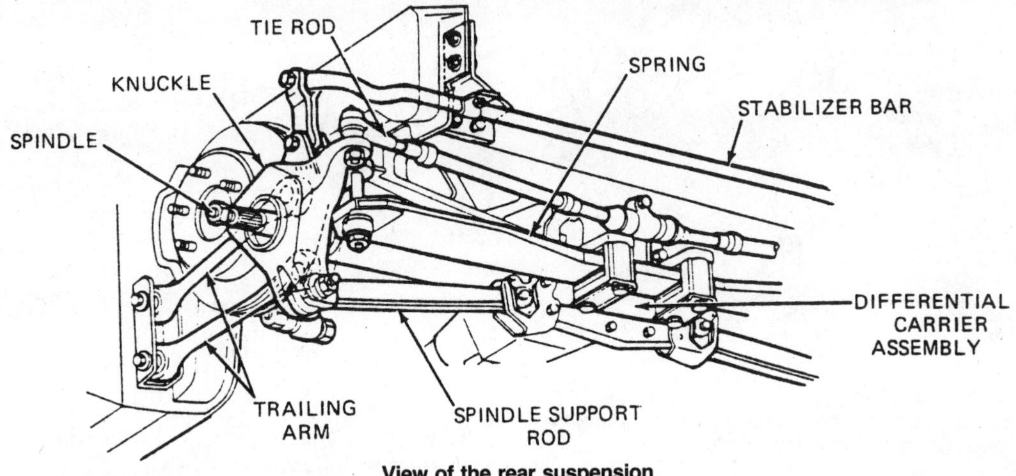

View of the rear suspension

for the brake caliper mounting, the rear spring link, shock absorber lower attachment and parking brake backing plate assembly.

Aside from the controlling wheel locations, each portion of the suspension has additional functions. The control arms and knuckle carries the brake caliper, thus, all brake torque and braking tractive forces are transmitted through the arms. The lateral links transmit side forces to the fixed differential and through the rubber bushings in the cover beam to the frame. The upper link or wheel drive shaft, transmits acceleration torque through the differential to the frame. The final duty of the lateral links is to maintain the camber angle of the wheel throughout its travel. Since the camber control support rod and the wheel drive shaft are of different lengths, a certain amount of camber change occurs through jounce and rebound. The overall result of the camber control support rod and wheel drive shaft geometry holds the wheel in a near vertical position at all times.

Direct double-acting shock absorbers are attached at the upper eye to a frame bracket and at the lower eye to the knuckle which has a threaded stud for the shock absorber lower eye. The transversely mounted spring is clamp bolted at the center section to a lower mounting surface on the differential carrier cover beam. The outer ends of the spring are provided with a hole through which the spring is link bolted to the rear of the knuckle. A stabilizer shaft is used which attaches to the section of the knuckle and extends rearward where it is connected to the frame by two rubber bushings and mounting brackets. A single unit hub/bearing assembly is bolted to each knuckle. A single unit hub/bearing assembly is bolted to each knuckle. The hub/bearing assembly supports the drive axle shaft and spindle allowing torque to be transferred from the differential carrier to the wheel and tire. This hub/bearing assembly is a sealed unit and no maintenance is required.

Transverse Leaf Spring

REMOVAL AND INSTALLATION

1. Raise and support the rear of the vehicle on jackstands. Remove the wheel/tire assembly.
2. At each spring-to-knuckle assembly, remove the cotter pins, the nuts, bushings and link bolt.
3. At the bottom of the differential carrier, remove the spring retainer bolts, spacers, insulators. Remove the transverse leaf spring from the vehicle.
4. To install, reverse the removal procedures. Torque the transverse leaf spring-to-differential cover beam bolts to 29–44 ft. lbs.

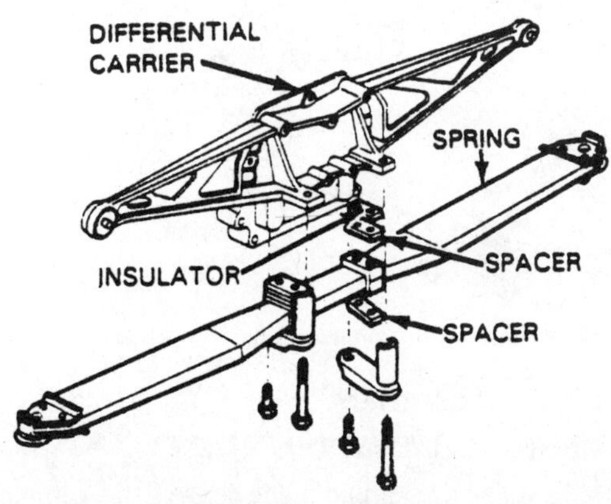

Rear leaf spring mounting assembly

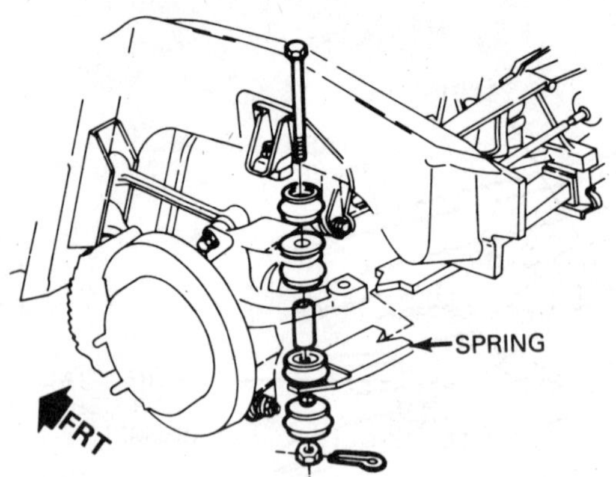

Exploded view of the transverse leaf spring-to-knuckle assembly—rear suspension

Spindle Support Rod

REMOVAL AND INSTALLATION

1. Raise and support the rear of the vehicle on jackstands.
2. Using a scribe, mark the cam adjusting bolt and the mounting bracket, so that they may be realigned during assembly.
3. Remove the cam bolt and separate the spindle support rod from the mounting bracket.
4. Remove the spindle support rod-to-knuckle bolt/nut and the spindle support rod from the vehicle.
5. To install, reverse the removal procedures. Torque the spindle support rod-to-knuckle bolt/nut to 95–118 ft. lbs. (130–160 Nm) and the spindle support rod cam bolt to 158–213 ft. lbs. (215–290 Nm). Check and/or adjust the rear suspension (as necessary).

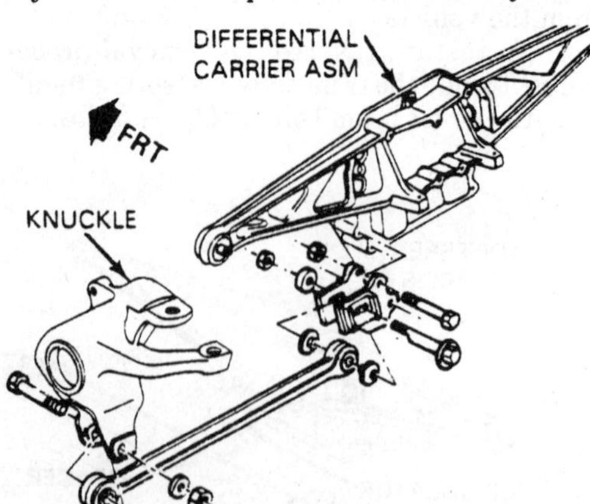

Spindle support rod assembly

Shock Absorbers

REMOVAL AND INSTALLATION

1. Raise and support the rear of the vehicle on jackstands.

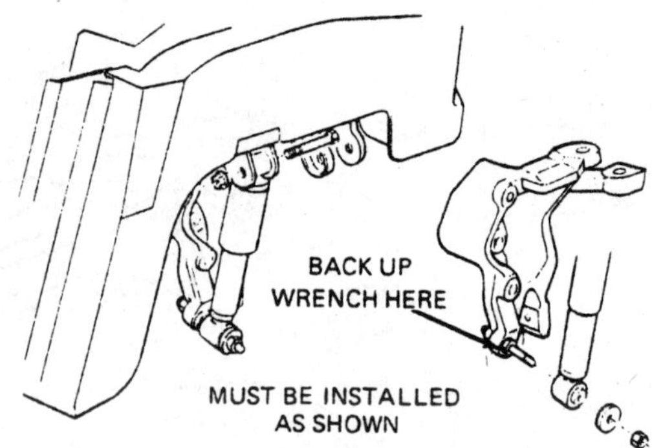

Rear shock absorber mounting

2. Remove the lower shock absorber-to-knuckle nut, bolt and washer.

NOTE: *When removing the shock absorber nut/bolt, be sure to use a back-up wrench.*

3. Remove the upper shock absorber-to-frame bolt/nut.
4. Remove the shock absorber from the vehicle.
5. To install, reverse the removal procedures. Torque the shock absorber-to-frame nut/bolt to 40–51 ft. lbs. (55–70 Nm) and the shock absorber-to-knuckle nut/bolt to 55–73 ft. lbs. (75–100 Nm).

BOUNCE TEST

Each shock absorber can be tested by bouncing the corner of the vehicle until maximum up and down movement is obtained. Release the car. It should stop bouncing in 1–2 bounces. Compare both front corners or both rear corners but do not compare the front to the rear. If one corner bounces longer than the other it should be inspected for damage and possibly be replaced.

DISPOSAL OF PRESSURIZED SHOCK ABSORBERS

Due to the high pressure of gas it is advised that, upon scrapping or disposal of these shock absorbers, the pressure be released. This is carried out as follows:

1. Clamp shock in a vise with piston rod pointing down.
2. Measure approx. 0.5 in. (10–15mm) from bottom of shock and drill an approx. 5mm hole so the gas can escape.
3. Measure approx. 5.5–6.0 in. (140–150mm) from first hole and drill an approx. 5mm hole to facilitate drainage of the oil. Drain shock completely, then dispose of in the normal manner.

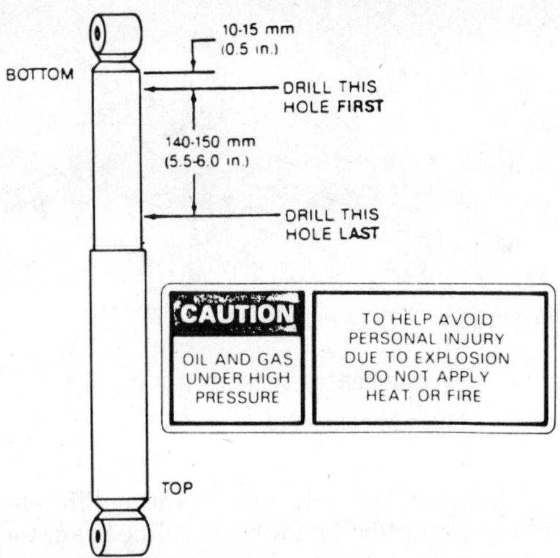

Drill holes as shown to relieve pressure in the gas-filled shock absorbers before disposal. Gas shocks can be recognized by the warning label attached

Upper And Lower Control Arms

REMOVAL AND INSTALLATION

1. Raise and support the rear of the vehicle on jackstands.
2. At each spring-to-knuckle assembly, remove the cotter pins, the nuts, bushings and link bolt.
3. Remove the control arm-to-knuckle bolts.
4. Remove the control arm-to-bracket bolts and the control arms from the vehicle.

NOTE: *When removing the nut/bolt assemblies, be sure to use a backup wrench.*

5. To install, reverse the removal procedures. Torque the control arm-to-bracket bolts to 55–70 ft. lbs. (75–95 Nm) and the control arm-to-knuckle bolts to 125–154 ft. lbs. (170–210 Nm).

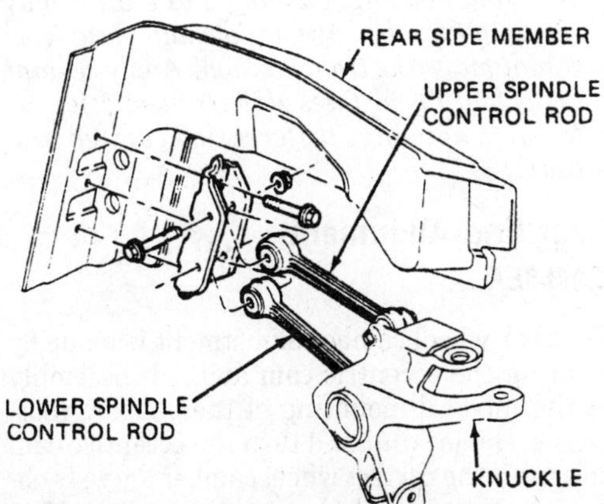

Control arms on 5-link rear suspension

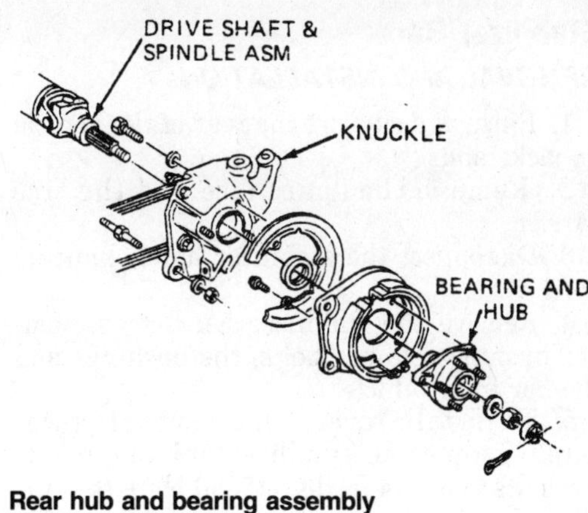

Rear hub and bearing assembly

Rear Axle Tie Rod Assembly

REMOVAL AND INSTALLATION

1. Raise and support the rear of the vehicle on jackstand. Remove the wheel/tire assembly.
2. Remove the cotter pin, the nut and washer from the tie rod end at the knuckle. Discard the cotter pin.
3. If removing the tie rod end from the assembly, loosen adjusting sleeve nut on the tie rod end.
4. Using tool No. J-24319-01 or equivalent, press the tie rod end out of the knuckle.

NOTE: *If removing the tie rod end from the adjusting sleeve, note the number of turns necessary to remove it; the same number of turns are necessary to install it.*

5. To install, reverse the removal procedures. Torque the tie rod assembly-to-differential carrier bolts to 47–61 ft. lbs. (64–84 Nm), the tie rod end adjusting sleeve nut to 39–53 ft. lbs. (54–72 Nm) and the tie rod end-to-knuckle nut to 29–36 ft. lbs. (40–50 Nm). Check and adjust the rear suspension alignment (as necessary).

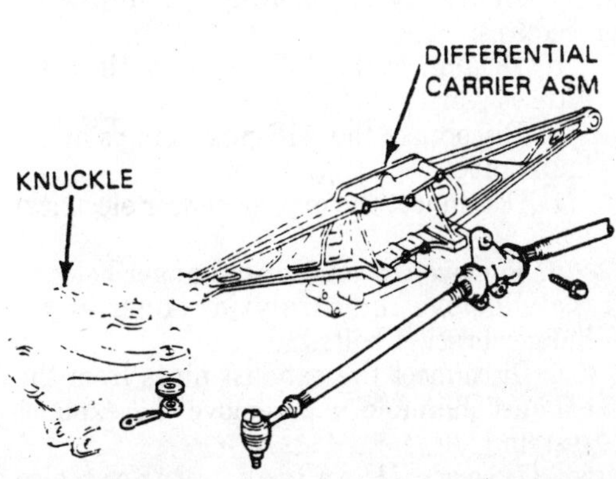

Rear suspension tie-rod assembly

Stabilizer Bar

REMOVAL AND INSTALLATION

1. Raise and support the rear of the vehicle on jackstands.
2. Remove the spare tire and the tire carrier.
3. Disconnect the stabilizer bar-to-knuckle bolts.
4. Remove the stabilizer bar-to-crossmember bushing retainer bolts, the bushings and the bar from vehicle.
5. To install, reverse the removal procedures. Torque the stabilizer link-to-bracket/bar bolts to 33–44 ft. lbs. (45–60 Nm), the stabilizer bar-to-crossmember bolts and the stabilizer bar-to-knuckle bolts to 14–22 ft. lbs. (20–30 Nm).

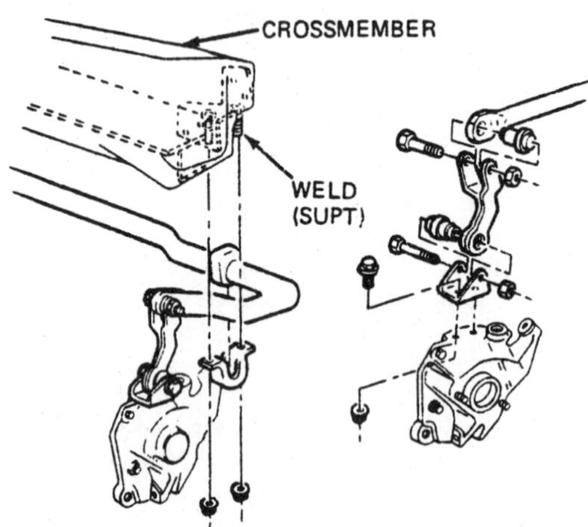

Rear stabilizer bar linkage

Driveline Beam

REMOVAL

1. Raise and support the rear of the vehicle on jackstands.
2. Remove the complete exhaust system as an assembly, by performing the following procedures:
   a. Disconnect the AIR pipe from the catalytic converter.
   b. Disconnect the AIR pipe clamps at exhaust pipe.
   c. Disconnect the oxygen sensor electrical lead.
   d. Remove the muffler-to-hanger bolts.
   e. Remove the catalytic converter-to-hanger bracket bolts.
   f. Disconnect the exhaust pipes from the exhaust manifold and remove the exhaust system
3. Using a floor jack, support the transmission.

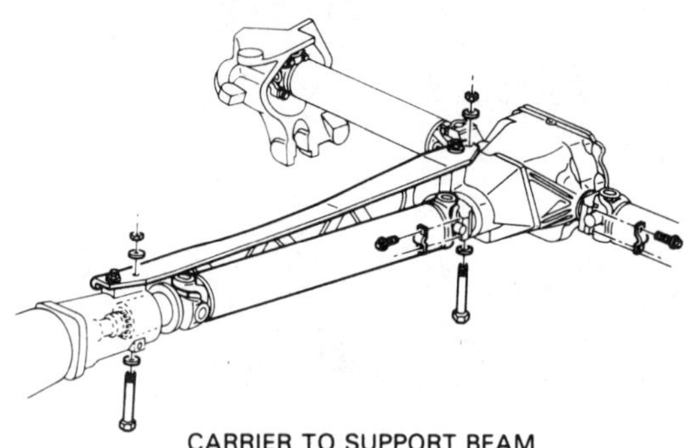

Driveline beam attachments

4. Remove the driveline beam-to-differential carrier nut/bolt and the driveline beam-to-transmission extension housing nut/bolt.
5. Remove the propeller shaft.
6. Using a medium pry bar, pry the transmission toward the driver's side of vehicle and remove the driveline beam from the vehicle.

   NOTE: *DO NOT use excessive force when prying transmission housing.*
7. To install, reverse the removal procedures, by performing the following procedures:
   a. Align the driveline components.
   b. To insure proper alignment of the driveline, a clearance of 1.520–2.020 in. (39–51mm) must be maintained between the top of the beam to the underbody and a clearance of 0.850–1.350 in. (22–34mm) from the right-side (passenger-side) of the beam to the side wall. Take these measurements directly above and to the right-side of the propeller shaft dampener.
   c. Torque the driveline beam-to-transmission nut/bolt to 47–55 ft. lbs. (65–75 Nm) the driveline beam-to-differential carrier nut/bolt to 51–66 ft. lbs. (70–90 Nm).

NOTE: *DO NOT over torque the bolts attaching the driveline beam to the transmission. Over torquing can damage the transmission extension housing, bushing and seal; it may result in fluid leakage. Inadequate fluid level can damage the transmission. Apply sealant to the mating surfaces of the transmission extension housing, differential carrier and beam.*

Rear End Alignment

CAMBER

The rear wheel camber adjustment is made by rotating the eccentric cam and bolt assembly at the inboard mounting of the support rods. Loosen the locknut and turn the eccentric cam bolt until the correct wheel camber angle is obtained. Secure the locknut and torque to 158–213 ft. lbs. (215–290 Nm).

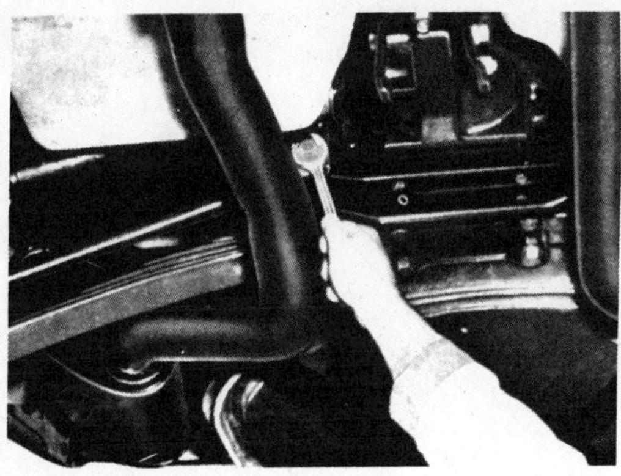
Adjusting camber

TOE-IN

The rear toe-in is adjusted by loosening lock nuts on the tie-rod ends and turning the adjusting sleeve.

STEERING

The steering system is a rack and pinion type with 2 adjustable tie-rods, connected to each steering arm through self-adjusting ball and socket joints.

These models have a Function Locking Energy Absorbing steering columns. With this design, the mast jacket and steering shaft are designed to collapse during conditions generated by a front end collision. The collapsible mast jacket consists of plastic pins, pressed between the upper and lower jackets. A predetermined load will collapse the assembly. The steering shaft collapses under predetermined loads, shearing the plastic pins.

Additionally, these columns contain an anti-theft ignition switch and ignition lock system. This system prevents the removal of the ignition key unless the automatic transmission is in Park or the manual transmission is in Reverse and the key is in the Lock position. In this position, a rod and lock plate mechanism lock the steering wheel and shift lever.

The power rack and pinion steering system has a rotary control valve which directs hydraulic fluid, coming from the hydraulic pump, to either side of the rack piston. The integral rack piston is attached to the rack and converts hydraulic pressure to a linear force which moves the rack left or right. The force is then transmitted through the inner and outer tie-rods to the steering knuckles which turn the wheels.

Lip seals, which seal rotating shaft, require special treatment. This type of seal is used on the steering rack and pinion at the rack, at the pinion and valve and on the drive shaft of the pump. When leakage occurs in one of these areas, always replace the seal(s), after inspecting and thoroughly cleaning the sealing surfaces. Replace the shaft only if very severe pitting is found except for the rack. If the rack shows evidence of corrosion, it should be replaced. If the corrosion in the lip seal contact zone is slight, clean the surface of the shaft with crocus cloth. Replace the shaft only if the leakage cannot be stopped by smoothing with crocus cloth first.

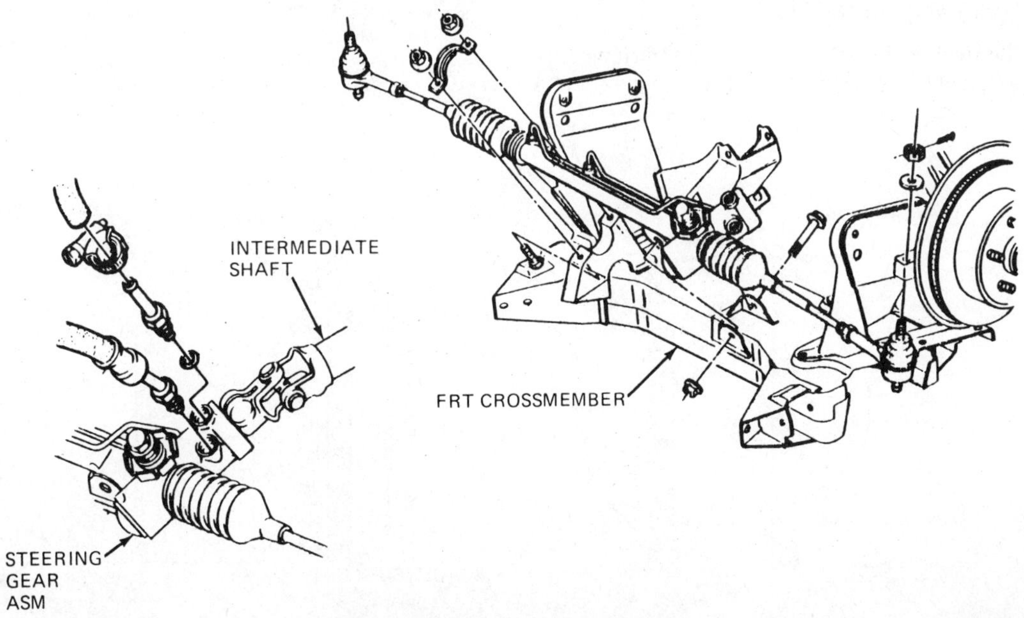

Power rack and pinion assembly

Steering wheel

REMOVAL AND INSTALLATION

1. Disconnect the negative battery cable.
2. Squeeze the horn button cap (top and bottom), disengage the locking fingers and remove the cap.
3. Carefully pull the horn contact plate from the steering wheel and disconnect the horn electrical connector.
4. Remove the telescoping adjusting lever assembly and the steering wheel nut.
5. Using the Steering Wheel Puller tool No. J-1859-03, press the steering wheel from the steering column.
6. To install, reverse the removal procedures. Torque the steering wheel-to-steering column nut to 30 ft. lbs. (40 Nm). Using two ¼" spacers, press the horn cap/horn plate assembly onto the steering wheel.

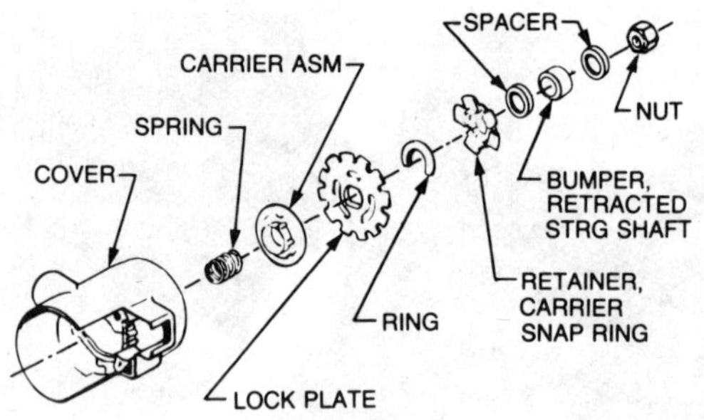

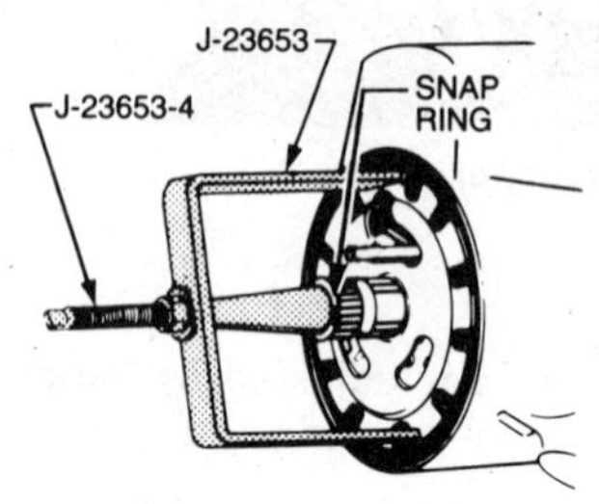

Remove and install shaft lock retainer snap ring

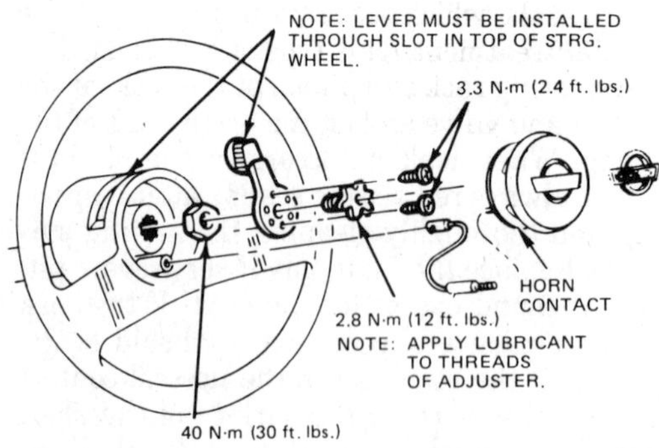

Exploded view of the steering wheel

Combination Switch

The combination switch is a combination of the turn signal, the dimmer and the cruise control switches.

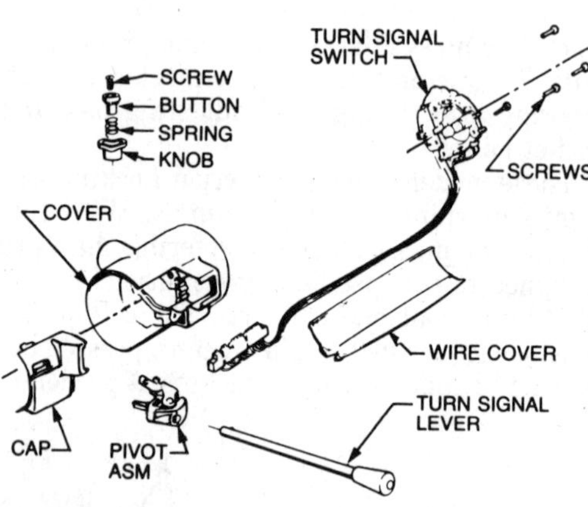

Removing the combination switch from the steering column

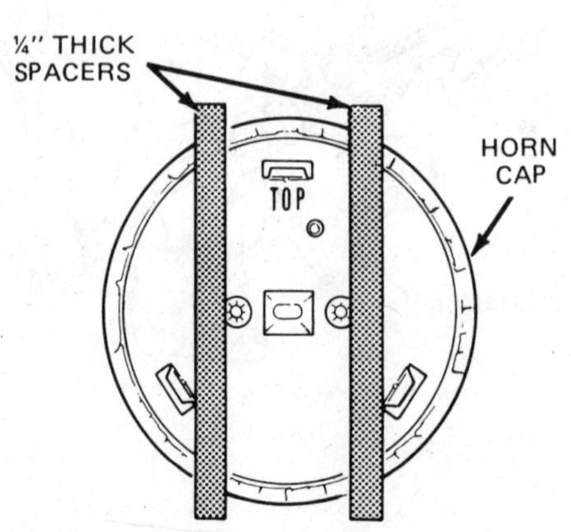

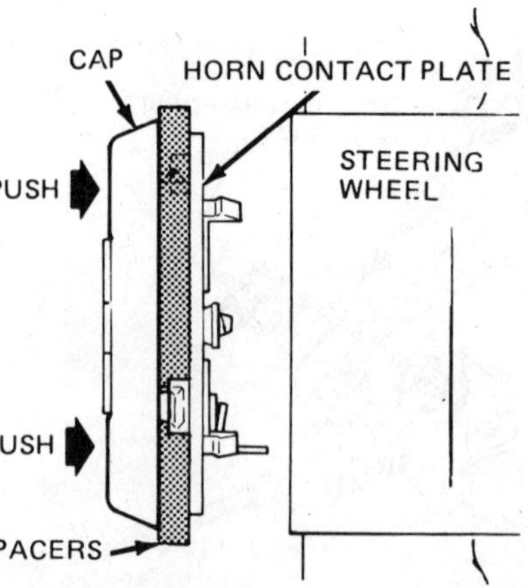

Installing the horn cap and horn contact plate

REMOVAL AND INSTALLATION

1. Refer to the "Steering Wheel, Removal and Installation" procedures in this section and remove the steering wheel.
2. Remove the steering column/dash trim cover.
3. Remove the C-ring plastic retainer.
4. Using the Lock Plate Depressing tools No. J-23653 and No. J-23653-A, install it onto the steering column shaft and compress the lock plate.
5. Using a small pry bar, pry the C-ring from the steering column shaft.
6. Remove the tool and lift out the lock plate, the contact carrier and the upper bearing preload spring.
7. Pull the switch connector out of the mast jacket and tape the upper part to facilitate the switch removal.
8. Remove the combination switch lever. Push the flasher button IN and unscrew it.
9. Position the combination switch and shifter housing in the central position. Remove the steering column cover, the wire cover and the pivot assembly.
10. Remove combination switch-to-column screws and pull the switch straight up, while guiding the wiring harness out of the housing.
11. To install, reverse the removal procedures. Torque the combination switch-to-steering column screws to 35 inch lbs. (4 Nm) and the steering wheel nut to 30 ft. lbs. (40 Nm).

NOTE: *The replacement switch is installed by working the harness connector down through the housing and under the mounting bracket.*

Ignition Switch

REMOVAL AND INSTALLATION

The ignition switch is located inside the channel section of the brake pedal support and is completely inaccessible without first lowering the steering column. The switch is actuated by a rod and rack assembly. A gear on the end of the lock cylinder engages the toothed upper end of the actuator rod.

1. Lower the steering column; be sure to properly support it.
2. Place the switch in the Off-Unlocked position. With the cylinder removed, the rod is in the Off-Unlocked position when it is in the next to the uppermost detent.
3. Remove the two ignition switch screws and the switch assembly.
4. Before installing, place the new switch in the Off-Unlocked position and make sure the lock cylinder and actuating rod are in the Off-Locked position (2nd detent from the top).
5. Install the activating rod into the switch and assemble the switch on the column. Tighten the mounting screws. Use only the specified screws since overlength screws could impair the collapsibility of the column.
6. Reinstall the steering column.

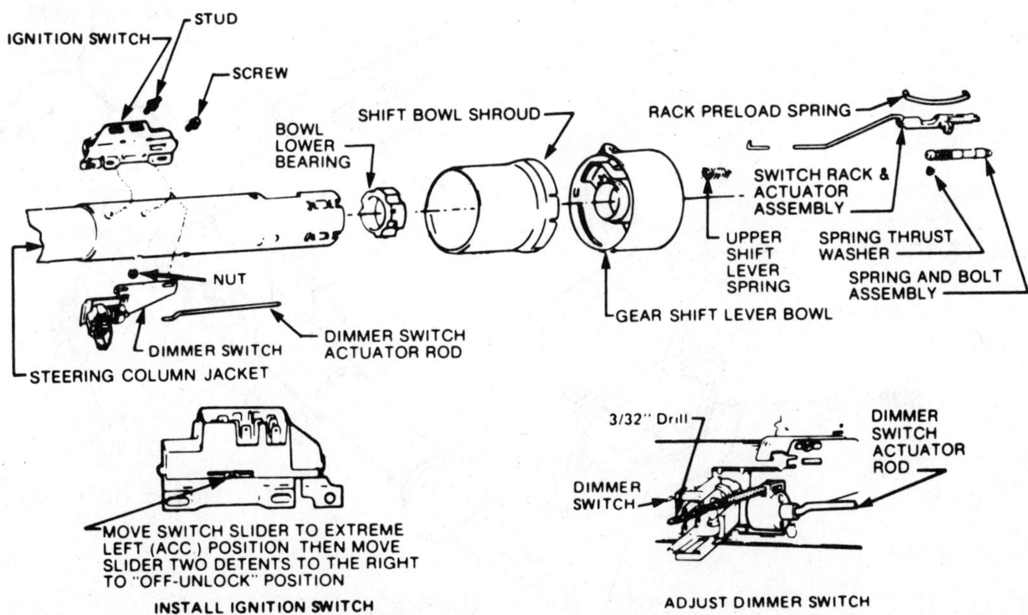

Exploded view of the steering column ignition and dimmer switches

Ignition Lock Cylinder

REMOVAL AND INSTALLATION

1. Refer to the "Combination Switch, Removal and Installation" procedures in this section and remove the combination switch.
2. Place the lock cylinder in the "Run" Position.
3. Remove the buzzer switch, the lock cylinder screw and the lock cylinder.

CAUTION: *If the screw is dropped on removal, it could fall into the column, requiring complete disassembly to retrieve the screw.*

4. Rotate the lock cylinder clockwise to align the cylinder key with the keyway in the housing.
5. Push the lock cylinder all the way in.
6. Install the screw. Tighten the screw to 14 inch lbs.

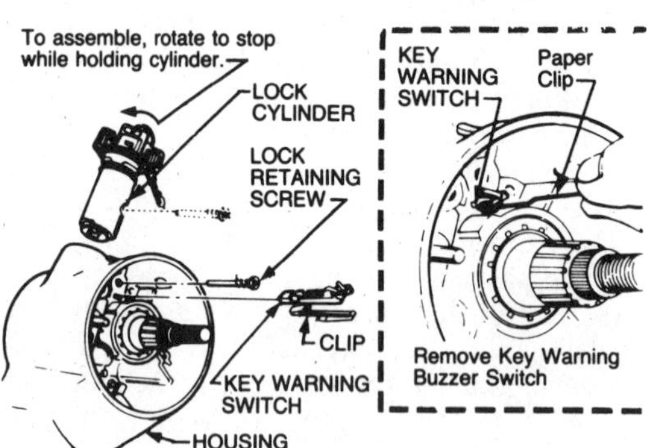

Exploded view of the ignition lock cylinder

Steering Column

CAUTION: *The newly designed collapsible steering column is extremely susceptible to damage; it should not subjected to hammering, leaning or dropping pressures.*

REMOVAL AND INSTALLATION

1. Disconnect the negative battery cable.
2. At the universal coupling (near the steering gear), remove the pinch bolt.
3. Remove the steering column-to-firewall nuts.
4. Remove the steering column-to-instrument panel bolts.

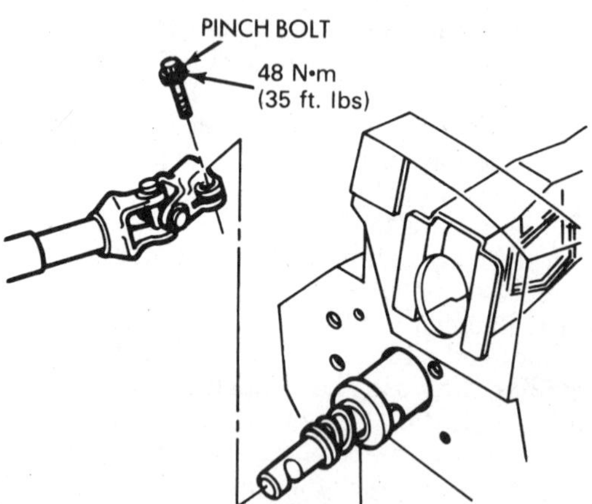

Removing the steering column pinch bolt

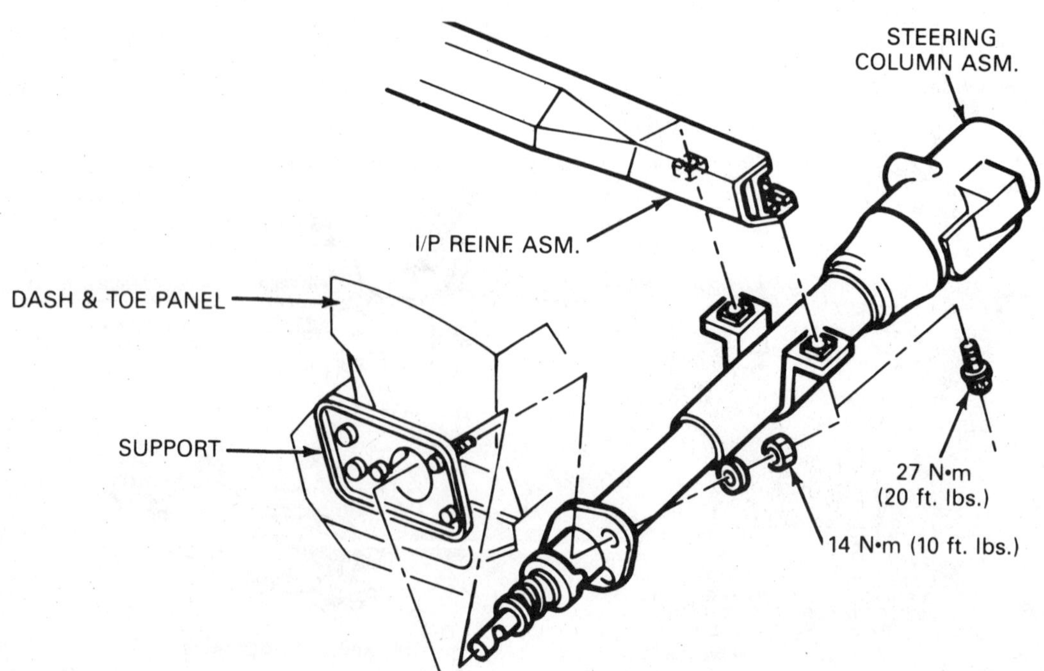

Removing the steering column from the vehicle

5. Disconnect all of the electrical harness connectors from the steering column.

6. Remove the steering column from the vehicle.

7. To install, reverse the removal procedures. Torque the steering column-to-instrument panel bolts to 20 ft. lbs. (27 Nm), the steering column-to-firewall nuts to 10 ft. lbs. (14 Nm) and the universal joint pinch bolt to 44 ft. lbs. (60 Nm).

Tie Rod Ends

The vehicle is equipped with two tie rods. Each rod is a two-piece assembly made up of the tie rod and a tie-rod ends. The ends screw onto the rod and are torqued into place with a jam nut. Right and left-hand threads are used to assist toe-in and centering adjustments. The ends are self adjusting and with the exception of periodic lubrication; no servicing is required.

REMOVAL AND INSTALLATION

1. Raise and support the front of the vehicle on jackstands.
2. At the tie rod-to-steering knuckle assembly, remove the cotter pin, the retaining nut.
3. Loosen the tie rod jam nut.
4. Using the Ball Joint Removal tool No. J-24319-01 or BT-7101, separate the tie rod end from the steering knuckle.

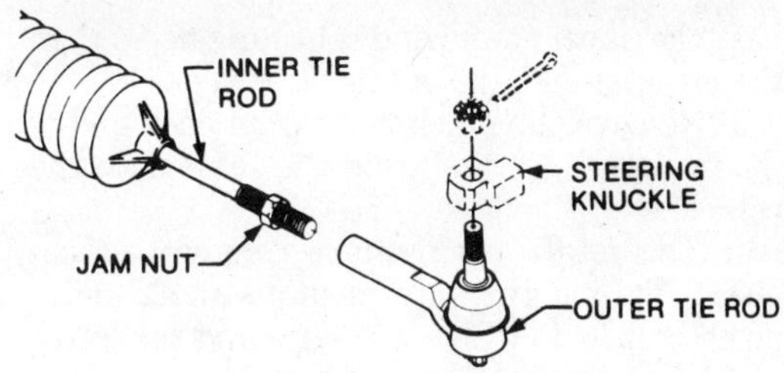

Exploded view of the tie-rod end

5. Unscrew the tie rod end from the tie rod; be sure to count the number of turns necessary to remove the tie rod end.

   NOTE: *When installing the tie rod end to the tie rod, be sure to install it with the correct number of turns necessary to remove it.*

6. To install, reverse the removal procedures. Torque the tie rod-to-steering knuckle nut to 33 ft. lbs. (45 Nm) and the tie rod jam nut to 50 ft. lbs. (70 Nm). Check and/or adjust the front wheel alignment.

Intermediate Shaft

REMOVAL AND INSTALLATION

1. Raise and support the front of the vehicle on jackstands.
2. At the intermediate steering shaft, disen-

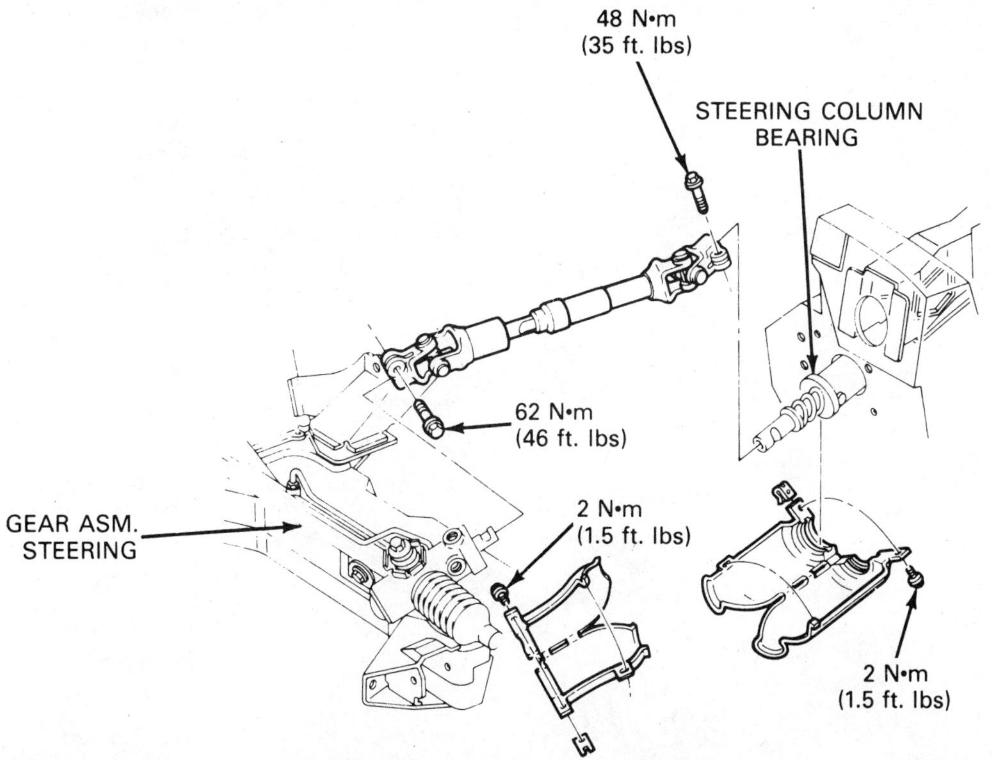

Exploded view of the intermediate steering shaft

gage the upper shield and retaining hook, then the lower shield and retaining hook.

3. Remove the pinch bolts from each end of the intermediate shaft and the shaft from the vehicle.

4. To install, reverse the removal procedures. Torque the intermediate shaft upper pinch bolt to 35 ft. lbs. (48 Nm) and the lower pinch bolt to 46 ft. lbs. (62 Nm).

Rack And Pinion Assembly

REMOVAL AND INSTALLATION

1. Raise and support the front of the vehicle on jackstands.

2. Remove the driver's side wheel/tire assembly.

3. Disconnect and plug the power steering hoses.

4. Remove the cotter pin and the retaining nut from the outer tie-rod ends (both sides).

5. Using the Ball Joint Removal tool No. J-24319-01 or BT-7101, separate the tie-rod end from the steering knuckle.

6. Remove the upper and lower mounting bolts from the passenger-side.

7. Remove the mounting bolt from the driver's-side.

8. Remove the intermediate shaft lower universal joint at the rack and pinion assembly.

9. Remove the stabilizer bar and the electric fan.

10. Remove the rack and pinion assembly from the vehicle.

11. To install, reverse the removal procedures. Torque the steering gear clamp bolts to 18 ft. lbs. (25 Nm), the steering gear-to-crossmember bolts to 25 ft. lbs. (34 Nm), the tie rod ends-to-steering knuckle nuts to 33 ft. lbs. (45 Nm) and the steering gear-to-intermediate bolt to 46 ft. lbs. (62 Nm). Check and/or refill the power steering reservoir. Bleed the power steering system. Check and/or adjust the toe-in, if necessary.

Power Steering Pump

REMOVAL AND INSTALLATION

1. Remove the serpentine drive belt from the power steering pump.

2. Disconnect and plug the power steering pump hoses and the pump fittings to keep the fluid in the pump.

3. Remove the pulley from the power steering pump. Loosen the bracket retaining nuts.

4. Remove the bracket-to-pump bolts and the pump from the vehicle.

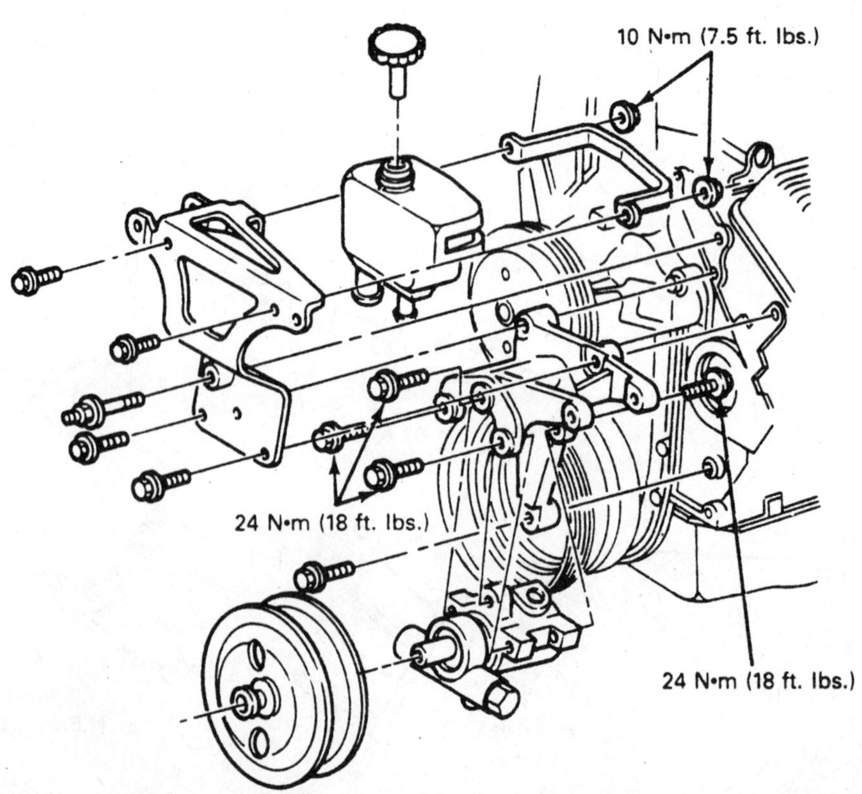

Power steering pump, reservoir and mounting brackets on engines with serpentine drive belt—1984

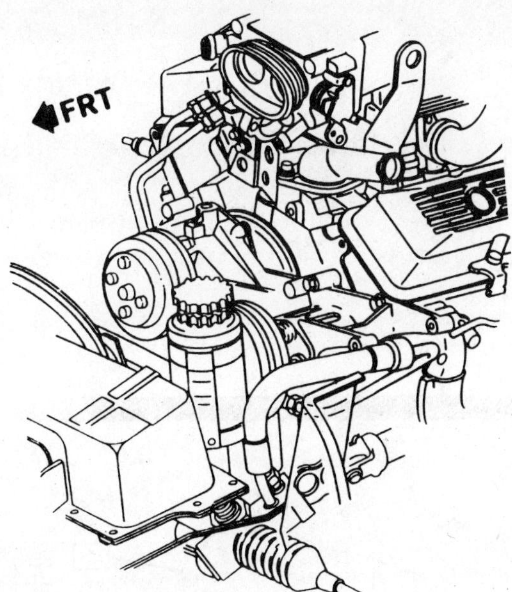

View of the power steering system—1985 and later

5. To install, reverse the removal procedures. Refill the pump reservoir; turn the pulley backward to bleed the pump. Bleed the hydraulic system.

BLEEDING

1. Run the engine until the power steering fluid reaches normal operating temperature, approximately 170°F (80°C), then shut the engine Off. Remove the reservoir filler cap and check the oil level.
2. If the oil level is low, add power steering fluid to proper level and replace the filler cap. When adding or making a complete fluid change, always us GM No. 1050017 or equivalent power steering fluid. DO NOT use transmission fluid.
3. Start the engine and turn the wheels in both directions (to the stops) several times. Stop the engine and add power steering fluid to level indicated on the reservoir.

NOTE: *Maintain the fluid level just above the internal pump casting. Fluid with air in it will have a light tan or milky appearance. This air must be eliminated from the fluid before normal steering action can be obtained.*

4. Return the wheels to the center position and continue to run it for 2–3 minutes, then shut the engine Off.
5. Road-test the vehicle to make sure the steering functions normally and is free from noise.
6. Allow the vehicle to stand for 2–3 hours, then recheck the power steering fluid.

Brakes

BRAKE SYSTEM

Adjustments

BRAKE PEDAL

1. With the brakes cold and the engine Off, pump the brake pedal a minimum of 3 times.

   NOTE: *Pumping the brake pedal exhausts the vacuum assist from the power booster.*

2. Apply approx. 70 lbs. (310 N) of force to the brake pedal (on the center of the pedal).
3. The pedal travel should not exceed 2.75 inches (70mm).
4. If the pedal exceeds 2.75 inches (70mm), adjust the push rod at the power booster.

Brake Light Switch

REMOVAL AND INSTALLATION

1. Disconnect the negative battery cable.
2. Remove the close out panel, then disconnect the courtesy light and the brake light switch electrical connectors.

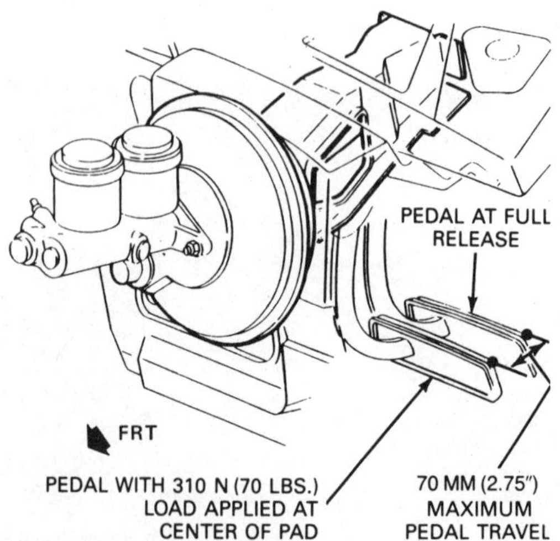

Checking the brake pedal travel

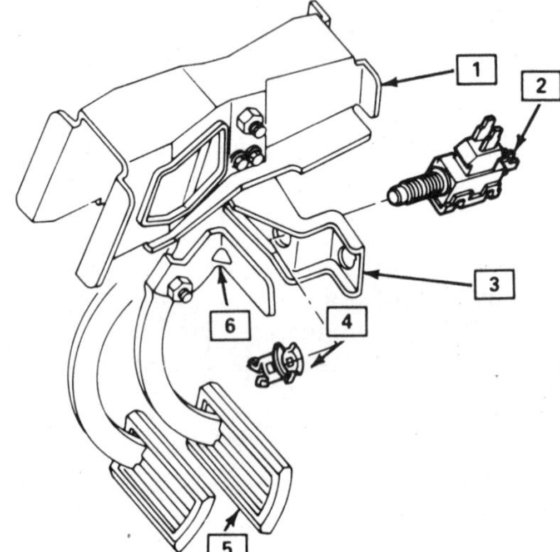

1. Brake pedal support
2. switch
3. Switch bracket
4. Clip
5. Brake pedal
6. Actuator

Exploded view of the brake light switch assembly

3. Depress the brake pedal, then remove or expand the brake light switch retaining clip.
4. Pull the brake light switch from the mounting bracket and remove it from the vehicle.
5. To install, depress the brake pedal and insert the brake light switch into the tubular clip, until it seats on the clip.

   NOTE: *An audible click is heard as the threaded portion of the switch is pushed through the clip (toward the brake pedal).*

6. Release the brake pedal, then pull it rearward until the clicking sounds can no longer be heard.

   NOTE: *When no more clicking sounds are heard, the switch is properly adjusted in the tube.*

CAUTION: *DO NOT apply excessive rearward force to the brake pedal, for damage may occur to the power booster.*

7. Repeat Step 6 to assure that no audible clicking sounds remain.

8. To complete the installation, reverse the removal procedures.

Master Cylinder

The master cylinder assembly is an aluminum and plastic composite with an integral proportioning valve/warning switch, individual reservoirs and a conventional front-to-rear split. Two outlets are provided for the frontal brakes, fed from the front reservoir and secondary piston; one outlet for the rear brakes, fed by the rear reservoir and primary piston.

REMOVAL AND INSTALLATION

1. Disconnect the electrical connector from the warning switch of the master cylinder.

2. Disconnect and plug the brake lines from the master cylinder.

NOTE: *Cap all of the brake lines during service procedures to prevent contamination of the hydraulic system with dirt, grease or water.*

3. Remove the master cylinder-to-power booster nuts and the master cylinder from the vehicle.

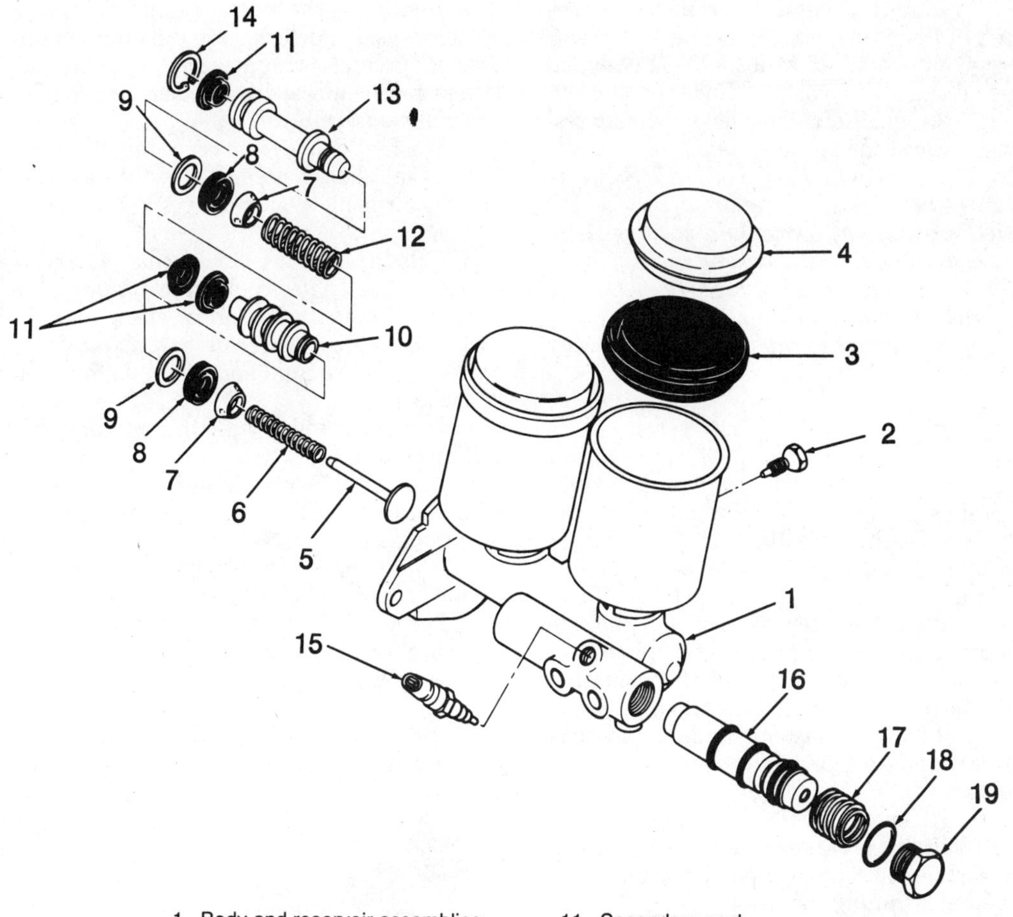

1. Body and reservoir assemblies
2. Stop bolt
3. Diaphragm
4. Cap
5. Spring locator
6. Secondary spring
7. Seal retainer
8. Primary seal
9. Seal washer
10. Secondary piston
11. Secondary seal
12. Primary spring
13. Primary piston
14. Retaining ring
15. Warning switch
16. Combination piston
17. Spring
18. O-ring
19. Plug

Exploded view of brake master cylinder—1984 and later

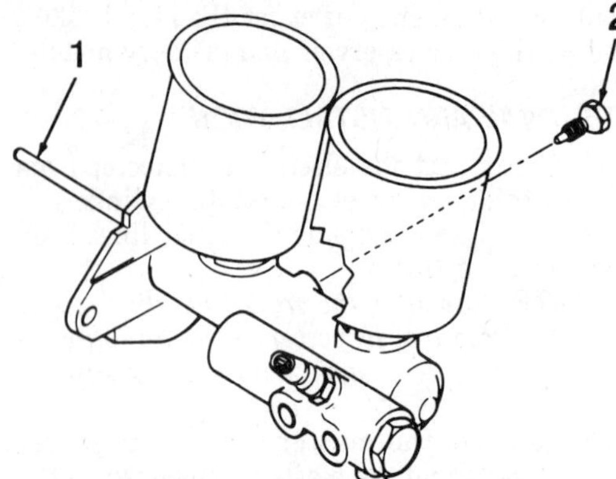

Bottom the piston in the bore with a brass or wood rod (1) before removing or installing stop bolt (2)

4. To install, reverse the removal procedures. Torque the master cylinder-to-power booster nuts to 15–25 ft. lbs. (20–34 Nm) and the brake tubes-to-master cylinder to 12–15 ft. lbs. (16–20 Nm). Refill the master cylinder reservoirs. Bleed the brake system.

NOTE: *Use ONLY DOT 3 or Delco Supreme No. 11 brake fluid in the brake system. DO NOT use silicone brake fluid such as Delco Supreme No. 24. Any type of silicone brake fluid may cause seal damage. DO NOT use lubricated compressed air to blow off brake parts, as damage to rubber components may occur.*

OVERHAUL

1. Remove master cylinder reservoir caps, separate the caps and diaphragms, then discard the diaphragms. Inspect the caps for cracks or damage and replace (if necessary). Drain and discard any remaining brake fluid.
2. Secure the master cylinder in a suitable holding fixture, like a piece of steel plate with holes drilled to accommodate the mounting bolts and piston bore clamped in a vise. Clamping the aluminum master cylinder in a vise is not recommended and may cause cracks or damage.
3. Fully depress the master cylinder pistons with a suitable brass rod or wooden dowel and remove the stop bolt. Using snapring pliers, remove the retaining snapring.

NOTE: *Never remove the stop bolt unless both pistons are fully bottomed in the bore.*

4. Remove the brass rod or dowel and primary piston.
5. Lightly tap the open end of the master cylinder body on a block of wood to dislodge the secondary piston.
6. Remove the primary piston spring.
7. Using a small pry bar, remove the seal retainer and discard it.
8. Remove and discard the primary seal and washer. Remove and discard the secondary seal.
9. Remove the spring locator and spring from the secondary piston.
10. Using a small pry bar, remove and discard the seal retainer.
11. Remove and discard the primary seal/washer and secondary seal.
12. Remove the switch assembly, be careful to retain the plastic body, spring and probe as an assembly.
13. Remove the end plug, then discard the O-ring.

NOTE: *The end plug O-rings should be replaced whenever the master cylinder is overhauled.*

14. Gently tap the master cylinder body on a block of wood to dislodge the combination piston with ground spring attached. The combination piston should be discarded and replaced as a complete assembly.
15. Wash all parts to be reused in clean, denatured alcohol. Use only dry, filtered compressed air to blow out passages in the master cylinder body.

NOTE: *DO NOT wash the replacement combination piston in any cleaning solution. New parts are coated with special grease.*

16. Lubricate the secondary piston/seals with clean brake fluid and assemble the seals to the piston.
17. Lubricate and install the primary seal washer and seal.
18. Install the seal retainer while making sure it seats properly in the groove in the secondary piston.
19. Install the secondary spring and spring locator in the secondary piston.
20. Lubricate the master cylinder bore with clean brake fluid and install the secondary piston spring assembly.
21. Lubricate the primary piston and piston seals with clean brake fluid and install the secondary seals.

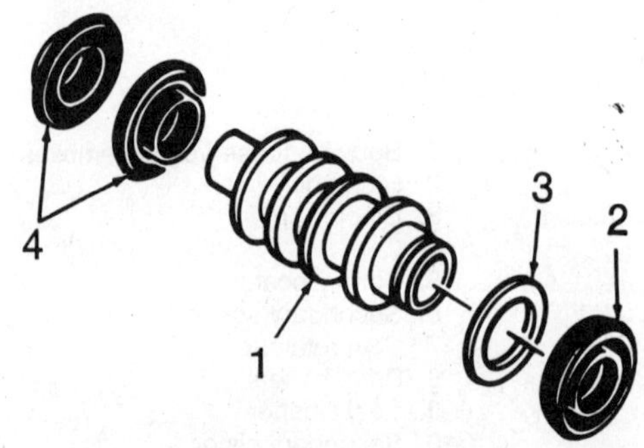

Secondary piston (1) showing location of primary seal (2), washer (3) and secondary seal (4)

Primary piston (1) showing location of primary seal (2), washer (3) and secondary seal (4)

22. Install the primary seal washer and seal. Install the seal retainer, making sure it is properly seated in the primary piston groove.
23. Install the primary piston spring, then install the primary piston spring assembly into the master cylinder bore.
24. Using a brass rod or wooden dowel, push on the primary piston until the primary and secondary pistons bottom in the bore. Once the pistons bottom, install the stop bolt and torque to 7–9 ft. lbs. (9–12 Nm).

CAUTION: *DO NOT install the stop bolt unless the pistons are fully bottomed in the master cylinder bore.*

25. Install a new snapring retainer in the master cylinder bore, making sure it is seated properly into the groove. Remove the brass rod or dowel.
26. Install the fine wire spring over the capped end of the new combination piston.
27. Lubricate both the bore and the combination piston with clean brake fluid and insert the piston open end first. Make sure the piston is fully bottomed in the bore.
28. Lubricate a new O-ring with clean brake fluid and install it over the threaded end of the end plug. Install the end plug and torque to 15–22 ft. lbs. (20–30 Nm).
29. Install new diaphragms on the reservoir caps and fill with the recommended brake fluid. Torque master cylinder-to-brake booster bolts to 15 ft. lbs. (21 Nm). Bleed the brake system and check for leaks after installation.

CAUTION: *The use of silicone brake fluid such as Delco Supreme No. 24 may damage the seals and rubber components in the brake system. Use brake fluid that meets or excels DOT 3 specifications, such as Delco Supreme No. 11.*

Power Brake Booster

REMOVAL AND INSTALLATION

1. Without disconnecting the brake lines from the master cylinder, remove the master cylinder-to-power brake booster nuts and move the master cylinder clear of the power brake booster.
2. At the power brake booster, remove the vacuum hose from the vacuum check valve.
3. From under the dash, disconnect the power brake booster push rod from the brake pedal and the power brake booster-to-firewall nuts.
4. Remove the power brake booster from the vehicle.
5. To install, reverse the removal procedures. Check and/or adjust the pedal height.

Combination Valve

The combination (proportioning) valve is an integral part of the master cylinder housing. The proportioning section of the combination valve proportions the outlet pressure to the rear brakes after a predetermined rear input pressure has been reached. This is done to prevent rear wheel lock-up. The valve is designed with a bypass feature which assures full system pressure to the rear brakes if the front brake system fails and full system pressure to the front brakes if the rear brake system fails.

The warning switch is designed to constantly compare the front and rear brake pressure from the master cylinder and turn ON the dash light in case of front or rear system failure. The warning light switch portion of the combination valve is not serviceable. If the switch is found defective the combination valve must be replaced.

REMOVAL AND INSTALLATION

Refer to the "Master Cylinder Overhaul" procedures in this section to replace the proportioning valve.

ADJUSTMENT AND/OR CENTERING

Refer to the "Master Cylinder Overhaul" procedures in this section to adjust and/or center the proportioning valve.

Bleeding

The hydraulic brake system must be bled any time one of the lines is disconnected or air enters the system. This may be done manually or by the pressure method. The correct bleeding sequence is: left rear, right rear, left front and right front wheel calipers.

The manufacturer recommends that the entire hydraulic system be thoroughly flushed with clean brake fluid whenever new parts are installed in the hydraulic system. Flushing is also recommended if there is any doubt as to

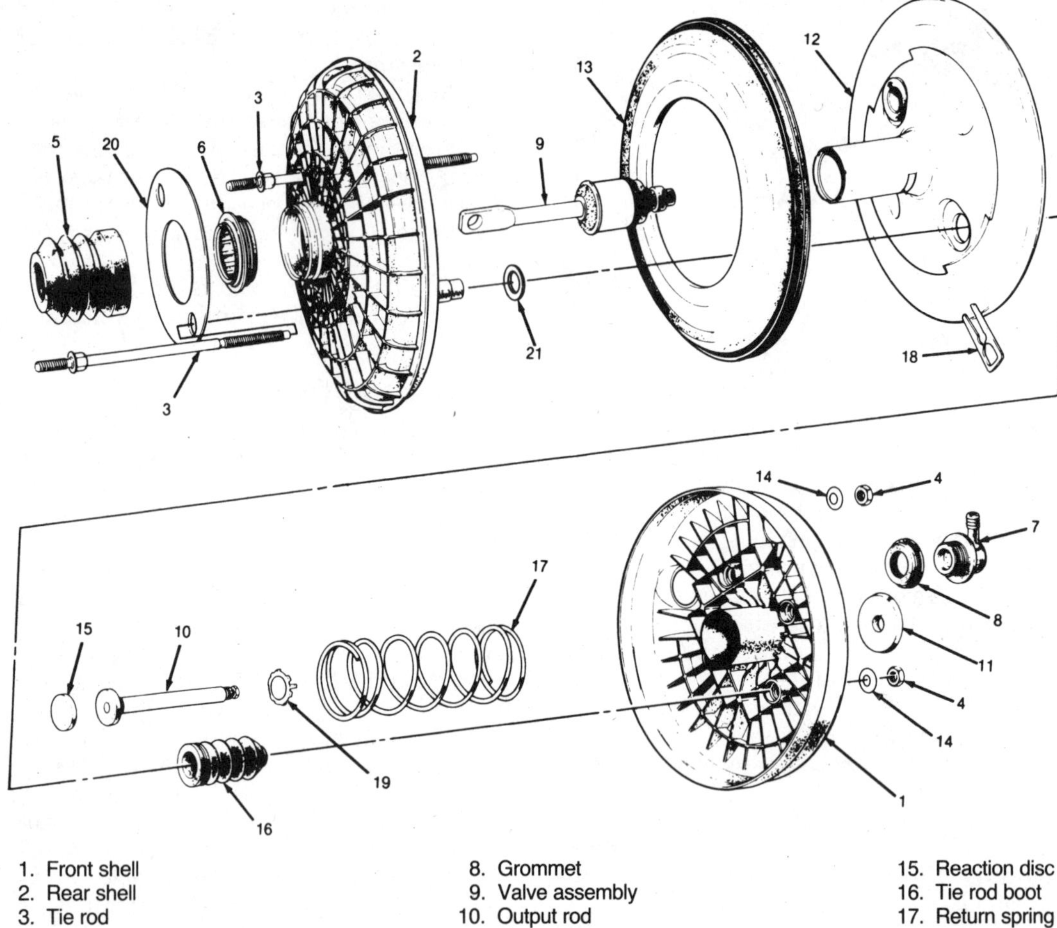

1. Front shell
2. Rear shell
3. Tie rod
4. Nut
5. Boot
6. Rear seal
7. Vacuum check valve
8. Grommet
9. Valve assembly
10. Output rod
11. Front seal
12. Vacuum piston
13. Diaphragm
14. Coned spring
15. Reaction disc
16. Tie rod boot
17. Return spring
18. Stop plate
19. Retainer
20. Gasket
21. Steel washer

Exploded view of the power brake booster

the grade of fluid in the system. If fluid has been used which contains the slightest trace of mineral oil, all rubber parts that have been subjected to the contaminated fluid should be replaced.

When bleeding the rear brake system, the front of the vehicle should be raised higher than the rear; in this position, the rear caliper bleeder screw will be near the 12 o'clock position to prevent air being trapped in the caliper.

PRESSURE BLEEDING

1. Clean the top of the master cylinder, remove the cover and attach the pressure bleeding adapter.
2. Check the pressure bleeder reservoir for correct pressure and fluid level, then open the release valve.
3. Fasten a bleeder hose to the wheel cylinder bleeder nipple and submerge the free end of the hose in a transparent receptacle. The receptacle should contain enough brake fluid to cover the open end of the hose.
4. Open the wheel cylinder bleeder nipple and allow the fluid to flow until all bubbles disappear and an uncontaminated flow exists.
5. Close the nipple, remove the bleeder hose and repeat the procedure on the other wheel cylinder according to the bleeding sequence.

MANUAL BLEEDING

An alternative to the pressure method of bleeding requires two people to perform: one to depress the brake pedal and the other to open the bleeder nipples.

1. Observe the cleaning operation of the pressure method, then remove the cover and fill the reservoir.

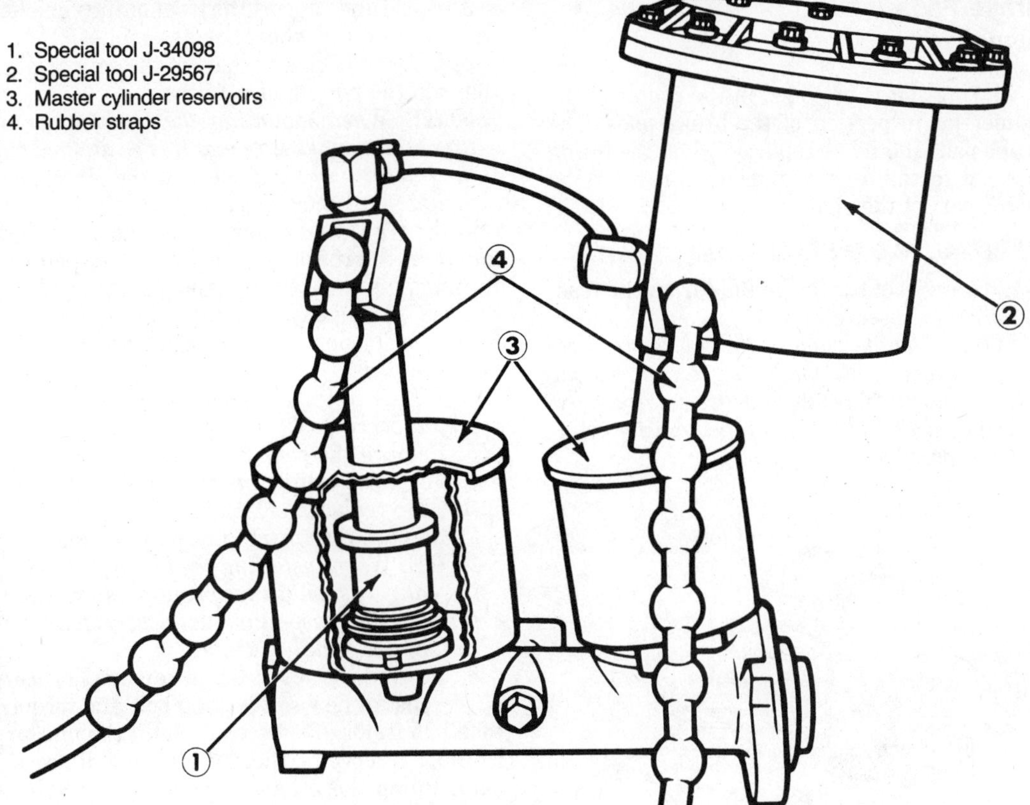

Using the power bleeder to bleed the brake system

Extracting the fluid from the brake caliper

2. Attach a bleeder hose and clear container as before.
3. Have the assistant depress the brake pedal to the floor, open the bleeder screw, pause until fluid flow ceases and close the bleeder screw.
4. Release the pedal, allow it to return and repeat the procedure until a steady, bubble-free flow is seen.
5. Secure the nipple and move to the other wheels in the correct sequence.
6. Periodically check the master cylinder for an adequate supply of fluid. If the reservoir runs dry, air will enter the system and bleeding will have to be done again.

FRONT DISC BRAKES

CAUTION: *Brake shoes contain asbestos, which has been determined to be a cancer causing agent. Never clean the brake surfaces with compressed air! Avoid inhaling any dust from any brake surface! When cleaning brake surfaces, use a commercially available brake cleaning fluid.*

Brake Pads

INSPECTION

A viewing slot is provided in the center of the caliper for inspection of the brake pads. The brake pads should be replaced when the lining is worn to the approximate thickness of the metal part of the shoe.

REMOVAL AND INSTALLATION

1. Drain ⅔ of the brake fluid from the master cylinder reservoirs.

NOTE: *The insertion of the thicker replacement brakes will push the caliper pistons back into their bores and the resulting hydraulic action will cause a full master cylinder to overflow.*

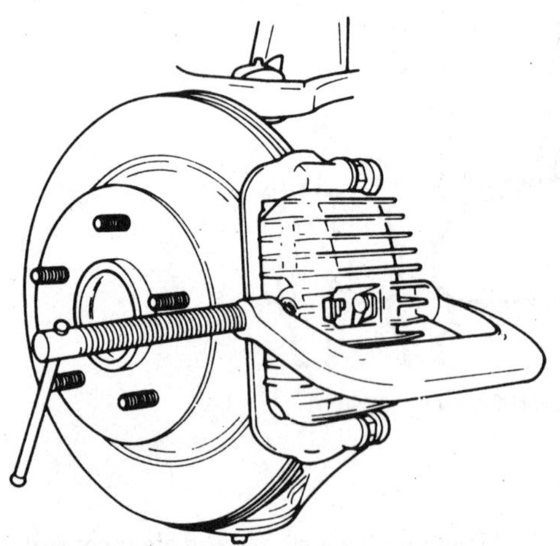

Using C-clamp to retract the caliper piston for pad removal

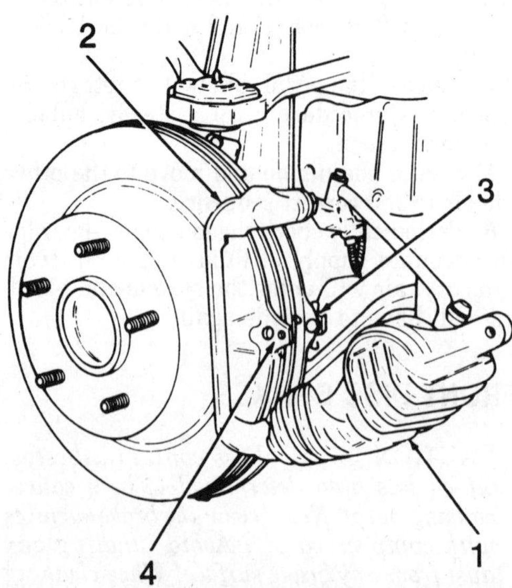

Pivot the caliper (1) on the mounting bracket (2) to expose the inboard (3) and outboard (4) brake pads

2. Raise and support the front of the vehicle, then remove the wheel/tire assemblies.

3. Using a C-clamp, squeeze the caliper piston into the bottom of it's bore.

NOTE: *When mounting the C-clamp onto the caliper, make sure that it is positioned on the inlet fitting head bolt and the other side against the outlet shoe.*

4. Extract and discard the shoe springs found on the inside edge of the brake pad retaining pins (two retaining pins on heavy duty brakes). Remove and discard the upper self-locking bolt, then rotate the caliper back to expose the pads.

NOTE: *A lining wear sensor is mounted on the outboard pad.*

5. Remove the pads from the calipers.

6. Force the caliper piston into it's bore and insert the replacement pads.

7. Replace the spring pins on the pads.

NOTE: *When installing the brake pads onto the caliper, should the spring pins protrude through the inspection window, rotate the caliper and readjust them.*

8. To install, reverse the removal procedures. Install new self-locking bolt and torque to 22–25 ft. lbs. (30–34 Nm). Refill the master cylinder reservoirs. Bleed the system, if necessary. Pump the brakes (firmly and slowly) 3 times to bring the pads in contact with the disc. Road test the vehicle.

Brake Caliper

REMOVAL AND INSTALLATION

1. Raise and support the front of the vehicle on jackstands. Remove the wheel/tire assemblies.

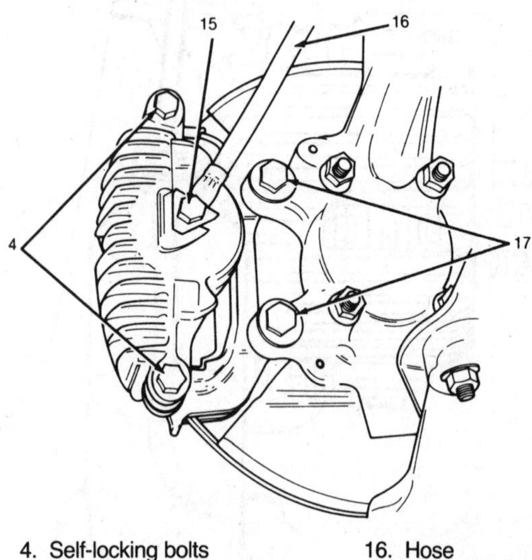

4. Self-locking bolts
15. Inlet fitting
16. Hose
17. Bracket bolts

View of the brake caliper mounting bolts and brake inlet fitting

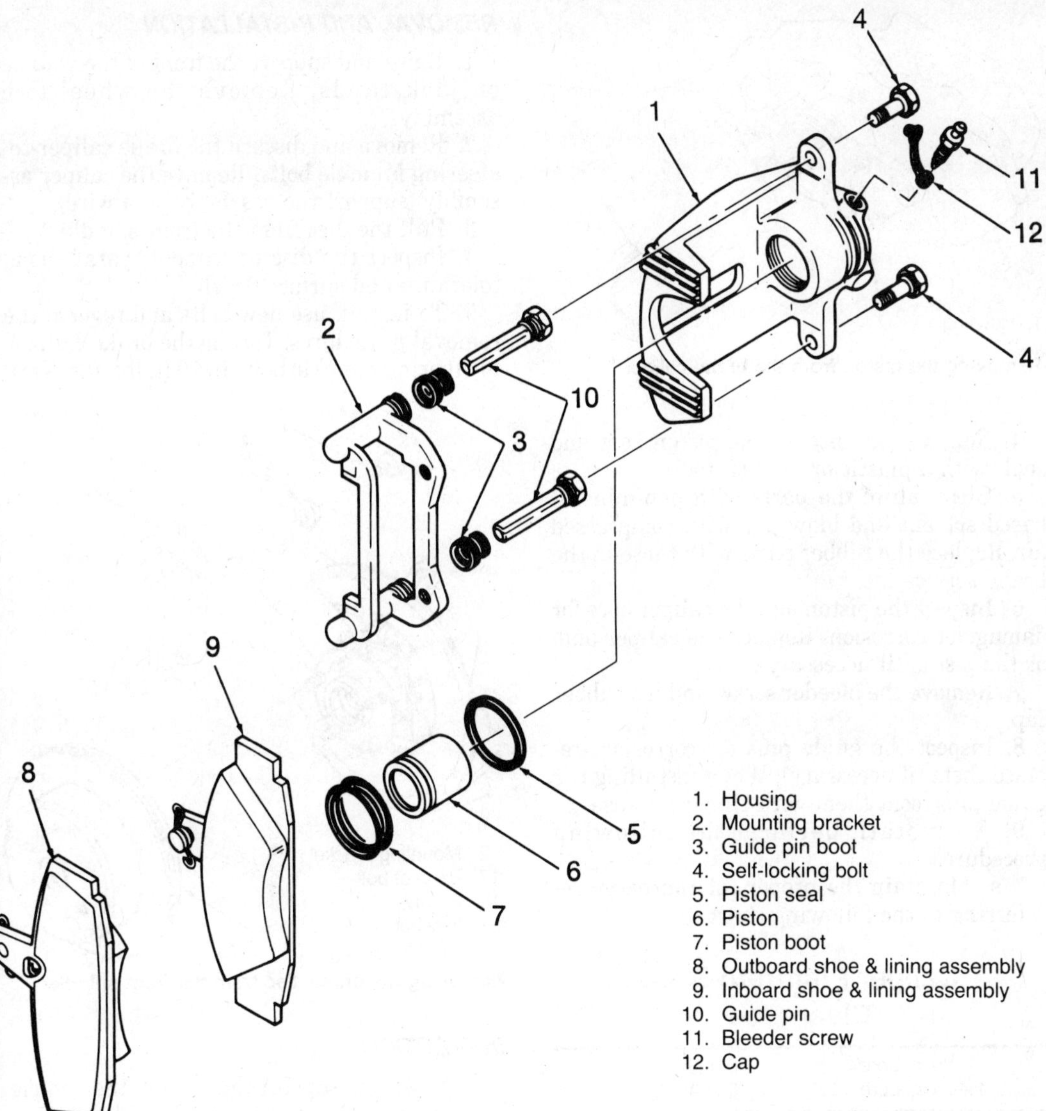

Exploded view of Girlock caliper assembly on 1984 and later models

2. Disconnect the front caliper's brake hose at it's support bracket. Plug each line to prevent dirt from entering the system.

NOTE: *If the caliper is not being removed from the vehicle, DO NOT disconnect the brake line.*

3. Remove and discard the 2 caliper-to-bracket self-locking bolts. Remove the caliper from it's mounting bracket.

4. To install, use 2 new self-locking bolts and reverse the removal procedures. Torque the caliper-to-mounting bracket bolts to 22–25 ft. lbs. (30–34 Nm).

NOTE: *If the caliper was removed from the vehicle, be sure to bleed the brake system.*

OVERHAUL

1. Refer to the "Brake Caliper, Removal and Installation" procedures in this section and remove the brake caliper from the vehicle.

2. Remove the inlet fitting from the brake caliper.

3. Position the caliper on a work bench and place clean shop cloths in the caliper opening. Using compressed air, force the piston from it's bore.

CAUTION: *DO NOT apply too much air pressure to the bore, for the piston may jump out, causing damage to the piston and/or the operator.*

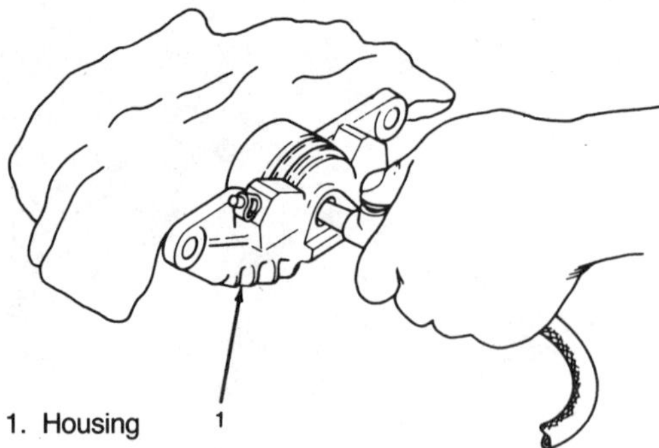

Removing the piston from the brake caliper

4. Remove and discard the piston boot and seal (with a plastic or wooden tool).
5. Clean all of the parts with non-mineral based solvent and blow dry with compressed air. Replace the rubber parts with those in the brake service kit.
6. Inspect the piston and the caliper bore for damage or corrosion. Replace the caliper and/or the piston (if necessary).
7. Remove the bleeder screw and it's rubber cap.
8. Inspect the guide pins for corrosion, replace them (if necessary). When installing the guide pins, coat them with silicone grease.
9. To install, perform the following procedures:
   a. Maintain the proper tolerances by referring to the following chart.

Caliper Piston-to-Bore Clearance

1—3/8 in. bore	0.0035–0.009
1—7/8 in. bore	0.0045–0.010

   b. Lubricate the piston, caliper and seal with clean brake fluid.
   NOTE: *When positioning the piston seal on the piston, it goes in the groove nearest the piston's flat end with the lap facing the largest end. If placement is correct, the seal lips will be in the groove and not extend over the groove's step.*
   c. Replace the self-locking bolts and torque to 22–25 ft. lbs. (30–40 Nm).
10. To complete the installation procedures, reverse the removal procedures. Bleed the brake system after installation.

Brake Disc (Rotor)

Refer the "Wheel Bearing, Removal and Installation" procedures in Chapter 1 to replace the wheel bearing.

REMOVAL AND INSTALLATION

1. Raise and support the front of the vehicle on jackstands. Remove the wheel/tire assembly.
2. Remove and discard the brake caliper-to-steering knuckle bolts. Remove the caliper assembly (support the assembly on a wire).
3. Pull the disc from the front spindle.
4. Inspect the disc for runout, parallelism, tolerance and surface finish.
5. To install, use new bolts and reverse the removal procedures. Torque the brake caliper-to-steering knuckle bolts to 70 ft. lbs. (95 Nm).

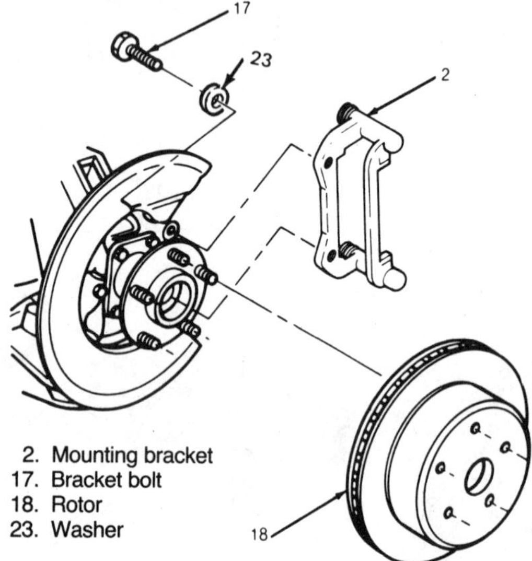

Removing the brake disc from the front spindle

INSPECTION

1. Raise and support the front of the vehicle on jackstands. Remove the wheel/tire assembly.
2. Install 2 lug nuts to ensure proper wheel alignment.
3. To check the disc runout, perform the following procedures:
   a. Using a dial indicator, secure and position it so that the button contacts the disc about 1/2" from the outer edge.
   b. Rotate the disc. The lateral reading should not exceed 0.006 in. (0.15mm). If the reading is excessive, recondition or replace the disc.
4. To check the disc parallelism, perform the following procedures:
   a. Using a micrometer, check the disc thickness at 4 locations around the disc, at the same distance from the edge.
   b. The thickness should not vary more than 0.0005 in. (0.013mm). If the readings are excessive, recondition or replace the disc.

Checking disc run-out

5. The surface finish must be relatively smooth to avoid pulling and erratic performance, also, to extend the lining life. Light rotor surface scoring of up to 0.015 in. (0.38mm) in depth, can be tolerated. If the scoring depths are excessive, refinish or replace the rotor.

REAR DISC BRAKES

CAUTION: *Brake shoes contain asbestos, which has been determined to be a cancer causing agent. Never clean the brake surfaces with compressed air! Avoid inhaling any dust from any brake surface! When cleaning brake surfaces, use a commercially available brake cleaning fluid.*

Brake Pads

INSPECTION

A viewing slot is provided in the center of the caliper for inspection of the brake pads; the brake pads should be replaced when the lining is worn to the approximate thickness of the metal part of the shoe.

REMOVAL AND INSTALLATION

1. Drain ⅔ of the brake fluid from the master cylinder reservoirs.

NOTE: *The insertion of the thicker replacement brakes will push the caliper pistons back into their bores and the resulting hydraulic action will cause a full master cylinder to overflow.*

2. Raise and support the rear of the vehicle, then remove the wheel/tire assemblies.

3. Using a C-clamp, squeeze the caliper piston into the bottom of it's bore.

NOTE: *When mounting the C-clamp onto the caliper, make sure that it is positioned on the inlet fitting head bolt and the other side against the outlet shoe.*

4. Extract and discard the shoe springs found on the inside edge of the brake pad retaining pins (two retaining pins on heavy duty brakes). Remove and discard the upper self-locking bolt, then rotate the caliper back to expose the pads.

NOTE: *A lining wear sensor is mounted on the outboard pad.*

5. Remove the pads from the calipers.

6. Force the caliper piston into it's bore and insert the replacement pads.

7. Replace the spring pins on the pads.

NOTE: *When installing the brake pads onto the caliper, should the spring pins protrude through the inspection window, rotate the caliper and readjust them.*

8. To install, reverse the removal procedures. Install new self-locking bolt and torque to 22–25 ft. lbs. (30–34 Nm). Refill the master cylinder reservoirs. Bleed the system, if necessary. Pump the brakes (firmly and slowly) 3 times to bring the pads in contact with the disc. Road test the vehicle.

Brake Caliper

REMOVAL AND INSTALLATION

1. Raise and support the rear of the vehicle on jackstands. Remove the wheel/tire assemblies.

2. Disconnect the rear caliper's brake hose at it's support bracket. Plug each line to prevent dirt from entering the system.

NOTE: *If the caliper is not being removed from the vehicle, DO NOT disconnect the brake line.*

3. Remove and discard the 2 caliper-to-bracket self-locking bolts. Remove the caliper from it's mounting bracket.

4. To install, use 2 new self-locking bolts and reverse the removal procedures. Torque the caliper-to-mounting bracket bolts to 22–25 ft. lbs. (30–34 Nm).

NOTE: *If the caliper was removed from the vehicle, be sure to bleed the brake system.*

OVERHAUL

1. Refer to the "Brake Caliper, Removal and Installation" procedures in this section and remove the brake caliper from the vehicle.

2. Remove the inlet fitting from the brake caliper.

3. Position the caliper on a work bench and place clean shop cloths in the caliper opening.

Using compressed air, force the piston from it's bore.

CAUTION: *DO NOT apply too much air pressure to the bore, for the piston may jump out, causing damage to the piston and/or the operator.*

4. Remove and discard the piston boot and seal (with a plastic or wooden tool).

5. Clean all of the parts with non-mineral based solvent and blow dry with compressed air. Replace the rubber parts with those in the brake service kit.

6. Inspect the piston and the caliper bore for damage or corrosion. Replace the caliper and/or the piston (if necessary).

7. Remove the bleeder screw and it's rubber cap.

8. Inspect the guide pins for corrosion, replace them (if necessary). When installing the guide pins, coat them with silicone grease.

9. To install, perform the following procedures:

a. Maintain the proper tolerances by referring to the following chart.

b. Lubricate the piston, caliper and seal with clean brake fluid.

NOTE: *When positioning the piston seal on the piston, it goes in the groove nearest the piston's flat end with the lap facing the largest end. If placement is correct, the seal lips will be in the groove and not extend over the groove's step.*

c. Replace the self-locking bolts and torque to 22–25 ft. lbs. (30–40 Nm).

10. To complete the installation procedures, reverse the removal procedures. Bleed the brake system after installation.

Brake Disc (Rotor)

Refer the "Wheel Bearing, Removal and Installation" procedures in Chapter 6 and replace the wheel bearing.

REMOVAL AND INSTALLATION

1. Raise and support the rear of the vehicle on jackstands. Remove the wheel/tire assembly.

2. Remove and discard the brake caliper-to-knuckle bolts. Remove the caliper assembly (support the assembly on a wire).

3. Pull the disc from the rear spindle.

4. Inspect the disc for runout, parallelism, tolerance and surface finish.

5. To install, use new bolts and reverse the removal procedures. Torque the brake caliper-to-knuckle bolts to 44 ft. lbs. (60 Nm).

INSPECTION

1. Raise and support the rear of the vehicle on jackstands. Remove the wheel/tire assembly.

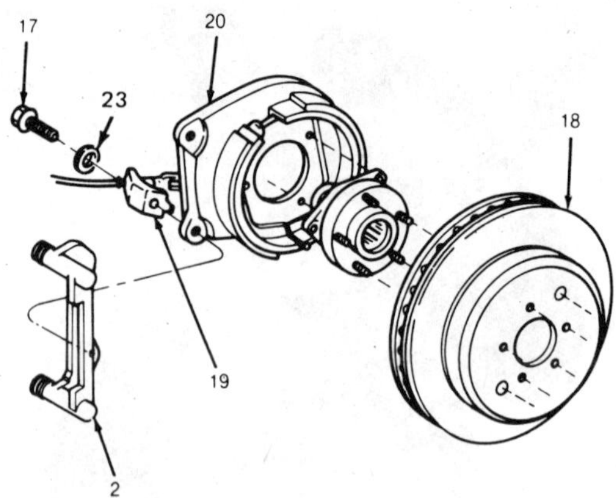

2. Mounting bracket
17. Bracket bolt
18. Rotor
19. Cable bracket
20. Mounting plate
23. Washer

Removing the rear brake disc

2. Install 2 lug nuts to ensure proper wheel alignment.

3. To check the disc runout, perform the following procedures:

a. Using a dial indicator, secure and position it so that the button contacts the disc about ½" from the outer edge.

b. Rotate the disc. The lateral reading should not exceed 0.006 in. (0.15mm). If the reading is excessive, recondition or replace the disc.

4. To check the disc parallelism, perform the following procedures:

a. Using a micrometer, check the disc thickness at 4 locations around the disc, at the same distance from the edge.

b. The thickness should not vary more than 0.0005 in. (0.013mm). If the readings are excessive, recondition or replace the disc.

5. The surface finish must be relatively smooth to avoid pulling and erratic performance, also, to extend the lining life. Light rotor surface scoring of up to 0.015 in. (0.38mm) in depth, can be tolerated. If the scoring depths are excessive, refinish or replace the rotor.

PARKING BRAKE

Cable

REMOVAL AND INSTALLATION

Front

1. Raise and support the front of the vehicle on jackstands.

2. Disconnect the left rear and the right rear cables from the equalizer.

3. Lower the vehicle half way.

4. At the driver's door, remove the lower door sill molding.

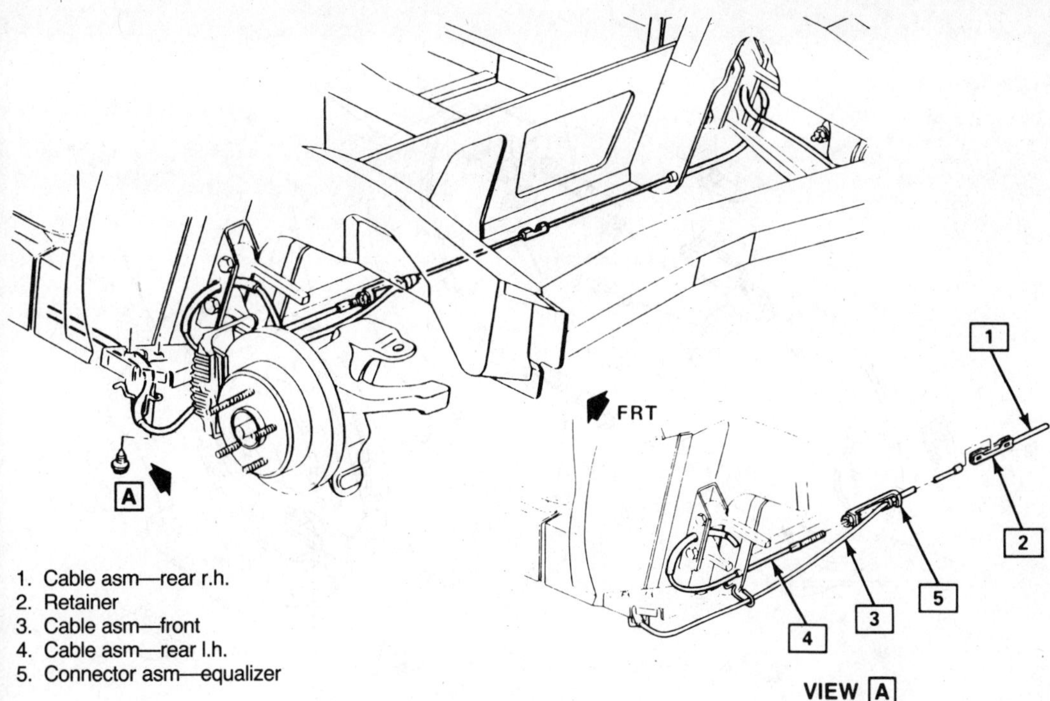

View of the parking brake cables

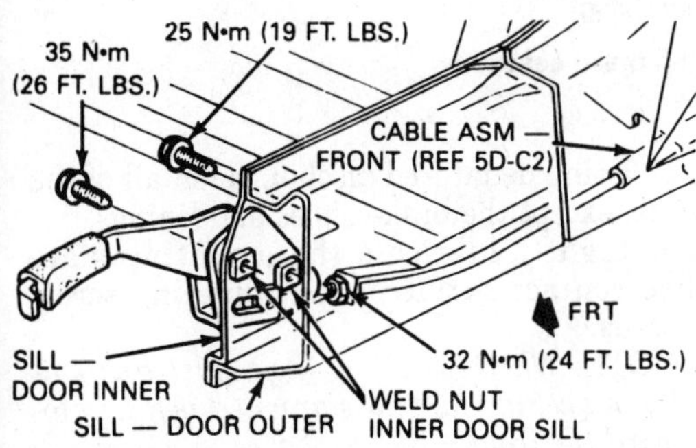

View of the parking brake lever

5. Remove the cable nut, the cable guide and the cable.

6. To install, reverse the removal procedures. Adjust the parking brake.

Left Rear

1. Raise and support the rear of the vehicle on jackstands.

2. Disconnect the left rear cable from the equalizer.

3. Remove the cable from the frame, the caliper mounting bracket and the parking brake lever (at the wheel).

4. To install, reverse the removal procedures. Adjust the parking brake.

Right Rear

1. Raise and support the rear of the vehicle on jackstands.

2. Disconnect the right rear cable from the equalizer.

3. Remove the cable from the frame, the caliper mounting bracket and the parking brake lever (at the wheel).

4. To install, reverse the removal procedures. Adjust the parking brake.

ADJUSTMENT

1. Refer to the "Parking Brake Shoe Adjustment" procedures in this section and adjust the parking brake shoes.

2. Apply the parking brake to the 2nd notch.

3. Tighten the cables at the equalizer to give a light drag with the wheel mounted.

4. Release the parking brake and check for a no drag condition.

Brake Shoes

The parking brake is a conventional (Duo Servo type) drum brake located in the rear wheel disc. Adjustments are similar to those for a regular drum brake.

REMOVAL AND INSTALLATION

CAUTION: *Brake shoes contain asbestos, which has been determined to be a cancer causing agent. Never clean the brake surfaces with compressed air! Avoid inhaling any dust from any brake surface! When cleaning brake surfaces, use a commercially available brake cleaning fluid.*

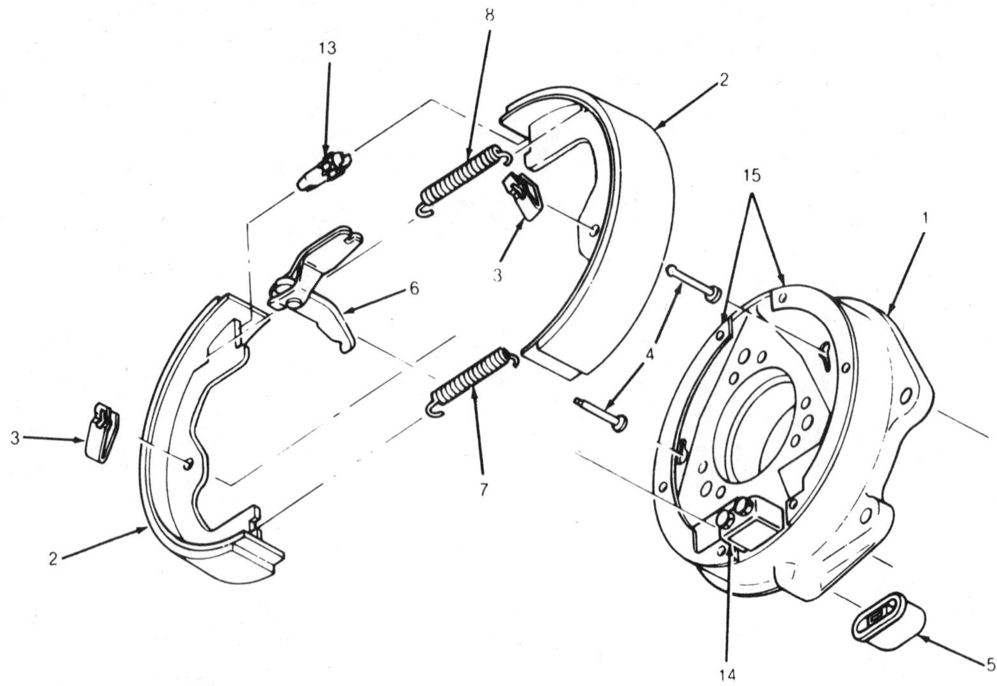

1. Mounting plate assembly
2. Shoe and lining
3. Hold-down spring
4. Hold-down pin
5. Boot
6. Lever and strut assembly
7. Shoe return spring
8. Adjuster return spring
13. Adjuster assembly
14. Wear bracket
15. Wear shim

Exploded view of the parking brake assembly

1. Refer to the "Rear Disc Brake, Removal and Installation" procedures in this section and remove the rear wheel disc.

NOTE: *When removing the brake caliper, DO NOT disconnect the brake line but hang the caliper above the disc with wire. Be careful not to damage the wear indicators on the mounting plate assembly, for it may be necessary to replace the entire assembly.*

2. Spread the brake shoes and remove the adjuster assembly and the return spring.
3. Disconnect the hold down spring and the anchor pins from the brake shoes.
4. Using a pair of pliers, remove the shoe return spring.
5. Remove the primary and the secondary shoes from the mounting plate assembly.
6. Inspect the various components:
   a. Disassemble and inspect the adjuster assembly threads for wear, burrs or damage, replace it (if necessary).
   b. Clean and inspect the wear bracket and the shims for wear, burrs or damage, replace mounting plate assembly (if necessary).
   c. Inspect the shift lever strut rubber boot for cracks or tears, replace it (if necessary).
   d. Inspect the springs for wear or damage, replace them (if necessary).
7. Using denatured alcohol, clean all of the parts, except the brake shoes and linings.
8. Lightly lubricate the mounting plate shoe contact surfaces and adjusting screw threads.

NOTE: *When installing the adjuster assembly, make sure that the star wheel is facing toward the front.*

9. To install, reverse the removal procedures. Adjust the parking brake.

NOTE: *After the installation of new parking brake linings, the shoes should be burnished. At a speed of 50 mph, apply the parking brakes until a slight drag is felt. Keep the brakes on for approximately 50–60 seconds.*

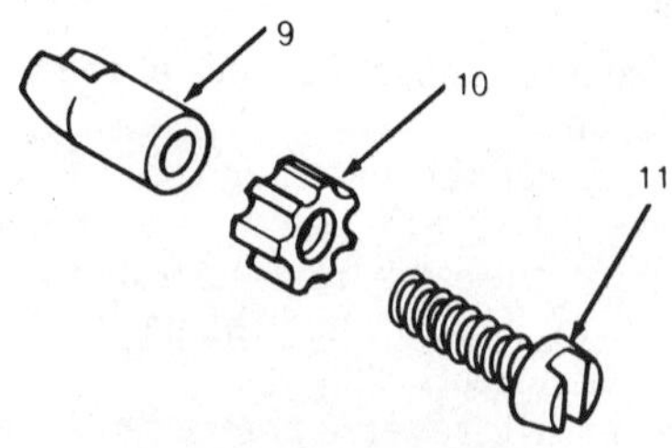

9. Adjuster socket
10. Adjuster nut
11. Adjuster screw

Exploded view of the adjuster assembly

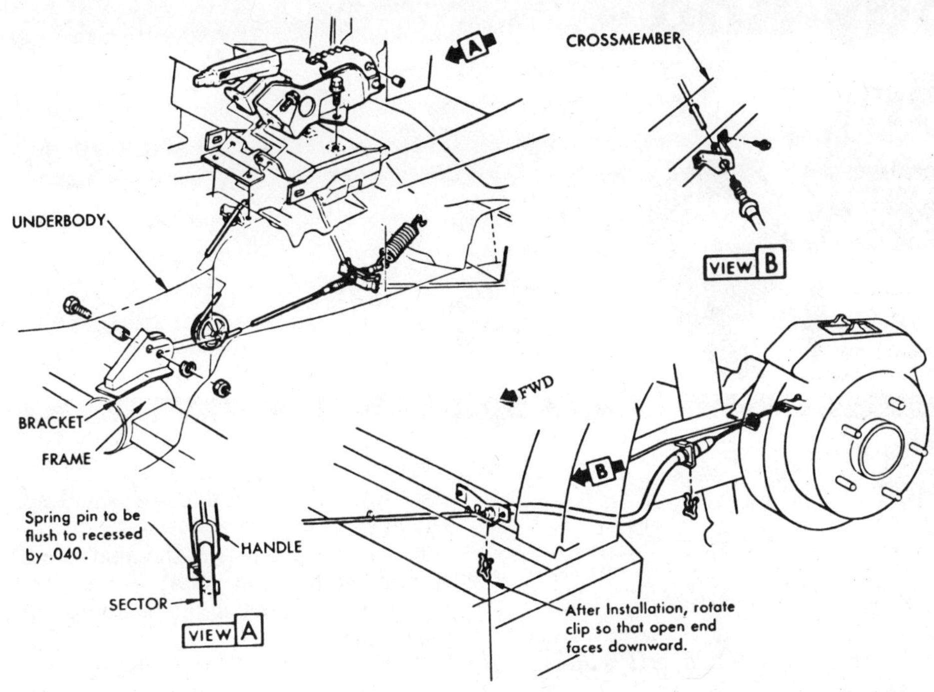

Disc brake parking brake cable assembly

ADJUSTMENTS

1. Block the front wheels. Raise and support the rear of the vehicle on jackstands. Remove the rear wheel/tire assemblies, then replace 2 wheel lug nuts to maintain the disc/drum alignment.
2. Release the handbrake and loosen the parking brake cable at the equalizer so that there is no tension on the parking brake shoes.
3. Rotate the disc until the adjusting screw can be seen through the hole in the disc/drum.
4. Insert a small pry bar into the adjusting hole and adjust the shoe position using the following procedures:
   a. On the driver's side, move the tool handle toward the ceiling to adjust the shoes outward and toward the floor to move the shoes inward.
   b. On the passenger's side, move the tool handle toward the floor to adjust the shoes outward and toward the ceiling to move the shoes inward.
5. Expand the shoes (one wheel at a time) until the wheel does not turn, then back off the star adjuster 5–7 notches; do the same for the opposite side.
6. Replace the rear wheel/tire assemblies.
7. Apply the parking brake to the 2nd notch. Tighten the cables at the equalizer to give a light drag with the wheel mounted.
6. Release the parking brake and check for a no drag condition.

Brake Specifications

Year	Lug Nut Torque (ft. lbs.)	Master Cylinder Bore	Front Brake Disc		Rear Brake Disc		Max Wear Limit	Minimum Lining Thickness	
			Minimum Thickness	Maximum Run-Out	Minimum Thickness	Maximum Run-Out		Front	Rear
1984	80	0.787	0.724	0.006	0.724	0.006	—	0.063	0.063
1985–86	80	0.875	0.724	0.006	0.724	0.006	—	0.063	0.063

Body and Trim

EXTERIOR

Doors

REMOVAL AND INSTALLATION

1. Refer to the "Door Panel, Removal and Installation" procedures in this section and remove the door panel.
2. Raise the hood and disconnect the negative battery cable.
3. Disconnect the door components electrical connectors and remove the electrical harness from the door.
4. To remove the front fender, perform the following procedures:
   a. Remove the fender-to-wheel splash shield screws.
   b. Remove the rear of the fender-to-brace screws and the fender seal.
   c. Remove the clips, the moldings and the fender brace.
   d. Remove the front fender from the vehicle.
5. Using a scribing tool, mark the door hinge-to-body pillar position.
6. Support the door (from the floor) and remove the door hinge-to-body pillar bolts.
7. Remove the door from the vehicle.
8. To install, align the door hinge-to-body pillar marks and reverse the removal proce-

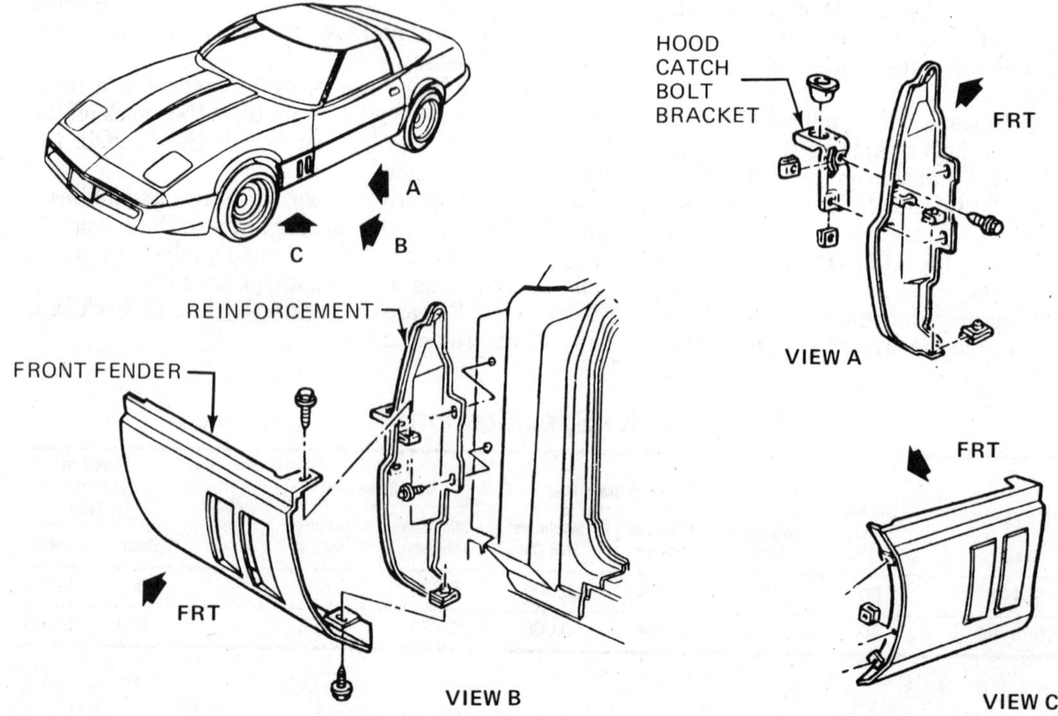

Exploded view of the fender assembly

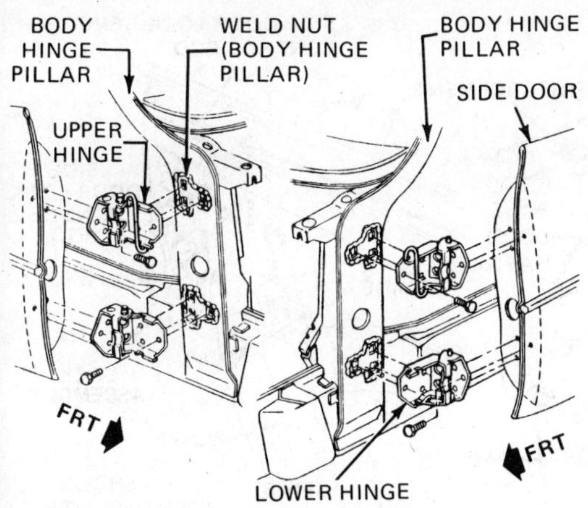

Exploded view of the door hinge assembly

dures. Torque the door hinge-to-body pillar bolts to 15–25 ft. lbs. (20–34 Nm).

ADJUSTMENT

The only adjustment necessary is the alignment of the door striker. The door striker consists of a single metal bolt/washer assembly, which is threaded into a floating plate located in the body lock pillar. The door is secured when the door lock fork-bolt snaps over and engages the striker bolt.

1. If adjustment is necessary, loosen the striker bolt and shift the striker as required, then tighten the bolt.
2. To determine the striker fore or aft adjustment, perform the following procedures:
   a. Make sure that the door is properly aligned.
   b. Using molding clay, apply some to the lock bolt opening.
   c. Close the door ONLY far enough to make an impression in the clay.

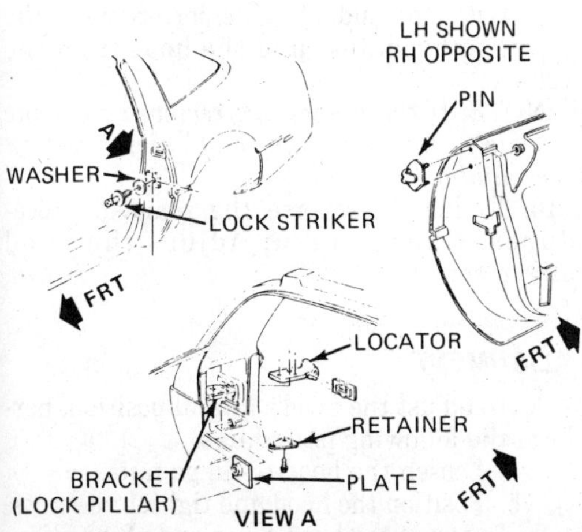

Exploded view of the door lock striker and locator

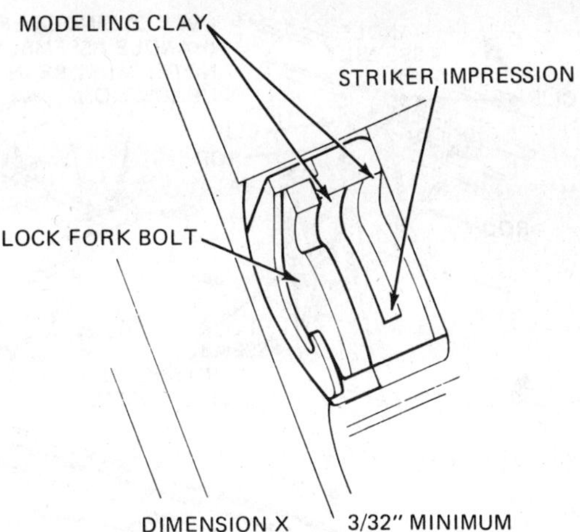

Using molding clay to check the alignment of the striker

   d. Measure the striker impression and adjust the fore and/or aft movement accordingly.
3. If spacers are needed to bring the striker within tolerance measurements, perform the following procedures:
   a. Using a pencil, mark the position of the striker on the body lock pillar.
   b. Using wrench tool No. J-23457, remove the striker bolt.
   c. Install the proper spacer or spacers, then reinstall the striker bolt. Make sure that the striker aligns with the pencil mark. NOTE: *Striker spacers are available in several thicknesses, they are: $^5/_{64}$", $^5/_{32}$", $^1/_4$" and $^5/_{16}$".*
4. Make sure that the door closes and properly engages the striker.

Door Locks

REMOVAL AND INSTALLATION

1. Disconnect the negative battery cable.
2. Remove the armrest, the speaker grille, the foam insulator and the door trim panel.
3. To remove the inner mounting plate, perform the following procedures:
   a. Disconnect the wiring harness rose bud clip.
   b. Remove the mounting plate screws and bolts.
   c. Disconnect the actuator rod. Remove the rod by pushing it down and pulling it out (slightly) to remove the clip.
   d. Remove the door lock mechanism screws.
   e. Disconnect the door lock cylinder rod.
   f. Lower the door lock mechanism by pushing the rod/plate assembly back into the door to access the door lock opening.

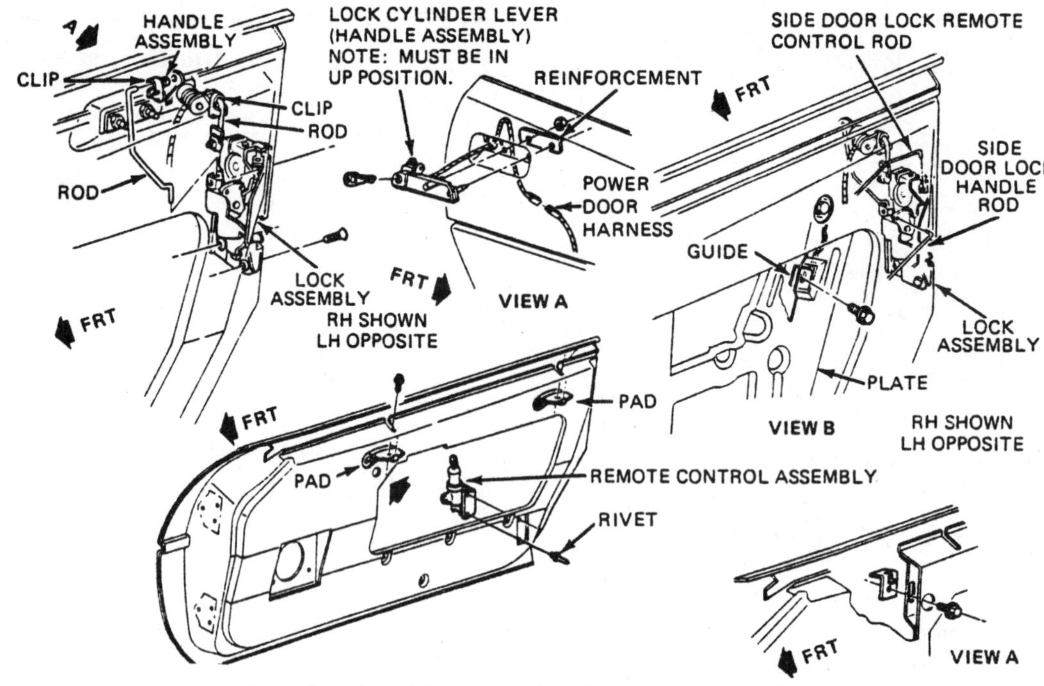

Exploded view of the door lock and remote control switch

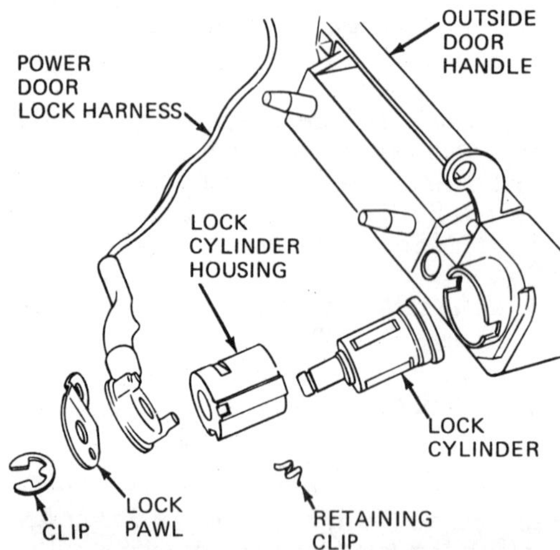

Exploded view of the door lock cylinder assembly

4. Remove the nuts and the backing plate from the handle. Replace the clips on the remote rod to facilitate the assembly.
5. Remove the handle from the vehicle.
6. To install, reverse the removal procedures.

Hood

REMOVAL AND INSTALLATION

1. Raise the hood and disconnect the negative battery cable.
2. Remove the upper wheel-to-hood panel screws from both sides.
3. Remove both underhood lamps and both hood-to-air cleaner ducts.
4. If necessary, remove the bolt and spring assemblies (3 screws) from each side of the hood.
5. At the headlamps, remove the electrical connectors and the lamps from the hood.
6. If necessary, remove the hood emblem nuts and the emblem.
7. Remove the hood support rod, then any necessary fasteners and clips.
8. Using a scribing tool, mark the hinge-to-hood location.
9. With the aid of a helper, remove the hinge-to-hood nuts and the hood from the vehicle.

NOTE: *If the hinges are removed from the vehicle, note the number of shims used on each hinge.*

10. To install, reverse the removal procedures. Check and/or adjust the hood alignment.

ALIGNMENT

1. To adjust the hood's lateral position, perform the following procedures:
   a. Loosen the hood-to-hinge nuts.
   b. Position the hood and tighten the nuts.
2. To adjust the hood's fore and aft position, perform the following procedures:

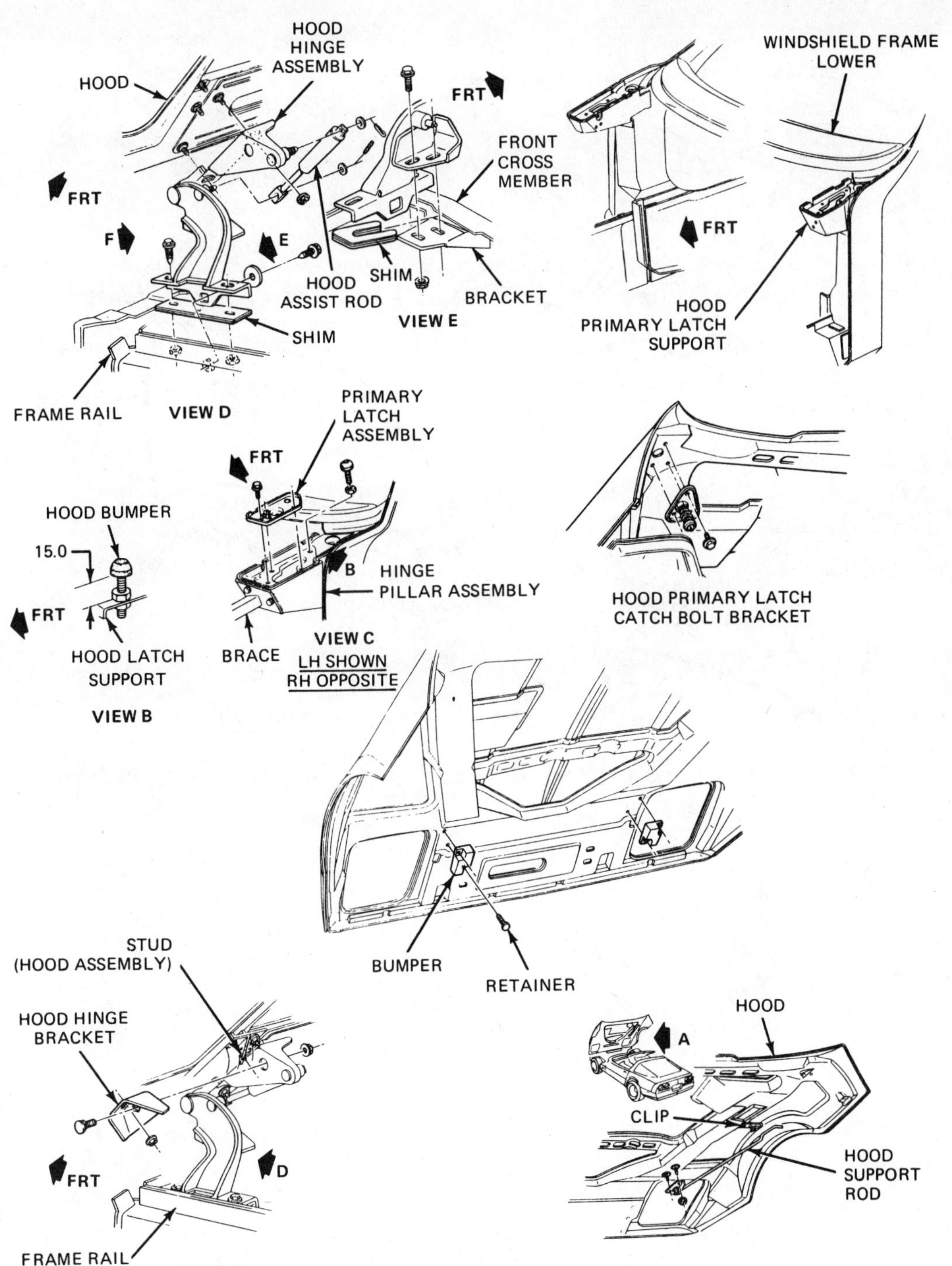

Exploded view of the hood assembly

a. Loosen the hood hinge-to-frame bolts.

b. Position the hood and tighten the bolts.

3. To adjust the hood's latch position, perform the following procedures:

a. At the rear of the hood, loosen either the lock/bolt assemblies or the latch/latch assembly.

b. Position the assembly(s) and tighten the bolts.

Hatch (Rear Window Glass)

The rear window upper hinge and glass are serviced as an assembly.

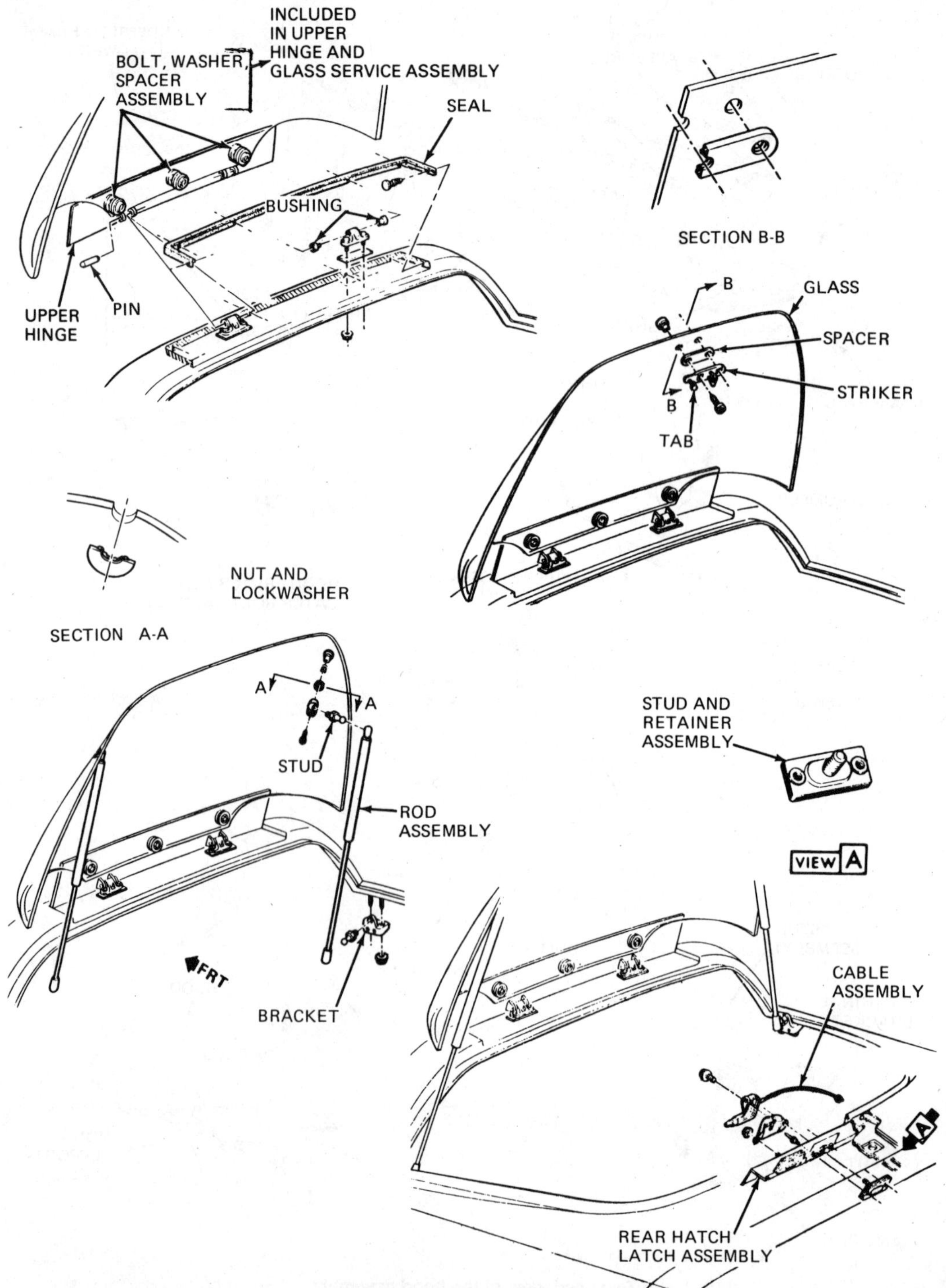

Exploded views of the rear hatch (window glass) assembly

REMOVAL AND INSTALLATION

1. Disconnect the negative battery cable.
2. Raise the hatch (rear window).
3. Remove the roof panel and the interior center roof trim panel.
4. At both sides of the hatch (glass), peel back the noise control patch. Disconnect the electric defogger ground wire.
5. Using a scribing tool, mark the position of the hinge to the body.
6. With the aid of a helper, remove the sup-

port rod-to-hatch (glass) nut (each side), the hatch (glass) hinge-to-body nuts/bolts and the hatch (glass) from the vehicle.

NOTE: *If replacing the hatch (glass), transfer the striker to the new hatch (glass).*

7. To install, reverse the removal procedures. Check and/or adjust the hatch-to-body positions.

ALIGNMENT

1. To adjust the hatch's lateral position, perform the following procedures:
   a. Loosen the hatch hinge assembly-to-body nuts.
   b. Position the hatch assembly and tighten the nuts.
2. To adjust the hatch's fore and aft position, perform the following procedures:
   a. Loosen the hatch hinge assembly-to-body nuts.
   b. Position the hatch assembly and tighten the bolts.
3. To adjust the hatch's latch position, perform the following procedures:
   a. At the rear of the hatch (glass), loosen the striker bolts and/or at the rear of the vehicle, loosen the latch assembly bolts.
   b. Position the assembly(s) and tighten the bolts.

Windshield

Several tools and supplies are necessary to replace the windshield, such as:

- A tube of self curing urethane adhesive.
- A Cold Knife tool No. J-24402, a piece of 0.020 in. diameter steel piano wire and 2 pieces of wood (for wire handles).
- Primers and primer applicator.
- Alcohol (to clean the glass edge).
- A dispensing gun and nozzle.
- A razor knife.
- A tube of black weatherstrip adhesive.

REMOVAL AND INSTALLATION

1. Raise the hood and remove the windshield wiper arms.
2. To remove the weatherstrip (both sides) from the frame, remove the mounting screws and pull the weatherstrip from the channel.
3. Remove both side retainer moldings by removing the screws from the frame.
4. Remove both side reveal moldings by removing the remaining screws.
5. Using tape, index the molding-to-header rail to insure proper reinstallation. Using a small non-metallic pry bar, raise the upper reveal molding (at the corner) and pull it out by hand.
6. To separate the windshield from the urethane seal, use a steel piano wire (with wooden handles) and the Cold Knife tool No. J-24402, then perform the following procedures:
   a. Using the razor knife, cut a slot through the urethane seal.
   b. Pass one end of the wire through the slot.
   c. Secure each end of the wire to a wooden handle.
   d. Using a sawing motion (with the aid of a helper), separate the bottom of the windshield from the frame.
   e. Using the Cold Knife tool No. J-24402, cut through the urethane material across the top and both sides of the windshield.
7. Remove the windshield from the frame.
8. Using a sharp scraper or a wooden chisel, remove the urethane material from the pinchweld flange.

NOTE: *Remove all of the loose urethane pieces from the frame. It is not necessary to remove all of the adhesive material.*

9. Carefully position the replacement windshield in the frame opening. Position the windshield so that a minimum of $^3/_{16}$" overlap exists around the perimeter of the glass.

NOTE: *When positioning the windshield, it may be necessary to place shims under the lower supports.*

10. Once the proper glass-to-pinchweld position has been attained, use a grease pencil to mark the locating position on the glass and the windshield pillar.
11. Remove the glass from the vehicle and place it on a protected table.
12. Using alcohol, thoroughly clean the adhesive bead perimeter of the glass and allow it to air dry.
13. To apply adhesive primers to the glass, thoroughly stir the primers and perform the following procedures:
   a. Apply primer to the inner glass surface (¼" from the edge) around the entire perimeter and allow it to dry for 5 minutes.
   b. Using the Glass Prep No. 1 (clear), apply it to the edge and inner surface of the glass, then wipe dry using a clean cloth.
   c. Using the Glass Prep No. 2 (black), apply it to any portion that requires painting and refinishing or any portion that was cleaned of former adhesive sufficiently to expose the painted surface. Allow it to dry for 5 minutes.
14. Using a caulking gun, carefully apply a continuous bead of urethane adhesive ⅛" high by $^3/_{16}$" wide (at the base) around the entire inside perimeter of the glass.
15. Using a helper, position the glass in the windshield opening and align the matchmarks.

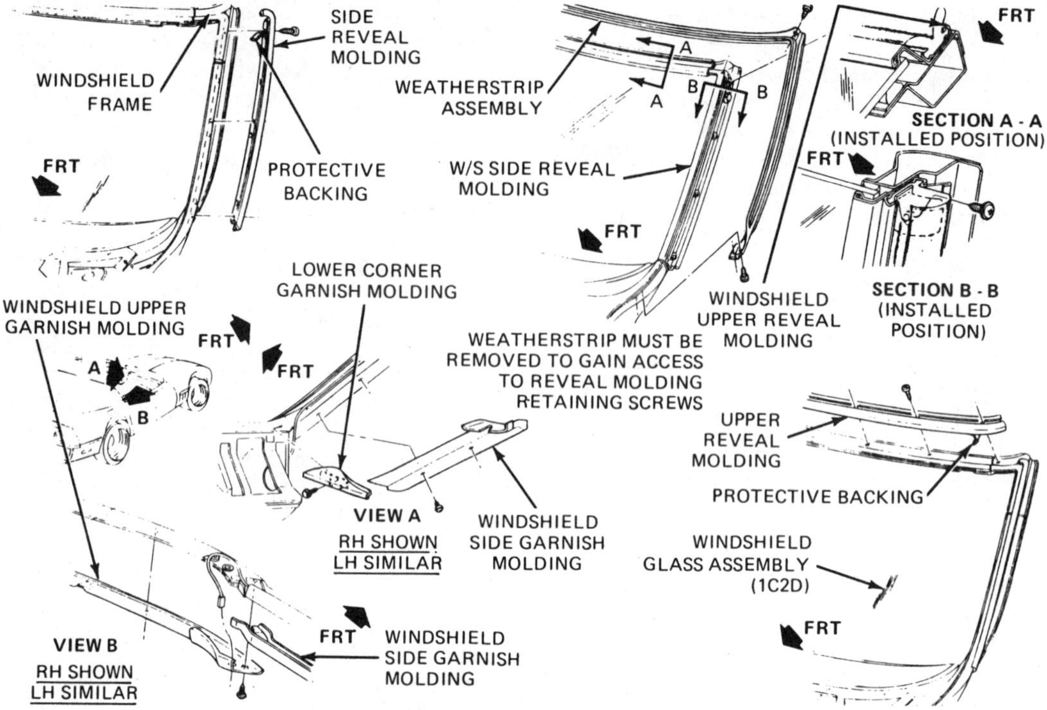

Replacing the widshield

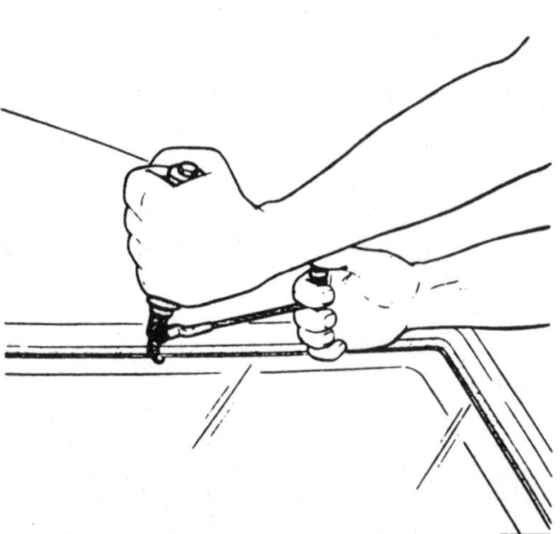

Using tool J-24402 to remove the windshield from the frame

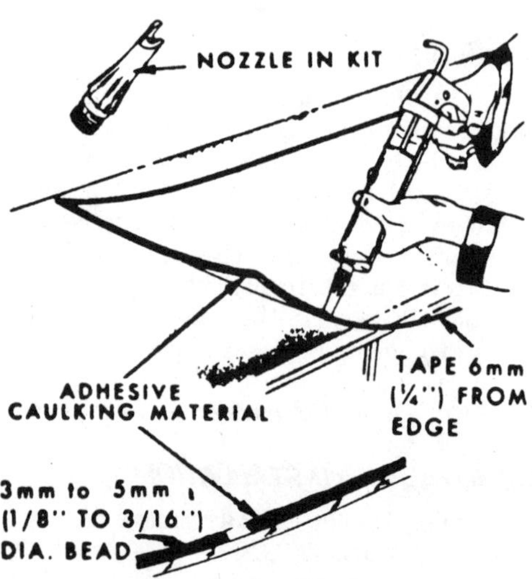

Applying adhesive to the windshield

16. Lightly press the glass to set the adhesive material. Paddle the extra material to insure proper sealing.
17. Immediately, using cold water, water test the seal. If leaks are detected, paddle adhesive material around the leak area.
18. To complete the installation, reverse the removal procedures.

INTERIOR

Door Panel

REMOVAL AND INSTALLATION

1. Raise the hood and disconnect the negative battery cable.
2. Remove the armrest-to-trim panel

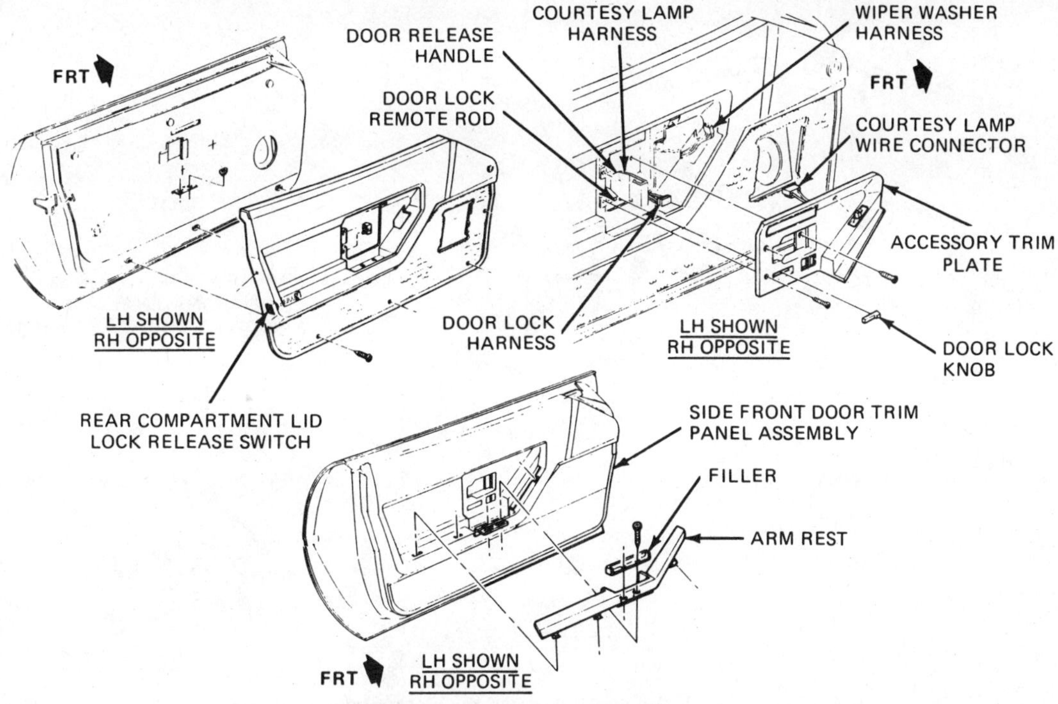

Exploded view of the door panel

screws. Push the armrest inward and remove the plastic hooks from the slot on the door trim panel.

3. Remove the speaker grille-to-door panel screws and the grille.

4. Remove the door trim panel-to-door screws. One screw is located behind the door handle.

5. Disconnect the electrical wiring connectors from the hatch lid release switch, the door lock courtesy light and the wipe/wash switch (driver's side ONLY).

6. Remove the remote control plate, the courtesy lamp and the door panel from the door.

7. To install, reverse the removal procedures.

Door Glass

REMOVAL AND INSTALLATION

1. Refer to the "Door Panel, Removal and Installation" procedures in this section and remove the door panel.

2. Remove the water separator.

3. Mark the location, then loosen and move the anti-rattle pads to facilitate the glass removal.

4. Move the regulator into position so that the glass nuts on the inner mounting plate are accessible.

5. Mark the position, then remove the stabilizing guide and the glass top.

6. Remove the glass-to-regulator nuts, the glass, the stud nuts and the stop (on the glass) through the slot at the top of the door.

NOTE: *If replacing the window glass, transfer the studs and the stop to the new glass.*

7. To install, reverse the removal procedures.

Electric Window Motor

REMOVAL AND INSTALLATION

1. Refer to the "Door Panel, Removal and Installation" procedures in this section and remove the door panel.

2. Remove the water separator.

3. To remove the inner mounting plate, perform the following procedures:

a. At the rear of the mounting plate, disconnect the electrical connectors.

b. Remove the mounting plate-to-door screws, then mark the position of the guide bolts.

c. Remove the mounting plate-to-motor bolt, the guide-to-mounting plate bolt and the guide-to-door bolt, then remove the guide.

d. Disconnect the rods from the remote control and the lock actuator (pull the rod

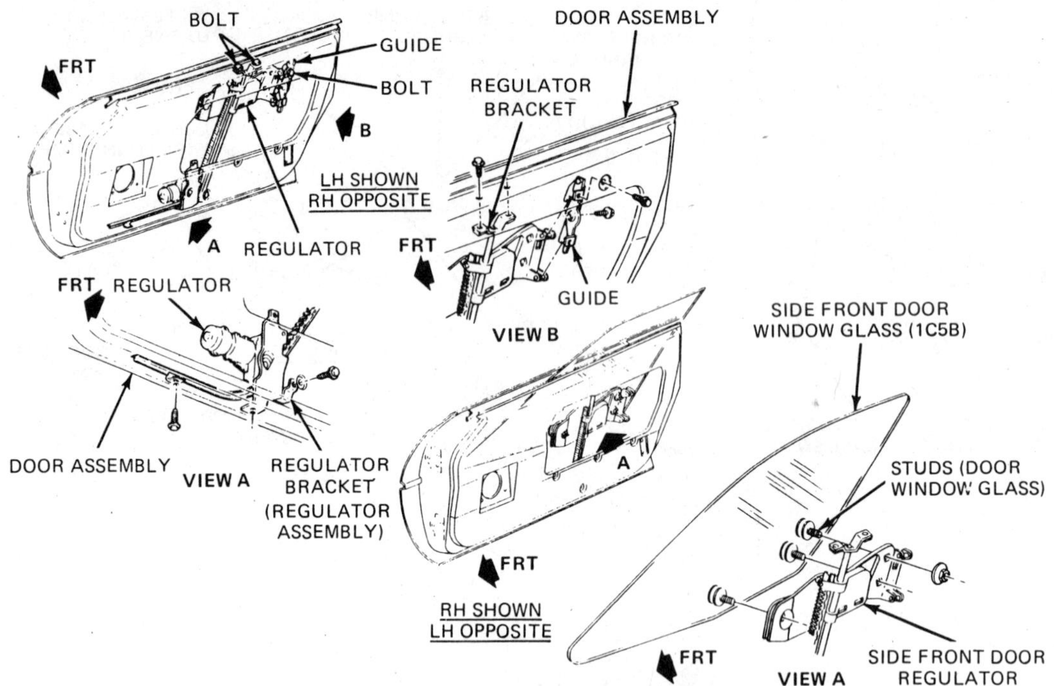

Exploded view of the door glass and the electric window motor

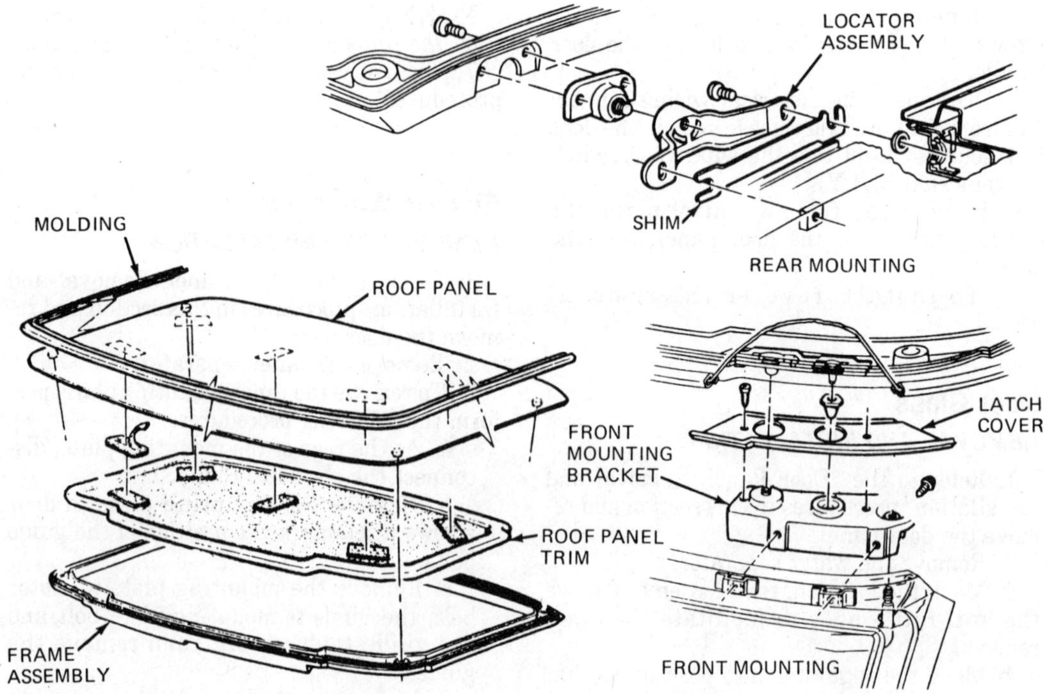

LOCATOR
ASSEMBLY
SHIM
REAR MOUNTING
MOLDING
ROOF PANEL
LATCH
COVER
FRONT
MOUNTING
BRACKET
ROOF PANEL
TRIM
FRAME
ASSEMBLY
FRONT MOUNTING

Exploded view of the roof panel assembly

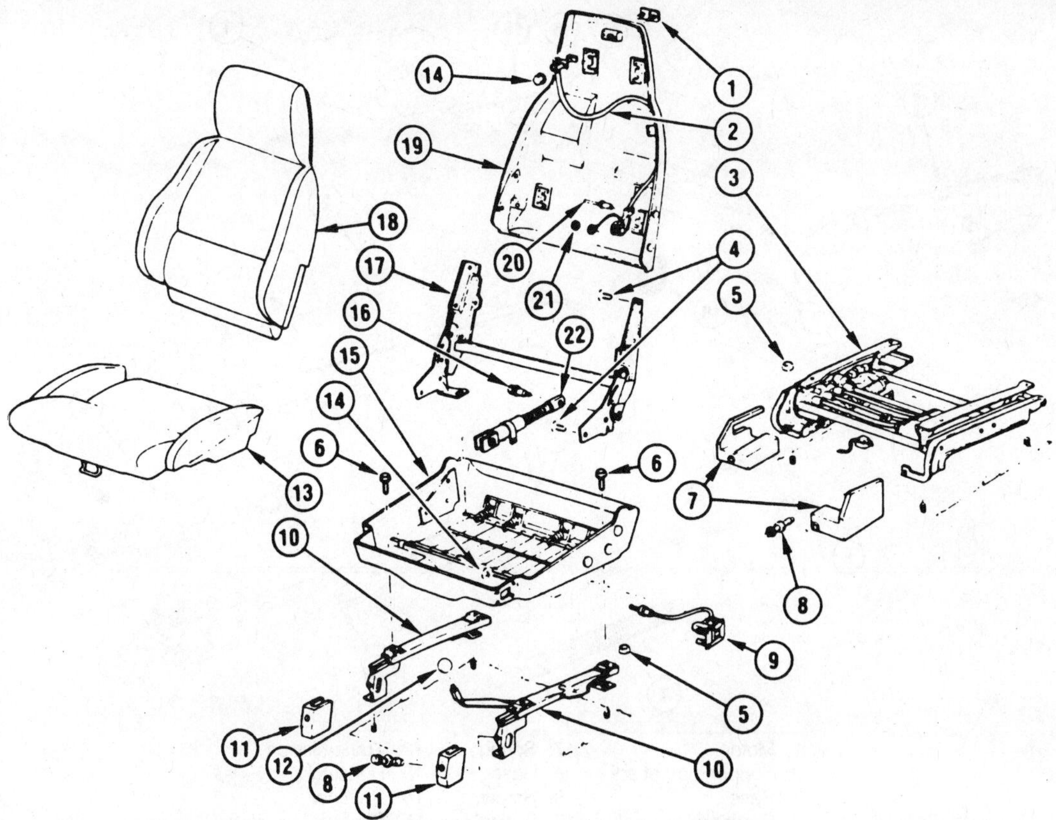

1. Bezel, seat back release handle
2. Release, seat back
3. Adjuster, driver's seat
4. Bolt, seat back hinge
5. Nut, washer
6. Bolt
7. Cover, driver seat adjuster, cover, passenger seat adjuster
8. Retainer, adjuster cover
9. Lever, back adjuster actuator
10. Adjuster, right and left hand seat
11. Cover, seat adjuster
12. Knob seat adjuster
13. Trim, cushion cloth
14. Nut
15. Frame, seat cushion
16. Bolt
17. Hinge seat back
18. Trim, seat back cloth
19. Frame, seat back
20. Rivet
21. Retainer
22. Actuator, seat back adjuster

Exploded view of the driver's seat

out of the rubber), push the plate down and pull the top out to gain access to the remote rod clip, then pop out the plastic guide.

e. Disconnect the electrical connector from the window regulator motor.

f. At the rear of the door, pull the plate out and allow it to hang from the lock rod.

4. Remove the weatherstrip-to-door (window opening) screws and the weatherstrip.

5. Mark the position and remove the glass stop bracket.

6. Mark the location, then loosen and move the anti-rattle pads to facilitate the glass removal.

7. Remove the glass-to-regulator nuts and the glass through the slot at the top of the door.

NOTE: *If replacing the window glass, transfer the studs and the stop to the new glass.*

8. Remove the regulator-to-door bolts and the regulator from the vehicle.

9. To install, reverse the removal procedures.

Power Seat Motor

Only the driver's seat is equipped with a six-way adjusting unit.

REMOVAL AND INSTALLATION

1. Disconnect the negative battery cable.
2. To gain access to the power seat adjuster bolts, remove the seat cushion.

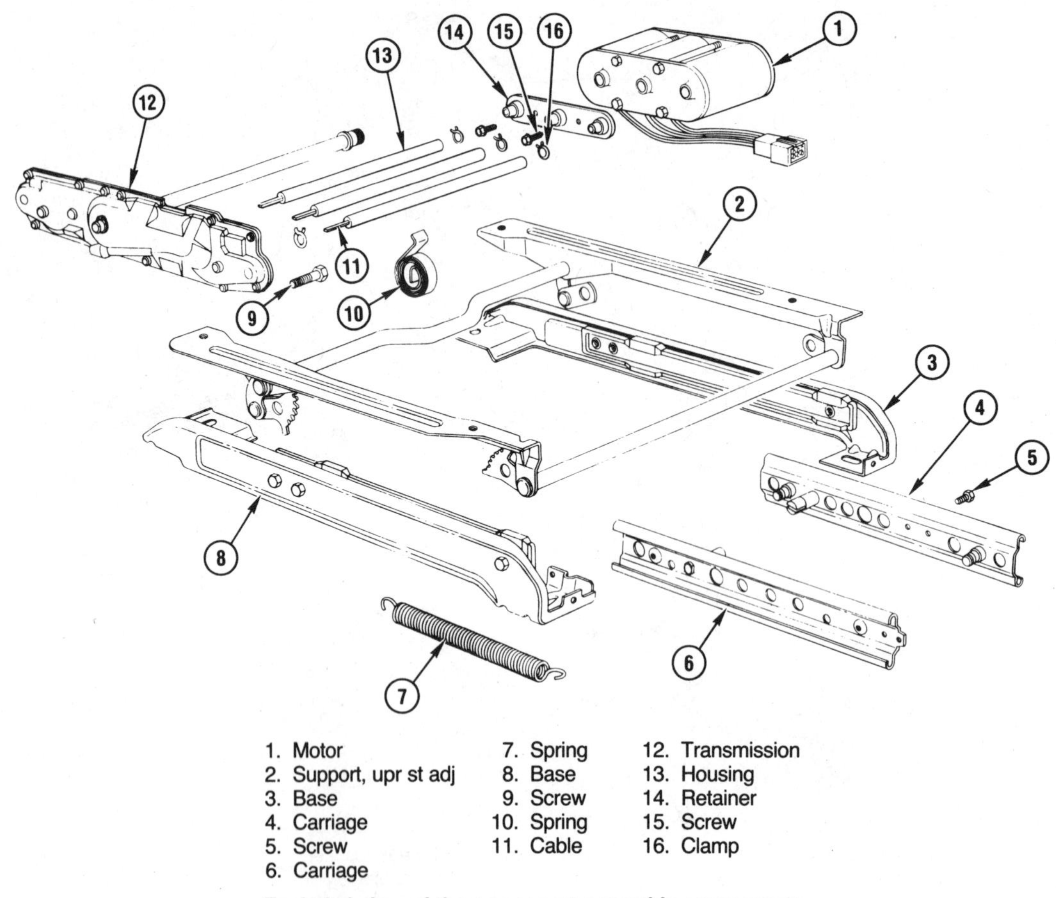

1. Motor
2. Support, upr st adj
3. Base
4. Carriage
5. Screw
6. Carriage
7. Spring
8. Base
9. Screw
10. Spring
11. Cable
12. Transmission
13. Housing
14. Retainer
15. Screw
16. Clamp

Exploded view of the power seat assembly components

3. Disconnect any necessary electrical connectors from the seat assembly.
4. Remove the seat assembly-to-power adjuster bolts and the seat assembly from the vehicle.
5. Align the access hole in the left-side rack and the mounting base.
6. Remove the mounting base-to-motor screws and the motor from the vehicle.
7. To install, reverse the removal procedures.

Roof Panel

REMOVAL AND INSTALLATION

1. Lower the side windows and move the sunvisors out of the way.
2. Using the tool provided in the compartment behind the driver's seat, loosen the 4 non-removable bolts. 2 bolts are located near the rear corners in the roof panel and 2 bolts are in the brackets of the front corner molding.

NOTE: *When using the tool, use the hooked end to break (turn counter-clockwise) the bolts loose, then the straight end.*

3. Remove the roof panel from the vehicle.
4. To install, reverse the removal procedures.

Troubleshooting 10

This section is designed to aid in the quick, accurate diagnosis of automotive problems. While automotive repairs can be made by many people, accurate troubleshooting is a rare skill for the amateur and professional alike.

In its simplest state, troubleshooting is an exercise in logic. It is essential to realize that an automobile is really composed of a series of systems. Some of these systems are interrelated; others are not. Automobiles operate within a framework of logical rules and physical laws, and the key to troubleshooting is a good understanding of all the automotive systems.

This section breaks the car or truck down into its component systems, allowing the problem to be isolated. The charts and diagnostic road maps list the most common problems and the most probable causes of trouble. Obviously it would be impossible to list every possible problem that could happen along with every possible cause, but it will locate MOST problems and eliminate a lot of unnecessary guesswork. The systematic format will locate problems within a given system, but, because many automotive systems are interrelated, the solution to your particular problem may be found in a number of systems on the car or truck.

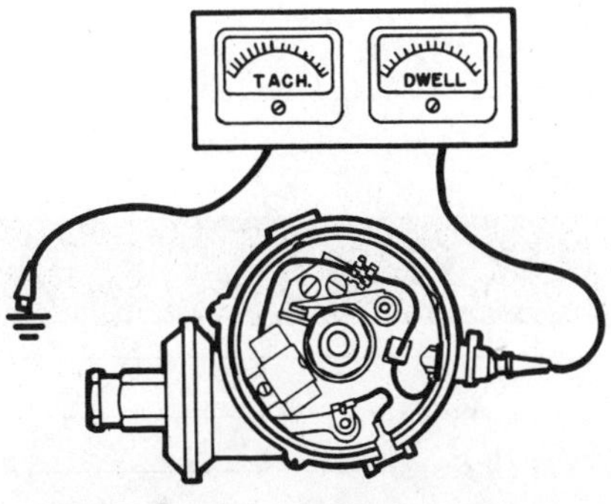

Tach-dwell hooked-up to distributor

USING THE TROUBLESHOOTING CHARTS

This book contains all of the specific information that the average do-it-yourself mechanic needs to repair and maintain his or her car or truck. The troubleshooting charts are designed to be used in conjunction with the specific procedures and information in the text. For instance, troubleshooting a point-type ignition system is fairly standard for all models, but you may be directed to the text to find procedures for troubleshooting an individual type of electronic ignition. You will also have to refer to the specification charts throughout the book for specifications applicable to your car or truck.

TOOLS AND EQUIPMENT

The tools illustrated in Chapter 1 (plus two more diagnostic pieces) will be adequate to troubleshoot most problems. The two other tools needed are a voltmeter and an ohmmeter. These can be purchased separately or in combination, known as a VOM meter.

In the event that other tools are required, they will be noted in the procedures.

Troubleshooting Engine Problems

See Chapters 2, 3, 4 for more information and service procedures.

Index to Systems

System	To Test	Group
Battery	Engine need not be running	1
Starting system	Engine need not be running	2
Primary electrical system	Engine need not be running	3
Secondary electrical system	Engine need not be running	4
Fuel system	Engine need not be running	5
Engine compression	Engine need not be running	6
Engine vacuum	Engine must be running	7
Secondary electrical system	Engine must be running	8
Valve train	Engine must be running	9
Exhaust system	Engine must be running	10
Cooling system	Engine must be running	11
Engine lubrication	Engine must be running	12

Index to Problems

Problem: Symptom	Begin at Specific Diagnosis, Number ___
Engine Won't Start:	
Starter doesn't turn	1.1, 2.1
Starter turns, engine doesn't	2.1
Starter turns engine very slowly	1.1, 2.4
Starter turns engine normally	3.1, 4.1
Starter turns engine very quickly	6.1
Engine fires intermittently	4.1
Engine fires consistently	5.1, 6.1
Engine Runs Poorly:	
Hard starting	3.1, 4.1, 5.1, 8.1
Rough idle	4.1, 5.1, 8.1
Stalling	3.1, 4.1, 5.1, 8.1
Engine dies at high speeds	4.1, 5.1
Hesitation (on acceleration from standing stop)	5.1, 8.1
Poor pickup	4.1, 5.1, 8.1
Lack of power	3.1, 4.1, 5.1, 8.1
Backfire through the carburetor	4.1, 8.1, 9.1
Backfire through the exhaust	4.1, 8.1, 9.1
Blue exhaust gases	6.1, 7.1
Black exhaust gases	5.1
Running on (after the ignition is shut off)	3.1, 8.1
Susceptible to moisture	4.1
Engine misfires under load	4.1, 7.1, 8.4, 9.1
Engine misfires at speed	4.1, 8.4
Engine misfires at idle	3.1, 4.1, 5.1, 7.1, 8.4

Sample Section

Test and Procedure	Results and Indications	Proceed to
4.1—Check for spark: Hold each spark plug wire approximately ¼″ from ground with gloves or a heavy, dry rag. Crank the engine and observe the spark.	→ If no spark is evident:	→ **4.2**
	→ If spark is good in some cases:	→ **4.3**
	→ If spark is good in all cases:	→ **4.6**

Specific Diagnosis

This section is arranged so that following each test, instructions are given to proceed to another, until a problem is diagnosed.

Section 1—Battery

Test and Procedure	Results and Indications	Proceed to
1.1—Inspect the battery visually for case condition (corrosion, cracks) and water level.	If case is cracked, replace battery:	**1.4**
	If the case is intact, remove corrosion with a solution of baking soda and water (**CAUTION:** ***do not get the solution into the battery***), and fill with water:	**1.2**

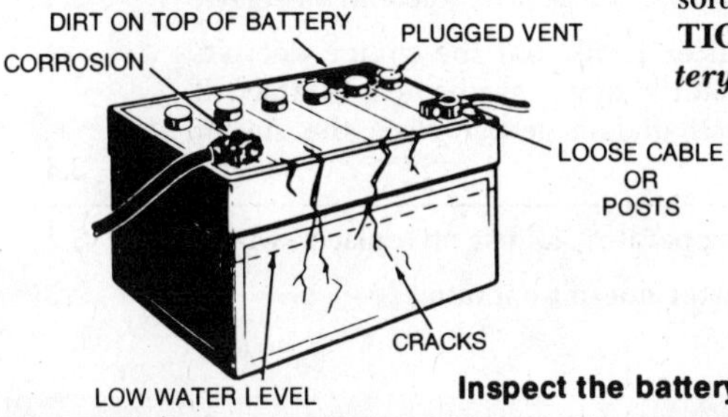

DIRT ON TOP OF BATTERY
PLUGGED VENT
CORROSION
LOOSE CABLE OR POSTS
CRACKS
LOW WATER LEVEL

Inspect the battery case

Test and Procedure	Results and Indications	Proceed to
1.2—Check the battery cable connections: Insert a screwdriver between the battery post and the cable clamp. Turn the headlights on high beam, and observe them as the screwdriver is gently twisted to ensure good metal to metal contact.	If the lights brighten, remove and clean the clamp and post; coat the post with petroleum jelly, install and tighten the clamp:	**1.4**
	If no improvement is noted:	**1.3**

TESTING BATTERY CABLE CONNECTIONS USING A SCREWDRIVER

Test and Procedure	Results and Indications	Proceed to
1.3—Test the state of charge of the battery using an individual cell tester or hydrometer.	If indicated, charge the battery. **NOTE:** ***If no obvious reason exists for the low state of charge (i.e., battery age, prolonged storage), proceed to:***	**1.4**

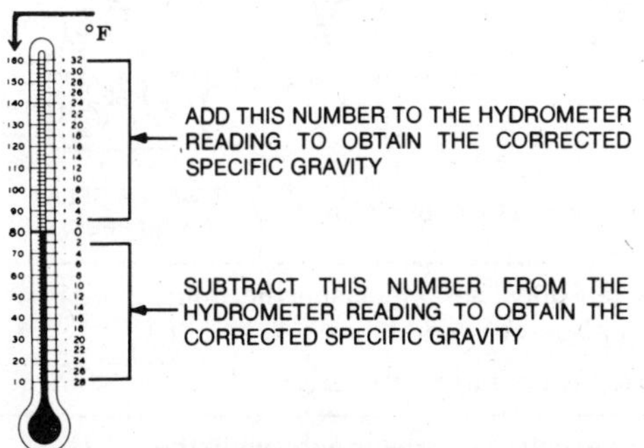

Specific Gravity (@ 80° F.)

Minimum	*Battery Charge*
1.260	100% Charged
1.230	75% Charged
1.200	50% Charged
1.170	25% Charged
1.140	Very Little Power Left
1.110	Completely Discharged

The effects of temperature on battery specific gravity (left) and amount of battery charge in relation to specific gravity (right)

Test and Procedure	Results and Indications	Proceed to
1.4—Visually inspect battery cables for cracking, bad connection to ground, or bad connection to starter.	If necessary, tighten connections or replace the cables:	**2.1**

Section 2—Starting System

See Chapter 3 for service procedures

Test and Procedure	Results and Indications	Proceed to
Note: Tests in Group 2 are performed with coil high tension lead disconnected to prevent accidental starting.		
2.1—Test the starter motor and solenoid: Connect a jumper from the battery post of the solenoid (or relay) to the starter post of the solenoid (or relay).	If starter turns the engine normally:	2.2
	If the starter buzzes, or turns the engine very slowly:	2.4
	If no response, replace the solenoid (or relay).	3.1
	If the starter turns, but the engine doesn't, ensure that the flywheel ring gear is intact. If the gear is undamaged, replace the starter drive.	3.1
2.2—Determine whether ignition override switches are functioning properly (clutch start switch, neutral safety switch), by connecting a jumper across the switch(es), and turning the ignition switch to "start".	If starter operates, adjust or replace switch:	3.1
	If the starter doesn't operate:	2.3
2.3—Check the ignition switch "start" position: Connect a 12V test lamp or voltmeter between the starter post of the solenoid (or relay) and ground. Turn the ignition switch to the "start" position, and jiggle the key.	If the lamp doesn't light or the meter needle doesn't move when the switch is turned, check the ignition switch for loose connections, cracked insulation, or broken wires. Repair or replace as necessary:	3.1
	If the lamp flickers or needle moves when the key is jiggled, replace the ignition switch.	3.3

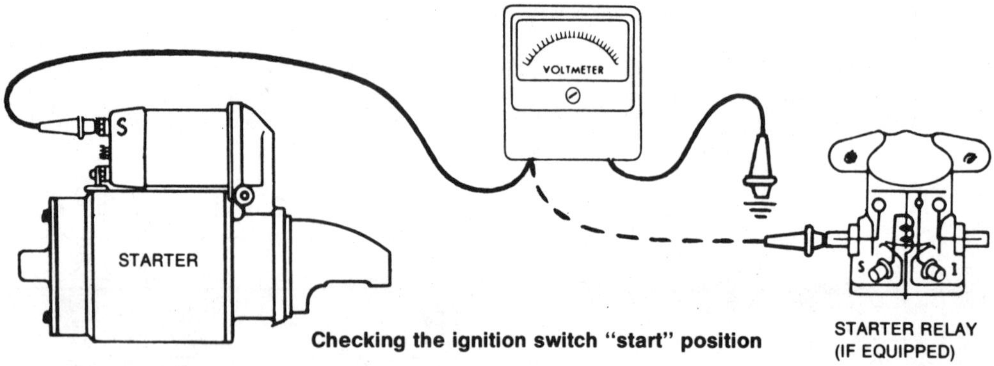

STARTER RELAY (IF EQUIPPED)

Checking the ignition switch "start" position

Test and Procedure	Results and Indications	Proceed to
2.4—Remove and bench test the starter, according to specifications in the engine electrical section.	If the starter does not meet specifications, repair or replace as needed:	3.1
	If the starter is operating properly:	2.5
2.5—Determine whether the engine can turn freely: Remove the spark plugs, and check for water in the cylinders. Check for water on the dipstick, or oil in the radiator. Attempt to turn the engine using an 18″ flex drive and socket on the crankshaft pulley nut or bolt.	If the engine will turn freely only with the spark plugs out, and hydrostatic lock (water in the cylinders) is ruled out, check valve timing:	9.2
	If engine will not turn freely, and it is known that the clutch and transmission are free, the engine must be disassembled for further evaluation:	Chapter 3

Section 3—Primary Electrical System

Test and Procedure	Results and Indications	Proceed to
3.1—Check the ignition switch "on" position: Connect a jumper wire between the distributor side of the coil and ground, and a 12V test lamp between the switch side of the coil and ground. Remove the high tension lead from the coil. Turn the ignition switch on and jiggle the key.	If the lamp lights:	3.2
	If the lamp flickers when the key is jiggled, replace the ignition switch:	3.3
	If the lamp doesn't light, check for loose or open connections. If none are found, remove the ignition switch and check for continuity. If the switch is faulty, replace it:	3.3

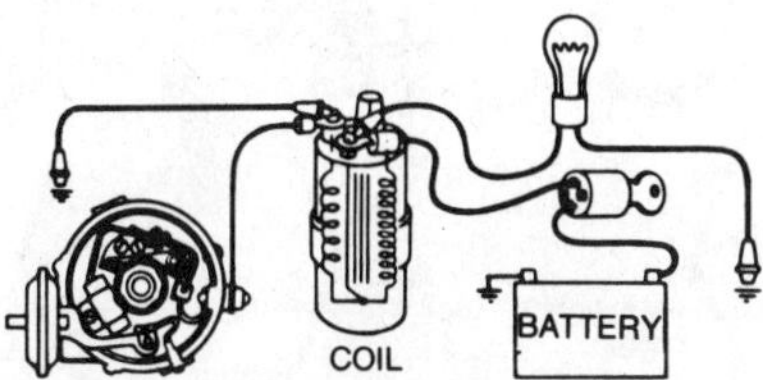

Checking the ignition switch "on" position

Test and Procedure	Results and Indications	Proceed to
3.2—Check the ballast resistor or resistance wire for an open circuit, using an ohmmeter. See Chapter 3 for specific tests.	Replace the resistor or resistance wire if the resistance is zero. **NOTE:** ***Some ignition systems have no ballast resistor.***	3.3

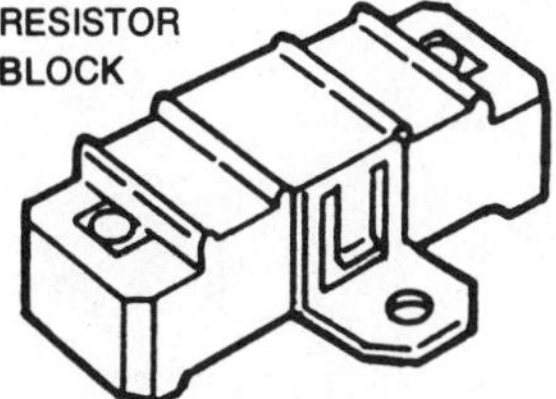

Two types of resistors

Test and Procedure	Results and Indications	Proceed to
3.3—On point-type ignition systems, visually inspect the breaker points for burning, pitting or excessive wear. Gray coloring of the point contact surfaces is normal. Rotate the crankshaft until the contact heel rests on a high point of the distributor cam and adjust the point gap to specifications. On electronic ignition models, remove the distributor cap and visually inspect the armature. Ensure that the armature pin is in place, and that the armature is on tight and rotates when the engine is cranked. Make sure there are no cracks, chips or rounded edges on the armature.	If the breaker points are intact, clean the contact surfaces with fine emery cloth, and adjust the point gap to specifications. If the points are worn, replace them. On electronic systems, replace any parts which appear defective. If condition persists:	3.4

Test and Procedure	Results and Indications	Proceed to
3.4—On point-type ignition systems, connect a dwell-meter between the distributor primary lead and ground. Crank the engine and observe the point dwell angle. On electronic ignition systems, conduct a stator (magnetic pickup assembly) test. See Chapter 3.	On point-type systems, adjust the dwell angle if necessary. **NOTE:** ***Increasing the point gap decreases the dwell angle and vice-versa.***	**3.6**
	If the dwell meter shows little or no reading;	**3.5**
	On electronic ignition systems, if the stator is bad, replace the stator. If the stator is good, proceed to the other tests in Chapter 3.	

Dwell is a function of point gap

3.5—On the point-type ignition systems, check the condenser for short: connect an ohmeter across the condenser body and the pigtail lead.	If any reading other than infinite is noted, replace the condenser	**3.6**

Checking the condenser for short

3.6—Test the coil primary resistance: On point-type ignition systems, connect an ohmmeter across the coil primary terminals, and read the resistance on the low scale. Note whether an external ballast resistor or resistance wire is used. On electronic ignition systems, test the coil primary resistance as in Chapter 3.	Point-type ignition coils utilizing ballast resistors or resistance wires should have approximately 1.0 ohms resistance. Coils with internal resistors should have approximately 4.0 ohms resistance. If values far from the above are noted, replace the coil.	**4.1**

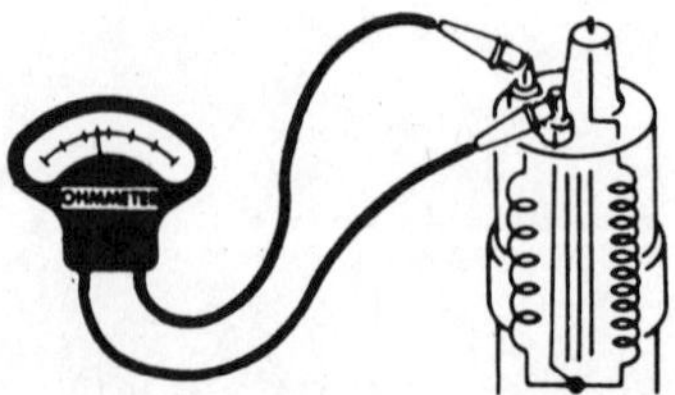

Check the coil primary resistance

Section 4—Secondary Electrical System

See Chapters 2–3 for service procedures

Test and Procedure	Results and Indications	Proceed to
4.1—Check for spark: Hold each spark plug wire approximately ¼″ from ground with gloves or a heavy, dry rag. Crank the engine, and observe the spark.	If no spark is evident:	**4.2**
	If spark is good in some cylinders:	**4.3**
	If spark is good in all cylinders:	**4.6**
 **Check for spark at the plugs**		
4.2—Check for spark at the coil high tension lead: Remove the coil high tension lead from the distributor and position it approximately ¼″ from ground. Crank the engine and observe spark. **CAUTION:** ***This test should not be performed on engines equipped with electronic ignition.***	If the spark is good and consistent:	**4.3**
	If the spark is good but intermittent, test the primary electrical system starting at 3.3:	**3.3**
	If the spark is weak or non-existent, replace the coil high tension lead, clean and tighten all connections and retest. If no improvement is noted:	**4.4**
4.3—Visually inspect the distributor cap and rotor for burned or corroded contacts, cracks, carbon tracks, or moisture. Also check the fit of the rotor on the distributor shaft (where applicable).	If moisture is present, dry thoroughly, and retest per 4.1:	**4.1**
	If burned or excessively corroded contacts, cracks, or carbon tracks are noted, replace the defective part(s) and retest per 4.1:	**4.1**
	If the rotor and cap appear intact, or are only slightly corroded, clean the contacts thoroughly (including the cap towers and spark plug wire ends) and retest per 4.1:	
	If the spark is good in all cases:	**4.6**
	If the spark is poor in all cases:	**4.5**
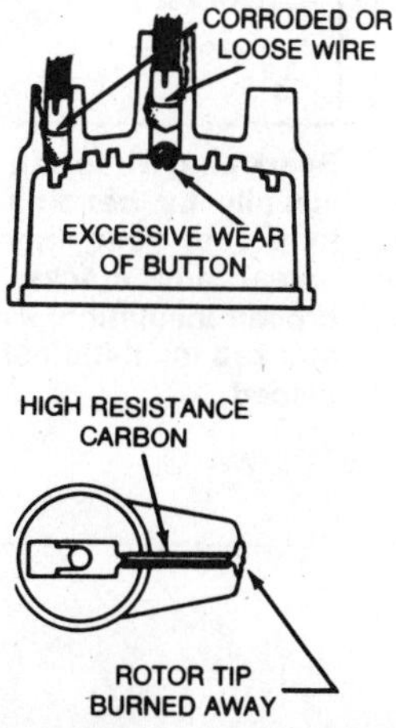 **Inspect the distributor cap and rotor**		

Test and Procedure	Results and Indications	Proceed to
4.4—Check the coil secondary resistance: On point-type systems connect an ohmmeter across the distributor side of the coil and the coil tower. Read the resistance on the high scale of the ohmmeter. On electronic ignition systems, see Chapter 3 for specific tests.	The resistance of a satisfactory coil should be between 4,000 and 10,000 ohms. If resistance is considerably higher (i.e., 40,000 ohms) replace the coil and retest per 4.1. **NOTE:** ***This does not apply to high performance coils.***	

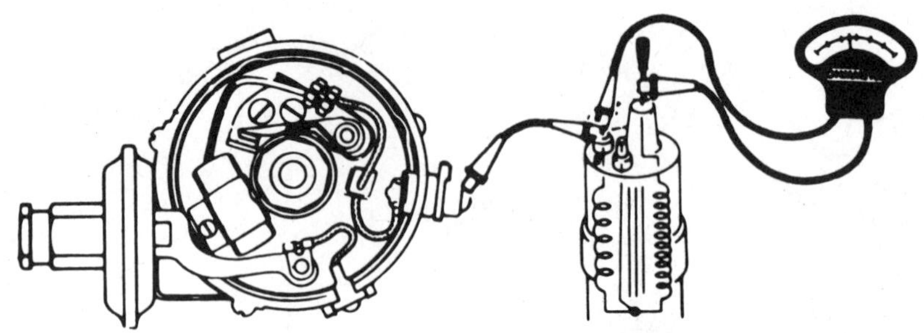

Testing the coil secondary resistance

Test and Procedure	Results and Indications	Proceed to
4.5—Visually inspect the spark plug wires for cracking or brittleness. Ensure that no two wires are positioned so as to cause induction firing (adjacent and parallel). Remove each wire, one by one, and check resistance with an ohmmeter.	Replace any cracked or brittle wires. If any of the wires are defective, replace the entire set. Replace any wires with excessive resistance (over 8000 Ω per foot for suppression wire), and separate any wires that might cause induction firing.	**4.6**

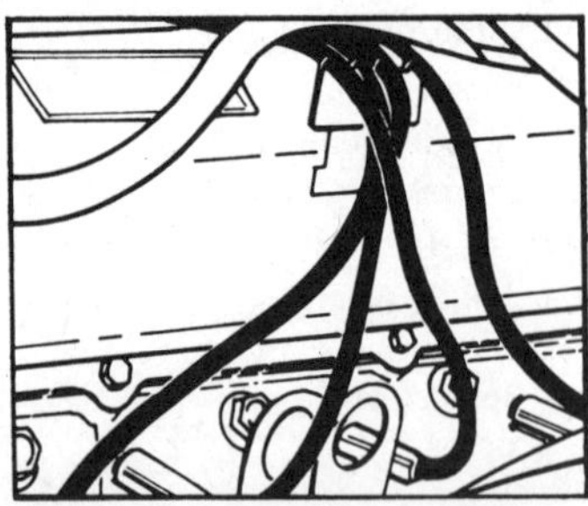

Misfiring can be the result of spark plug leads to adjacent, consecutively firing cylinders running parallel and too close together

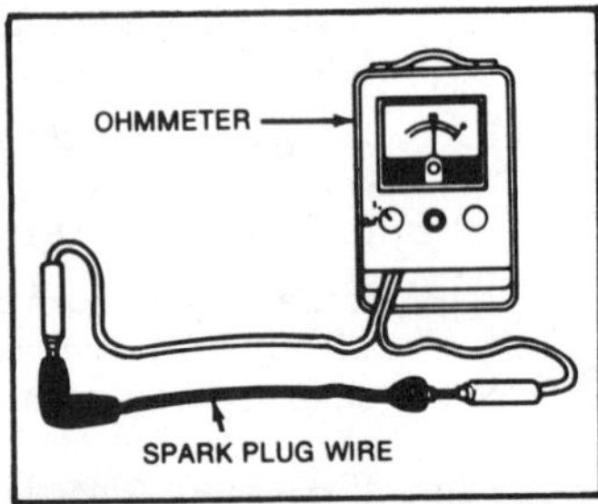

On point-type ignition systems, check the spark plug wires as shown. On electronic ignitions, do not remove the wire from the distributor cap terminal; instead, test through the cap

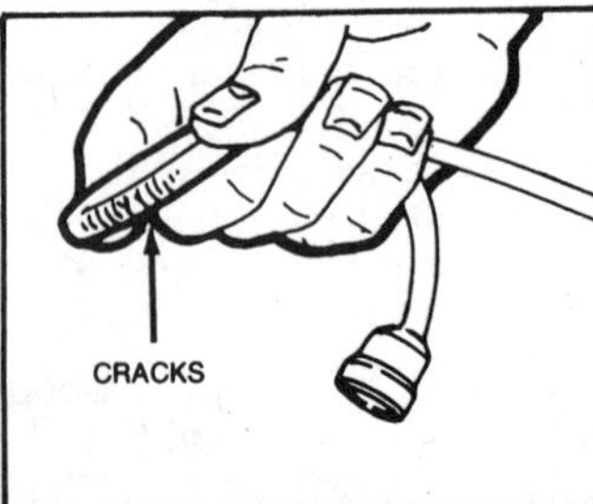

Spark plug wires can be checked visually by bending them in a loop over your finger. This will reveal any cracks, burned or broken insulation. Any wire with cracked insulation should be replaced

Test and Procedure	Results and Indications	Proceed to
4.6—Remove the spark plugs, noting the cylinders from which they were removed, and evaluate according to the color photos in the middle of this book.	See following.	**See following.**

Test and Procedure	Results and Indications	Proceed to
4.7—Examine the location of all the plugs.	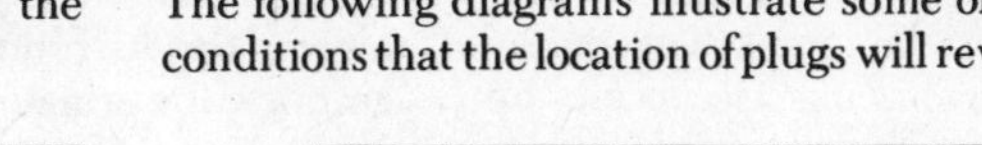 The following diagrams illustrate some of the conditions that the location of plugs will reveal.	**4.8**

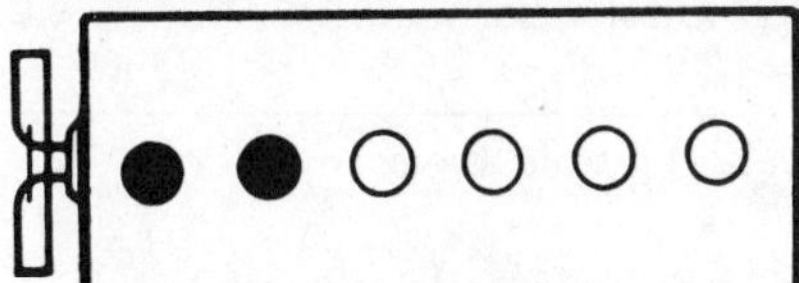

Two adjacent plugs are fouled in a 6-cylinder engine, 4-cylinder engine or either bank of a V-8. This is probably due to a blown head gasket between the two cylinders

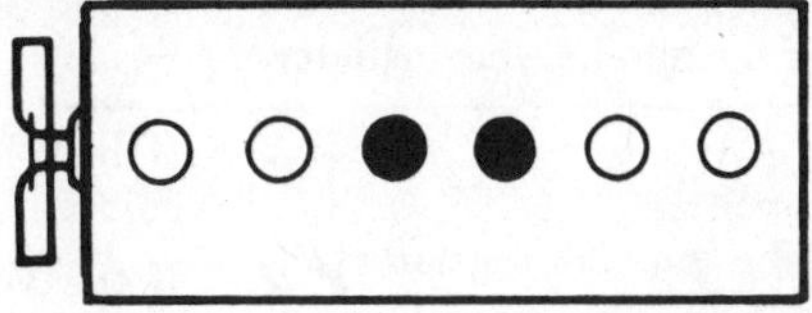

The two center plugs in a 6-cylinder engine are fouled. Raw fuel may be "boiled" out of the carburetor into the intake manifold after the engine is shut-off. Stop-start driving can also foul the center plugs, due to overly rich mixture. Proper float level, a new float needle and seat or use of an insulating spacer may help this problem

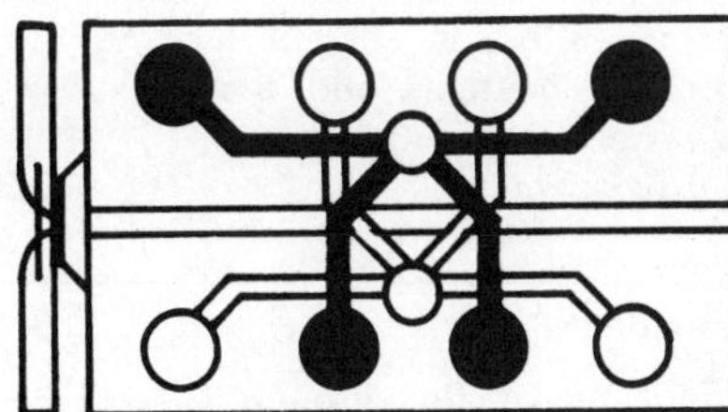

An unbalanced carburetor is indicated. Following the fuel flow on this particular design shows that the cylinders fed by the right-hand barrel are fouled from overly rich mixture, while the cylinders fed by the left-hand barrel are normal

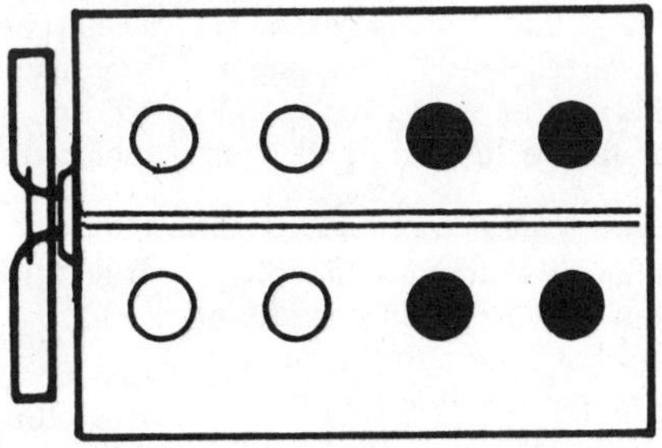

If the four rear plugs are overheated, a cooling system problem is suggested. A thorough cleaning of the cooling system may restore coolant circulation and cure the problem

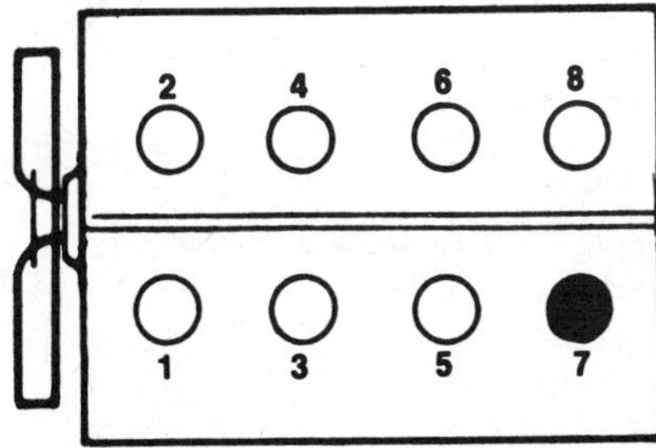

Finding one plug overheated may indicate an intake manifold leak near the affected cylinder. If the overheated plug is the second of two adjacent, consecutively firing plugs, it could be the result of ignition cross-firing. Separating the leads to these two plugs will eliminate cross-fire

Occasionally, the two rear plugs in large, lightly used V-8's will become oil fouled. High oil consumption and smoky exhaust may also be noticed. It is probably due to plugged oil drain holes in the rear of the cylinder head, causing oil to be sucked in around the valve stems. This usually occurs in the rear cylinders first, because the engine slants that way

Test and Procedure	Results and Indications	Proceed to
4.8—Determine the static ignition timing. Using the crankshaft pulley timing marks as a guide, locate top dead center on the compression stroke of the number one cylinder.	The rotor should be pointing toward the No. 1 tower in the distributor cap, and, on electronic ignitions, the armature spoke for that cylinder should be lined up with the stator.	4.8
4.9—Check coil polarity: Connect a voltmeter negative lead to the coil high tension lead, and the positive lead to ground (**NOTE:** ***Reverse the hook-up for positive ground systems***). Crank the engine momentarily.	If the voltmeter reads up-scale, the polarity is correct:	5.1
	If the voltmeter reads down-scale, reverse the coil polarity (switch the primary leads):	5.1
	Checking coil polarity	

Section 5—Fuel System

See Chapter 4 for service procedures

Test and Procedure	Results and Indications	Proceed to
5.1—Determine that the air filter is functioning efficiently: Hold paper elements up to a strong light, and attempt to see light through the filter.	Clean permanent air filters in solvent (or manufacturer's recommendation), and allow to dry. Replace paper elements through which light cannot be seen:	5.2
5.2—Determine whether a flooding condition exists: Flooding is identified by a strong gasoline odor, and excessive gasoline present in the throttle bore(s) of the carburetor.	If flooding is not evident:	5.3
	If flooding is evident, permit the gasoline to dry for a few moments and restart. If flooding doesn't recur:	5.7
	If flooding is persistent:	5.5
	If the engine floods repeatedly, check the choke butterfly flap	
5.3—Check that fuel is reaching the carburetor: Detach the fuel line at the carburetor inlet. Hold the end of the line in a cup (not styrofoam), and crank the engine.	If fuel flows smoothly:	5.7
	If fuel doesn't flow (**NOTE:** ***Make sure that there is fuel in the tank***), or flows erratically:	5.4
	Check the fuel pump by disconnecting the output line (fuel pump-to-carburetor) at the carburetor and operating the starter briefly	

Test and Procedure	Results and Indications	Proceed to
5.4—Test the fuel pump: Disconnect all fuel lines from the fuel pump. Hold a finger over the input fitting, crank the engine (with electric pump, turn the ignition or pump on); and feel for suction.	If suction is evident, blow out the fuel line to the tank with low pressure compressed air until bubbling is heard from the fuel filler neck. Also blow out the carburetor fuel line (both ends disconnected):	**5.7**
	If no suction is evident, replace or repair the fuel pump:	**5.7**
	NOTE: ***Repeated oil fouling of the spark plugs, or a no-start condition, could be the result of a ruptured vacuum booster pump diaphragm, through which oil or gasoline is being drawn into the intake manifold (where applicable).***	
5.5—Occasionally, small specks of dirt will clog the small jets and orifices in the carburetor. With the engine cold, hold a flat piece of wood or similar material over the carburetor, where possible, and crank the engine.	If the engine starts, but runs roughly the engine is probably not run enough.	
	If the engine won't start:	**5.9**
5.6—Check the needle and seat: Tap the carburetor in the area of the needle and seat.	If flooding stops, a gasoline additive (e.g., Gumout) will often cure the problem:	**5.7**
	If flooding continues, check the fuel pump for excessive pressure at the carburetor (according to specifications). If the pressure is normal, the needle and seat must be removed and checked, and/or the float level adjusted:	**5.7**
5.7—Test the accelerator pump by looking into the throttle bores while operating the throttle. 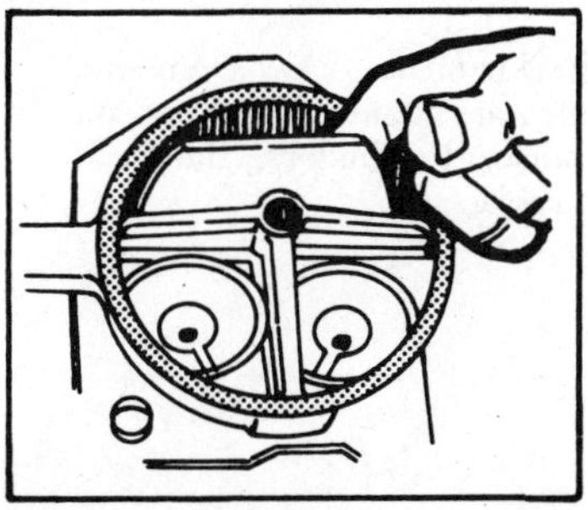	If the accelerator pump appears to be operating normally:	**5.8**
Check for gas at the carburetor by looking down the carburetor throat while someone moves the accelerator	If the accelerator pump is not operating, the pump must be reconditioned. Where possible, service the pump with the carburetor(s) installed on the engine. If necessary, remove the carburetor. Prior to removal:	**5.8**
5.8—Determine whether the carburetor main fuel system is functioning: Spray a commercial starting fluid into the carburetor while attempting to start the engine.	If the engine starts, runs for a few seconds, and dies:	**5.9**
	If the engine doesn't start:	**6.1**

Test and Procedure	Results and Indications	Proceed to
5.9—Uncommon fuel system malfunctions: See below:	If the problem is solved:	6.1
	If the problem remains, remove and recondition the carburetor.	

Condition	Indication	Test	Prevailing Weather Conditions	Remedy
Vapor lock	Engine will not restart shortly after running.	Cool the components of the fuel system until the engine starts. Vapor lock can be cured faster by draping a wet cloth over a mechanical fuel pump.	Hot to very hot	Ensure that the exhaust manifold heat control valve is operating. Check with the vehicle manufacturer for the recommended solution to vapor lock on the model in question.
Carburetor icing	Engine will not idle, stalls at low speeds.	Visually inspect the throttle plate area of the throttle bores for frost.	High humidity, 32–40° F.	Ensure that the exhaust manifold heat control valve is operating, and that the intake manifold heat riser is not blocked.
Water in the fuel	Engine sputters and stalls; may not start.	Pump a small amount of fuel into a glass jar. Allow to stand, and inspect for droplets or a layer of water.	High humidity, extreme temperature changes.	For droplets, use one or two cans of commercial gas line anti-freeze. For a layer of water, the tank must be drained, and the fuel lines blown out with compressed air.

Section 6—Engine Compression

See Chapter 3 for service procedures

Test and Procedure	Results and Indications	Proceed to
6.1—Test engine compression: Remove all spark plugs. Block the throttle wide open. Insert a compression gauge into a spark plug port, crank the engine to obtain the maximum reading, and record.	If compression is within limits on all cylinders:	7.1
	If gauge reading is extremely low on all cylinders:	6.2
	If gauge reading is low on one or two cylinders: (If gauge readings are identical and low on two or more adjacent cylinders, the head gasket must be replaced.)	6.2
6.2—Test engine compression (wet): Squirt approximately 30 cc. of engine oil into each cylinder, and retest per 6.1.	If the readings improve, worn or cracked rings or broken pistons are indicated:	See Chapter 3
	If the readings do not improve, burned or excessively carboned valves or a jumped timing chain are indicated: **NOTE:** ***A jumped timing chain is often indicated by difficult cranking.***	7.1

Checking compression

Section 7—Engine Vacuum

See Chapter 3 for service procedures

Test and Procedure	*Results and Indications*	*Proceed to*
7.1—Attach a vacuum gauge to the intake manifold beyond the throttle plate. Start the engine, and observe the action of the needle over the range of engine speeds.	See below.	**See below**

INDICATION: normal engine in good condition

Proceed to: 8.1

Normal engine

Gauge reading: steady, from 17–22 in./Hg.

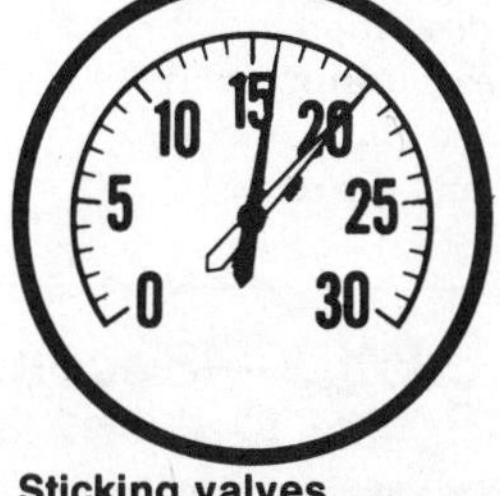

INDICATION: sticking valves or ignition miss

Proceed to: 9.1, 8.3

Sticking valves

Gauge reading: intermittent fluctuation at idle

INDICATION: late ignition or valve timing, low compression, stuck throttle valve, leaking carburetor or manifold gasket

Proceed to: 6.1

Incorrect valve timing

Gauge reading: low (10–15 in./Hg) but steady

INDICATION: improper carburetor adjustment or minor intake leak.

Proceed to: 7.2

Carburetor requires adjustment

Gauge reading: drifting needle

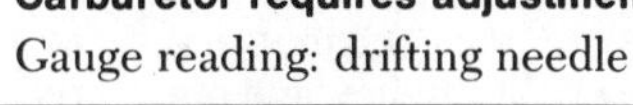

INDICATION: ignition miss, blown cylinder head gasket, leaking valve or weak valve spring

Proceed to: 8.3, 6.1

Blown head gasket

Gauge reading: needle fluctuates as engine speed increases

INDICATION: burnt valve or faulty valve clearance: Needle will fall when defective valve operates

Proceed to: 9.1

Burnt or leaking valves

Gauge reading: steady needle, but drops regularly

INDICATION: choked muffler, excessive back pressure in system

Proceed to: 10.1

Clogged exhaust system

Gauge reading: gradual drop in reading at idle

INDICATION: worn valve guides

Proceed to: 9.1

Worn valve guides

Gauge reading: needle vibrates excessively at idle, but steadies as engine speed increases

White pointer = steady gauge hand

Black pointer = fluctuating gauge hand

Test and Procedure	Results and Indications	Proceed to
7.2—Attach a vacuum gauge per 7.1, and test for an intake manifold leak. Squirt a small amount of oil around the intake manifold gaskets, carburetor gaskets, plugs and fittings. Observe the action of the vacuum gauge.	If the reading improves, replace the indicated gasket, or seal the indicated fitting or plug:	**8.1**
	If the reading remains low:	**7.3**
7.3—Test all vacuum hoses and accessories for leaks as described in 7.2. Also check the carburetor body (dashpots, automatic choke mechanism, throttle shafts) for leaks in the same manner.	If the reading improves, service or replace the offending part(s):	**8.1**
	If the reading remains low:	**6.1**

Section 8—Secondary Electrical System

See Chapter 2 for service procedures

Test and Procedure	Results and Indications	Proceed to
8.1—Remove the distributor cap and check to make sure that the rotor turns when the engine is cranked. Visually inspect the distributor components.	Clean, tighten or replace any components which appear defective.	**8.2**
8.2—Connect a timing light (per manufacturer's recommendation) and check the dynamic ignition timing. Disconnect and plug the vacuum hose(s) to the distributor if specified, start the engine, and observe the timing marks at the specified engine speed.	If the timing is not correct, adjust to specifications by rotating the distributor in the engine: (Advance timing by rotating distributor opposite normal direction of rotor rotation, retard timing by rotating distributor in same direction as rotor rotation.)	**8.3**
8.3—Check the operation of the distributor advance mechanism(s): To test the mechanical advance, disconnect the vacuum lines from the distributor advance unit and observe the timing marks with a timing light as the engine speed is increased from idle. If the mark moves smoothly, without hesitation, it may be assumed that the mechanical advance is functioning properly. To test vacuum advance and/or retard systems, alternately crimp and release the vacuum line, and observe the timing mark for movement. If movement is noted, the system is operating.	If the systems are functioning:	**8.4**
	If the systems are not functioning, remove the distributor, and test on a distributor tester:	**8.4**
8.4—Locate an ignition miss: With the engine running, remove each spark plug wire, one at a time, until one is found that doesn't cause the engine to roughen and slow down.	When the missing cylinder is identified:	**4.1**

Section 9—Valve Train

See Chapter 3 for service procedures

Test and Procedure	Results and Indications	Proceed to
9.1—Evaluate the valve train: Remove the valve cover, and ensure that the valves are adjusted to specifications. A mechanic's stethoscope may be used to aid in the diagnosis of the valve train. By pushing the probe on or near push rods or rockers, valve noise often can be isolated. A timing light also may be used to diagnose valve problems. Connect the light according to manufacturer's recommendations, and start the engine. Vary the firing moment of the light by increasing the engine speed (and therefore the ignition advance), and moving the trigger from cylinder to cylinder. Observe the movement of each valve.	Sticking valves or erratic valve train motion can be observed with the timing light. The cylinder head must be disassembled for repairs.	**See Chapter 3**
9.2—Check the valve timing: Locate top dead center of the No. 1 piston, and install a degree wheel or tape on the crankshaft pulley or damper with zero corresponding to an index mark on the engine. Rotate the crankshaft in its direction of rotation, and observe the opening of the No. 1 cylinder intake valve. The opening should correspond with the correct mark on the degree wheel according to specifications.	If the timing is not correct, the timing cover must be removed for further investigation.	**See Chapter 3**

Section 10—Exhaust System

Test and Procedure	Results and Indications	Proceed to
10.1—Determine whether the exhaust manifold heat control valve is operating: Operate the valve by hand to determine whether it is free to move. If the valve is free, run the engine to operating temperature and observe the action of the valve, to ensure that it is opening.	If the valve sticks, spray it with a suitable solvent, open and close the valve to free it, and retest.	
	If the valve functions properly:	**10.2**
	If the valve does not free, or does not operate, replace the valve:	**10.2**
10.2—Ensure that there are no exhaust restrictions: Visually inspect the exhaust system for kinks, dents, or crushing. Also note that gases are flowing freely from the tailpipe at all engine speeds, indicating no restriction in the muffler or resonator.	Replace any damaged portion of the system:	**11.1**

Section 11—Cooling System

See Chapter 3 for service procedures

Test and Procedure	Results and Indications	Proceed to
11.1—Visually inspect the fan belt for glazing, cracks, and fraying, and replace if necessary. Tighten the belt so that the longest span has approximately ½″ play at its midpoint under thumb pressure (see Chapter 1).	Replace or tighten the fan belt as necessary: **Checking belt tension**	**11.2**
11.2—Check the fluid level of the cooling system.	If full or slightly low, fill as necessary:	**11.5**
	If extremely low:	**11.3**
11.3—Visually inspect the external portions of the cooling system (radiator, radiator hoses, thermostat elbow, water pump seals, heater hoses, etc.) for leaks. If none are found, pressurize the cooling system to 14–15 psi.	If cooling system holds the pressure:	**11.5**
	If cooling system loses pressure rapidly, reinspect external parts of the system for leaks under pressure. If none are found, check dipstick for coolant in crankcase. If no coolant is present, but pressure loss continues:	**11.4**
	If coolant is evident in crankcase, remove cylinder head(s), and check gasket(s). If gaskets are intact, block and cylinder head(s) should be checked for cracks or holes. If the gasket(s) is blown, replace, and purge the crankcase of coolant:	**12.6**
	NOTE: ***Occasionally, due to atmospheric and driving conditions, condensation of water can occur in the crankcase. This causes the oil to appear milky white. To remedy, run the engine until hot, and change the oil and oil filter.***	
11.4—Check for combustion leaks into the cooling system: Pressurize the cooling system as above. Start the engine, and observe the pressure gauge. If the needle fluctuates, remove each spark plug wire, one at a time, noting which cylinder(s) reduce or eliminate the fluctuation.	Cylinders which reduce or eliminate the fluctuation, when the spark plug wire is removed, are leaking into the cooling system. Replace the head gasket on the affected cylinder bank(s).	

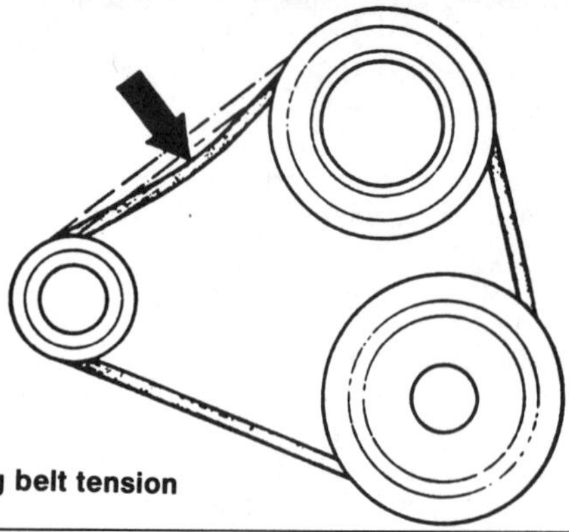

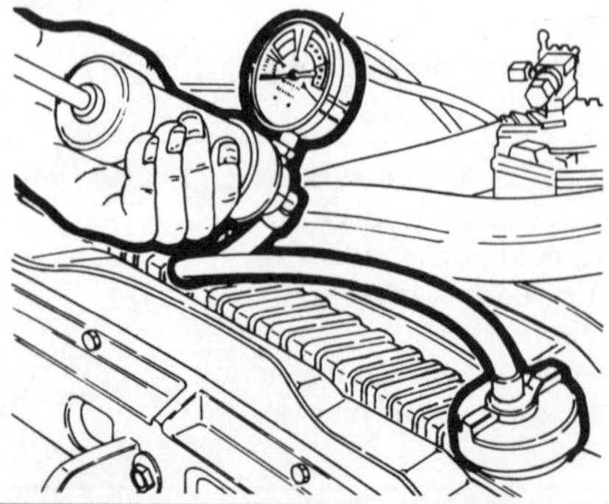

Pressurizing the cooling system

Test and Procedure	Results and Indications	Proceed to
11.5—Check the radiator pressure cap: Attach a radiator pressure tester to the radiator cap (wet the seal prior to installation). Quickly pump up the pressure, noting the point at which the cap releases.	If the cap releases within ± 1 psi of the specified rating, it is operating properly:	**11.6**
	If the cap releases at more than ± 1 psi of the specified rating, it should be replaced:	**11.6**

Checking radiator pressure cap

Test and Procedure	Results and Indications	Proceed to
11.6—Test the thermostat: Start the engine cold, remove the radiator cap, and insert a thermometer into the radiator. Allow the engine to idle. After a short while, there will be a sudden, rapid increase in coolant temperature. The temperature at which this sharp rise stops is the thermostat opening temperature.	If the thermostat opens at or about the specified temperature:	**11.7**
	If the temperature doesn't increase: (If the temperature increases slowly and gradually, replace the thermostat.)	**11.7**
11.7—Check the water pump: Remove the thermostat elbow and the thermostat, disconnect the coil high tension lead (to prevent starting), and crank the engine momentarily.	If coolant flows, replace the thermostat and retest per 11.6:	**11.6**
	If coolant doesn't flow, reverse flush the cooling system to alleviate any blockage that might exist. If system is not blocked, and coolant will not flow, replace the water pump.	

Section 12—Lubrication

See Chapter 3 for service procedures

Test and Procedure	Results and Indications	Proceed to
12.1—Check the oil pressure gauge or warning light: If the gauge shows low pressure, or the light is on for no obvious reason, remove the oil pressure sender. Install an accurate oil pressure gauge and run the engine momentarily.	If oil pressure builds normally, run engine for a few moments to determine that it is functioning normally, and replace the sender.	—
	If the pressure remains low:	**12.2**
	If the pressure surges:	**12.3**
	If the oil pressure is zero:	**12.3**
12.2—Visually inspect the oil: If the oil is watery or very thin, milky, or foamy, replace the oil and oil filter.	If the oil is normal:	**12.3**
	If after replacing oil the pressure remains low:	**12.3**
	If after replacing oil the pressure becomes normal:	—

Test and Procedure	Results and Indications	Proceed to
12.3—Inspect the oil pressure relief valve and spring, to ensure that it is not sticking or stuck. Remove and thoroughly clean the valve, spring, and the valve body.	If the oil pressure improves:	—
	If no improvement is noted:	**12.4**
12.4—Check to ensure that the oil pump is not cavitating (sucking air instead of oil): See that the crankcase is neither over nor underfull, and that the pickup in the sump is in the proper position and free from sludge.	Fill or drain the crankcase to the proper capacity, and clean the pickup screen in solvent if necessary. If no improvement is noted:	**12.5**
12.5—Inspect the oil pump drive and the oil pump:	If the pump drive or the oil pump appear to be defective, service as necessary and retest per 12.1:	**12.1**
	If the pump drive and pump appear to be operating normally, the engine should be disassembled to determine where blockage exists:	**See Chapter 3**
12.6—Purge the engine of ethylene glycol coolant: Completely drain the crankcase and the oil filter. Obtain a commercial butyl cellosolve base solvent, designated for this purpose, and follow the instructions precisely. Following this, install a new oil filter and refill the crankcase with the proper weight oil. The next oil and filter change should follow shortly thereafter (1000 miles).		

TROUBLESHOOTING EMISSION CONTROL SYSTEMS

See Chapter 4 for procedures applicable to individual emission control systems used on specific combinations of engine/transmission/model.

TROUBLESHOOTING THE CARBURETOR

See Chapter 4 for service procedures

Carburetor problems cannot be effectively isolated unless all other engine systems (particularly ignition and emission) are functioning properly and the engine is properly tuned.

Condition	Possible Cause
Engine cranks, but does not start	1. Improper starting procedure 2. No fuel in tank 3. Clogged fuel line or filter 4. Defective fuel pump 5. Choke valve not closing properly 6. Engine flooded 7. Choke valve not unloading 8. Throttle linkage not making full travel 9. Stuck needle or float 10. Leaking float needle or seat 11. Improper float adjustment
Engine stalls	1. Improperly adjusted idle speed or mixture **Engine hot** 2. Improperly adjusted dashpot 3. Defective or improperly adjusted solenoid 4. Incorrect fuel level in fuel bowl 5. Fuel pump pressure too high 6. Leaking float needle seat 7. Secondary throttle valve stuck open 8. Air or fuel leaks 9. Idle air bleeds plugged or missing 10. Idle passages plugged **Engine Cold** 11. Incorrectly adjusted choke 12. Improperly adjusted fast idle speed 13. Air leaks 14. Plugged idle or idle air passages 15. Stuck choke valve or binding linkage 16. Stuck secondary throttle valves 17. Engine flooding—high fuel level 18. Leaking or misaligned float
Engine hesitates on acceleration	1. Clogged fuel filter 2. Leaking fuel pump diaphragm 3. Low fuel pump pressure 4. Secondary throttle valves stuck, bent or misadjusted 5. Sticking or binding air valve 6. Defective accelerator pump 7. Vacuum leaks 8. Clogged air filter 9. Incorrect choke adjustment (engine cold)
Engine feels sluggish or flat on acceleration	1. Improperly adjusted idle speed or mixture 2. Clogged fuel filter 3. Defective accelerator pump 4. Dirty, plugged or incorrect main metering jets 5. Bent or sticking main metering rods 6. Sticking throttle valves 7. Stuck heat riser 8. Binding or stuck air valve 9. Dirty, plugged or incorrect secondary jets 10. Bent or sticking secondary metering rods. 11. Throttle body or manifold heat passages plugged 12. Improperly adjusted choke or choke vacuum break.
Carburetor floods	1. Defective fuel pump. Pressure too high. 2. Stuck choke valve 3. Dirty, worn or damaged float or needle valve/seat 4. Incorrect float/fuel level 5. Leaking float bowl

Condition	Possible Cause
Engine idles roughly and stalls	1. Incorrect idle speed 2. Clogged fuel filter 3. Dirt in fuel system or carburetor 4. Loose carburetor screws or attaching bolts 5. Broken carburetor gaskets 6. Air leaks 7. Dirty carburetor 8. Worn idle mixture needles 9. Throttle valves stuck open 10. Incorrectly adjusted float or fuel level 11. Clogged air filter
Engine runs unevenly or surges	1. Defective fuel pump 2. Dirty or clogged fuel filter 3. Plugged, loose or incorrect main metering jets or rods 4. Air leaks 5. Bent or sticking main metering rods 6. Stuck power piston 7. Incorrect float adjustment 8. Incorrect idle speed or mixture 9. Dirty or plugged idle system passages 10. Hard, brittle or broken gaskets 11. Loose attaching or mounting screws 12. Stuck or misaligned secondary throttle valves
Poor fuel economy	1. Poor driving habits 2. Stuck choke valve 3. Binding choke linkage 4. Stuck heat riser 5. Incorrect idle mixture 6. Defective accelerator pump 7. Air leaks 8. Plugged, loose or incorrect main metering jets 9. Improperly adjusted float or fuel level 10. Bent, misaligned or fuel-clogged float 11. Leaking float needle seat 12. Fuel leak 13. Accelerator pump discharge ball not seating properly 14. Incorrect main jets
Engine lacks high speed performance or power	1. Incorrect throttle linkage adjustment 2. Stuck or binding power piston 3. Defective accelerator pump 4. Air leaks 5. Incorrect float setting or fuel level 6. Dirty, plugged, worn or incorrect main metering jets or rods 7. Binding or sticking air valve 8. Brittle or cracked gaskets 9. Bent, incorrect or improperly adjusted secondary metering rods 10. Clogged fuel filter 11. Clogged air filter 12. Defective fuel pump

TROUBLESHOOTING FUEL INJECTION PROBLEMS

Each fuel injection system has its own unique components and test procedures, for which it is impossible to generalize. Refer to Chapter 4 of this Repair & Tune-Up Guide for specific test and repair procedures, if the vehicle is equipped with fuel injection.

TROUBLESHOOTING ELECTRICAL PROBLEMS

See Chapter 5 for service procedures

For any electrical system to operate, it must make a complete circuit. This simply means that the power flow from the battery must make a complete circle. When an electrical component is operating, power flows from the battery to the component, passes through the component causing it to perform its function (lighting a light bulb), and then returns to the battery through the ground of the circuit. This ground is usually (but not always) the metal part of the car or truck on which the electrical component is mounted.

Perhaps the easiest way to visualize this is to think of connecting a light bulb with two wires attached to it to the battery. If one of the two wires attached to the light bulb were attached to the negative post of the battery and the other were attached to the positive post of the battery, you would have a complete circuit. Current from the battery would flow to the light bulb, causing it to light, and return to the negative post of the battery.

The normal automotive circuit differs from this simple example in two ways. First, instead of having a return wire from the bulb to the battery, the light bulb returns the current to the battery through the chassis of the vehicle. Since the negative battery cable is attached to the chassis and the chassis is made of electrically conductive metal, the chassis of the vehicle can serve as a ground wire to complete the circuit. Secondly, most automotive circuits contain switches to turn components on and off as required.

Every complete circuit from a power source must include a component which is using the power from the power source. If you were to disconnect the light bulb from the wires and touch the two wires together (don't do this) the power supply wire to the component would be grounded before the normal ground connection for the circuit.

Because grounding a wire from a power source makes a complete circuit—less the required component to use the power—this phenomenon is called a short circuit. Common causes are: broken insulation (exposing the metal wire to a metal part of the car or truck), or a shorted switch.

Some electrical components which require a large amount of current to operate also have a relay in their circuit. Since these circuits carry a large amount of current, the thickness of the wire in the circuit (gauge size) is also greater. If this large wire were connected from the component to the control switch on the instrument panel, and then back to the component, a voltage drop would occur in the circuit. To prevent this potential drop in voltage, an electromagnetic switch (relay) is used. The large wires in the circuit are connected from the battery to one side of the relay, and from the opposite side of the relay to the component. The relay is normally open, preventing current from passing through the circuit. An additional, smaller, wire is connected from the relay to the control switch for the circuit. When the control switch is turned on, it grounds the smaller wire from the relay and completes the circuit. This closes the relay and allows current to flow from the battery to the component. The horn, headlight, and starter circuits are three which use relays.

It is possible for larger surges of current to pass through the electrical system of your car or truck. If this surge of current were to reach an electrical component, it could burn it out. To prevent this, fuses, circuit breakers or fusible links are connected into the current supply wires of most of the major electrical systems. When an electrical current of excessive power passes through the component's fuse, the fuse blows out and breaks the circuit, saving the component from destruction.

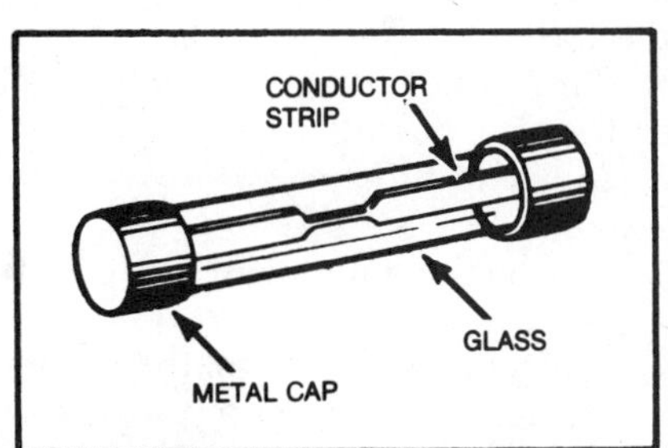

Typical automotive fuse

A circuit breaker is basically a self-repairing fuse. The circuit breaker opens the circuit the same way a fuse does. However, when either the short is removed from the circuit or the surge subsides, the circuit breaker resets itself and does not have to be replaced as a fuse does.

A fuse link is a wire that acts as a fuse. It is normally connected between the starter relay and the main wiring harness. This connection is usually under the hood. The fuse link (if installed) protects all the

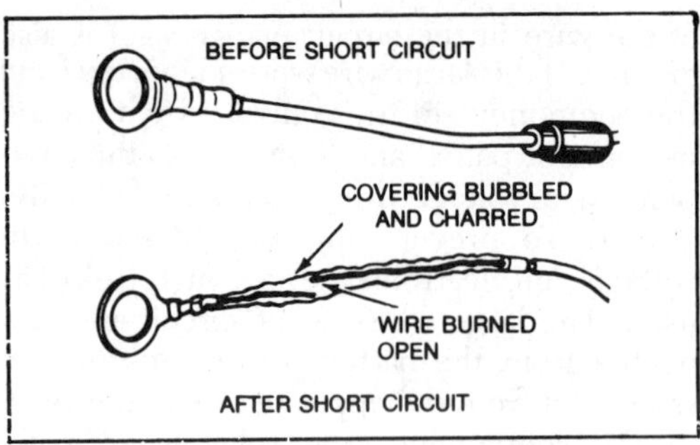

Most fusible links show a charred, melted insulation when they burn out

chassis electrical components, and is the probable cause of trouble when none of the electrical components function, unless the battery is disconnected or dead.

Electrical problems generally fall into one of three areas:

1. The component that is not functioning is not receiving current.
2. The component itself is not functioning.
3. The component is not properly grounded.

The electrical system can be checked with a test light and a jumper wire. A test light is a device that looks like a pointed screwdriver with a wire attached to it and has a light bulb in its handle. A jumper wire is a piece of insulated wire with an alligator clip attached to each end.

If a component is not working, you must follow a systematic plan to determine which of the three causes is the villain.

1. Turn on the switch that controls the inoperable component.
2. Disconnect the power supply wire from the component.
3. Attach the ground wire on the test light to a good metal ground.
4. Touch the probe end of the test light to the end of the power supply wire that was disconnected from the component. If the component is receiving current, the test light will go on.

NOTE: ***Some components work only when the ignition switch is turned on.***

If the test light does not go on, then the problem is in the circuit between the battery and the component. This includes all the switches, fuses, and relays in the system. Follow the wire that runs back to the battery. The problem is an open circuit between the battery and the component. If the fuse is blown and, when replaced, immediately blows again, there is a short circuit in the system which must be located and repaired. If there is a switch in the system, bypass it with a jumper wire. This is done by connecting one end of the jumper wire to the power supply wire into the switch and the other end of the jumper wire to the wire coming out of the switch. If the test light lights with the jumper wire installed, the switch or whatever was bypassed is defective.

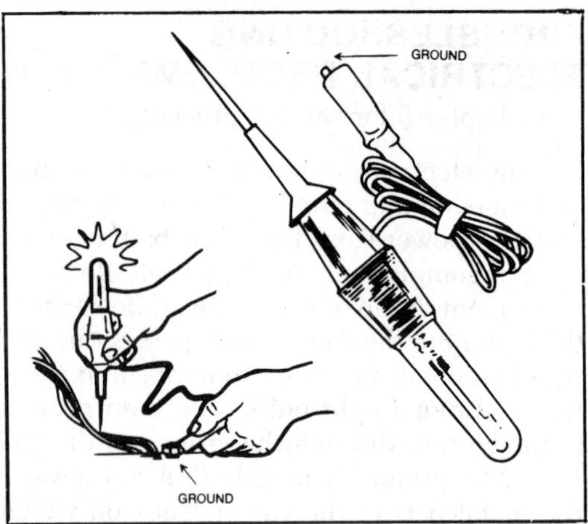

The test light will show the presence of current when touched to a hot wire and grounded at the other end

NOTE: ***Never substitute the jumper wire for the component, since it is required to use the power from the power source.***

5. If the bulb in the test light goes on, then the current is getting to the component that is not working. This eliminates the first of the three possible causes. Connect the power supply wire and connect a jumper wire from the component to a good metal ground. Do this with the switch which controls the component turned on, and also the ignition switch turned on if it is required for the component to work. If the component works with the jumper wire installed, then it has a bad ground. This is usually caused by the metal area on which the component mounts to the chassis being coated with some type of foreign matter.
6. If neither test located the source of the trouble, then the component itself is defective. Remember that for any electrical system to work, all connections must be clean and tight.

Troubleshooting Basic Turn Signal and Flasher Problems

See Chapter 5 for service procedures

Most problems in the turn signals or flasher system can be reduced to defective flashers or bulbs, which are easily replaced. Occasionally, the turn signal switch will prove defective.

F = Front R = Rear ● = Lights off ○ = Lights on

Condition		Possible Cause
Turn signals light, but do not flash	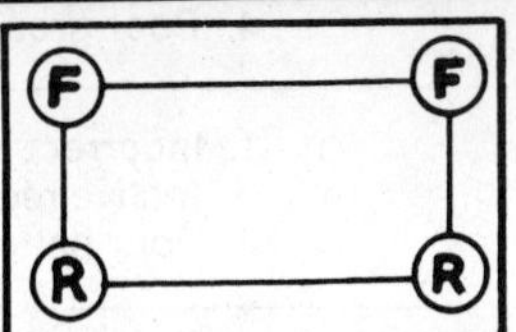	Defective flasher
No turn signals light on either side	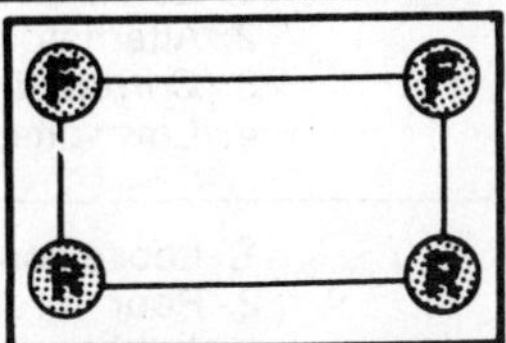	Blown fuse. Replace if defective. Defective flasher. Check by substitution. Open circuit, short circuit or poor ground.
Both turn signals on one side don't work	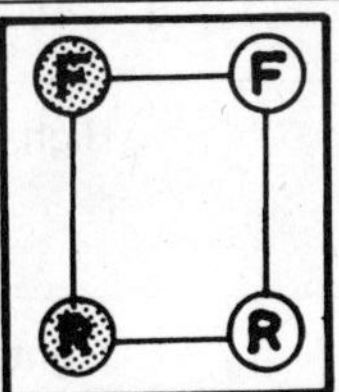	Bad bulbs. Bad ground in both (or either) housings.
One turn signal light on one side doesn't work	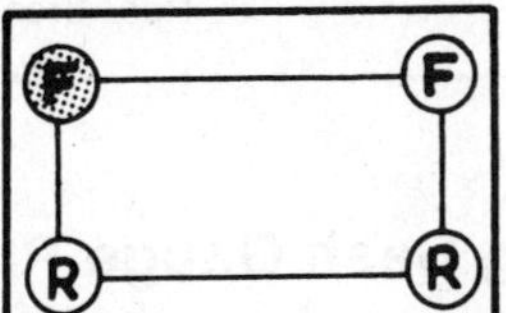	Defective bulb. Corrosion in socket. Clean contacts. Poor ground at socket.
Turn signal flashes too fast or too slowly	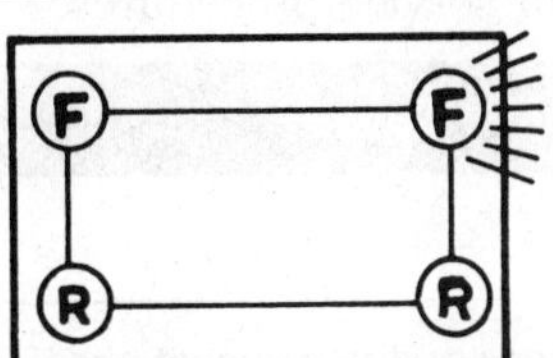	Check any bulb on the side flashing too fast. A heavy-duty bulb is probably installed in place of a regular bulb. Check the bulb flashing too slowly. A standard bulb was probably installed in place of a heavy-duty bulb. Loose connections or corrosion at the bulb socket.
Indicator lights don't work in either direction		Check if the turn signals are working. Check the dash indicator lights. Check the flasher by substitution.
One indicator light doesn't light		On systems with one dash indicator: See if the lights work on the same side. Often the filaments have been reversed in systems combining stoplights with taillights and turn signals. Check the flasher by substitution. On systems with two indicators: Check the bulbs on the same side. Check the indicator light bulb. Check the flasher by substitution.

Troubleshooting Lighting Problems

See Chapter 5 for service procedures

Condition	Possible Cause
One or more lights don't work, but others do	1. Defective bulb(s) 2. Blown fuse(s) 3. Dirty fuse clips or light sockets 4. Poor ground circuit
Lights burn out quickly	1. Incorrect voltage regulator setting or defective regulator 2. Poor battery/alternator connections
Lights go dim	1. Low/discharged battery 2. Alternator not charging 3. Corroded sockets or connections 4. Low voltage output
Lights flicker	1. Loose connection 2. Poor ground. (Run ground wire from light housing to frame) 3. Circuit breaker operating (short circuit)
Lights "flare"—Some flare is normal on acceleration—If excessive, see "Lights Burn Out Quickly"	High voltage setting
Lights glare—approaching drivers are blinded	1. Lights adjusted too high 2. Rear springs or shocks sagging 3. Rear tires soft

Troubleshooting Dash Gauge Problems

Most problems can be traced to a defective sending unit or faulty wiring. Occasionally, the gauge itself is at fault. See Chapter 5 for service procedures.

Condition	Possible Cause
COOLANT TEMPERATURE GAUGE	
Gauge reads erratically or not at all	1. Loose or dirty connections 2. Defective sending unit. 3. Defective gauge. To test a bi-metal gauge, remove the wire from the sending unit. Ground the wire for an instant. If the gauge registers, replace the sending unit. To test a magnetic gauge, disconnect the wire at the sending unit. With ignition ON gauge should register COLD. Ground the wire; gauge should register HOT.
AMMETER GAUGE—TURN HEADLIGHTS ON (DO NOT START ENGINE). NOTE REACTION	
Ammeter shows charge Ammeter shows discharge Ammeter does not move	1. Connections reversed on gauge 2. Ammeter is OK 3. Loose connections or faulty wiring 4. Defective gauge

Condition	Possible Cause
OIL PRESSURE GAUGE	
Gauge does not register or is inaccurate	1. On mechanical gauge, Bourdon tube may be bent or kinked. 2. Low oil pressure. Remove sending unit. Idle the engine briefly. If no oil flows from sending unit hole, problem is in engine. 3. Defective gauge. Remove the wire from the sending unit and ground it for an instant with the ignition ON. A good gauge will go to the top of the scale. 4. Defective wiring. Check the wiring to the gauge. If it's OK and the gauge doesn't register when grounded, replace the gauge. 5. Defective sending unit.
ALL GAUGES	
All gauges do not operate	1. Blown fuse 2. Defective instrument regulator
All gauges read low or erratically	3. Defective or dirty instrument voltage regulator
All gauges pegged	4. Loss of ground between instrument voltage regulator and frame 5. Defective instrument regulator
WARNING LIGHTS	
Light(s) do not come on when ignition is ON, but engine is not started	1. Defective bulb 2. Defective wire 3. Defective sending unit. Disconnect the wire from the sending unit and ground it. Replace the sending unit if the light comes on with the ignition ON.
Light comes on with engine running	4. Problem in individual system 5. Defective sending unit

Troubleshooting Clutch Problems

It is false economy to replace individual clutch components. The pressure plate, clutch plate and throwout bearing should be replaced as a set, and the flywheel face inspected, whenever the clutch is overhauled. See Chapter 6 for service procedures.

Condition	Possible Cause
Clutch chatter	1. Grease on driven plate (disc) facing 2. Binding clutch linkage or cable 3. Loose, damaged facings on driven plate (disc) 4. Engine mounts loose 5. Incorrect height adjustment of pressure plate release levers 6. Clutch housing or housing to transmission adapter misalignment 7. Loose driven plate hub
Clutch grabbing	1. Oil, grease on driven plate (disc) facing 2. Broken pressure plate 3. Warped or binding driven plate. Driven plate binding on clutch shaft
Clutch slips	1. Lack of lubrication in clutch linkage or cable (linkage or cable binds, causes incomplete engagement) 2. Incorrect pedal, or linkage adjustment 3. Broken pressure plate springs 4. Weak pressure plate springs 5. Grease on driven plate facings (disc)

Troubleshooting Clutch Problems (cont.)

Condition	Possible Cause
Incomplete clutch release	1. Incorrect pedal or linkage adjustment or linkage or cable binding 2. Incorrect height adjustment on pressure plate release levers 3. Loose, broken facings on driven plate (disc) 4. Bent, dished, warped driven plate caused by overheating
Grinding, whirring grating noise when pedal is depressed	1. Worn or defective throwout bearing 2. Starter drive teeth contacting flywheel ring gear teeth. Look for milled or polished teeth on ring gear.
Squeal, howl, trumpeting noise when pedal is being released (occurs during first inch to inch and one-half of pedal travel)	Pilot bushing worn or lack of lubricant. If bushing appears OK, polish bushing with emery cloth, soak lube wick in oil, lube bushing with oil, apply film of chassis grease to clutch shaft pilot hub, reassemble. NOTE: Bushing wear may be due to misalignment of clutch housing or housing to transmission adapter
Vibration or clutch pedal pulsation with clutch disengaged (pedal fully depressed)	1. Worn or defective engine transmission mounts 2. Flywheel run out. (Flywheel run out at face not to exceed 0.005") 3. Damaged or defective clutch components

Troubleshooting Manual Transmission Problems

See Chapter 6 for service procedures

Condition	Possible Cause
Transmission jumps out of gear	1. Misalignment of transmission case or clutch housing. 2. Worn pilot bearing in crankshaft. 3. Bent transmission shaft. 4. Worn high speed sliding gear. 5. Worn teeth or end-play in clutch shaft. 6. Insufficient spring tension on shifter rail plunger. 7. Bent or loose shifter fork. 8. Gears not engaging completely. 9. Loose or worn bearings on clutch shaft or mainshaft. 10. Worn gear teeth. 11. Worn or damaged detent balls.
Transmission sticks in gear	1. Clutch not releasing fully. 2. Burred or battered teeth on clutch shaft, or sliding sleeve. 3. Burred or battered transmission mainshaft. 4. Frozen synchronizing clutch. 5. Stuck shifter rail plunger. 6. Gearshift lever twisting and binding shifter rail. 7. Battered teeth on high speed sliding gear or on sleeve. 8. Improper lubrication, or lack of lubrication. 9. Corroded transmission parts. 10. Defective mainshaft pilot bearing. 11. Locked gear bearings will give same effect as stuck in gear.
Transmission gears will not synchronize	1. Binding pilot bearing on mainshaft, will synchronize in high gear only. 2. Clutch not releasing fully. 3. Detent spring weak or broken. 4. Weak or broken springs under balls in sliding gear sleeve. 5. Binding bearing on clutch shaft, or binding countershaft. 6. Binding pilot bearing in crankshaft. 7. Badly worn gear teeth. 8. Improper lubrication. 9. Constant mesh gear not turning freely on transmission mainshaft. Will synchronize in that gear only.

Condition	*Possible Cause*
Gears spinning when shifting into gear from neutral	1. Clutch not releasing fully. 2. In some cases an extremely light lubricant in transmission will cause gears to continue to spin for a short time after clutch is released. 3. Binding pilot bearing in crankshaft.
Transmission noisy in all gears	1. Insufficient lubricant, or improper lubricant. 2. Worn countergear bearings. 3. Worn or damaged main drive gear or countergear. 4. Damaged main drive gear or mainshaft bearings. 5. Worn or damaged countergear anti-lash plate.
Transmission noisy in neutral only	1. Damaged main drive gear bearing. 2. Damaged or loose mainshaft pilot bearing. 3. Worn or damaged countergear anti-lash plate. 4. Worn countergear bearings.
Transmission noisy in one gear only	1. Damaged or worn constant mesh gears. 2. Worn or damaged countergear bearings. 3. Damaged or worn synchronizer.
Transmission noisy in reverse only	1. Worn or damaged reverse idler gear or idler bushing. 2. Worn or damaged mainshaft reverse gear. 3. Worn or damaged reverse countergear. 4. Damaged shift mechanism.

TROUBLESHOOTING AUTOMATIC TRANSMISSION PROBLEMS

Keeping alert to changes in the operating characteristics of the transmission (changing shift points, noises, etc.) can prevent small problems from becoming large ones. If the problem cannot be traced to loose bolts, fluid level, misadjusted linkage, clogged filters or similar problems, you should probably seek professional service.

Transmission Fluid Indications

The appearance and odor of the transmission fluid can give valuable clues to the overall condition of the transmission. Always note the appearance of the fluid when you check the fluid level or change the fluid. Rub a small amount of fluid between your fingers to feel for grit and smell the fluid on the dipstick.

If the fluid appears:	*It indicates:*
Clear and red colored	Normal operation
Discolored (extremely dark red or brownish) or smells burned	Band or clutch pack failure, usually caused by an overheated transmission. Hauling very heavy loads with insufficient power or failure to change the fluid often result in overheating. Do not confuse this appearance with newer fluids that have a darker red color and a strong odor (though not a burned odor).
Foamy or aerated (light in color and full of bubbles)	1. The level is too high (gear train is churning oil) 2. An internal air leak (air is mixing with the fluid). Have the transmission checked professionally.
Solid residue in the fluid	Defective bands, clutch pack or bearings. Bits of band material or metal abrasives are clinging to the dipstick. Have the transmission checked professionally.
Varnish coating on the dipstick	The transmission fluid is overheating

TROUBLESHOOTING DRIVE AXLE PROBLEMS

First, determine when the noise is most noticeable.

Drive Noise: Produced under vehicle acceleration.

Coast Noise: Produced while coasting with a closed throttle.

Float Noise: Occurs while maintaining constant speed (just enough to keep speed constant) on a level road.

External Noise Elimination

It is advisable to make a thorough road test to determine whether the noise originates in the rear axle or whether it originates from the tires, engine, transmission, wheel bearings or road surface. Noise originating from other places cannot be corrected by servicing the rear axle.

ROAD NOISE

Brick or rough surfaced concrete roads produce noises that seem to come from the rear axle. Road noise is usually identical in Drive or Coast and driving on a different type of road will tell whether the road is the problem.

TIRE NOISE

Tire noise can be mistaken as rear axle noise, even though the tires on the front are at fault. Snow tread and mud tread tires or tires worn unevenly will frequently cause vibrations which seem to originate elsewhere; *temporarily, and for test purposes only,* inflate the tires to 40–50 lbs. This will significantly alter the noise produced by the tires, but will not alter noise from the rear axle. Noises from the rear axle will normally cease at speeds below 30 mph on coast, while tire noise will continue at lower tone as speed is decreased. The rear axle noise will usually change from drive conditions to coast conditions, while tire noise will not. Do not forget to lower the tire pressure to normal after the test is complete.

ENGINE/TRANSMISSION NOISE

Determine at what speed the noise is most pronounced, then stop in a quiet place. With the transmission in Neutral, run the engine through speeds corresponding to road speeds where the noise was noticed. Noises produced with the vehicle standing still are coming from the engine or transmission.

FRONT WHEEL BEARINGS

Front wheel bearing noises, sometimes confused with rear axle noises, will not change when comparing drive and coast conditions. While holding the speed steady, lightly apply the footbrake. This will often cause wheel bearing noise to lessen, as some of the weight is taken off the bearing. Front wheel bearings are easily checked by jacking up the wheels and spinning the wheels. Shaking the wheels will also determine if the wheel bearings are excessively loose.

REAR AXLE NOISES

Eliminating other possible sources can narrow the cause to the rear axle, which normally produces noise from worn gears or bearings. Gear noises tend to peak in a narrow speed range, while bearing noises will usually vary in pitch with engine speeds.

Noise Diagnosis

The Noise Is:	Most Probably Produced By:
1. Identical under Drive or Coast	Road surface, tires or front wheel bearings
2. Different depending on road surface	Road surface or tires
3. Lower as speed is lowered	Tires
4. Similar when standing or moving	Engine or transmission
5. A vibration	Unbalanced tires, rear wheel bearing, unbalanced driveshaft or worn U-joint
6. A knock or click about every two tire revolutions	Rear wheel bearing
7. Most pronounced on turns	Damaged differential gears
8. A steady low-pitched whirring or scraping, starting at low speeds	Damaged or worn pinion bearing
9. A chattering vibration on turns	Wrong differential lubricant or worn clutch plates (limited slip rear axle)
10. Noticed only in Drive, Coast or Float conditions	Worn ring gear and/or pinion gear

Troubleshooting Steering & Suspension Problems

Condition	Possible Cause
Hard steering (wheel is hard to turn)	1. Improper tire pressure 2. Loose or glazed pump drive belt 3. Low or incorrect fluid 4. Loose, bent or poorly lubricated front end parts 5. Improper front end alignment (excessive caster) 6. Bind in steering column or linkage 7. Kinked hydraulic hose 8. Air in hydraulic system 9. Low pump output or leaks in system 10. Obstruction in lines 11. Pump valves sticking or out of adjustment 12. Incorrect wheel alignment
Loose steering (too much play in steering wheel)	1. Loose wheel bearings 2. Faulty shocks 3. Worn linkage or suspension components 4. Loose steering gear mounting or linkage points 5. Steering mechanism worn or improperly adjusted 6. Valve spool improperly adjusted 7. Worn ball joints, tie-rod ends, etc.
Veers or wanders (pulls to one side with hands off steering wheel)	1. Improper tire pressure 2. Improper front end alignment 3. Dragging or improperly adjusted brakes 4. Bent frame 5. Improper rear end alignment 6. Faulty shocks or springs 7. Loose or bent front end components 8. Play in Pitman arm 9. Steering gear mountings loose 10. Loose wheel bearings 11. Binding Pitman arm 12. Spool valve sticking or improperly adjusted 13. Worn ball joints
Wheel oscillation or vibration transmitted through steering wheel	1. Low or uneven tire pressure 2. Loose wheel bearings 3. Improper front end alignment 4. Bent spindle 5. Worn, bent or broken front end components 6. Tires out of round or out of balance 7. Excessive lateral runout in disc brake rotor 8. Loose or bent shock absorber or strut
Noises (see also "Troubleshooting Drive Axle Problems")	1. Loose belts 2. Low fluid, air in system 3. Foreign matter in system 4. Improper lubrication 5. Interference or chafing in linkage 6. Steering gear mountings loose 7. Incorrect adjustment or wear in gear box 8. Faulty valves or wear in pump 9. Kinked hydraulic lines 10. Worn wheel bearings
Poor return of steering	1. Over-inflated tires 2. Improperly aligned front end (excessive caster) 3. Binding in steering column 4. No lubrication in front end 5. Steering gear adjusted too tight
Uneven tire wear (see "How To Read Tire Wear")	1. Incorrect tire pressure 2. Improperly aligned front end 3. Tires out-of-balance 4. Bent or worn suspension parts

HOW TO READ TIRE WEAR

The way your tires wear is a good indicator of other parts of the suspension. Abnormal wear patterns are often caused by the need for simple tire maintenance, or for front end alignment.

Excessive wear at the center of the tread indicates that the air pressure in the tire is consistently too high. The tire is riding on the center of the tread and wearing it prematurely. Occasionally, this wear pattern can result from outrageously wide tires on narrow rims. The cure for this is to replace either the tires or the wheels.

This type of wear usually results from consistent under-inflation. When a tire is under-inflated, there is too much contact with the road by the outer treads, which wear prematurely. When this type of wear occurs, and the tire pressure is known to be consistently correct, a bent or worn steering component or the need for wheel alignment could be indicated.

Feathering is a condition when the edge of each tread rib develops a slightly rounded edge on one side and a sharp edge on the other. By running your hand over the tire, you can usually feel the sharper edges before you'll be able to see them. The most common causes of feathering are incorrect toe-in setting or deteriorated bushings in the front suspension.

When an inner or outer rib wears faster than the rest of the tire, the need for wheel alignment is indicated. There is excessive camber in the front suspension, causing the wheel to lean too much putting excessive load on one side of the tire. Misalignment could also be due to sagging springs, worn ball joints, or worn control arm bushings. Be sure the vehicle is loaded the way it's normally driven when you have the wheels aligned.

Cups or scalloped dips appearing around the edge of the tread almost always indicate worn (sometimes bent) suspension parts. Adjustment of wheel alignment alone will seldom cure the problem. Any worn component that connects the wheel to the suspension can cause this type of wear. Occasionally, wheels that are out of balance will wear like this, but wheel imbalance usually shows up as bald spots between the outside edges and center of the tread.

Second-rib wear is usually found only in radial tires, and appears where the steel belts end in relation to the tread. It can be kept to a minimum by paying careful attention to tire pressure and frequently rotating the tires. This is often considered normal wear but excessive amounts indicate that the tires are too wide for the wheels.

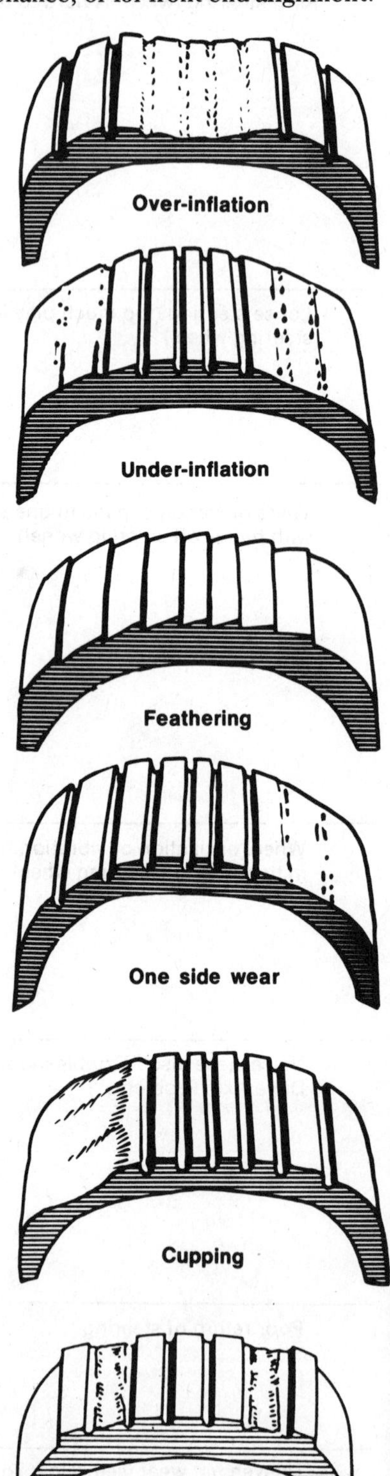

Troubleshooting Disc Brake Problems

Condition	Possible Cause
Noise—groan—brake noise emanating when slowly releasing brakes (creep-groan)	Not detrimental to function of disc brakes—no corrective action required. (This noise may be eliminated by slightly increasing or decreasing brake pedal efforts.)
Rattle—brake noise or rattle emanating at low speeds on rough roads, (front wheels only).	1. Shoe anti-rattle spring missing or not properly positioned. 2. Excessive clearance between shoe and caliper. 3. Soft or broken caliper seals. 4. Deformed or misaligned disc. 5. Loose caliper.
Scraping	1. Mounting bolts too long. 2. Loose wheel bearings. 3. Bent, loose, or misaligned splash shield.
Front brakes heat up during driving and fail to release	1. Operator riding brake pedal. 2. Stop light switch improperly adjusted. 3. Sticking pedal linkage. 4. Frozen or seized piston. 5. Residual pressure valve in master cylinder. 6. Power brake malfunction. 7. Proportioning valve malfunction.
Leaky brake caliper	1. Damaged or worn caliper piston seal. 2. Scores or corrosion on surface of cylinder bore.
Grabbing or uneven brake action—Brakes pull to one side	1. Causes listed under "Brakes Pull". 2. Power brake malfunction. 3. Low fluid level in master cylinder. 4. Air in hydraulic system. 5. Brake fluid, oil or grease on linings. 6. Unmatched linings. 7. Distorted brake pads. 8. Frozen or seized pistons. 9. Incorrect tire pressure. 10. Front end out of alignment. 11. Broken rear spring. 12. Brake caliper pistons sticking. 13. Restricted hose or line. 14. Caliper not in proper alignment to braking disc. 15. Stuck or malfunctioning metering valve. 16. Soft or broken caliper seals. 17. Loose caliper.
Brake pedal can be depressed without braking effect	1. Air in hydraulic system or improper bleeding procedure. 2. Leak past primary cup in master cylinder. 3. Leak in system. 4. Rear brakes out of adjustment. 5. Bleeder screw open.
Excessive pedal travel	1. Air, leak, or insufficient fluid in system or caliper. 2. Warped or excessively tapered shoe and lining assembly. 3. Excessive disc runout. 4. Rear brake adjustment required. 5. Loose wheel bearing adjustment. 6. Damaged caliper piston seal. 7. Improper brake fluid (boil). 8. Power brake malfunction. 9. Weak or soft hoses.

Troubleshooting Disc Brake Problems (cont.)

Condition	Possible Cause
Brake roughness or chatter (pedal pumping)	1. Excessive thickness variation of braking disc. 2. Excessive lateral runout of braking disc. 3. Rear brake drums out-of-round. 4. Excessive front bearing clearance.
Excessive pedal effort	1. Brake fluid, oil or grease on linings. 2. Incorrect lining. 3. Frozen or seized pistons. 4. Power brake malfunction. 5. Kinked or collapsed hose or line. 6. Stuck metering valve. 7. Scored caliper or master cylinder bore. 8. Seized caliper pistons.
Brake pedal fades (pedal travel increases with foot on brake)	1. Rough master cylinder or caliper bore. 2. Loose or broken hydraulic lines/connections. 3. Air in hydraulic system. 4. Fluid level low. 5. Weak or soft hoses. 6. Inferior quality brake shoes or fluid. 7. Worn master cylinder piston cups or seals.

Troubleshooting Drum Brakes

Condition	Possible Cause
Pedal goes to floor	1. Fluid low in reservoir. 2. Air in hydraulic system. 3. Improperly adjusted brake. 4. Leaking wheel cylinders. 5. Loose or broken brake lines. 6. Leaking or worn master cylinder. 7. Excessively worn brake lining.
Spongy brake pedal	1. Air in hydraulic system. 2. Improper brake fluid (low boiling point). 3. Excessively worn or cracked brake drums. 4. Broken pedal pivot bushing.
Brakes pulling	1. Contaminated lining. 2. Front end out of alignment. 3. Incorrect brake adjustment. 4. Unmatched brake lining. 5. Brake drums out of round. 6. Brake shoes distorted. 7. Restricted brake hose or line. 8. Broken rear spring. 9. Worn brake linings. 10. Uneven lining wear. 11. Glazed brake lining. 12. Excessive brake lining dust. 13. Heat spotted brake drums. 14. Weak brake return springs. 15. Faulty automatic adjusters. 16. Low or incorrect tire pressure.

Condition	Possible Cause
Squealing brakes	1. Glazed brake lining. 2. Saturated brake lining. 3. Weak or broken brake shoe retaining spring. 4. Broken or weak brake shoe return spring. 5. Incorrect brake lining. 6. Distorted brake shoes. 7. Bent support plate. 8. Dust in brakes or scored brake drums. 9. Linings worn below limit. 10. Uneven brake lining wear. 11. Heat spotted brake drums.
Chirping brakes	1. Out of round drum or eccentric axle flange pilot.
Dragging brakes	1. Incorrect wheel or parking brake adjustment. 2. Parking brakes engaged or improperly adjusted. 3. Weak or broken brake shoe return spring. 4. Brake pedal binding. 5. Master cylinder cup sticking. 6. Obstructed master cylinder relief port. 7. Saturated brake lining. 8. Bent or out of round brake drum. 9. Contaminated or improper brake fluid. 10. Sticking wheel cylinder pistons. 11. Driver riding brake pedal. 12. Defective proportioning valve. 13. Insufficient brake shoe lubricant.
Hard pedal	1. Brake booster inoperative. 2. Incorrect brake lining. 3. Restricted brake line or hose. 4. Frozen brake pedal linkage. 5. Stuck wheel cylinder. 6. Binding pedal linkage. 7. Faulty proportioning valve.
Wheel locks	1. Contaminated brake lining. 2. Loose or torn brake lining. 3. Wheel cylinder cups sticking. 4. Incorrect wheel bearing adjustment. 5. Faulty proportioning valve.
Brakes fade (high speed)	1. Incorrect lining. 2. Overheated brake drums. 3. Incorrect brake fluid (low boiling temperature). 4. Saturated brake lining. 5. Leak in hydraulic system. 6. Faulty automatic adjusters.
Pedal pulsates	1. Bent or out of round brake drum.
Brake chatter and shoe knock	1. Out of round brake drum. 2. Loose support plate. 3. Bent support plate. 4. Distorted brake shoes. 5. Machine grooves in contact face of brake drum (Shoe Knock). 6. Contaminated brake lining. 7. Missing or loose components. 8. Incorrect lining material. 9. Out-of-round brake drums. 10. Heat spotted or scored brake drums. 11. Out-of-balance wheels.

Troubleshooting Drum Brakes (cont.)

Condition	*Possible Cause*
Brakes do not self adjust	1. Adjuster screw frozen in thread. 2. Adjuster screw corroded at thrust washer. 3. Adjuster lever does not engage star wheel. 4. Adjuster installed on wrong wheel.
Brake light glows	1. Leak in the hydraulic system. 2. Air in the system. 3. Improperly adjusted master cylinder pushrod. 4. Uneven lining wear. 5. Failure to center combination valve or proportioning valve.

Mechanic's Data

General Conversion Table

Multiply By	To Convert	To	
	LENGTH		
2.54	Inches	Centimeters	.3937
25.4	Inches	Millimeters	.03937
30.48	Feet	Centimeters	.0328
.304	Feet	Meters	3.28
.914	Yards	Meters	1.094
1.609	Miles	Kilometers	.621
	VOLUME		
.473	Pints	Liters	2.11
.946	Quarts	Liters	1.06
3.785	Gallons	Liters	.264
.016	Cubic inches	Liters	61.02
16.39	Cubic inches	Cubic cms.	.061
28.3	Cubic feet	Liters	.0353
	MASS (Weight)		
28.35	Ounces	Grams	.035
.4536	Pounds	Kilograms	2.20
—	To obtain	From	Multiply by

Multiply By	To Convert	To	
	AREA		
.645	Square inches	Square cms.	.155
.836	Square yds.	Square meters	1.196
	FORCE		
4.448	Pounds	Newtons	.225
.138	Ft./lbs.	Kilogram/meters	7.23
1.36	Ft./lbs.	Newton-meters	.737
.112	In./lbs.	Newton-meters	8.844
	PRESSURE		
.068	Psi	Atmospheres	14.7
6.89	Psi	Kilopascals	.145
	OTHER		
1.104	Horsepower (DIN)	Horsepower (SAE)	.9861
.746	Horsepower (SAE)	Kilowatts (KW)	1.34
1.60	Mph	Km/h	.625
.425	Mpg	Km/1	2.35
—	To obtain	From	Multiply by

Tap Drill Sizes

National Coarse or U.S.S.

Screw & Tap Size	Threads Per Inch	Use Drill Number
No. 5	40	39
No. 6	32	36
No. 8	32	29
No. 10	24	25
No. 12	24	17
1/4	20	8
5/16	18	F
3/8	16	5/16
7/16	14	U
1/2	13	27/64
9/16	12	31/64
5/8	11	17/32
3/4	10	21/32
7/8	9	49/64

National Coarse or U.S.S.

Screw & Tap Size	Threads Per Inch	Use Drill Number
1	8	7/8
1 1/8	7	63/64
1 1/4	7	1 7/64
1 1/2	6	1 11/32

National Fine or S.A.E.

Screw & Tap Size	Threads Per Inch	Use Drill Number
No. 5	44	37
No. 6	40	33
No. 8	36	29
No. 10	32	21

National Fine or S.A.E.

Screw & Tap Size	Threads Per Inch	Use Drill Number
No. 12	28	15
1/4	28	3
6/16	24	1
3/8	24	Q
7/16	20	W
1/2	20	29/64
9/16	18	33/64
5/8	18	37/64
3/4	16	11/16
7/8	14	13/16
1 1/8	12	1 3/64
1 1/4	12	1 11/64
1 1/2	12	1 27/64

Drill Sizes In Decimal Equivalents

Inch	Decimal	Wire	mm
1/64	.0156		.39
	.0157		.4
	.0160	78	
	.0165		.42
	.0173		.44
	.0177		.45
	.0180	77	
	.0181		.46
	.0189		.48
	.0197		.5
	.0200	76	
	.0210	75	
	.0217		.55
	.0225	74	
	.0236		.6
	.0240	73	
	.0250	72	
	.0256		.65
	.0260	71	
	.0276		.7
	.0280	70	
	.0292	69	
	.0295		.75
	.0310	68	
1/32	.0312		.79
	.0315		.8
	.0320	67	
	.0330	66	
	.0335		.85
	.0350	65	
	.0354		.9
	.0360	64	
	.0370	63	
	.0374		.95
	.0380	62	
	.0390	61	
	.0394		1.0
	.0400	60	
	.0410	59	
	.0413		1.05
	.0420	58	
	.0430	57	
	.0433		1.1
	.0453		1.15
	.0465	56	
3/64	.0469		1.19
	.0472		1.2
	.0492		1.25
	.0512		1.3
	.0520	55	
	.0531		1.35
	.0550	54	
	.0551		1.4
	.0571		1.45
	.0591		1.5
	.0595	53	
	.0610		1.55
1/16	.0625		1.59
	.0630		1.6
	.0635	52	
	.0650		1.65
	.0669		1.7
	.0670	51	
	.0689		1.75
	.0700	50	
	.0709		1.8
	.0728		1.85

Inch	Decimal	Wire	mm
	.0730	49	
	.0748		1.9
	.0760	48	
	.0768		1.95
5/64	.0781		1.98
	.0785	47	
	.0787		2.0
	.0807		2.05
	.0810	46	
	.0820	45	
	.0827		2.1
	.0846		2.15
	.0860	44	
	.0866		2.2
	.0886		2.25
	.0890	43	
	.0906		2.3
	.0925		2.35
	.0935	42	
3/32	.0938		2.38
	.0945		2.4
	.0960	41	
	.0965		2.45
	.0980	40	
	.0981		2.5
	.0995	39	
	.1015	38	
	.1024		2.6
	.1040	37	
	.1063		2.7
	.1065	36	
	.1083		2.75
7/64	.1094		2.77
	.1100	35	
	.1102		2.8
	.1110	34	
	.1130	33	
	.1142		2.9
	.1160	32	
	.1181		3.0
	.1200	31	
	.1220		3.1
1/8	.1250		3.17
	.1260		3.2
	.1280		3.25
	.1285	30	
	.1299		3.3
	.1339		3.4
	.1360	29	
	.1378		3.5
	.1405	28	
9/64	.1406		3.57
	.1417		3.6
	.1440	27	
	.1457		3.7
	.1470	26	
	.1476		3.75
	.1495	25	
	.1496		3.8
	.1520	24	
	.1535		3.9
	.1540	23	
5/32	.1562		3.96
	.1570	22	
	.1575		4.0
	.1590	21	
	.1610	20	

Inch	Decimal	Wire & Letter	mm
	.1614		4.1
	.1654		4.2
	.1660	19	
	.1673		4.25
	.1693		4.3
	.1695	18	
11/64	.1719		4.36
	.1730	17	
	.1732		4.4
	.1770	16	
	.1772		4.5
	.1800	15	
	.1811		4.6
	.1820	14	
	.1850	13	
	.1850		4.7
	.1870		4.75
3/16	.1875		4.76
	.1890		4.8
	.1890	12	
	.1910	11	
	.1929		4.9
	.1935	10	
	.1960	9	
	.1969		5.0
	.1990	8	
	.2008		5.1
	.2010	7	
13/64	.2031		5.16
	.2040	6	
	.2047		5.2
	.2055	5	
	.2067		5.25
	.2087		5.3
	.2090	4	
	.2126		5.4
	.2130	3	
	.2165		5.5
7/32	2188		5.55
	.2205		5.6
	.2210	2	
	.2244		5.7
	.2264		5.75
	.2280	1	
	.2283		5.8
	.2323		5.9
	.2340	A	
15/64	.2344		5.95
	.2362		6.0
	.2380	B	
	.2402		6.1
	.2420	C	
	.2441		6.2
	.2460	D	
	.2461		6.25
	.2480		6.3
1/4	.2500	E	6.35
	.2520		6.
	.2559		6.5
	.2570	F	
	.2598		6.6
	.2610	G	
	.2638		6.7
17/64	.2656		6.74
	.2657		6.75
	.2660	H	
	.2677		6.8

Inch	Decimal	Letter	mm
	.2717		6.9
	.2720	I	
	.2756		7.0
	.2770	J	
	.2795		7.1
	.2810	K	
9/32	.2812		7.14
	.2835		7.2
	.2854		7.25
	.2874		7.3
	.2900	L	
	.2913		7.4
	.2950	M	
	.2953		7.5
19/64	.2969		7.54
	.2992		7.6
	.3020	N	
	.3031		7.7
	.3051		7.75
	.3071		7.8
	.3110		7.9
5/16	.3125		7.93
	.3150		8.0
	.3160	O	
	.3189		8.1
	.3228		8.2
	.3230	P	
	.3248		8.25
	.3268		8.3
21/64	.3281		8.33
	.3307		8.4
	.3320	Q	
	.3346		8.5
	.3386		8.6
	.3390	R	
	.3425		8.7
11/32	.3438		8.73
	.3445		8.75
	.3465		8.8
	.3480	S	
	.3504		8.9
	.3543		9.0
	.3580	T	
	.3583		9.1
23/64	.3594		9.12
	.3622		9.2
	.3642		9.25
	.3661		9.3
	.3680	U	
	.3701		9.4
	.3740		9.5
3/8	.3750		9.52
	.3770	V	
	.3780		9.6
	.3819		9.7
	.3839		9.75
	.3858		9.8
	.3860	W	
	.3898		9.9
25/64	.3906		9.92
	.3937		10.0
	.3970	X	
	.4040	Y	
13/32	.4062		10.31
	.4130	Z	
	.4134		10.5
27/64	.4219		10.71

Inch	Decimal	mm
	.4331	11.0
7/16	.4375	11.11
	.4528	11.5
29/64	.4531	11.51
15/32	.4688	11.90
	.4724	12.0
31/64	.4844	12.30
	.4921	12.5
1/2	.5000	12.70
	.5118	13.0
33/64	.5156	13.09
17/32	.5312	13.49
	.5315	13.5
35/64	.5469	13.89
	.5512	14.0
9/16	.5625	14.28
	.5709	14.5
37/64	.5781	14.68
	.5906	15.0
19/32	.5938	15.08
39/64	.6094	15.47
	.6102	15.5
5/8	.6250	15.87
	.6299	16.0
41/64	.6406	16.27
	.6496	16.5
21/32	.6562	16.66
	.6693	17.0
43/64	.6719	17.06
11/16	.6875	17.46
	.6890	17.5
45/64	.7031	17.85
	.7087	18.0
23/32	.7188	18.25
	.7283	18.5
47/64	.7344	18.65
	.7480	19.0
3/4	.7500	19.05
49/64	.7656	19.44
	.7677	19.5
25/32	.7812	19.84
	.7874	20.0
51/64	.7969	20.24
	.8071	20.5
13/16	.8125	20.63
	.8268	21.0
53/64	.8281	21.03
27/32	.8438	21.43
	.8465	21.5
55/64	.8594	21.82
	.8661	22.0
7/8	.8750	22.22
	.8858	22.5
57/64	.8906	22.62
	.9055	23.0
29/32	.9062	23.01
59/64	.9219	23.41
	.9252	23.5
15/16	.9375	23.81
	.9449	24.0
61/64	.9531	24.2
	.9646	24.5
31/64	.9688	24.6
	.9843	25.0
63/64	.9844	25.0
1	1.0000	25.4

Index

continued on next page

RTUG Title	Part No.
1983-85 Marquis, Montego, 1980-85 XR-7; LINCOLN 1982-85 Continental, 1984-85 Mark VII, 1978-80 Versailles	
Ford Pick-Ups 1965-86 Covers all 1/2, 3/4 and 1 ton, 2- and 4-wheel drive U.S. and Canadian pick-up, chassis cab and camper models, including diesel engines	6913
Ford Pick-Ups 1965-82 Spanish	7469
Ford Ranger 1983-84 Covers all U.S. and Canadian models	7338
Ford Vans 1961-86 Covers all U.S. and Canadian 1/2, 3/4 and 1 ton van and cutaway chassis models, including diesel engines	6849
GM A-Body 1982-85 Covers all front wheel drive U.S. and Canadian models of BUICK Century, CHEVROLET Celebrity, OLDSMOBILE Cutlass Ciera and PONTIAC 6000	7309
GM C-Body 1985 Covers all front wheel drive U.S. and Canadian models of BUICK Electra Park Avenue and Electra T-Type, CADILLAC Fleetwood and deVille, OLDSMOBILE 98 Regency and Regency Brougham	7587
GM J-Car 1982-85 Covers all U.S. and Canadian models of BUICK Skyhawk, CHEVROLET Cavalier, CADILLAC Cimarron, OLDSMOBILE Firenza and PONTIAC 2000 and Sunbird	7059
GM N-Body 1985-86 Covers all U.S. and Canadian models of front wheel drive BUICK Somerset and Skylark, OLDSMOBILE Calais, and PONTIAC Grand Am	7657
GM X-Body 1980-85 Covers all U.S. and Canadian models of BUICK Skylark, CHEVROLET Citation, OLDSMOBILE Omega and PONTIAC Phoenix	7049
GM Subcompact 1971-80 Covers all U.S. and Canadian models of BUICK Skyhawk (1975-80), CHEVROLET Vega and Monza, OLDSMOBILE Starfire, and PONTIAC Astre and 1975-80 Sunbird	6935
Granada/Monarch 1975-82 Covers all U.S. and Canadian models	6937
Honda 1973-84 Covers all U.S. and Canadian models	6980
International Scout 1967-73 Covers all U.S. and Canadian models	5912
Jeep 1945-87 Covers all U.S. and Canadian CJ-2A, CJ-3A, CJ-3B, CJ-5, CJ-6, CJ-7, Scrambler and Wrangler models	6817
Jeep Wagoneer, Commando, Cherokee, Truck 1957-86 Covers all U.S. and Canadian models of Wagoneer, Cherokee, Grand Wagoneer, Jeepster, Jeepster Commando, J-100, J-200, J-300, J-10, J20, FC-150 and FC-170	6739
Laser/Daytona 1984-85 Covers all U.S. and Canadian models	7563
Maverick/Comet 1970-77 Covers all U.S. and Canadian models	6634
Mazda 1971-84 Covers all U.S. and Canadian models of RX-2, RX-3, RX-4, 808, 1300, 1600, Cosmo, GLC and 626	6981
Mazda Pick-Ups 1972-86 Covers all U.S. and Canadian models	7659
Mercedes-Benz 1959-70 Covers all U.S. and Canadian models	6065
Mereceds-Benz 1968-73 Covers all U.S. and Canadian models	5907
Mercedes-Benz 1974-84 Covers all U.S. and Canadian models	6809
Mitsubishi, Cordia, Tredia, Starion, Galant 1983-85 Covers all U.S. and Canadian models	7583
MG 1961-81 Covers all U.S. and Canadian models	6780
Mustang/Capri/Merkur 1979-85 Covers all U.S. and Canadian models	6963
Mustang/Cougar 1965-73 Covers all U.S. and Canadian models	6542
Mustang II 1974-78 Covers all U.S. and Canadian models	6812
Omni/Horizon/Rampage 1978-84 Covers all U.S. and Canadian models of DODGE omni, Miser, 024, Charger 2.2; PLYMOUTH Horizon, Miser, TC3, TC3 Tourismo; Rampage	6845
Opel 1971-75 Covers all U.S. and Canadian models	6575
Peugeot 1970-74 Covers all U.S. and Canadian models	5982
Pinto/Bobcat 1971-80 Covers all U.S. and Canadian models	7027
Plymouth 1968-76 Covers all U.S. and Canadian models	6552
Pontiac Fiero 1984-85 Covers all U.S. and Canadian models	7571
Pontiac Mid-Size 1974-83 Covers all U.S. and Canadian models of Ventura, Grand Am, LeMans, Grand LeMans, GTO, Phoenix, and Grand Prix	7346
Porsche 924/928 1976-81 Covers all U.S. and Canadian models	7048
Renault 1975-85 Covers all U.S. and Canadian models	7165
Roadrunner/Satellite/Belvedere/GTX 1968-73 Covers all U.S. and Canadian models	5821
RX-7 1979-81 Covers all U.S. and Canadian models	7031
SAAB 99 1969-75 Covers all U.S. and Canadian models	5988
SAAB 900 1979-85 Covers all U.S. and Canadian models	7572
Snowmobiles 1976-80 Covers Arctic Cat, John Deere, Kawasaki, Polaris, Ski-Doo and Yamaha	6978
Subaru 1970-84 Covers all U.S. and Canadian models	6982
Tempest/GTO/LeMans 1968-73 Covers all U.S. and Canadian models	5905
Toyota 1966-70 Covers all U.S. and Canadian models of Corona, MkII, Corolla, Crown, Land Cruiser, Stout and Hi-Lux	5795
Toyota 1970-79 Spanish	7467
Toyota Celica/Supra 1971-85 Covers all U.S. and Canadian models	7043
Toyota Trucks 1970-85 Covers all U.S. and Canadian models of pick-ups, Land Cruiser and 4Runner	7035
Valiant/Duster 1968-76 Covers all U.S. and Canadian models	6326
Volvo 1956-69 Covers all U.S. and Canadian models	6529
Volvo 1970-83 Covers all U.S. and Canadian models	7040
VW Front Wheel Drive 1974-85 Covers all U.S. and Canadian models	6962
VW 1949-71 Covers all U.S. and Canadian models	5796
VW 1970-79 Spanish	7081
VW 1970-81 Covers all U.S. and Canadian Beetles, Karmann Ghia, Fastback, Squareback, Vans, 411 and 412	6837

Chilton's Repair & Tune-Up Guides are available at your local retailer or by mailing a check or money order for **$13.95** plus **$3.25** to cover postage and handling to:

Chilton Book Company
Dept. DM
Radnor, PA 19089

NOTE: When ordering be sure to include your name & address, book part No. & title.